American History

Sixth Edition

Jack Abramowitz

Follett Social Studies

Allyn and Bacon, Inc.

Boston · Rockleigh, N.J. · Atlanta · Dallas · San Jose
London · Sydney · Toronto

Contents

ISBN 0-205-09259-4 (Previously ISBN 0-695-27890-8)

Library of Congress Catalog Card Number 83-71112

Printed in the United States of America

6 7 8 9 10   91 90 89 88

4

PART 1 New Life in a New Land: Prehistory to 1789

unit
1

Æatis suæ 21. Aᵒ 1616.

Matoaks als Rebecka daughter to the mighty Prince Powhatan Emperour of Attanoughkomouck als Virginia converted and baptized in the Christian faith, and Wife to the worᵗᵗ Mʳ Tho: Rolff.

Pocahontas by unidentified artist, National Portrait Gallery, Smithsonian Institution

Penn's Treaty with the Indians by Benjamin West, Pennsylvania Academy of the Fine Arts, Joseph and Sarah Harrison Collection

The
People of
Early America

In 1492, America was changed forever. Indian met European.
Relations between the two would often be difficult. Yet people
on both sides tried to keep peace, among them Pocahontas
(left) and William Penn (above). But with or without peace, the
New World colonies grew.

Lesson 1   The First People of America

WORDS TO UNDERSTAND
Discuss the meanings of these words.

descendants   advanced

cultures   civilizations

NEW WORDS IN SENTENCES
1. Your **descendants** are your children, your children's children, and so on.

2. The beliefs, activities, and all the other things that are part of life in groups of people are what make up **cultures.**

3. Later Mound Builders were more **advanced** because they had developed more skills.

4. The **civilizations** in Mexico and Peru were cultures with highly developed skills, arts, and beliefs.

AS YOU READ
As you read this selection, try to answer these questions.

1. Who were the first people of the Americas and where did they come from?

2. How did people change their ways of life after the big game animals died out?

3. What kinds of mounds were built in the Eastern culture area?

THE READING SELECTION
When Columbus landed in America in 1492, he thought he had reached the Indies. So he called the people living in the new land "Indians." These Native Americans had already lived in this part of the world for thousands of years. They had developed a variety of ways of life.

Thousands of years ago, Alaska was linked to northeastern Asia. At that time, there was a wide bridge of land between the two. Today, this land bridge is under water. Sometime between 20,000 and 40,000 years ago, the first people came to the Americas by crossing this bridge. They were probably following the herds of large animals that they hunted.

Over thousands of years, many groups of people moved over the land bridge. Slowly, groups began to move south. Most of them moved along a route east of the Rocky Mountains. By 6,000 to 10,000 years ago, people had reached the tip of South America. They had spread over both North and South America. These people were the first Americans. Their **descendants** would be called Native Americans, or Indians.

For thousands of years, most Indians continued to hunt big game, as they had done in Asia. They moved with the herds of huge mammals that existed at that time. They lived in caves or built camps. They made tools and weapons from rock, wood, and bone.

But after many thousands of years, the big animals of America died out. The people who hunted them had to change their way of life. They had to find other kinds of food. This started a new period in the history of people in America.

The early Indians of the Southwest built clay and stone pueblos in the cliffs. As many as 400 people could live in one village. Mesa Verde, below, was probably built around 1100.

U.S. Department of the Interior, National Park Service photo by Red E. Mang, Jr.

During this period, most people in North America had some things in common. They gathered wild plants for food. But they also began to farm. They trapped small animals. In some places, they also fished. People began to build homes in which they lived for the whole year. They slowly began to use pottery, jewelry, and tools.

People who lived in different areas began to develop different ways of life. There were two main **cultures.** One was the Desert culture of the west and southwest areas. The other was the Eastern culture of the central and eastern areas.

The groups of Eastern people about whom we know the most built large mounds of earth. We now call these people the Mound Builders. They lived in what is now the Midwest. At first, they built two kinds of mounds. One kind was shaped like an animal—a snake, for example. Another kind was round or oval. This was used to bury the dead.

The last Mound Builder culture developed around the Mississippi River and in the South. It was more **advanced** than the earlier cultures. Mounds were the bases for wooden temples and homes of important people. Farming was well established. Ornaments and other objects were made with more skill than in earlier cultures.

In the centuries before Europeans arrived, advanced cultures developed in Mexico and Peru. The Mayas, Aztecs, and Incas have become famous for their **civilizations.** In North America, other Indian cultures also grew. They developed into a number of different groups. These were the people who met the first European explorers.

COMPREHENSION CHECK

A. Recognizing the Main Idea

This selection as a whole tells you that

1. there were always people living in the Americas.
2. the first people of the Americas were the Eskimos.
3. over thousands of years, people in America developed various cultures.
4. people crossed the land bridge from Asia about 1,000 years ago.

B. Selecting Important Details

Choose the ending that best completes each statement.

1. The first groups of people who came across the land bridge
   a. were probably following herds of big game.
   b. built mounds of earth.
   c. worked out systems for bringing water to their crops.
   d. moved north.
2. The people of the Desert culture
   a. lived in the eastern part of the continent.
   b. built mounds for temples.
   c. were just like the people of the Eastern culture.
   d. lived in the west and southwest areas.
3. Some of the Mound Builders
   a. lived in what is now the Midwest.
   b. built mounds to bury the dead.
   c. built animal-shaped mounds.
   d. all of the above.

4. Before Columbus landed, people in America
   a. did not know how to hunt or farm.
   b. had developed many cultures.
   c. lived only in Mexico and Peru.
   d. called themselves "Indians."

C. True or False

Decide whether each of these statements is true or false.

1. There were no civilizations in the Americas when the Europeans arrived.
2. The descendants of people who crossed the land bridge built civilizations in Mexico and Peru.
3. As the large animals in America died out, the people who hunted them had to look for other kinds of food.
4. The mounds were all built to bury the dead.

D. Vocabulary

Match the words with the definitions.

Words	Definitions
1. descendant	a. your grandmother, for example
2. culture	b. the beliefs and activities of a group of people
3. advanced	c. a highly developed group of people
4. civilization	d. your grandchild, for example
	e. developed ahead of others
	f. a language

12

The First Europeans in America

Indians had lived in North and South America for thousands of years before the first Europeans landed in the New World. But who was the first European to arrive?

Columbus often gets the credit. His voyage was a great achievement. It was his trips that led to later European explorations and settlements. But he was not the first.

In the North Atlantic lies a series of "stepping stones" between Europe and North America. These islands provided stopping places to make the long voyage easier. Norse sailors made this voyage hundreds of years before Columbus did.

The Norse were a seagoing people from northern Europe—what is now Norway, Sweden, and Denmark. By the early ninth century, they had sailed to and settled Iceland. Around the year 985, Eric the Red landed in Greenland. He later brought groups of settlers there. The Greenland colony lasted for a few hundred years.

Eric's son, Leif the Lucky, was sailing to Greenland around the year 1000. His ship was blown off course by a storm. He landed in a place to the west of Greenland. He named it Vinland (or vine-land). Vinland was probably in what we now call Newfoundland.

About twenty years later, around 250 Norse men and women established a settlement in Vinland. But the Norse settlers did not get along well with the Eskimos already living there. In fact, the settlement was saved during one Eskimo attack by Freydis, a settler who was the daughter of Eric the Red. After trying unsuccessfully to get the Norse men to fight back, she picked up a sword herself and chased the attackers off.

Yet, after two winters, the Norse decided that Vinland was too dangerous. They sailed back to Greenland. But the Norse were still the first Europeans to find, and live in, North America.

The early Viking explorers often fought with the Native Americans.

Culver Pictures, Inc.

13

Lesson 2 Indian Life in America

WORDS TO UNDERSTAND

Discuss the meanings of these words.

environment   clans
political   confederacies

NEW WORDS IN SENTENCES

1. People who live in a desert **environment** have a different way of life from people who live surrounded by lakes.

2. Groups of people usually have some kind of **political** structure to organize and govern themselves.

3. The tribe was made up of several family **clans** in which everyone was related by birth or marriage.

4. Some Indian tribes formed **confederacies** to join themselves together for a common purpose.

AS YOU READ

As you read this selection, try to answer these questions.

1. What were some differences in the ways Indian groups got food and clothing?

2. What were some differences in Indian political systems?

THE READING SELECTION

The Indians of North America had settled in many different kinds of places. Each group developed a way of life fitted to its **environment.** One area might have good soil and rain for farming. Another area might be very dry or full of mountains. The food, houses, clothing, and tools of Indian groups depended on the materials of their areas.

The main farming areas were east of the Mississippi River and in the Southwest. Indians in these areas usually depended on farming, plus hunting or fishing, for food. Clothing was made from animal skins or woven fabrics. In areas with forests, wood was used to build houses. Stone, brush, and clay were used in other areas.

Hunting and fishing became much more important as sources of food in the plains, in mountain areas, and along the coasts. Indians in many western areas also depended more on gathering wild plants or shellfish than the farmers did. There were, however, many Indian groups who did raise some crops. In areas where large animals were hunted, skins were used for homes. In other areas, wood or brush was used to build shelters. Clothing was usually made from skins.

Indian **political** systems were not all alike. Indians in the plains and eastern areas were usually the ones organized into tribes. In other regions, the most important group might be a village, a band, or a family. Even within tribes, family **clans** were often important.

The arrival of Europeans changed the Indian political systems. Smaller groups began to form larger groups. Villages joined with other villages of the tribe. Tribes began to form **confederacies.** The Iroquois Confederacy in the Northeast was made up of five, and later six, tribes. It was a strong group that new white settlers had to deal with.

The arrival of Europeans also tended to decrease warfare between Indian groups. In some areas, warfare was not very common. California and northwest Indians often settled disagreements by exchanging gifts or making payments. But in the Northeast, the Southeast, and on the Plains, war was important. However, faced with a new problem—whites who wanted land—Indians tended more to ignore their own disagreements.

The map and chart in this lesson will tell you more about the ten main Indian groups in what is now the United States.

Use this map with the chart on the following pages. The map helps you locate the Indian culture areas listed on the chart. The map also gives you the names of some of the Indian tribes in each culture area.

Major American Indian Tribes and Culture Areas in the 1600s

Culture Areas
- Arctic
- Sub-Arctic
- California
- Northwest Coast
- Plateau
- Great Basin
- Southwest
- Plains
- Eastern Woodlands
- Southeast

NATIVE AMERICAN CULTURE GROUPS

	EASTERN WOODLANDS	SOUTHEAST	PLAINS	SOUTHWEST	GREAT BASIN
FOOD SUPPLY	Farming and Hunting Fishing	Farming and Hunting Fishing	Large-Game Hunting or Farming and Hunting	Farming and Hunting Gathering	Gathering and Hunting
HOUSING	Bark Skins Wood	Wood Grasses Mud/Earth	Skins Earth	Clay-Stone Brush	Brush
CLOTHING	Skins	Skins	Skins	Skins Fibers	Skins Fibers
ART	Iroquois False Face Mask	Seminole Bead-work	Sioux Painted Buffalo Robe	Zuni Water Jar	Paiute Gathering Basket

PLATEAU	NORTHWEST COAST	CALIFORNIA	SUB-ARCTIC	ARCTIC	
Hunting Gathering	Fishing Hunting (Sea Animals) and Gathering	Gathering and Hunting Fishing	Fishing Hunting	Fishing Hunting Sea Animals	FOOD SUPPLY
Wood Brush Earth	Wood	Brush Wood Earth	Skins Wood	Snow Skins Earth	HOUSING
Furs Skins	Fibers	Fibers Skins	Furs Skins	Furs Skins	CLOTHING
Klickitat Basket	Tlingit Raven Hat	Pomo Basket	Mic-Mac Quill and Bark Box	Eskimo Ivory Carving	ART

COMPREHENSION CHECK

A. Recognizing the Main Idea

This selection as a whole tells you that

1. war was important to Indians of the Northeast, the Southeast, and the Plains.

2. there were many different Indian political and cultural groups.

3. most of the Indians of North America had settled in one kind of place.

4. the Indian farming areas were east of the Mississippi River and in the Southwest.

B. Selecting Important Details

Choose the ending that best completes each statement.

1. Indian life varied from area to area
   a. only in the kinds of political systems.
   b. in every way except food and clothing.
   c. very little.
   d. depending on the environment.

2. The Iroquois Confederacy was
   a. a European organization.
   b. made up of five or six tribes.
   c. a small hunting tribe.
   d. made up of large game hunters.

3. Indian political systems
   a. included tribes, family clans, villages, and confederacies.
   b. varied from area to area.
   c. were changed by the arrival of the Europeans.
   d. all of the above.

4. The arrival of Europeans
   a. caused warfare among the Indian tribes.
   b. made Indians tend to ignore their own disagreements.
   c. made large Indian groups form smaller groups.
   d. taught the Indians to settle their disagreements by exchanging gifts.

C. Vocabulary

Match the words with the definitions.

Words	Definitions
1. environment	a. groups joined together
2. political	b. surroundings
3. clan	c. having to do with government
4. confederacy	d. a secret plan
	e. an Indian house
	f. a family group

D. Map Work

Use the map in this lesson to answer this question.

Tribes in the Great Basin area made houses out of brush. What were the names of some of these tribes?

Iroquois Women

In some Indian tribes, women held important positions. An outstanding example of the power of Indian women was found in the Iroquois Confederacy. The Iroquois Confederacy included the Mohawk, Oneida, Onondaga, Cayuga, and Seneca tribes. The Tuscarora tribe joined the league later.

The Iroquois engaged in large-scale farming and lived in permanent villages. Within the village areas, the Iroquois built their family longhouses. The Iroquois family was more than a set of parents and their children. It was an "extended" family that might include uncles, aunts, married daughters and their husbands, and others. The family of the Iroquois was based upon relation to the women. An Iroquois man who married left his parents. He joined the family of his wife's mother.

This put an Iroquois man under the rule of the woman's family and clan. Women ran the longhouses. If a man displeased his wife, he could be ordered to leave the longhouse.

The power of Iroquois women also extended into tribal affairs. Each tribe was ruled by a council of chiefs, or sachems (say-kems). Each sachem was the leader of a clan, or family. The sachems were men. But the family or clan line was traced through the women. The women decided which men would be sachems.

When a sachem died, another had to be selected. The women of the clan gathered under the leadership of the head woman to pick the new sachem. Their selection was then sent for approval to the two main tribal groups. The women kept watch over the work of each sachem and warned of any shortcomings. The women only gave the sachem three warnings. If the sachem did not change, he could be removed from office by the women. He was sent back to the ranks as a common warrior. The women then picked a new sachem. Thus, although the Iroquois men ruled, the women appointed and could remove these rulers.

The powers of the women reached everything in Iroquois life. They owned the longhouses and the tools used in the fields. Women also owned and worked the small fields, or gardens, where food was grown. All property was inherited through the woman's side of the family. This was the exact opposite of the system of inheriting in Europe. In all these ways and in others, the Iroquois women had much more power than most European women of the time.

Lesson 3 Living in America: Indian Customs

WORDS TO UNDERSTAND
Discuss the meanings of these words.

treaty   retribution

justice   customs

NEW WORDS IN SENTENCES
1. The Indians thought the government would keep its part of the agreement when they signed a **treaty.**

2. Every culture has its own system of **justice** to punish crimes or decide disagreements.

3. In the Indian system of justice, the criminal could expect **retribution,** or punishment, from the family of the victim.

4. Indians had their own **customs,** or usual ways of doing things.

AS YOU READ
As you read this selection, try to answer these questions.

1. What were some of the important differences between the Indian and European cultures?

2. Why did the differences in cultures lead to conflicts?

THE READING SELECTION
Christopher Columbus found more than a new world in 1492. He and the Europeans who followed also found a new kind of culture, or way of life. They found the culture of the Native Americans, whom they called Indians. This culture was as strange to Europeans as the European culture was to the Indians. Neither the Europeans nor the Indians ever really understood one another. In the end it was the Europeans who crushed the Indian way of life.

What was Indian culture? How did it differ from the European culture of the white settlers? To begin, there was no one Indian culture. There was no single Indian nation. Indian people lived in different ways all across the lands of North, Central, and South America. But despite many differences, they were alike in some striking ways. In North America, the Indians' ways of living were different from those of the white settlers.

These settlers came from a society that included the idea of private property. The farmlands, forests, animals, and even some waterways could be owned by individuals. The same was true of homes, tools, and other things. Landowners could work the land, rent it, or sell it. They could even leave the land unused if they wished. To the settlers, nature and land could be part of private property.

Games were popular with the Cheyennes, shown here, and with other tribes. The games in this winter painting include kickball, tobogganing, and a kind of field hockey.

Indians generally looked at nature in a very different way. They saw themselves as one with nature. They used it to live, because the parts of nature worked together. But they did not own land. They did not buy and sell it. It belonged to all Indians, to the Great Spirit. The Nez Percé chief, Joseph, said "The one who has the right to dispose of [the land] is the one who has created it."

Tribes had a variety of landholding systems. But in general, the rights of the user of the land were most important. Land used by a tribe for hunting was often shared with other tribes. A plot of land used for farming was under the control of the family working it. Once the family stopped working it, it could be used by anyone else. An Indi-

an would usually not buy a piece of land, fence it in, and leave it unused.

This difference in cultures led to many disputes between new settlers and Indians. Indians were already using land that new settlers wanted to buy or take for private use. Indian ways did not allow for signing a **treaty** to sell land that was being used by the tribe.

Sharing was important in Indian cultures. Crops were often shared by the whole tribe. Sometimes, hunters were unlucky and might fail to bring back food from their hunt. In such cases, luckier or more skilled hunters shared their food supply. Those who helped others expected help for themselves if they ever needed it. The European settlers did not always work this way.

21

Most Plains tribes hunted buffalo for food and clothing.

Their crops and game were private property. They did not share when Indians expected them to.

Indians gave great importance to gift-giving and to sharing. Gift-giving often was almost a form of trade among Indians. In some places, it had a special meaning. The "potlatch" of the Northwest Indians was an unusual example of gift-giving. Chiefs and others would arrange great feasts for their tribespeople. At these feasts, they would give gifts as a way of bringing honor to themselves. Often, the failure by white settlers to give gifts at proper times offended the Indians. On the other hand, these settlers often thought the Indians were simply greedy.

Another difference between the white settlers and Indians was in their ideas of **justice.** The settlers' justice called for trials in a court of law. Lawyers, judges, witnesses, and juries argued, listened, and made decisions. The process was often slow. Sometimes a good lawyer might win freedom for a guilty person. Also, the same crime could bring different punishments. An Indian might be punished and a settler go free, though both had committed the same crime. To the Indian, that justice seemed slow and unfair.

Indian justice was based upon **retribution.** Someone who committed a crime was punished, but not by courts of law. It was the duty of the victims or their families to punish the guilty. Tribal **customs** decided what were crimes and what the punishments should be. The Indian system of justice by retribution was personal and often swift. To the settlers, such justice seemed cruel. But Indians did not want to leave justice to outsiders. They felt the settlers' justice favored the settlers over the Indians. For this reason, they kept using retribution as a way of justice. This brought them into disagreement with the settlers' law.

Indians and settlers also differed in many other ways. In the Indian culture, a person's word was sacred. Indians expected others also to keep their word. They were shocked when settlers broke their promises. Indian chiefs could not understand a government that broke the terms of a treaty. Time and again, Indians tried to shame different governments for breaking treaties. Their efforts brought them no results.

COMPREHENSION CHECK

A. Recognizing the Main Idea

This selection as a whole tells you that

1. the Indian justice system was different from the justice system of the settlers.

2. the Indians and the settlers learned to understand each other.

3. treaties meant the same things to Indians as they did to the settlers.

4. the culture of the American Indians was different in important ways from the culture of the European settlers.

B. Selecting Important Details

Choose the ending that best completes each statement.

1. White settlers
   a. found the Indian cultures to be similar to their own.
   b. felt that land could not be bought and sold.
   c. came from a society in which property ownership was important.
   d. all of the above.

2. Indian culture did not allow for treaties by which they lost their land because
   a. land belonged to the Great Spirit.
   b. land could not be bought and sold.
   c. the rights of the user of the land were most important.
   d. all of the above.

3. In the Indian system of justice
   a. decisions were made by judges and juries.
   b. punishment was usually slow to come.
   c. retribution was considered unfair.
   d. families of the victims punished the person who did the crime.

4. All the following were important to Indians EXCEPT
   a. gift-giving.
   b. private ownership of land.
   c. caring for nature.
   d. keeping one's promise.

C. True or False

Decide whether each of these statements is true or false.

1. The Indians got results by shaming the American government when it broke treaties.

2. Differences in sharing and gift-giving led to disputes between the settlers and the Indians.

3. The potlatch was the settlers' gift-giving feast.

4. Indians would buy land, fence it in, and leave it unused.

D. Vocabulary

Match the words with the definitions.

Words	Definitions
1. treaty	a. punishment
2. justice	b. an agreement
3. retribution	c. usual way of doing something
4. custom	d. a crime
	e. a change
	f. a system for deciding fair treatment

Lesson 4 The Beginning of European Exploration

WORDS TO UNDERSTAND
Discuss the meanings of these words.
**imported   navigator   circumnavigate
continent   isthmus**

NEW WORDS IN SENTENCES
1. Most Asian goods were **imported,** or brought to Europe, by Italian merchants.
2. The United States is located on the **continent** of North America.
3. The **navigator** guided the ship in the right direction.
4. An **isthmus** is a narrow strip of land connecting two larger land areas.
5. The ships that sailed completely around the world were the first to **circumnavigate** the earth.

AS YOU READ
As you read this selection, try to answer these questions.
1. Why did Europeans start exploring the world?
2. Who were some of the early explorers, and where did they travel?

THE READING SELECTION
When Europeans came to America in the late 1400s, they were not looking for a new world. They were looking for a new way to get to Asia. They wanted the new route for their trading ships to travel.

Europeans had been using Asian goods for several hundred years. But Italians controlled most of the trade with Asia. Almost all Asian goods were **imported** by Italian merchants. The goods were then resold to the other countries of Europe. The other important countries in Europe were Portugal, Spain, France, and England. After the Crusades of the 1100s, Europeans wanted Asian goods and riches more than ever. Italian control of trade, however, meant high prices for the Asian goods. The merchants of Europe did not want to pay high prices. So they were forced to look for a new way to get to Asia.

The usual way to get to Asia from Europe was to travel east over land and water. But overland travel was slow. So Europeans began looking for an all-water route to Asia.

Portugal led the way. In the mid-1400s, Portugal began sending ships down the coast of Africa. They were hoping to find this new route.

Christopher Columbus was an Italian navigator serving under Portugal. He had another plan. Like others of the time, Columbus believed the world was round.

This painting shows Christopher Columbus as he probably looked in 1492, though it was painted much later, in 1519.

He thought that he could reach Asia by sailing west across the Atlantic Ocean. However, Portugal would not agree to pay for the voyage. Finally, Columbus persuaded Spain to support the trip. In August 1492, he set sail. Two months later, he landed in what he thought was Asia. Actually, Columbus had landed in America—in what is now the West Indies. Columbus thought he was in Asia because he had misjudged the size of the world. He thought that after sailing west from Spain, he would next touch Asia. He had no idea there was another **continent** between Europe and Asia. Columbus made three more trips to the new lands. Toward the end of his life, he began to realize that he had landed on a "new" continent.

After Columbus's successful voyage, others started to look for a new way to reach Asia. In 1497, the English hired an Italian **navigator,** Giovanni Cabato. They sent him to find new routes to India. John Cabot, as the English called him, landed in Labrador. He claimed that area for England.

In 1498, Vasco da Gama, a Portuguese, sailed around Africa and on to India. Two years later, Pedro Cabral sailed west and landed in Brazil. He claimed it for Portugal.

An Italian named Amerigo Vespucci wrote about the new lands to the west. He realized these lands were not Asia but a new continent. The new lands—America—were named for him.

Many others explored the lands of North America and South America after 1500. A Spaniard named Balboa landed on the narrow **isthmus** of Panama in 1513. He pushed westward across the land and reached the eastern end of the Pacific Ocean.

In 1519, Ferdinand Magellan decided to try to sail around the world. Magellan was a Portuguese sailing for Spain. In November 1519, he set sail with five ships and several hundred men. The trip took a long time, and Magellan himself was killed in the Philippine Islands. But three years later, one ship and eighteen sailors returned to Spain. They were the first to **circumnavigate,** or sail around, the earth.

In 1492, Europeans were familiar only with their own continent and parts of Asia and Africa. Much of their knowledge of Asia and Africa was a result of the Crusades.

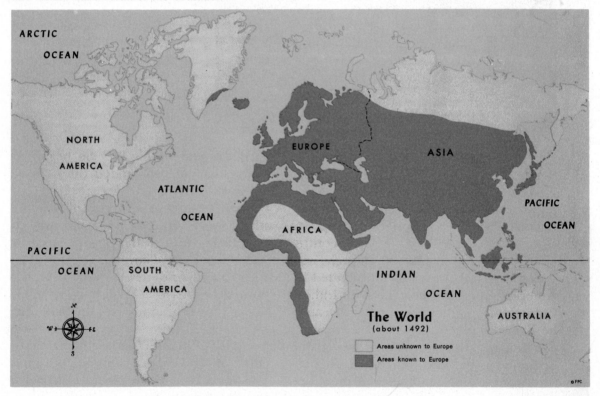

COMPREHENSION CHECK

A. Recognizing the Main Idea

This selection as a whole tells you

1. why explorers decided to stay home after Columbus's voyage.

2. how the new land came to be called America.

3. why Columbus thought he had reached Asia.

4. about the beginnings of the European exploration of the New World.

B. Selecting Important Details

Choose the ending that best completes each statement.

1. Europeans wanted
   a. to find a new world.
   b. to give control of Asian trade to the Italians.
   c. a land route to Asia.
   d. a water route to Asia.

2. Columbus
   a. circumnavigated the earth.
   b. was sent by France to look for a new continent.
   c. sailed down the coast of Africa looking for a new route to Asia.
   d. sailed west and landed in what is now the West Indies.

3. All of the following statements are true EXCEPT
   a. Magellan set out to circumnavigate the earth.
   b. Balboa crossed the isthmus of Panama.
   c. Pedro Cabral claimed Brazil for Portugal.
   d. Amerigo Vespucci thought the new lands to the west were Asia.

4. Explorers
   a. stopped sailing after 1500.
   b. knew the exact size of the world.
   c. did not always sail for their own country.
   d. all of the above.

C. True or False

Decide whether each of these statements is true or false.

1. Trade with Asia stopped after the Crusades of the 1100s.

2. Columbus was the only person who thought the world was round.

3. Vasco da Gama claimed Labrador for England.

4. John Cabot crossed the isthmus of Panama.

D. Vocabulary

Match the words with the definitions.

Words	Definitions
1. import	a. to go completely around something
2. continent	b. one who plans a course of travel
3. navigator	c. not connected to anything
4. isthmus	d. to bring in from a foreign place
5. circumnavigate	e. a strip of land connecting two larger areas of land
	f. one of the large land areas of the world
	g. to move in a straight line

The Crusades and Islam

Europeans became interested in trade with Asia long before Columbus set sail. This interest was partly a result of the Crusades. The Crusades were wars between Europeans and Muslims.

Muslims, or Mohammedans, were the followers of a religion called Islam. The religion was founded in Arabia around A.D. 622 by a man named Mohammed. Muslims believed that God, or Allah, had spoken through Mohammed. The ideas of Allah and of Islam were written down in the *Koran,* a holy book. It was important to Muslims to spread their religion. They believed in the idea of a "holy war" against non-Muslims. To a Muslim, it was good to die while fighting for Allah.

Muslims became great warriors. The religion spread through what is now the Middle East and North Africa. By 732, Muslims also controlled a large part of Spain. By 1095, it looked as if they would conquer Constantinople. This was an important city in eastern Europe.

In 1095, the Christian Pope called for a Crusade against the Muslims. Christian crusaders were to defend Constantinople. They were also to try to win back the Holy Land, or Palestine. During the next 125 years, there were at least five Crusades. The crusaders did not win back the Holy Land. However, they did bring many changes to Europe. Christians returning from the wars brought back spices and other new foods from Asia. They also brought silk, clothing, perfume, and tools.

Europeans liked the new goods. A great demand arose for more of them. An easier and cheaper trade route to Asia became much more important. Several European countries began sending explorers to look for such a route. Christopher Columbus was one of them.

This painting shows a fight between a Christian and a Muslim during the Crusades.

Lesson 5 Spain in the New World

WORDS TO UNDERSTAND
Discuss the meanings of these words.

colonies   **empire**
demarcation   **missionaries**

NEW WORDS IN SENTENCES

1. **Colonies** are groups of people living in new territories while keeping ties with their home country.

2. The river was the **demarcation** line showing the limits of the property.

3. The Spanish **empire** controlled land and people in many parts of the world.

4. **Missionaries** were sent by the Church to bring Christianity to the Native Americans.

AS YOU READ

As you read this selection, try to answer these questions.

1. Who were some of the Spanish explorers? What were they looking for, and what did they find?

2. What were some characteristics of the Spanish colonies in the New World?

THE READING SELECTION

Review. In 1492, Christopher Columbus sailed west across the Atlantic Ocean. He was looking for an all-water route to Asia. Asian goods were in demand. Europeans wanted a faster route to Asia—one that would not be controlled by Italians. When Columbus landed, he thought he was in Asia. At the time, he did not realize there was another continent between Europe and Asia. After Columbus's voyage, other explorers began to look for a water route to Asia. ☆

The New World continued to attract the attention of most European nations in the 1500s and 1600s. Spain and Portugal were the first to set up **colonies** in the New World. In fact, in 1494 Spain and Portugal decided on a line of **demarcation.** This imaginary line divided the world in half. Spain was to control trade in one half, and Portugal in the other. Before long, however, Portugal lost much of its power. Soon France, England, and Holland were also setting up colonies in the New World.

The Spaniards set up colonies in Central and South America and in California. Spain was interested mainly in Central and South America because of the gold and silver found there.

One of the first Spanish explorers was Juan Ponce de León. In 1513, he explored Florida.

Another Spaniard, Hernando Cortés, explored Mexico. Cortés was a hero in Spain. He proved to be an enemy of the Aztec Indians of Mexico. In 1519, Cortés and about 500 well-armed soldiers conquered the Aztec **Empire.** Cortés seized gold and silver from the Aztecs. He shipped these riches back to Spain. This made more people want to search for riches in the area of the Gulf of Mexico.

Ten years later, Francisco Pizarro sailed to Peru. He found that the Inca Indians of Peru had much gold and silver. Pizarro tricked the Inca Indians, captured their leader, and killed many of the people. Pizarro took over the Inca Empire. Hernando de Soto had served with Pizarro in Peru but wanted to explore new lands on his own. In 1539, de Soto landed in present-day Florida. He explored the lands from Florida to the Mississippi River.

In 1540, Francisco Coronado sailed from Spain. He explored Mexico and the Southwest. He got as far north as the Kansas plains but found no precious metals.

The Spanish empire in the New World was spread out across many hundreds of miles. The discovery of precious metals and the work of the **missionaries** kept Spain interested in these new lands.

The Spanish colonies, however, did not attract many settlers. The average Spanish farmer or worker had little reason to come to America. Spain allowed no self-government and little religious freedom. Also, Spain did not allow any industries in its colonies. Settlers were not allowed to trade with countries other than Spain.

From the beginning, the Spanish colonies in America did not give all members equal rights. The colonists often mistreated the Indians. They used them as slaves in the mines and fields.

Because of the strict rules, Spanish settlements remained small in size. The main task of the Spanish colonists was to collect gold and silver. These treasures were shipped back to Spain. From 1520 to 1660, the Spanish settlers sent about 200 tons of gold and 18,000 tons of silver back to Spain.

Although he was the first European to reach the Mississippi River, Hernando de Soto was discouraged by his explorations in the Southeast. He had not found the gold he had sought.

Collection of State Historical Society of Wisconsin

30

COMPREHENSION CHECK

A. Recognizing the Main Idea

This selection as a whole tells you

1. why Spain was not interested in the gold and silver in the New World.

2. how Portugal became a more powerful nation.

3. how Spain and Portugal divided the world in half.

4. about Spanish explorers and Spanish colonies in the New World.

B. Selecting Important Details

Choose the ending that best completes each statement.

1. The line of demarcation was
   a. a colony in South America.
   b. the border between France and England.
   c. the army led by Cortés.
   d. supposed to divide world trade between Spain and Portugal.

2. Hernando Cortés
   a. explored Peru.
   b. was a missionary.
   c. did not find gold or silver.
   d. conquered the Aztec Empire.

3. Francisco Pizarro
   a. discovered Florida.
   b. was tricked by the Inca Indians.
   c. took over an empire in Peru.
   d. set up a colony in California.

4. Spanish colonies
   a. treated everyone equally.
   b. allowed religious freedom.
   c. attracted many Spanish farmers.
   d. shipped gold and silver back to Spain.

C. Vocabulary

Match the words with the definitions.

Words	Definitions
1. colony	a. to go downward
2. demarcation	b. person doing religious work
3. empire	c. a powerful ruler
4. missionary	d. a number of territories and people under a single government
	e. to go upward
	f. group of people living in a new territory while keeping ties with the old country
	g. marking the limits of

D. Using Your Knowledge

Match each main idea with two details about it.

Main Ideas	Details
1. Spanish explorers were looking for gold and silver.	a. Spanish colonies had no self-government.
2. Spain kept strong control of its colonies.	b. Francisco Pizarro conquered the Inca Empire and sent riches back to Spain.
	c. The success of Hernando Cortés made more people want to explore the area of the Gulf of Mexico.
	d. Spanish colonies were not allowed to trade with other countries.

Bartolomé de Las Casas

Bartolomé de Las Casas, a Spanish priest and missionary, sailed with Columbus on one of his trips. His description of the journey tells much about what the Spaniards found in the new lands. But more important is his description of the explorers' treatment of Indians.

Las Casas spent many years in the New World and became a bishop in Mexico. From there, he sent dozens of letters to the queen and king of Spain. He urged them to do something to help the Indians. The Spaniards were using the Indians as slaves. The Indians were forced to work long, hard hours mining gold and silver to send back to Spain. Thousands of Indians died as a result of this treatment.

Las Casas bitterly protested the cruelty of the Spanish officials. He claimed that almost 12 million Indians had died of starvation, disease, and overwork. This is a great exaggeration, but there is no doubt that the Indian population of the Caribbean Islands was wiped out less than a hundred years after the first landing of Columbus. Thousands of mainland Indians died, too.

Las Casas lived to the age of ninety-two. For most of his life, he worked to help the Indians.

D. FR. BARTHOLOME DE LAS CASAS
Del Orden de Predicadores, Obispo de Chiapa
Varon apostolico, y el mas zeloso de la felicidad
de los Indios.
Nació en Sevilla el año de 1474, y murió en Ma
el de 1566.

Library of Congress

Lesson 6   France in the New World

WORDS TO UNDERSTAND

Discuss the meanings of these words.

strait   **encouraged**   **methods**

NEW WORDS IN SENTENCES

1. The explorers were looking for a **strait,** or passageway of water, between the Atlantic Ocean and the Pacific Ocean.

2. Stories of the New World **encouraged** more Frenchmen to explore America.

3. The Indians knew how to trap animals, and they taught their trapping **methods** to the French explorers.

AS YOU READ

As you read this selection, try to answer these questions.

1. Who were some of the French explorers? What were they looking for and what did they find?

2. What were some characteristics of the French colonies?

THE READING SELECTION

France was a little behind Spain, Portugal, and England in sending explorers to the New World. One of the first explorers for France was Giovanni da Verrazano, an Italian. He hoped to find a **strait** through the new land that would lead to Asia. Verrazano crossed the Atlantic in 1524 and landed on the coast of present-day North Carolina. He then sailed along the Atlantic coast to Newfoundland, Canada. From there, he returned to France. Verrazano was certain that he had found the beginning of a new route to Asia.

More French explorers now were **encouraged** to go to the New World. Jacques Cartier sailed from France and in 1534 explored the St. Lawrence River in Canada. He found that he could not get to Asia by this water route since the river was blocked on the western end. Cartier made another trip to America, once again in hopes of finding a route to Asia. This time, he met Indians of the area. From them, he learned **methods** of fur trapping.

Another Frenchman, Samuel de Champlain, explored the Atlantic coast from Nova Scotia to Cape Cod. During his explorations, he became good friends with the Huron Indians. In 1608, he founded the colony of Quebec.

Other French explorers were Jacques Marquette, Louis Joliet, and Robert de La Salle. Marquette, a priest, and Louis Joliet, a trader, explored the Mississippi

In 1682, Robert de La Salle was met by the Taensa Indians near what is now Natchez, Mississippi.

River in 1672. By this time, the French explorers realized that these new lands would not lead them to Asia. However, they continued to look for treasures in America.

In 1682, Robert de La Salle explored from the Illinois River to the Gulf of Mexico. He named the territory Louisiana and claimed it for France.

France, like Spain, was interested mainly in finding treasure. Most French colonies were located in Canada. There they found a new sort of treasure— furs. The fur trade became one of the main French activities in America. It often controlled French relations with Indian tribes. The tribes were often the sources of furs for the French. The French would trade guns and other goods for beaver and other animal skins. This trade increased Indian hunting and led to the disappearance of some animals, like the beaver, from several areas. The fur trade also affected relations among the tribes themselves, since it brought the gun into the area for the first time. Some tribes had guns before others did. This helped cause some wars, and changed the outcome of others.

The French colonies did not attract many settlers. France allowed no freedom of religion. It allowed almost no self-government. In addition, the French did not permit their settlers to trade with any other country. The result was that the French colonies grew very slowly. As late as 1750, there were fewer than 100,000 settlers in the French lands.

3. French explorers in the New World were mainly interested in
    a. exploring the Pacific Coast.
    b. finding treasure.
    c. building colonies.
    d. selling slaves to the Spanish explorers.
4. Most French colonies
    a. were located in Canada.
    b. attracted many settlers.
    c. governed themselves.
    d. traded with countries other than France.

COMPREHENSION CHECK

A. Recognizing the Main Idea
This selection as a whole tells you
1. how Marquette and Joliet explored the Mississippi River.
2. about Indian methods of trapping animals for furs.
3. about French explorers and French colonies in the New World.
4. about Champlain and the Huron Indians.

B. Selecting Important Details
Choose the ending that best completes each statement.
1. Verrazano was all of the following EXCEPT
    a. an explorer for France.
    b. an Italian.
    c. an explorer who thought he found a route to Asia.
    d. the founder of Quebec.
2. Samuel de Champlain
    a. was an enemy of the Huron Indians.
    b. founded the colony of Quebec.
    c. explored the Mississippi River.
    d. all of the above.

C. Completion
Fill in the word or words that best complete each sentence.
1. The Mississippi River was explored by _____ and _____.
2. La Salle named _____ and claimed it for France.
3. The explorer who became friends with the Huron Indians and founded the colony of Quebec was _____.
4. Cartier explored the _____.

D. Vocabulary
Match the words with the definitions.

Words	Definitions
1. strait	a. to give hope to
2. encourage	b. a passageway of water connecting two large bodies of water
3. method	c. to be happy
	d. a way of doing something
	e. a narrow strip of land connecting two large land areas

Lesson 7 England in the New World

WORDS TO UNDERSTAND

Discuss the meanings of these words.

dominant   indentured
proprietary   prejudice

NEW WORDS IN SENTENCES

1. Spain used to be the **dominant** European nation, a world power.

2. The **proprietary** colonies were under the rule of their owners, or proprietors.

3. The **indentured** servants had a contract to work for their masters for seven years.

4. Many English people came to the New World for religious freedom, to avoid religious **prejudice.**

AS YOU READ

As you read this selection, try to answer these questions.

1. Why did English people come to the New World?

2. What three different types of English colonies existed in America?

THE READING SELECTION

During the 1500s and 1600s several European nations established New World colonies. Spain was the **dominant** nation for a time, but it gradually became less of a world power. In 1588, England defeated the great Spanish Armada, or fleet of warships. England, with its powerful navy, became a leading nation in world affairs.

England began to set up colonies in the New World in 1585. Some English colonists came to America hoping to find silver and gold. However, most colonists came for other reasons. Some people wanted to find religious freedom. Others came because they hoped for a better life. Some settlers did not like the laws of their home country. They moved to America for more political freedom.

For more than 100 years, the English colonial system spread along the Atlantic coast from the border of Florida to Canada. These colonies were organized as **proprietary,** royal, or self-governing colonies.

Proprietary colonies were those belonging to a person or group of people. They were actually large grants of land given to owners, or proprietors. The proprietor held the colony's charter and controlled its government. Most proprietary colonies soon became royal colonies.

The royal colonies were controlled by English rulers and the English government.

Self-governing colonies were ruled by the colonists living in them. Only Rhode Island and Connecticut were self-governing colonies.

The first successful English colony in the New World was Jamestown, Virginia, in 1607. It was started as a business investment by an English group. They called themselves "Gentlemen Adventurers." At first, few of the settlers considered their settlement a new home. They had hoped to find gold and precious stones and to bring these riches back to Europe. Later, the settlers organized into a society. Many of the Jamestown settlers were **indentured** servants. In return for their passage to America, they agreed to work as servants for two to seven years. At the end of their service, they became free citizens.

Plymouth and Massachusetts Bay Colony were started by religious groups. Plymouth was settled in 1620 by Pilgrims. The Puritans founded the Massachusetts Bay Colony in 1629. Both groups came to America to escape religious **prejudice.** The two settlements joined together to form the colony of Massachusetts in 1631.

Maryland was founded in 1634 by Lord Baltimore. It was a colony for Catholics who wanted to escape religious prejudice.

Rhode Island was founded in 1636 by Roger Williams. He had been forced to leave Massachusetts because he did not accept the religion of that colony.

North and South Carolina were founded in 1663. They were personal landholdings for a group of British nobles.

New York was called New Amsterdam when it belonged to the Dutch. In 1664, the English took it from the Dutch and changed its name in honor of the Duke of York.

Pennsylvania was founded in 1682 by William Penn. He started the colony as a place for Quakers, a religious group in England. Pennsylvania offered freedom of religion to its settlers.

Georgia was started in 1733. Some of its early settlers had been in English prisons. Many had been in prison for not paying their debts. They were given their freedom for settling in Georgia.

English Colonies in America

Area settled by 1750

NORTH AMERICA
© FPC

NIEUW AMSTERDAM OFTE NUE NIEUW IORX OPT TEYLANT MAN

Above is the colony of New Amsterdam. The picture was painted in 1653, a few years before the colony became British. At right, women arrive at the Jamestown colony. The first English women came to America in 1619.

COMPREHENSION CHECK

A. Recognizing the Main Idea

This selection as a whole tells you that

1. there were fewer English colonies than Spanish colonies in North America.
2. English colonists were mainly interested in gold and silver.
3. English colonists settled in the New World for many reasons other than the desire for gold and silver.
4. Jamestown was the last successful English colony.

B. Selecting Important Details

Choose the ending that best completes each statement below.

1. The English colonies in America were located mainly
   a. in Canada.
   b. along the Atlantic coast from the border of Florida to Canada.
   c. in South America.
   d. along the entire Atlantic coast in North and South America.
2. Many colonists came to the English colonies to find
   a. religious freedom.
   b. political freedom.
   c. gold.
   d. all of the above.
3. Royal colonies were
   a. ruled by the colonists living in them.
   b. controlled by the English government.
   c. large grants of land given to proprietors.
   d. ruled by indentured servants.

4. Jamestown was
   a. the first successful English colony in the New World.
   b. started by Quakers.
   c. settled entirely by indentured servants.
   d. all of the above.

C. True or False

Decide whether each of these statements is true or false.

1. England became a leading nation after defeating the Spanish Armada.
2. Plymouth and Massachusetts Bay Colony were started by people hoping to find silver and gold.
3. New York was called New Amsterdam when it belonged to Spain.
4. Pennsylvania was started by Quakers who had been in English prisons for not paying their debts.

D. Vocabulary

Match the words with the definitions.

Words	Definitions
1. dominant	a. a slave
2. proprietary	b. owned by someone
3. indentured	c. stronger than others
4. prejudice	d. bound by contract to a master
	e. an opinion against something
	f. self-ruled

E. Ask Yourself

If you had come to America in 1690, would you have chosen a Spanish, French, or English colony for your home? Why?

The Mayflower Compact

Late in November 1620, a small boat neared the Cape Cod shore. Aboard were fifty men, twenty women, and thirty-four children. These new settlers faced a strange land, approaching winter, and political problems.

Aboard the ship were many who were known as Pilgrims. These people were English, but they disagreed with the Church of England. As a result, they made long journeys in search of religious freedom. Many had moved to Holland in 1609. But by 1620, they were finding it hard to keep their English language and ways. They made an agreement with a merchant to seek a new home in English territory across the sea. In 1620, they set sail aboard the *Mayflower*.

However, members of the Church of England were also on board the *Mayflower*. Serious trouble broke out between the two groups. Strange as it may seem, the Pilgrims did not extend their own religious freedom to others. Although they wanted the right to follow their own beliefs, they tried to force others to accept the Pilgrim view.

With the *Mayflower* lying offshore, the settlers decided to draw up some rules for the colony. The Mayflower Compact, as these rules are called, was one of the first European efforts at self-government in the New World. In our words of today it would say:

> We combine ourselves into a group to better serve our purposes, and by virtue of this pledge, to pass equal laws as shall be best for the good of all in the colony.

L. C. Handy Studios

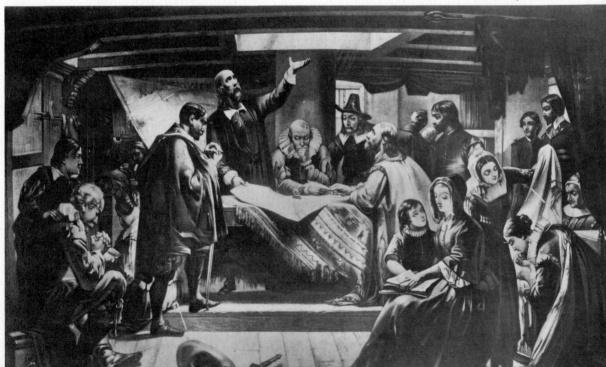

Lesson 8 The Success of English Colonies in the New World

WORDS TO UNDERSTAND

Discuss the meanings of these words.

legislature   **libel**

NEW WORDS IN SENTENCES

1. Laws for a state are made by the state **legislature**.

2. His damaging statement was not true, and he could be sued for **libel** for having made the remark.

AS YOU READ

As you read this selection, try to answer these questions.

1. What are some examples of the democratic liberties enjoyed by the English colonies in America?

2. How did the farming of the southern colonies differ from the farming of the other colonies?

THE READING SELECTION

Review. Spain was mainly interested in sending missionaries to the New World and in bringing back gold and silver. Spanish colonies did not grow large because they had no self-government and little religious freedom. They had no industries, and no trade with countries other than Spain. French colonies remained small for the same reasons. However, the French found their treasure in furs. The English came to America for many reasons. Some colonies were started as business investments. Others were started by religious groups. They were organized as proprietary, royal, or self-governing colonies. ☆

Spain, France, and England set up colonies in the New World. Each of them hoped to develop a new empire in America. However, it was England that developed the richest, most populated colonies in the New World. By 1773, the English had established thirteen colonies along the Atlantic coast.

The success of the English colonies can be seen when they are compared to the French colonies. In 1750, France had fewer than 100,000 settlers in America. By this time, English colonies had over a million settlers. French settlers were mainly interested in hunting, trading, and fishing. The English settlers had wider interests and choices.

The New England colonies were engaged in lumbering, shipping, and fish-

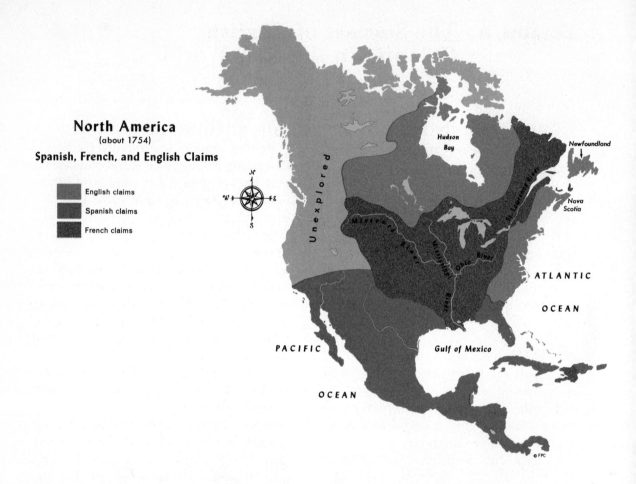

North America
(about 1754)

Spanish, French, and English Claims

English claims

Spanish claims

French claims

Unexplored

Hudson Bay

Newfoundland

Nova Scotia

Mission River

Mississippi River

Ohio River

St. Lawrence River

ATLANTIC

OCEAN

PACIFIC

OCEAN

Gulf of Mexico

© FPC

ing. The central, or middle, colonies had many small, family farms. Because of their large-scale wheat farming, the middle colonies were called the "bread colonies."

There was a different kind of farming in the southern colonies. Southern farmers grew rice, tobacco, and indigo plants. Some southern colonists had large farms, or plantations. These plantations made use of indentured servants and of slaves from Africa. By this time, almost all indentured servants were white Europeans. The slaves were black Africans.

Jobs and the cheap farmland in the English colonies attracted many settlers. But settlers were also interested in the promise of democracy and human rights. The English colonies in America provided for self-rule and many democratic rights for the people.

All English colonists were guaranteed the Rights of Englishmen. These rights included trial by jury, freedom to assemble, and some freedom of speech. There also was much self-government in the colonies. Self-government began as early as 1619. In that year, the House of Burgesses was set up in Virginia. It was the first **legislature** in the New World.

Some rules of life and government were established early in the English colonies. The Pilgrims aboard the *Mayflower* signed the Mayflower Compact in 1620. They agreed to make and obey needed laws. In 1639, the Fundamental Orders of Connecticut was written. This was the first written constitution in America. It explained the role of government.

Settlers in many English colonies were active in pressing for democratic rights. Town meetings were a regular part of life in New England during the 1600s and 1700s. At these meetings, the settlers voiced their opinions on local government. However, most democratic rights did not apply to women. Colonial women worked as hard as the men and faced as many dangers. But women were given few rights under the law.

Some English colonists wanted more rights. The Rights of Englishmen did not, for example, generally include much freedom of the press. However, freedom of the press was established in the colonies after the Zenger case in 1735. John Peter Zenger was a New York newspaper publisher. He was put in jail for printing criticism of the governor of New York. The governor claimed that any criticism, even if it was true, was a **libel.** This idea was accepted in England at the time. Zenger fought against the libel rule. He demanded the right to print truthful criticism. At his trial, the judge demanded that he be found guilty. However, the jury ruled that Zenger was innocent. The decision formed the legal basis for a free press in the English colonies.

A problem in some English colonies was little religious freedom, against which Anne Hutchinson (top) fought. There was also some conflict with Indians. In Jamestown, the marriage of Pocahontas and John Rolfe eased this problem for a time.

COMPREHENSION CHECK

A. Recognizing the Main Idea

This selection as a whole tells you that

1. English colonists were attracted by economic and democratic advantages.
2. English colonies had fewer settlers than French colonies.
3. there were no economic advantages in the English colonies.
4. none of the English colonies was self-governing.

B. Selecting Important Details

Choose the ending that best completes each statement.

1. By 1750, the English colonies in the New World
   a. had fewer than 100,000 settlers.
   b. had over a million settlers.
   c. were all located in the New England area.
   d. were all engaged in large-scale farming.
2. The name "bread colonies" was used for
   a. all the English colonies.
   b. the English colonies in the New England area.
   c. the English colonies in the South.
   d. the English colonies in the middle area.
3. Women in the English colonies
   a. had the same rights as men under the law.
   b. were guaranteed the Rights of Englishmen.
   c. had few rights under the law.
   d. did not have to work very hard.
4. Freedom of the press in the New World was helped by the
   a. Fundamental Orders of Connecticut.
   b. Mayflower Compact.
   c. John Peter Zenger case.
   d. town meetings of New England.

C. True or False

Decide whether each of these statements is true or false.

1. The Rights of Englishmen did not include much freedom of the press.
2. Plantation farming was carried on in New England.
3. The House of Burgesses was the first legislature in the New World.
4. The Mayflower Compact was the first written constitution in America.

D. Vocabulary

Match the words with the definitions.

Words	Definitions
1. legislature	a. a damaging falsehood
2. libel	b. to be afraid
	c. a lawmaking body
	d. a court of law

E. Ask Yourself

Which Rights of Englishmen are today also the rights of Americans? What do you consider to be your most precious liberty?

Roger Williams and Anne Hutchinson: Workers for Freedom

The Puritans came to America because they had no religious freedom in England. But once they were settled in Massachusetts, they did not allow others to have religious freedom. Those who did not accept the Puritans' beliefs were punished or forced to leave Massachusetts.

Anne Hutchinson and Roger Williams were two New England colonists who sought freedom and justice for all people.

Roger Williams, a minister, came to the Massachusetts Colony in 1631. He settled in Salem. Soon he created a stir with his views on Indians, the church, and government. Many leaders of the colony were shocked by his words and actions.

Roger Williams spoke out for greater fairness to Indians. He also preached that no government should punish people for their religious views. He favored religious liberty in a colony where the leaders limited religious freedom. In the Massachusetts Colony, government leaders were closely tied to religious leaders. Taxes paid by the colony's people helped support the church. Roger Williams believed that churches should not receive government money. He believed that churches should not be controlled by government officials.

His views angered many of the colony's Puritan officials. They ordered Roger Williams to return to England. Instead, with the aid of the Narragansett Indians, he left Massachusetts. Together with a few followers, he settled near what is now Rhode Island. Before long, the area became a center for those favoring the separation of the government and the church. Roger Williams was the leader of the people for almost fifty years. He continued to speak out for religious freedom and fair treatment of Indians until his death in 1683.

Anne Hutchinson came to Massachusetts with her family in 1634. The Hutchinsons soon learned that there was little religious freedom in the colony. Anne Hutchinson stated her religious views clearly and forcefully. She questioned the views of the colony's ministers. She challenged their power. She began holding separate Sunday meetings, teaching the sermon in her own way.

Anne Hutchinson's actions angered the Puritan leaders. At that time, women were expected only to work in the home and be followers, not leaders. In most cases, Puritan ministers were men. Also, ministers were usually college educated. Few women had the opportunity to go to college.

Because Anne Hutchinson preached her own religious views, she and her family were forced to leave Massachusetts in 1638. She and a few others founded the town of Pocasset. Today, this town is Portsmouth, New Hampshire. She was a leader in Pocasset for the next five years. Anne Hutchinson was the first woman to serve in an American government.

Lesson 9   The French and Indian War

WORDS TO UNDERSTAND
Discuss the meanings of these words.

rivals   **allies**   **ceded**

NEW WORDS IN SENTENCES
1. Spain and Portugal were **rivals** in the race for colonies.
2. A weak nation needs **allies** in a war with a strong country.
3. France **ceded** Canada to England and never regained that territory.

AS YOU READ
As you read this selection, try to answer these questions.
1. What were some of the reasons for the outbreak of the French and Indian War?
2. What were some results of the French and Indian War?

THE READING SELECTION
England often fought France for world leadership. They fought four wars between the years of 1689 and 1763. The troops of the two **rivals** fought in Europe, India, Canada, and the Ohio Valley in North America.

The last of the wars between Britain and France began in North America. Colonial rivalry in America led to open warfare. In this fighting, the French had many Indian **allies.** This gave France great strength. The war in America lasted from 1754 to 1763. It is called the French and Indian War. This name is used because the British fought both the French and the Indians allied with the French.

The French and Indian War began in the Ohio Valley. This large area was claimed by both the French and British. In 1754, a young Virginian, George Washington, led a force into that area. His job was to strengthen the British position. However, Washington was attacked by French troops and had to surrender. A year later he was involved in another British defeat. This time the colonial and British forces, led by General Braddock, lost nearly 1,000 men against a force of French and Indian fighters.

The war went badly for Britain until 1757. In that year, the great British statesman William Pitt was put in charge of the war. He reorganized the army and drew up new battle plans. Pitt decided to make use of Britain's powerful navy and to attack the French in Canada.

In 1758, the British advanced in both Canada and the Ohio Valley. The next year they seized the important French city of Quebec. Although the war dragged on, it was clear the British had the advantage. A peace treaty was finally signed in 1763. France was forced to agree to several terms.

1. France **ceded** all its Canadian lands to Britain.

2. France also ceded to Britain all its lands east of the Mississippi River, except for New Orleans.

3. France ceded New Orleans and all its lands west of the Mississippi River to Spain.

As a result of the French and Indian War, France lost its power in North America. Britain became not only the major American power but a world leader. Britain had begun what soon would be the greatest of all colonial empires.

Defeat in the French and Indian War cost France its land in North America. The lands were ceded to England and Spain.

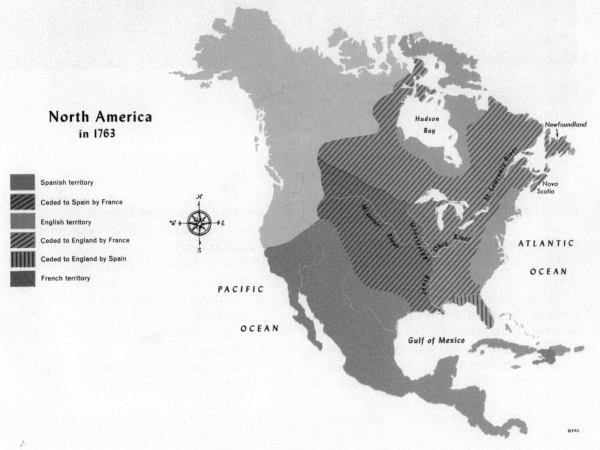

North America
in 1763

Spanish territory

Ceded to Spain by France

English territory

Ceded to England by France

Ceded to England by Spain

French territory

Hudson Bay

Newfoundland

Nova Scotia

St. Lawrence River

Missouri River

Mississippi River

Ohio River

ATLANTIC

OCEAN

PACIFIC

OCEAN

Gulf of Mexico

©FPC

The British were badly defeated at the Battle of the Wilderness
in the Ohio Valley in 1755. British redcoats were easy targets
for the French and Indian forces, who took cover on higher
ground. British General Edward Braddock died from the
wounds he received. His twenty-three-year-old aide, George
Washington, survived.

COMPREHENSION CHECK

A. Recognizing the Main Idea

This selection as a whole tells you
that

1. the French and Indian War was
part of the fight for world leadership
between France and Britain.

2. the French and Indian War was
caused by Indian attacks on the French.

3. there was no winner in the French
and Indian War.

4. the peace treaty of 1763 gave Canada to France.

B. Selecting Important Details

Choose the ending that best completes each statement.

1. A major cause of the French and
Indian War was the

  a. Indians' struggle for world leadership.

  b. French desire for trade with
Britain.

  c. struggle between Britain and
France for control of the Ohio
Valley.

  d. desire of the British to win Indian allies.

2. In the fighting in the French and Indian War, the British
    a. were successful from the beginning.
    b. suffered defeats at first but won in the end.
    c. won many victories at first but lost in the end.
    d. were completely successful.

3. All the following were results of the French and Indian War EXCEPT that
    a. Britain became the major power in America.
    b. France ceased to be a major power in North America.
    c. the Indians came out of the war as world leaders.
    d. Britain came out of the war as a world leader.

4. As a result of the French and Indian War, Britain won
    a. no new lands.
    b. all of Canada and Florida.
    c. New Orleans and lands west of the Mississippi River.
    d. Canada and all French lands east of the Mississippi River except New Orleans.

C. True or False

Decide whether each of these statements is true or false.

1. During the French and Indian War, the Indians were mainly on the side of the British.

2. The force led by General Braddock was badly defeated.

3. William Pitt organized the French army and drew up battle plans.

4. As a result of the French and Indian War, Spain received New Orleans and French lands west of the Mississippi.

D. Vocabulary

Match the words with the definitions.

Words	Definitions
1. rival	a. to give up
2. allies	b. a friend
3. cede	c. to make complete
	d. one who tries to defeat another
	e. friends or supporters

E. Map Skills

This map shows North America in 1763. Certain areas are labeled with letters. Match each description below with the correct letter. There is one extra letter.

1. The lands given by France to Spain after 1763.

2. The lands given by France to Britain after 1763.

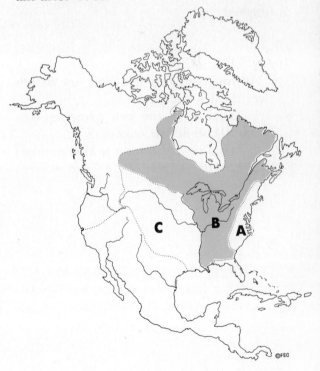

49

Lesson 10　Living in America: Life in the Colonies

Discuss the meanings of these words.
immigrants　　　**leisure**
apprenticeships

NEW WORDS IN SENTENCES
1. When the **immigrants** arrived from foreign countries, they hoped to become Americans.
2. People would take **apprenticeships** in order to be trained as doctors.
3. Colonists found ways to use the **leisure** time they had when work was finished.

AS YOU READ
As you read this selection, try to answer these questions.
1. What were the two growing economic classes in the colonies?
2. What was education in the colonies like?

THE READING SELECTION
European settlers in the New World had brought European cultures and ways of life with them. However, life in America was different in some ways from life in the older European nations.

Population. The population of the British colonies was changing. By the mid-1700s, more people were being born in America than were arriving from Europe. The **immigrants** came from different nations. By 1763, only half of the people in the British colonies were English. The other half were Irish, Scottish, German, Dutch, African, or other nationalities.

Almost all the Africans in America were slaves. Slavery existed in all the colonies. There were some free blacks. They were usually the descendants of indentured servants or of slaves who had bought freedom. However, even free blacks had few rights.

The colonial population was also growing. In early years a high death rate had limited growth. In later years, food and water supplies, shelter, and health care improved. This lowered the death rate.

Economic life. Many Europeans came to the New World to find greater opportunity. In Europe, people in the lower and middle classes often had little chance to improve their lives. In America, they could get a fresh start.

By the mid-1700s, cities in the colonies were growing. They were helped along by a general population increase. This picture shows Baltimore in 1752.

Land was easier to get in America than it was in Europe. Some colonists owned large amounts of land, especially in New York and the southern colonies. However, in most colonies, the land was divided into small plots owned by free farmers. By 1763, nearly all colonial farmers owned their own land. There was a growing class of independent farmers.

There was also a small but growing class of merchants in the colonies. Many merchants traded in tobacco, furs, and grain. There were often several steps in trading. Merchants might buy furs and trade them for horses. The horses were then traded for grain. The grain was sold to a British merchant.

Education. The colonies differed in the schooling they provided. New England colonies often required the teaching of reading and writing. More New Englanders could read and write than could people in any other section. The middle colonies also had many schools. These schools were often begun by churches or religious groups. The southern colonies had fewer schools. The wealthy often hired private teachers.

Apprenticeships were important in many fields. An apprentice learned a trade, skill, or art by working with an experienced person. Most doctors, for example, learned medicine in this way. Yet colleges were growing in the colonies. By the Revolution, there were nine of them.

Education in the colonies was intended for white males. Women and slaves usually received little schooling. It was thought unnecessary for their work.

Social life. Life in the colonies was hard work. Much time was spent just getting food and clothing. However,

leisure time did begin to increase. Work was often combined with fun. The church was often the center of social life. Barn raisings, corn huskings, quilting bees, and taffy pulls were common activities. They were an opportunity for people to get together and have fun while they worked. Horseback riding and hunting became popular, especially in the southern colonies. Music and dancing were also popular.

COMPREHENSION CHECK

A. Recognizing the Main Idea

This selection as a whole tells you that

1. colonists did not have time for leisure activities.
2. colonists continued to feel like Europeans.
3. religion played a small part in the lives of the colonists.
4. colonial life differed in some ways from life in Europe.

B. Selecting Important Details

Choose the ending that best completes each statement.

1. The population of the colonies began to increase because
   a. colleges started attracting students.
   b. education became available to everyone.
   c. doctors were always required to go to medical school.
   d. there was improved health care and better food supplies.
2. Land in the colonies was owned
   a. only by wealthy planters.
   b. usually by small farmers.
   c. only by the British monarch.
   d. by the Indian tribes.
3. Blacks in America
   a. were all slaves.
   b. were all free in some colonies.
   c. had equal rights after buying freedom from slavery.
   d. had few rights even if they were not slaves.
4. Education in schools was
   a. the same in all colonies.
   b. usually given only to white males.
   c. necessary for the work of slaves.
   d. necessary for learning trades.

C. Vocabulary

Match the words with the definitions.

Words	Definitions
1. immigrants	a. free time
2. apprenticeship	b. type of boat
3. leisure	c. working with a trained person to learn a skill
	d. type of book
	e. new settlers who come from a foreign country

D. Chronology

Arrange these events in the order in which they happened.

1. Jamestown established
2. First people arrive in America
3. French and Indian War
4. House of Burgesses established
5. Columbus lands
6. Beginning of Mound Builder cultures

The Atlantic Slave Trade

In 1619, a Dutch ship sold twenty African workers to Jamestown colony planters. These twenty Africans were sold as indentured servants. But it was not long before Africans were being brought in and sold as slaves. The indentured servant could hope to be freed after about seven years of service. But the slave had little hope of ever gaining freedom.

It is likely that about 10 million black Africans were brought to the New World as slaves during the seventeenth and eighteenth centuries. They were usually kidnapped, chained, and taken to America in slave ships under conditions unfit for human beings. Because of these unhealthy conditions, millions are believed to have died making the trip.

One visitor to a slave ship described the treatment of the blacks in these words: "human beings . . . packed up and wedged together as tight as they could cram, in low cells three feet high. . . . The height sometimes between decks was only eighteen inches, so that the unfortunate beings could not turn round or even on their sides. . . . A living man was sometimes dragged up, and his companion [chained to him] was a dead body. . . . Many took the first opportunity of leaping overboard and getting rid, in this way, of an intolerable life."

Thus, while millions of people came to America in search of freedom and a new life, millions of others were brought as slaves.

Before slaves were bought, they were checked carefully to make sure they were healthy and could work hard. The sale in this picture was probably in Africa. The buyer would take the slave to America and sell him again.

Culver Pictures, Inc.

Unit 1 Summary   The People of Early America

The First People in America

Sometime between 20,000 and 40,000 years ago, people began coming to America. They crossed a land bridge that then connected Asia and Alaska. Many groups of people crossed the bridge over a period of thousands of years. They hunted big game for food. They slowly moved across North and South America.

As the big game died out, farming was developed. The two main cultures were the Desert and the Eastern. In the eastern areas, the Mound Builders had a highly developed civilization.

By the time Europeans arrived, the Mayas, Aztecs, and Incas had developed advanced civilizations in Mexico and Peru. The Indians of North America had developed different ways of life fitted to different environments. There were ten main Indian cultural areas in what is now the United States. Depending on the environment, food was obtained by hunting, fishing, gathering, or farming.

Clothes and houses were made out of the materials available in the different areas. Political systems also differed.

The various Indian cultures were alike in some ways. But they differed greatly from the European cultures of the white settlers. The white settlers and the Indians had different ideas about owning land, sharing, keeping promises, and justice. The differences brought them into conflict.

Europeans in the New World

In 1492, Christopher Columbus sailed west across the Atlantic Ocean. He was looking for an all-water route to Asia. Asian goods were in demand. Europeans wanted a faster route to Asia that would not be controlled by Italians. When Columbus landed, he thought he was in Asia. He did not realize there was another continent between Europe and Asia. He called the Native Americans "Indians."

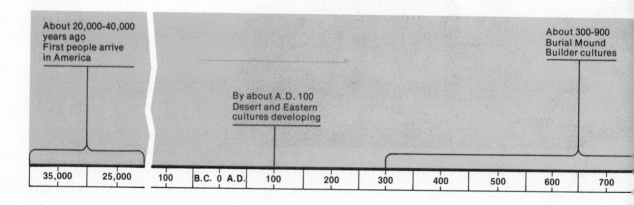

About 20,000-40,000 years ago
First people arrive in America

By about A.D. 100
Desert and Eastern cultures developing

About 300-900
Burial Mound Builder cultures

| 35,000 | 25,000 | 100 | B.C. 0 A.D. | 100 | 200 | 300 | 400 | 500 | 600 | 700 |

After Columbus's voyage, other explorers were encouraged to sail west to look for a water route to Asia. European explorers searched the continent for a strait that would connect the Atlantic and Pacific oceans.

One of the Spanish explorers was Juan Ponce de León, who explored Florida. Hernando Cortés explored Mexico and conquered the Aztec civilization. The Spanish had colonies in Central and South America and in California. Spanish colonies did not grow large because there was little freedom and few ways of making a living. Spain was mainly interested in sending missionaries to the New World and in bringing back gold and silver.

French explorers included Jacques Cartier, who explored the St. Lawrence River in Canada, and Samuel de Champlain, who founded Quebec. Most French colonies were located in Canada. Like the Spanish colonies, French colonies remained small. The French found their treasure in furs. They learned trapping methods from the Indians.

English Colonies in America

England had established thirteen colonies along the Atlantic coast by 1773. Some were started as business investments. Others were started by religious groups. They were organized as proprietary, royal, or self-governing colonies. The colonists engaged in various kinds of industries and farming.

English colonies were the richest and most populated. They allowed religious freedom, self-government, and many democratic rights. Many people settled in the colonies to find religious or political freedom. Settlers were also attracted by jobs and cheap land. Some people came as indentured servants. Others were brought from Africa as slaves.

The French and Indian War was fought from 1754 to 1763. The British defeated the French and the Indians allied with the French. France was forced to cede most of its North American lands. France lost its power in the New World, and Britain began its powerful colonial empire.

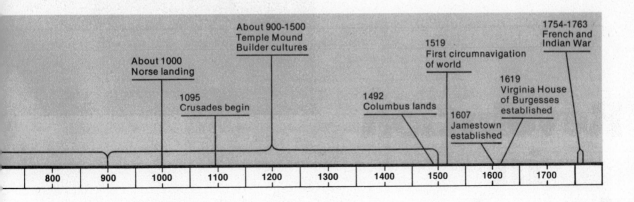

unit
2

Pulling Down the Statue of George III by Johannes A. Oertel, courtesy New York Historical Society

Revolution in America

Change was coming to the English colonies. Popular feeling
against England rose—one crowd even pulled down a statue of
the king (left). In the end, the decision was made to sign the
Declaration of Independence (above). The war that followed
made independence a reality.

Lesson 1 Disputes Between England and Colonial America

WORDS TO UNDERSTAND

Discuss the meanings of these words.

mercantilism **enumerated** **repealed**
enforce **financial**

NEW WORDS IN SENTENCES

1. Under **mercantilism,** colonies were supposed to help build up trade and industry in the ruling country.

2. Additional troops arrived to help **enforce** the new laws.

3. The items that were listed, or **enumerated,** included many badly needed things.

4. Increasing debt caused the family **financial** problems.

5. The new law caused so many problems that the government **repealed** it.

AS YOU READ

As you read this selection, try to answer these questions.

1. In what ways did mercantilism and the Navigation Acts hurt the colonists?

2. Why did Britain issue the Proclamation of 1763?

3. What were the major points of the Grenville program?

THE READING SELECTION

After the French and Indian War, the American colonists felt safer. They felt more able to take care of themselves. The British had a large debt after the war. They felt that money should come from the colonies they protected. Between 1763 and 1774, two methods were used to get this money. One was placing taxes on items in use in the colonies. The other was **mercantilism,** a policy under which colonial trade was controlled. Neither of these methods was really new. What was new was the British decision to strictly **enforce** old laws, as well as to add new ones.

Under mercantilism, the American colonies lost money in trade with Britain. They shipped raw materials to Britain and got manufactured goods back from Britain. For example, a colony might ship out raw lumber and receive back finished furniture. Since the furniture cost more than the raw lumber, the colonies had to pay the price difference in gold. This helped build British trade and industry. But it kept the colonists short of money.

Another example of mercantilism was the Navigation Acts. These had been in effect since the 1600s. But in the 1760s, they were strictly enforced. One of these acts stated that only ships owned by Britain or its American colonies could carry goods to the colonies. This provided more business for British and

A crowd of angry colonists hang a British tax collector from a pole.

colonial shipbuilders and owners. But it often raised prices for colonial merchants.

Another of the Navigation Acts **enumerated** certain materials that could be exported only to England. These included sugar, cotton, tobacco, and wool. This helped keep British industry supplied with raw materials. But it hurt colonists who might have received better prices from other nations.

At the same time, there was disagreement over relations with the Indians. In 1763, Pontiac, an Ottawa chief, led an Indian uprising. Soon after this fighting started, the British issued the Proclamation of 1763. This set the boundary for white settlements at the Appalachian Mountains. The proclamation was supposed to end fighting with the Indians. Colonists who owned land west of the mountains, or wanted to move there, protested. This became one more British-American disagreement.

In 1764, economic policy was again the center of attention. In that year, the British government was led by George Grenville. He prepared a **financial** program that included taxes on goods produced within the colonies. The main parts of his program included these.

The Sugar Act of 1764. Molasses imported from the British West Indies was not taxed. All other imported molasses was taxed. The act also raised duties and lowered limits on some other imports and exports.

The Currency Act of 1764. This law banned the printing of paper money in the colonies. This decreased the amount of money in circulation. As a result, it was harder to get loans or credit.

The Stamp Act of 1765. This law required that stamps be bought from the British. These were to be placed on all legal documents and other printed materials.

The Quartering Act of 1765. This was not part of Grenville's program, but it had a great effect on the colonies. It required colonists to provide housing and supplies for British troops. It reduced costs for England, and increased those for America.

The Grenville program combined stricter enforcement of old mercantilist policy with new taxes. It caused great protest in the colonies. The colonists, and even some British merchants, demanded that the Stamp Act be **repealed.** Parliament did repeal the act. But it also issued another act. This declared that the British government had a right to make any law it wished for the colonies. It was a warning to the colonists of things to come.

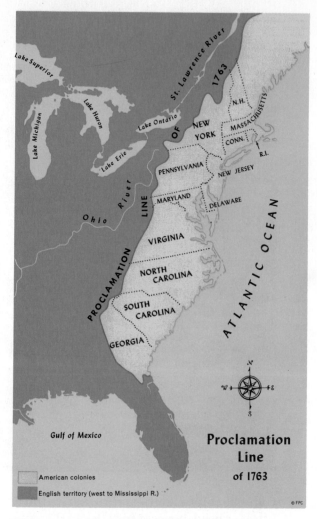

Proclamation Line of 1763

American colonies

English territory (west to Mississippi R.)

© FPC

The Proclamation of 1763 fixed the western boundary of the American colonies along the Appalachian Mountains. Colonists were forbidden to settle west of this line.

COMPREHENSION CHECK

A. Recognizing the Main Idea

This selection as a whole tells you that

1. conditions in the English colonies encouraged growth and independence.

2. the Grenville program succeeded.

3. mercantilism and taxes caused disputes between England and the colonies.

4. most colonists were afraid of the British rulers.

B. Selecting Important Details

Choose the ending that best completes each statement.

1. Mercantilism had the effect of making the colonists
   a. richer.
   b. poorer.
   c. more in favor of England.
   d. more in favor of taxes.

2. The Navigation Acts
   a. had long been in effect.
   b. were new laws.
   c. had nothing to do with trade.
   d. were favored by the colonists.

3. The Proclamation of 1763 closed off western lands in order to
   a. stop wars with Indian tribes.
   b. end England's control of the area.
   c. take land from the Indians.
   d. collect taxes in the area.

4. The new British economic policy included all of the following EXCEPT
   a. the purchase of special stamps for documents.
   b. stricter enforcement of mercantilist policy.
   c. the encouragement of American trade with other countries.
   d. new taxes.

C. True or False

Decide whether each of these statements is true or false.

1. Mercantilism and taxation of colonists were not new English policies in 1763.

2. After 1763, the Navigation Acts were strictly enforced.

3. The Ottawa chief who led the 1763 war against the British was Powhatan.

4. Grenville's program included no new taxes.

5. Under mercantilism, the colonies lost money.

D. Vocabulary

Write your own sentence for each of these words.

mercantilism   enumerate   repeal
enforce   financial

The Sons of Liberty

In 1765, the British government had put the Stamp Act into effect. The Stamp Act was only one part of the Grenville program, but it seemed to rouse greater bitterness than many of the other Grenville proposals.

It was not long before the English discovered that passing a tax was one thing and collecting that tax was something else. There was much protest against the Stamp Act. The home of Governor Hutchinson of Massachusetts was attacked and partly destroyed by a mob.

It was apparent that the colonists' protest was part of some organized movement. But who were the organizers? Soon, word began to emerge of a group called the Sons of Liberty. Their aim was to force the British to withdraw the hated Stamp Act. To do this, they tried to discourage stamp agents from doing their duty. They tried to stop Americans from buying stamps. They also helped to spread word of patriotic activities among the colonies.

To the British, the Sons of Liberty were a lawless band. To Americans, they were a group of patriots. What is the truth? The truth would seem to be that they were people devoted to the task of preventing the British from collecting a legal tax. To do this, they had to resort to breaking the law. Is it right for people to break the law to achieve even the most worthwhile results?

One thing is sure. The Sons of Liberty helped prepare the American colonists for the day when action would be needed to win independence from England.

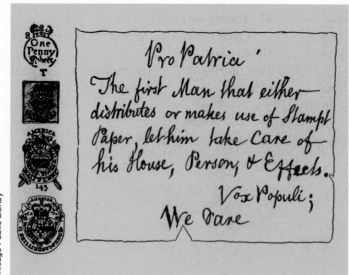

The Sons of Liberty used signs such as this one to make people afraid to obey the Stamp Act. At left are examples of British tax stamps.

Lesson 2 More Trouble for the Colonies: The Townshend Acts

WORDS TO UNDERSTAND

Discuss the meanings of these words.

revenue	writ of assistance
internal taxes	boycott
external taxes	

NEW WORDS IN SENTENCES

1. Taxes are used to raise **revenue** for the government.

2. **Internal taxes** are placed on goods produced within a country.

3. Taxes on items imported into a country are called **external taxes.**

4. A British **writ of assistance** permitted officials to search any place or person at any time.

5. The townspeople began a **boycott** of the store, refusing to buy anything there.

AS YOU READ

As you read this selection, try to answer these questions.

1. How did Townshend's plan differ from Grenville's?

2. Why did the colonists object to the Townshend Acts?

3. What caused the Boston Massacre?

THE READING SELECTION

In 1765, George Grenville fell from power in Britain. The next year, Charles Townshend led the government. He proposed a new plan to bring in **revenue** from the colonies.

Grenville's program had placed taxes on some items produced in the colonies themselves. These **internal taxes** failed. To replace them, Townshend proposed **external taxes.** These taxes were placed on imported goods before they arrived in the colonies. Thus, the colonists paid the tax indirectly, simply by buying the items. These items were glass, lead, paper, paints, and tea.

Townshend and Parliament thought that the new plan, called the Townshend Acts, would be accepted. But it was not. The colonists did not want to pay any taxes to support the British government. Tax dodging and smuggling became common in many colonies.

The British were determined to stop the smuggling. They issued special permission to search colonists and their property. This kind of special permission was called a **writ of assistance.** Writs of assistance allowed British officials to search anywhere at any time. The colonists felt that writs of assistance denied them their rights.

In addition, the British took other steps to enforce the Townshend Acts. When a writ of assistance was used to

The BLOODY MASSACRE perpetrated in King — Street — on March — by a party of the 29th Reg.t

Engrav'd Printed & Sold by Paul Revere Boston

Unhappy Boston! see thy Sons deplore,
Thy hallow'd Walks besmear'd with guiltless Gore.
While faithless P——n and his savage Bands,
With murd'rous Rancour stretch their bloody Hands;
Like fierce Barbarians grinning o'er their Prey,
Approve the Carnage, and enjoy the Day.

If scalding drops from Rage from Anguish Wrung
If speechless Sorrows lab'ring for a Tongue
Or if a weeping World can ought appease
The plaintive Ghosts of Victims such as these;
The Patriot's copious Tears for each are shed,
A glorious Tribute which embalms the Dead.

But know, Fate summons to that awful Goal,
Where Justice strips the Murd'rer of his Soul:
Should venal C——ts the scandal of the Land,
Snatch the relentless Villain from her Hand,
Keen Execrations on this Plate inscrib'd,
Shall reach a Judge who never can be brib'd.

The unhappy Sufferers were Mess.rs Sam.l Gray, Sam.l Maverick, Jam.s Caldwell, Crispus Attucks & Pat.k Carr
Killed. Six wounded; two of them (Christ.r Monk & John Clark) Mortally

Published in 1770 by Paul Revere Boston

64

make an arrest for smuggling, the person arrested was not tried by a jury. Such a case was tried by a judge alone. Many Americans felt that this denied them their right to a trial by jury.

The Townshend Acts angered many colonists. Movements to **boycott** the taxed goods were begun in Boston, New York, Philadelphia, and other important cities. Boycotts had been used successfully to fight the Stamp Act. But soon, violence broke out in some cities. Mobs attacked customs officers carrying out their jobs.

The outbreaks of violence angered the British. They felt the colonists were being unreasonable. Since British citizens paid taxes, it seemed only fair that the colonists pay their share. The colonial leaders replied that the British Parliament had no right to tax America simply to raise revenue. Furthermore, since the colonists had no representatives in the British Parliament, they should not be taxed at all. "No taxation without representation" became the cry of many colonial leaders. British leaders pointed out that many parts of Britain did not have direct representation in Parliament. The Parliament was supposed to represent all British subjects everywhere.

The actions of colonists in Boston were especially violent. A special British military force from Canada was sent to the Boston area. Soldiers and colonists soon were involved in quarrels. In March 1770, a force of soldiers fired on a crowd. Five Americans were killed in the "Boston Massacre," as the colonists soon named it. Among them was a runaway slave, Crispus Attucks, who had been active in anti-British work along the waterfront.

Americans and British were both shocked by the Boston Massacre. The British soldiers went on trial and were defended by two Americans. They were John Adams (later the second president of the United States) and Josiah Quincy, Jr. These American lawyers opposed the British policies but believed the soldiers deserved a fair trial. Only two soldiers received any punishment.

The day of the Boston Massacre, Parliament had taken the first steps toward repealing the Townshend Acts. Only the tax on tea was kept. The Townshend plan was one of many policies that the British later changed or repealed. The colonists had begun to feel that their protests could force the British to change laws. But the issue of taxation and representation now went beyond a single law. The colonists were outgrowing their loyalty to England. New leaders were bringing forward new ideas.

Opposite, the British fire into a crowd of colonists in Paul Revere's picture of the Boston Massacre. The picture was published in 1770, the same year as the shooting. The names of the colonists who were killed were listed below a poem that mourned their deaths.

COMPREHENSION CHECK

A. Recognizing the Main Idea

This selection as a whole tells you that

1. Townshend's program was different from Grenville's, but no more successful.
2. Townshend's program was aimed at helping the colonists.
3. Townshend proposed the same taxes as Grenville.
4. Townshend's program was very successful.

B. Selecting Important Details

Choose the ending that best completes each statement.

1. After 1763, England's plan of taxation for the colonists was to
   a. reduce colonial taxes.
   b. make the colonies richer.
   c. have the colonists pay more taxes.
   d. give writs of assistance to the colonists.
2. Charles Townshend's tax plan was based on the use of
   a. internal taxes.
   b. neither internal nor external taxes.
   c. both internal and external taxes.
   d. external taxes.
3. Writs of assistance were used to allow
   a. the collection of taxes.
   b. smuggling.
   c. jury cases.
   d. searches by officers of the law.

4. As a result of the Boston Massacre and other actions
   a. the Townshend Acts were strengthened.
   b. the Townshend Acts were repealed.
   c. British troops were sent to Boston.
   d. a special tax was placed on tea.

C. True or False

Decide whether each of these statements is true or false.

1. The Townshend Acts placed taxes on glass, lead, paint, and other items produced in the colonies.
2. Movements to buy out the taxed items began in many cities.
3. All cases of smuggling were tried before juries.
4. Many colonial leaders argued, "No taxation without representation."
5. Five Americans were killed by British soldiers in the Boston Massacre.

D. Vocabulary

Match the words with the definitions.

Words	Definitions
1. revenue	a. refusal to buy a product
2. internal taxes	b. unlimited permission to search
3. external taxes	c. income
4. writ of assistance	d. tax on imported goods
5. boycott	e. a loan
	f. tax on goods produced within a country

Lesson 3   The Colonists and Their Leaders

WORDS TO UNDERSTAND
Discuss the meanings of these words.

radical   **moderate**   **Loyalists**

NEW WORDS IN SENTENCES

1. The **radical** leaders did not want any compromise with England.

2. The **moderate** leaders wanted to settle the disagreement without war against England.

3. Colonists who still supported England were called **Loyalists.**

AS YOU READ

As you read this selection, try to answer these questions.

1. How did many colonial leaders regard the question of independence?

2. Who were some of the outstanding colonial leaders of protest?

3. Who were the Loyalists? What was their position?

THE READING SELECTION

Review. Britain and the American colonists drew apart between 1763 and 1774. One reason for this was a growing colonial sense of independence. Another reason was the British effort to put tighter controls on the colonies.

There were many reasons for colonial resentment. Americans were angered by the Proclamation of 1763, which closed the western lands to colonists. They were also against the Grenville and Townshend tax programs. Meetings, boycotts, and other forms of action were used against the British government. The British felt they were losing control and sent soldiers to keep order. In 1770, British soldiers fired on a Boston crowd and killed five men. This was called the Boston Massacre.

The changing nature of British control made matters worse. British policies began as strict laws but were later changed or repealed. This led the colonists to challenge the laws and added to the problems. ☆

Colonial protests against British policies were led by different kinds of people. Some leaders were rich and some were quite poor. The leaders included merchants, farmers, plantation owners, and lawyers. Some were well educated, and others were self-taught. There were **radical** leaders who wanted many changes made quickly. Other leaders favored a **moderate** approach, with changes coming slowly. Still other colonists remained loyal to Britain.

At first, most colonial leaders did not want to break away from Britain. Their main idea was to gain changes, or reforms. It was only later that the idea of independence became popular. The leaders of colonial protest included many people.

John Dickinson. He wrote the book *Letters from a Farmer in Pennsylvania.* Dickinson argued that colonists should oppose both internal and external taxes. He also believed that Parliament had no power to tax the colonists simply to raise money for Britain.

Samuel Adams. He was a radical leader in the Boston area. He stressed the need for the colonists to work together against Britain. Adams led the way in setting up the Committees of Correspondence. These committees kept the colonists in touch with one another in organizing their protests.

Benjamin Franklin. He was an older man and was well known and respected in both the colonies and Britain. In 1754, at Albany, New York, he put forward a new plan for governing the colonies. His Albany Plan proposed a president-general appointed by the king. This official would rule with the aid of a council of delegates. The council of delegates would be chosen by the colonial legislatures. Franklin's plan was not accepted. However, it became the basis of later British colonial policy in other parts of the world.

Patrick Henry. He was a radical leader from Virginia. Henry was also well known as a fiery speaker. His words "Give me liberty or give me death"

Benjamin Franklin (top) suggested the Albany Plan for British rule of the colonies. Samuel Adams organized the Committees of Correspondence. Patrick Henry (opposite) is shown before the Virginia Assembly, arguing for independence.

became a slogan of the more radical American colonists.

John Hancock. He was a Boston merchant who had a reputation for smuggling goods to avoid paying taxes. Hancock and Samuel Adams led the radicals in the Boston area.

Another leader of protest was George Washington of Virginia. He was wealthy and highly respected in the South. He had served in the British army during the French and Indian War. He resigned because he disagreed with British army policy.

Women were expected to stay out of public affairs. During these years, they managed farms and businesses and gave support in other indirect ways. Many were committed to independence. Abigail Adams, for example, whose husband, John, was a colonial leader, argued for revolution well before he did. (She also managed the family farm very successfully for ten years. John Adams once

wrote to her that he was afraid the neighbors would think she did a better job of it than he did.) In general, however, women stayed in the background. Many black people also worked for independence. Some slaves later won their freedom by fighting in the Revolutionary War. But the protest did not include the eastern Indian tribes. They were not involved in the quarrel at this time.

There were colonists who were not involved at all in the movement for independence. These men and women were called **Loyalists.** They were against separation from Britain. They tended to support British policies in the colonies, even if they did not always like them. About one-third of the colonists were Loyalists.

Conflict between Loyalists and patriots increased. The disagreements showed the strength of feeling on both sides. A crisis was coming.

69

COMPREHENSION CHECK

Recognizing the Main Idea

This selection as a whole tells you that

1. all colonial leaders were radicals.
2. all the colonial leaders favored independence.
3. there were many different types of leaders of colonial protest.
4. only the colonial merchants favored independence.

B. Selecting Important Details

Choose the ending that best completes each statement.

1. At first the leaders of colonial protest wanted to
   a. win independence.
   b. end all taxes.
   c. gain some changes, or reforms.
   d. smuggle in goods without paying taxes.
2. Benjamin Franklin's Albany Plan proposed
   a. a new boycott of taxed goods.
   b. the first Committees of Correspondence.
   c. a new plan for governing the colonies.
   d. a radical form of opposition.
3. Loyalists were
   a. the women who wanted more rights.
   b. involved in the movement for independence.
   c. the people who felt strong ties to Britain.
   d. people who agreed with the patriots.

4. Opposition to Britain included all the following EXCEPT
   a. local Indian tribes.
   b. slaves.
   c. the poor.
   d. the wealthy.

C. Matching

Match the names with the descriptions.

Names	Descriptions
1. John Dickinson	a. author of a plan for governing the colonies
2. Samuel Adams	b. Boston merchant and radical leader
3. Benjamin Franklin	c. opponent of both internal and external taxes
4. John Hancock	d. leader of Committees of Correspondence
5. Patrick Henry	e. radical leader in Virginia

D. Vocabulary

Match the words with the definitions.

Words	Definitions
1. radical	a. extreme or excessive
2. moderate	b. afraid
3. Loyalist	c. courageous
	d. one who remained faithful to the established government
	e. middle-of-the-road

Lesson 4 Events That Began the American Revolution

WORDS TO UNDERSTAND
Discuss the meanings of these words.

illegal   **rumor**   **intolerable**

NEW WORDS IN SENTENCES
1. It is **illegal** to drive through a red light.
2. Though no official would admit it, there was a **rumor** that a new school was soon to be built.
3. The new laws were **intolerable** to those expected to obey them.

AS YOU READ
As you read this selection, try to answer these questions.
1. Why did the Boston merchants resent the Tea Act?
2. How did the British react to the Boston Tea Party?

THE READING SELECTION
Review. Members of the colonial protest movement were called patriots. Some patriot leaders were radical. Others were moderate. But many Americans still supported England. They were called Loyalists.

The patriot leaders included Samuel Adams, John Hancock, Patrick Henry, John Dickinson, and Benjamin Franklin. By 1772, Samuel Adams had organized the Committees of Correspondence. These committees made it possible for colonists to work closely together. ☆

A Tea Act was passed in 1773. It permitted the British East India Company to sell tea directly to colonial merchants who were agents of the company. These merchants could then sell tea for a lower price than other merchants. Some tea smugglers had been bringing in tea without paying the tax on it, and then selling it cheaply. The East India Company merchants now could sell tea for less than the **illegal,** smuggled tea.

There were many protests against the Tea Act in American cities. On December 16, 1773, a group of Boston citizens disguised themselves as Indians and went to the harbor. These "Indians" seized a cargo of tea on a British ship and threw it overboard. There was a strong **rumor** that John Hancock and Samuel Adams were behind the "Boston Tea Party." There was even a belief that Hancock had been one of the "Indians."

The Boston Tea Party was, of course, illegal. Colonists had seized and destroyed property that was not theirs. The British government was angered by the American protests. Parliament quickly passed a series of laws to punish the colonists. Boston Harbor was to be closed until payment was made for the destroyed tea. In addition, severe limits were put on the right of self-government in the Massachusetts Colony. The colonists complained that the laws were **intolerable.** In fact, they called them the "Intolerable Acts."

British soldiers were ordered to the Boston area to enforce law and order.

The troops were quartered in private homes. The British also acted to protect their own officials in Massachusetts. British officials accused of serious crimes were to be tried in Britain, or in a colony other than Massachusetts. The British said this would protect officials from revenge by local colonists. Many colonists feared these officials would never be punished for any wrongdoing.

The British actions led to growing colonial sympathy for the people of Boston. Meetings were held and petitions were signed in many colonies. The protest movement gained many new supporters. In September 1774, the

The Revolution began on April 19, 1775, as minutemen and British soldiers battled at Lexington, Massachusetts.

colonial leaders called the First Continental Congress. This congress asked the king for a change in British policy. At the same time, the congress organized a boycott of British goods.

The actions of the First Continental Congress show the differences of opinion within the colonies. On the one hand, they asked the king for changes, but on the other hand, they organized a boycott. Americans disagreed among themselves about what they ought to do. Most leaders urged caution and care. A few spoke of the need for complete independence for the colonies. Some Americans felt it unwise to press the British too hard at this time. Other Americans believed it was time for action and self-defense.

Those who favored action began gathering arms and ammunition. The British commander in the Boston area, General Thomas Gage, heard that the arms were being collected in Concord, near Boston. He sent soldiers to seize the arms and ammunition. The soldiers were also to arrest John Hancock and Samuel Adams in the nearby village of Lexington.

The movement of British troops was seen by patriots. A warning was sent out. A group of colonists who had been secretly training to fight ran to meet the troops. These Americans were called "minutemen." On April 19, 1775, fighting broke out at Lexington and Concord between the minutemen and British troops. This was the beginning of the American Revolution.

Library of Congress

Thomas Paine wrote pamphlets that called for independence for the colonies.

COMPREHENSION CHECK

A. Recognizing the Main Idea
This selection as a whole tells you that
1. British efforts to control the colonies led to conflicts.
2. Americans favored the Tea Act because it lowered the cost of tea.
3. Britain blamed Indians for the destruction of the tea in Boston.
4. Americans were not to blame for the conflicts with England.

B. Selecting Important Details
Choose the ending that best completes each statement.
1. The Tea Act was resented by some colonists because it
   a. enabled East India Company agents to undersell colonial merchants.
   b. raised the price of all tea.
   c. forced Americans to drink tea.
   d. encouraged smuggling in the colonies.

2. The Boston Tea Party was all of the following EXCEPT

    a. one of many protests in American cities.

    b. one of the results of the Intolerable Acts.

    c. an illegal destruction of property.

    d. one of the causes of the Intolerable Acts.

3. All the following were part of the Intolerable Acts EXCEPT that

    a. soldiers were quartered in private homes.

    b. self-government in Massachusetts was limited.

    c. Americans accused of crimes would be tried in England.

    d. Boston was closed to shipping until it paid for the tea destroyed.

4. The movement of British troops to Lexington and Concord was for the purpose of

    a. collecting taxes there.

    b. stopping a meeting of the Continental Congress.

    c. seizing the arms of the colonists and arresting Hancock and Adams.

    d. starting a fight with the minutemen.

C. Vocabulary

Match the words with the definitions.

Words	Definitions
1. illegal	a. to be tolerant
2. rumor	b. an unproved story or statement
3. intolerable	c. not lawful
	d. unbearable
	e. factual

D. Using Your Knowledge

List the errors in this "newspaper story" that might have been printed in 1775.

BRITISH TROOPS CLASH WITH COLONISTS

A clash occurred between British regular troops and some colonial "minutemen" in the New York towns of Lexington and Concord.

The British forces had been sent for the purpose of fixing the roads and were attacked by farmers who thought they came to collect taxes. The British commander blamed leaders of the First Continental Congress for the fighting. He declared that in the ten years since the establishment of this congress, it had been the cause of many difficulties.

Lesson 5   The Ideas Behind the American Revolution

WORDS TO UNDERSTAND

Discuss the meanings of these words.

self-rule   compromise   abolished
extremists   inalienable

NEW WORDS IN SENTENCES

1. The people wanted **self-rule;** they wanted to govern themselves.

2. The **extremists** refused to listen to suggestions for moderate action.

3. They tried to **compromise** between those who wanted action and those who favored doing nothing.

4. The right to be free is **inalienable** and therefore cannot rightfully be taken away.

5. They **abolished** the bad law and replaced it with a new one.

AS YOU READ

As you read this selection, try to answer these questions.

1. What was the basic difference of opinion between England and the colonies?

2. How did extremism help bring on the American Revolution?

3. What were the main ideas of the Declaration of Independence?

THE READING SELECTION

The shots fired at Lexington and Concord marked the start of the American Revolution. This revolution was a struggle between two armies. But it was a result of a clash of ideas. Generally, the British felt that the colonies existed to benefit the British. The colonists felt that they existed for their own benefit. They thought they had a right to do things for their own good. These two different ideas affected both economic and political issues.

Economic. British policy in the colonies was based on the idea of mercantilism. Mercantilism meant controlling the economy in a colony to help the home country. England used taxation and other controls to limit industry and commerce in the colonies.

The colonists felt they should be able to grow economically. They thought they should develop industry and commerce to provide for themselves. They did not want to be held back to make England richer.

Political. If England wanted to control the colonies economically, it had to make all the laws for them. But the colonists felt that laws affecting the colonies should be made by colonists. The cry of "no taxation without representation" was heard. This meant that the colonies ought to be represented in the British Parliament. Actually, this would not have satisfied all the colonists. What many col-

Americans raise a liberty pole to celebrate the adoption of the Declaration of Independence in July 1776.

onists really wanted was the right to rule themselves. They felt that it would not help them to elect a few representatives to Parliament. These representatives would be outvoted and would have no power to change British policies. Only **self-rule** could really protect the interests of the colonists. This is why many colonial leaders began to favor independence and self-rule.

The disagreements between England and the colonies were made worse by

76

the fact that there were **extremists** on both sides. The extremists would not agree to **compromise** in order to settle problems. Americans like Samuel Adams and John Hancock did not trust the British. No matter what the British offered, these people would have been dissatisfied. They wanted independence from Britain.

There were also extremists in England. King George III felt that the power of the monarchy was slipping away. Much of the power of government was in the hands of Parliament. He often had little control over the leaders of that body. Now the colonists also wanted to take away his power. The king felt it was his duty to preserve the power of the throne for future monarchs. George III may have believed that crushing the colonists would solve his problems with both them and Parliament.

Not all colonists favored radical forms of protest. Many favored reforms based on greater British respect for colonial rights. There were people in Britain who also favored a moderate approach to problems. Many of these British people did not want the king to crush the colonists. Moderates in Britain and America favored reform rather than the use of force.

After the battles of Lexington and Concord, the idea of independence gained strength in the American colonies. The Second Continental Congress met and adopted the Declaration of Independence in July 1776. This declaration was drawn up by Thomas Jefferson of Virginia. There were several main ideas in the Declaration of Independence.

1. All people are created equal.

2. People have certain **inalienable** rights, or rights that cannot be taken away. They include life, liberty, and the pursuit of happiness.

3. Governments are organized to get these rights for the people.

4. Governments get their powers from the people they govern. George III and other European kings believed they had "divine" rights that they received from God.

5. A government may not always live up to the purposes for which it was created. Such a government should be changed or **abolished** by the people.

The colonists had a right to do things for their own good. If the English government did not let them do this, they had a right to revolt. These were radical ideas in 1776. It was the start of a new era in history.

COMPREHENSION CHECK

A. Recognizing the Main Idea

This selection as a whole tells you that

1. the British and Americans agreed on colonial policy.

2. the British and Americans disagreed about the definition of mercantilism.

3. the British and Americans disagreed about the purpose and rights of the colonies.

4. the British and Americans agreed on the necessity for the Declaration of Independence.

B. Selecting Important Details

Choose the ending that best completes each statement.

1. The colonists believed that
   a. colonies had a right to do things for their own good.
   b. England had a right to control the colonies.
   c. all forms of government were bad.
   d. England should never have established colonies.

2. The British believed that
   a. colonies had a right to do things for their own good.
   b. England had a right to control the colonies.
   c. all forms of government were bad.
   d. England should never have established colonies.

3. King George's view was that he
   a. had to share power with the colonists.
   b. needed the colonists to help him against Parliament.
   c. was theatened by both the colonists and Parliament.
   d. had more power than he needed.

4. Extremists in America felt the solution was
   a. tighter control of colonies by England.
   b. colonial representation in Parliament.
   c. a movement to abolish the colonies.
   d. complete self-rule.

C. True or False

These are statements about the Declaration of Independence. Decide whether each is true or false.

1. It states that all men are created equal.

2. It states that governments get their power from God.

3. It states that a government can take away all rights of the people, if necessary.

4. It states that people may abolish a government.

5. The ideas in it were radical for the time.

D. Vocabulary

Use a word from this list to complete each sentence.

self-rule   extremist   compromise
intolerable   inalienable   abolish
              revenue

1. An _____ right is one that cannot be taken away.

2. The two sides worked out a _____ that satisfied both of them.

3. _____ meant that the colony completely governed itself.

4. She decided to do away with, or _____, the group.

5. An _____ is one who holds a radical point of view.

E. Ask Yourself

Do you think the differences between England and the colonies could have been settled without the Revolution? How?

Lesson 6   The American Revolution

WORDS TO UNDERSTAND
Discuss the meanings of these words.

oppose   **neutral**   **mercenaries**

NEW WORDS IN SENTENCES
1. Did Sue **oppose** the plan because she did not think it would work?
2. They did not take sides in the war, but remained **neutral.**
3. There were **mercenaries** — German soldiers being paid by England — in the war.

AS YOU READ
As you read this selection, try to answer these questions.
1. What factors weakened the colonial cause in the Revolution?
2. What were some factors that aided the colonists?

THE READING SELECTION
Today it may seem that American colonists had no choice but to fight the Revolution. But at the time, the decision to **oppose** the British must have seemed foolish. England was a wealthy, strong, well-established nation. The American colonies were none of these things.

The colonists had to overcome a number of real disadvantages.

1. England had a strong government. The Continental Congress in the colonies was weak. It did little to back up armies in the field. The Articles of Confederation, the system of government adopted in 1781, was also weak.

2. England had a large treasury. There was little money in America to pay for the war. For example, Haym Salomon, a Jewish immigrant, gave or lent his own money to the government. Because of the shortages of money and industry, the colonial army was often short of supplies.

3. The British had a well-trained regular army. Some Americans had fought in the French and Indian War, but many were untrained.

4. The British navy commanded the oceans. There was almost no colonial navy.

5. Not all the colonists supported the cause of independence. About one-third of the colonists were **neutral** in the war. Another third really supported the Brit-

ish, though few of these fought for them. Only about one-third of colonial America supported the revolution against Britain.

In spite of all these weaknesses, the colonists had a number of advantages.

1. The colonists were fighting on their own soil for their own liberties. Many of the British troops were hired soldiers, or **mercenaries,** from Germany. They did not have the commitment of the Americans. Also, British troops and supplies had to be shipped all the way from England.

2. The Americans received support from some European nations. France gave large sums of money to aid the colonists against its old enemy, Britain. After 1777 the French entered the war. Their fleet played an important part in the final victory. Spain and Holland also gave some aid to the colonies. The American army was also aided by many foreign volunteers. These volunteers included Lafayette of France, von Steuben of Germany, and Kosciusko and Pulaski of Poland.

3. American military leadership was better than many had thought possible. Washington was a skilled leader who saved his armies time and again. General Gates and General Arnold defeated the British armies at Saratoga. George Rogers Clark swept the British out of the Northwest Territory. On the high seas, the daring John Paul Jones defeated the British in a number of naval battles.

4. Americans were well acquainted with firearms. In addition, the rifles used by the colonial army were more effective than British muskets.

5. Public opinion in Britain was never completely against the Americans. Some British leaders actually favored the American cause. They felt that a British victory would hurt the cause of liberty in Britain as well as in the colonies. Both William Pitt and Edmund Burke spoke in Parliament on behalf of the colonists. The Whig party in Britain was also in sympathy with the colonists. Thus, the British were not united in their efforts to put down the revolt.

The Americans got off to a good start in 1775. They made a brave showing against trained British soldiers at the Battle of Bunker (Breed's) Hill in Boston. From then on, however, the colonial armies suffered many defeats. George Washington had been appointed commander in chief of the colonial armies. One of his main problems was to keep the army from deserting. The years from 1776 to 1781 were filled with defeat for

Thaddeus Kosciusko, a Pole, was one of many foreign volunteers who served with the American army.

BOSTON

CHARLES TOWN

British soldiers left their ships to attack Breed's Hill and then Bunker Hill. The Americans forced them back twice. But the British had more soldiers and ammunition and were able to win the battle.

Attack on Bunker's Hill, with the Burning of Charles Town American School, National Gallery of Art, Washington, Gift of Edgar William and Bernice Chrysler Garbisch

Washington and his little army. But daring actions by Washington brought victories in the battles of Trenton and Princeton. These victories came at a time when American hopes were low. The major American victory of the war came in 1777. An American army defeated a British army at Saratoga, New York. The victory convinced France to enter the war on the side of the colonists.

The turning point came in 1781. Washington managed to trap General Cornwallis's army at Yorktown. The surrender of Cornwallis led the British to see that they could not easily defeat the colonists. The war went on for another two years, but there were no major battles. In 1783, a peace treaty was signed. Britain agreed that the colonists were to be free and independent.

COMPREHENSION CHECK

A. Recognizing the Main Idea

This selection as a whole tells you that

1. the colonists were able to win the war because they were better trained soldiers than the British.

2. the colonists won the war in spite of the many problems that faced them.

3. the colonists won the war only because of the aid they received from France.

4. the colonists won the war because they had a strong government supporting their armies.

B. Selecting Important Details

Choose the ending that best completes each statement.

1. During the Revolution,
   a. almost all the colonists were in favor of the revolt.
   b. most of the colonists actively opposed the revolt.
   c. only about one-third of the colonists supported the revolt.
   d. very few colonists opposed the revolt.

2. The Battle of Saratoga was
   a. a major defeat for the British.
   b. of no great importance in the war.
   c. a major defeat for the colonists.
   d. won because the French aided the Americans.

3. During the Revolution, the colonists lacked all the following EXCEPT
   a. money to pay for the costs of war.
   b. a commander in chief for the colonial armies.
   c. strong public support.
   d. a strong central government.

4. All the following were advantages for Americans EXCEPT
   a. the experience and organization of the army.
   b. support from European nations.
   c. sympathetic public opinion in Britain.
   d. the location of the war on their own soil.

C. Vocabulary

Write your own sentences for each of these words.

oppose   neutral   mercenary

D. Ask Yourself

The American Revolution occurred even though only one-third of the colonists actively supported it. How do you think this could happen? How does this fit with the ideal of democratic government and with the ideas of the Declaration of Independence?

Burning the Stamps.

Black patriots were among the people who protested the Stamp Act by burning the stamps in public.

Black Men in the Revolution

On June 17, 1775, the British sent 2,400 men to force American troops off the heights of Breed's Hill near Boston. The fighting that followed has come to be known as the Battle of Bunker Hill.

Major Pitcairn had commanded British troops at the battles of Lexington and Concord, and he now led one of the charges against the hill. Among the 1,600 Americans at the top of the hill were such black patriots as Cuff Hayes, Caesar Dickerson, Prince Hall (later a famous abolitionist), Salem Poor, and Peter Salem. Peter Salem, recently freed from slavery, celebrated his freedom in the fighting that day. His musket is believed to have fired the shot that killed the British commander, Major Pitcairn.

Black men were at the Boston Massacre and at Lexington and Concord, as well as at Bunker Hill, but American commanders often refused to accept them as soldiers. Washington, a slaveowner, hesitated to use black soldiers. He feared that blacks who fought for the American cause would later have to be given their freedom from slavery.

As early as 1775, the British had offered to free any slave who served in their armies. Thousands of black men and women fled to the British lines, and some fought in the British army. Washington and other American officers gradually became willing to accept black men as soldiers, and before the war ended, more than 5,000 blacks had served in the army.

Lesson 7 The Results of the American Revolution

WORDS TO UNDERSTAND
Discuss the meanings of these words.

restored   **restrictions**   **aristocracy**

NEW WORDS IN SENTENCES
1. Everything they had lost during the war was to be **restored,** or given back, to them.

2. The **restrictions** on their actions meant that they could do almost nothing.

3. The **aristocracy** was made up of nobles who held much of the power in the country.

AS YOU READ
As you read this selection, try to answer these questions.

1. What were the main provisions of the Treaty of Paris in 1783?

2. What were the main results of the American Revolution?

THE READING SELECTION
Review. From 1775 to 1783, the American colonists fought against Britain for their independence. It often seemed impossible for them to defeat the mighty British. The colonists' skill and courage, European aid, and the lack of British unity brought colonial victory. In 1783, a treaty of peace was signed. ☆

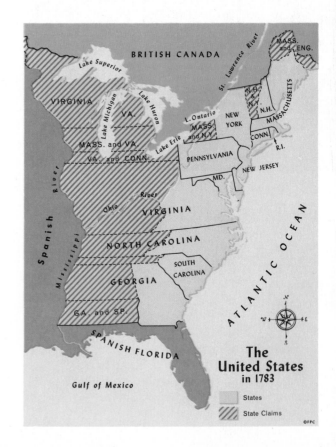

The United States in 1783

States

State Claims

The Treaty of Paris fixed the western boundary of the United States at the Mississippi River. Large territories in the west were claimed by various states. In some cases, two different states claimed the same area.

General Washington offers a hand to the dying Colonel Rall, who led the fight for the British at Trenton, New Jersey. This American victory brought new hope to the American army.

Capture of the Hessians at Trenton by Trumbull, Yale University Art Gallery

The Treaty of Paris included these main points.

1. Britain recognized the independence of the thirteen colonies.

2. The boundaries of the new nation were established. It would extend from Canada and the Great Lakes in the north to the border of Florida, and from the Atlantic Ocean to the Mississippi River.

3. The Continental Congress was to recommend to the states that the rights of Loyalists be **restored.** Their property seized during the war was to be paid for.

4. Americans would keep the right to fish off the Canadian banks of Newfoundland.

American success in the Revolution affected the entire world. The mightiest nation of Europe had been forced to grant independence to its American colonies. The world was never the same after 1783. There were several important results of the Revolution.

1. A new, independent nation was formed. Its thirteen states were tied together by the Articles of Confederation. This provided a form of national government for the states.

2. The Revolution ended mercantilist **restrictions** upon the colonists. American industry and trade were now free to develop and expand.

3. The independent states drafted new state constitutions. These gave greater rights to white males. Five northern states abolished slavery, or gradually freed the slaves. The slave trade was outlawed or taxed in eleven states.

4. The ideas of **aristocracy,** or nobility, in America died out.

5. The ideas of the American Revolution spread throughout the world. There was a growth of revolutionary ideas in many parts of Europe. Within a few years, the people of France rose in revolt against the aristocracy. The American and French revolutions also encouraged Latin American colonies to seek freedom from European nations.

Even the British were affected by the ideas of the American Revolution. Belief in the "divine right of kings" died out. From that time on, the power of Parliament grew steadily. The American Revolution also taught Britain the need for changes in its policy towards other colonies.

COMPREHENSION CHECK

A. Recognizing the Main Idea

This selection as a whole tells you that

1. the Revolution resulted in many changes, both in America and in other countries.

2. the Revolution brought no new freedoms to the colonists.

3. the Revolution had no great effect upon the rest of the world.

4. the Revolution was to be of great help to the kings of France and Spain.

B. Selecting Important Details

Choose the ending that best completes each statement.

1. The victory of the colonists in the Revolution
   a. led to better treatment of other English colonies.
   b. resulted in greater powers for the British kings.
   c. weakened the powers of Parliament.
   d. encouraged the idea of "divine right of kings."

2. All the following were results of the American Revolution EXCEPT
   a. the growth and extension of mercantilism.
   b. the drafting of new state constitutions giving greater rights to Americans.
   c. the spread of the ideas of the Revolution throughout the world.
   d. the formation of a new, independent nation.

3. The western boundary of the new, independent nation was the
    a. Great Lakes.
    b. Canadian border.
    c. Mississippi River.
    d. Florida border.

4. The ideas of the American Revolution encouraged all of the following EXCEPT
    a. revolution in France.
    b. revolution in Latin America.
    c. changes in British colonial policies.
    d. stronger belief in the "divine right of kings."

C. True or False

Decide whether each of these statements is true or false.

1. England did not continue the war after its troops were defeated at Saratoga.

2. The peace treaty set the United States' western border at the Mississippi River.

3. Congress was to recommend that rights be restored to Loyalists.

4. Americans had been encouraged to rebel by the success of the French Revolution.

5. All the new state constitutions abolished slavery.

D. Vocabulary

Match the words with the definitions.

Words	Definitions
1. restore	a. to become smaller
2. restriction	b. to give back
3. aristocracy	c. to attack
	d. nobility
	e. limitation

E. Map Skills

This map shows part of North America in 1783, when the Treaty of Paris was signed. Certain areas are labeled with letters. Match each description below with the correct letter. There are two extra letters.

1. Lands west of the Mississippi River
2. The southern states
3. The New England states
4. The Great Lakes
5. The Atlantic Ocean
6. Florida

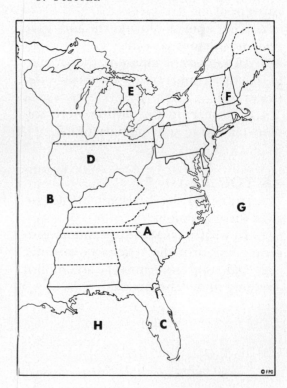

Lesson 8 The Articles of Confederation

WORDS TO UNDERSTAND
Discuss the meanings of these words.

consent   inflation

unanimous   militia

NEW WORDS IN SENTENCES
1. They could not begin without the **consent** of the Congress.

2. The women all agreed and gave their **unanimous** consent.

3. In periods of **inflation,** the amount of currency and credit increases, and prices rise.

4. The men in the **militia** were soldiers trained in state military units.

AS YOU READ
As you read this selection, try to answer these questions.

1. In what ways was the national government set up in the Articles a weak one?

2. Did the government accomplish anything under the Articles?

THE READING SELECTION
The Treaty of Paris ended the Revolutionary War in 1783. A new nation existed. But was it really a nation? The Articles of Confederation had been adopted in 1781. They provided a weak national government at a time when the new nation needed a strong one.

The Americans had remembered what a strong national government in England had done to them. As a result, when they wrote the Articles of Confederation, they refused to give the national government much power.

There was a national Congress, in which each state had one vote. No law could be passed without the **consent** of nine states. It was difficult to get nine to agree on any law, since they all had different interests. And any effort to change the Articles needed the **unanimous** approval of all the states. This was almost impossible to get.

The weakness of the national government caused trouble in a number of ways.

1. There were no national officials to enforce laws. Only the states could enforce laws. A law passed by Congress could be completely useless if the states did not enforce it.

2. Finances were confused and awkward. The national government had no way to raise the money needed to pay its debts and perform its duties. It could not tax the people. It could only ask the states for money, and the states

could easily refuse. In addition, there was no national system of money. Each state printed its own. This led to **inflation** and rising prices.

3. There was no national army or navy. Each state took care of its own defense with its **militia,** or volunteers. If the national government needed troops, it had to ask the states to supply them. They could refuse.

4. There was no national system of courts or other means for settling disputes between states. The states argued about land claims beyond the Appalachian Mountains. They also argued about taxes on goods shipped from state to state. There were no national agencies to prevent these disputes or to settle differences.

5. The national government had little power in foreign affairs. Most European governments expected the United States to fall apart, with the states fighting among themselves.

Under the Articles, the national government did do a few useful things. One example was the passage of the Northwest Ordinance in 1787. The ordinance set up rules for governing the Northwest Territory. It provided an orderly system for converting the land into new states.

Many Americans became dissatisfied with the Articles of Confederation. They felt the country needed a stronger central government. Such a government could strengthen the value of money. It could provide armed forces for defense, and settle arguments among the states. It could encourage the growth of industry and trade. By 1787, many leaders of the nation thought a change was necessary.

Indians paddle or pole their canoes past a newly cleared farm. This 1791 plan of an American farm shows long fences made from felled trees. The forest still stands behind the barns and houses.

COMPREHENSION CHECK

A. Recognizing the Main Idea

This selection as a whole tells you that

1. the new nation solved most of its problems in the early years.

2. the problems of the new nation were mostly due to lack of money.

3. the new nation faced many problems due to lack of a strong central government.

4. the new nation's main problem was the strong central government which took over the authority of the states.

B. Selecting Important Details

Choose the ending that best completes each statement.

1. All the following were lacking in the new nation EXCEPT
   a. an army and navy.
   b. a means of raising funds.
   c. a strong foreign policy.
   d. independence from England.

2. It was thought that a strong central government could do all the following EXCEPT
   a. provide armed forces.
   b. strengthen the value of money.
   c. give the states more power.
   d. settle disputes between the states.

3. The lack of national officials to enforce laws under the Articles of Confederation meant that
   a. the states could not enforce laws.
   b. Congress's laws could become useless.
   c. laws could not be passed.
   d. both the states and the Congress had power to enforce laws.

4. A serious weakness of the Articles of Confederation was the fact that they could be changed only
   a. if nine states agreed to the change.
   b. if all thirteen states agreed to the change.
   c. if a majority of the states agreed to the change.
   d. if any one state wished a change.

C. True or False

Decide whether each of these statements is true or false.

1. By 1783, all western land had been clearly divided up among the states.

2. At first, Americans wanted to set up a national government exactly like England's.

3. By 1783, most of the states favored a government with a strong central authority.

4. A major weakness of the Articles of Confederation was that they required all thirteen states to give their consent to any new laws.

5. Under the Articles of Confederation, the Congress had to ask the states for whatever money it needed.

D. Vocabulary

Write your own sentence for each of these words.

consent   inflation
unanimous   militia

E. Ask Yourself

Suppose you are a newspaper editor in the United States in 1787. You are working on an editorial arguing against the Articles of Confederation. What would you consider the three major problems with them? Why?

The Northwest Ordinance

Probably the outstanding achievement of the years 1783 to 1789 was the Northwest Ordinance. This law set up a way of governing the Northwest Territory.

The lands of this Northwest Territory at various times were claimed by Virginia, Connecticut, Massachusetts, and New York. By 1784, all these states had settled their claims. The Northwest Territory then belonged to the whole United States as public domain. In 1785, a law established the way in which the land would be surveyed and sold to settlers. As the land was sold, the government would set aside one square mile out of every thirty-six square miles to finance free public education.

On July 13, 1787, the Northwest Ordinance for the government of the territory was passed. It contained the following provisions:

1. Three to five states were to be formed out of the Northwest Territory.

2. When 5,000 free males of voting age had settled in any part of the territory, they could elect a territorial legislature. This legislature would govern with the aid of a governor appointed by Congress.

3. When 60,000 free settlers lived in the new territory, the legislature could adopt a constitution and apply for statehood "on an equal footing" with the original states.

4. A bill of rights was adopted by the territory, which guaranteed free speech, a free press, and other liberties.

5. Slavery was forbidden in all the new territory.

6. Schools and education were to be encouraged.

Eventually, the states of Illinois, Indiana, Ohio, Michigan, and Wisconsin were formed from the Northwest Territory. The Northwest Ordinance was the American solution to a problem the British had failed to solve: how to govern colonial territories. It set the basic policy of the United States for bringing new lands into the Union.

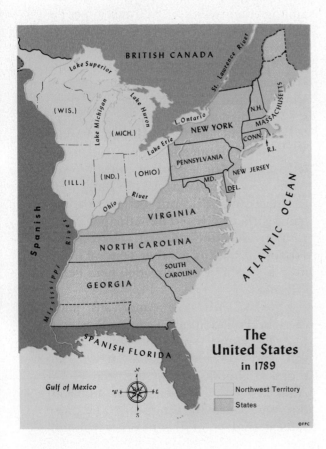

The United States in 1789

Northwest Territory

States

©FPC

Lesson 9 Debate Over the Constitution

WORDS TO UNDERSTAND

Discuss the meanings of these words.

interpret   **ratify**   **republic**

NEW WORDS IN SENTENCES

1. He found the scientist's language difficult to **interpret.**

2. Nine states had to approve, or **ratify,** the Constitution before it could go into effect.

3. A **republic** is a government in which people elect representatives to govern for them according to law.

AS YOU READ

As you read this selection, try to answer these questions.

1. What were some of the important issues in the Constitutional Convention?

2. Who were some of the leaders of the Constitutional Convention?

THE READING SELECTION

Review. From 1781 to 1788, the newly independent nation was governed under the Articles of Confederation. But the Articles did not provide for a national government with the power to unite the states. The states had more power than the national government did. There was no national power to enforce laws, to raise money or troops, or to control trade. The states argued among themselves. And many people felt a new government was needed. ☆

Two early meetings helped pave the way for changes in the American government. In 1785, representatives of Virginia and Maryland met to try to settle a dispute. They met at George Washington's home at Mount Vernon, Virginia. This meeting was a success. It led to a call for a general convention at Annapolis, Maryland. All the states were to meet to work out better relations among themselves. The Annapolis convention did not succeed. However, it sent out a call for another general meeting to be held in Philadelphia, Pennsylvania.

In 1787, fifty-five Americans gathered in Philadelphia. George Washington, Benjamin Franklin, James Madison, and Alexander Hamilton were all there. (Thomas Jefferson and John Adams were away, serving as ambassadors to France and England.) The more radical leaders of the recent revolution

George Washington addresses the Constitutional Convention.
Can you recognize Benjamin Franklin seated at the left?

did not attend. This meeting had been called to revise the Articles of Confederation. It was the beginning of a long debate about the structure of the new country.

The Constitutional Convention lasted for four months. George Washington served as its president. The delegates decided to design a completely new government rather than make a few changes in the old one. All the discussion was kept secret. By September, the constitution setting up this new government was ready to be presented to the people. The new constitution had several major features.

1. A central, or national, government was to be established.

2. The national government was to share powers with the states. But it would also have special powers of its own.

93

3. The national government was to consist of three branches. The legislative branch would make laws. The executive branch would enforce the laws. The judicial branch would help **interpret** the meaning of the laws.

The system of representation in the national government grew out of a compromise. The large states favored Virginia's plan to allow representation in Congress according to population. Thus, the larger states would have more representatives than the smaller states. The smaller states preferred New Jersey's plan of equal representation for all states. The Great Compromise allowed for two houses in Congress. The Senate would have two representatives from each state. In the House of Representatives, the number of members from each state would be based on population.

Of course, this meant the people would have to be counted. The South wanted to count slaves. This would give the South more members in Congress. The North objected. The Three-Fifths Compromise settled the debate. In each state, every five slaves would count as three persons in deciding representation. White women were counted equally with men. Indians were not counted at all.

This was largely because they were not considered part of the United States. They were considered separate nations.

Nine states had to **ratify,** or approve, the Constitution before it could go into effect. The arguments for and against the new government began. Many people were afraid of a strong central government. They feared it would become like the government in England. Instead, they wanted the states to remain strong.

To persuade them, a series of essays arguing for the Constitution were published. These were written by Hamilton, Madison, and John Jay. The essays reminded people of the problems in the Articles of Confederation. They argued that a strong central government was needed. And they tried to prove that the Constitution followed the best principles of government in a **republic.**

The promise of a bill of rights helped win ratification of the Constitution. In June 1788, New Hampshire became the ninth state to ratify the Constitution. The last state, Rhode Island, finally approved it in 1790. By that time, the first president of the United States had begun his term of office under the Constitution. The new government had been established.

COMPREHENSION CHECK

A. Recognizing the Main Idea

This selection as a whole tells you that

1. the Constitutional Convention sought to change the Articles of Confederation.
2. the Constitutional Convention made few changes in the Articles of Confederation.
3. the Constitutional Convention decided not to change the Articles of Confederation, but to write a new constitution for the nation.
4. the Constitutional Convention gave all governing powers to the central government.

B. Selecting Important Details

Choose the ending that best completes each statement.

1. All the following were leaders of the Constitutional Convention EXCEPT
   a. Alexander Hamilton.
   b. Thomas Jefferson.
   c. George Washington.
   d. James Madison.
2. The Great Compromise provided for
   a. a federal executive.
   b. two houses of Congress.
   c. a Supreme Court.
   d. a central authority.
3. The Three-Fifths Compromise related to
   a. giving citizenship to slaves.
   b. giving more power to Congress.
   c. the functions of the president.
   d. the way in which slaves were to be counted for purposes of representation.

4. The basic reason many people did not like the Constitution was
   a. fear of a strong central government.
   b. fear of taxes.
   c. preference for European systems.
   d. preference for a system exactly like the Iroquois Confederacy.

C. Vocabulary

Use a word from this list to complete each sentence.

unanimous   ratify   republican
interpret   inflation

1. She hoped that the delegates would _____ her proposal.
2. The way the essay was written made it difficult to _____ the author's meaning.
3. Voting for officials is an important part of a _____ government.

D. Chronology

Arrange these events in the order in which they happened.

1. Articles of Confederation adopted
2. Battles of Lexington and Concord fought
3. Constitution adopted
4. Townshend Acts take effect
5. Declaration of Independence adopted
6. Treaty of Paris signed

James Madison and the Constitution

James Madison was a small man who did not enjoy good health. At first glance, he scarcely seemed a man who could fight hard for anything. But he was a good fighter and more. He was an intelligent man who understood the need for properly organizing the new government.

James Madison was born in Virginia in 1751. During the Revolution, he served in the Continental Congress. Later he was a member of the Virginia state legislature. When the Constitutional Convention met, he was sent by the people of Virginia as a delegate. Madison played a major part in writing the Constitution.

When it appeared that the new constitution might not win approval, James Madison showed what a fighter he was. He joined with John Jay and Alexander Hamilton in writing a series of papers and articles. These came to be known as the Federalist Papers. In the Federalist Papers are many arguments for adopting the Constitution.

James Madison's efforts helped to win ratification of the Constitution. Later, Madison served as secretary of state when Thomas Jefferson was president. In 1808, Madison was himself elected president and served for two terms. But it was his work on the Constitution that had made his later career possible.

James Madison gave deep thought to the problems of organizing a government. No one knew whether the Constitution would work when it was written. But Madison believed in it and worked for its ratification.

Lesson 10 Living in America: The Postrevolutionary Period

WORDS TO UNDERSTAND
Discuss the meanings of these words.

rural   **urban**   **sanitary**

NEW WORDS IN SENTENCES
1. Before the growth of cities, **rural** life was much more common in America.
2. Many **urban** people enjoy the excitement of living in the city.
3. Poor **sanitary** conditions can spread germs and disease.

AS YOU READ
As you read this selection, try to answer these questions.
1. What were some changes in American life during this period?
2. What were some ways in which American life was still tied to Europe?

THE READING SELECTION
While British troops surrendered at Yorktown, their bands played the tune "The World Turned Upside Down." The American political world may have turned upside down. But American culture and society were still connected to Europe in many ways.

Population. One change that did occur was a growth of population. In 1770, there were about 2 million whites in the American colonies. By 1810, there were more than 7 million. The number of black slaves increased from about 600,000 in 1775 to 1,200,000 in 1810. At the same time, the Indian population east of the Mississippi River was decreasing quickly.

The United States was a **rural** nation. In 1810, nearly 93 percent of the population lived outside cities. Nearly 84 percent worked in agriculture. Yet the **urban** population was growing. In 1790, both New York City and Charleston, South Carolina, had four times as many people as they had had in 1730.

It was not a time for great social changes. Women, slaves, and free blacks had few rights. Indians and whites clashed frequently over the differences between them.

Daily life. Furniture and clothing were made by hand. Working people made simple furniture from local materials. This is what is now called "Early

Flax is a plant that was used to make cloth. After harvesting, fibers were separated by a process called "scutching." In this scene, colonists work at a flax scutching bee, or party.

Flax Scutching Bee, Linton Park, National Gallery of Art, Washington, Gift of Edgar William and Bernice Chrysler Garbisch

American" style. Some people also made their own clothes. They spun thread at home from flax or wool. Wealthier people often imported furniture and clothing from Europe. They could also have European styles copied at home, using local or imported materials.

Food was usually plentiful. Corn was a favorite food. Meat was obtained by hunting or by raising livestock. City people could get fresh foods from nearby farms. Food storage for the winter was the major problem. There was no refrigeration or canning at the time. Meats were salted or smoked. Vegetables were dried, or stored in cool cellars.

Medical care was poor. **Sanitary** conditions were also poor. Epidemics killed many Americans. Smallpox was a major killer. There were few hospitals or college-educated doctors.

Education and work. The number of schools and colleges was growing. Doctors and lawyers were beginning to receive some college training in the United States. But education was not as important to most people then as it is now. Most workers entered trades through apprenticeships. In the 1790s, some workers began to form unions. There were even some strikes—a completely new event.

Women were generally limited in what they were allowed to do. But some women were farmers, teachers, midwives, and shopkeepers. A small number of women entered the trades. One of these was Mary Katherine Goddard. She was the printer who first published the signed Declaration of Independence.

Transportation and communication. The horse was the main means of carrying mail or people. But the horse was slow and not very dependable. In the 1790s, a system of paved turnpikes was begun. Riders on horseback carried the mail. One big change at this time was the growth of newspapers. At the end of the Revolution, only 43 were being published. But by 1810, there were 359. Most of these were founded in order to publish a particular point of view. But the change did mean that more Americans were reading and becoming aware of events.

Religion. In 1775, there were almost 2 million Protestants in the colonies. There were only about 25,000 Catholics and 2,000 Jews. There was often prejudice against Catholics and Jews. The number of Christians increased because many slaves converted to the religion of their owners. However, efforts to convert Indians to Christianity had only limited success. After the Revolution, American churches became more independent of Europe. They began to run their own affairs with their own leaders.

New York State Historical Association, Cooperstown

Abigail Adams was a remarkably independent woman for her time. A letter she sent to her husband at the Constitutional Convention strongly suggested that women be given more rights under the new government. Her husband, John, and her son, John Quincy, both became presidents of the United States.

Courtesy Pennsylvania Academy of the Fine Arts

Gary Kulik, flax spinning wheel, Slater Mill Historic Site

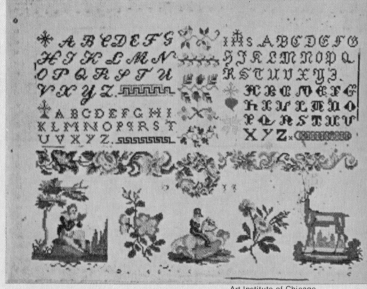

Art Institute of Chicago

Paul Revere by J. S. Copley, Gift of Joseph W., William B., and Edward H. R. Revere, Courtesy Museum of Fine Arts, Boston

LIFE IN THE NEW NATION

The large picture at left shows an early Fourth of July celebration in Philadelphia. Below are some objects from the time. Spinning wheels were used to spin thread. Samplers were used to teach children how to sew. The pitcher has a patriotic design that was popular at the time. Monticello (above), Thomas Jefferson's home, is a good example of buildings of the period. Paul Revere (top right) was a well-known silversmith. Charles W. Peale was a well-known painter who established a popular natural history exhibit.

Courtesy Pennsylvania Academy of the Fine Arts

COMPREHENSION CHECK

A. Recognizing the Main Idea

This selection as a whole tells you that

1. American society was totally changed after 1775.

2. there were no changes in America except the political.

3. American society did not break completely with Europe after the Revolution.

4. Europe itself changed greatly after 1775.

B. Selecting Important Details

Choose the ending that best completes each statement.

1. After the Revolution, all the following changed greatly EXCEPT
   a. the population.
   b. the rights of women.
   c. the number of newspapers.
   d. the number of unions for workers.

2. Furniture and clothing of working people were often
   a. different in style from those of wealthier people.
   b. made in Europe.
   c. made by machine.
   d. made in factories.

3. All the following were true of medical care during this time EXCEPT that
   a. epidemics were common.
   b. sanitary conditions were poor.
   c. smallpox was a serious problem.
   d. most doctors had college educations.

4. After the Revolution, communication improved because of
   a. paved turnpikes for cars.
   b. airmail.
   c. the publishing of more newspapers.
   d. the invention of telephones.

C. Vocabulary

Use a word from this list to complete each sentence.

sanitary   neutral   rural
republican   urban

1. _____ areas often have much noise and pollution.

2. Some people find _____ life satisfying because it is close to nature.

3. Before doctors became concerned with _____ conditions in surgery, infection was common.

D. Using Your Knowledge

Match each main idea with two details about it.

Main Ideas	Details
1. Population	a. trade unions
2. Education and work	b. population increase
	c. women in trades
3. Transportation and communication	d. horseback riders carrying mail
	e. newspapers
	f. voting rights for minorities

Unit 2 Summary   Revolution in America

Colonial Discontent

After the French and Indian War, the colonists did not feel they needed England's protection. They felt more confident of their own powers because they had served with the English armies against the French. England, on the other hand, found that the war had left it heavily in debt. England felt that the colonists ought to help pay the costs of the war. Mercantilism was the system England used for this purpose.

Under mercantilism, the colonies existed to enrich and strengthen the home country. Under this belief, the British sought to impose many taxes for the purpose of raising money and controlling the economic life of their colonies. This policy brought much resentment and led, finally, to the American Revolution.

The American Revolution had other causes, also. The demand of the colonists for greater self-rule was a very important cause. The colonists wanted to be governed by their own colonial assemblies rather than by the British Parliament. Extremism on both sides was still another factor in the break with the home country.

The Establishment of a New Nation

The victory of the colonists in 1783 led to the establishment of a new nation. The Articles of Confederation, under which the new nation was governed, had many weaknesses. The confederation government lacked any executive power or any strong central authority.

This weakness led to demands for change. A convention met in 1787 to draw up a new plan for government—the Constitution. The Constitutional Convention was led by Washington, Hamilton, Franklin, and Madison. The proposed new government would share power with the state governments. The national government would consist of a legislative branch to make laws, an executive branch to enforce the laws, and a judicial branch to interpret the meaning of laws. The new Constitution was presented to the states for ratification and went into effect in 1788. A president and Congress were elected.

The population of the new nation grew quickly. Some areas of American life—education and communication, for example—saw real changes. But changes in others—such as transportation and medical care—were yet to come.

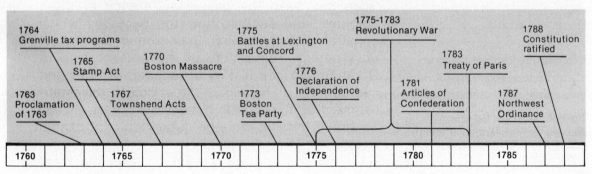

THE DECLARATION OF INDEPENDENCE

The opening paragraph explains that when people decide to free themselves from political ties with another country, they ought to explain their actions to the rest of the world.

This paragraph contains ideas at the heart of American democracy. All people are created equal. All people have certain natural, God-given rights. Governments are set up to protect these natural rights. If a government fails to do this, the people have the right to change or abolish their government. However, the reasons for such drastic action must be very serious.

The colonists then list what the king and his government have done to cause them to break away from British rule.

When, in the course of human events, it becomes necessary for one people to dissolve the political bands which have connected them with another, and to assume, among the powers of the earth, the separate and equal station to which the laws of nature and of nature's God entitle them, a decent respect to the opinions of mankind requires that they should declare the causes which impel them to the separation.

We hold these truths to be self-evident: that all men are created equal; that they are endowed by their Creator with certain inalienable rights; that among these are life, liberty, and the pursuit of happiness. That, to secure these rights, governments are instituted among men, deriving their just powers from the consent of the governed; that, whenever any form of government becomes destructive of these ends, it is the right of the people to alter or to abolish it, and to institute new government, laying its foundation on such principles, and organizing its powers in such form, as to them shall seem most likely to effect their safety and happiness. Prudence, indeed, will dictate that governments long established should not be changed for light and transient causes; and accordingly, all experience hath shown, that mankind are more disposed to suffer, while evils are sufferable, than to right themselves by abolishing the forms to which they are accustomed. But, when a long train of abuses and usurpations, pursuing invariably the same object, evinces a design to reduce them under absolute despotism, it is their right, it is their duty, to throw off such government, and to provide new guards for their future security. Such has been the patient sufferance of these colonies, and such is now the necessity which constrains them to alter their former systems of government. The history of the present King of Great Britain is a history of repeated injuries and usurpations, all having, in direct object, the establishment of an absolute tyranny over these States. To prove this, let facts be submitted to a candid world.

He has refused his assent to laws the most wholesome and necessary for the public good.

He has forbidden his governors to pass laws of immediate and pressing importance, unless suspended in their operation till his assent should be obtained; and, when so suspended, he has utterly neglected to attend to them.

He has refused to pass other laws for the accommodation of large districts of people, unless those people would relinquish the right of representation in the legislature—a right inestimable to them and formidable to tyrants only.

He has called together legislative bodies at places unusual, uncomfortable, and distant from the depository of their public records, for the sole purpose of fatiguing them into compliance with his measures.

He has dissolved representative houses repeatedly, for opposing, with manly firmness, his invasions on the rights of the people.

He has refused, for a long time after such dissolutions, to cause others to be elected; whereby the legislative powers, incapable of annihilation, have returned to the people at large for their exercise; the State remaining, in the meantime, exposed to all the dangers of invasions from without and convulsions within.

He has endeavored to prevent the population of these States; for that purpose obstructing the laws for naturalization of foreigners, refusing to pass others to encourage their migrations hither, and raising the conditions of new appropriations of lands.

He has obstructed the administration of justice, by refusing his assent to laws for establishing judiciary powers.

He has made judges dependent on his will alone for the tenure of their offices and the amount and payment of their salaries.

He has erected a multitude of new offices, and sent hither swarms of officers to harass our people, and eat out their substance.

He has kept among us, in times of peace, standing armies, without the consent of our legislatures.

He has affected to render the military independent of, and superior to, the civil power.

He has combined with others to subject us to a

The king and his government interfered with self-government in the colonies.

They tried to limit the growth and expansion of the colonies. This refers, though not by name, to the Proclamation of 1763.

The king and his government interfered with justice in the colonies by appointing British judges and British-controlled courts.

They quartered British soldiers in colonial homes at the expense and inconvenience of the colonists.

They replaced civilian rule and law with harsh military rule.

The king and his government interfered with the trade of the colonies.

They taxed colonists without allowing them to have any say about it.

They took away the right of trial by jury.

They extended British rule into lands claimed by colonial governments.

They used paid foreign soldiers, or mercenaries, on American soil. The use of hired foreign soldiers was quite common at this time, but it was a sore point with many colonists.

jurisdiction foreign to our constitution, and unacknowledged by our laws, giving his assent to their acts of pretended legislation:

For quartering large bodies of armed troops among us;

For protecting them, by a mock trial, from punishment for any murders which they should commit on the inhabitants of these States;

For cutting off our trade with all parts of the world;

For imposing taxes on us without our consent;

For depriving us, in many cases, of the benefits of trial by jury;

For transporting us beyond seas to be tried for pretended offences;

For abolishing the free system of English laws in a neighboring province, establishing therein an arbitrary government, and enlarging its boundaries, so as to render it at once an example and fit instrument for introducing the same absolute rule into these colonies;

For taking away our charters, abolishing our most valuable laws, and altering fundamentally the forms of our governments;

For suspending our own legislatures, and declaring themselves invested with power to legislate for us in all cases whatsoever.

He has abdicated government here, by declaring us out of his protection and waging war against us.

He has plundered our seas, ravaged our coasts, burnt our towns, and destroyed the lives of our people.

He is, at this time, transporting large armies of foreign mercenaries to complete the works of death, desolation, and tyranny already begun, with circumstances of cruelty and perfidy scarcely paralleled in the most barbarous ages, and totally unworthy the head of a civilized nation.

He has constrained our fellow-citizens, taken captive on the high seas, to bear arms against their country, to become the executioners of their friends and brethren, or to fall themselves by their hands.

He has excited domestic insurrections amongst

us, and has endeavored to bring on the inhabitants of our frontiers, the merciless Indian savages, whose known rule of warfare is an undistinguished destruction of all ages, sexes, and conditions.

In every stage of these oppressions, we have petitioned for redress, in the most humble terms; our repeated petitions have been answered only by repeated injury. A prince, whose character is thus marked by every act which may define a tyrant, is unfit to be the ruler of a free people.

Nor have we been wanting in attentions to our British brethren. We have warned them, from time to time, of attempts by their legislature to extend an unwarrantable jurisdiction over us. We have reminded them of the circumstances of our emigration and settlement here. We have appealed to their native justice and magnanimity, and we have conjured them, by the ties of our common kindred, to disavow these usurpations, which would inevitably interrupt our connections and correspondence. They, too, have been deaf to the voice of justice and of consanguinity. We must, therefore, acquiesce in the necessity, which denounces our separation, and hold them, as we hold the rest of mankind, enemies in war; in peace, friends.

We, therefore, the representatives of the United States of America, in General Congress assembled, appealing to the Supreme Judge of the world for the rectitude of our intentions, do, in the name, and by authority of the good people of these colonies, solemnly publish and declare: That these United Colonies are, and of right ought to be, free and independent States; that they are absolved from all allegiance to the British Crown, and that all political connection between them and the state of Great Britain is, and ought to be, totally dissolved; and that, as free and independent States, they have full power to levy war, conclude peace, contract alliances, establish commerce, and to do all other acts and things which independent States may of right do. And, for the support of this declaration, with a firm reliance on the protection of Divine Providence, we mutually pledge to each other our lives, our fortunes, and our sacred honor.

The king and his government used Indians as allies against the colonists. This was a common complaint of many western colonists.

After listing their complaints, the colonists then mention their many attempts to settle these issues peacefully.

The colonists argue that all appeals to the king and to the people of Britain have failed.

In the last paragraph, the colonists declare that the colonies are now free and independent. They owe no loyalty to the king or to Britain. In taking this action, the colonists feel that they have the protection of God. In conclusion, the colonists pledge their lives, property, and honor to their cause.

unit
3

The Old House of Representatives by Samuel B. Morse, in the Collection of the Corcoran Gallery of Art

A New Plan
for
Government

We the People

Article I.

Section 1.

Section 2.

Section 3.

Section 4.

Section 5.

Section 6.

Fresh from the Revolution, the new nation needed a new government. It found this through the Constitution, which set up a practical democracy. This history-making document set up three branches of government: legislative (left), executive, and judicial.

Lesson 1   The Ideas Behind the Constitution

WORDS TO UNDERSTAND

Discuss the meanings of these words.

modification	legislative
federal	executive
residual	judicial

NEW WORDS IN SENTENCES

1. There was some **modification** of the program, but the changes were not great.

2. The **federal** government ties the individual states together.

3. Those powers not granted to the federal government and not denied to the state governments are the states' **residual** powers.

4. The chief lawmaking, or **legislative,** body in the United States is the Congress.

5. The president, our chief **executive,** must promise to make sure all laws are faithfully carried out.

6. The Supreme Court is the highest **judicial** body in the United States.

AS YOU READ

As you read this selection, try to answer these questions.

1. What system did the founders of the nation propose to prevent one branch of the government from becoming too powerful?

2. What were the six major purposes of the Constitution?

THE READING SELECTION

A British statesman once described the Constitution of the United States as "the most remarkable work . . . to have been produced by the human intellect, at a single stroke." This may seem an exaggerated statement. But the fact that the Constitution has existed in almost original form since 1787 is proof of its unique nature. This document has kept pace with our growing nation and changing times. It has undergone little **modification** over the years. Our Constitution has remained effective for nearly 200 years.

Since the writing of the Constitution, our nation has expanded from thirteen states to fifty. Its population has grown from less than 4 million in 1790 to more than 226 million in the 1980s. The United States has changed from an agricultural society to an industrial nation. Our ways of thinking, working, and living have changed. But the Constitution, written in 1787, remains very much the same. This "most remarkable" document continues to work in modern times because its writers planned well for the future.

The Constitution achieves six major purposes.

1. It establishes a republic. A republic is a form of government in which the power is in the hands of citizens qualified to vote. The voters elect representatives who make the laws and govern the country.

The writers of the Constitution wanted this republican form of government to work within a **federal** system. In a federal system, individual states join together in a union. In addition to the state governments, therefore, there is a national, or federal, government to tie the states together. The federal government makes laws for the union of the states.

2. It establishes a division of power between the state and federal governments. The Constitution grants certain specific powers to the federal government. It also specifically denies certain powers to the state governments. It does not, however, name the specific powers that the states do have. There are some powers that are not given to the federal government and not denied to the states. These are known as the states' **residual** powers, because they reside, or remain, with the state governments or with the people. For example, the control of education is not granted to the federal government and not denied to the states. This power, then, resides with the state governments. States also control matters of health, police, and fire protection.

3. It provides for a separation of powers among the branches of the federal government. The three branches of federal authority are the **legislative** (Congress), **executive** (president), and **judicial** (federal courts). The Constitution gives each of these branches the power to control, or check, the authority of the other two. No one branch of the government can control the others. Each has enough power to make sure that no one branch becomes too powerful. This system of checks and balances has worked well throughout our history.

4. It establishes the qualifications and duties of members of the various branches of government.

5. It provides a means for amending, or changing, the Constitution.

6. It provides for future needs by making it possible to enlarge the meaning of the Constitution. The "elastic clause" of the Constitution (Article I, Section 8, Clause 18) achieves this purpose. The elastic clause gives Congress the authority "to make all laws . . . necessary and proper" to carry out its duties. This clause gives Congress the means to handle unknown future problems.

The authors of the Constitution did not specifically set out to establish a democracy. The word *democracy* does not appear in the Constitution. But the Constitution did provide the means by which a democracy could be established, expanded, and preserved. It is a "living Constitution" that can be expanded and revised by several methods.

1. amendments.

2. court rulings on laws.

3. new laws passed by Congress.

4. traditions that develop through the years.

The Constitution has adjusted to the needs of the growing nation. For this reason, it remains the basis of the American democratic spirit.

COMPREHENSION CHECK

A. Recognizing the Main Idea

This selection as a whole tells you that

1. the Constitution was not intended to last forever.

2. the Constitution can adjust to and grow with the changing times.

3. the Constitution was written for the specific purpose of setting up a democracy.

4. the Constitution does not easily adjust to changing times.

B. Selecting Important Details

Choose the ending that best completes each statement.

1. In a federal system, individual states
   a. have no powers of their own.
   b. are united by a central, national government.
   c. are completely independent.
   d. may not have their own governments.

2. The purpose of the division of power is to divide governing power
   a. among the various federal agencies.
   b. between the state and federal governments.
   c. between the president and Congress.
   d. among all the agencies of government.

3. No one branch of the federal government can become too powerful
   a. according to the amendments.
   b. under the system of checks and balances.
   c. under the system of division of power.
   d. except the executive branch.

4. The Constitution
   a. cannot be amended.
   b. states that the government is a democracy.
   c. can be expanded and revised.
   d. does not include the elastic clause.

C. Vocabulary

Match the words with the definitions.

Words	Definitions
1. modification	a. corroding
2. federal	b. change; alteration
3. legislative	c. judge
4. executive	d. lawmaking branch of the government
5. judicial	e. central force uniting individual states
	f. branch of government that interprets laws
	g. branch of government that carries out laws

D. Ask Yourself

Why do you think the writers of the Constitution chose to divide power between the federal and state governments?

Slavery and the Constitution

The American Revolution had been fought to win greater freedom. But black Americans generally, and slaves especially, were not included in this new-found freedom.

The issue of slavery arose several times during the Constitutional Convention. In the matter of counting the population, the southern states wanted slaves to be counted equally with whites. This would give greater representation to the South in Congress. Northern states opposed this because of the greater power it would give the South, and also because there was feeling against giving blacks any sort of equal standing with whites. The "three-fifths compromise" finally settled the issue by counting five slaves as three persons for purposes of taxation and representation.

Another matter brought before the convention was the slave trade. There was strong opposition in the North to the slave trade. Even some southerners wanted to end the trade, because they felt that if no more slaves were brought into the country, the value of the slaves they now owned would increase. The compromise which was finally worked out stated that Congress would pass no laws restricting the slave trade for twenty years.

The final action of the convention regarding slavery was the passage of a provision requiring the return of runaway slaves. It declared that any slave escaping from one state to another must be returned upon the claim of the slave's owner.

Negroes for Sale.

A Cargo of very fine stout Men and Women, in good order and fit for immediate service, just imported from the Windward Coast of Africa, in the Ship Two Brothers.—

Conditions are one half Cash or Produce, the other half payable the first of January next, giving Bond and Security if required.

The Sale to be opened at 10 o'Clock each Day, in Mr. Bourdeaux's Yard, at No, 48, on the Bay.

May 19, 1784.   JOHN MITCHELL.

Thirty Seasoned Negroes

To be Sold for Credit, at Private Sale.

AMONGST which is a Carpenter, none of whom are known to be dishonest.

Also, to be sold for Cash, a regular tred young Negroe Man-Cook, born in this Country, who served several Years under an exceeding good French Cook abroad, and his Wife a middle aged Washer-Woman, (both very honest) and their two Children. Likewise, a young Man a Carpenter.

For Terms apply to the Printer.

Slavery in the former colonies was not ended by either American independence or the new government of the Constitution. These signs advertised slave sales only a year after the Revolution ended. (In the 1700s, a small s was often represented by a letter that looked like an f without the crossbar.)

113

Lesson 2   The Organization of the Constitution

WORDS TO UNDERSTAND
Discuss the meanings of these words.

impeach	**jurisdiction**	**extradition**
convicted	**treason**	**allegiance**

NEW WORDS IN SENTENCES
1. Before the House of Representatives votes to **impeach** an official, there must be sufficient grounds for the accusation.
2. The suspect was **convicted** by the jury because all the evidence pointed to his guilt.
3. Traffic courts cannot hear divorce cases because they have **jurisdiction** only over violations of traffic laws.
4. People who commit acts aimed at overthrowing the government can be charged with the crime of **treason.**
5. According to the laws of **extradition,** the suspect captured in California was returned for trial to Nevada, where the crime had been committed.
6. Each new club member had to take an oath of **allegiance** and pledge loyalty to the club.

AS YOU READ
As you read this selection, try to answer these questions.
1. What is the only crime that is defined in the Constitution?
2. What does the Constitution say about cases in which a state law and a federal law conflict?

THE READING SELECTION
Review. The Constitution sought to establish

1. a republican form of government based on a federal system.
2. a division of power between state and federal governments.
3. a separation of powers among the legislative, executive, and judicial branches of the federal government.
4. the qualifications and duties of members of the branches of the federal government.
5. a system for amending the Constitution.
6. the right of Congress to handle unforeseen future events. The elastic clause gives Congress authority "to make all laws . . . necessary and proper" to carry out its duties.   ☆

The Constitution is made up of a preamble, seven articles, and a number of amendments.

The preamble, or introduction, states the general purposes of the Constitution. These purposes include establishing a union of states and a principle of justice. In addition, the Constitution seeks to ensure peace and promote the well-being and liberty of people in the United States.

Article I. Article I establishes Congress. Congress is the legislative, or lawmaking, branch of the federal government. It is composed of two houses, the Senate and the House of Representatives. Article I gives the duties and qualifications of senators and representatives.

Article I also describes the manner in which laws must be passed by Congress. It names the powers given to Congress as well as the powers denied to Congress. While Article I is mainly about the legislative branch of the federal government, it also lists the powers denied to the states. Those powers not specifically granted to the federal government or denied to the state governments are the states' residual powers.

Article II. Article II establishes the executive branch of government. It provides that the executive power shall be given to a president. It also provides for the office of vice-president. The vice-president assumes the duties of president if the president dies, is removed from office, or cannot perform the duties of the office. Article II also outlines the duties and qualifications of the president. It makes provisions for the removal of federal officers by Congress. It grants Congress the power to **impeach** an official, or make a formal accusation that could lead to a trial. The House of Representatives has the power to make an accusation. But the trial must be before the Senate. The Senate decides the verdict in the impeached official's case. An official **convicted,** or found guilty of wrongdoing, is removed from office and may face a criminal trial. Article II also sets up a method for electing the president and vice-president. This method, however, has been changed by the Twelfth Amendment.

Article III. Article III concerns the judicial branch of government, or the federal courts. It provides for a Supreme Court and such lower courts as Congress may decide to set up. The article outlines the cases over which the Supreme Court and other federal courts have **jurisdiction,** or authority. It also declares that criminal cases must be tried before juries.

Article III is the only part of the Constitution that defines a specific crime. That crime is **treason.** The Constitution declares that only those citizens who go to war against the United States or who aid its enemies can be charged with treason. The charge of treason can be established only in two ways. One is by open confession. The other is by the testimony of two witnesses to the same act of treason. Since treason is such a serious crime, the writers of the Constitution were careful to define it exactly.

Article IV. Article IV covers the relation of states to each other and to the Union. It provides that the legal actions of any state must be recognized as legal in all the other states. This provision protects the rights of citizens when they leave their state for any other state. The article also covers the treatment of criminals fleeing from the state in which they committed a crime. They are subject to **extradition,** or return to the authorities in the state from which they fled. One part of Article IV discusses the return of runaway slaves. This part has not been in effect since 1865, when the Thirteenth Amendment ended slavery in the United States.

An important part of Article IV outlines the way new states are to be admitted to the Union. It also specifies the authority of Congress over territories of the United States. Territories are areas owned by the United States that are not part of the fifty states. Article IV further guarantees every state an elected, republican form of government. It promises each state protection from invasion and riots that threaten the national security.

Article V. Article V establishes the method of amending the Constitution.

Article VI. Article VI ties together a number of loose ends. This article covers the problem of debts owed by the new government at the time the Constitution was written. Article VI also declares that the Constitution, the federal laws, and all treaties made by the United States are the supreme laws of the land. When state laws conflict with federal or treaty laws, the state laws are overruled. Article VI also requires federal and state officials to take an oath of **allegiance** to the Constitution. But it forbids religious requirements for any federal officeholder.

Article VII. Article VII states that when nine states (of the thirteen that existed in 1787) ratified, or accepted, the Constitution, it would be considered in effect for those nine states.

The rest of our Constitution consists of the amendments that have been added since 1787. The first ten amendments, called the Bill of Rights, were ratified in 1791. This was only three years after the Constitution itself had been adopted. The Bill of Rights pleased those states that had been unwilling to ratify the Constitution without it.

ORGANIZATION of the CONSTITUTION

Constitution of the United States

Preamble	General purposes
Article I	Legislative Branch
Article II	Executive Branch
Article III	Judicial Branch
Article IV	Relations of states to each other and to federal government
Article V	Method of amending Constitution
Article VI	General provisions: supreme law of the land, oaths of allegiance
Article VII	Method of ratifying Constitution

Amendments to the Constitution

THE BILL OF RIGHTS (1791)

1 Freedom of religion, speech, and press
2 Right of states to have militia
3 Freedom from having to quarter soldiers during peace time
4 No unreasonable searches and arrests
5 Grand jury, double jeopardy, due process
6 Right to a fair trial by jury in criminal cases
7 Right to a trial by jury in most civil cases
8 Reasonable bails, fines, and punishments
9 Protection of rights not named in Constitution
10 Residual powers of states and people

11 Protection of states from being sued in federal court (1795)
12 Separate ballots for president and vice-president (1804)
13 Abolition of slavery (1865)
14 Citizenship for blacks (1868)
15 Voting rights for blacks (1870)
16 Income tax (1913)
17 Direct election of senators (1913)
18 Prohibition of liquor (1919)
19 Voting rights for women (1920)
20 Lame Duck Amendment (1933)
21 Repeal of prohibition (1933)
22 Two-term limit for president (1952)
23 Voting rights in presidential elections for residents of District of Columbia (1961)
24 Anti-poll tax Amendment (1964)
25 Presidential succession (1967)
26 Eighteen-year-old vote (1971)

COMPREHENSION CHECK

A. Recognizing the Main Idea

This selection as a whole tells you that

1. the Constitution is not a democratic document.

2. the Constitution is divided into articles that describe the various parts of the government.

3. the articles of the Constitution do not outline the different branches of the government.

4. the amendments are more important than parts of the original Constitution.

B. Selecting Important Details

Choose the ending that best completes each statement.

1. The Constitution declares that the supreme law of the land is
   a. decided by the Supreme Court.
   b. decided only by the state governments.
   c. the Constitution.
   d. the Congress and its laws.

2. The residual powers of states are powers that are
   a. denied to the state governments.
   b. not given to the federal government or denied to the state governments.
   c. given to both the state and federal governments.
   d. granted to the state governments.

3. The only specific crime defined in the Constitution is
   a. murder.
   b. extradition.
   c. treason.
   d. felony.

4. The Constitution does not include
   a. a provision for amending the Constitution.
   b. a division of power between state and federal governments.
   c. the powers granted to the state governments.
   d. qualifications for members of the executive and legislative branches.

C. True or False

Decide whether each of these statements is true or false.

1. The Constitution describes the way in which Congress may remove the president from office.

2. The Constitution provides for federal courts but not specifically for a Supreme Court.

3. According to the Constitution, the legal actions of one state do not need to be recognized in another state.

4. The Constitution guarantees a republican form of government in each state.

5. The Constitution describes how laws are to be passed by Congress.

D. Vocabulary

Match the words with the definitions.

Words	Definitions
1. impeach	a. acquitted
2. convicted	b. accuse an official of wrongdoing
3. treason	c. loyalty
4. extradition	d. secrecy
5. allegiance	e. the return of a suspect to authorities
	f. action against one's government
	g. found guilty

Lesson 3   The Powers of the Legislative Branch

WORDS TO UNDERSTAND

Discuss the meanings of these words.

proceedings   commerce
uniform   copyright
interstate   patent

NEW WORDS IN SENTENCES

1. When the meeting was called to order, the **proceedings** began.

2. Divorce laws are not **uniform** throughout the country, since each state has different laws on divorce.

3. Airplanes help speed **interstate** travel.

4. The federal government regulates trade, or **commerce,** with foreign countries.

5. The author applied for a **copyright** for the new book.

6. Other companies began to copy the invention after the **patent** on it expired.

AS YOU READ

As you read this selection, try to answer these questions.

1. What special powers are given to each of the houses of Congress?

2. In what ways do the powers of Congress assure equal treatment of all states?

THE READING SELECTION

Review. The preamble of the Constitution states the general purposes of the document. Articles I, II, and III set up the legislative, executive, and judicial branches of the government. Article IV covers the relation of states to each other and to the Union. Article V provides the means for amending the Constitution. Article VI declares the Constitution the supreme law of the land, and Article VII explains when the Constitution may go into effect. ☆

The legislative branch, or Congress, is the lawmaking body of the federal government. It consists of the House of Representatives (the lower house) and the Senate (the upper house). The House of Representatives has 435 members, elected on the basis of state population. States with large populations have more representatives than states with smaller populations. Each member of the House serves a two-year term of office. The Senate has 100 members, two senators from each of the fifty states. Each senator serves a six-year term of office. No member of Congress may hold any other federal office during the time that he or she is serving in Congress.

The Constitution grants many powers to Congress. For example, Congress has the general power to run its own **proceedings.** It also has the power to impeach federal officials. The House of Representatives has the power to make

THE ORGANIZATION OF THE LEGISLATIVE BRANCH

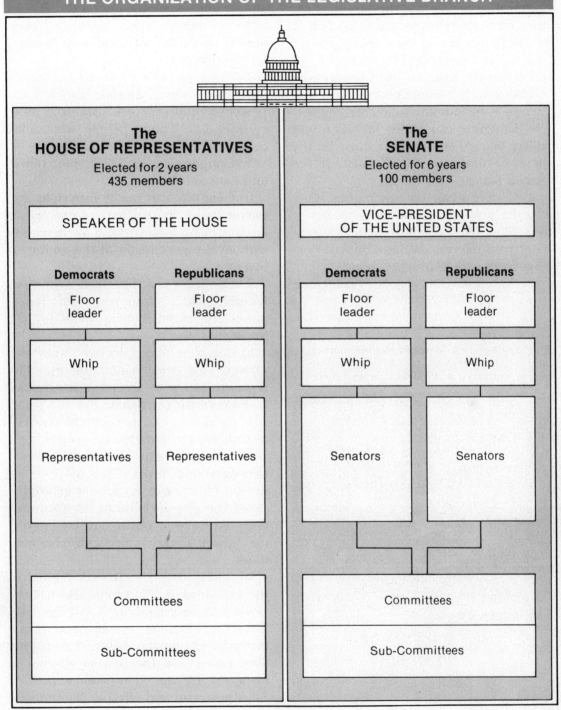

The
HOUSE OF REPRESENTATIVES
Elected for 2 years
435 members

SPEAKER OF THE HOUSE

Democrats

Floor leader

Whip

Representatives

Republicans

Floor leader

Whip

Representatives

Committees

Sub-Committees

The
SENATE
Elected for 6 years
100 members

VICE-PRESIDENT
OF THE UNITED STATES

Democrats

Floor leader

Whip

Senators

Republicans

Floor leader

Whip

Senators

Committees

Sub-Committees

a formal accusation of official wrong-doing. The Senate has the power to try impeached officials. Article I, Section 8, of the Constitution lists more powers granted to Congress. This section is often called the heart of the Constitution.

The powers enumerated in Article I, Section 8, include the following.

1. Congress can make tax laws and collect taxes. Federal taxes must be the same, or **uniform,** for all parts of the United States.

2. Congress can borrow money. One way the government borrows money is by selling federal bonds. The government pays interest on the money it borrows from people who buy bonds.

3. Congress can regulate **interstate** trade. Congress regulates the buying and selling of goods among the various states. Congress also regulates **commerce,** or trade, with Indian tribes and foreign nations.

4. Congress can print paper money and issue coins. Congress also has the power to punish people who issue money illegally. These people are called counterfeiters.

5. Congress can establish post offices and national roads.

6. Congress can make **copyright** and **patent** laws. These laws prevent people from copying a book, song, or invention without the permission of the author or inventor.

7. Congress can set up a system of federal courts. Congress also determines the number of justices on the Supreme Court.

8. Congress can declare war and provide for the armed forces. The power to ratify, or accept, peace treaties is reserved for the Senate.

9. Congress can govern the District of Columbia, the nation's capital.

10. Congress can "make all laws . . . necessary and proper" to perform its duties. This power is granted in what is called the elastic clause of the Constitution. The elastic clause gives Congress the power to keep up with changing times.

In addition to the powers named in the Constitution, Congress also has the power of investigation. Congress may investigate matters to obtain information that will help in future lawmaking. This power and the powers granted to Congress by the Constitution provide for a powerful and effective legislature.

The Senate and the House of Representatives meet in joint session on special occasions. Shown here is an address by President Jimmy Carter.

Dev O'Neill, K. Jewell

120

COMPREHENSION CHECK

A. Recognizing the Main Idea

This selection as a whole tells you that

1. there are no limits to the powers of Congress.

2. many of the powers given to Congress are enumerated in the Constitution.

3. the powers of Congress enumerated in the Constitution are not very important.

4. Congress has less power than the president.

B. Selecting Important Details

Choose the ending that best completes each statement.

1. Members of the House of Representatives are elected on the basis of
    a. an equal number from each state.
    b. special acts of Congress.
    c. the population of each state.
    d. the size of each state.

2. All of the following powers are granted to Congress in Section 8 of Article I EXCEPT the power to
    a. regulate interstate commerce.
    b. make tax laws and collect taxes.
    c. run its own proceedings.
    d. regulate religion.

3. The purpose of the investigating power of Congress is to
    a. punish those who break the laws.
    b. get information for future law-making.
    c. check up on the work of other government agencies.
    d. help the president enforce the laws.

4. All the following are powers given to Congress EXCEPT
    a. power to set up a system of federal courts.
    b. power to borrow money.
    c. power to impeach federal officials.
    d. power to regulate education.

C. True or False

Decide whether each of these statements is true or false.

1. States have the power to set up post offices.

2. The House of Representatives has the power to try an impeached official.

3. The Senate has the power to ratify peace treaties.

4. Senators serve four-year terms.

5. Congress cannot declare war.

D. Vocabulary

Use a word from this list to complete each sentence.

proceedings   commerce
uniform   copyright
interstate   patent

1. The _____ of last week's meeting were summed up in the secretary's report.

2. Congress regulates _____ with foreign nations.

3. She applied for a _____ to protect her invention.

4. The _____ highways make travel across the country much faster.

5. The _____ date of the book was 1974.

Lesson 4 The Powers Denied to the Federal Government

WORDS TO UNDERSTAND

Discuss the meanings of these words.

habeas corpus   *ex post facto*
bail   exports
bills of attainder

NEW WORDS IN SENTENCES

1. A writ, or legal order, of *habeas corpus* demands that a prisoner be brought before a judge to be told why he or she was put in jail.

2. When the prisoner's family delivered the amount of money set by the judge as **bail,** the prisoner was released from jail until the trial.

3. **Bills of attainder** are illegal because they deny a person's right to trial.

4. If *ex post facto* laws were allowed, many people could be punished for acts that were not illegal at the time they were done.

5. American **exports** are sold to countries all around the world.

AS YOU READ

As you read this selection, try to answer these questions.

1. Why are some powers denied to the federal government?

2. Why were the founders of the nation fearful of such things as bills of attainder and *ex post facto* laws?

THE READING SELECTION

Review. The Constitution contains a preamble, seven articles, and over twenty-five amendments. Article I is devoted to the legislative branch of the federal government. It provides for a two-house federal legislature composed of a House of Representatives and a Senate. The House of Representatives has 435 members, elected on the basis of population. The Senate has 100 members, two senators from each of the fifty states. ☆

Article I, Section 8, of the Constitution states the things Congress may do. But the Constitution also lists the things that Congress may not do. These powers that are denied the federal government are outlined in Article I, Section 9, of the Constitution.

Denying certain powers to the federal government guarantees basic rights to individuals. One right is that no person can be kept in jail without having been charged with a specific crime. Each prisoner has a right to a writ of *habeas corpus.* A writ of *habeas corpus* is a court order for a prisoner to be brought before a judge. The prisoner must then be charged with a specific crime. The judge can set **bail** and a date for trial. Without the power of a writ of *habeas corpus,* accused persons could be kept in jail for years. They might never learn what crimes they were accused of committing. Congress may deny this important right

only in the case of extreme emergency.

The Constitution also forbids Congress to pass **bills of attainder.** Bills of attainder declare a person guilty without a court trial. The federal government may not deny anyone the right to a trial in court. The Constitution also forbids the federal government to pass *ex post facto* laws. These laws would allow a person to be punished for past actions that were not considered crimes at the time they were done. European rulers had used bills of attainder and *ex post facto* laws in the past. They used these laws to get rid of people who opposed the government. The writers of the Constitution wanted no part of such unfair laws.

In addition to protecting personal rights, Article I, Section 9, also seeks to protect the rights and privileges of American manufacturers. The Constitution forbids Congress to tax goods leaving any state for foreign shores or for another state. Such goods are called **exports.**

The Constitution also denies the federal government the power to take money from the national treasury without the permission of Congress. Records of income and expenses must be kept and published by the government. The federal government may not make use of secret funds. Congress must also keep and publish a record of its own proceedings. The federal government does, however, use some money for purposes that are not specifically explained in reports. In government records, some expenses are listed under a general heading without specific information about their use. Some secrecy, especially about spying and atomic research, is considered important to the national security.

The Constitution also forbids Congress to issue any titles of nobility. There are no titled persons such as queens, princes, countesses, and dukes in the United States.

COMPREHENSION CHECK

A. Recognizing the Main Idea

This selection as a whole tells you that

1. the federal government is rarely denied any powers.

2. *ex post facto* laws are forbidden.

3. the Constitution lists the powers denied to the federal government.

4. the federal government can favor one state over another.

B. Selecting Important Details

Choose the ending that best completes each statement.

1. All of the following powers are denied the federal government EXCEPT
   a. the power to borrow money.
   b. the power to keep prisoners in jail indefinitely.
   c. the power to take money from the treasury without approval of Congress.
   d. the power to tax exports.

2. Bills of attainder are unfair because they
   a. punish people for crimes.
   b. punish people for acts committed in the past.
   c. declare people guilty before they have a trial.
   d. do not permit a prisoner to post bail.

3. Money can be taken from the national treasury only with the permission of the
   a. president.
   b. treasurer.
   c. Congress.
   d. courts.

4. The purpose of a writ of *habeas corpus* is to
   a. keep a prisoner in jail.
   b. require a specific charge to be brought against a prisoner.
   c. avoid bail.
   d. set a prisoner free without a trial.

C. True or False

Decide whether each of these statements is true or false.

1. The Constitution guarantees each person the right to a writ of *habeas corpus.*

2. The Constitution does not permit the government to tax exports.

3. Congress may not remove the president from office.

4. *Ex post facto* laws may not be passed by the federal government.

5. Congress can issue titles of nobility to important federal officials.

D. Vocabulary

Use a term from this list to complete each sentence.

habeas corpus	*ex post facto*
bail	exports
bills of attainder	

1. _____ deny a person's right to a trial.

2. A writ of _____ guarantees that prisoners be brought before a judge to be told why they were arrested.

3. If prisoners have enough money for _____, they can go free until their trial.

4. Japanese _____ are sold to many countries.

5. An _____ law allows a person to be punished for an act that was not illegal at the time it was done.

Lesson 5   The Members of Congress

WORDS TO UNDERSTAND

Discuss the meanings of these words.

proportion   qualifications

census   presides

residents

NEW WORDS IN SENTENCES

1. The **proportion** of students to teachers in the school was fifty to one.

2. When the government conducts a **census,** each family must report the number of people in the household.

3. The **residents** of Belleville did not want to see a shopping center built in their town.

4. She got the job because she met all of the company's **qualifications.**

5. The principal **presides** over most faculty meetings.

AS YOU READ

As you read this selection, try to answer these questions.

1. How do the qualifications for U.S. representatives and senators differ?

2. How does the system of electing senators differ from that of electing representatives?

THE READING SELECTION

Review. According to the Constitution, Congress is denied the power to

1. refuse anyone a writ of *habeas corpus.*

2. condemn a person without a trial.

3. pass *ex post facto* laws.

4. tax exports or favor one state's commerce.

5. issue titles of nobility.   ☆

Article I of the Constitution states that the legislative powers of the federal government are to be given to a "Congress of the United States, which shall consist of a Senate and House of Representatives."

The membership of the Senate is fixed by the Constitution. Each state is entitled to two senators, regardless of its size or population. At the present time, we have 100 senators, since there are fifty states.

The Constitution does not fix the size of the House of Representatives. It states only that representatives must be chosen by the states "according to their respective numbers." It is up to Congress to determine the size of the House of Representatives, based on each state's population. Each state elects representatives in **proportion** to its population. The representation from each state is adjusted after each national **census.** There are now 435 members in the House of Representatives.

Originally, the Constitution contained the so-called three-fifths compromise. It

125

stated that every five slaves would count as three persons when states figured their population for purposes of representation. This part of the Constitution has not applied since 1868, when the Fourteenth Amendment was passed. The Fourteenth Amendment granted full citizenship to former slaves.

The House of Representatives. The House of Representatives is called the lower house. Each state today is entitled to one representative for about every 490,000 people living in the state. However, each state must have at least one representative, even if it has fewer than 490,000 people.

A representative must be at least twenty-five years of age. He or she must have been a United States citizen for at least seven years. Representatives must also be **residents** of the state from which they are elected. Members of the House of Representatives are elected to serve two-year terms. There are elections for all 435 seats every two years.

The Senate. The Senate is known as the upper house. All senators must be at least thirty years of age. They must have been citizens of the United States for at least nine years. Senators must also be residents of the state from which they are elected.

Members of the Senate serve six-year terms. The system of electing senators is different from that of electing representatives. Senators are divided into three groups, according to the year in which they were elected. One-third of the senators run for election every second year. Two senators from the same state never run for a full six-year term of office in the same year. This stag-

gered system of electing senators was put into the Constitution to prevent great changes of power in both houses of Congress in any one election year. In a single election, control of the House of Representatives can shift from one political party to another. In the Senate, however, it is more difficult for political power to shift so completely. This is because only one-third of the members are elected at one time.

Senators were originally elected by an indirect method. Each state legislature chose the senators for its state. The Seventeenth Amendment changed this indirect method in 1913. Today, senators as well as representatives are elected directly by the voters in each state.

Each house judges the **qualifications** of those who have been elected to it. Each house determines whether or not to seat new members. Each house of Congress has its own rules for its members and its proceedings. The House of Representatives elects its own officers, including the Speaker. The Speaker **presides** over sessions of the House. The vice-president of the United States presides over the Senate but cannot vote except in the case of a tie. Both houses of Congress must approve all new laws.

COMPREHENSION CHECK

A. Recognizing the Main Idea

This selection as a whole tells you

1. that both houses of Congress are chosen in the same year.

2. that the Senate is more democratically chosen than the House.

3. about the qualifications of and method of electing members of Congress.

4. that the size of both houses of Congress is fixed by the Constitution.

B. Selecting Important Details

Choose the ending that best completes each statement.

1. A candidate for the House of Representatives must be
   - a. at least thirty years of age.
   - b. a citizen of the United States for at least nine years.
   - c. a native-born citizen of the United States.
   - d. at least twenty-five years of age.

2. Members of the Senate are elected for
   - a. two-year terms.
   - b. three-year terms.
   - c. four-year terms.
   - d. six-year terms.

3. It is difficult for political power in the Senate to shift suddenly because
   - a. senators are elected for six-year terms.
   - b. the entire Senate runs for office every two years.
   - c. only one-third of the Senate runs for office every two years.
   - d. senators are elected for life.

4. The three-fifths compromise in the Constitution provided that
   - a. the House have three-fifths as much power as the Senate.
   - b. every five slaves be counted as three persons for purposes of representation.
   - c. every three slaves be counted as five persons for purposes of representation.
   - d. only three-fifths of all people be counted to decide representation.

C. Vocabulary

Match the words with the definitions.

Words	Definitions
1. census	a. half of something
2. residents	b. requirements
3. qualifications	c. to move away
4. presides	d. official population count
	e. people who live in a certain area
	f. leads or conducts a meeting

D. Chart Skills

Make a chart like the one below, comparing the qualifications of senators with those of representatives.

	senators	representatives
minimum age		
residency		
citizenship		

John Quincy Adams in Congress

The powers of the federal government are divided among three different branches. Each of these branches—legislative, executive, and judicial—has its part to play. The question often arises, "Which branch of government is most important?" Our answer usually is that each branch has its own important part to play and that no one branch is more important than any other. Yet most Americans would agree that the presidency is the highest position in the nation.

John Quincy Adams had been president from 1825 to 1829. When he was defeated by Andrew Jackson in the election of 1828, it seemed that his career was at an end. However, Adams was then only beginning a new and more brilliant period of service to his country. In 1830, he ran for the office of member of the House of Representatives from Massachusetts. His friends had felt that he ought not to run for this position after having been president. Adams replied that no position in the service of the American people was beneath the dignity of any American.

John Quincy Adams was the son of a president and had, himself, served in that high office. For the next seventeen years, until his death in 1848, he made a brilliant record as a congressman. John Quincy Adams showed that a person could offer as much to the country in the legislative as in the executive branch of our government.

Lesson 6　The Business of Congress

WORDS TO UNDERSTAND

Discuss the meanings of these words.

majority　　　　duplicates
confirm　　　　adjourn
ambassadors　　veto

NEW WORDS IN SENTENCES

1. Since fewer than half of the senators voted for the bill, it failed to win a **majority** vote.

2. The Senate showed its approval by voting to **confirm** the president's choice of cabinet officers.

3. United States **ambassadors** around the world help establish good relations with foreign governments.

4. He made **duplicates** of his letter so that everyone at the meeting would have an exact copy.

5. The judge will **adjourn** the court when it finishes its business for the day.

6. If the president rejects a bill, Congress may still approve it over the president's **veto** if two-thirds of both houses vote for it.

AS YOU READ

As you read this selection, try to answer these questions.

1. What is the purpose of congressional committees?

2. How may Congress pass a law without the approval of the president?

THE READING SELECTION

Review. The Constitution states that all legislative powers of the federal government are to be given to the Congress of the United States. The Congress consists of a Senate and a House of Representatives. The Senate is known as the upper house. The House of Representatives is called the lower house. Both houses of Congress make laws, but each has certain specific jobs, or functions.　☆

The House of Representatives is responsible for starting all revenue, or money, bills. The House must also begin any impeachment proceedings against the president or other officials if there is evidence of wrongdoing. In addition, the House must elect a president if no presidential candidate receives a **majority** of the necessary votes.

The Senate has different duties. It must **confirm,** or approve, all treaties and all presidential appointments. These include appointments of cabinet officers and **ambassadors** sent to other countries. The Senate also tries impeachment cases sent to it by the House of Representatives. The Senate elects a vice-president if no candidate for that office receives a majority of electoral-college votes.

In addition to these special functions, both houses of Congress pass laws to govern the United States. To aid them in this work, both houses have a number of committees. The committees weed out useless bills, and bills that may be **duplicates** of each other. Much of the work of Congress takes place in the committees.

All proposed laws must be approved by both houses of Congress. For this reason, it is important that both houses be in session at the same time. The Constitution states that neither house can **adjourn** for more than three days without the consent of the other house.

A bill becomes a law in the following way.

1. A member of one of the houses (we will assume that it is the House of Representatives) draws up a bill. Sometimes this bill is the result of work done by a congressional investigating committee. Sometimes it is the idea of a single member of the House.

2. The bill is filed with the clerk of the House. Then it goes to one of the committees.

3. The committee then studies the bill. It may hold special hearings to gather information about the bill. During the hearings, private citizens can speak for or against the bill. Then the members of the committee vote on whether or not to send the bill to the entire House. About nine out of every ten bills die in committee. They never get to the full House for a vote.

4. If the bill goes to the full House, it is debated and perhaps amended. It is then put to a vote. If a majority of representatives present in the House vote for the bill, it passes and goes on to the Senate for consideration.

5. The Senate may offer more changes or amendments to the bill. If the Senate makes any changes, the bill must go back to the House for approval in its changed form. Both houses of Congress must agree on one form of the bill. If the two houses cannot agree on a bill, it goes to a conference committee, which considers the changes. This conference committee is made up of members from both houses. They try to agree upon a single version of the bill.

6. When a bill is passed by both houses, it goes to the president. The president may either sign the bill into law or **veto** it. If the president vetoes, or rejects, a bill, it can still become law.

HOW A BILL BECOMES A LAW

1.	2.	3.	4.
The bill is introduced into either house, given a number, and sent to the proper committee.	The committee holds discussions and hearings on the bill. It makes its recommendations to the full house.	The bill is debated, amended, and voted upon. If it is passed, it is sent to the other house.	If the other house approves the bill, but in a different form, it goes to a joint committee. A compromise bill is worked out.

The powerful Ways and Means Committee in the House of Representatives often makes news. Here, Chairman Al Ullman is questioned about committee business by reporters.

Dev O'Neill

This happens if each house approves the bill by a two-thirds majority vote.

A bill passed by both houses and approved by the president becomes a law. However, all laws can be challenged. They can be taken before the courts on the grounds that they are not proper under the Constitution. Such cases may reach the Supreme Court. The Supreme Court can then uphold the law or declare it unconstitutional (against the Constitution). If the Court decides a law is unconstitutional, that law is no longer in effect.

5.

Both houses vote on the new compromise bill.

6.

If the bill is passed by both houses, it is sent to the president. The bill becomes a law if the president signs it.

7.

If the president does not sign the bill (if the president vetoes it), the bill goes back to the Congress.

8.

Both houses of Congress vote again. If two-thirds of both houses pass the bill after the president's veto, the bill becomes a law.

COMPREHENSION CHECK

A. Recognizing the Main Idea
This selection as a whole tells you
1. that all bills need the approval of the president to become laws.
2. how bills become laws.
3. that Congress must vote a second time on bills that the president signs.
4. how the president may veto the bills passed by Congress.

B. Selecting Important Details
Choose the ending that best completes each statement.
1. If the president vetoes a bill, it can still become a law if
   a. the Senate passes it by a two-thirds majority.
   b. both houses pass it by a simple majority.
   c. Congress appeals to the Supreme Court.
   d. it passes both houses by a two-thirds majority.
2. In the event that no candidate in a presidential election receives a majority of votes,
   a. both houses of Congress must choose a president.
   b. the Supreme Court chooses who will be president.
   c. the House of Representatives chooses a president.
   d. the Senate must choose a president.
3. All revenue, or money, bills
   a. must start in the House of Representatives.
   b. must start in the Senate.
   c. must be approved by the president.
   d. are started by joint committees of both houses.
4. A law passed by Congress
   a. can never be questioned.
   b. automatically comes before the Supreme Court for approval.
   c. must come to the Supreme Court if the president desires it.
   d. may reach the Supreme Court for a decision on whether or not it violates the Constitution.

C. Vocabulary
Match the words with the definitions.

Words	Definitions
1. majority	a. two-thirds
2. confirm	b. representatives to other countries
3. ambassadors	
4. adjourn	c. appoint a judge
5. veto	d. approve; accept
	e. reject; refuse to approve
	f. more than half
	g. close a session or meeting

D. Using Your Knowledge
The steps by which a bill introduced in the House becomes a law are listed out of order below. On a separate sheet of paper, list them in the proper order.

Bill sent to president
Bill filed with clerk of the House
Bill sent to Senate
Bill sent to House
Bill sent to House committee

Lesson 7   The Election of the President

WORDS TO UNDERSTAND

Discuss the meanings of these words.

candidate   slate
electoral college   registered
nominate   popular vote

NEW WORDS IN SENTENCES

1. Although she was a **candidate** for governor three times, she was never elected.

2. Many people feel that presidents should be elected by direct vote rather than by the **electoral college.**

3. Each party will **nominate** a qualified person to run for the office of president.

4. The party needed one more name on the list to complete the **slate** of presidential electors for the state.

5. Only those people who had **registered** in advance were allowed to vote.

6. The general public liked the young candidate, and he received a majority of the **popular vote.**

AS YOU READ

As you read this selection, try to answer these questions.

1. How is it possible for presidential candidates to lose elections even though they receive more votes than their opponents?

2. What qualifications must a candidate for president of the United States meet?

THE READING SELECTION

Review. Article I of the Constitution describes the duties and qualifications of members of Congress. It also outlines the method Congress uses to pass laws.

Congress has two houses: the Senate and the House of Representatives. The people of each state elect two members of the Senate. Each state also elects members to the House of Representatives in proportion to its population. There are now 435 members in the House.

Article I gives all lawmaking power to the Congress. Both houses have committees that study proposed laws. These committees do much of the work of Congress. They begin the process by which a bill becomes a law.   ☆

Article II of the Constitution outlines the executive branch of the federal government. The executive branch enforces the laws passed by Congress. The Constitution places the executive power in a president. It also provides for a vice-president. The vice-president replaces the president if the president dies, resigns, or is unable to perform the duties of the office.

The president is elected for a four-year term and must meet certain qualifications. A president must be a native-born citizen of the United States and at least thirty-five years of age. The president must have been a resident of the

133

United States for at least fourteen years.

The Constitution does not mention how many terms a president may serve. According to a custom begun by George Washington, presidents served for no more than two terms. President Franklin D. Roosevelt, however, was reelected to a third and a fourth term of office. In 1951, the Twenty-second Amendment was passed. It limits a president to two full terms in office.

The president is elected by an indirect voting method. The writers of the Constitution did not favor letting the people vote directly for the president. They thought that the people should choose qualified citizens from each state as presidential electors. These electors would then meet to select a president. The **candidate** receiving the largest number of electoral votes would become president. The candidate with the next largest number of votes would be vice-president. The Twelfth Amendment changed this system in 1804. It

The 1976 Democratic National Convention included more minority and women delegates than ever before. Changes in the methods used to select delegates helped make this possible.

Democratic National Committee

provided that electors vote for the president and vice-president on separate ballots.

The presidential electors are called the **electoral college.** They still elect the president and vice-president, but not in the original way. The rise of political parties has brought changes in this method. Now, political parties hold national conventions to **nominate** candidates for president and vice-president.

The political parties in each state draw up a **slate** of presidential electors. Each state is entitled to as many electors as it has members in both houses of Congress. The District of Columbia is also granted electors. For the nation, the total number of electors in the electoral college is 538. Of these, 435 equal the number of representatives, 100 equal the number of senators, and 3 are electors for the District of Columbia. A candidate must win a majority (270 or more) of the total electoral votes to become president.

On election day, **registered** voters cast their ballots. While they vote for a candidate by name, they are really voting for the electors chosen by the candidate's political party. That is, the voter who votes for Candidate A for president is really voting for electors for A for president.

When the votes are counted at the end of election day, there are two totals. One total is the **popular vote.** This shows how many people voted for each candidate. The other total is the electoral vote. It is the electoral vote that decides who will be president.

The electoral vote in each state is decided by the popular vote. If a majority of the people in a state vote for Candidate A, then A's electors are the ones chosen from the state to elect the president. Members of the electoral college are free to vote for anyone. But it has become the custom that they vote for the candidate of their political party.

The candidate who gets a majority of the total electoral vote is the one who will be the president. The official notice of election comes weeks after the popular voting takes place. In each state, the electors chosen must meet and vote for their candidate. Their votes are sent to Washington, D.C. There they are officially recorded in the Senate, and the result is announced.

Sometimes, there are more than two candidates for president. If none of them receives a majority of the electoral-college votes, the Constitution provides for the decision to be made by the House of Representatives. Each state is allowed a single vote. The House chooses a president from the top three candidates. In a similar way, if the electors cannot choose a vice-president, the decision goes to the Senate. The Senate chooses a vice-president from the two candidates receiving the most electoral votes.

This method of electing a president has sometimes resulted in problems. In the presidential election of 1888, for example, Grover Cleveland received more popular votes than his opponent. But Cleveland lost the election. His opponent, Benjamin Harrison, carried most of the states with large populations by a slim margin. These states had more electoral votes than less populated states, so Harrison was able to win a majority of the electoral votes.

COMPREHENSION CHECK

A. Recognizing the Main Idea

This selection as a whole tells you

1. the qualifications a presidential candidate must meet.

2. that the selection of a president is left to Congress if not enough people vote.

3. how the president is nominated and elected.

4. about problems in the electoral-college system of electing the president.

B. Selecting Important Details

Choose the ending that best completes each statement.

1. The selection of candidates by political nominating conventions is
   a. part of the Constitution.
   b. out of date.
   c. the result of the rise of political parties.
   d. the result of an amendment.

2. The number of electors for each state is determined by
   a. the political parties.
   b. agreement among the states.
   c. its representation in both houses of Congress.
   d. the number of people eligible to vote.

3. A candidate for the presidency must be at least
   a. twenty-five years old.
   b. thirty-five years old.
   c. forty years old.
   d. forty-five years old.

4. A candidate for the presidency must
   a. be a native-born citizen of the U.S.
   b. have been a resident of the U.S. for seven years.
   c. be a lawyer.
   d. be the child of native-born citizens.

C. True or False

Decide whether each of these statements is true or false.

1. There is no mention of political parties in the Constitution.

2. The candidate who wins a majority of electoral votes is the one who will be president.

3. The popular vote does not directly determine who has been elected president.

4. No candidate has ever won a majority of the popular vote but failed to gain a majority in the electoral college.

5. The Twenty-second Amendment limits a president to three full terms in office.

D. Vocabulary

Write your own sentence for each of these words.

candidate   slate
electoral college   registered

Lesson 8 The Powers of the President

WORDS TO UNDERSTAND
Discuss the meanings of these words.

vested   source

inaugurated   tyranny

NEW WORDS IN SENTENCES
1. The powers **vested** in the president are those granted by the Constitution as well as by custom and tradition.

2. The governor does not officially begin her duties until she is **inaugurated.**

3. The **source** of the fire was an exposed wire.

4. The people treated harshly by the king rebelled against his **tyranny.**

AS YOU READ
As you read this selection, try to answer these questions.

1. How have the president's powers been expanded beyond those listed in Article II of the Constitution?

2. How does the president share responsibility for foreign affairs with Congress?

THE READING SELECTION
The executive branch is the department of government that enforces the laws passed by Congress. In Article II, the Constitution states that "the executive power shall be **vested** in a president of the United States of America." The president, then, is the chief executive of the United States. The president comes to power through the vote of the electoral college. According to the provisions of the Twentieth Amendment, the president is **inaugurated** on January 20.

The writers of the Constitution believed that the new nation needed a strong president to keep it together. But they also knew that many people feared a strong executive. The **source** of these fears was the memory of bitter struggles with the British government in colonial times. Many people feared the **tyranny** of a strong ruler like King George III of England.

Nevertheless, the Constitution created an executive with great powers. Like the other branches, the executive branch is subject to checks and balances on its power. Article II of the Constitution includes the following powers and duties for the president.

1. The president is commander in chief of all armed forces at all times.

2. The president appoints the heads of all executive departments. These include all cabinet officers, postmasters, tax collectors, and the officers of our

armed forces. Some of these appointments require approval by a majority of the Senate.

3. The president has the power to make treaties. However, all treaties must be approved by a two-thirds majority of the Senate.

4. The president appoints all U.S. ambassadors to other countries and all federal judges, including the judges of the Supreme Court. These appointments require the approval of a majority of the Senate.

5. The president must, from time to time, give a report to Congress on the problems and progress of the country. This report is now called the State of the Union Address.

6. The president must "take care that the laws be faithfully executed." This gives the president a good deal of power in enforcing laws. It gives a sort of elastic power to the president.

These are the powers specifically granted to the president by the Constitution. But the president's power actual-

THE ORGANIZATION OF THE EXECUTIVE BRANCH

The President

Executive Office	Cabinet	Agencies and Commissions
Office of Management and Budget	State Department (1789)	Federal Reserve System
National Security Council	Treasury Department (1789)	Federal Communications Commission
Council on Economic Policy	War Department (1789) (renamed Defense Department)	Federal Trade Commission
Council of Economic Advisers	Department of the Interior (1849)	Interstate Commerce Commission
White House Office	Department of Agriculture (1862)	United States Information Agency
Community Services Administration	Department of Justice (1870)	Environmental Protection Agency
Special Action Office for Drug Abuse Prevention	Department of Labor (1888)	Veterans Administration
Energy Resources Council	Department of Commerce (1903)	(and many others)
Council on Wage and Price Stability	Health, Education, and Welfare (1953)	
(and many others)	Housing and Urban Development (1965)	
	Department of Transportation (1966)	
	Department of Energy (1977)	

President John Kennedy exercises his power to sign legislation into law.

ly extends further. The customs and traditions of our nation have broadened the powers and duties of the president. As a result of custom and tradition, we now expect a president also to

1. be the leader and chief representative of a political party.

2. be responsible for keeping the nation at peace.

3. be responsible for the economic health of the nation.

4. be the representative for the whole nation on all matters.

5. be directly responsible for our foreign policy.

The powers of the executive branch have grown over the years. The president is a powerful figure. To make certain that presidents do not misuse their powers, the Constitution (Article II, Section 4) warns that presidents may be removed from office if they commit treason, bribery, or other serious crimes. No president has ever been removed from office. President Andrew Johnson was impeached by the House in 1868. But the Senate failed by one vote to convict him, so he was not re-moved from office. In 1974, the House began an investigation to decide whether or not to impeach President Richard Nixon. When it seemed likely that the House would vote to impeach him, Nixon resigned his office. He was the first president ever to resign.

Article II also provides for a vice-president. The vice-president, like the president, is chosen by the electoral college in a regular election.

If a president resigns, is removed, or dies while in office, the vice-president becomes president. When the vice-president takes over as president, a new vacancy is created in the vice-presidency. A vacancy is also created when a vice-president resigns, is removed, or dies. The Twenty-fifth Amendment explains how this vacancy is to be filled. The president nominates a new vice-president. Congress must approve the new vice-president by a majority of both houses.

Two vice-presidents came to office through this process. In 1973, Vice-President Spiro Agnew resigned. President Nixon then nominated Representative Gerald Ford to be vice-president. Both houses of Congress approved, and Gerald Ford became vice-president. When President Nixon resigned in 1974, Vice-President Ford became president. President Ford then nominated Nelson Rockefeller, former governor of New York, to be vice-president. Both houses of Congress voted to accept the nomination, and Nelson Rockefeller became vice-president. Thus, neither the president nor the vice-president of the United States at the end of 1974 had been elected to office.

COMPREHENSION CHECK

A. Recognizing the Main Idea

This selection as a whole tells you that

1. the president has less power than Congress.

2. the president has more power than Congress.

3. the powers of the president are listed in the Constitution and have grown through custom and tradition.

4. the Constitution does not specifically list the presidential powers.

B. Selecting Important Details

Choose the ending that best completes each statement.

1. The president is commander in chief of the armed forces
   a. in time of emergency.
   b. during war only.
   c. at all times.
   d. when a general dies or resigns.

2. The Constitution provides that the president
   a. cannot be removed from office.
   b. may be removed from office only by the Supreme Court.
   c. may be removed from office for treason, bribery, or other serious crimes.
   d. may be removed from office by the consent of the cabinet.

3. Custom and tradition have added all the following presidential duties EXCEPT
   a. leading a political party.
   b. interpreting the laws.
   c. representing the nation in matters of foreign policy.
   d. guarding the economic health of the country.

4. If a vice-president becomes president, the new vice-president is
   a. elected by popular vote.
   b. nominated by Congress and approved by the president.
   c. elected by the electoral college.
   d. nominated by the president and approved by Congress.

C. Vocabulary

Match the words with the definitions.

Words	Definitions
1. vested	a. sworn into office formally
2. inaugurated	b. an elected representative
3. source	c. appointed to office
4. tyranny	d. harsh and unfair rule
	e. placed in the authority of
	f. starting place

D. Using Your Knowledge

Choose the name that best completes each sentence.

Spiro Agnew   Richard Nixon
Gerald Ford   Nelson Rockefeller

1. In 1973, _____ resigned, leaving the office of vice-president vacant.

2. _____ nominated Representative Gerald Ford to be vice-president.

3. In 1974, President Nixon resigned and _____ became president.

4. President Ford nominated _____ to be vice-president.

E. Ask Yourself

Both the president and the vice-president in the Ford administration were appointed rather than elected. Why do you think people were disturbed by this?

The President as Commander in Chief

In 1951, the seventy-one-year-old General Douglas MacArthur was one of the great military heroes of the United States. He had been a brilliant graduate of West Point, a hero of World War I, a brave and skilled commander of American and Allied forces in the Pacific in World War II, and the commander of occupation forces in Japan after the war.

Since 1950, General MacArthur had been commander of American and United Nations forces fighting in Korea. He believed that our position was in danger because of aid the North Koreans were receiving from their allies in Communist China. General MacArthur wanted to bomb supply areas in China, even at the risk of involving the United States in a nuclear war with Communist China and the Soviet Union.

President Truman disagreed. As commander in chief, he told MacArthur to keep his views to himself. The general's talk about bombing China might endanger American foreign-policy decisions. But MacArthur insisted on speaking out. In April 1951, President Truman used his authority as commander in chief of the armed forces to remove General MacArthur from command in Korea.

Most Americans were shocked at Truman's actions. They supported the popular general, and Truman was booed in public. But opinions changed. It became clear that MacArthur's strategy was not supported by other military leaders. And Truman's decision to use his authority over the military may have avoided a third world war.

President Truman (left) confers with General MacArthur.

Wide World

Lesson 9   The Judicial Branch of Government

WORDS TO UNDERSTAND

Discuss the meanings of these words.

appealed   **precedent**
judicial review

NEW WORDS IN SENTENCES

1. The lawyer **appealed** the case to a higher court when the lower court found his client guilty.

2. The Supreme Court used its power of **judicial review** when it declared the law unconstitutional.

3. She set a **precedent** by being the first woman tennis player to beat a man in a professional match.

AS YOU READ

As you read this selection, try to answer these questions.

1. How does the function of the judicial branch differ from those of the executive branch and the legislative branch?

2. What is the right of judicial review?

THE READING SELECTION

The powers of the federal government are separated into three parts. These are the legislative, executive, and judicial branches. The legislative branch makes the laws, the executive branch enforces the laws, and the judicial branch interprets the laws.

Articles I and II of the Constitution outline the legislative and executive branches of the federal government. Article III outlines the judicial branch. It states that "the judicial power of the United States shall be vested in one Supreme Court and in such inferior courts as the Congress may . . . establish." In other words, Congress is given the power to set up a system of federal courts. It also determines the number of Supreme Court justices. From time to time, Congress passes judiciary acts. These acts affect the system of federal courts.

Judges of the federal judiciary are appointed, not elected, to office. Federal judges, including the members of the Supreme Court, are nominated by the president. They must all be approved by a majority in the Senate.

The founders of this nation wanted federal judges to be independent of politics. For this reason, the Constitution states that federal judges "shall hold their offices during good behavior." They are, in other words, appoint-

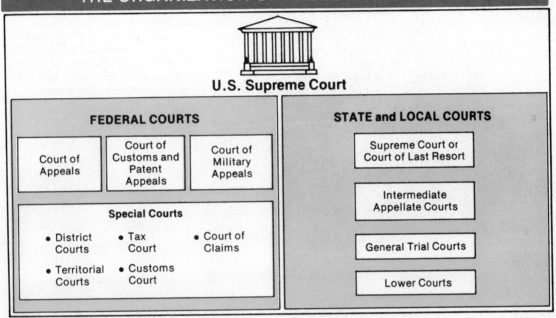

THE ORGANIZATION OF THE JUDICIAL SYSTEM

U.S. Supreme Court

FEDERAL COURTS

Court of Appeals

Court of Customs and Patent Appeals

Court of Military Appeals

Special Courts

- District Courts
- Tax Court
- Court of Claims
- Territorial Courts
- Customs Court

STATE and LOCAL COURTS

Supreme Court or Court of Last Resort

Intermediate Appellate Courts

General Trial Courts

Lower Courts

ed for life, as long as they perform their duties well. They need not depend on gaining political favor in order to hold their high offices.

This nation has local and state court systems as well as federal courts. To prevent conflicts with the other courts, the Constitution spells out the jurisdiction of the federal courts. In general, the federal courts handle six types of cases. They are

1. cases in which federal laws have been violated.

2. cases involving treaties with other nations.

3. cases involving ships on the high seas.

4. cases in which the United States government is involved.

5. cases between two or more states.

6. cases involving ambassadors of other nations.

The federal judiciary has three levels of courts: district courts, courts of appeal, and the Supreme Court. The decisions of the district courts may be **appealed** to a federal court of appeal, the next highest level. An appeal from this court may go on to the Supreme Court, the highest level. The Supreme Court usually serves as the court of last appeal from decisions of lower federal or state courts. However, the Supreme Court does more than rule on cases that have been appealed to it from lower courts. Certain cases can be brought directly to the Supreme Court. Cases involving ambassadors and cases in which a state is a party go directly to the Supreme Court.

John Marshall served as chief justice of the Supreme Court for thirty-four years. When he began his term in 1801, the judicial branch was very weak. He led the fight to establish the power of the courts. He also helped establish the power of the young national government over the states.

Library of Congress

The number of federal judges is determined by Congress in various judiciary acts. Judiciary acts also set the number of Supreme Court justices. At the present time, the Supreme Court has nine members. There are eight associate justices and one chief justice. The president, with the approval of the Senate, appoints a new justice whenever one dies or retires.

The Constitution does not specifically give the Supreme Court the right to declare any laws unconstitutional. But a case arose in the early 1800s that established the right of **judicial review.** The night before leaving office in 1801, President John Adams appointed William Marbury justice of the peace in Washington, D.C. When President Thomas Jefferson took office the next day, he refused to honor this and other judicial appointments made by Adams.

He ordered James Madison, secretary of state, not to deliver the papers appointing Marbury. Marbury sued Madison, and asked the Supreme Court to order Jefferson to honor the appointments. One section of the Judiciary Act of 1789 gave the Supreme Court the power to do so. Although Chief Justice John Marshall did declare Marbury's appointment legal, he refused to order Jefferson to honor it. In a unanimous decision, the Supreme Court declared the section of the Judiciary Act of 1789 unconstitutional. The justices argued that only the Constitution, not acts of Congress, can grant powers to the Supreme Court. The decision in the *Marbury* v. *Madison* case established a **precedent** for future Supreme Court justices. The power of judicial review is now an important part of the system of checks and balances.

COMPREHENSION CHECK

A. Recognizing the Main Idea

This selection as a whole tells you

1. why the federal judiciary is less important than the executive branch.

2. how the federal judiciary enforces the laws of the Constitution.

3. what the powers of the federal judiciary are.

4. how precedents expand the powers of the judiciary.

B. Selecting Important Details

Choose the ending that best completes each statement.

1. The laws of the nation are interpreted by

   a. the executive branch.

   b. the judicial branch.

   c. the police department.

   d. the legislative branch.

2. The term of office for judges of the federal judiciary is

   a. set by Congress.

   b. decided by the president.

   c. limited to six years.

   d. for life, during good behavior.

3. The right of the Supreme Court to declare laws unconstitutional is

   a. stated in the Constitution.

   b. different from the right of judicial review.

   c. not part of the system of checks and balances.

   d. not stated in the Constitution.

4. The number of justices on the Supreme Court is established by

   a. the president.

   b. Congress.

   c. the Supreme Court.

   d. district courts.

C. True or False

Decide whether each of these statements is true or false.

1. The size of the Supreme Court is fixed by the Constitution.

2. No federal judge can be removed from office for any reason.

3. The case of *Marbury* v. *Madison* set a precedent for the right of judicial review.

4. Any case can be brought directly to the Supreme Court if there is doubt about the constitutionality of the law involved.

5. Supreme Court justices are expected to be very involved in politics.

D. Vocabulary

Use a term from this list to complete each sentence.

appealed   judicial review   precedent

1. The lawyer _____ the case to a higher court for another ruling.

2. John Marshall set a _____ for the Supreme Court's power of _____ in the *Marbury* v. *Madison* decision.

Lesson 10 The Separation of Powers and Checks and Balances

WORDS TO UNDERSTAND
Discuss the meanings of these words.
concentrate appropriation patronage

NEW WORDS IN SENTENCES
1. He hoped to **concentrate** all his efforts on achieving his main goal.
2. The president asked Congress for an **appropriation** of $2 billion for medical research.
3. Many workers in the executive branch got jobs through the **patronage** of the president.

AS YOU READ
As you read this selection, try to answer these questions.
1. What is the purpose of the system of checks and balances?
2. Why is the executive branch often regarded as the strongest branch of our government?

THE READING SELECTION
The authors of the Constitution did not want to give too much power to the government. They especially did not want to **concentrate** power in any one branch of the government. For this reason, they provided for the separation of powers among the branches of government.

The division of power between state and federal governments left certain residual powers with the states. However, a great deal of power still remained with the federal government. What if the Congress used this power unwisely? What if the federal courts assumed more and more power as time went on? How could such a concentration of power be prevented?

One way to prevent a concentration of power was to separate the federal government's power into three branches. Each branch could then check the power of the others. By checking one another, the three branches would establish a balance of power in government. Such a balance would keep any one branch from becoming too powerful.

The executive branch can check the power of Congress through the president's right to veto bills. The executive branch also has some control over the judiciary, since the president appoints all federal judges.

Congress, in turn, has several ways to

check, or control, the president's power. Congress can pass bills over the president's veto by a two-thirds majority. Congress can also check the president's power by using its power to pass revenue and **appropriation** bills. Revenue bills are the tax bills that raise money. Appropriation bills give money to the government for its spending needs. The president needs these money bills to pay for government programs. Congress, then, has some control over the president's spending because of its power to pass or defeat money bills.

Congress can check both the president and the judiciary in another way. The Senate must approve the president's nomination of federal judges. In addition, Congress passes judiciary acts.

These acts control the system of federal courts.

The judicial branch also has checks and balances on the other branches of government. The judiciary has the power of judicial review. This is the power to rule on whether or not a law follows the guidelines of the Constitution.

Also, because the federal judges are appointed for life, they do not have to worry about political pressures. For this reason, judges can decide on cases on the basis of their own judgments. Judges are not necessarily tied to any political party. An independent judiciary is necessary to our system of checks and balances.

The separation of powers, with its system of checks and balances, keeps any one branch from having too much

SEPARATION OF POWERS

The Legislative Branch
has the power to:

1. Write laws
2. Approve presidential appointments
3. Impeach the president

The Executive Branch
has the power to:

1. Enforce laws
2. Veto bills
3. Appoint ambassadors, judges, other officials

The Judicial Branch
has the power to:

1. Interpret laws
2. Review executive decisions
3. Declare laws unconstitutional

CHECKS ON GOVERNING POWER

Presidential Limits

1. Congress can remove the president by impeachment.

2. Congress can pass a bill over the president's veto.

3. Congress must approve presidential appointments.

4. Congress determines how much money can be spent.

5. Supreme Court can declare an executive action unconstitutional.

Congressional Limits

1. President can veto bills of Congress.

2. Supreme Court can declare a law unconstitutional.

Judicial Limits

1. President appoints Supreme Court and other judges.

2. Congress must approve judicial appointments.

3. Congress can remove a judge by impeachment.

power. However, in recent times, the executive branch has become somewhat more powerful than the other branches. The following reasons help explain why.

1. The president is elected by a majority of the people in the country. Members of Congress, on the other hand, are elected only by the people of a given district or state. The president, then, has a wider and more powerful popular support.

2. The president is leader of a political party. As leader, the president has some control over fellow party members in Congress. This control helps to pass laws favorable to the president's programs.

3. The president has the power to fill thousands of jobs in the executive branch. This power of appointment is known as political **patronage.** It gives the president great influence within the political party.

4. The president, with the consent of Congress, appoints the members of many agencies and commissions of the executive branch. These agencies and commissions perform specific duties. For example, the Interstate Commerce Commission (ICC) regulates fares, safety, and other aspects of interstate com-

merce. The president has the power to appoint the eleven members who direct the ICC. But even here the president's power is somewhat checked. The act creating the ICC states that no more than six of the eleven members may belong to the same political party.

In spite of the growing power of the executive branch, power remains divided among the three branches of the federal government. Congress still guards its "power of the purse." This is the power to appropriate money for the needs of government. Without the money appropriated by the legislative branch, the executive branch cannot carry out its plans. The powerful independent judiciary also keeps its power to interpret and review laws. It can declare a law unconstitutional even though Congress and the president have approved it.

COMPREHENSION CHECK

A. Recognizing the Main Idea

This selection as a whole tells you that

1. the separation of powers enables the three branches of government to check and balance each other.

2. the separation of powers makes the states equal in power to the federal government.

3. the purpose of the separation of powers is to make the states more powerful than the federal government.

4. the separation of powers protects the residual powers of the states.

B. Selecting Important Details

Choose the ending that best completes each statement.

1. The separation of powers concerns
    a. state and local governments.
    b. state and federal governments.
    c. the three branches of the federal government.
    d. the state governments only.

2. The president can check the power of Congress through the executive power to
    a. appropriate money.
    b. veto legislation.
    c. determine whether or not a law is constitutional.
    d. impeach officials.

3. The federal judiciary may check the power of Congress through its power of
    a. impeachment.
    b. veto.
    c. judicial review.
    d. appointment.

4. Congress exercises one of its most important checks on the president through its power to
  a. interpret the laws.
  b. veto bills.
  c. pass revenue and appropriation bills.
  d. appoint federal judges.

C. True or False

Decide whether each of these statements is true or false.

1. The Interstate Commerce Commission is part of the legislative branch.

2. Political patronage weakens the president's power.

3. The president has greater popular support than senators or representatives.

4. Appropriation bills give money to the government for its expenses.

5. Federal judges have strong ties to political parties.

D. Vocabulary

Match the words with the definitions.

Words	Definitions
1. concentrate	a. expel
2. appropriation	b. system of filling government jobs by appointment
3. patronage	c. approve
	d. condense or collect in one place
	e. money set aside for certain uses

E. Ask Yourself

How can the voters of the United States exercise their own checks and balances on the government?

Checks and Balances in Action

How does the American system of checks and balances work in real life? Let's look at an example of a conflict between the executive and judicial branches of government.

The conservative Supreme Court was an annoyance to President Franklin D. Roosevelt in the 1930s. Congress passed most of the liberal legislation requested by President Roosevelt. But many of these laws were challenged in the Supreme Court and declared unconstitutional. President Roosevelt was angry and threatened to ask Congress to increase the size of the Supreme Court. This would have allowed him to appoint more justices who would see things his way. Roosevelt's threat proved harmful politically to himself and his party. The nation wanted the Supreme Court to be free from threats and interference. Roosevelt dropped his idea of a larger Court. In time, some of the conservative Supreme Court justices retired. By 1945, eight of the nine justices had been appointed by President Roosevelt. But the justices he appointed did not always decide cases as he wished. The system of checks and balances prevented the executive branch from gaining too much power. The Supreme Court remained independent of the president. And the powers of the judicial and executive branches of government remained separate.

Lesson 11 Powers of the State Governments

WORDS TO UNDERSTAND
Discuss the meanings of these words.
minimum **concurrent** **alliance**

NEW WORDS IN SENTENCES
1. The lowest hourly pay that employers may legally pay their workers is called the **minimum** wage.
2. The power to collect taxes is a **concurrent** power of the federal and state governments, since both levels of government hold this power at the same time.
3. The two nations formed an **alliance** to work together and defeat the enemy.

AS YOU READ
As you read this selection, try to answer these questions.
1. What are the residual powers of the states?
2. What powers are held concurrently by the federal and state governments?

THE READING SELECTION
When the United States won its independence from Britain in 1783, the new country was a loose association of states. The states were joined together under the Articles of Confederation. The Articles of Confederation placed most of the governing power with the states.

The Constitution changed this distribution of power. It gave power to both the federal and state governments. Except for the powers specifically given to the federal government or specifically denied to the states, all powers reside with the states or with the people. Such powers are called residual powers.

Each state's residual powers control such matters as education, marriage, and divorce. Each state, for example, controls the money that supports its schools. It decides on the attendance requirements and the courses that are to be taught. In addition, each state controls requirements for marriage. The state decides the **minimum** age people must be before they can legally marry in that state. The state has the power to require its citizens to have blood tests and a marriage license before they marry. Individual states also establish the grounds for divorce in the state.

The states also have the power to establish the requirements for voting in all elections. The only federal restriction on this state power is that voting requirements must apply equally to all the people in the state. Until recently, some states set twenty-one years as the minimum voting age, although other states allowed people to vote at the age of eighteen. The Twenty-sixth Amendment, passed in 1971, did away with these differences. Now, all citizens of the United States who are eighteen years old or older can register and vote.

States also have powers **concurrent** with the federal government's powers. Concurrent powers are those that both the federal and state governments hold at the same time. Concurrent powers of the federal and state governments include the power to pass tax laws and to collect these taxes. The powers to borrow money and to build roads are also held concurrently. Police power is still another concurrent power. Federal, state, and local governments all have the power to protect the health, safety, and general welfare of the people. Under its police power, each state controls a state police force, traffic safety divisions, and motor-vehicle licensing. Each state may also set up a health department and other departments to protect the people's welfare.

FEDERAL POWERS	SHARED POWERS	STATE POWERS
To regulate foreign and interstate commerce. To pass naturalization and immigration laws. To provide for the common defense and the general welfare. To coin money. To fix weights and measures. To punish counterfeiters. To establish post offices. To grant patents and copyrights. To declare war and make peace. To maintain the armed forces. To govern the District of Columbia. To make all laws "necessary and proper" to carry out the provisions of the Constitution.	To lay and collect taxes. To borrow money. To establish courts. To promote programs of agriculture, industry, and science. To cooperate in programs promoting the health, welfare, and education of the people. To acquire property for public purposes.	To establish local governments. To conduct elections. To ratify constitutional amendments. To regulate commerce within a state. To provide for and maintain schools. To care for the handicapped and mentally ill. To use the residual powers not granted to the federal government and not prohibited to the states.

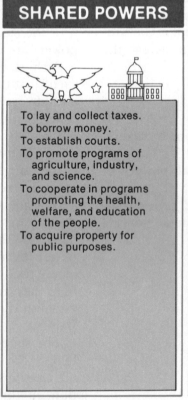
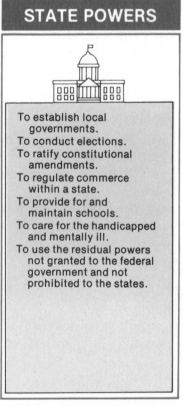

Article I of the Constitution does deny some powers to the state governments.

1. No state may make any treaty or **alliance** with another state or with a foreign country.

2. No state may coin money.

3. No state may pass bills of attainder or *ex post facto* laws. (This power is denied to the federal government also.)

4. No state may grant titles of nobility. (This power is also denied to the federal government.)

5. No state may fight a war without the permission of Congress unless it is invaded or is in extreme danger.

Despite these limitations, the state governments were given considerable strength. Over the years, however, state governments have lost power and the federal government has gained power. When the Constitution first went into effect, most of our trade and commerce was between cities or towns of one state. Such trade was then naturally controlled by the states. Today, much of our trade is with other states or nations. Therefore, most commerce today is controlled by the federal government. The federal government has also taken over the regulation of old-age-benefit plans, unemployment insurance, and minimum wages. In addition, the federal government has gained power through its efforts to eliminate inequalities among people because of their sex, age, race, or beliefs.

Although the powers of the federal government have grown, the residual powers of the states today remain strong in such areas as education, marriage, divorce, and police protection.

United Press International

Ella Grasso, the first woman elected governor who did not follow her husband into the office, won two terms as the chief executive of Connecticut.

COMPREHENSION CHECK

A. Recognizing the Main Idea

This selection as a whole tells you that

1. all state powers are listed in the Constitution.

2. the Constitution removes the residual powers that the states had years ago.

3. powers not given to the federal government or denied to the state governments are called concurrent powers.

4. some of the powers of the states are listed in the Constitution, and some, called residual powers, are not.

B. Selecting Important Details

Choose the ending that best completes each statement.

1. Before the Constitution went into effect, the power of government rested mainly with
   a. the federal government.
   b. the states.
   c. both the federal and state governments.
   d. the executive departments.

2. Among the concurrent powers is the power to
   a. coin money.
   b. control trade between states.
   c. establish federal courts.
   d. collect taxes.

3. The police power of the states refers to their power to
   a. borrow money.
   b. call out the armed forces.
   c. protect the health, safety, and welfare of the people.
   d. overrule the federal government.

4. The states' power to control voting requirements stems from
   a. their residual power.
   b. their enumerated powers.
   c. court rulings.
   d. a constitutional amendment.

C. True or False

Decide whether each of these statements is true or false.

1. The federal government demands that voting requirements apply equally to all people in a state.

2. The concurrent powers of state and federal governments are those powers that are held by both at the same time.

3. Under the Articles of Confederation, the power of government was concentrated in the federal government.

4. Marriage and divorce laws are controlled by the state governments.

5. The powers of state governments have decreased over the years.

D. Vocabulary

Match the words with the definitions.

Words	Definitions
1. minimum	a. at the same place
2. concurrent	b. the lowest or least possible
3. alliance	c. held at the same time
	d. legal voting age
	e. agreement to work together for a common goal

E. Using Your Knowledge

Make a chart comparing some of the powers of the federal government with those of the state governments. Start by making two columns. Label one column "Powers of the Federal Government." Label the other column "Powers of State Governments." Then put each of the following powers in the correct column.

Tax goods from other countries
Control interstate commerce
Control schools
Control police departments
Tax all U.S. citizens
Raise an army and a navy
Coin and print money
Make marriage and divorce laws

Indian Land Claims

There was a time when Indians were the only people living on the land that is now the United States. The white settlers' law was used to take land from the Indians. Time and again, treaties were signed giving white settlers vast sections of land.

The federal government and the state governments operated against the interests of the Indians. In the 1960s, protests and television reports helped alert other Americans to the problems of Indians. At the same time, many Indian tribes took the issues to court.

Several Indian tribes won important victories in the courts. Perhaps the most unusual case brought by Indians involved the state of Maine. Eastern Maine had once been held by a number of Indian tribes, including the Penobscots and the Passamaquoddies. A federal law passed in 1790 stated that Congress had to approve all Indian land deals. But the state of Maine violated this law in 1796. The Indians had been left with two small reservation areas.

In order to regain their land in Maine, the Passamaquoddy tribe brought suit against the federal government. They claimed that the federal government had not protected the Indians' rights. The Indians argued that they still owned about 50 percent of Maine. They claimed the state violated federal law by taking the land without congressional approval. In 1975, the case was ruled in favor of the Passamaquoddies.

Terence Moore

In recent years, Indian tribes across the nation have fought for their treaty and land rights.

This ruling meant two things. First of all, it gave the Indians a basis for a suit against the state of Maine. They could sue to claim either the land or payment for the land. Second, the court ruled that the federal government is trustee for the Indians. This means that the federal government is responsible for the protection of Indian tribal rights.

Other successful lawsuits include those brought by the Narraganset in Rhode Island and the Sioux in South Dakota. In addition to winning lands or payment, some Indians have also won the right to control the use of valuable natural resources on their lands.

Lesson 12   Amendments to the Constitution

WORDS TO UNDERSTAND

Discuss the meanings of these words.

prohibits   **income taxes**
double jeopardy   **succeeds**
sue

NEW WORDS IN SENTENCES

1. A city law **prohibits** smoking in elevators.

2. Because of the protection against **double jeopardy,** she could not be tried twice for the same crime.

3. She decided to **sue** the driver of the car that hit her fence since he refused to settle out of court.

4. In addition to other taxes, people pay **income taxes** on the money that they earn.

5. She **succeeds** to the position of manager when the present manager resigns.

AS YOU READ

As you read this selection, try to answer these questions.

1. How does an amendment become part of the Constitution?

2. What is the Bill of Rights?

3. How have amendments changed the Constitution?

THE READING SELECTION

The writers of the United States Constitution provided a means for amending, or changing, it. This has helped the Constitution meet the needs of a changing nation. Article V provides two ways to propose an amendment. One way is for both houses of Congress to pass a proposed amendment by a two-thirds majority. The second way is for two-thirds of the state legislatures to apply to Congress for a convention. At this convention, an amendment can be proposed. In either case, the proposed amendment must be ratified, or approved, by three-fourths of the states. If ratified, the amendment becomes part of the Constitution.

The first ten amendments are called the Bill of Rights. They were all ratified in 1791. The Bill of Rights guarantees freedom of religion, speech, and press. It protects people from unreasonable searches of person or property. It **prohibits** excessive fines or bail and cruel or unusual punishment. It also guarantees each person the right to trial by jury, and protection of personal and property rights.

The Fifth Amendment has several especially important clauses. One provides that no person can be tried twice for the same crime. This is the protection against **double jeopardy.** The Fifth Amendment also states that no person can be forced to be a witness against

The First Amendment forbids Congress to outlaw freedom of speech, assembly, and petition. Thus, the right to protest is guaranteed in the U.S.

himself or herself. One purpose of this clause is to prevent the police from forcing confessions from prisoners.

The Tenth Amendment limits federal power and grants residual powers to the states and people. It provides that powers not given to the federal government or denied to the states must reside with the states or with the people.

The amendments passed after the Bill of Rights are the following.

Amendment 11 (1798) changed part of Article III, Section 2, of the Constitution. According to the Eleventh Amendment, a citizen of one state may not **sue** another state in a federal court.

Nor may a foreigner sue a state in a federal court.

Amendment 12 (1804) changed the system of electing a president and vice-president. The Twelfth Amendment provides that electors should cast separate ballots for president and vice-president.

Amendment 13 (1865) abolished slavery in the United States.

Amendment 14 (1868) provides that all United States citizens are automatically citizens of the state in which they reside. No state may pass laws depriving citizens of their personal and property rights. The Fifth Amendment prohibited the federal government from passing such laws. The Fourteenth Amendment extends this prohibition to state governments as well.

Amendment 15 (1870) declares that no state can deprive American citizens of the right to vote because of their race or color, or because they had been slaves.

Amendment 16 (1913) declares that Congress has the right to collect **income taxes.** A federal income tax had been declared unconstitutional in the 1890s. The purpose of the Sixteenth Amendment was to make new income-tax laws legal.

Amendment 17 (1913) provides for the direct election of senators. Before 1913, senators had been chosen by state legislatures.

Amendment 18 (1919) made it illegal to manufacture or sell alcoholic beverages.

Amendment 19 (1920) gave women the right to vote.

Amendment 20 (1933) provides for newly elected presidents to take office on January 20 instead of March 4, named in Amendment 12. It also provides that Congress begin its new session in the January following the election. Amendment 20 therefore shortens the time of service of "lame ducks." These were members of Congress defeated in November, who once continued to serve in Congress until March.

Amendment 21 (1933) repealed Amendment 18. This is the only amendment that repeals another amendment.

Amendment 22 (1951) limits presidents of the United States to two full four-year terms. A vice-president who **succeeds** to the presidency in the first two years of the term, may serve only one more term after that. A vice-president who succeeds during the second two years, may serve two more full terms.

Amendment 23 (1961) permits citizens of the federal area of the District of Columbia to vote in national elections.

Amendment 24 (1964) declares that no citizen is required to pay a poll tax (a state-imposed voting tax) to vote in federal elections.

Amendment 25 (1967) outlines the way in which vacancies in the presidency and vice-presidency are to be filled.

Amendment 26 (1971) gives citizens eighteen years of age or older the right to vote in all states.

In 1972, Congress passed a resolution proposing another constitutional amendment, the Equal Rights Amendment (ERA). If ratified by three-quarters of the states by 1982, the Twenty-seventh Amendment would guarantee equal rights under the law regardless of sex.

The amendments have not changed the structure of the government as outlined in the Constitution. Some of the amendments seek to make clear the general terms of the Constitution. Others were adopted in response to changing times, events, and attitudes. Basically, however, the Constitution has remained unchanged.

COMPREHENSION CHECK

A. *Recognizing the Main Idea*

This selection as a whole tells you about

1. the Bill of Rights.
2. how an amendment becomes ratified.
3. how constitutional amendments serve to make clear the Constitution and to respond to changing times.
4. the Equal Rights Amendment.

B. *Selecting Important Details*

Choose the ending that best completes each statement.

1. An important part of the Fifth Amendment states that
   a. a person must confess to crimes.
   b. a person must be a witness if called into court.
   c. a person must be tried in court for a crime.
   d. no person can be forced to testify against himself or herself.
2. The Fourteenth Amendment
   a. protects the states against being sued.
   b. protects the rights of citizens of states.
   c. is the same as the Fifth Amendment.
   d. says that states may deprive people of their civil rights in some cases.
3. The Twenty-sixth Amendment
   a. was ratified in 1972.
   b. prohibits poll taxes.
   c. has not yet been ratified by three-quarters of the states.
   d. gives eighteen-year-olds the right to vote.

4. The Twenty-second Amendment limits the president of the United States to
   a. three full terms in office.
   b. four full terms in office.
   c. no more than eight years in office.
   d. no more than ten years in office, including two full terms.

C. *True or False*

Decide whether each of these statements is true or false.

1. Amendments need to be ratified by two-thirds of the state legislatures.
2. Newly elected members of Congress are called lame ducks.
3. Before the Seventeenth Amendment, U.S. senators were elected by the legislatures of states.
4. The Sixteenth Amendment was necessary in order to allow Congress to pass income-tax laws.
5. The Bill of Rights expands the power of the federal government.

D. *Vocabulary*

Write your own sentence for each of these words.

prohibits   income taxes
double jeopardy   succeed
sue

Equal Rights for Women

Two hundred years ago, women could not vote, own property, or make contracts. Most women had to depend completely on their fathers, husbands, brothers, or sons. Abigail Adams was one of the women who felt change was needed. She wrote to her husband, John Adams, in 1777 and said:

> In the new code of laws which I suppose it will be necessary for you to make, I desire you would remember the ladies and be more generous and favorable to them than were your ancestors. . . . If particular care and attention are not paid to the ladies we are determined to foment a rebellion, and will not hold ourselves bound to obey any laws in which we have no voice or representation.

John Adams put up a brief fight for more rights for women, but then backed down. Ten years later, the Constitution was written with voting rights limited to men.

It was not until 1920 that the Nineteenth Amendment extended this right to women. Winning the right to vote was a big step forward for American women. However, there remained many other things that tended to make women second-class citizens. Women still were limited in the kinds of jobs they were offered and the pay they received. Often, men were paid more than women for the same job.

In 1971, the Supreme Court ruled that unequal treatment based on the sex of a person violated the Fourteenth Amendment. That same year, Congress introduced the Equal Rights Amendment, which was passed in 1972. It states:

> Equality of rights under the law shall not be denied or abridged by the United States or by any state on account of sex.

Congress provided that the amendment had to be ratified by March 1979. Approval by thirty-eight states was needed for it to be ratified. Strong opposition to the Equal Rights Amendment arose. The charge was made that the amendment would remove special protections needed by women. It was also said that women would lose their sense of femininity and might be drafted as soldiers if the amendment passed. Supporters of the Equal Rights Amendment answered that women would not lose their femininity if they had equal rights. They argued that if women need special protections, men should probably have those protections as well. Supporters of the amendment won an extension of the approval deadline to June 1982. But hopes for its passage seemed dim.

Lesson 13   The Living Constitution

WORDS TO UNDERSTAND
Discuss the meanings of these words.

outmoded   **flexible**   **caucus**

NEW WORDS IN SENTENCES
1. The new designs of cars make last year's models seem **outmoded.**
2. Any product that will be bent or stretched needs to be **flexible** if it is to last.
3. A congressional **caucus** was held, and this meeting lasted all afternoon.

AS YOU READ
As you read this selection, try to answer these questions.

1. What are three examples of the unwritten Constitution?
2. How has the unwritten Constitution helped to keep the written Constitution up to date?

THE READING SELECTION
The Constitution was ratified in 1788, nearly 200 years ago. Since that time, only twenty-six amendments, or changes, have been added to the original document. The first ten amendments (the Bill of Rights) were passed within three years after the Constitution was ratified. The Eighteenth Amendment was repealed by the Twenty-first. The Constitution, then, has, in effect, been changed only fourteen times in more than 185 years. Because the amendments represent only a small number of changes, they alone do not explain why the Constitution remains up to date today.

The amending process is only one way in which change has come to the Constitution. Equally important are the other ways of changing the Constitution. Decisions of the courts, customs, and the elastic clause have all helped change the meaning of the Constitution. All of these have kept our Constitution from becoming **outmoded,** or out of date.

When Congress passes certain laws under its power "to make all laws necessary and proper," it often extends the original meaning of the Constitution. Such extension helps to make the Constitution **flexible.** It makes the Constitution better able to cover the needs of a changing country.

Federal courts often interpret legal questions. This also helps extend the original meaning of the Constitution. Court decisions, the changing nature of the executive branch, and the elastic clause are parts of the "living Constitution." A living constitution is a constitution that grows with the changing times.

Several customs and traditions have developed alongside the written Constitution. These make up the so-called unwritten Constitution. They help form the idea of a living Constitution. Some features of the unwritten Constitution include the following.

Party system. There were no political parties in 1788, when the Constitution was ratified. Since then, however, a two-party system of politics has developed in our country.

Party leader. The president is considered the leader of the party in power. The president is also the chief person who speaks for the party.

Nominating conventions. Presidential candidates are named at national nominating conventions. Each party holds its own convention to nominate a candidate. The first nominating conventions were held in 1832. Before that time, the presidential candidates were named by members of Congress. Senators and representatives in each political party met together in a **caucus** to nominate a candidate for their party.

Supreme Court. The Supreme Court has the right to declare laws unconstitutional in cases that are appealed to the Court. The Supreme Court assumed this right in 1803. It has remained a tradition, although the Constitution makes no mention of it.

Cabinet. George Washington established the custom of meeting with the heads of major executive departments to decide policies of government. These department heads form the cabinet.

Electoral college. It became a custom for presidential electors to cast their votes for the candidate of their political party. When the electoral college was set up in 1788, there were no political parties. The electors were free to vote for any person qualified for the office of president. Today, the members of the electoral college are pledged to vote for specific candidates.

Congressional committees. Both houses of Congress use committees. Committees help speed up the process of lawmaking. They eliminate useless bills and duplication of legislation.

Federal agencies. Administrative agencies were established to work within the framework set up by Congress. Such agencies as the Interstate Commerce Commission are set up by acts of Congress. However, they are under the control of the executive branch.

The great power of the Constitution does not rest only in what it actually says. Of equal importance is the ability of the Constitution to expand and grow by amendment, interpretation, and custom. The living Constitution provides strength for the present as well as promise for the future.

COMPREHENSION CHECK

A. Recognizing the Main Idea

This selection as a whole tells you that

1. the Constitution can only be expanded by amendment.

2. amendments are not important in expanding the Constitution.

3. amendments, court decisions, and customs help make a living Constitution.

4. a living constitution is one that does not need change.

B. Selecting Important Details

Choose the ending that best completes each statement.

1. The elastic clause of the Constitution
    a. limits the powers of the president.
    b. extends the power of Congress.
    c. extends the power of the courts.
    d. stretches the power of state governments.

2. The two-party system of politics in the United States
    a. has always existed.
    b. is provided for in the Constitution's amendments.
    c. stems from the elastic clause of the Constitution.
    d. is a part of the unwritten Constitution.

3. Before 1832, presidential candidates were nominated by
    a. national conventions.
    b. the electoral college.
    c. the state legislatures.
    d. a congressional caucus.

4. The right of the Supreme Court to declare laws unconstitutional
    a. was established in 1788.
    b. has never been accepted by the states.
    c. has been part of the unwritten Constitution since 1803.
    d. is now approved by a constitutional amendment.

C. True or False

Decide whether each of these statements is true or false.

1. The interpretation of laws by the courts is part of the process that makes up the living Constitution.

2. When the Constitution was ratified in 1788, there were two political parties.

3. Members of the electoral college today are pledged to vote for specific candidates.

4. Congressional committees were created to speed up legislative work.

5. The Interstate Commerce Commission is under the control of the legislative branch.

D. Vocabulary

Match the words with the definitions.

Words	Definitions
1. outmoded	a. capable of being changed; easily adapted
2. flexible	b. out of date
3. caucus	c. more than half
	d. compromise
	e. meeting of members of Congress or other political leaders

Brown v. Board of Education of Topeka

During the 1880s and 1890s, laws were passed that said black people and white people would have to use separate public facilities. In 1896, a black man asked the Supreme Court to rule on a Louisiana law requiring segregation on trains. In this case, known as *Plessy* v. *Ferguson,* the Supreme Court held that laws which called for "separate but equal accommodations for the white and colored races" did not violate the Constitution.

This "separate but equal" decision was later used in many states to justify segregation in the public schools. Although schools for blacks and whites were indeed separate, there was little effort to make schools for black children equal to those for white children. For the next fifty-eight years, people fought against segregation in the public schools. Finally, in 1952, a group of cases was presented to the Supreme Court. After two years of study, the Supreme Court ruled in the case known as *Brown* v. *Board of Education of Topeka:*

"In these days, it is doubtful that any child may reasonably be expected to succeed in life if he is denied the opportunity of an education. Such an opportunity, where the state has undertaken to provide it, is a right which must be made available to all on equal terms. . . . Separate educational facilities are inherently unequal. . . . We have now announced that such segregation is a denial of the equal protection of the laws. . . ."

The decision of the Supreme Court meant that segregation in public schools could no longer be practiced anywhere in the United States.

As a result of the Supreme Court's landmark decision in the *Brown* case, Linda Brown and other black children were able to attend integrated schools.

Unit 3 Summary   A New Plan for Government

The Purposes of the Constitution

The Constitution of the United States was written in 1787. It was ratified and adopted in 1788. The Constitution has been changed only a few times in almost 200 years.

The Constitution achieves six major purposes.

1. It establishes a republican form of government based on a federal system.

2. It provides for a *division of power* between state and federal governments.

3. It establishes a *separation of powers* among the executive, legislative, and judicial branches of the federal government.

4. It outlines the qualifications and duties of the members of the various branches of the government.

5. It provides a means for amending the Constitution.

6. It provides for the expansion of power to meet future needs. The elastic clause plays a major part in accomplishing this purpose.

The Constitution makes no mention of democracy. But the way in which the new government was to be established provided the basis for democracy. The election of key officials and the Bill of Rights help create a democracy. The ability of the Constitution to expand by interpretation, by new laws, and by customs accepted by the people provides a further basis for democracy in our government.

The Contents of the Constitution

The Constitution consists of a preamble, seven articles, and a number of amendments. The preamble states the general purposes of the Constitution. The seven articles describe the three branches of the federal government, the relation of the states to the federal government, and the means for amending the Constitution.

Article I of the Constitution provides for a legislative branch with two houses of Congress. These are the House of Representatives and the Senate. There are now 435 representatives, chosen on the basis of the population of each state. Members of the House serve two-year terms. The entire House must stand for election every two years. The Senate is made up of 100 members. There are two senators from each of the fifty states. Members of the Senate serve six-year terms. Only one-third of the Senate stands for election every second year. Article I also lists the powers granted to Congress and the powers denied to the federal and state governments.

Article II of the Constitution outlines the powers of the executive branch. It describes the manner of electing the president and vice-president and the qualifications for these offices. Presidents are chosen by an indirect method. Voters select an electoral college which, in turn, elects a president. Originally, the electoral college was supposed to be free to choose any qualified person. Today, members of the electoral college are pledged to cast their votes for specific candidates. When the people vote for a presidential candidate, they are really voting for electors pledged to cast a vote for that candidate.

Article III describes the judicial branch of the government. The judiciary consists of a Supreme Court and such other, lower, federal courts as Congress may set up. Federal judges are appointed for life in order that they may be free from political pressures. The Supreme Court is the court of last appeal in the United States. The Constitution does not specifically give the Supreme Court the power to declare laws unconstitutional. But since 1803, the Supreme Court has used that power many times.

The separation of powers among the executive, legislative, and judicial branches sets up a system of checks and balances. This system guarantees that no single branch of the government will become too powerful. The Constitution also provides for a division of power between the federal and state governments.

The rest of the Constitution takes up such matters as the relation of state governments to each other and to the federal government, and the means for amending the Constitution. It also declares that the Constitution and the federal laws are the supreme law of the land.

The Living Constitution

Amendments to the Constitution are only one means of keeping that document up to date. The ability of the Constitution to expand to meet the needs of the nation makes it a living Constitution. Such things as court decisions, the use of the elastic clause by Congress, and the customs of the people are part of our unwritten Constitution. The unwritten Constitution plays a major part in keeping the entire Constitution up to date.

The Meaning of the Constitution

The Constitution is the foundation of our ideas of freedom and personal security. It is the guarantee that no single agency of government can become the master of the nation. It assures us that government will remain the servant of the people who created it.

Guided by the broad outlines of the Constitution and the unwritten Constitution, the legislative branch occupies itself with making laws. The executive branch enforces these laws, and the judicial branch interprets the laws in court cases that come before it. Within this framework of the Constitution, democracy can develop, expand, and become part of the life and thought of the entire nation.

THE CONSTITUTION OF THE UNITED STATES OF AMERICA

To help you understand the Constitution we are presenting the original words in the wider column with some explanations in the margin. Parts of the Constitution that have been changed by amendments or that are no longer in effect have been crossed out. Spelling and punctuation have been updated.

Preamble

We the people of the United States, in order to form a more perfect union, establish justice, insure domestic tranquility, provide for the common defense, promote the general welfare, and secure the blessings of liberty to ourselves and our posterity, do ordain and establish this Constitution for the United States of America.

The Preamble explains why the Constitution was written.

Article I [Legislative Branch]

SECTION 1 [Congress in general]

All legislative powers herein granted shall be vested in a Congress of the United States, which shall consist of a Senate and House of Representatives.

The power to make laws is given to the Senate and the House of Representatives.

SECTION 2 [The House of Representatives]

1) The House of Representatives shall be composed of members chosen every second year by the people of the several states, and the electors in each state shall have the qualifications requisite for electors of the most numerous branch of the state legislature.

The members of the House are elected every two years. The electors (voters) are those qualified to vote for the lower house of their state legislature.

2) No person shall be a representative who shall not have attained to the age of twenty-five years, and been seven years a citizen of the United States, and who shall not, when elected, be an inhabitant of that state in which he shall be chosen.

Members of the House must be at least twenty-five years old, United States citizens for at least seven years, and residents of the states that elect them.

3) Representatives and direct taxes shall be apportioned among the several states which may be included within this Union, according to their

The number of representatives allowed each state shall be determined by the state's population.

This is the "three-fifths compromise," which settled the problem of how slaves were to be counted in determining a state's representation. It no longer applies.

The population of the states shall be determined by a federal census taken every ten years.

respective numbers, [~~which shall be determined by adding to the whole number of free persons, including those bound to service for a term of years, and excluding Indians not taxed, three-fifths of all other persons~~]. The actual enumeration shall be made within three years after the first meeting of the Congress of the United States, and within every subsequent term of ten years, in such manner as they shall by law direct. The number of representatives shall not exceed one for every thirty thousand, but each state shall have at least one representative; [~~and until such enumeration shall be made, the state of New Hampshire shall be entitled to choose 3, Massachusetts 8, Rhode Island and Providence Plantations 1, Connecticut 5, New York 6, New Jersey 4, Pennsylvania 8, Delaware 1, Maryland 6, Virginia 10, North Carolina 5, South Carolina 5, and Georgia 3~~].

Vacancies in the House are filled by special elections.

4) When vacancies happen in the representation from any state, the executive authority thereof shall issue writs of election to fill such vacancies.

The House chooses its own officers. It has the power of impeachment (the power to accuse a government official of a crime).

5) The House of Representatives shall choose their speaker and other officers; and shall have the sole power of impeachment.

Section 3 [The Senate]

Each state is allowed two senators. Senators, originally elected by the state legislatures, are now elected directly by the people of each state. (See Amendment 17.) Senate elections are arranged so that one-third of the senators are elected every two years for six-year terms.

1) The Senate of the United States shall be composed of two senators from each state, chosen [~~by the legislature thereof,~~] for six years; and each senator shall have one vote.

2) Immediately after they shall be assembled in consequence of the first election, they shall be divided as equally as may be into three classes. [~~The seats of the senators of the first class shall be vacated at the expiration of the second year, of the second class at the expiration of the fourth year, and of the third class at the expiration of the sixth year,~~] so that one-third may be chosen every second year; [~~and if vacancies happen by resignation, or otherwise, during the recess of the legislature of any state, the executive thereof may make temporary appointments until the next meeting of the legislature, which shall then fill such vacancies.~~]

Originally, vacancies in the Senate were filled through appointment by the governor of the state. This was changed by Amendment 17.

3) No person shall be a senator who shall not have attained to the age of thirty years, and been nine years a citizen of the United States, and who shall not, when elected, be an inhabitant of that state for which he shall be chosen.

Senators must be at least thirty years old, United States citizens for at least nine years, and residents of the states that elect them.

4) The vice-president of the United States shall be president of the Senate, but shall have no vote, unless they be equally divided.

The vice-president is president of the Senate but has no vote except in case of a tie.

5) The Senate shall choose their other officers, and also a president pro tempore, in the absence of the vice-president, or when he shall exercise the office of president of the United States.

The Senate elects its own officers, including a president pro tempore (*pro tempore* means "for the time being") who presides when the vice-president is not in the chair.

6) The Senate shall have the sole power to try all impeachments. When sitting for that purpose, they shall be on oath or affirmation. When the president of the United States is tried, the chief justice shall preside; and no person shall be convicted without the concurrence of two-thirds of the members present.

The Senate tries all impeachment cases. A two-thirds vote is necessary for conviction.

7) Judgment in cases of impeachment shall not extend further than to removal from office, and disqualification to hold and enjoy any office of honor, trust, or profit under the United States; but the party convicted shall, nevertheless, be liable and subject to indictment, trial, judgment, and punishment, according to law.

The Senate can remove from office those it convicts on impeachment charges, but any further punishment must come by way of trial in regular courts of law.

SECTION 4 [The electoral process]

1) The times, places, and manner of holding elections for senators and representatives shall be prescribed in each state by the legislature thereof; but the Congress may at any time by law make or alter such regulations, except as to the places of choosing senators.

Election regulations are left to the states, though Congress may pass certain laws concerning elections.

2) The Congress shall assemble at least once in every year, [and such meeting shall be on the first Monday in December,] unless they shall by law appoint a different day.

Congress must meet at least once a year. (Amendment 20 sets January 3 as the date for a session to begin.)

SECTION 5 [Rules of procedure]

1) Each House shall be the judge of the elections, returns, and qualifications of its own members, and a majority of each shall constitute a quorum to do business; but a smaller number

Each house of Congress has the right to judge the elections and qualifications of its members. In order to conduct official business, each house must have a majority of its members present.

may adjourn from day to day, and may be authorized to compel the attendance of absent members, in such manner, and under such penalties, as each House may provide.

Each house may make rules governing the conduct of its members. Members may be expelled by a two-thirds vote.

2) Each House may determine the rules of its proceedings, punish its members for disorderly behavior, and, with the concurrence of two-thirds, expel a member.

Each house of Congress must keep a journal and publish a record of its activities.

3) Each House shall keep a journal of its proceedings, and from time to time publish the same, excepting such parts as may in their judgment require secrecy; and the yeas and nays of the members of either House on any question shall, at the desire of one-fifth of those present, be entered on the journal.

Neither house may adjourn for more than three days without the permission of the other house.

4) Neither House, during the session of Congress, shall, without the consent of the other, adjourn for more than three days, nor to any other place than that in which the two Houses shall be sitting.

SECTION 6 [Compensation, privileges, and restrictions]

1) The senators and representatives shall receive a compensation for their services, to be ascertained by law, and paid out of the Treasury of the United States. They shall in all cases, except treason, felony, and breach of the peace, be privileged from arrest during their attendance at the session of their respective Houses, and in going to and returning from the same; and for any speech or debate in either House, they shall not be questioned in any other place.

Members of Congress are paid a salary. With certain exceptions, members cannot be sued or arrested for anything they say in Congress.

Members of Congresss may not hold any other federal office while serving in Congress.

2) No senator or representative shall, during the time for which he was elected, be appointed to any civil office under the authority of the United States, which shall have been created, or the emoluments whereof shall have been increased during such time; and no person holding any office under the United States shall be a member of either House during his continuance in office.

SECTION 7 [Method of passing laws]

All money bills must begin in the

1) All bills for raising revenue shall originate in

the House of Representatives; but the Senate may propose or concur with amendments as on other bills.

2) Every bill which shall have passed the House of Representatives and the Senate shall, before it become a law, be presented to the president of the United States; if he approve he shall sign it, but if not he shall return it with his objections to that House in which it shall have originated, who shall enter the objections at large on their journal, and proceed to reconsider it. If after such reconsideration two-thirds of that House shall agree to pass the bill, it shall be sent, together with the objections, to the other House, by which it shall likewise be reconsidered, and if approved by two-thirds of that House, it shall become a law. But in all such cases the votes of both Houses shall be determined by yeas and nays, and the names of the persons voting for and against the bill shall be entered on the journal of each House respectively. If any bill shall not be returned by the president within ten days (Sundays excepted) after it shall have been presented to him, the same shall be a law, in like manner as if he had signed it, unless the Congress by their adjournment prevent its return, in which case it shall not be a law.

3) Every order, resolution, or vote, to which the concurrence of the Senate and House of Representatives may be necessary (except on a question of adjournment), shall be presented to the president of the United States; and before the same shall take effect, shall be approved by him, or being disapproved by him, shall be repassed by two-thirds of the Senate and House of Representatives, according to the rules and limitations prescribed in the case of a bill.

SECTION 8 [Powers granted to Congress]

The Congress shall have power:

1) To lay and collect taxes, duties, imposts, and excises, to pay the debts and provide for the common defense and general welfare of the United States; but all duties, imposts, and excises shall be

House. The Senate may amend such bills.

A bill passed by both houses of Congress goes to the president. If the president approves the bill, it becomes a law. If the president vetoes a bill, it goes back to Congress. Congress may pass a bill into law over the president's veto by a two-thirds vote.

A bill becomes a law if the president holds it unsigned for ten days (Sundays excepted). But if Congress adjourns during this ten-day period, the bill is killed.

Every order or resolution of Congress should be presented to the president. (Actually, many congressional resolutions do not go to the president. But any bill that is to become a law must be sent to the president.)

CONGRESS HAS THE POWER TO: collect taxes and pay debts, provide for the defense and welfare of the United States.

uniform throughout the United States;

borrow money,

2) To borrow money on the credit of the United States;

regulate commerce,

3) To regulate commerce with foreign nations, and among the several states, and with the Indian tribes;

establish uniform laws of naturalization and bankruptcy,

4) To establish a uniform rule of naturalization, and uniform laws on the subject of bankruptcies throughout the United States;

coin money and fix standards of weights and measures,

5) To coin money, regulate the value thereof, and of foreign coin, and fix the standard of weights and measures;

fix punishment for counterfeiting,

6) To provide for the punishment of counterfeiting the securities and current coin of the United States;

establish post offices and roads, issue patents and copyrights,

7) To establish post offices and post roads;

8) To promote the progress of science and useful arts by securing for limited times to authors and inventors the exclusive right to their respective writings and discoveries;

set up federal courts,

9) To constitute tribunals inferior to the Supreme Court;

punish piracies,

10) To define and punish piracies and felonies committed on the high seas, and offenses against the law of nations;

declare war,

11) To declare war, grant letters of marque and reprisal, and make rules concerning captures on land and water;

raise and support armies,

12) To raise and support armies; but no appropriation of money to that use shall be for a longer term than two years;

maintain a navy

13) To provide and maintain a navy;

make regulations for the armed forces,

14) To make rules for the government and regulation of the land and naval forces;

provide, in case of emergency, for calling out the militia (national guard),

15) To provide for calling forth the militia to execute the laws of the union, suppress insurrections, and repel invasions;

maintain and train the national guard,

16) To provide for organizing, arming, and disciplining the militia, and for governing such part of them as may be employed in the service of the United States, reserving to the states respectively, the appointment of the officers, and the authority of

training the militia according to the discipline prescribed by Congress;

17) To exercise exclusive legislation in all cases
whatsoever, over such district — not exceeding ten
miles square — as may, by cession of particular
states, and the acceptance of Congress, become
the seat of the government of the United States,
and to exercise like authority over all places purchased by the consent of the legislature of the state
in which the same shall be, for the erection of forts,
magazines, arsenals, dockyards, and other needful
buildings; — And

*make laws for the District of Colum-
bia and other federal properties,*

18) To make all laws which shall be necessary
and proper for carrying into execution the forego-
ing powers, and all other powers vested by this
Constitution in the government of the United
States, or in any department or officer thereof.

*make all laws "necessary and prop-
er." (This is the "elastic clause,"
which allows Congress to make
laws not specifically mentioned in
the Constitution.)*

SECTION 9 [Powers denied to the federal
government]

1) [The migration or importation of such persons as any of the states now existing shall think
proper to admit, shall not be prohibited by the
Congress prior to the year one thousand eight
hundred and eight, but a tax or duty may be imposed on such importation, not exceeding ten dollars for each person.]

*This clause, referring to the slave
trade until 1808, has no effect today.*

2) The privilege of the writ of *habeas corpus*
shall not be suspended, unless when in cases of
rebellion or invasion the public safety may require it.

*CONGRESS MAY NOT:
deny the right of habeas corpus
except in emergency,*

3) No bill of attainder or *ex post facto* law shall
be passed.

4) No capitation, or other direct, tax shall be
laid, unless in proportion to the census or enumeration herein before directed to be taken.

*pass a law that punishes a person
without trial or makes a crime of an
act that was committed before the
law was passed,*

*pass any direct tax unless it is in
proportion to population (except
the income tax, which is allowed by
Amendment 16), tax exports,*

5) No tax or duty shall be laid on articles exported from any state.

6) No preference shall be given by any regulation of commerce or revenue to the ports of one
state over those of another; nor shall vessels
bound to, or from, one state be obliged to enter,
clear, or pay duties in another.

*pass any law that would favor the
trade of a particular state,*

spend money that has not been authorized by law,

grant any title of nobility.

STATE GOVERNMENTS MAY NOT: make treaties or alliances, coin money, give bills of credit, grant titles of nobility.

tax imports or exports without the consent of Congress,

tax ships without the consent of Congress, keep a regular army (though they may keep a militia), make agreements with other states or with foreign countries, or engage in war, unless invaded or in grave danger.

The executive power is given to the president, who holds office for a four-year term.

7) No money shall be drawn from the Treasury, but in consequence of appropriations made by law; and a regular statement and account of the receipts and expenditures of all public money shall be published from time to time.

8) No title of nobility shall be granted by the United States; and no person holding any office of profit or trust under them shall, without the consent of the Congress, accept of any present, emolument, office, or title, of any kind whatever, from any king, prince, or foreign state.

SECTION 10 [Powers denied to the states]

1) No state shall enter into any treaty, alliance, or confederation; grant letters of marque and reprisal; coin money; emit bills of credit; make anything but gold and silver coin a tender in payment of debts; pass any bill of attainder, *ex post facto* law, or law impairing the obligation of contracts, or grant any title of nobility.

2) No state shall, without the consent of Congress, lay any imposts or duties on imports or exports, except what may be absolutely necessary for executing its inspection laws; and the net produce of all duties and imposts, laid by any state on imports or exports, shall be for the use of the Treasury of the United States; and all such laws shall be subject to the revision and control of the Congress.

3) No state shall, without the consent of Congress, lay any duty of tonnage, keep troops, or ships of war in time of peace, enter into any agreement or compact with another state, or with a foreign power, or engage in war, unless actually invaded, or in such imminent danger as will not admit of delay.

Article II [Executive Branch]

SECTION 1 [President and vice-president]

1) The executive power shall be vested in a president of the United States of America. He shall hold his office during the term of four years, and together with the vice-president, chosen for the same term, be elected as follows:

2) Each state shall appoint, in such manner as the legislature thereof may direct, a number of electors, equal to the whole number of senators and representatives to which the state may be entitled in the Congress; but no senator or representative, or person holding an office of trust or profit under the United States, shall be appointed an elector.

The president is elected by an electoral college made up of electors appointed by the states. The number of electors given to each state equals the number of its senators and representatives.

3) [The electors shall meet in their respective states, and vote by ballot for two persons, of whom one at least shall not be an inhabitant of the same state with themselves. And they shall make a list of all persons voted for, and of the number of votes for each; which list they shall sign and certify, and transmit sealed to the seat of the government of the United States, directed to the president of the Senate. The president of the Senate shall, in the presence of the Senate and House of Representatives, open all the certificates, and the votes shall then be counted. The person having the greatest number of votes shall be the president, if such number be a majority of the whole number of electors appointed; and if there be more than one who have such a majority, and have an equal number of votes, then the House of Representatives shall immediately choose by ballot one of them for president; and if no person have a majority, then from the five highest on the list the said House shall in like manner choose the president. But in choosing the president, the votes shall be taken by states, the representation from each state having one vote; a quorum for this purpose shall consist of a member or members from two-thirds of the states, and a majority of all the states shall be necessary to a choice. In every case, after the choice of the president, the person having the greatest number of votes of the electors shall be the vice-president. But if there should remain two or more who have equal votes, the Senate shall choose from them by ballot the vice-president.]

This method of electing a president and vice-president has been changed by Amendment 12.

4) The Congress may determine the time of choosing the electors, and the day on which they shall give their votes; which day shall be the same throughout the United States.

Congress determines when electors are chosen and the day on which they cast their votes.

The president must be a natural-born citizen of the United States, at least thirty-five years old, and a resident of the United States for at least fourteen years.

5) No person except a natural-born citizen, [or a citizen of the United States at the time of the adoption of this Constitution], shall be eligible to the office of president; neither shall any person be eligible to that office who shall not have attained to the age of thirty-five years, and been fourteen years a resident within the United States.

This section has been replaced by Amendment 25.

6) In case of the removal of the president from office, or of his death, resignation, or inability to discharge the powers and duties of the said office, the same shall devolve on the vice-president, and the Congress may by law provide for the case of removal, death, resignation, or inability, both of the president and vice-president, declaring what officer shall then act as president, and such officer shall act accordingly, until the disability be removed, or a president shall be elected.

The president receives a salary, which cannot be lowered or raised while the president is serving a term.

7) The president shall, at stated times, receive for his services, a compensation, which shall neither be increased nor diminished during the period for which he shall have been elected, and he shall not receive within that period any other emolument from the United States, or any of them.

Before taking office, the president takes this oath, usually administered by the chief justice of the Supreme Court.

8) Before he enter on the execution of his office, he shall take the following oath or affirmation: —"I do solemnly swear (or affirm) that I will faithfully execute the office of president of the United States, and will to the best of my ability, preserve, protect, and defend the Constitution of the United States."

SECTION 2 [Powers of the president]

The president is commander in chief of the armed forces.

1) The president shall be commander in chief of the army and navy of the United States, and of the militia of the several states, when called into the actual service of the United States; he may require the opinion, in writing, of the principal officer in each of the executive departments, upon any subject relating to the duties of their respective offices, and he shall have power to grant reprieves and pardons for offenses against the United States, except in cases of impeachment.

The president can grant reprieves and pardons for offenses against the United States, except in impeachment cases.

2) He shall have power, by and with the advice

176

and consent of the Senate, to make treaties, provided two-thirds of the senators present concur; and he shall nominate, and by and with the advice and consent of the Senate, shall appoint ambassadors, other public ministers and consuls, judges of the Supreme Court, and all other officers of the United States, whose appointments are not herein otherwise provided for, and which shall be established by law; but the Congress may by law vest the appointment of such inferior officers, as they think proper, in the president alone, in the courts of law, or in the heads of departments.

The president has the power to make treaties and to appoint ambassadors and other officers. The Senate must approve such appointments. (Minor appointments may be made without Senate approval.)

3) The president shall have power to fill up all vacancies that may happen during the recess of the Senate, by granting commissions which shall expire at the end of their next session.

When the Senate is not in session, the president may make temporary appointments to office.

Section 3 [Duties of the president]

He shall from time to time give to the Congress information of the state of the union, and recommend to their consideration such measures as he shall judge necessary and expedient; he may, on extraordinary occasions, convene both Houses, or either of them, and in case of disagreement between them with respect to the time of adjournment, he may adjourn them to such time as he shall think proper; he shall receive ambassadors and other public ministers; he shall take care that the laws be faithfully executed, and shall commission all the officers of the United States.

The president is required to report to Congress on the state of the Union, to receive ambassadors, to see that all laws are executed, and to commission all officers of the United States. He also has the power to call special sessions of Congress.

Section 4 [Impeachment]

The president, vice-president, and all civil officers of the United States shall be removed from office on impeachment for, and conviction of, treason, bribery, or other high crimes and misdemeanors.

The president and all other civil officers of the United States may be removed from office if convicted of treason, bribery, or other high crimes.

Article III [Judicial Branch]

Section 1 [The federal courts]

The judicial power of the United States shall be vested in one Supreme Court, and in such inferior courts as the Congress may from time to time or-

Judicial power is given to a Supreme Court and other lesser courts authorized by Congress. Federal judges hold office for life during good behavior.

dain and establish. The judges, both of the Supreme and inferior courts, shall hold their offices during good behavior, and shall, at stated times, receive for their services a compensation, which shall not be diminished during their continuance in office.

SECTION 2 [Jurisdiction of the federal courts]

The federal courts try all cases involving the Constitution, federal laws, and treaties. Lawsuits involving the federal government, two states, or citizens of different states are tried in federal courts. (See Amendment 11 for cases involving a state and citizens of another state.)

1) The judicial power shall extend to all cases in law and equity, arising under this Constitution, the laws of the United States, and treaties made, or which shall be made, under their authority; — to all cases affecting ambassadors, other public ministers and consuls; — to all cases of admiralty and maritime jurisdiction; — to controversies to which the United States shall be a party; — to controversies between two or more states; [—between a state and citizens of another state;] — between citizens of different states; — between citizens of the same state claiming lands under grants of different states, and between a state, or the citizens thereof, and foreign states, citizens, or subjects.

Cases involving ambassadors or officials of foreign nations or those involving states are tried in the Supreme Court. Other cases begin in lesser courts but may be appealed to the Supreme Court.

2) In all cases affecting ambassadors, other public ministers and consuls, and those in which a state shall be a party, the Supreme Court shall have original jurisdiction. In all the other cases before mentioned, the Supreme Court shall have appellate jurisdiction, both as to law and fact, with such exceptions, and under such regulations as the Congress shall make.

All crimes, except in cases of impeachment, shall be tried by jury.

3) The trial of all crimes, except in cases of impeachment, shall be by jury; and such trial shall be held in the state where the said crimes shall have been committed; but when not committed within any state, the trial shall be at such place or places as the Congress may by law have directed.

SECTION 3 [Treason]

It is an act of treason to wage war against the United States or to give aid to its enemies.

1) Treason against the United States shall consist only in levying war against them, or in adhering to their enemies, giving them aid and comfort. No person shall be convicted of treason unless on the testimony of two witnesses to the same overt act, or on confession in open court.

2) The Congress shall have power to declare the punishment of treason, but no attainder of treason shall work corruption of blood, or forfeiture except during the life of the person attainted.

Congress may fix the punishment for treason, but it may not punish the families of those found guilty of treason.

Article IV [The States and the Federal Government]

SECTION 1 [State records]

Full faith and credit shall be given in each state to the public acts, records, and judicial proceedings of every other state. And the Congress may by general laws prescribe the manner in which such acts, records, and proceedings shall be proved, and the effect thereof.

The official acts of one state must be recognized as legal by all other states.

SECTION 2 [Privileges and immunities of citizens]

1) The citizens of each state shall be entitled to all privileges and immunities of citizens in the several states.

States must treat citizens of another state as fairly as their own citizens.

2) A person charged in any state with treason, felony, or other crime, who shall flee from justice, and be found in another state, shall, on demand of the executive authority of the state from which he fled, be delivered up, to be removed to the state having jurisdiction of the crime.

Criminals who flee to another state must be returned to the state in which they committed a crime.

3) [No person held to service or labor in one state, under the laws thereof, escaping into another shall, in consequence of any law or regulation therein, be discharged from such service or labor, but shall be delivered up on claim of the party to whom such service or labor may be due.]

This provision for the return of runaway slaves has had no effect since Amendment 13 was adopted in 1865.

SECTION 3 [New states and territories]

1) New states may be admitted by the Congress into this union; but no new state shall be formed or erected within the jurisdiction of any other state; nor any state be formed by the junction of two or more states, or parts of states, without the consent of the legislatures of the states concerned, as well as of the Congress.

New states may be admitted into the Union by Congress.

2) The Congress shall have power to dispose of and make all needful rules and regulations respecting the territory or other property belonging to the

Congress has power to make rules and regulations for territories and federal property.

United States; and nothing in this Constitution shall be so construed as to prejudice any claims of the United States, or of any particular state.

SECTION 4 [Guarantees to the states]

The federal government guarantees to each state a republican form of government, protection against invasion, and protection against disturbances within the state.

The United States shall guarantee to every state in this union a republican form of government, and shall protect each of them against invasion; and on application of the legislature, or of the executive — when the legislature cannot be convened — against domestic violence.

Article V [Method of Amendment]

Amendments to the Constitution may be proposed by either two-thirds of both houses of Congress or by two-thirds of the states. Amendments may be ratified by either the legislatures of three-fourths of the states or by conventions in three-fourths of the states.

This clause has not been in effect since 1808.

The Congress, whenever two-thirds of both Houses shall deem it necessary, shall propose amendments to this Constitution, or, on the application of the legislatures of two-thirds of the several states, shall call a convention for proposing amendments, which, in either case shall be valid to all intents and purposes, as part of this Constitution, when ratified by the legislatures of three-fourths of the several states, or by conventions in three-fourths thereof, as the one or the other mode of ratification may be proposed by the Congress; provided that [no amendment which may be made prior to the year one thousand eight hundred and eight shall in any manner affect the first and fourth clauses in the ninth section of the first article, and that] no state, without its consent, shall be deprived of its equal suffrage in the Senate.

Article VI [General Provisions]

The money borrowed by the United States under the Articles of Confederation is to be paid back by the government established by the Constitution.

The Constitution, federal laws, and the treaties of the United States are the supreme law of the land. This means that state or local laws may not conflict with federal law.

1) All debts contracted and engagements entered into, before the adoption of this Constitution, shall be as valid against the United States under this Constitution, as under the Confederation.

2) This Constitution, and the laws of the United States which shall be made in pursuance thereof; and all treaties made, or which shall be made, under the authority of the United States, shall be the supreme law of the land; and the judges in every state shall be bound thereby, anything in the con-

stitution or laws of any state to the contrary not-withstanding.

3) The senators and representatives before mentioned, and the members of the several state legislatures, and all executive and judicial officers, both of the United States and of the several states, shall be bound by oath or affirmation, to support this Constitution; but no religious test shall ever be required as a qualification to any office or public trust under the United States.

All federal and state officials must take an oath of office promising to support the Constitution. There can be no religious requirement for holding office.

Article VII [Ratification of the Constitution]

The ratification of the conventions of nine states shall be sufficient for the establishment of this Constitution between the states so ratifying the same.

The Constitution will take effect when it is approved by nine states.

Amendments to the Constitution

The first ten amendments to the Constitution are known as the Bill of Rights. The dates on which these and the other amendments were declared ratified are shown in parentheses.

Amendment 1 (1791)

Congress shall make no law respecting an establishment of religion, or prohibiting the free exercise thereof; or abridging the freedom of speech, or of the press; or the right of the people peaceably to assemble, and to petition the government for a redress of grievances.

The Congress may not make laws interfering with the freedoms of religion, speech, the press, assembly, and petition.

Amendment 2 (1791)

A well-regulated militia, being necessary to the security of a free state, the right of the people to keep and bear arms, shall not be infringed.

The states have the right to maintain an armed militia (national guard).

Amendment 3 (1791)

No soldier shall, in time of peace, be quartered in any house, without the consent of the owner, nor in

Troops cannot be lodged in private homes during peacetime.

time of war, but in a manner to be prescribed by law.

Amendment 4 (1791)

People are protected against unreasonable searches and arrests.

The right of the people to be secure in their persons, houses, papers, and effects, against unreasonable searches and seizures, shall not be violated, and no warrants shall issue but upon probable cause, supported by oath or affirmation, and particularly describing the place to be searched, and the persons or things to be seized.

Amendment 5 (1791)

A person cannot be tried for a serious crime unless charged by a grand jury. A person may not be tried twice for the same crime, nor may a person be forced to testify against himself or herself. A person may not be deprived of life, liberty, or property except by lawful means. The government must pay a fair price for private property taken for public use.

No person shall be held to answer for a capital, or otherwise infamous crime, unless on a presentment or indictment of a grand jury, except in cases arising in the land or naval forces, or in the militia, when in actual service in time of war or public danger; nor shall any person be subject for the same offense to be twice put in jeopardy of life or limb; nor shall be compelled in any criminal case to be a witness against himself, nor be deprived of life, liberty, or property, without due process of law; nor shall private property be taken for public use without just compensation.

Amendment 6 (1791)

A person accused of a crime has a right to a speedy public trial by jury, information about the accusation, help from the court in bringing favorable witnesses to the trial, and the aid of a lawyer.

In all criminal prosecutions, the accused shall enjoy the right to a speedy and public trial, by an impartial jury of the state and district wherein the crime shall have been committed, which district shall have been previously ascertained by law, and to be informed of the nature and cause of the accusation; to be confronted with the witnesses against him; to have compulsory process for obtaining witnesses in his favor, and to have the assistance of counsel for his defense.

Amendment 7 (1791)

In civil lawsuits involving more than twenty dollars, the right to a jury trial is guaranteed.

In suits at common law, where the value in controversy shall exceed twenty dollars, the right of trial by jury shall be preserved, and no fact tried by a jury shall be otherwise re-examined in any court of the United States than according to the rules of the common law.

Amendment 8 (1791)

Excessive bail shall not be required, nor excessive fines imposed, nor cruel and unusual punishments inflicted.

Bails, fines, and punishments cannot be unreasonable.

Amendment 9 (1791)

The enumeration in the Constitution of certain rights, shall not be construed to deny or disparage others retained by the people.

The basic rights of the people cannot be denied even if those rights are not named in the Constitution.

Amendment 10 (1791)

The powers not delegated to the United States by the Constitution, nor prohibited by it to the states, are reserved to the states respectively, or to the people.

The powers not given to the federal government are to be held by the states or the people.

Amendment 11 (1798)

The judicial power of the United States shall not be construed to extend to any suit in law or equity, commenced or prosecuted against one of the United States by citizens of another state, or by citizens or subjects of any foreign state.

Federal courts do not have the power to hear suits brought against a state by the citizens of another state or by foreigners.

Amendment 12 (1804)

The electors shall meet in their respective states and vote by ballot for president and vice-president, one of whom, at least, shall not be an inhabitant of the same state with themselves; they shall name in their ballots the person voted for as president, and in distinct ballots the person voted for as vice-president, and they shall make distinct lists of all persons voted for as president, and of all persons voted for as vice-president, and of the number of votes for each, which lists they shall sign and certify, and transmit sealed to the seat of the government of the United States, directed to the president of the Senate; — the president of the Senate shall, in

The members of the electoral college vote for the president and vice-president on separate ballots. If no person receives a majority of the electoral votes for president, the House of Representatives elects the president. In such an election, the representatives from each state have one vote between them. A majority of these votes is necessary to elect the president.

the presence of the Senate and House of Representatives, open all the certificates and the votes shall then be counted; — the person having the greatest number of votes for president, shall be president, if such number be a majority of the whole number of electors appointed; and if no person have such majority, then from the persons having the highest numbers not exceeding three on the list of those voted for as president, the House of Representatives shall choose immediately, by ballot, the president. But in choosing the president, the votes shall be taken by states, the representation from each state having one vote; a quorum for this purpose shall consist of a member or members from two-thirds of the states, and a majority of all the states shall be necessary to a choice. And if the House of Representatives shall not choose a president whenever the right of choice shall devolve upon them, [before the fourth day of March next following,] then the vice-president shall act as president, as in the case of the death or other constitutional disability of the president. — The person having the greatest number of votes as vice-president, shall be the vice-president, if such number be a majority of the whole number of electors appointed, and if no person have a majority, then from the two highest numbers on the list, the Senate shall choose the vice-president; a quorum for the purpose shall consist of two-thirds of the whole number of senators, and a majority of the whole number shall be necessary to a choice. But no person constitutionally ineligible to the office of president shall be eligible to that of vice-president of the United States.

This amendment was brought about as a result of the election of 1800, when Jefferson and Burr, candidates of the same party, received the same number of votes. Although it was understood that Burr was the candidate for vice-president, he could have been named president by the House of Representatives.

The reference to March 4 does not apply today, since the president takes office in January (See Amendment 20).

If no person receives a majority of the votes for vice-president, the Senate elects the vice-president. A majority vote is necessary.

Amendment 13 (1865)

SECTION 1 [Abolition of slavery]

Neither slavery nor involuntary servitude, except as a punishment for crime whereof the party shall have been duly convicted, shall exist within the United States, or any place subject to their jurisdiction.

Slavery is prohibited. Congress is given the power to enforce the abolition of slavery.

184

SECTION 2 [Enforcement]

Congress shall have power to enforce this article by appropriate legislation.

Amendment 14 (1868)

SECTION 1 [Definition of citizenship]

All persons born or naturalized in the United States, and subject to the jurisdiction thereof, are citizens of the United States and of the state wherein they reside. No state shall make or enforce any law which shall abridge the privileges or immunities of citizens of the United States; nor shall any state deprive any person of life, liberty, or property, without due process of law; nor deny to any person within its jurisdiction the equal protection of the laws.

All people born or naturalized in the United States are citizens. No state may infringe on the rights of citizens of the United States. (This extended the civil rights protection of Amendment 5 to include the citizens of individual states.)

SECTION 2 [Apportionment of representatives]

Representatives shall be apportioned among the several states according to their respective numbers, counting the whole number of persons in each state, excluding Indians not taxed. But when the right to vote at any election for the choice of electors for president and vice-president of the United States, representatives in Congress, the executive and judicial officers of a state, or the members of the legislature thereof, is denied to any of the male inhabitants of such state, being twenty-one years of age, and citizens of the United States, or in any way abridged, except for participation in rebellion, or other crime, the basis of representation therein shall be reduced in the proportion which the number of such male citizens shall bear to the whole number of male citizens twenty-one years of age in such state.

If a state prevents certain citizens from voting, that state's representation in Congress may be reduced. (This amendment was passed to guarantee newly freed slaves the right to vote. Congress has never applied this penalty.)

SECTION 3 [Disability resulting from insurrection]

No person shall be a senator or representative in Congress, or elector of president and vice-president, or hold any office, civil or military, under the United States, or under any state, who, having previously taken an oath, as a member of Congress, or as an officer of the United States, or as a member of any state legislature, or as an executive or judi-

This section was aimed at keeping former Confederate officials from holding public office on the grounds that they had not lived up to their oath to support the Constitution. In later years, Congress passed laws pardoning these officials.

cial officer of any state, to support the Constitution of the United States, shall have engaged in insurrection or rebellion against the same, or given aid or comfort to the enemies thereof. But Congress may by a vote of two-thirds of each House, remove such disability.

SECTION 4 [Confederate debt void]

All debts of the Confederate states are declared invalid and may not be paid.

The validity of the public debt of the United States, authorized by law, including debts incurred for payments of pensions and bounties for services in suppressing insurrection or rebellion, shall not be questioned. But neither the United States nor any state shall assume or pay any debt or obligation incurred in aid of insurrection or rebellion against the United States, or any claim for the loss or emancipation of any slave; but all such debts, obligations, and claims shall be held illegal and void.

SECTION 5 [Enforcement]

The Congress shall have power to enforce, by appropriate legislation, the provisions of this article.

Amendment 15 (1870)

SECTION 1 [The suffrage]

No citizen can be denied the right to vote because of race or color, or because he or she was formerly a slave.

The right of citizens of the United States to vote shall not be denied or abridged by the United States or by any state on account of race, color, or previous condition of servitude.

SECTION 2 [Enforcement]

The Congress shall have power to enforce this article by appropriate legislation.

Amendment 16 (1913)

Congress has the right to pass an income tax law.

The Congress shall have power to lay and collect taxes on incomes, from whatever source derived, without apportionment among the several states, and without regard to any census or enumeration.

Amendment 17 (1913)

Senators are to be elected directly by the voters rather than by state legislatures. A vacancy in the Sen-

1) The Senate of the United States shall be composed of two senators from each state, elected by the people thereof for six years; and each senator

shall have one vote. The electors in each state shall have the qualifications requisite for electors of the most numerous branch of the state legislatures.

2) When vacancies happen in the representation of any state in the Senate, the executive authority of such state shall issue writs of election to fill such vacancies; provided, that the legislature of any state may empower the executive thereof to make temporary appointments until the people fill the vacancies by election as the legislature may direct.

3) This amendment shall not be so construed as to affect the election or term of any senator chosen before it becomes valid as part of the Constitution.

ate is to be filled by a special election called by the governor. The governor may be given power by the state legislature to appoint someone to fill the vacancy until a special election is held.

Amendment 18 (1919)

SECTION 1 [Prohibition of intoxicating liquors]

[After one year from the ratification of this article the manufacture, sale, or transportation of intoxicating liquors within, the importation thereof into, or the exportation thereof from the United States and all territory subject to the jurisdiction thereof for beverage purposes is hereby prohibited.]

This entire amendment (forbidding the manufacture, sale, or transporting of alcoholic beverages) was repealed by Amendment 21.

SECTION 2 [Enforcement]

[The Congress and the several states shall have concurrent power to enforce this article by appropriate legislation.]

SECTION 3 [Limited time for ratification]

[This article shall be inoperative unless it shall have been ratified as an amendment to the Constitution by the legislatures of the several states as provided in the Constitution, within seven years from the date of the submission hereof to the states by the Congress.]

Amendment 19 (1920)

The right of citizens of the United States to vote shall not be denied or abridged by the United States or by any state on account of sex.

The Congress shall have power to enforce this article by appropriate legislation.

Women have the right to vote.

Amendment 20 (1933)

This is the "lame duck" amendment. The terms of senators and representatives end on January 3 instead of March 4, and the terms of the president and vice-president end on January 20 rather than March 4. By specifying earlier dates for starting new terms of office, this amendment assured that officials who were defeated in an election would not continue to serve (as "lame ducks") for a long period of time.

SECTION 1 [Terms of president, vice-president, and Congress]

The terms of the president and vice-president shall end at noon on the 20th day of January, and the terms of senators and representatives at noon on the third day of January, of the years in which such terms would have ended if this article had not been ratified; and the terms of their successors shall then begin.

SECTION 2 [Sessions of Congress]

The Congress shall assemble at least once in every year, and such meeting shall begin at noon on the third day of January, unless they shall by law appoint a different day.

SECTION 3 [Presidential succession]

If, at the time fixed for the beginning of the term of the president, the president elect shall have died, the vice-president elect shall become president. If a president shall not have been chosen before the time fixed for the beginning of his term, or if the president elect shall have failed to qualify, then the vice-president elect shall act as president until a president shall have qualified; and the Congress may by law provide for the case wherein neither a president elect nor a vice-president elect shall have qualified, declaring who shall then act as president, or the manner in which one who is to act shall be selected, and such person shall act accordingly until a president or vice-president shall have qualified.

SECTION 4 [Choice of president by House]

The Congress may by law provide for the case of the death of any of the persons from whom the House of Representatives may choose a president whenever the right of choice shall have devolved upon them, and for the case of the death of any of the persons from whom the Senate may choose a vice-president whenever the right of choice shall have devolved upon them.

SECTION 5 [Date effective]

Sections 1 and 2 shall take effect on the 15th day of October following the ratification of this article.

SECTION 6 [Limited time for ratification]

This article shall be inoperative unless it shall have been ratified as an amendment to the Constitution by the legislatures of three-fourths of the several states within seven years from the date of its submission.

Amendment 21 (1933)

SECTION 1 [Repeal of Amendment 18]

The eighteenth article of amendment to the Constitution of the United States is hereby repealed.

Amendment 18 is repealed.

SECTION 2 [States protected]

The transportation or importation into any state, territory, or possession of the United States for delivery or use therein of intoxicating liquors, in violation of the laws thereof, is hereby prohibited.

SECTION 3 [Limited time for ratification]

This article shall be inoperative unless it shall have been ratified as an amendment to the Constitution by convention in the several states, as provided in the Constitution, within seven years from the date of the submission hereof to the states by the Congress.

Amendment 22 (1951)

SECTION 1 [Presidential term limited]

No person shall be elected to the office of the president more than twice, and no person who has held the office of president, or acted as president, for more than two years of a term to which some other person was elected president shall be elected to the office of the president more than once. But this article shall not apply to any person holding the office of president when this article was proposed by the Congress, and shall not prevent any person who may be holding the office of president, or acting as president, during the term within which this article becomes operative from holding the office

The president is limited to two terms of office.

189

of president or acting as president during the remainder of such term.

SECTION 2 [Limited time for ratification]

This article shall be inoperative unless it shall have been ratified as an amendment to the Constitution by the legislatures of three-fourths of the several states within seven years from the date of its submission to the states by the Congress.

Amendment 23 (1961)

SECTION 1 [Voting rights of residents of the District of Columbia]

The residents of the District of Columbia are given the right to vote for president and vice-president.

The District constituting the seat of government of the United States shall appoint in such manner as the Congress may direct: A number of electors of president and vice-president equal to the whole number of senators and representatives in Congress to which the district would be entitled if it were a state, but in no event more than the least populous state; they shall be in addition to those appointed by the states, but they shall be considered, for the purposes of the election of president and vice-president, to be electors appointed by a state; and they shall meet in the district and perform such duties as provided by the twelfth article of amendment.

SECTION 2 [Enforcement]

The Congress shall have power to enforce this article by appropriate legislation.

Amendment 24 (1964)

SECTION 1 [Abolition of poll taxes]

No citizen can be made to pay a tax for the right to vote in a federal election.

The right of citizens of the United States to vote in any primary or other election for president or vice-president, for electors for president or vice-president, or for senator or representative in Congress, shall not be denied or abridged by the United States or any state by reason of failure to pay any poll tax or other tax.

SECTION 2 [Enforcement]

The Congress shall have the power to enforce this article by appropriate legislation.

190

Amendment 25 (1967)

SECTION 1 [Presidential succession]

In case of the removal of the president from office or his death or resignation, the vice-president shall become president.

The vice-president becomes president if the president is impeached, dies, or resigns.

SECTION 2 [Appointment of new vice-president]

Whenever there is a vacancy in the office of the vice-president, the president shall nominate a vice-president who shall take the office upon confirmation by a majority vote of both houses of Congress.

If the office of vice-president is vacant, the president shall appoint and the Congress approve a new vice-president.

SECTION 3 [Creation of acting president]

Whenever the president transmits to the president pro tempore of the Senate and the Speaker of the House of Representatives his written declaration that he is unable to discharge the powers and duties of his office, and until he transmits to them a written declaration to the contrary, such powers and duties shall be discharged by the vice-president as acting president.

If the president declares himself unable to continue as president for a period of time, the vice-president becomes acting president during that period.

SECTION 4 [Provisions for presidential disability]

Whenever the vice-president and a majority of either the principal officers of the executive departments, or of such other body as Congress may by law provide, transmit to the president pro tempore of the Senate and the Speaker of the House of Representatives their written declaration that the president is unable to discharge the powers and duties of his office, the vice-president shall immediately assume the powers and duties of the office as acting president.

Whenever the vice-president and a majority of other officers declare that the president is disabled, the vice-president becomes acting president.

Thereafter, when the president transmits to the president pro tempore of the Senate and the Speaker of the House of Representatives his written declaration that no inability exists, he shall resume the powers and duties of his office unless the vice-president and a majority of either the principal officers of the executive department, or of such other body as Congress may by law provide, transmit within four days to the president pro tempore of the Senate and the Speaker of the House of Representatives their written declaration that the president is

When the president declares that he is again able, he resumes his duties. But if the vice-president and other officers disagree, Congress decides whether or not the president is able to resume the powers and duties of the office.

unable to discharge the powers and duties of his office. Thereupon Congress shall decide the issue, assembling within forty-eight hours for that purpose if not in session. If the Congress, within twenty-one days after receipt of the latter written declaration, or, if Congress is not in session, within twenty-one days after Congress is required to assemble, determines by two-thirds vote of both houses that the president is unable to discharge the powers and duties of his office, the vice-president shall continue to discharge the same as acting president; otherwise, the president shall resume the powers and duties of his office.

Amendment 26 (1971)

SECTION 1 [Voting age lowered]

Eighteen-year-olds are given the right to vote.

The right of citizens of the United States, who are eighteen years of age or older, to vote shall not be denied or abridged by the United States or by any state on account of age.

SECTION 2 [Enforcement]

The Congress shall have the power to enforce this article by appropriate legislation.

Proposed Equal Rights Amendment

As of late 1981, the necessary three-fourths of the state legislatures had not yet approved this amendment.

[This amendment was proposed in 1972. It has not yet been ratified by three-fourths of the states.]

SECTION 1 [Equal rights for both sexes]

Equality of rights under the law shall not be denied or abridged by the United States or by any state on account of sex.

Section 2 [Enforcement]

The Congress shall have the power to enforce, by appropriate legislation, the provisions of this article.

SECTION 3 [Date effective]

This amendment shall take effect two years after the date of ratification.

PART 2 Growth and Crisis: 1789 to Reconstruction

unit
4

Thomas Jefferson by Rembrandt Peale,
courtesy New York Historical Society

Fairview Inn by Thomas C. Ruckle. Maryland Historical Society

The Growing
Nation:
1789–1814

The thirteen former colonies were facing an important test.
Could they make one strong nation? The time was full of
challenges: new government, new politics, new foreign policy,
new land. The country did meet the challenges. Trade and
commerce increased. Towns and farms grew quickly, linked to
one another by newly built turnpikes (above). The success was a
credit to strong, determined Americans, such as Thomas
Jefferson (left), a revolutionary leader and third president of
the nation.

Lesson 1 President Washington and the New Government

WORDS TO UNDERSTAND
Discuss the meanings of these words.

assume   excise tax
obligation   tariffs

NEW WORDS IN SENTENCES
1. He decided he would **assume** the responsibility of paying the family's debts.
2. He had borrowed the money and now had to pay off his **obligation.**
3. Congress raised money through an **excise tax** on goods manufactured in this country.
4. Revenue also came from **tariffs,** or taxes on imported goods.

AS YOU READ
As you read this selection, try to answer these questions.
1. Who were the men President Washington named to his cabinet?
2. What were Hamilton's proposals to solve the financial problems of the new nation?

THE READING SELECTION
The new Constitution of the United States was to go into effect as soon as nine states ratified it. By 1788, eleven had done so. As a result of debates over ratification, ten amendments were added to the Constitution. They were meant to protect the rights of individuals and of the states.

One of the first things to be done under the new Constitution was the election of a president. Under the Constitution, the voters chose members of the electoral college. In turn, the electoral college chose George Washington as the first president. The vote was unanimous. Washington was inaugurated in April 1789.

A Congress made up of a Senate and a House had also been elected. In 1789, the Congress passed the first judiciary act. This provided for a Supreme Court of six judges and for a system of lower federal courts. President Washington named five associate justices of the Supreme Court and John Jay as chief justice. The newly elected Senate approved the president's nominations. The United States now had legislative, executive, and judicial branches. The new government was ready to function.

Washington served as president for two terms, from 1789 to 1797. During these years, Washington established many precedents, or customs, for future presidents. One important act was the

This drawing shows the inauguration of George Washington as the first president of the United States. At bottom right, Washington takes the oath of office. The main part of the drawing shows the crowd that gathered on Wall Street in New York City to greet the new president. Washington is standing on the balcony.

appointment of people to head various executive departments. Together, these people were referred to as the cabinet. To his first cabinet, Washington named Thomas Jefferson as secretary of state. Henry Knox was the first secretary of war. Alexander Hamilton became secretary of the treasury. The cabinet members also served as advisors to the president.

The Constitution had made no provision for a cabinet. But Washington set the precedent, and his actions became the custom. Future presidents also had cabinets. So from the start, the Constitution was expanded by custom.

Washington's new administration faced serious financial problems. Finding answers to these problems was the task of the new secretary of the treasury, Alexander Hamilton. He took strong steps to save the new government from ruin. He pointed out that the new nation was heavily in debt. It had no system of taxes to bring in the money it needed. The government could not borrow money, because it had no established credit. As a result, Hamilton proposed the following program.

1. The new national government was to promise to pay all its debts in full. These included the old debts of the

FUNCTIONS of the BANK of the UNITED STATES

Bank of the United States

Accepted deposits	Made loans	Transferred funds	Provided sound national currency
from individuals	to individuals	from state to state	by issuing bank notes backed by gold or silver
from government tax collection	to national government	by issuing drafts, rather than by shipping gold or silver	by controlling amount of currency in circulation

Hamilton's national bank was to serve several functions. But there was disagreement for many years over whether or not the government had the power to establish the bank.

national government under the Articles of Confederation.

2. The government was to **assume,** or take over, the debts of the states. Many of these debts were the result of expenses the states had during the Revolution. Hamilton argued that the federal government should assume that **obligation.**

3. The government was to raise funds through taxes. Hamilton proposed an **excise tax** on liquor produced within the country. There would also be additional revenue from **tariffs,** or taxes on imports. The tariffs were also meant to encourage American manufacturing. They did this by raising the prices of foreign goods.

4. The government was to charter a national bank. The bank would be privately owned. However, the government would provide 2 million of the 10 million dollars needed to set up the bank. The Bank of the United States would provide credit to the new federal government. It would also help provide a strong currency in the United States.

Hamilton's program met with some strong opposition. One issue was over the federal government's assuming state debts. Northern states with heavy unpaid debts favored the idea. But southern states, which had already arranged to pay their debts, did not like it. They did not want to be taxed to pay northern debts.

There was also disagreement over whether the government had the power to set up a Bank of the United States. Thomas Jefferson and his supporters argued that the Constitution did not mention this power. Hamilton and his supporters replied that the power went along with other financial powers the Constitution gave to Congress. As time went on, people began to take sides on these and other issues.

These disputes finally led to something completely new in this country. It was the forming of political parties.

COMPREHENSION CHECK

A. Recognizing the Main Idea

This selection as a whole tells you

1. of the problems facing the new nation.
2. how Washington became president.
3. about the beginnings of the first American government under the Constitution.
4. why Washington was elected President.

B. Selecting Important Details

Choose the ending that best completes each statement.

1. The Judiciary Act of 1789
   a. selected Washington as president.
   b. provided for the Supreme Court and other federal courts.
   c. set up the legislative branch of the government.
   d. named John Jay as chief justice of the Supreme Court.
2. The selection of George Washington as president by the electoral college
   a. was by a majority vote.
   b. was by a unanimous vote.
   c. was not constitutional.
   d. was made under the Judiciary Act of 1789.
3. All the following were parts of Hamilton's program EXCEPT the
   a. payment of state debts by the federal government.
   b. passage of an excise tax by Congress.
   c. purchase of lands from France.
   d. passage of a tariff on imported goods.
4. Southern states opposed part of Hamilton's program because
   a. they felt it would be expensive.
   b. they had already arranged to pay their debts.
   c. excise taxes would hurt them greatly.
   d. it made slavery too expensive.

C. True or False

Decide whether each of these statements is true or false.

1. The Constitution went into effect after it had been ratified by all thirteen states.
2. Among the important appointments made by President Washington was his selection of John Jay as secretary of state.
3. A major problem of the new government was the many debts it had to pay.
4. The Constitution was amended to allow for a cabinet.
5. The Bank of the United States was owned by the government.

D. Vocabulary

Match the words with the definitions.

Words	Definitions
1. assume	a. strong and un-changing
2. obligation	b. responsibility or debt
3. excise tax	c. collections
4. tariff	d. past action that becomes a custom
	e. tax on manufacture of goods
	f. tax on imported goods
	g. take over

Mr. President

In 1789, the new United States was preparing to inaugurate its first president, George Washington. All New York, a bustling city of 30,000 people, was astir with preparation. New York was the temporary capital of the United States. At a building called Federal Hall, the new president would take the oath of office.

But how should the new president be addressed? What should be his proper title? After all, judges were addressed as "Your Honor," and governors were called "Excellency." What title could be given to the president of the United States to show his special place in the new nation?

A Senate committee suggested using the title "His Highness." But the House of Representatives had addressed the president as "the President of the United States." This simple form of address seemed to suit the feelings of most Americans.

A great revolution had been fought against England. In part, this revolution had been directed against British interference in the economic life of the colonists. In part, too, it had been a demand for greater political rights. But it also represented a revolt against the aristocratic ways of European society. There seemed no better way for Americans to show their firm attachment to a new spirit in government than to address their chief officer with the simple but impressive title "Mr. President."

George Washington (Vaughan Portrait) by Gilbert Stuart, National Gallery of Art, Washington, Andrew W. Mellon Collection

Lesson 2   The Formation of Political Parties

WORDS TO UNDERSTAND
Discuss the meanings of these words.
economic   interpretation   provisions

NEW WORDS IN SENTENCES
1. Increasing debts brought **economic** problems for the family.
2. Each person had his or her own **interpretation** of the meaning of the law.
3. There were no **provisions** in the law that prevented that particular action.

AS YOU READ
As you read this selection, try to answer these questions.
1. How did Federalists and Anti-Federalists differ in their views on a central government?
2. Why did the Anti-Federalists oppose Hamilton's financial plan?

THE READING SELECTION
Alexander Hamilton's **economic** program raised such strong feelings that two parties were formed. One was the Federalist, led by Hamilton. The other was the Anti-Federalist, or Republican, led by Thomas Jefferson.

The Federalists and Anti-Federalists differed sharply on many issues. One issue on which they disagreed was the sort of government the United States needed. The parties also were very far apart on how much democracy ought to exist in the new nation. They were in complete disagreement about who ought to be the leaders of the new nation.

Federalists generally favored a strong national government and a loose **interpretation** of the Constitution. They believed that the Constitution gave broad powers to the national government. These powers could be interpreted according to the country's needs. The Federalists also believed that only those actions specifically forbidden by the Constitution were unconstitutional. Federalists did not want to give too much power to ordinary people.

The Federalists wanted to encourage finance, industry, and trade. They believed that agriculture alone could not provide a strong economy. As a rule, they were supported by trading and manufacturing people in the North.

Most Anti-Federalists favored a different system of government. They

FEDERALISTS vs. ANTI-FEDERALISTS

Support for Hamilton's Program by Federalists	Opposition to Hamilton's Program by Anti-Federalists
1. Government to pay off all debts of the federal authority. This would make the new government more reliable.	1. Payment of debts favored *speculators* who had bought up government bonds at reduced prices from ex-soldiers and farmers who were hard up for money after the Revolutionary War.
2. Government to assume state debts left over from the Revolutionary War. This would help unify different interest groups.	2. Some states had paid their debts, and it was unfair to tax the citizens of these states a second time.
3. Government funds to be raised by tariffs on imports and by excise tax on whiskey. Tariffs would encourage business. Revenue from whiskey was needed.	3. Tariffs meant higher prices on imports. Excise tax on whiskey hurt the farmers of the West, who used their surplus grain to make whiskey.
4. Private bank, supported by national government, to be set up. This would help control the economy and provide reliable currency. "Hard" money also favored business interests.	4. Bank law stretches the Constitution, which has no specific provision for such a bank. "Hard money" hurt farmers and other debtors, who favored "cheap money."

Political disagreements over Hamilton's financial program helped form the first American political parties. These parties became a permanent part of American political life.

wanted power left in the hands of the states. The Anti-Federalists opposed strong national authority at the expense of states' rights. In addition, they believed in a strict interpretation of the Constitution. This meant that actions of the national government had to be based on powers specifically listed in the Constitution. The Anti-Federalists favored extending voting rights to more people. Not all white males could vote at this time. There were property or money restrictions.

The Anti-Federalists also favored farming interests over those of business. They believed agriculture was the basis of the economy. They were usually supported by southern plantation owners, other farmers, and the poorer classes.

The two parties disagreed strongly in their views of Hamilton's financial program. It was strongly favored by the Federalists and was opposed by the Anti-Federalists. The chart on this page outlines the main **provisions** of the program and the reasons for Anti-Federalist opposition. This chart shows there were serious differences between

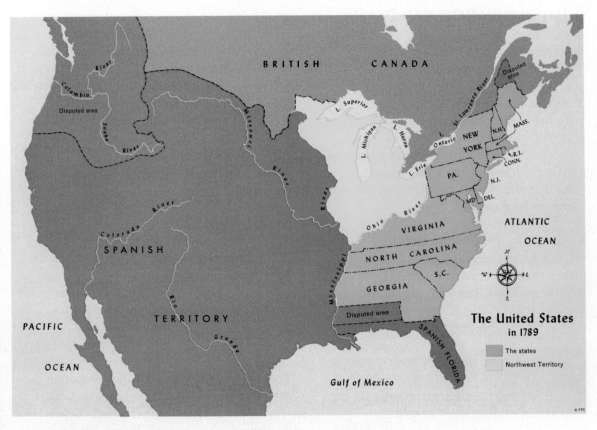

In 1789, the United States was a very small nation. Most of
North America was claimed by Britain and Spain.

the two parties. These differences often
centered on "hard" and "cheap" money.

Money is called cheap when there is
a large amount of currency and credit
available. It is called hard when these
things are difficult to get. When money
is cheap, prices tend to rise. When it is
hard, prices tend to stay the same or
fall. Hamilton's program would affect
whether money was hard or cheap. The
Federalists and their business supporters
favored hard money. The Anti-Federalists and their farm supporters favored
cheap money.

President Washington did not fully
agree with either side. But he tended to
favor Hamilton. During Washington's
first administration, the Federalists
seemed to gain in strength. Hamilton's
program became law over the opposition of the Anti-Federalists.

In his address at the end of his second
term as president, Washington warned
the nation of the dangers of political
parties. But parties had already begun,
and they would continue to affect American politics in many ways.

COMPREHENSION CHECK

A. Recognizing the Main Idea
This selection as a whole tells you

1. that the Federalists were stronger than the Anti-Federalists.

2. how the Federalists and Anti-Federalists differed on many issues.

3. that both political parties in the early republic had the same ideas.

4. that the rise of political parties was bad for the nation.

B. Selecting Important Details
Choose the ending that best completes each statement.

1. Federalists favored all the following EXCEPT
   a. loose interpretation of the Constitution.
   b. business interests over farming interests.
   c. strong national government.
   d. extending voting rights.

2. Anti-Federalists favored all the following EXCEPT
   a. strict interpretation of the Constitution.
   b. farming interests.
   c. hard money.
   d. extending voting rights.

3. In the new political parties,
   a. Hamilton led the Anti-Federalists, and Jefferson led the Federalists.
   b. Hamilton and Jefferson were both Federalists.
   c. Hamilton led the Federalists, and Jefferson led the Anti-Federalists.
   d. Hamilton and Jefferson were both Anti-Federalists.

4. The Federalists did not want to extend voting rights because they
   a. did not want ordinary people to have too much power.
   b. wanted to establish a monarchy.
   c. felt it would create hard money.
   d. believed it would increase debt.

C. Vocabulary
Write your own sentence for each of these words.

economic   provision
interpretation

D. Ask Yourself
You have learned how the political parties differed in 1796. How do today's parties—the Democratic and the Republican—differ on economic issues?

E. Map Study
This map shows the United States in 1789. Certain areas are labeled with letters. Match each description below with the correct letter. There are two extra letters.

1. The territory of Spanish Florida
2. The Louisiana Territory
3. Canada
4. The Northwest Territory
5. The New England area

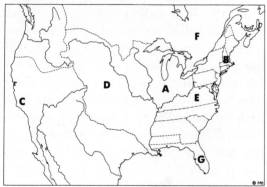

Lesson 3 Foreign Affairs and American Politics

WORDS TO UNDERSTAND
Discuss the meanings of these words.

executed   **criticized**   **negotiate**

NEW WORDS IN SENTENCES
1. French revolutionaries **executed** people by beheading them.
2. He **criticized** the government's actions by speaking out loudly against them.
3. To settle their differences, the countries began to **negotiate** a treaty.

AS YOU READ
As you read this selection, try to answer these questions.

1. Why did many Americans change in their attitude toward the French Revolution after 1792?
2. How did Americans feel about Jay's Treaty? about Pinckney's Treaty?

THE READING SELECTION
Review. In 1788, George Washington was unanimously elected the first president of the United States. He established the first government under the new Constitution. One of his decisions was to appoint Alexander Hamilton, Thomas Jefferson, and others to be the first cabinet. Hamilton's financial program brought disagreements to the surface. Finally, two political parties formed. One was the Federalist, which favored a strong national government. The other was the Anti-Federalist, or Republican, which favored strong state governments. These parties disagreed about many things, including the Constitution, voting rights, and the importance of business and industry. ☆

As political disagreements grew, the Anti-Federalists came to call themselves Republicans. The Federalist and Republican parties disagreed about foreign as well as domestic affairs. The Federalists usually favored Britain. The Republicans preferred France. The French Revolution soon brought political conflict to America.

The French Revolution broke out in 1789 and won the support of most Americans. They saw it as a revolt against the tyranny of the French king. This American support lasted until about 1792. Then Austria and Prussia tried to stop the revolt by going to war with France. Leaders of the French

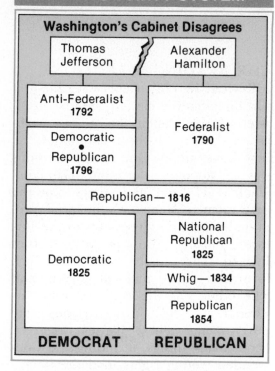

DEVELOPMENT OF TWO-PARTY SYSTEM

Washington's Cabinet Disagrees

Thomas Jefferson	Alexander Hamilton

Anti-Federalist 1792	
Democratic Republican 1796	Federalist 1790

Republican— 1816	

	National Republican 1825
Democratic 1825	Whig— 1834
	Republican 1854

DEMOCRAT **REPUBLICAN**

Does the program of today's Democratic party remind you in any ways of that of the old Anti-Federalist party? Do today's Republicans remind you at all of the early Federalists?

Revolution feared that supporters of the French king might aid the Austrians and Prussians. To prevent this, they began what was called the Reign of Terror. The king and queen of France and many nobles were **executed.** France was declared a republic. But before long, anyone who **criticized** the government was also in danger.

The Reign of Terror troubled most Americans. Many lost their enthusiasm for the aims of the French Revolution. Hamilton and the Federalists became bitter opponents of the Revolution.

They even said that supporters of the Revolution wanted to bring a Reign of Terror to the United States. Jefferson and the Republicans denied this charge. They continued to support the ideas behind the Revolution—"liberty, equality, fraternity." The political disagreement in America became worse after France and England went to war in 1793. Federalists again supported the British, while the Republicans supported the French.

President Washington declared that the United States would be neutral in the wars between France and other European nations. In 1794, Congress passed a neutrality act. But United States neutrality was ignored by both Britain and France.

By 1794, the British were seizing American ships and sailors engaged in trade in the French West Indies. This problem was added to others remaining from the Revolutionary War. The British refused to give up forts in the American Northwest Territory. Americans claimed that the British were supplying arms to Indians who raided frontier settlements.

President Washington sent John Jay, a leading Federalist, to Britain to **negotiate** these issues. In the treaty he obtained, the British agreed to leave the Northwest forts by 1796. But the treaty also contained agreements for trade and payment of American debts. Many Republicans felt that these provisions favored Britain. In addition, Britain did not promise to stop seizing American ships. Jay's Treaty was very unpopular. But after much bitterness and debate, the Senate ratified it.

Problems with Spain were settled more easily. In 1795, Pinckney's Treaty settled boundary disputes between Spain and the United States. It also gave Americans the right to use the Mississippi River freely. They could also use New Orleans for storing and shipping goods. This could be done without paying a tariff to Spain. This right was called the "right of deposit." Pinckney's Treaty was hailed by all Americans.

So, American political parties did not disagree about all foreign affairs. But party influence was being felt in many areas. This was especially true as 1796 approached. President Washington was finishing his second term and would leave office. The coming election would be a full-scale political conflict.

Charles Pinckney's treaty with Spain was popular with Americans. This was a contrast to the unpopular treaty with Britain worked out by John Jay.

Free Library of Philadelphia

COMPREHENSION CHECK

A. Recognizing the Main Idea
This selection as a whole tells you that
1. Americans liked both Jay's Treaty and Pinckney's Treaty.
2. foreign affairs did not affect politics.
3. foreign affairs increased political disagreements.
4. Pinckney's Treaty was rejected by all Americans.

B. Selecting Important Details
Choose the ending that best completes each statement.
1. In matters of foreign policy,
   a. both political parties favored France.
   b. the Federalists favored France, and the Republicans favored Britain.
   c. both parties favored Britain.
   d. the Federalists favored Britain, and the Republicans favored France.
2. The wars raging between France and its European neighbors
   a. led the United States to give aid to France.
   b. led to the declaration of American neutrality and the neutrality act.
   c. led the United States to give aid to France's enemies.
   d. had no effect upon American foreign policy.

207

3. Jay's Treaty
   a. opened the Mississippi River to American ships.
   b. forced the British to stop their seizure of American ships.
   c. was unpopular because it seemed to favor Britain more than it favored the United States.
   d. settled all the issues between Britain and the United States.
4. Pinckney's Treaty accomplished all the following EXCEPT
   a. opening the Mississippi River to American ships.
   b. establishing the right to store goods in New Orleans.
   c. settling boundary disputes with Spain.
   d. making the Spaniards agree to sell Florida.

C. Vocabulary

Use a word from this list to complete each sentence.

execute   criticize   negotiate
obligation   assume

1. A bad government can find many ways to silence those who _____ it.
2. Bad feelings on both sides made it hard to _____ a settlement.
3. It is difficult to believe that people want liberty when they _____, or put to death, those who oppose them.

D. Essay-type Question

For each headline below, write a few sentences that explain why it represents the feeling of Republicans or Federalists.

1. JAY'S TREATY A SELLOUT!
2. FREEDOM BECOMES A BLOODBATH IN FRANCE!

Washington's Farewell Address

In 1796, President Washington's second term of office was drawing to a close. The nation had to choose a new president. There could be no thought of President Washington's serving a third term. He had agreed to serve a second term only because the nation was passing through its most difficult times.

With the people preparing to choose a new president and facing many problems, President Washington prepared a farewell address. In it, he gave advice for the years to come.

The two main ideas stressed in the farewell address concerned internal affairs and foreign policy. In internal affairs, President Washington warned against the rise of political parties. He felt there was much harm in "the baneful effects of the spirit of party." Washington was fearful that strife between the newly formed Federalist and Anti-Federalist parties would disrupt the unity of the nation.

In the field of foreign policy, the president said that the policy of the United States should be "to steer clear of permanent alliances with any portion of the foreign world." He pointed out that "Europe has a set of primary interests which to us have none or a very remote relation."

President Washington's words cannot, of course, apply to our nation today. But they represent his sincere effort to give worthwhile advice to the young nation in 1796. He wanted the United States to remain united and to maintain its independence.

Lesson 4 The Federalists Come to Power

WORDS TO UNDERSTAND
Discuss the meanings of these words.

aliens   sedition

deported   null and void

NEW WORDS IN SENTENCES
1. They were **aliens** who had come from Europe and were not yet citizens of the United States.

2. The government **deported** the aliens to the countries from which they had come.

3. His efforts to overthrow the government were acts of **sedition.**

4. A law that is **null and void** is not in effect and has no power.

AS YOU READ
As you read this selection, try to answer these questions.

1. What was the main issue of the XYZ affair?

2. Why did the major provisions of the Alien and Sedition Acts seem unfair or unconstitutional?

THE READING SELECTION
Review. During Washington's years as president, two political parties had developed. They were the Federalist party and the Anti-Federalist, or Republican, party. Washington had remained above the party battles, though he favored the Federalists. In 1796, Washington was near the end of his second and last term in office. The way was open for full-scale political conflict in the coming election. ☆

In 1796, the Federalists nominated John Adams to follow George Washington as president. Adams had served as vice-president under Washington. He had been a leader in the Revolution. The Republicans nominated Thomas Jefferson, another revolutionary leader. Jefferson had served as Washington's secretary of state. Each party also chose vice-presidential candidates.

The electoral college vote in the 1796 election showed a weakness in the Constitution. The writers of the Constitution did not know that political parties would arise. The Constitution did not allow for two parties, each choosing separate candidates for president and vice-president. The Constitution stated that each member of the electoral college would vote for two candidates. Members did not indicate a choice of president or vice-president. The person who received the most votes would be president, provided that person had a

John Adams was the nation's first vice-president and its second president. This painting of him was done by Gilbert Stuart, one of the best-known artists of the time. Stuart painted many famous public figures, including Thomas Jefferson, James Madison, and James Monroe. In fact, the picture of George Washington on page 200 is also by Stuart.

John Adams by Gilbert Stuart, National Gallery of Art, Washington, Gift of Mrs. Robert Homans

majority of the votes. The person who received the next highest number of votes would be vice-president.

Under this system, Adams was elected president. However, Jefferson, the Republican, was elected vice-president. The Federalists did win a majority in Congress. Having won the Congress and the presidency, the Federalists were in power.

In foreign policy, the Federalists continued to keep America neutral in Europe's wars. However, the French government was displeased by the Jay Treaty. French warships began seizing American ships and cargoes. In 1797, President Adams sent representatives to France to work out a treaty. They re-

ported back that French officials were demanding bribes and a loan to France. These officials were identified only as X, Y, and Z. American feelings now rose against the French because of the XYZ affair. The whole nation supported the president in refusing to pay any bribes. A popular cry was "millions for defense, but not one cent for tribute." Congress repealed the former treaties with France. So, in 1798, an undeclared naval war began between France and the United States. By 1800, the French were interested in a new treaty. When it was completed, it ended the threat of full-scale war with France.

The XYZ affair added to the Federalist strength. However, the Federalists feared they might lose the congressional elections of 1798. They also deeply resented the attacks by Republican newspapers on President Adams and Federalist members of Congress. It was this fear and resentment that led to the passage of the Alien and Sedition Acts in 1798.

These acts had two main purposes. One was to end criticism of the Federalist party. The other was to make it more difficult for **aliens** to become citizens. The Federalists felt that most immigrants to America favored the Republicans. The provisions of the acts included the following.

1. Aliens had to live in this country for fourteen years (instead of five) before they could become citizens.

2. Aliens considered "dangerous" could be **deported** or jailed.

3. Those who opposed laws or wrote false or harmful statements about the president or Congress were guilty of **sedition.** They faced fines and jail sentences.

The Republicans protested strongly against these laws. They pointed out that the laws against aliens were unfair. The sedition laws meant that anyone who merely criticized the government might face imprisonment. This, they said, violated the First Amendment to the Constitution.

The passage of the Alien and Sedition Acts harmed the Federalists. No aliens were deported. Only a few people were jailed under the Sedition Acts. But many Americans agreed that the acts were unconstitutional.

The Virginia legislature passed special resolutions prepared by James Madison. These declared that a state had the right to keep the federal government from misusing its authority. Madison's criticisms of the Federalists were taken very seriously by many Americans.

Virginia's action was soon followed by the Kentucky Resolutions. They were drawn up secretly by Thomas Jefferson, the vice-president. In them, Jefferson declared that the Alien and Sedition Acts were **null and void.** This meant they had no effect in any state that believed them unconstitutional.

The acts expired in a few years. But the Virginia and Kentucky resolutions were important. In them, state governments claimed they could declare a federal law unconstitutional. In 1799, it was not yet established that only the Supreme Court could do this. In fact, this issue of states' rights would not be settled until after the Civil War.

The Federalists' term of office had been eventful for the new nation. But now it was time for the Republicans. The Alien and Sedition Acts would be an issue in the election of 1800.

COMPREHENSION CHECK

A. Recognizing the Main Idea

This selection as a whole tells you

1. how the Republicans took office in 1796.

2. of the major actions and events of the Adams administration.

3. about the electoral college system.

4. why the Alien and Sedition Acts were unfair.

B. Selecting Important Details

Choose the ending that best completes each statement.

1. In the election of 1796,
   a. the Federalists elected the president and vice-president.
   b. the Republicans won a great victory.
   c. a Federalist was chosen president, and a Republican was chosen vice-president.
   d. the electoral college could not select a president.

2. Americans were angry about the XYZ affair because they
   a. did not want to pay bribes.
   b. did not want to keep the old treaties.
   c. did not like the way President Adams handled it.
   d. preferred to side with Spain.

3. The Alien and Sedition Acts did all of the following EXCEPT
   a. make it harder for aliens to become citizens.
   b. make it easier to criticize the government.
   c. make it easier to deport aliens.
   d. make it easier to silence criticism.

4. The right of a state to declare a federal law unconstitutional was
   a. supported by most Federalists.
   b. approved by the Supreme Court.
   c. opposed by Jefferson.
   d. the argument of the Virginia and Kentucky resolutions.

C. Completion

Fill in the word or words that best complete each sentence.

1. The XYZ affair strengthened the _____ party.

2. The Federalist candidate for president to follow Washington was _____.

3. The Sedition Acts provided jail terms for those who _____ the laws.

4. The Kentucky Resolutions claimed that a state could declare a federal law _____ and _____.

5. The men who wrote the Virginia and Kentucky resolutions were _____ and _____.

D. Vocabulary

Match the words with the definitions.

Words	Definitions
1. alien	a. a new citizen
2. sedition	b. to send out of a country
3. deport	c. not in effect and without power
4. null and void	d. misuse
	e. one who comes from another country
	f. disloyal actions

E. Using Your Knowledge

The main idea of a paragraph is often given in a single sentence. This sentence is usually at the beginning or the end of the paragraph. Find the third and fifth paragraphs of the Reading Selection (include the Review when you count). In each, choose the sentence that you think gives the paragraph's main idea. For each choice, write a short explanation of why you picked that sentence.

212

Lesson 5 The Revolution of 1800

WORDS TO UNDERSTAND

Discuss the meanings of these words.

foe   expire
duel   spoils system

NEW WORDS IN SENTENCES

1. She considered John her **foe** and fought him at every opportunity.

2. When one man insulted another, they often settled the matter in a **duel** with pistols.

3. The law would **expire** at the end of a year and would no longer be in effect.

4. In a **spoils system,** political loyalty alone can buy a job.

AS YOU READ

As you read this selection, try to answer these questions.

1. How did the election of 1800 point out a weakness in the Constitution?

2. What actions by Jefferson and his party after 1800 were referred to as a revolution?

THE READING SELECTION

Review. In 1796, John Adams became the first Federalist president. Shortly after he took office, Adams tried to solve problems with France. But the XYZ affair turned Americans against the French. It was not until 1800 that the threat of war with France was ended. The XYZ affair had strengthened the Federalists. To protect themselves, they passed the Alien and Sedition Acts. These made it harder to become a citizen. They also created serious punishments for criticizing the government. Many people argued that the acts were unconstitutional. Virginia and Kentucky claimed the right to set aside these laws. These Federalist actions were issues in the next election. ☆

In 1796, Thomas Jefferson was the Republican candidate for president. But the electoral college vote made him vice-president. In 1800, he was again nominated for president. Aaron Burr was his running mate for vice-president. The Federalists chose John Adams for president and Charles Pinckney for vice-president.

The system of having each elector cast two votes without showing a choice for president and vice-president again created problems. The final vote came out as follows:

Jefferson (Republican)	73
Burr (Republican)	73
Adams (Federalist)	65
Pinckney (Federalist)	64

213

Cities in the new nation were continuing to grow quickly in Jefferson's time. This picture shows Second Street in Philadelphia, probably about 1800. What can you tell from it about the buildings of the period? The clothing? The transportation?

It had been understood that Jefferson was to be president and Burr vice-president. But neither candidate had the necessary majority. So the election had to be decided in the House of Representatives. Each state cast one vote for either Jefferson or Burr, the two leading candidates.

Burr could have withdrawn from the election and become vice-president, as was planned. Yet Burr wanted the presidency. He knew that many of the Federalists hated Jefferson. The Federalist states, therefore, would cast votes for Burr. However, Hamilton, one of the leading Federalists, worked for Jefferson's election. He had long been a political **foe** of Jefferson, but he believed that the election of Burr would be bad for the nation.

Thirty-five separate votes were taken in the House. And in each vote, neither of the two candidates got a majority. Finally, on the thirty-sixth vote, Jefferson won and became president. Burr became vice-president. Burr never forgot how Hamilton had worked against his election. Four years later, Burr killed Hamilton in a pistol **duel.**

The election of 1800, like that of 1796, showed the weakness in the electoral system. As a result, the Twelfth Amendment to the Constitution was passed by Congress and ratified by the states. This amendment provided that electors should cast separate ballots for president and vice-president.

The election of Jefferson brought the Republicans to power in the years from 1801 to 1809. The many changes made by Jefferson have led some people to call the election of 1800 the "revolution of

1800." The changes included these actions.

1. The national debt was lowered. There also was a reduction in spending by the federal government.

2. The excise tax on whiskey was repealed. This tax had been part of Hamilton's financial program. It had been strongly opposed by western farmers, who were Republicans. They sold their extra grain to the whiskey makers, and the tax hurt their business.

3. The Alien and Sedition Acts ended. These laws were allowed to **expire** after the two-year period of their legal effectiveness had passed.

4. The first **spoils system** was introduced in government. That is, the Republicans gained the "spoils of victory" and replaced many Federalist officeholders with Republicans.

5. The vast region of Louisiana was purchased from France. This was one of the most important of Jefferson's actions.

COMPREHENSION CHECK

A. *Recognizing the Main Idea*

This selection as a whole tells you

1. about the Federalist victory in 1800.

2. how the electoral system was changed.

3. about the election of 1800 and the changes that came in Jefferson's administration.

4. that Hamilton favored Jefferson for president.

B. *Selecting Important Details*

Choose the ending that best completes each statement.

1. The problem arising out of the presidential election of 1800 was that
   a. Jefferson and Adams had the same number of electoral votes.
   b. Jefferson and Burr had the same number of electoral votes.
   c. Burr had more votes than Jefferson.
   d. Hamilton did not want Burr to become president.

2. Since the electoral college could not select a president,
   a. the issue was left to the Senate.
   b. the issue was left to the Supreme Court.
   c. the Republicans had to decide between Burr and Jefferson.
   d. the House of Representatives had to select a president.

3. An important result of the election of 1800 was
   a. the election of Hamilton to office.
   b. the passage of the Eleventh Amendment to the Constitution.
   c. the election of a Federalist president.
   d. the passage of the Twelfth Amendment to the Constitution.

4. All the following were actions taken during Jefferson's administration EXCEPT the
   a. purchase of Louisiana from France.
   b. introduction of the first spoils system.
   c. introduction of an excise tax to raise funds.
   d. reduction of the national debt.

Decide whether each of these statements is true or false.

1. In 1800, the Republican electors cast equal numbers of votes for Jefferson and Adams.

2. When the electoral college could not choose a president in 1800, the decision was left to the Senate.

3. The election of Jefferson led to actions referred to as a revolution.

4. An important action of the Republicans during Jefferson's administration was the passage of the excise tax on whiskey.

5. The Twelfth Amendment to the Constitution provided that electors would cast separate votes for president and vice-president.

D. Vocabulary

Write your own sentence for each of these words.

foe	expire
duel	spoils system

E. Essay-type Question

For each of these presidents, write a few sentences describing two major events of his administration.

1. Washington
2. Adams
3. Jefferson

The Midnight Judges

Early in 1801, the Federalists were preparing to go out of office. The Republicans had won the presidency and control of Congress in the election of 1800.

Thomas Jefferson would become president on March 4, 1801. Suppose President Jefferson was able to make a large number of appointments to the federal courts? This would give the Republicans complete control over all three branches of government. The Federalists were very much worried by this possibility.

The Federalists moved quickly to maintain some control over the courts in the years ahead. While Congress was still under Federalist control, it passed the Judiciary Act of 1801, creating a large number of new judgeships. The bill was approved by President Adams just before he was to leave office. In fact, the official commissions appointing judges to their positions had, in many cases, still not been signed by March 3, the day before Adams was to leave office.

Because President Adams sat up late into the night signing commissions for the new judges, they came to be known as "midnight judges." The Republicans protested bitterly against these appointments. One of the midnight judges, William Marbury, did not receive his commission from Madison, Jefferson's secretary of state. This led to the *Marbury* v. *Madison* case. This was the case that led to the Supreme Court's first declaring a law unconstitutional.

Lesson 6 The Louisiana Purchase

WORDS TO UNDERSTAND

Discuss the meanings of these words.

interfere   **justified**

NEW WORDS IN SENTENCES

1. It would be easy to **interfere** with shipping by stopping boats or demanding taxes.

2. She claimed her actions were **justified** under the law that established legal limits.

AS YOU READ

As you read this selection, try to answer these questions.

1. Why did Napoleon decide to sell the Louisiana Territory?

2. What were the purposes of Lewis and Clark's expedition?

THE READING SELECTION

The purchase of Louisiana was one of the most important actions of the Jefferson administration. Louisiana had been ceded by Spain to France in a secret treaty. This worried the Americans. Napoleon Bonaparte, the ruler of France in 1800, was trying to build an empire in Europe. Americans feared he would try to reestablish a French empire in North America. They also feared that the French would **interfere** with Americans' right of deposit in New Orleans. This could ruin western farmers.

In fact, these fears were **justified.** Napoleon was planning on a new French empire. But his plans ran into trouble in the Americas. At the time, there was a black revolution on Santo Domingo, a Caribbean island owned by France. The former slaves were being led by Toussaint L'Ouverture. Napoleon sent an army to put down the revolt. He wanted the army to continue to New Orleans and occupy it. But fighting and disease killed too many French soldiers. Napoleon faced a new war with England, and he was afraid England might seize Louisiana. So he decided to sell the area.

In 1803, Jefferson sent representatives to France to try to buy New Orleans. Instead, the French offered to sell all of Louisiana for $15 million. However, there was no time to consult with President Jefferson. The representa-

Lewis and Clark began exploring the Louisiana Territory in 1804. They spent the winter of 1804–05 at a Mandan village, where they were joined by Sacajawea. She is shown with them at the center of this detail from a painting.

tives agreed to the sale and then returned home to tell the president.

When Jefferson learned of the purchase, he was worried. He believed that the Constitution did not give the national government the power to make such purchases. He was also afraid that the area was too large and too far away from the rest of the United States. This would make it difficult to govern. But he approved the purchase. The Senate quickly ratified the treaty.

Jefferson had approved the treaty with the hope that a new constitutional amendment would be passed. This amendment would clearly give the national government the power to make land purchases. However, no such amendment was ever passed. Nor was it needed. Jefferson and later presidents accepted the idea that the national government did have the right to purchase territory.

The Louisiana Purchase decreased the threat of a new French empire in America. The territory also doubled the size of the United States. But very little was known about this huge land. So the president sent a small group of soldiers to learn more. They were led by Meriwether Lewis and William Clark. The Lewis and Clark expedition spent two

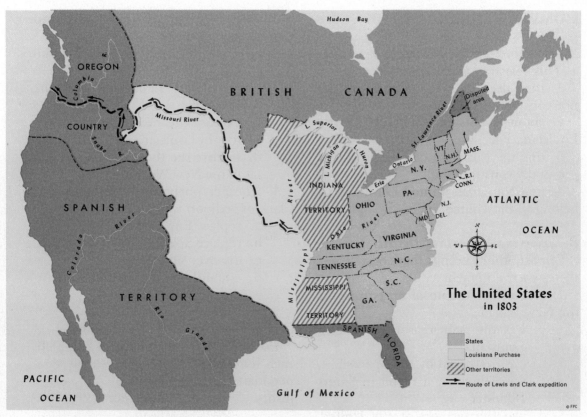

Compare the route of Lewis and Clark shown with a current
U.S. map. Through which present-day states did they travel?

and a half years on its journey to the
west and back. They traveled up the
Missouri River, crossed the Continental
Divide, and followed the Columbia
River to the Pacific Ocean.

There were a large number of Indian
tribes living in the Louisiana Territory.
Many of them had met British fur traders or Spanish traders before. Part of
the mission was to establish good relations between these tribes and the
United States. Lewis and Clark carried
with them various goods to trade and
present as gifts. Among the items were
eighty-seven silver medals to be presented to chiefs of different tribes. Lew-

is and Clark generally established good
relations with the tribes they met. They
were honest and fair, and they respected the ways of life they saw. Their work
was made easier by Sacajawea, a Shoshoni woman traveling with them as a
translator and go-between.

By the time they returned in 1806,
Lewis and Clark had learned a great
deal about the new area. It seemed that
it had been a very wise purchase for the
United States. But for the Indians living
there, it meant the start of great changes
in their lives.

COMPREHENSION CHECK

A. Recognizing the Main Idea

This selection as a whole tells you

1. that the Louisiana Territory was not considered valuable.

2. about events at the time of the Louisiana Purchase.

3. that the purchase of Louisiana was not really constitutional.

4. that Napoleon wanted Louisiana to belong to the United States.

B. Selecting Important Details

Choose the ending that best completes each statement.

1. Napoleon's dream of an empire in the New World
   a. was his main reason for selling Louisiana.
   b. was destroyed by the Spanish.
   c. was ruined by a revolt in Santo Domingo.
   d. had the support of the United States.

2. When Jefferson learned of the purchase of Louisiana, he
   a. approved it, though he felt he lacked constitutional authority to make the purchase.
   b. refused to approve it, because he lacked authority to make the purchase.
   c. approved it with the hope that a constitutional amendment would not be passed.
   d. refused to send the treaty to the Senate.

3. One purpose of the Lewis and Clark expedition was to
   a. drive the Indians out of Louisiana.
   b. try to buy Louisiana from the French.
   c. explore the newly bought territory of Louisiana.
   d. remove the threat of the French in the New World.

4. Another purpose of the Lewis and Clark expedition was to
   a. replace English fur traders.
   b. replace Spanish traders.
   c. discover silver deposits.
   d. establish good relations with Indian tribes.

C. Vocabulary

Use a word from this list to complete each sentence.

negotiate   criticize
justify   interfere

1. It was difficult to _____ the decision when we looked at the bad results of it.

2. Americans did not want other nations to _____ with local affairs.

D. Ask Yourself

Pretend you are one of the representatives who bought the Louisiana Territory from Napoleon. What reasons would you give to President Jefferson for making the purchase?

Lesson 7 The War of 1812

WORDS TO UNDERSTAND

Discuss the meanings of these words.

blockade	impressed	patriotism
embargo	deserters	

NEW WORDS IN SENTENCES

1. British ships set up a **blockade** of the port and kept vessels from entering or leaving it.

2. The **embargo** on shipping prevented any ships from sailing.

3. The British **impressed** American sailors, forcing them to serve on British ships.

4. The **deserters** had left the army without official permission.

5. Pride in their nation gave Americans a spirit of **patriotism.**

AS YOU READ

As you read this selection, try to answer these questions.

1. What were the main causes of the War of 1812?

2. What were the results of the War of 1812?

THE READING SELECTION

Review. In 1800, Thomas Jefferson, a Republican, won the presidency from the Federalists. During his term of office, the national debt was lowered, and the Alien and Sedition Acts were ended. In addition, the Louisiana Territory was purchased from France in 1803. Lewis and Clark then led an expedition to chart the new land and establish good relations with the Indian tribes living there. ☆

From 1793 to 1814, many European nations, led by Britain, were at war with Napoleon's France. Napoleon tried to fight back by forbidding any nation to trade with Britain. The British, in turn, blocked trade between other nations and French lands. American shipping was soon caught in the middle of this system of **blockade.**

In 1793, President Washington issued a proclamation of neutrality. President Jefferson also wanted to keep the United States out of the European conflict. In 1807, he asked Congress to pass an **embargo** act. The embargo outlawed any American trade with foreign nations. But this had bad effects on the American economy. Ships had to stay in port, and the United States lost millions of dollars in trade. The embargo act was amended to permit trade with other neutral nations. But British ships still seized American shipping. They argued that goods shipped to neutral countries could later be shipped to France.

The Battle of Lake Erie was one of the bloodiest naval battles of the War of 1812. It was an important victory for the Americans. In this painting, Captain Oliver H. Perry is forced to leave his badly damaged ship for another one. After the battle, Perry sent the famous message, "We have met the enemy and they are ours."

James Madison, also a Republican, was elected president in 1808. He found the nation drifting toward war with Britain. There were several issues involved.

1. Americans wanted freedom of the seas. The British **impressed** American sailors as well as ships. These sailors were forced to serve on British ships. The British claimed they were former British citizens or **deserters** from the navy.

2. Americans felt resentment against Britain, dating back to the Revolution. Also, the British still illegally held some lands in the Northwest. British agents carried on illegal fur trade with the Indians of the Northwest Territory.

3. Some Americans had ambitions to take over lands in Canada and Florida. These "War Hawks," as they were called, favored a war to expand American boundaries. The War Hawks were mainly southern and western Republican politicians.

All these things brought on the war that Jefferson and Madison had hoped to avoid. The War of 1812 between Great Britain and the United States probably was not necessary. The United States declared war two days after the British withdrew their blockade against neutral nations. Speedier communications might have prevented the war's outbreak. However, the news of the British action did not reach America until the war was well under way.

Fortunately for the United States, the British were busy fighting Napoleon in Europe during the War of 1812. Even so, the Americans suffered several defeats. An American invasion of Canada failed, though the Americans did capture and burn the city of York. The British fleet blockaded many American cities. A British force captured Washington, D.C., and burned the White House as revenge for the burning of York.

The major American successes were won on the water. American ships won victories on Lake Erie and Lake Champlain. These victories blocked any British invasion from Canada. The greatest victory on land was won at New Orleans by troops under General Andrew Jackson. But once again, the lack of quick communications was involved. The battle was actually fought after the peace treaty had ended the war in 1814. The news had not yet reached America.

This peace treaty did not really produce changes for Americans. But the war itself did.

1. It led to final recognition of the United States as an independent power. For this reason, the War of 1812 is sometimes called the "Second War of American Independence."

2. It led to the end of the Federalist party, which had strongly opposed the war. Federalists were now charged with "disloyalty."

3. It encouraged the growth of American industry. The British blockade of American ports had cut off trade. The nation had to develop its own industries to make up for shortages in goods from Europe.

4. It led to a growing feeling of **patriotism** and pride in this country.

COMPREHENSION CHECK

A. Recognizing the Main Idea

This selection as a whole tells you

1. that the United States was wrong in fighting Britain.

2. why the United States became involved in the War of 1812 and about some of the results of that war.

3. that the United States won its freedom of the seas as a result of the War of 1812.

4. that the United States won a great victory over Britain in the War of 1812.

B. Selecting Important Details

Choose the ending that best completes each statement.

1. Britain justified its seizure of American shipments to neutrals

    a. because such goods were needed in Britain.

    b. because such goods might later be sent on to France.

    c. because its navy was strong enough to make the seizures.

    d. because Americans still owed money to Britain.

2. The British claimed that they impressed American sailors in order to

    a. force the United States to stop shipping goods to France.

    b. force the United States to pay for their release.

    c. force a war upon the United States.

    d. force deserters and former British subjects to serve in the British navy.

3. The Battle of New Orleans was an unnecessary battle because
   a. very few men were involved in the battle.
   b. the treaty of peace was signed before the battle.
   c. neither side was able to win a victory.
   d. the New Orleans territory was of no importance.

4. All of the following were results of the War of 1812 EXCEPT
   a. it led to the downfall of the Federalists.
   b. it greatly encouraged American industry.
   c. it led to the British occupation of Florida.
   d. it led to greater patriotism and pride.

C. True or False

Decide whether each statement is true or false. If it is false, rewrite it so that it is true.

1. The British blockade during the War of 1812 destroyed American industry.

2. The embargo act that was passed during Jefferson's administration prohibited trade between Americans and Britain only.

3. The War Hawks were mainly politicians from New England.

4. During the War of 1812, the Americans won only land battles.

5. An important result of the War of 1812 was the growth of patriotism in the United States.

D. Vocabulary

Match the words with the definitions.

Words	Definitions
1. blockade	a. fighting spirit
2. embargo	b. feeling of loyalty to a country
3. impressed	c. to step up trade
4. deserter	d. forced someone to serve
5. patriotism	e. an order halting trade
	f. a naval patrol to keep ships from entering or leaving port
	g. one who leaves military service without permission

E. Chronology

Arrange these events in the order in which they happened.

1. Revolution of 1800 begins
2. XYZ affair
3. War of 1812
4. Washington's inauguration
5. Alien and Sedition Acts passed
6. Louisiana Purchase

Tecumseh Fights Back

During the War of 1812, the United States was not only fighting the British. It was also fighting Indian tribes who were allied with the British. These Indians were part of a movement led by Tecumseh, a Shawnee chief. He hoped to stop white Americans from taking Indian lands in the Northwest.

Since 1790, millions of acres of Indian land had been taken over by new settlers. The white population in the East was expanding rapidly. Many people were becoming land hungry. So various methods were being used to persuade or force tribes into signing away their lands.

Chicago Natural History Museum

Tecumseh argued for the Indian idea of landholding. The land, he said, belonged to all tribes in common. No person or tribe could sell a part of it without the consent of all Indians. "Sell a country! Why not sell the air, the great sea, as well as the earth? Did not the Great Spirit make them all for the use of his children?"

Many Indians agreed. A new Indian unity grew, with its center at the old Indian town of Kithtippecanoe (later called Tippecanoe). This was a major challenge to territorial Governor William Henry Harrison. He rejected Tecumseh's argument against land sales and opened more Indian lands to new settlers.

While Tecumseh was away, Harrison led a force toward the Indian lands. In the battle at Tippecanoe, the Shawnees were defeated and their village was destroyed. Tecumseh was now ready to accept the help of the British against the United States. When the War of 1812 broke out, he led the Indian allies of the British in the fighting in the Northwest Territory.

But in the battle of Thames, in 1813, Tecumseh was killed. Without him, Indian unity fell apart. The struggle to keep Indian lands east of the Mississippi River was almost over.

No certain portrait of Tecumseh is known to exist. However, this painting is believed to be of the Shawnee chief.

Unit 4 Summary The Growing Nation: 1789–1814

The New Federal Government

In 1788, the new federal Constitution went into effect. By unanimous choice, the electoral college selected George Washington to be the first president.

George Washington took office in 1789 and organized the first administration under the new Constitution. The Congress passed the Judiciary Act of 1789, which established the nation's federal court system, including the Supreme Court. Washington, with the consent of the Senate, named the six Supreme Court judges. He also selected the cabinet. Among the members of his cabinet were Alexander Hamilton, secretary of the treasury, and Thomas Jefferson, secretary of state.

The Rise of Political Parties

Soon after Washington took office, disagreements led to the formation of political parties. The Federalists were led by Hamilton. The Anti-Federalists were led by Jefferson. The first issue on which the parties disagreed was Hamilton's financial program. Fresh cause for American political strife came with the outbreak of the French Revolution in 1789. The Federalists opposed the Revolution, while the Anti-Federalists supported the ideas behind it.

In 1796, John Adams, a Federalist leader, was elected president. Jefferson, the Anti-Federalist leader, was chosen vice-president. The political struggles continued. Adams and the Federalists

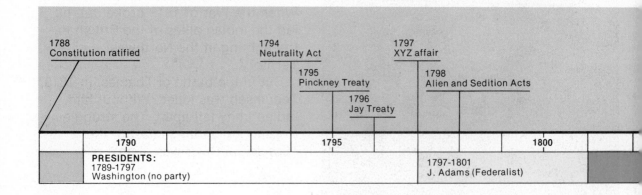

1788
Constitution ratified

1794
Neutrality Act

1797
XYZ affair

1795
Pinckney Treaty

1798
Alien and Sedition Acts

1796
Jay Treaty

1790   1795   1800

PRESIDENTS:
1789-1797
Washington (no party)

1797-1801
J. Adams (Federalist)

won support in the nation as a result of the XYZ affair with France. But the Federalists lost much support when they pushed through the Alien and Sedition Acts. The Anti-Federalists, or Republicans, as they were now called, answered with the Virginia and Kentucky resolutions, which argued that states could declare federal laws unconstitutional.

Jefferson and the Revolution of 1800

In 1800, Jefferson was chosen president. As a result of confusion in the 1796 and 1800 elections, the Twelfth Amendment was added to the Constitution. This required that electors cast separate votes for president and vice-president.

Under Jefferson's administration, the national debt was reduced, the excise tax repealed, and the Alien and Sedition Acts allowed to expire. In addition, Jefferson purchased the Louisiana Territory from France. This purchase more than doubled the territory of the new nation.

The War of 1812

Presidents Washington, Jefferson, and Madison tried to keep the United States out of European wars. But in 1812, war began with Britain. Two of the causes were the issue of freedom of the seas and the desire to expand American borders. The war ended in 1814. Some of its results were the growth of American industry, a growth of American patriotism, the end of the Federalist party, and the recognition of the United States as an independent power.

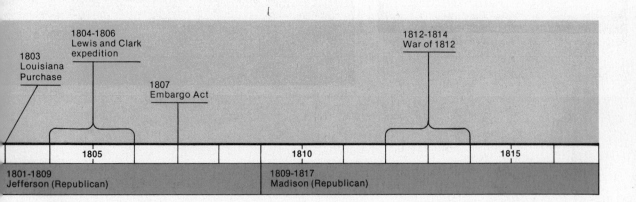

1803
Louisiana
Purchase

1804-1806
Lewis and Clark
expedition

1807
Embargo Act

1812-1814
War of 1812

1805   1810   1815

1801-1809
Jefferson (Republican)

1809-1817
Madison (Republican)

unit
5

An Early Challenge:
Nationalism
versus Sectionalism

It seemed the nation was firmly established. The government and the economy grew stronger and stronger. The country expanded westward. But along with the growth came divisions. The South depended on plantations worked by black slaves. It came to seem less and less like the bustling North (above). And both North and South came to seem even less like the frontier West with its open land (left). Was the United States really one nation? Or was it a weak collection of very different sections?

Lesson 1 The Roots of American Nationalism

WORDS TO UNDERSTAND
Discuss the meanings of these words.

nationalism   **domestic**   **decline**

NEW WORDS IN SENTENCES
1. The rise of **nationalism** meant that Americans were more concerned about their own country.
2. Americans spent their money at home, to help the **domestic** economy.
3. The loss of business meant a **decline** in profits.

AS YOU READ
As you read this selection, try to answer these questions.
1. How did the War of 1812 change Americans' attitudes about the United States?
2. What were the five kinds of change related to nationalism?

THE READING SELECTION
The second war between the United States and England lasted only two years. The treaty that ended it said nothing about the issues that had caused the war. But the War of 1812 marked one turning point in American history. It led to the growth of **nationalism** in the United States.

Nationalism is a feeling of patriotism towards one's country. It is based on people's sharing political and social ideas, customs, and goals. Nationalism involves a strong feeling for a country and a desire to see it grow strong.

After the Revolution ended, Americans often felt closely tied to Europe. The War of 1812 made Americans realize that their interests might be very different from Europe's. Nationalism for Americans meant thinking of the United States as independent of Europe.

It also meant thinking of the whole United States, rather than of only one section or state. Different sections or states often had had different interests. What was good for one was opposed by another. During the period just after the War of 1812, these differences seemed less important. The war showed that American strength lay in unity. Americans became more loyal to the national government and the country as a whole than to one section.

There was a great deal of growth after 1812. Industry grew as a result of the

Patriotism was part of nationalism. July 4th, the national holiday, was celebrated with pride all over the nation. Parades, picnics, games, and speeches marked the occasion. This celebration is in Philadelphia in 1819. The pictures hung on the tents at left and right are reminders of the War of 1812. That war had done much to develop nationalism in the United States.

Historical Society of Pennsylvania

war. The area held by white settlers grew, while that held by Indians shrank. The power of the federal government grew. Nationalism was involved in many of these changes. Sometimes, this was direct involvement, as in the growth of national government. Sometimes, it was indirect, as in the new settlement of lands further west.

There were five main areas of change related to nationalism. Four of these were **domestic** changes. One involved foreign policy.

1. There was a **decline** in political party struggles. The Federalist party died out after the War of 1812. No other strong party developed at that time to replace it. From 1816 to 1824, only one strong party existed—the Republican party. This period of political peace is called the Era of Good Feelings. Actually, there were still many political differences. However, most Americans were united by a feeling of pride in what the nation had achieved.

2. The national government gained more power through legislation. One event was the chartering of the second Bank of the United States in 1816. (The first bank had been allowed to die.) Also in 1816, a tariff bill was passed. Both ideas had originally been proposed by Alexander Hamilton in the 1790s. The Republicans, who opposed strong national government, had opposed them. Now, Hamilton's Federalist party was gone, but the Republicans passed the proposals. This was because they felt they were in the best interests of the nation.

3. The national government was also strengthened by the decisions of the Supreme Court. Chief Justice John Marshall led the Court in issuing a number of decisions that set important precedents.

4. The population of the United States began to move west. The population west of the Appalachian Mountains rose quickly. This also helped bring about changes in methods of transportation.

5. In foreign policy, the United States began to assert itself as a power in the Western Hemisphere. The nation saw that it had interests in the Americas. As a result, it began to limit European power in the area.

COMPREHENSION CHECK

A. Recognizing the Main Idea

This selection as a whole tells you that

1. nationalism was harmful to the nation.

2. national spirit in the United States increased after 1814.

3. nationalism had always existed in the United States.

4. national spirit in the United States declined after 1814.

B. Selecting Important Details

Choose the ending that best completes each statement.

1. The War of 1812 had all the following effects EXCEPT
   a. the knowledge that unity was important for American strength.
   b. the growth of industry.
   c. less American nationalism.
   d. the knowledge that the United States had interests different from those of Europe.

2. All the following are characteristics of nationalism EXCEPT
   a. an increase in loyalty to the nation as a whole.
   b. a desire to see the nation grow strong.
   c. a realization of the importance of the national government.
   d. an increase in arguments among sections of a country.

3. The Era of Good Feelings is the name given to the time when there was
   a. not much pride in the nation.
   b. no longer any danger of war.
   c. strong national feeling and only one important political party.
   d. bitter political fighting.

4. All the following were changes connected with nationalism EXCEPT
   a. the spirit of the Era of Good Feelings.
   b. the chartering of the second Bank of the United States.
   c. greater European involvement in the Western Hemisphere.
   d. passage of the Tariff of 1816.

C. Completion

Fill in the word or words that best complete each sentence.

1. Nationalism for Americans meant realizing that their interests might be different from those of _____.

2. Nationalism also meant thinking of the whole nation, rather than of one _____.

3. Nationalism involved the realization that all Americans share the same _____ and social systems.

4. The power of the _____ government grew during this period.

5. Nationalism affected both foreign and _____ affairs.

D. Vocabulary

Write your own sentence for each of these words.

nationalism   domestic   decline

E. Ask Yourself

What are some examples of the spirit of nationalism in the United States today?

Lesson 2 Nationalism and Domestic Affairs

WORDS TO UNDERSTAND
Discuss the meanings of these words.

commission   vast

invalid   temporary

NEW WORDS IN SENTENCES
1. She held a **commission** as a captain in the army.
2. A law that has become **invalid** no longer has any legal force.
3. The **vast** western lands stretched thousands of miles to the Pacific Coast.
4. Since the treaty had not been approved, the peace was only **temporary**.

AS YOU READ
As you read this selection, try to answer these questions.
1. How did nationalism help increase the federal government's power?
2. In what other ways did nationalism affect domestic affairs?

THE READING SELECTION
The nationalism resulting from the War of 1812 affected domestic affairs in the United States. It was associated with the Era of Good Feelings, the growth of the national government, and the westward movement.

After the War of 1812, the Federalist party lost power. In 1820, the Federalists did not even have a candidate for president. There were still political differences, but only the Republicans had much power.

At this time, the Republicans became more like the Federalists. They had once opposed a strong national government and a national bank. As a result, the first Bank of the United States was allowed to die in 1811. This led to inflation and confusion. The Republicans saw the need for national control of currency. So the second Bank of the United States was set up in 1816.

The Republicans had also opposed tariffs in the 1790s. But now, the new industries built during the war demanded protection. By 1816, the Republicans saw that protecting industry in America could help all Americans. They passed a new tariff, and the government gained more tax power.

The bank and the Tariff of 1816 increased the national government's power. Both resulted from one part of nationalism—a concern for the national economy.

Federal powers also grew as a result of nationalism in Supreme Court decisions. In 1801, John Marshall became chief justice. He helped make a weak federal court into a strong one.

In an 1803 case, *Marbury* v. *Madison,* the Court first declared a law passed by Congress unconstitutional. Marbury, a Federalist, had been appointed a justice of the peace by President Adams. But Jefferson's Republican administration refused to give him his **commission.** Marbury asked the Supreme Court to order Secretary of State Madison to do so. The Judiciary Act of 1789 gave the Court power to do this.

Marshall delivered the Court's decision. He said that Madison should have delivered the commission. But the Supreme Court could not order him to do it. Marshall pointed out that the Constitution did not give such power to the Court. The Constitution was the highest law in the land. Congress could not give the Court more power than the Constitution had given to it. Therefore, Marshall said that part of the 1789 Judiciary Act was unconstitutional, or **invalid.**

The Supreme Court established its right to declare both state and federal laws unconstitutional. In many cases, it also increased the power of the federal government over the states. Concern for a workable government for the country was a part of these decisions. It was also a part of nationalism. Thus, nationalism had again resulted in an increase in the national government's power.

More people began to depend on the federal government, rather than on the states. This was particularly true for people who settled in the **vast** lands west of the Appalachian Mountains. Local governments were not set up right away. When they existed, they often had little money or power. So the new settlers looked to the nation's capital for their needs. The importance of the national government increased as these needs increased.

The settlers needed military protection against Indian tribes they often fought. They needed money to build "internal improvements." These included new roads and canals for transportation to the East. Settlers also wanted low-cost farmland. The federal government sold millions of acres of government-owned land cheaply.

Nationalism was also connected to the growing westward movement. Between 1810 and 1820, the population west of the Appalachian Mountains doubled. Six new states were added to the Union between 1816 and 1821. Traders now met regularly with Indian tribes in the Far West, and the Santa Fe Trail was opened in 1821. Most eastern Indian tribes had already left their land. The rest were under pressure to do so. After the War of 1812, tribes no longer received aid from European nations. The United States had begun to stretch west of the Mississippi River. National pride and the desire to grow encouraged this westward movement.

Thus, nationalism affected domestic affairs in several ways. It encouraged a **temporary** political peace, based on common concerns. There was also an increase in the power of the national government. And pride encouraged the increase in western settlement.

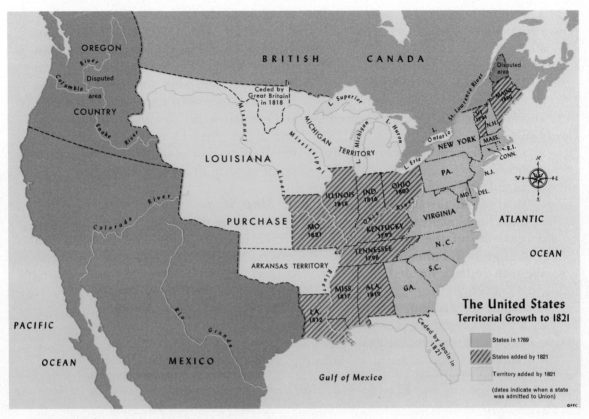

The movement to the frontier west began before the Revolution. It continued until nearly 1900. Which states were added between 1791 and 1812? Between 1816 and 1821?

COMPREHENSION CHECK

A. Recognizing the Main Idea

This selection as a whole tells you how nationalism

1. was created in this country.
2. affected domestic affairs.
3. affected foreign affairs.
4. lost power.

B. Selecting Important Details

Choose the ending that best completes each statement.

1. Republicans supported the second Bank of the United States for all the following reasons EXCEPT

   a. they had always favored strong national government.
   b. the first bank no longer existed.
   c. loss of the first bank caused inflation and confusion.
   d. the party saw the need for national control of currency.

2. The Tariff of 1816 gave more power to
   a. the states.
   b. the Supreme Court.
   c. the federal government.
   d. merchants.
3. In *Marbury* v. *Madison,* the Supreme Court ruled
   a. that a federal law was constitutional.
   b. against the state laws.
   c. that it had no authority to declare laws unconstitutional.
   d. that one of the laws passed by Congress was unconstitutional.
4. Western settlers needed all of the following EXCEPT
   a. military protection.
   b. a weaker federal government.
   c. money for developing transportation.
   d. low-cost farmland.

C. Vocabulary
Match the words with the definitions.

Words	Definitions
1. commission	a. huge
2. invalid	b. strictly limited
3. vast	c. without legal force
4. temporary	d. an accomplishment
	e. written authority to perform a duty
	f. not permanent

D. Essay-type Question
The end of the War of 1812 brought an end to European aid to American Indian tribes. These tribes could no longer get weapons and other supplies from Europeans to fight against the new settlers. How do you think the Indians felt about this? How do you think the new settlers felt about it? Describe each point of view in several sentences.

E. Map Study
This map shows the United States in 1821. Certain areas are labeled with letters. Match each name below with the correct letter. There are two extra letters.
1. the new state of Missouri
2. the new state of Alabama
3. the new state of Illinois
4. the new state of Indiana
5. the new state of Mississippi

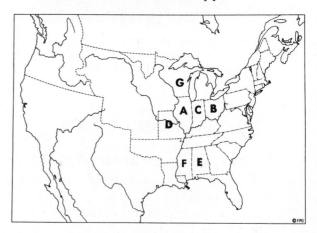

Santa Fe and the Trail

Mexican culture was important in New Mexico, Texas, and California. These dancers were painted in San Antonio, Texas.

In the early 1600s, the English were founding Jamestown, in Virginia, and the Spanish were founding Santa Fe, in what is now New Mexico. While the English colonies expanded east of the Mississippi River, Santa Fe remained a Spanish–Indian center. Under Spanish rule, it was isolated. Located far from Mexico City, it was closed to all foreign trade. When Mexico became independent in 1821, Santa Fe was quiet and well established in the midst of ranches, missions, and Indian pueblos.

At the center of Santa Fe was the Plaza de la Constitución. This was a large dusty square in dry weather, a sea of mud in wet. It was the social and commercial area. Buildings along the plaza were often two stories, with verandas. Their flat roofs and thick adobe walls kept out the summer heat.

This plaza became the end of the Santa Fe Trail. In 1822, an American trader, William Becknell, arrived with goods to sell. Officials of New Mexico welcomed him. They wanted to end the old isolation. The trade route known as the Santa Fe Trail had opened, and it grew rapidly.

Trade caravans heading west to Santa Fe began in Independence, Missouri. There, they were outfitted for the 780-mile trip. It would be two or three months before their return. A caravan was made up of 50 to 100 covered wagons, owned by several trading companies. The trip was hard and often dangerous. The country traveled was often rocky and dry. It often belonged to Indian tribes trying to defend their land against both Mexicans and easterners.

When the caravan finally sighted the Rocky Mountains, it would send a runner ahead to announce its arrival. People turned out in Santa Fe to watch it arrive. The wagons would often parade through the streets to advertise their goods. They finally unloaded near the Plaza de la Constitución. People crowded around to watch, and several days of bargaining followed.

The time in Santa Fe was a chance for the traders to rest and take on supplies for the return trip. It was also an opportunity for different cultures to meet. In Santa Fe, and the Southwest in general, it was the Spanish who won control from the Indians. The United States later won it from the Spanish. But both the Indian and the Spanish–Mexican cultures have continued, right alongside that of the "newcomers."

Lesson 3 Nationalism and Foreign Affairs

WORDS TO UNDERSTAND
Discuss the meanings of these words.
isolationism demilitarization regain

NEW WORDS IN SENTENCES
1. Because the government favored **isolationism,** it tried to avoid contact with other nations.
2. Under the **demilitarization** agreement, both countries removed their forts and troops from the border.
3. After its defeat, the nation began to **regain** its former strength.

AS YOU READ
As you read this selection, try to answer these questions.
1. How did nationalism affect American border disputes with European nations?
2. What were the main points of the Monroe Doctrine?

THE READING SELECTION
Review. The War of 1812 led to the growth of American nationalism. Americans felt more independent of Europe. They also felt more unified as a nation. Sectional differences seemed less important. Americans became more interested in their own problems and progress.

Nationalism affected domestic affairs. Political party struggles decreased after the Federalist party lost power. The national government gained more power through laws. The government also gained power through decisions of the Supreme Court. Nationalism was also part of the westward movement. The population west of the Appalachian Mountains doubled, and new states were added. The new settlers looked to Washington for help. In all these ways, nationalism helped change the country after the War of 1812. ☆

American nationalism involved an attention to the nation's own problems and progress. Americans tended to turn their backs on other countries in a growing feeling of **isolationism.** Foreign policy during this period was limited to protecting the interests of the United States at home. There were steps taken to settle boundary disputes with European nations. Efforts were also made to avoid other involvements with Europe.

There were several treaties to establish clear boundaries.

The Rush-Bagot Agreement of 1817.
This was an agreement between the United States and Britain. The two nations agreed to remove forts and warships from the Great Lakes area. This **demilitarization** was extended in later years. It finally included the entire 3,000-mile border between Canada and the United States.

The Convention of 1818. This was an agreement between the United States and Britain. It settled disputes concerning the border between Canada and the United States. (See the map on page 235.)

The Adams-Onis Treaty of 1819. Spain ceded Florida to the United States, which in turn gave up its claims to Texas. This treaty also formally established the western limit of the Louisiana Purchase.

Under these treaties, the United States gained more land. There also was less chance of war with Europe over boundaries. However, Europe was still interested in the Western Hemisphere. Many of Spain's colonies in the New World had won independence. It was feared that Spain might try to conquer them again. The United States was also concerned about any such action by a European power. President James Monroe and Secretary of State John Quincy Adams worked out a declaration that was sent to Congress in 1823. This Monroe Doctrine made four main points.

1. Europe could establish no new colonies in the Western Hemisphere.

2. European attempts to colonize or control countries in the Americas would be considered unfriendly by the United States.

3. The United States would not interfere in the affairs of Europe or its existing colonies.

4. Europe must not interfere with any country in the Western Hemisphere.

The Monroe Doctrine warned that the United States was ready to protect its interests in the Western Hemisphere. Actually, the United States had no power to enforce the Monroe Doctrine. It knew, however, that the British supported the American action. Great Britain did not want Spain to **regain** its power in the Americas. The powerful British navy was a force that Europeans could not easily overcome. No European nation attempted to challenge the Monroe Doctrine until the 1860s. By then, the United States was strong enough to enforce it.

COMPREHENSION CHECK

A. Recognizing the Main Idea

This selection as a whole tells you how

1. American foreign policy tried to ally us with Britain.

2. American foreign policy sought to protect American interests in the Western Hemisphere.

3. American foreign policy sought to avoid war at any cost.

4. boundary disputes remained a big problem even after 1840.

B. Selecting Important Details

Choose the ending that best completes each statement.

1. The Rush-Bagot Agreement of 1817 resulted in
    a. an alliance between the United States and Canada.
    b. the purchase of Florida from Spain.
    c. the building of American forts on the Canadian border.
    d. the demilitarization of the United States–Canadian border.

2. The Monroe Doctrine was issued because the United States
    a. wished to take over Spanish possessions.
    b. feared British influence in the New World.
    c. wanted to gain influence in Europe.
    d. wished to limit European influence in the Western Hemisphere.

3. The Monroe Doctrine stated all the following EXCEPT
    a. the United States would not interfere in European affairs.
    b. Europeans must give up all colonies in the Western Hemisphere.
    c. Europe was not to interfere in the Western Hemisphere.
    d. no further colonization by Europeans was to be allowed in the Western Hemisphere.

4. The Monroe Doctrine was made possible by the
    a. strength of the United States.
    b. support given the United States by Great Britain.
    c. support given to it by France.
    d. War of 1812.

C. Completion

Fill in the word or words that best complete each sentence.

1. The Rush-Bagot Agreement of 1817 demilitarized the area of the _____.

2. In 1819, the United States obtained Florida from _____.

3. The Convention of 1818 fixed the boundary between the United States and _____.

4. The Monroe Doctrine is the name given to the declaration sent by President Monroe to _____ in 1823.

5. The Monroe Doctrine closed the Western Hemisphere to any further colonization by _____.

D. Vocabulary

Use a word from this list to complete each sentence.

demilitarization   regain   isolationism
nationalism   decline   internal

1. After that illness, it was difficult to _____ his strength.

2. The peace treaty required a _____ of the armed border.

3. Many nations try to practice _____ when they are tired of wars with other lands.

E. Ask Yourself

If you were a Latin American, how would you have felt about the Monroe Doctrine in 1823? Would you feel differently about the Monroe Doctrine today? If so, what would have caused you to change your mind?

The Monroe Doctrine

In December 1823, President James Monroe sent a message to Congress. Contained within it was the famous "Monroe Doctrine," which would be one of the key features of American foreign policy from then on.

The president's message was delivered at a time when great dangers existed for the United States. Two years earlier, the Russian czar had claimed control of the Pacific coast of North America as far south as the fifty-first parallel, into the area that is now Oregon. At the same time, several nations in Europe were ready to help Spain regain its former South American colonies.

The United States wanted to keep European countries from establishing colonies in the Western Hemisphere for several reasons. For one thing, trade with Spanish colonies in South America had been tightly controlled by Spain. The United States economy benefited from independent nations in South America that were open to trade with other countries. Second, keeping European countries out of the Western Hemisphere would make it easier for the United States to stay out of European wars.

How could the young, relatively weak United States prevent European involvement in the Western Hemisphere? Fortunately, the British were also interested in keeping Russia, France, Austria, and Spain out of the New World. Like the United States, Britain wanted trade with South American countries. Britain was willing to aid the United States in preventing further colonization in the Americas.

For a time, the United States considered issuing a joint statement with Britain. However, Secretary of State John Quincy Adams favored a declaration by the United States alone. The Monroe Doctrine was issued as an American statement. It declared the Western Hemisphere closed to further European colonization. Behind this policy of the United States was the support of the mighty British government with its powerful fleet. In later years, the United States would be able to back up the Monroe Doctrine with its own power.

Lesson 4 The Roots of American Sectionalism

WORDS TO UNDERSTAND
Discuss the meanings of these words.

sectionalism   immigration
protective   unity

NEW WORDS IN SENTENCES
1. **Sectionalism** increased as each section became more determined to get what it wanted.
2. Nations are usually very **protective** about their people.
3. **Immigration** provides a country with new people who have different ideas and strengths.
4. The new spirit of **unity** bound all the sections of the nation together as one.

AS YOU READ
As you read this selection, try to answer these questions.
1. What is meant by sectionalism?
2. What were some characteristics of the three main sections?
3. What were some of the major issues the sections disagreed about?

THE READING SELECTION
Review. The growth of American nationalism meant that Americans paid most attention to their own domestic affairs. They felt more isolated from foreign countries. Foreign policy aimed at keeping the United States out of disputes with Europe. As a result, treaties were signed settling several border disagreements. Foreign policy also tried to protect United States interests in the Western Hemisphere. In 1823, the Monroe Doctrine warned Europe to stay out of affairs in the Americas. ☆

Just after the War of 1812, nationalism grew stronger in the United States. Americans put aside many sectional differences. However, the three main sections of the nation remained different. The nationalist period was one of growth, and the sections grew in different ways. Each one needed different things. In addition, each section felt strongly about many issues that were to be decided. So in the 1820s, **sectionalism** began to grow again. Sectionalism is the favoring of the interests of one section over those of the nation as a whole. The three main sections were the North, the South, and the West.

The North. This section included New England and such "middle states" as Pennsylvania and New York. Most people of the section were farmers. However, the national centers of commerce and industry were also in the North. The

BRITISH CANADA

Disputed area

MAINE

L. Superior

MICHIGAN TERRITORY

L. Michigan

L. Huron

St. Lawrence River

VT.

N.H.

L. Ontario

N.Y.

MASS.

R.I.

CONN.

L. Erie

PA.

N.J.

ILL. IND. OHIO

MD. DEL.

MO.

KY.

VA.

ARKANSAS TERRITORY

TENN.

N.C.

S.C.

ATLANTIC

MISS. ALA. GA.

OCEAN

MEXICO

LA.

FLORIDA TERRITORY

Gulf of Mexico

North — West (northern)
South — West (southern)

© FPC

Areas considered the West in 1822 joined either the North or the South by 1860. Which areas probably joined the North? The South?

area was developing industry and transportation. Immigrants from Europe would soon begin to arrive to work in the factories.

The South. This section had almost no industry. It depended on raising cotton, tobacco, and sugar cane. These products were sent to northern and European factories. The invention of the cotton gin in 1793 led to greater cotton production. This, in turn, led to a greater demand for slave labor. Most

white southerners [...] but much of the [...] from slave labo[...] The plantation [...] economy and [...]

The West. This [...] tion than the other tw[...] had been the area between [...] chian Mountains and the Missi[...] River. In 1800, there were only two states in the area. By 1821, seven more had joined the Union. The northwestern areas were settled by northeasterners and European immigrants. They usually had small farms. Grains and other food products were their major crops. Southwestern areas had been settled in large slave plantations by southerners who needed fresh soil for cotton. Thus, the West could actually be divided into the South West and the North West. Generally, however, it was agricultural. The people were concerned with developing its new settlements and linking them to the older areas.

The sections differed on most issues of the day.

Protective tariffs. The North favored high tariffs to protect its industry. The South opposed them, since it had to buy the manufactured goods it used. The West was divided on the issue.

The Bank of the United States. The North favored the bank, because the bank's hard money policies helped business and industry. The South and West opposed the bank. Hard money made it difficult to get loans and credit farmers needed.

Internal improvements. The West favored this program, since the section needed roads and canals. The North

ed feelings. The South did not
▢ pay taxes to build roads it did
▢eed.

▢mmigration. The North and West
▢vored increased immigration. This
would provide more labor in factories
and more settlers on the frontier. The
South saw no need for more immigrants.

Expansion of the frontiers. The
South and West wanted new land for
more plantations and settlements. The
North feared this could take away its
labor supply.

Slavery. The South favored taking
slaves into new areas to establish plantations. The North opposed extending
slavery any further. The West was divided, with the South West supporting
the expansion of slavery.

In 1824, Henry Clay, a representative
from Kentucky, proposed what he called
the "American system." He suggested
that the South and West support protective tariffs to aid the industrial North.
In return, the North would support a
system of internal improvements. The
whole program would tie the different
sections together in economic **unity.** But
Clay's idea failed. The nationalist spirit
could not overcome the growing sectionalism. For the next forty years, the
division of the people along sectional
lines would be part of American life.

Sectional differences could sometimes be obvious.
Both paintings above are of homes in the West
section. At top is a plantation in Louisiana
(South West). Below it is a homestead in
Indiana (North West). What might be some
differences between the two ways of life? How
might these ways of life affect the political views
of the people?

COMPREHENSION CHECK

A. Recognizing the Main Idea

This selection as a whole tells you

1. of a major issue on which sectional feeling developed.
2. about the growth of sectionalism in the United States.
3. that sectionalism helped to promote nationalist feeling.
4. that nationalism replaced sectionalism.

B. Selecting Important Details

Choose the ending that best completes each statement.

1. Political differences between the sections were partly the result of
   a. the nationalist spirit.
   b. Clay's American system.
   c. economic unity.
   d. economic differences.
2. All the following statements are true EXCEPT
   a. the South and West opposed the Bank of the United States.
   b. the North and South favored high tariffs.
   c. the North and West favored continued immigration.
   d. the South and West favored expansion of American frontiers.
3. Clay's plan for an American system
   a. succeeded because of sectional feeling.
   b. would have limited national feeling.
   c. failed because of the developing sectional feelings.
   d. was based mainly on aid to the South.

4. The industrial North was strongly in favor of
   a. high protective tariffs.
   b. the sale of western lands to settlers.
   c. low tariffs.
   d. special aid to the West and South.

C. True or False

Decide whether each of these statements is true or false.

1. The South was trying to develop industry and commerce.
2. The North had given up farming entirely.
3. The West was settled partly by immigrants.
4. The North favored immigration because it provided labor for the factories.
5. The West was unified in support of extending slavery to new areas.

D. Vocabulary

Write your own sentence for each of these words.

sectionalism   immigration
protective   unity

E. Essay-type Question

For each item below, write one or two sentences identifying which section (North, South, West) it describes. Include in your sentences the reasons for your choice.

1. This section preferred hard money policies.
2. This section was interested in new ways of shipping grain quickly.
3. This section would be badly hurt by any limitation on exports to Europe.

The Great Compromiser: Henry Clay

Henry Clay was a leader who seemed to fall just short of his goals. In his seventy-five years, he served as state legislator, United States senator, Speaker of the House of Representatives, secretary of state, and presidential candidate. Many times in those years, he seemed on the point of reaching his great ambition—to become president. But he never reached that goal.

As a young congressman, he had been a "war hawk," favoring war to expand American boundaries. In 1824, he helped John Quincy Adams win the presidency when the election was thrown into the House of Representatives. This earned him the ill will of Andrew Jackson, who won his revenge by defeating Clay in the presidential election of 1832.

By this time, Clay had begun to see more clearly the need to unite the nation. He became more concerned about the issues of the day. In 1820, he had helped promote the Missouri Compromise. But this turned out to be only a temporary solution to the slavery problem. Later, he proposed the "American system." This was a plan to unite all sections in a system of high tariffs and internal improvements. The "American system" failed to win approval, and

Chicago Historical Society

the sections of the nation pulled ever further apart.

In 1850, Henry Clay, then seventy-three years old, made one more effort to find a compromise settlement of the slavery issue. He worked out the Compromise of 1850 and earned the title the Great Compromiser. But this plan failed to prevent the Civil War. His efforts at compromise, however, earned Clay his place in the nation's history.

Lesson 5   Sectionalism and the Tariff

WORDS TO UNDERSTAND
Discuss the meanings of these words.

revenue   rate
discourage   competition

NEW WORDS IN SENTENCES
1. Governments must have enough **revenue** to pay their expenses.
2. Traffic tickets are intended to **discourage** people from driving illegally.
3. The telephone company wanted to increase the **rate** for long distance calls.
4. The owner of the small grocery store was worried about **competition** from the supermarket.

AS YOU READ
As you read this selection, try to answer these questions.
1. What is the difference between a revenue tariff and a protective tariff?
2. Why did the North strongly favor a high tariff?

THE READING SELECTION
Review. Sectionalism, which had been put aside just after the War of 1812, began to grow in the 1820s. There were three main sections, which were different in their ways of life and political goals. The North was developing industry and commerce. The South was depending more and more on cotton plantations run with slave labor. The West was a frontier area, settled by people from both North and South. The issues on which the sections disagreed included slavery, a protective tariff, and internal improvements. ☆

One issue dividing the sections during the 1820s was the question of tariffs. A tariff is a tax on imports. The tariff is paid to the government when an item enters the country. An equal amount is added to the selling price of the item so that the seller does not lose money.

There are two kinds of tariffs. They are the **revenue** tariff and the protective tariff. A revenue tariff aims only at gaining income for the government. It is usually a small amount, which will not hurt the sale of the item in this country. A protective tariff, however, aims at helping American industry. It seeks to **discourage** foreign industry from competing with American manufacturers. To do this, the protective tariff places a very high **rate** of tax on the imported item. When that amount is added to the price of the item, imported goods are

The North led the other sections in developing industry and commerce. This picture shows a busy New York City port in 1828. How is this a contrast to the pictures on page 244?

much more expensive. The imported item does not sell, and soon it is not imported any longer. The government does not get much income from a protective tariff, but American industry has less **competition.**

The first American tariffs on imports were quite low. Their main aim was to bring in revenue. From 1790 to 1812, the tariffs on imports were increased. However, the main purpose of tariffs was still to raise revenue. During the War of 1812, tariff rates were doubled. This helped raise money needed for the war. It was expected that the tariff rates would be reduced after the war. The growth of industry as a result of the war changed the ideas of many people about the purpose of tariffs.

American industry had greatly expanded during the war. Trade with Europe had been stopped. Americans were forced to produce their own goods. When the War of 1812 ended, foreign goods flooded the American markets. These goods were cheaper than American products. They were a real threat to the new industries. These American industries, mostly located in the North, argued for protection by the government.

The Tariff of 1816 was a high protective tariff. Most Americans supported this tariff. It was passed during the nationalistic period, when sectional differences were less important. In addition, non-industrial sections like the South hoped at that time to develop industries. They felt that the tariff might benefit more than just the North.

In the 1820s, sectional differences increased. The South saw that it would not develop enough industry to benefit from the tariff. Southerners were paying higher prices for goods because of the protective tariff. Also, the South was an exporting section. It sold much of its cotton in Europe. If protective tariffs kept foreign goods out of the United States, European nations would buy fewer American products, including cotton. This would hurt southern planters.

The North benefited most from the high tariffs. Other sections demanded something in return. President Madison and Congress tried to do something for the West. Congress passed bills to provide money for finishing the Cumberland Road. This road would greatly benefit the western farmers. President Madison knew the delegates to the Constitutional Convention had not wanted Congress to pass such bills. But Madison realized the Constitution had to grow to meet the changing needs of the country. He therefore approved the money for the Cumberland Road, which was completed in 1818.

The tariff measures were good for the North. The Cumberland Road was a benefit to the West. Only the South felt it was being shortchanged by the Congress. By the time the Congress was ready to pass the Tariff of 1824, the South was organized against further protective tariffs. The election of 1824 showed the nation that sectionalism was one of the main problems it faced.

COMPREHENSION CHECK

A. Recognizing the Main Idea
This selection as a whole tells you that
1. the North and the South were in agreement about the need for tariffs.
2. tariffs cannot protect American industry.
3. tariffs became an important issue because of sectional differences.
4. tariffs encourage foreign countries to buy American goods.

B. Selecting Important Details
Choose the ending that best completes each statement.
1. Revenue tariffs
   a. are paid to industry.
   b. discourage foreign competition in the United States.
   c. were the first tariffs to be placed on imports.
   d. have the same rates as protective tariffs.
2. Protective tariffs
   a. increased the sale of cotton to foreign countries.
   b. benefited the North more than the South.
   c. helped non-industrial sections in the South.
   d. are no different from revenue tariffs.
3. The Tariff of 1816
   a. was opposed in the South.
   b. made foreign goods cheaper than American goods.
   c. was a revenue tariff.
   d. protected American industry.

4. The South's claim that it was being ignored by the government was based on all of the following facts EXCEPT

    a. American industry was being protected.

    b. federal funds were being used to build the Cumberland Road.

    c. Southern industry was strengthened by the tariffs.

    d. American cotton exports might decrease.

C. Completion

Fill in the word that best completes each sentence.

1. The War of 1812 helped American industry to _____.

2. Just after the War of 1812, foreign goods cost _____ than American goods.

3. The industrial North was in favor of high _____ tariffs.

4. The South did not develop enough _____ to benefit from protective tariffs.

5. Southern planters felt they would be hurt by protective tariffs because foreign nations would buy less _____.

D. Vocabulary

Write your own sentence for each of these words.

revenue   rate
discourage   competition

E. Ask Yourself

Do you think the United States has any need for high protective tariffs today? If so, what might be some industries that would want tariff protection?

The Missouri Compromise

The sectionalism of the 1820s and 1830s involved several specific issues. Perhaps the most important was slavery.

During the 1800s, the cotton gin made cotton even more profitable, and production increased greatly. More land was used to grow cotton, and more land was wanted. With this growth came an increase in the number of slaves. Plantation owners began to settle in the southern areas of the West. These lands are now Louisiana, Mississippi, and Alabama. The new settlers brought slavery with them.

Opposition to slavery in the North and parts of the West increased. This opposition was gaining strength in the government. The population of the North and West was rising faster than that in the South. Thus, anti-slavery members in the House of Representatives also increased. In 1820, the South controlled 90 House seats. The North and the northern part of the West controlled 123.

The South was determined to protect its interests. It aimed at the Senate, where each state had two seats, regardless of population. By 1818, there were eleven free states and eleven slave states. Each group had twenty-two senators. Southern leaders were determined to keep the number of slave states equal to the number of free states. In that way, the South would have some control over the Senate.

In 1819, Missouri applied for admission to the Union as a slave state. Northerners wanted to change the bill of admission to forbid slavery in Missouri. Neither side wanted the other to gain a majority in the Senate.

When Maine requested statehood at the end of 1819, Henry Clay was able to work out a compromise to admit both states. The Missouri Compromise of 1820 had three main points. First, Missouri would be admitted as a slave state. Second, Maine would be admitted as a free state. Third, the Louisiana Territory north of the parallel 36°30' was to be closed forever to slavery.

The Missouri Compromise kept the balance within the Senate. Now there were twelve free states and twelve slave states. However, the sectional feelings that had created the crisis still existed.

Northerners feared slavery would spread throughout the Louisiana Territory. But the Missouri Compromise set the northern boundary for slavery at the 36°30' parallel. Find this line on the map below. Which is larger, the territory open to slavery or the territory closed to it?

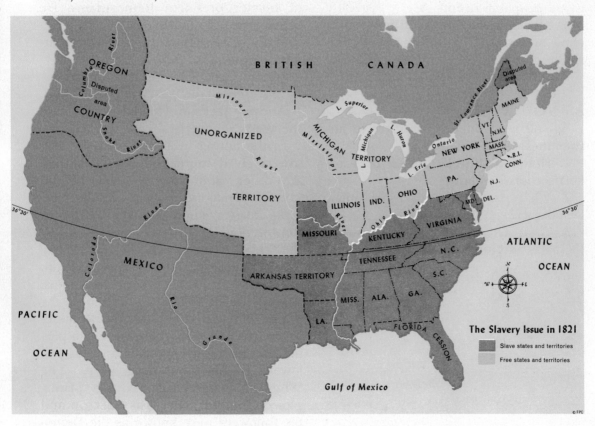

The Slavery Issue in 1821

Slave states and territories

Free states and territories

Lesson 6 Jackson's Administration: A Time of Change

WORDS TO UNDERSTAND

Discuss the meanings of these words.

contenders   humanitarian   abolition

NEW WORDS IN SENTENCES

1. There were several **contenders** for the office who were well qualified and well liked.

2. The **humanitarian** societies worked to aid people in need.

3. Members of the **abolition** movement were working to do away with slavery.

AS YOU READ

As you read this selection, try to answer these questions.

1. How did the election of 1824 reflect sectional feelings?

2. What is meant by Jacksonian Democracy?

3. What changes happened during Jackson's administration?

THE READING SELECTION

In the election of 1824, sectional differences broke into the open. Four separate candidates were nominated to run for the presidency. No party had replaced the Federalists as yet, so all the candidates were Republicans. But each candidate represented the views of a particular section. The candidates were:

John Quincy Adams. He was the son of former president John Adams. He represented the North.

William H. Crawford. He represented the South.

Henry Clay. The Great Compromiser represented the West.

Andrew Jackson. He also represented the West.

In the voting in 1824, Andrew Jackson received more popular votes than any other candidate. However, he did not win a majority of votes in the electoral college. Therefore, the House of Representatives had to choose among the three leading **contenders.** They were Adams, Crawford, and Jackson. When Clay threw his support to Adams, Adams was elected.

The bitter election split the Republican party. By 1828, there were two parties in the country. Adams and his followers formed the Whig party. The Whigs in general followed the principles of the old Federalists. Jackson and his followers were known as the Demo-

cratic party. They followed the old Republican principles.

In 1828, Jackson defeated Adams for the presidency. Andrew Jackson had been known as a representative of the common people. His two terms in office are often called the era of Jacksonian Democracy. This name is based on the idea that Jackson served the average person. He was disliked by special interest groups, such as bankers. Democratic rights were increased for many, but not all, Americans. Some of these changes were due to Jackson's policies, and some were the result of work by others. Changes during Jackson's administration included the following.

1. The people played a greater role in the political process. More state officials were elected rather than appointed. Many states dropped property or religious requirements for voters and officials. (Jews and Catholics had often been denied full political rights.) In addition, presidential candidates were selected by delegates to political party conventions. (They had been chosen by each party's congressional representatives.) In general, more people had more real power over the government.

2. There were many movements for social reform. Women could not vote or play an active role in politics. However, they played an important part in **humanitarian** movements. There were organizations to improve treatment of the mentally ill and to increase free education. There were others to improve conditions for factory workers and, later, to gain more rights for women. The **abolition** movement also began to gain strength at this time. Many of these activities continued for many years.

3. The spoils system in politics was expanded. Jackson fired large numbers of federal officials appointed by previous presidents. He replaced them with his own supporters. He intended, he said, to remove officials favoring wealthy northern interests. Their jobs were to be taken by people who would protect the average person. Jackson was the first president to use the spoils system so heavily. This did bring "new blood" into government. However, it often produced untrained officials who bought their jobs with votes.

4. The office of the president became more powerful. Jackson was a strong president. He fought and won battles with both Congress and the Supreme Court. He expanded the actions a president could take.

5. The position of American Indian tribes was weakened. They lost their remaining lands east of the Mississippi River and were forced westward.

COMPREHENSION CHECK

A. Recognizing the Main Idea

This selection as a whole tells you

1. how the election of Jackson reduced sectional strife.

2. that all the changes that came during the era of Jacksonian Democracy were brought about by Jackson personally.

3. that Jackson's administration was a time of many political and social changes.

4. that Jackson's election brought few changes to the United States.

B. Selecting Important Details

Choose the ending that best completes each statement.

1. In the election of 1824
   a. Jackson received the largest number of popular votes, but Adams was chosen by the electoral college.
   b. Adams won both the popular vote and the electoral vote.
   c. Jackson was elected by the House of Representatives.
   d. Jackson received the largest number of popular votes, but Adams was chosen by the House of Representatives.

2. All of the following statements about the spoils system are true EXCEPT that
   a. Jackson expanded the system.
   b. the new officials usually disagreed with the president.
   c. some officials bought their jobs with votes.
   d. "new blood" came into the government.

3. The candidates in 1824 represented
   a. the South and West.
   b. the South, West, and North.
   c. the North, West, and Southwest.
   d. the North, South, and Northwest.

4. All of the following are examples of the growing democracy under Jackson EXCEPT
   a. the selection of presidential candidates at party conventions.
   b. the election, rather than appointment, of most state officials.
   c. the end of many state religious qualifications for voters or officeholders.
   d. the gain of the vote by women.

C. True or False

Decide whether each of the following statements is true or false.

1. There were four candidates for the presidency in the election of 1824.

2. The Whig party, formed after 1824, was based on the principles of the old Republican party.

3. Jackson was a strong president who made the office more powerful.

4. American Indians gained land under Jackson.

5. Andrew Jackson favored northern bankers over the common people.

D. Vocabulary

Match the words with the definitions.

Words	Definitions
1. contender	a. something far off
2. humanitarian	b. person competing for a position
3. abolition	c. system of taxation
	d. helpful to people
	e. ending

Lesson 7 American Indians in the Jacksonian Era

WORDS TO UNDERSTAND

Discuss the meanings of these words.

uncivilized   **removal**   **trustee**

NEW WORDS IN SENTENCES

1. Because white people did not understand Indian cultures, they thought that Indians were **uncivilized.**

2. For the Indian tribes, **removal** meant the loss of their old homelands.

3. As **trustee** for the Indian nations, the national government was responsible for them.

AS YOU READ

As you read this selection, try to answer these questions.

1. What attitudes were the basis for Jackson's Indian policy?

2. What were the two Supreme Court decisions regarding the tribes?

3. What was the policy of removal? How was it carried out?

THE READING SELECTION

Review. Andrew Jackson was inaugurated as president in 1829. His eight years in office saw many changes in American life. Citizens played a greater role in government, yet the power of the president increased. It was the beginning of great efforts for social change. It was a period of conflict between sectionalism and nationalism. ☆

For American Indians, the 1830s was an important period. During Andrew Jackson's presidency, relations between the tribes and the United States came to national attention. There were two different issues. One involved the takeover of Indian lands by new settlers. The other issue centered on which level of government should deal with the tribes — state or federal.

Andrew Jackson had built a reputation on the frontier as an Indian fighter. As president, his policy toward Indians was based on attitudes shared by many others.

To Jackson, Indians stood in the way of progress by the United States. This was a common idea at the time. Indians were often called savages and thought of as **uncivilized.** Therefore, white settlers felt they had the right to take over Indian lands. To these settlers, Indian land claims were something to be gotten around or gotten rid of.

Most land had been taken over from tribes through treaties. Often the treaties were unfair or illegal. The tribes

Since the 1830s, many artists and writers have used the Trail of Tears as a subject. This modern painting was done by Jerome Tiger, a Creek-Seminole Indian from Oklahoma.

often had no choice. When they freely and legally sold their land, they did so in exchange for benefits promised to them.

By the 1820s, few tribes held much land east of the Mississippi River. The exceptions were the Cherokee, Creek, Choctaw, and Chickasaw in the South and Southeast. They still held land as a result of earlier federal treaties. In 1829, Jackson recommended the **removal** of all Indians to lands west of the Mississippi River. The Removal Act was passed and signed a year later. In 1834, a special Indian Territory, later called Oklahoma, was set aside.

Most white Americans saw removal as a way of easily getting more land. Even some Indians and their supporters saw it as the only way out of a war that the tribes could not win. Andrew Jackson did not invent the idea of removal. However, he was the president who asked for and signed the act.

Removal of the Indians was begun during Jackson's term of office. It continued for many years. The Cherokees were removed by the army during the winter of 1838–39. This six-month forced march over hundreds of miles has become known as the Trail of Tears. About one-fourth of the Indians died of cold, hunger, or disease. They were a defeated people when they arrived in the lands of the still-free Plains Indians.

The issue of which level of government

should deal with the Indians was not settled with a new law. It was settled by decisions of the Supreme Court. Earlier relations with tribes had been handled by the federal government. This was because the Constitution gave Congress the power to control commerce with the tribes. Congress had also passed a law in 1790 that declared that all treaties not approved by Congress were null and void.

Jackson felt that affairs with the tribes could be handled by the states. He did not generally believe that the states could act independently of the national government. But he felt it would be easier to obtain land if the tribes were dealt with separately by each state.

The last Indian war east of the Mississippi was in 1832. A group of Sauk-Fox led by Black Hawk fought to keep their land in Illinois.

Library of Congress

In 1831 and 1832, Chief Justice John Marshall delivered important Supreme Court decisions. These came in suits against the state of Georgia. In one lawsuit, he said the tribes were "domestic dependent nations." The federal government was a **trustee** for the Indians. In the second decision, the Court ruled that the states could not interfere with affairs on Indian reservations. Marshall clearly gave the power to deal with Indian tribes to the federal government.

Jackson did not support Marshall's decisions. When Georgia openly disobeyed the rulings, he refused to enforce them. Jackson is reported to have said, "John Marshall made his decision, now let him enforce it!"

In the long run, Marshall's decision did settle the question of who should deal with Indian tribes. However, the takeover of Indian lands remained an issue. Tribes west of the Mississippi River still held their land. This would lead to more conflict with new settlers in the future.

COMPREHENSION CHECK

A. Recognizing the Main Idea
This selection as a whole tells you

1. how the Supreme Court stopped Indian removal.

2. how the national government acted as trustee for the Indian nations.

3. why the Indians were not civilized.

4. about the conflicts between tribes and the government in the Jacksonian era.

B. Selecting Important Details

Choose the ending that best completes each statement.

1. Jackson did not believe
   a. in the Supreme Court decisions of 1831 and 1832.
   b. that state governments should handle tribal affairs.
   c. that Indians stood in the way of progress.
   d. in removal.

2. Treaties between tribes and the government were
   a. often unfair and illegal.
   b. a way of getting land for white people.
   c. sometimes a free and legal exchange.
   d. all of the above.

3. The Trail of Tears refers to the
   a. sufferings of many white settlers in the West.
   b. decision of the Supreme Court against the state of Georgia regarding Indians.
   c. many wars that took place between Indians and settlers.
   d. forced march of the Cherokees.

4. All of the following statements about the Supreme Court decisions of 1831 and 1832 are true EXCEPT that
   a. they involved the state of Georgia.
   b. they ruled that states had no power on Indian reservations.
   c. they ruled that the national government was the trustee for the Indian nations.
   d. they defined Indian tribes as "foreign independent nations."

C. True or False

Decide whether each of the following statements is true or false. Rewrite the false statements so that they are true.

1. Andrew Jackson invented the idea of removal.

2. The Constitution gives Congress power to regulate commerce with the Indian tribes.

3. The Removal Law said that the states had no power in Indian affairs.

4. The four tribes that still held land in the South and Southeast when Jackson took office were the Creek, Chickasaw, Choctaw, and Hopi.

5. Jackson agreed with Marshall's ideas about which level of government should deal with Indian tribes.

D. Vocabulary

Match the words with the definitions.

Words	Definitions
1. uncivilized	a. an Indian tribe
2. removal	b. taking away
3. trustee	c. a rich person
	d. untamed
	e. the responsible person or organization

E. Essay-type Question

Choose one of the statements below and defend it in four or five sentences.

1. Removal was justified. It was necessary to permit progress by advanced white civilization.

2. Removal was unfair. Indians had a right to live in their own ways on their land.

Lesson 8 Economic Issues and Jackson's Government

WORDS TO UNDERSTAND
Discuss the meanings of these words.

abominations **nullification**
fundamental **secede**

NEW WORDS IN SENTENCES

1. Actions that are extremely shameful and wrong are called **abominations.**

2. It is difficult to get a job without the **fundamental** skills of reading and writing.

3. According to the theory of **nullification,** a state had the right to declare a federal law null and void.

4. States cannot **secede,** or withdraw from the United States, when they disagree with national policies.

AS YOU READ

As you read this selection, try to answer these questions.

1. What law did South Carolina try to nullify, and how did Jackson handle the threat to secede?

2. Why did Jackson oppose the Bank of the United States?

THE READING SELECTION

Sectionalism often involved economic issues. During Andrew Jackson's presidency, two of these issues caused serious clashes. They were tariffs and banking.

Tariffs had already caused arguments. Northern factories were aided by higher tariff rates, which hurt southern plantations. An 1824 rate increase had upset the South. Another increase, in 1828, was called the Tariff of **Abominations** by southerners. John C. Calhoun, a senator and later vice-president, led the protest. His own South Carolina legislature adopted a formal protest he had written.

In the protest, Calhoun returned to the theory of states' rights. He believed that states were the **fundamental** system of government. He argued that the federal government had been given limited powers by a contract among the states. If the federal government went beyond its powers, each state had the right to declare a federal law null and void. This action is called **nullification.** In other words, Calhoun argued that states shared the Supreme Court's power to decide whether a law was constitutional.

Nullification was debated for the next several years. In 1830, President Jackson made it clear that he did not support the southern position. The real test came in 1832. In that year, a new tariff was passed. Although it reduced the rates, it did not please the South. South Carolina declared the new tariff law null and void. The state threatened to **secede** if the federal government tried to enforce the law there.

Jackson reacted quickly and forcefully in a proclamation to the people of South Carolina. "To say that any state may at pleasure secede from the Union is to say that the United States is not a nation." Jackson then asked Congress for a bill allowing him to send an army to enforce the law.

While Congress debated this Force Bill, Henry Clay worked out another compromise. This compromise was passed as the Tariff of 1833. It would gradually decrease tariff rates to the level of the Tariff of 1816. South Carolina was satisfied. It felt it had proved that a state could change federal policy by threatening to secede. Some people feared that this success would encourage more states to use the same method.

Jackson soon had to turn his attention to the Bank of the United States. It was a private bank in which the national government owned 20 percent of the stock. The bank held federal funds and made loans to the government. It also controlled state banks and the supply of currency. (See the chart on page 198.) The first bank had been allowed to die in 1811. A new one had been chartered in 1816, but its charter would end in 1836.

By 1832, the bank was powerful, but it had a great deal of opposition. State banks disliked being controlled. Farmers and planters in the West and South disliked the bank's hard money policies. They wanted more currency and loans available.

Jackson himself opposed the bank. He felt the government did not have the constitutional power to establish a bank. He also felt that the bank favored wealthy northern interests. In 1832, Congress passed a bill granting the bank a new charter. Jackson vetoed the bill, and the bank became the main issue of his reelection campaign. However, Jackson won the election.

Jackson felt that his reelection showed that most Americans did not want the bank. Federal money was slowly withdrawn. New funds were put into state banks, called "pet banks" by Jackson's enemies.

The immediate effects of Jackson's actions were bad. Without the Bank of the United States to control them, state banks freely issued currency and lent money. This made money lose value and led to an economic slump. But in the long run, the end of the Bank of the United States encouraged competition in banking. This did help the public.

Jackson's tariff action showed his belief in the power of the national government. His banking action showed that he believed that this power should be limited. He seemed to govern on the basis of a limited nationalism.

THE DOWNFALL OF MOTHER BANK.

Jackson's action against the Bank of the U.S. caused much argument. Do you think the artist of this cartoon supported or opposed Jackson's action? How can you tell?

COMPREHENSION CHECK

A. Recognizing the Main Idea

This selection as a whole tells you

1. how Jackson destroyed the Bank of the United States.

2. that tariff laws led to a dispute about nullification.

3. about sectionalism and economic disputes during Jackson's administration.

4. that Jackson wanted states to have the right to secede.

B. Selecting Important Details

Choose the ending that best completes each statement.

1. The Bank of the United States was

a. supported by Jackson because it favored wealthy northern interests.

b. favored by state banks because it gave them more control.

c. not very powerful.

d. disliked by farmers and planters because they opposed hard money.

2. John C. Calhoun argued for all of the following EXCEPT
   a. the states have the right to nullify laws.
   b. the states give limited power to the federal government.
   c. the federal government is the fundamental system of government.
   d. the federal government results from a contract among the states.

3. Jackson asked Congress for a Force Bill that would
   a. compromise on the tariff issue.
   b. allow him to send an army to enforce federal law.
   c. give states the power of nullification.
   d. give states the right to secede.

4. Jackson's actions against the Bank of the United States
   a. caused him to lose the election.
   b. made the federal government more powerful.
   c. immediately improved the economy.
   d. encouraged competition in banking.

C. True or False
Decide whether each of the following statements is true or false.

1. Calhoun argued that states had the right to secede.

2. The tariff law passed in 1832 lowered the rates.

3. Henry Clay worked out a compromise over the Tariff of Abominations.

4. Jackson wanted money withdrawn from state banks and put into the Bank of the United States.

5. Jackson called the Bank of the United States a "pet bank."

D. Vocabulary
Match the words with the definitions.

Words	Definitions
1. abomination	a. to regret
2. fundamental	b. to withdraw or leave
3. nullification	c. something shameful or wrong
4. secede	d. the act of making a law void
	e. to come between
	f. basic

E. Essay-type Question
Write a few sentences telling why each of the following statements is true.

1. In his actions during the tariff clash, President Jackson proved himself a representative of the entire nation.

2. In his actions against the Bank of the United States, Jackson proved he was in favor of limiting the power of the national government.

Our Federal Union—
It Must Be Preserved

On April 13, 1830, the Democratic party arranged an anniversary dinner to celebrate Jefferson's birthday. Jefferson had died just four years earlier, and many present at the dinner remembered him well. They gathered to honor him and his ideas. One of the ideas they sought to honor was the necessity of limiting the power of the central government.

The organizers of the dinner, to be held in Washington, D.C., were led by Vice-President Calhoun. They intended to use the dinner to express their belief in the right of the states to limit federal power. The recent debate between Senators Webster and Hayne over nullification had sharpened public interest in the issue of state versus federal power.

The committee arranging the meeting proposed that President Jackson should help them set the tone of the meeting. The program had allowed full expression of states' rights and nullification ideas by leading Democrats. Then all attention was turned to President Jackson, who was to deliver the main toast of the evening.

Vice-president John Calhoun had long supported states' rights. He had argued for nullification in the 1820s.

President Jackson well knew what Calhoun and the others wanted him to say. They expected him to support their views. Instead, the president, with his eyes fixed firmly on Vice-President Calhoun, proposed the toast, "Our federal Union—it must be preserved." Andrew Jackson had spoken. He had told the nation he proposed to support the federal Union at all costs.

263

Lesson 9 The Two-Party System Returns

WORDS TO UNDERSTAND
Discuss the meanings of these words.

authority   crisis

overrule   solutions

NEW WORDS IN SENTENCES
1. She did not have the **authority,** or power, to carry out her ideas.

2. Some people wanted states to have the right to **overrule** federal laws and do things their own way.

3. The conflict finally came to a **crisis,** or turning point.

4. Some **solutions** are only short-term answers to problems.

AS YOU READ
As you read this selection, try to answer these questions.

1. Who belonged to the Democratic party, and what was its program?

2. Who belonged to the Whig party, and what was its program?

THE READING SELECTION
During the period of strong American nationalism, there was only one political party. That was the Republican party. However, sectional differences increased in the 1820s and 1830s. With these differences, there was a gradual return to two parties.

The Republican party went through a number of steps on its way to becoming two parties. In 1820, James Monroe, the Republican, had been elected president overwhelmingly. He had received all electoral votes except one. By 1824, sectional differences had produced four different candidates. However, they all still called themselves Republicans. In 1828 and 1832, the Republicans were split into two branches—the National-Republicans and the Democratic-Republicans. By 1834, these branches had become two separate parties with different names. They became the Whig party and the Democratic party. The Whigs followed the ideas of the old Federalist party. The Democrats followed the ideas of the old Republicans.

The Democratic party was Jackson's party. It was made up largely of small farmers, southern slaveowners, and some northern interests. It supported the following program.

1. A low tariff. This would help farmers and planters who bought imported goods.

2. A cheap money policy. The sup-

BORN TO COMMAND.

OF VETO MEMORY.

HAD I BEEN CONSULTED.

KING ANDREW THE FIRST.

Compare this cartoon with the one on page 261. How does this artist feel about Jackson?

ply of money in circulation would be large, prices would be high, but interest rates would be low. This would help farmers and planters who borrowed from banks.

3. A pro-slavery policy. New lands would be opened to slavery. Laws would be passed to make it easier to bring back runaway slaves.

4. A states' rights policy. The national government would recognize the **authority** of the states as higher than its own.

The Whig party included western farmers and northern commercial and industrial interests. It also had some anti-slavery interests. The Whigs supported the following program.

1. A high protective tariff. This would help northern interests.

2. A hard money policy. The supply of money in circulation would be small, prices would be low, but interest rates would be high. This would protect northern bankers who loaned money.

3. No slavery policy. Whigs were divided on the issue, so the party usually tried not to take a position.

4. A policy supporting the federal government as the final authority over the states.

Of the two parties, the Democrats were more united. The Whigs had many good leaders, but they differed on many issues. Between 1829 and 1861, the Whigs were in control of the national government for only two short periods of time. During the rest of the time, there were Democratic administrations in Washington.

By 1840, there were two different views of the American system of government. One view was that the states had the right to **overrule** the federal authority. They could even withdraw from the United States. The other view was that the federal authority was the highest in the land. In this view, no state could withdraw from the Union.

By 1840, a strong national pride had developed. But alongside this national pride there existed also pride in a state or a section. The issues of slavery and tariffs still divided the nation. The Compromise of 1820 had helped overcome the slavery **crisis** for a time. The compromise Tariff of 1833 had helped solve the crisis caused by South Carolina's threat to secede. But would there continue to be compromise **solutions?**

COMPREHENSION CHECK

A. Recognizing the Main Idea

This selection as a whole tells you that

1. the issues of slavery and tariffs had been solved with compromises.
2. Southern slaveowners and western farmers agreed on most issues.
3. the Whig party disliked Jackson.
4. sectionalism led to the development of two parties by 1834 — the Whigs and the Democrats.

B. Selecting Important Details

Choose the ending that best completes each statement.

1. There was a gradual return to two parties
   a. in the 1820s and 1830s.
   b. as sectional differences increased.
   c. after the Era of Good Feelings.
   d. all of the above.
2. The Republican party
   a. won the election of 1820 overwhelmingly.
   b. had four candidates in the election of 1824.
   c. split into the National-Republicans and the Democratic-Republicans in the elections of 1828 and 1832.
   d. all of the above.
3. The Whigs favored all the following EXCEPT
   a. a high protective tariff.
   b. the recognition of federal authority over the states.
   c. a strong position against slavery.
   d. a policy of hard money.
4. The Democrats favored all the following EXCEPT
   a. recognition of states' rights.
   b. a policy of cheap money.
   c. an anti-slavery policy.
   d. a low tariff.
5. The Whig party
   a. included northern industrial interests, western farmers, and some anti-slavery interests.
   b. was a tight collection of groups united on most issues.
   c. liked Andrew Jackson and his policy toward the Bank of the United States.
   d. was in control of the national government for most of the time between 1829 and 1861.

C. Vocabulary

Write your own sentence for each of these words.

authority	crisis
overrule	solutions

D. Chronology

Arrange these events in the order in which they happened.

1. Monroe Doctrine
2. South Carolina's threat to secede
3. End of the War of 1812
4. Missouri Compromise
5. Beginning of Era of Good Feelings
6. Indian Removal Act

Make a chart of the membership and programs of either the Whig or the Democratic party.

1. Divide a sheet of paper into two sections. In one section, write the different kinds of members in the party (southern slaveowners, for example). In the other section, write the different parts of the party's program (pro-slavery, for example).

2. Draw arrows from each part of the party's program to the group of people it would serve.

July 4, 1826: The Passing of an Era

On July 4, 1826, both Thomas Jefferson and John Adams died. The passing of two former presidents on the fiftieth anniversary of the Declaration of Independence held special meaning for Americans.

Both men had been leaders of the American Revolution. They had been relatively young men when the United States won its independence. Jefferson had been forty and Adams only eight years older. They had both been members of the Continental Congress, which in 1776 adopted the Declaration of Independence written by Jefferson and revised by Adams.

Adams and Jefferson were close friends then, but after the Revolution they took different political paths. Adams was a leader of the Federalist party, Jefferson the leader of the Republicans. In 1800, Jefferson defeated Adams for the presidency. Political bitterness kept them apart for years. But when Jefferson left the presidency, the two old friends renewed their former friendly relations.

They had helped form a new nation during their youth. As they passed into old age, they saw the young nation grow to full stature. The letters exchanged by these two elder statesmen reflect their wisdom and pride in their nation and each other.

On July 4, 1826, in Massachusetts, the ninety-one-year-old John Adams whispered his last words, "Thomas Jefferson still lives." But a few hours earlier, eighty-three-year-old Thomas Jefferson had died in Virginia.

Lesson 10 Living in America: Economic Revolution, 1800–1850

WORDS TO UNDERSTAND
Discuss the meanings of these words.

manufactured   **inventions**

technical   **textile**

NEW WORDS IN SENTENCES
1. Many items that were once made by people are now **manufactured** by machines.

2. In order to understand a **technical** book about cars, a person must have special knowledge about machines.

3. Progress has often been based on the development of new machines, or **inventions.**

4. Nylon is often used as a **textile** for today's clothing.

AS YOU READ
As you read this selection, try to answer these questions.

1. How did the growth of land area and of population influence the American economy?

2. What are some examples of technical progress and of changes in transportation and communication?

THE READING SELECTION
The first half of the nineteenth century was a period of great change in the United States. Between 1800 and 1850, the new nation grew rapidly in size and in population. During this period, it also grew greatly in economic strength.

The United States expanded steadily westward. The Louisiana Purchase, in 1803, added a vast territory to the young nation. Later additions included Texas, California, and the Oregon Territory. By 1850, the United States stretched from the Atlantic to the Pacific, from Canada to Mexico.

The number of people in the United States also grew rapidly. The native-born population increased, and ever greater numbers of new immigrants arrived. Immigration from western Europe continued. Large numbers of German and Irish immigrants began to come to America in the 1820s and 1830s.

Cities were also growing rapidly. In 1800, there were only 33 towns and cities with more than 2,500 people. By 1850, there were 236 cities that large.

These changes in size and population were linked to important changes in the nation's economy.

Agriculture. American farm production rose steadily. Between 1800 and 1850, the production of corn, wheat, and cotton more than doubled. The vast increases in territory made much

The expanding textile mills of the North spun thread from the South's cotton. Here, even the child at lower left is working.

more land available for farming. Many of the new immigrants settled the frontier farmlands. At the same time, the increase in population made it necessary to grow more food. The area that is now the Middle West began to develop into a "grain belt." In the South, cotton, sugarcane, and tobacco plantations were growing and expanding further west. Changes in industry were helping to make cotton an even more important southern product.

Industry. Between 1800 and 1850, the United States economy was still largely based on agriculture. However, industry was becoming more and more important, especially in the North. The growing population provided more workers. It also provided more buyers for **manufactured** goods. Many of the new immigrants found work in the mills and factories in the growing cities.

Technical progress helped both industry and agriculture to expand. This period saw many new **inventions.** These included the typewriter, sewing ma-chine, telegraph, and safety pin. New and improved machines helped to expand factory and farm production. More farmland meant that more farm tools were necessary. Increased production in the northern **textile** mills led to a greater demand for the South's cotton.

Transportation and communications. Progress in transportation was linked to changes in other areas of the economy. Better methods were needed to bring food from the farms to the cities. More raw materials had to be shipped to the factories. More manufactured goods had to be shipped out of factories. As the nation grew, better and faster means of travel became necessary.

Steamboats began running on the rivers. New canals were built, linking other waterways. The Erie Canal, one of the first completed, was finished in 1825.

New roads were built. Regular routes were established for carrying mail. Stagecoaches and wagons carried passengers and freight to the areas further west.

Steam railroads began running in the 1830s. By 1850, more than 9,000 miles of railroad track had been completed. Railway construction provided jobs for thousands of people, including many new immigrants.

These were only some of the changes in American economic life between 1800 and 1850. The once weak nation had grown strong and had begun to gain the respect of other nations. Americans felt a new sense of strength and confidence.

COMPREHENSION CHECK

A. Recognizing the Main Idea

This selection as a whole tells you how

1. transportation and communication became more dependable as the American economy developed.

2. machines were invented to increase factory and farm production.

3. labor unions grew stronger as the number of factories increased.

4. the American economy developed in several areas between 1800 and 1850.

B. Selecting Important Details

Choose the ending that best completes each statement.

1. Between 1800 and 1850, all of the following were true EXCEPT
   a. production of corn, wheat, and cotton more than doubled.
   b. cotton, sugarcane, and tobacco were being grown in the northern states.
   c. the Middle West produced grain, dairy products, and meat.
   d. the amount of land devoted to farming increased.

2. Between 1800 and 1850, American industry was helped by all the following EXCEPT
   a. an expanded population.
   b. a better transportation system.
   c. a number of new inventions.
   d. a slump in agriculture.

3. Industrial production increased partly because of
   a. more workers.
   b. the invention of new machinery.
   c. a greater need for farm tools.
   d. all of the above.

4. Transportation and communication became faster and more dependable when
   a. steam railroads started running on the rivers.
   b. the Erie Canal was built for the use of wagons carrying mail.
   c. the amount of shipping was reduced.
   d. more than 9,000 miles of railroad track were completed.

C. True or False

The statements below are about the years between 1800 and 1850. Decide whether each one is true or false.

1. The economy stayed pretty much as it had been since the Revolution.

2. The typewriter, the sewing machine, the telegraph, and the safety pin were invented.

3. Agriculture quickly took a back seat to industry.

4. New territory in the West discouraged the development of transportation.

5. Water transportation was ignored in order to develop land transportation.

D. Vocabulary

Match the words with the definitions.

Words	Definitions
1. manufactured	a. cloth
2. technical	b. a new item or process
3. invention	c. lively
4. textile	d. goods produced, especially by machine
	e. medicine
	f. scientific or industrial

These women graduated from Oberlin College in 1855.

Oberlin College: The New American Education

In 1834, a dispute broke out in Lane Seminary, a religious school in Ohio. Disputes in schools were nothing new, but this time the issue was not religious. This time the issue was slavery.

The president of Lane Seminary had decided to limit discussion of slavery. The opposition to slavery by many teachers and students disturbed him. His reaction was to limit the anti-slavery activity of students and faculty.

As a protest against the president's action, a group of teachers and students decided to found their own school. They left the seminary and went to Oberlin, Ohio. There they established Oberlin College. Before long, the new college had won nationwide attention for its religious and anti-slavery views. Freedom of expression became the basis of education at Oberlin. Such freedom was quite unusual on college campuses at that time.

Oberlin led the way in other fields as well as in freedom of expression. In 1837, the college admitted women students. From the outset, it had admitted blacks. Oberlin College was, and is, a great American college. It was founded on a belief in freedom of expression.

Lesson 11 Living in America: Reforming Society, 1800–1850

WORDS TO UNDERSTAND
Discuss the meanings of these words.

utopia   colonization

NEW WORDS IN SENTENCES

1. Many people wanted to leave the cities and establish a perfect society, or **utopia**.

2. The **colonization** movement hoped to establish new homes in Africa for former American slaves.

AS YOU READ

As you read this selection, try to answer these questions.

1. What are some examples of changes in the areas of labor and education?

2. What efforts were being made to improve the lives of women and slaves?

THE READING SELECTION

Review. Between the end of the Revolution and 1850, the United States had changed dramatically. New land opened up new resources and new markets. A growing population—much of it from new immigration—provided new workers and farmers. Industry began to grow and expand. American farms doubled their crops. New and improved systems of transportation and communications were developed. Americans were feeling a new sense of strength and confidence. ☆

By 1850, life in the United States was quite different from what it had been following the Revolution. The nation's western border reached the Pacific Ocean. The number of states grew to thirty-one. The nation's economy was growing and changing.

The lives of the American people were changing, too. There were many changes in American social life. Many of these social changes were concerned with reform movements.

Workers. As factories expanded and the number of workers increased, so did labor problems. Working conditions were often poor. Hours were long and wages were low. In the late eighteenth and early nineteenth centuries, skilled workers began to form craft unions. Later, other workers began to band together in unions. By the late 1850s, workers were organizing national trade

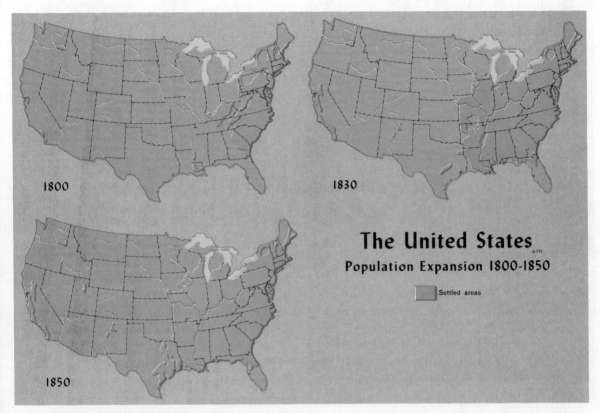

The United States
Population Expansion 1800-1850

Settled areas

1800

1830

1850

In which states was there a great growth of population between 1800 and 1830? Between 1830 and 1850?

unions. At first, these unions were very weak and had few members. As they grew, they demanded better wages, shorter hours, and better working conditions. Unions asked the government to pass laws that would protect workers.

Utopian societies. There were other reformers who objected to the evils connected with the growth of industry. Thousands of people had moved into cities to work in the new factories. Many of these people had to live in crowded, dirty slums. Some reformers tried to set up models of a "perfect" society. Such a society is called a **utopia.**

A number of such utopian societies were set up in the period from 1800 to 1850. They attempted to avoid the bad aspects of life at that time. They wanted to abolish private ownership of property. The workers themselves would share in the ownership of factories, farms, and other property. All would work together for the good of the community. The utopian societies failed, but they were a good example of the spirit of reform at that time.

Health care. In the first half of the 1800s, health care slowly began to improve. Doctors began to be better trained, and fewer people died from poor medical treatment. But medical

By the 1850s, new cities like Chicago sprang up in the Midwest.

science was still a long way from what we know today.

One important improvement in health care was in the treatment of the mentally ill. People with mental problems were usually just thrown into jails and mistreated. Reformers such as Dorothea Dix fought this kind of treatment. She worked to gain better living conditions and real medical help for the mentally ill.

Education. In the American colonies, as in Europe, education had been mainly for the wealthy. As the spirit of democracy grew, Americans began educating more people. They believed that free public education would help to prepare people as citizens.

Horace Mann was one of the leaders in the movement for free public education. Many new public grammar schools were set up between 1800 and 1850. In the later part of this period, public high schools were established as well.

At first, there was little good education for girls. This began to change in the 1820s. In the 1830s, Oberlin College and Mount Holyoke College began providing college education for women. However, most women had few chances for a good education. Black slaves were also not included in the expanding education system.

Abolition. Anti-slavery feelings also increased during this period. In the early 1800s, these feelings led to a **colonization** movement. It was proposed that slaveholders free their slaves and return them to colonies in Africa. The colonization idea was not a success. It was replaced by a movement to free all slaves and abolish slavery totally.

The abolition movement was the largest social reform effort of the period. It included such white people as William Lloyd Garrison, Lucretia Mott, Theodore Weld, and Sarah and Angelina Grimké. Black abolitionist leaders included Frederick Douglass, Sojourner Truth, and Henry H. Garnet.

Women's rights. In some ways, women had fewer rights and freedoms in the early 1800s than in earlier years. In colonial days, women shared the hard work with men, and they were often regarded more as equals. This was still largely true on the frontier in the early 1800s. But in the more settled areas, and in the growing cities, many of the kinds of work women had shared began to be closed to them. There were fewer women working as shopkeepers, for example, than there had been in colonial times.

Women could not vote or hold public office. If a woman had any property of her own, it went to her husband when she married. In most families, the father of the house was the absolute ruler of the wife and children.

In the 1800s, many women began to work for greater women's rights. Emma Willard, Catharine Beecher, and Mary Lyon began three of the earliest good schools for girls and women. In 1849, Elizabeth Blackwell became the first woman graduate of an American medical school. Many women became active in the abolition movement and worked for an end to slavery as well as for women's rights. In 1848, the first women's rights convention was held. Led by Elizabeth Cady Stanton, it demanded equal rights for women, including the vote. It would be a long time before this goal was met, but it was a start.

By permission of the Houghton Library, Harvard University

Women were responsible for much of the reform work of this period. Elizabeth Cady Stanton (far left) was one of the founders of the women's rights movement. She and Lucretia Mott (bottom left) were active in both that and the abolition movement. Dorothea Dix (top left) worked to improve care for the mentally ill.

of Congress

Library of Congress

COMPREHENSION CHECK

A. Recognizing the Main Idea

This selection as a whole tells you that between 1800 and 1850

1. there were many reform movements.

2. utopian societies were established to further the growth of industry.

3. slaves were freed and women gained equal rights.

4. reforms were accomplished overnight.

B. Selecting Important Details

Choose the ending that best completes each statement.

1. The craft and trade unions aimed at all of the following EXCEPT
   a. lower wages.
   b. shorter hours.
   c. more influence on government.
   d. laws to protect workers.

2. Utopian societies formed for all of the following reasons EXCEPT
   a. to share property and work for a common purpose.
   b. to avoid the big city problems of poor living and working conditions.
   c. to take care of the mentally ill.
   d. to create "perfect" societies.

3. The abolition movement
   a. was the largest social reform effort of the time.
   b. wanted slaves freed and sent back to Africa.
   c. was supported by most southerners.
   d. worked to give women the right to vote.

4. Women on the frontier
   a. were educated with the men.
   b. led the abolition movement.
   c. could hold public office.
   d. were treated more as men's equals than Eastern women.

C. Completion

Use a term from this list to complete each sentence.

Frederick Douglass   education
Elizabeth Blackwell   abolition
Elizabeth Cady Stanton   1848
Lucretia Mott   health
Dorothea Dix   1798

1. A person who worked for better living conditions and treatment for the mentally ill was _____.

2. Horace Mann was a leader in the area of _____.

3. The first women's rights convention was led by _____ in _____.

4. William Lloyd Garrison, Lucretia Mott, Sarah and Angelina Grimké, Frederick Douglass, and Sojourner Truth were leaders of _____.

5. The first female graduate of an American medical school was _____.

D. Vocabulary

Write your own sentence for each of these words.

technical   colonization
utopia   invention

E. Using Your Knowledge

Below are three main ideas. Under each one, list two details about it that are given in the reading selection.

1. education
2. women's rights
3. abolition

The Convention at Seneca Falls

In the first fifty years after the American Revolution, the role of American women had grown smaller. They still had few legal rights and no political rights. Their choice of work and their freedom to work at all had been decreased. The new ideal of the "lady" was setting strict rules for women's appearance and actions. Clearly, women's status was not improving by itself.

Strong, independent women began to take action. One of the first was Elizabeth Cady Stanton. Stanton had believed in women's rights for years. In fact, when she was married, she omitted the word "obey" from the marriage vows. She was already involved in the abolition movement, as was a friend, Lucretia Mott. But they found prejudice against women even there. For example, Stanton and Mott were denied their seats at an abolition convention—because they were women. Many abolition leaders felt that women's rights should be postponed until the slavery issue was settled. Stanton and Mott felt that women should not wait. In 1848, they organized the first women's rights convention, held in Seneca Falls, N.Y. That convention approved a Declaration of Women's Rights based on the Declaration of Independence.

We hold these truths to be self-evident: that all men and women are created equal . . . that the history of mankind is a history of repeated injuries . . . on the part of man toward woman, having in direct object the establishment of an absolute tyranny over her. . . .

Resolved, that woman is man's equal—was intended to be so by the Creator, and the highest good of the race demands that she be recognized as such . . . .

Resolved, that it is the duty of the women of this country to secure to themselves their sacred right to the elective franchise [the vote] . . . .

Resolved, that the speedy success of our cause depends upon . . . the securing to women an equal participation with men in the various trades, professions, and commerce.

The declaration contained the first formal demand for the vote by women. Even Mott felt they might be going too far. She warned Stanton, "Lizzie, thee will make us ridiculous."

But the demand for the right to vote was an issue for the next seventy-two years. Other women, such as Lucy Stone and Susan B. Anthony—who worked closely with Stanton—helped turn the 1848 demand into the Nineteenth Amendment to the Constitution. But it took a long time. Stanton, Mott, and Anthony all died without knowing that their work was finally successful.

Unit 5 Summary

An Early Challenge: Nationalism versus Sectionalism

The Rise of Nationalism

The War of 1812 helped create a strong feeling of nationalism in the United States. Americans saw their nation as independent of Europe. They valued the national good over that of a section or state. This was a period of great growth and change for the nation. Nationalism was involved with three main domestic changes.

1. During the Era of Good Feelings, there was a lack of political conflicts. Only the Republican party had much power.

2. The power of the national government was increased through legislation and decisions of the Supreme Court, led by John Marshall.

3. The population of the United States began to move westward in large numbers.

In foreign affairs, nationalism produced isolationism. The nation's main goal was to protect its interests in the Americas. It signed several treaties to settle boundary disputes with European nations. It also issued the Monroe Doctrine. This doctrine, supported by the British, aimed at keeping Europe out of the Western Hemisphere.

The Rise of Sectionalism

Nationalism was challenged in the 1820s by increasing sectionalism — concern for the interests of one section over those of the nation. The North became the center of trade and industry. The South remained dependent on slave labor and large plantations. The West, a frontier area, was settled by people from both North and South. The sections clashed over many issues. The North favored a high protective tariff and the Bank of the United States. The South favored the extension of slavery. The West favored internal improvements.

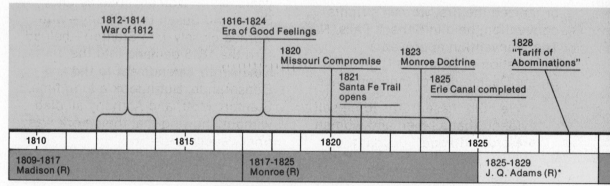

| 1812-1814 War of 1812 | 1816-1824 Era of Good Feelings | 1820 Missouri Compromise | 1821 Santa Fe Trail opens | 1823 Monroe Doctrine | 1825 Erie Canal completed | 1828 "Tariff of Abominations" |

| 1810 | 1815 | 1820 | 1825 |

| 1809-1817 Madison (R) | 1817-1825 Monroe (R) | 1825-1829 J. Q. Adams (R)* |

*After the Era of Good Feelings, party politics rose again. The new Republicans—and, for a time, the Whigs—replaced the old Federalists. The new Democrats replaced the old Republicans.

Andrew Jackson's Administration

Andrew Jackson was elected president in 1828. His administration was marked by a number of changes.

1. More people played a greater role in the political process. This was called Jacksonian democracy.

2. Social reform movements increased.

3. The spoils system was expanded.

4. The office of the president became stronger.

5. The eastern Indian tribes were removed to lands west of the Mississippi.

During Jackson's term, a high protective tariff was passed. South Carolina issued a declaration of nullification and threatened to secede. Jackson threatened to use force to settle the issue. But a compromise tariff was worked out. In another sectional dispute, Jackson vetoed a new charter for the second Bank of the United States.

In the 1830s, sectionalism led to the return of two parties. The Democrats, led by Jackson, followed the principles of the old Republican party. The Whigs, led by opponents of Jackson, followed the ideas of the old Federalists.

Economic and Social Changes

During this time, the land area of the United States expanded greatly. The population also expanded. Many new immigrants came from Europe. Americans also produced many inventions to aid technical progress. These changes helped produce economic growth. Both industrial and agricultural production expanded. New systems of transportation, such as the railroad and canals, were established.

Among the important social movements of the period were those for free education and better care for the mentally ill. Labor unions began to gain real strength, as did the abolition movement, which aimed at outlawing slavery. The women's rights movement also began in this period.

All in all, the United States was going through a period of great change and growth. It was becoming a strong, established nation.

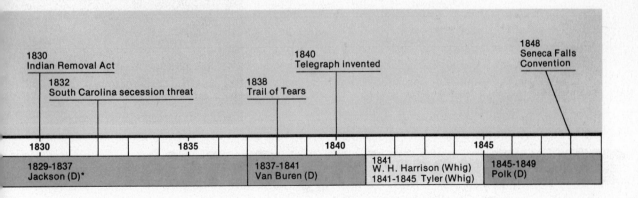

1830
Indian Removal Act

1832
South Carolina secession threat

1840
Telegraph invented

1838
Trail of Tears

1848
Seneca Falls Convention

1830   1835   1840   1845

1829-1837
Jackson (D)*

1837-1841
Van Buren (D)

1841
W. H. Harrison (Whig)
1841-1845 Tyler (Whig)

1845-1849
Polk (D)

unit
6

STOCKHOLDERS
OF THE UNDERGROUND
R. R. COMPANY
Hold on to Your Stock!!

The market has an upward tendency. By the express train which arrived this morning at 3 o'clock, fifteen thousand dollars worth of human merchandise, consisting of twenty-nine able bodied men and women, fresh and sound, from the Carolina and Kentucky plantations, have arrived safe at the depot on the other side, where all our sympathising colonization friends may have an opportunity of expressing their sympathy by bringing forward donations of ploughs, &c., farming utensils, pick axes and hoes, and not old clothes; as these emigrants all can till the soil. N. B.—Stockholders don't forget, the meeting to-day at 2 o'clock at the ferry on the Canada side. All persons desiring to take stock in this prosperous company, be sure to be on hand. By Order of the

Detroit, April 19, 1853. BOARD OF DIRECTORS.

Poster, courtesy Burton Historical Collection, Detroit Public Library

After the Sale: Slaves Going South from Richmond by Eyre Crowe, Chicago Historical Society

The Growing Crisis: Slavery

Human slavery was the issue that would rip the nation apart. To some Americans, the buying and selling of black slaves (above) was necessary. To others, it was a terrible evil to be fought (left). During the 1800s, the conflict grew. There was to be no peaceful solution.

Lesson 1 The Argument Over Slavery

WORDS TO UNDERSTAND

Discuss the meanings of these words.

profitable   **inferior**   **secession**

NEW WORDS IN SENTENCES

1. Cotton was a **profitable** crop because it brought a good price.

2. Some slaveowners felt that black Africans were **inferior** people who were beneath them in ability and intelligence.

3. The southern states spoke of **secession,** or formal withdrawal from the Union.

AS YOU READ

As you read this selection, try to answer these questions.

1. Why was slavery important to the South?

2. What were the arguments of the northerners against slavery? What were the arguments of the southerners in favor of slavery?

Steamboats carried mail, freight, and passengers quickly and cheaply to towns and plantations along the Mississippi River. The invention of steamboats in the early 1800s made the river a busy and important waterway.

THE READING SELECTION

In 1619, twenty black Africans were brought to Jamestown, Virginia. They came as indentured servants. However, after 1640, most Africans came to America as slaves. Black slavery spread through the colonies.

Most American slaves worked on the plantations and farms of the South. There were fewer slaves in the North and West. The small farms of these sections had less need for slaves. After the Revolution, most northern states reduced or prohibited slavery. The Northwest Ordinance of 1787 also prohibited slavery in the Northwest Territory.

At one time, it seemed that slavery would die out. Many Americans were freeing their slaves. However, the invention of the cotton gin in 1793 made slavery even more important to the South. The cotton gin separated cotton seed from the fibers. This difficult job had been done by hand. The cotton gin thus made cotton an even more **profitable** crop. More land was planted in cotton. More people were needed to work the new cotton fields. To fill the need, more slaves were brought from Africa. The slave trade had been outlawed by 1808, but the law was not enforced. Slaves also came from plantations that made money by raising slaves for sale.

By 1860, there were about 3.5 to 4 million black slaves working in the South. This does not mean that all southern white families owned slaves. Only about

25 percent of them had any slaves at all. Most of these families owned fewer than ten to twenty slaves each. Only a few thousand planters owned more than fifty slaves each. However, this small group of rich planters tightly controlled southern political life.

Those who favored slavery said that it was not an evil thing. Slaveowners often argued that Africans were **inferior** people, suited to the work done under slavery. They were said to be better off in the United States, where they were exposed to American civilization. Slaveowners also pointed out that slavery was mentioned in the Bible.

Slaveowners often claimed that slaves were treated better than factory workers in the North were. They said factory workers worked twelve and fourteen hours a day. Factories often were poorly lighted, dirty, and unsafe. Southerners declared that slaves worked in a healthier climate than northern workers did. They also argued that slavery allowed southern leaders to devote themselves to law, politics, and government.

Many Americans opposed slavery. They pointed out that the slavery in the Bible was different from the slavery of the South. The anti-slave societies doubted that slaves were better treated than factory workers. Slaves worked long hours and were often badly punished. They were not free to leave their masters even when they were poorly treated. Northerners also declared that slavery was opposed to the American ideals of equality and freedom. How could slavery be accepted when the Declaration of Independence declared that "all men are created equal"?

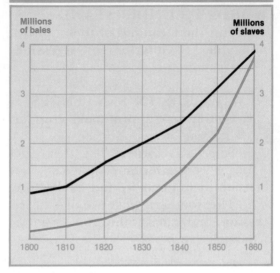

COTTON PRODUCTION and the GROWTH of SLAVERY 1800-1860

Millions of bales / Millions of slaves

What relationship does this chart show between cotton production and slave population? How could you explain this relationship?

There were northerners who felt that slavery was an economic threat. They felt that millions of slave workers hurt a free economic system. The North needed buyers for its factory products. Four million slaves had no wages with which to buy goods. This did not help the northern economy to grow.

By 1830, slavery was threatening the unity of the nation. As the southern states began losing control of the Congress, they spoke more frequently of **secession.** For the next thirty years, the debate over slavery continued. Compromise, persuasion, and threats were used to try to solve the problem. But slavery proved to be too difficult to solve by these methods.

COMPREHENSION CHECK

A. Recognizing the Main Idea

This selection as a whole tells you

1. how the cotton gin made cotton a more profitable crop.

2. why northern states prohibited slavery.

3. about the growing argument over slavery in the 1800s.

4. how southerners felt about slavery.

B. Selecting Important Details

Choose the ending that best completes each statement.

1. The slave trade in the United States
   a. was outlawed by 1808, but the law was not enforced.
   b. was prohibited in the North and the Northwest Territory.
   c. was under way after 1640.
   d. all of the above.

2. The invention of the cotton gin
   a. had little effect on slavery.
   b. made slavery less important to the North.
   c. made slavery less important to the South.
   d. made slavery more important to the South.

3. Some northerners did not like slavery because
   a. they believed that Africans were inferior.
   b. black slaves were no worse off than factory workers in the North.
   c. slaves could leave their masters when they were poorly treated.
   d. they felt that slavery hurt the economy.

4. In the South
   a. almost everyone owned slaves.
   b. most families owned more than twenty slaves.
   c. there were about 3.5 to 4 million slaves by 1860.
   d. all of the above.

C. True or False

Decide whether each of these statements is true or false.

1. The first black Africans arrived in America in the Northwest Territory.

2. The argument over slavery was solved when the South seceded.

3. Slavery helped the northern economy because it meant there were more people to buy factory products.

4. Some slaveowners argued that blacks were better off in America than in Africa.

5. A small group of rich planters controlled southern politics.

D. Vocabulary

Match the words with the definitions.

Words	Definitions
1. profitable	a. money-making
2. inferior	b. a meeting
3. secession	c. withdrawal
	d. more than
	e. less important or valuable

E. Ask Yourself

If you were a cotton planter who owned many slaves, why would you want to believe the arguments that black people were inferior? If you did not accept the idea that blacks were inferior, what arguments would you use to defend your position?

Frederick Douglass Asks, "Am I a Man?"

In 1841, a young black laborer attended an abolition meeting in Massachusetts. The speech he delivered that day set him upon a new career. To the abolitionists, he was the perfect example of what blacks might make of themselves if they were given a chance. That young black man was Frederick Douglass, whose name soon became known to the entire nation.

Frederick Douglass was born a slave in Maryland. He learned to read and write, though it was against the law for slaves to be taught. He began teaching other slaves to read and was punished for this crime. But no punishment could kill the young man's desire to learn and to be free.

In 1838, the twenty-one-year-old Douglass escaped to freedom. He found his way to Massachusetts, where he was working as a laborer when he made his first anti-slavery speech. For the next twenty-five years, his voice rang out in America and Europe against slavery. And what a voice it was! Ringing and clear, it held audiences spellbound and made him one of the leading speakers of the day. He had an imposing appearance,

standing over six feet tall. He was completely self-taught and had mastered foreign languages, history, and philosophy.

Those arguing for slavery claimed that black people were inferior human beings, something less than real men and women. Now the voice of this magnificent man boomed across the nation. "Am I a man?" he cried out. And other Americans saw proof that a person once held in slavery could rise above it.

Lesson 2 Life Under Slavery

WORDS TO UNDERSTAND
Discuss the meanings of these words.

overseer   **ceremony**   **fugitives**
ration   **abuse**

NEW WORDS IN SENTENCES
1. The **overseer** might whip the slaves if he saw them working slowly.
2. The **ration** of food was supposed to last a week.
3. Owners sometimes invented their own **ceremony** for slave marriages.
4. Physical **abuse,** such as whipping, was used to control slaves.
5. The **fugitives** swam the river to escape.

AS YOU READ
As you read this selection, try to answer these questions.
1. What was daily life like for slaves?
2. What were the rules for slaves?
3. In what ways did slaves try to help themselves?

THE READING SELECTION
While the debate over slavery raged, the system itself continued. Millions of black people were living as slaves. What was the life of a slave like? To some extent, it varied. Slaves on a small farm might actually work and eat with the owner. On a large plantation with many slaves, slaves were separated from the owner's family. There was generally an **overseer,** whose job was to boss the slaves. Usually the overseer was a white man. Sometimes he was black or had black assistants, often slaves themselves.

Food for the slaves was usually raised on the plantation itself. Each slave or family was given a **ration** of food every month or week. This ration was often pickled or salt pork and cornmeal. Vegetables, coffee, or other items might be added. Clothing for slaves was also produced at home. A single set of clothes sometimes had to last a slave for a whole year. Shoes were often supplied only in the winter.

On large plantations, the slave cabins were separated from the main house. A lucky slave might have a cabin with windows and a floor and a small garden outside. A slave might have a bed, chest, stool, and some cooking pots. Most slaves slept on blankets or straw on dirt floors.

A plantation overseer grouped the slaves into gangs to work in the fields. Hours were long, and slaves who did not work hard enough were often whipped. The luckier slaves worked in the main house, cooking and cleaning for the owner's family. This was an easier life, and many field slaves were jealous of house slaves.

Teaching a slave was against the law. A few schools existed, and some owners taught their slaves themselves. But generally, slaves had little free time for anything like books. The little time not spent working was often spent on religion. Religion became important to slaves, often as an escape from their hard lives. There were illegal gatherings known to slaves as "hush-harbor" meetings. Religion was often an issue in a marriage **ceremony.** Some slaveowners permitted a religious ceremony. In other cases, slaveowners invented their own ceremony. One former slave recalled,

> We slaves knowed them words wasn't binding. Don't mean nothing unless you say, "What God done joined, can't no man pull asunder." But they never would say that. Just say, "Now you married."

Of course, any slave marriage could be "pulled asunder." Slaveowners sold any slave they wished to. Slave families were often broken up. A former slave remembered,

> They used to give us passes to come in to town on Saturday sometimes and that is how I got to see the sale. Sometimes, when the ol' auctioneer was selling off a mother, she would call out to those that was looking on, "Buy my children, Master!" She was

Slaves pick the cotton crop in this southern plantation scene. Every available slave was sent to the fields during harvest time.

trying to fix it so they all be together. Sometimes Ol' Master would say, "I don't want your children." Then the mother would give such a pitiful cry. Lord, Lord, child, I don't like to recollect those days.

The "passes" this ex-slave remembered were part of the "slave codes." These codes were rules for slaves. Slaves could not make contracts, own property, or hit a white person. Slaves needed passes to leave the plantations. A newspaper in Paris, Kentucky, printed this notice in 1852.

> Notice is hereby given, that from and after this date, no slave will be permitted to come to Paris, day or night, without a written pass . . . and all slaves living in town will be required to retire from the streets at nine o'clock

P.M. Refusal to obey the above orders will be punished with stripes.

"Stripes" meant whipping, usually by the patrols. These groups of armed men rode about making sure the slave codes were obeyed. Whipping and other physical **abuse** of slaves were common under slavery.

The slaves had no legal protection from the evils of the system. There were only a few ways for slaves to help themselves. In earlier years, it was possible for slaves to buy their own freedom. But it became harder and harder for slaves to earn any money on the side.

Slaves did revolt. There were revolts as early as 1663. The most famous revolt was led by Nat Turner, in Virginia, in 1831. He and his followers killed 60 whites before the revolt was put down. About 100 slaves were killed in this revolt. Turner himself was caught and hanged.

Many slaves ran away. These **fugitives** tried to reach safety in the North. They were chased by owners and slave hunters. By the 1830s, the Underground Railroad was helping fugitive slaves to escape. The runaways traveled at night, stopping at "stations" located every ten to twenty miles. There they were given food and shelter during the day. Money for the Underground Railroad came from Quakers and other antislavery groups. Whites and blacks from both North and South helped thousands of slaves to escape. This loss of slaves increased the South's anger at the North. The national conflict over slavery was growing.

COMPREHENSION CHECK

A. Recognizing the Main Idea
This selection as a whole tells you
1. about the Underground Railroad.
2. about slave revolts.
3. what the "slave codes" were.
4. what life was like for slaves in the South and how they reacted to it.

B. Selecting Important Details
Choose the ending that best completes each statement.
1. The slave codes
   a. allowed slaves to own property.
   b. gave legal protection to slaves.
   c. allowed slaves to go to school.
   d. were rules for slaves.
2. Slaves
   a. could always buy their own freedom.
   b. never ran away.
   c. were sometimes whipped.
   d. could always keep their families together.
3. The most famous slave revolt
   a. was successful.
   b. resulted in the death of more whites than blacks.
   c. was led by Nat Turner.
   d. all of the above.
4. The Underground Railroad
   a. helped thousands of slaves to escape to the North.
   b. was run by slave hunters.
   c. eased the conflict over slavery between the North and the South.
   d. was a religious marriage ceremony.

C. True or False

Decide whether each of these statements is true or false.

1. Teaching slaves to read was against the law.

2. "Hush-harbor" meetings were punishment for slaves who did not obey the slave codes.

3. Slave children could not be sold separately from their mothers.

4. The lives of slaves were the same on big plantations and small farms.

5. House slaves usually felt that field slaves had easier lives.

D. Vocabulary

Match the words with the definitions.

Words	Definitions
1. overseer	a. without
2. ration	b. someone trying to escape
3. ceremony	c. a boss
4. abuse	d. an allowance
5. fugitive	e. a formal activity
	f. a railroad
	g. bad treatment

E. Essay Question

Write six to eight sentences answering the following question.

How was each of the following a kind of escape for slaves?

religion   the Underground Railroad
revolts   working in an owner's house

The Runaways

How did black people react to being kept as slaves? Here are portions of letters from plantation overseers written in 1833–1834 to owner James Polk, later to be president of the United States:

Dec. 22, 1833.

". . . I am sorry to tell you that Jack and Ben hath left the plantation. . . . I want them both brought back if they aint the rest will leave me also."

[The runaways were caught, and a white overseer wrote to Mr. Polk.]

"They say that Jack was very badly whip'd indeed, that Beanland salted him four or five times during the whipping, that Ben was also whip'd but not so badly. . . ."

Feb. 13, 1834.

". . . on this day a week ago Hardy left his teams standing in the field and on last night I got him home and on this morning Jim and Wally when I called them they both answered me . . . and I have not heard of them since. . . ."

Mar. 7, 1834.

". . . I have all the negroes at home but Jim. I have got Jack and I have got Hardy and I went to the iron works and got Ben and on last Monday I got Wally which they have been runaway and I have got them all back. . . ."

Mar. 18, 1834.

". . . your negroes have been doing very bad. Jim and Wally both have been run away two or three weeks. . . ."

Lesson 3 Texas and the Mexican War

WORDS TO UNDERSTAND
Discuss the meanings of these words.

annexed   **manifest destiny**

NEW WORDS IN SENTENCES
1. The southerners wanted Texas **annexed** as a slave state.
2. Many Americans believed that it was the **manifest destiny,** or unavoidable future, of their country to occupy land from the Atlantic to the Pacific Ocean.

AS YOU READ
As you read this selection, try to answer these questions.
1. What were the major reasons for hard feelings between Mexico and the Americans in Texas?
2. What were the terms of the treaty that ended the war with Mexico?

THE READING SELECTION
Review. By the 1800s, slavery had become important to the South. Slaves were needed to work the profitable cotton fields. The South argued that slavery was needed. The lives of slaves varied. In general, they worked long hours under an overseer. They had the bare necessities of life. Slaves had no rights. They were controlled by the slave codes or with whippings by their owners. Some slaves rebelled against this treatment. Others escaped to the North, using the Underground Railroad. ☆

Slavery and the sectionalism that went with it grew in importance through the 1830s and the 1840s. They began to affect many other issues. One of these other issues was the future of the territory of Texas.

By 1821, Mexico had won its independence from Spain. The Mexican government wanted to develop Texas, its northern territory. Therefore, it opened the area to settlement by Americans. By 1830, there were about 20,000 Americans living in Texas. Many of the new settlers were from the South. They brought with them slaves to work their new cotton plantations.

The Mexican government did not permit slavery in Texas. Hard feelings began to develop between the Mexican government and the Americans in Texas. There were additional causes for these hard feelings.

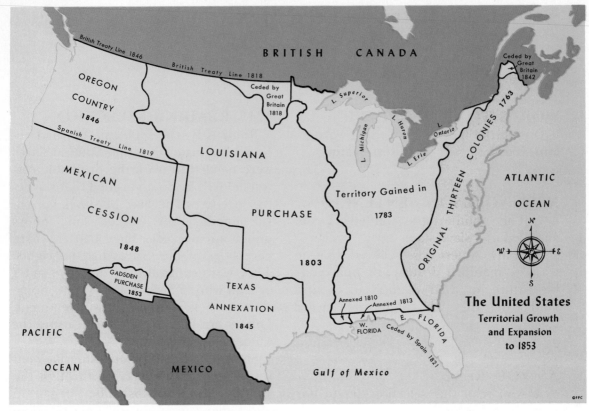

The Mexican War ended in 1848. Mexico ceded the Southwest and California to the United States. With this cession, the territory of the United States reached from sea to sea.

1. In 1830, Mexico prohibited any further immigration of Americans into Texas. Mexico feared it had let in too many Americans. It now wanted to bring more Mexicans into the territory.

2. The Mexican government limited self-government in Texas.

3. The Americans who came to Texas were supposed to become Mexican citizens. However, many of them continued to regard themselves as citizens of the United States.

The hard feelings between Texans and the Mexican government led to civil war. The Texans were led by Sam Houston. The Mexican army was led by Antonio de Santa Anna. After a defeat at the old mission, the Alamo, the Texans began to win the struggle. In 1836, they won independence from Mexico. The Lone Star Republic of Texas was founded.

Texas applied for admission to the United States in 1836. The South wanted Texas admitted. However, the North was afraid that the huge area might be broken up into as many as ten slave states. These states would give the South a majority in the Senate. However, in 1845, Texas was finally **annexed** to the United States by a joint resolution of Congress.

Trouble soon began over the border between Mexico and Texas. This and other disputes led to war between the United States and Mexico, lasting from 1846 to 1848. During the Mexican War, American forces took over the Southwest and California. In the Treaty of Guadalupe-Hidalgo, signed in 1848, these areas were ceded to the United States. The treaty also set the border between Mexico and the United States at the Rio Grande.

The United States settled its territorial quarrel with Mexico by using force. By contrast, the dispute with Britain over the Oregon Territory was settled by compromise. In 1846, the two nations agreed on the forty-ninth parallel as the boundary between Canada and the United States.

It was in the discussions over Texas and Oregon that the idea of **"manifest destiny"** appeared. It meant that nothing could stop Americans from settling the continent all the way to the Pacific. And in fact, by 1853, the nation had obtained all the land that would become the first forty-eight states.

The slavery issue had fed the dispute over Texas. It would also affect the new lands obtained under the treaty with Mexico. Slavery was already prohibited in Oregon. But the new California territory would be the center of another major conflict between the South and the North.

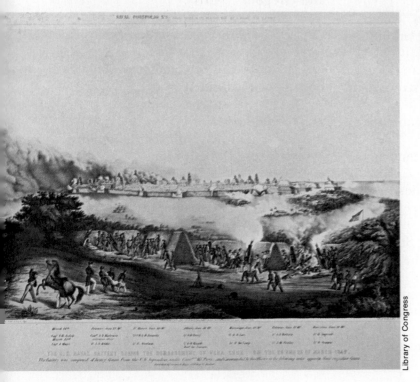

In 1847, the United States invaded Mexico at the port of Vera Cruz and occupied the city. United States forces then pushed inland. After six months of bloodshed, hardship, and disease, they captured Mexico City.

COMPREHENSION CHECK

A. Recognizing the Main Idea

This selection as a whole tells you

1. how the Mexican and American governments settled their disputes by compromise.

2. why slavery was not an issue in Texas.

3. about the issues surrounding Texas and the Mexican War.

4. why Americans moved to Texas.

B. Selecting Important Details

Choose the ending that best completes each statement.

1. The Mexican government invited Americans to settle in Texas to
   a. set up an independent state.
   b. bring slavery to Texas.
   c. govern themselves.
   d. help develop the area.

2. Northerners opposed admitting Texas to the Union because
   a. it had too many Mexican citizens.
   b. its admission might strengthen slavery.
   c. Texas had not yet become independent.
   d. the Mexican government might object.

3. The Treaty of Guadalupe-Hidalgo
   a. started the war between Texas and Mexico.
   b. had Mexico cede the Southwest and California to the United States.
   c. set the border between Mexico and the United States at the forty-ninth parallel.
   d. ended the dispute over the Oregon Territory.

4. During the civil war between the Texans and the Mexican government
   a. the Texans were led by Sam Houston.
   b. the Mexicans were led by Antonio de Santa Anna.
   c. the Texans were defeated at the Alamo.
   d. all of the above.

C. True or False

Decide whether each of these statements is true or false.

1. The refusal of the Mexican government to permit slavery in Texas caused hard feelings.

2. Most Americans living in Texas became Mexican citizens.

3. The idea of manifest destiny appeared in the discussions over Texas and Oregon.

4. The dispute with Britain over the Oregon Territory was settled by using force.

5. The Treaty of Guadalupe-Hidalgo ended the Mexican War.

D. Vocabulary

Match the words with the definitions.

Words	Definitions
1. annex	a. to lose
2. manifest destiny	b. a religious meeting
	c. an unavoidable future
	d. to attach

E. Ask Yourself

What might have happened if Texas had been annexed to the United States and then had broken up into a number of slave states?

Abraham Lincoln and the Mexican War

In 1846, Abraham Lincoln was thirty-seven years old. He had a growing reputation as a lawyer and had served as a state legislator in Illinois from 1834 to 1842. In 1846, Lincoln had been elected to Congress as a member of the Whig party. His political future seemed bright.

New representatives are rarely heard from during their first term in office. But Lincoln felt he had a duty to speak up about the war with Mexico. Lincoln was not impressed with the American claim to the Rio Grande as the boundary between Texas and Mexico. He agreed with the Mexican claim that the boundary was the Nueces River, farther east. Like many anti-slavery Whigs, he felt that the dispute with Mexico was being pushed by southern slaveowners who wanted to gain new lands.

Some Americans said that patriotism required everyone to support the government when the country was at war. Lincoln, and many others, felt that it was a misuse of patriotism to blindly support a war against Mexico. He believed it was the duty of those who disagreed with their government to speak out freely.

The war with Mexico had been brought on by fighting in the disputed border area. President Polk told the nation that Mexico was responsible for shedding American blood on American soil. Congressman Lincoln argued that the dispute had actually taken place on Mexican soil. He challenged the president to name the spot where American blood had been shed.

Lincoln's challenge went unanswered, and the United States won a victory over Mexico. Lincoln's failure to support the war cast a cloud over his future. His reputation was badly damaged. In fact, for a time, it seemed he would never succeed in politics.

Lesson 4 The Compromises Fail

WORDS TO UNDERSTAND

Discuss the meanings of these words.

realistic   tension
popular sovereignty   violence

NEW WORDS IN SENTENCES

1. They had to face the facts in order to come up with a **realistic** solution to the problem.

2. In the territories with **popular sovereignty,** the people decided the slavery issue themselves.

3. When an argument is very important to both sides, there is a great deal of **tension.**

4. There is usually bloodshed when **violence** is used to solve a problem.

AS YOU READ

As you read this selection, try to answer these questions.

1. What compromises were made on the slavery issue?

2. What were the results of these compromises?

THE READING SELECTION

By the 1850s, it was clear that earlier efforts to avoid the issue of slavery, or to compromise on it, had failed. The belief that the system would die out as slaves were slowly freed was no longer **realistic.** The colonization movement, which had intended to send slaves back to Africa, had largely failed. The importance of cotton meant that few southerners were willing to part with their slaves.

At the same time, the abolition movement gained support. Its members were determined to end slavery completely. Its membership increased. More people read William Lloyd Garrison's abolitionist newspaper, *The Liberator.* More people went to hear anti-slavery speakers like Garrison, Frederick Douglass, and Sojourner Truth. This increased support for abolition made any new compromises on slavery even harder.

More fuel was added to the fire as new lands were added to the nation. These additions, like earlier ones, raised the question of the spread of slavery. The 1820 Missouri Compromise had settled one debate. It kept the balance between North and South in the Senate. It also prohibited slavery in the new land north of the 36° 30′ parallel.

However, the Mexican War had added more land to the nation. California and the Southwest were now the center of attention. An 1846 resolution, the Wilmot Proviso, would have prohibited

Still a powerful speaker at age seventy-two, Henry Clay
explains his ideas for the Compromise of 1850 to the Senate.

slavery in these areas. It passed the
House of Representatives but failed in
the Senate.

In 1850, the problem came to a head
when California applied for admission
as a free state. The people of the state
had already adopted a constitution outlawing slavery. The admission of California would give the North an edge in
the Senate. Therefore, the South opposed it.

Henry Clay, the author of the Missouri Compromise, tried yet another
compromise. There was no way to avoid
giving the North the additional Senate

votes. So he proposed that other favors
be given to the South in his Compromise of 1850.

1. California would be admitted as a
free state.

2. The new lands in the Southwest
would be divided into the territories of
New Mexico and Utah. In these territories, the settlers would decide the issue
of slavery for themselves. This idea was
called **popular sovereignty.**

3. Slavery would remain legal in
Washington, D.C., but the trading of
slaves would be prohibited there.

4. A stricter Fugitive Slave Act would

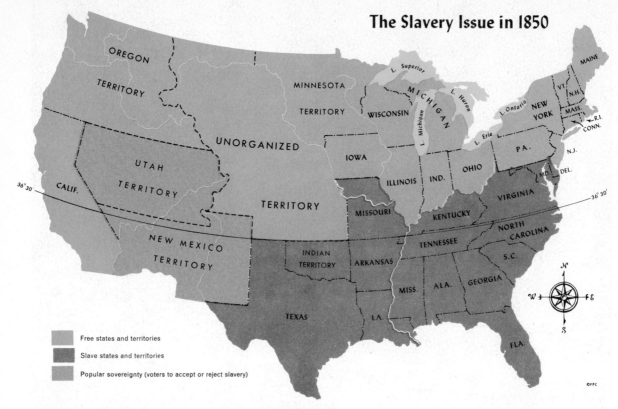

The Slavery Issue in 1850

Free states and territories

Slave states and territories

Popular sovereignty (voters to accept or reject slavery)

Which territories had popular sovereignty according to the Compromise of 1850? How was the area with popular sovereignty changed in 1854, as shown on the map opposite?

be passed. This would please the South. The new law made it easier to claim runaway slaves. It even required that bystanders help capture runaways. The new law upset the North. It led to several riots. It also led to some state laws barring slave hunters.

The Compromise of 1850 did not decrease the **tension** between the sections. In 1854, Senator Stephen A. Douglas of Illinois introduced the Kansas-Nebraska Act. The act would organize these two areas as territories. Both Kansas and Nebraska were north of the 36° 30′ parallel set up as a boundary for slavery

in the Missouri Compromise. But slavery would not be prohibited in these areas. It would be decided by popular sovereignty. Thus, the act actually repealed the Missouri Compromise. It passed despite opposition from many northerners.

Slavery would clearly not be profitable in Nebraska. But Kansas was another matter. Both the North and the South used **violence** to try to win that area. The territory came to be called "Bleeding Kansas." The slavery issue was causing bloodshed. Peaceful compromise seemed impossible.

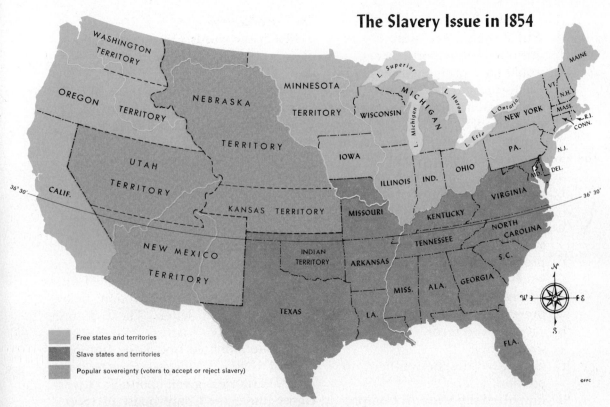

The Slavery Issue in 1854

WASHINGTON TERRITORY

OREGON TERRITORY

MINNESOTA

L. Superior

MICHIGAN

MAINE

NEBRASKA

TERRITORY

MINNESOTA TERRITORY

WISCONSIN

L. Huron

L. Michigan

VT.

N.H.

MASS.

NEW YORK

L. Ontario

L. Erie

R.I.

CONN.

UTAH TERRITORY

IOWA

ILLINOIS

IND.

OHIO

PA.

N.J.

DEL.

MD.

CALIF.

36° 30'

KANSAS TERRITORY

MISSOURI

KENTUCKY

VIRGINIA

36° 30'

NEW MEXICO TERRITORY

INDIAN TERRITORY

ARKANSAS

TENNESSEE

NORTH CAROLINA

S.C.

TEXAS

MISS.

ALA.

GEORGIA

LA.

FLA.

Free states and territories

Slave states and territories

Popular sovereignty (voters to accept or reject slavery)

©FPC

How did the Kansas-Nebraska Act of 1854 affect those two
areas? How did this act differ from the Missouri Compromise,
which prohibited slavery north of the 36° 30′ parallel?

COMPREHENSION CHECK

A. Recognizing the Main Idea

This selection as a whole tells you

1. how the addition of new lands to
the nation eased the tension in the
slavery conflict.

2. about compromises that solved
the problem of slavery.

3. how California applied for admission to the Union as a free state.

4. about the failure of compromises
to resolve the slavery issue.

B. Selecting Important Details

Choose the ending that best completes each statement.

1. Compromise on the slavery conflict
became more difficult as

a. the abolition movement grew
weaker.

b. new lands were added to the nation.

c. cotton became less important to
the South.

d. the colonization movement became successful.

2. The Wilmot Proviso
   a. settled the slavery issue.
   b. was opposed by northerners.
   c. would have prohibited slavery in California and the Southwest.
   d. was passed despite southern opposition.
3. All of the following were part of the Compromise of 1850 EXCEPT
   a. a stricter Fugitive Slave Act.
   b. popular sovereignty for Utah and New Mexico.
   c. admission of California as a free state.
   d. prohibition of slavery in new land north of the 36° 30′ parallel.
4. The Kansas-Nebraska Act
   a. prevented bloodshed.
   b. gave the two territories popular sovereignty.
   c. was passed despite southern opposition.
   d. supported the Missouri Compromise.

C. True or False

Decide whether each of these statements is true or false.

1. William Lloyd Garrison, Frederick Douglass, and Sojourner Truth supported compromises on the slavery issue.

2. The Missouri Compromise prohibited slavery in new land north of the 36° 30′ parallel.

3. The stricter Fugitive Slave Act caused some northern states to bar slave hunters.

4. The North and the South used violence to try to win Kansas.

5. The Compromise of 1850 and the Kansas-Nebraska Act were passed in the same year.

D. Vocabulary

Match the words with the definitions.

Words
1. realistic
2. popular sovereignty
3. tension
4. violence

Definitions
a. easily fooled
b. use of physical force against someone
c. based on fact
d. self-rule
e. understanding between two groups
f. strain between two groups

E. Map Skills

This map shows the United States in the 1850s. Certain areas are labeled with letters. Match each description below with the correct letter. There is one extra letter.

1. State admitted under the Compromise of 1850.

2. Territories given popular sovereignty under the Compromise of 1850.

3. The South before 1845.

4. State that won independence from Mexico.

5. Territories given popular sovereignty under act in 1854.

6. The North.

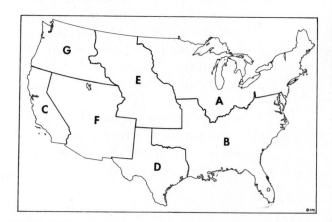

William Lloyd Garrison

No American was more closely associated with abolition than William Lloyd Garrison. He was first active as a printer and publisher in Baltimore. Feeling that northerners had to be convinced that slavery was wrong, he moved to Boston in 1830. There he established the newspaper *The Liberator.* In it, he wrote, "I *will be* as harsh as truth. . . . On this subject, I do not wish to think, to speak, or write with moderation. . . . I am in earnest . . . I will not retreat a single inch—AND I WILL BE HEARD."

Garrison did, indeed, make himself heard in the years that followed. His views earned him the hatred of the slaveowners. Even in Boston, he had many enemies, who regarded him as a danger to the nation. In 1834, a mob of Bostonians, including many wealthy people, resorted to mob action. An eyewitness reported:

"It was a mob of gentlemen. There were hundreds, then thousands. Mr. Garrison was writing at his desk. He was very calm about it. The whole fury of the crowd . . . seemed in one instant to turn upon the editor of *The Liberator. . . .* Garrison unwillingly consented to escape and took refuge in a carpenter's shop, only to be dragged out and carried into the midst of the mob, where it seemed he would be torn in pieces. I saw him, his hat off, his bald head shining, his scanty locks flying, his face pale, and his clothes torn and dusty, with a rope around his neck."

Garrison was rescued from the mob, but he faced other mobs, and even jail sentences, during his long fight against slavery. By 1865, however, he had lived to see his ideas win and himself an American hero.

Lesson 5 The Sections Grow Further Apart

WORDS TO UNDERSTAND
Discuss the meanings of these words.

emotional   status

emancipated   disappointing

NEW WORDS IN SENTENCES

1. An **emotional** book may arouse many feelings in the reader.

2. Abolitionists wanted slaves to be **emancipated,** or given their freedom.

3. In the eyes of the law, slaves had no **status,** or position, as people.

4. The court ruling was **disappointing** to the abolitionists because they had hoped for something different.

AS YOU READ

As you read this selection, try to answer these questions.

1. How did *Uncle Tom's Cabin* increase the conflict between the North and the South?

2. What were the main points of the Dred Scott decision?

THE READING SELECTION

Review. By the 1850s, earlier compromises on slavery had failed. In addition, the growth of the abolition movement made new compromises even harder. California's admission to the Union caused a crisis that was settled by the Compromise of 1850. This compromise provided for a stronger Fugitive Slave Act. It also provided that slavery would be decided in the New Mexico and Utah territories by popular sovereignty. The Kansas-Nebraska Act of 1854 extended popular sovereignty to those two territories. Both of these efforts at compromise finally led to increased tension between North and South, including actual bloodshed in Kansas. ☆

Popular feeling was running high in both the North and South in the 1850s. The anger was increased by both the Compromise of 1850 and the Kansas-Nebraska Act. Actions by the Congress were not the only causes of tension.

The Fugitive Slave Act was part of the Compromise of 1850. It was protested by many northerners. One of them was Harriet Beecher Stowe, who wrote *Uncle Tom's Cabin,* published in 1852. Her book is an **emotional** description of the lives of slaves on a southern plantation. The book sold over 300,000 copies the first year. For many Americans, it was almost a call to battle.

In the book, the old and kindly slave, Uncle Tom, is sold from one planta-

This poster advertises a stage play of *Uncle Tom's Cabin*.

tion to another. He ends up in the hands of a cruel owner, Simon Legree. The book describes Tom's suffering under slavery. It describes how he dies from a beating after he refuses to tell Legree where two escaped slaves are hiding. The slave Eliza, her husband, and child flee to the North. In a famous scene, Eliza escapes from slave catchers by running across the frozen Ohio River.

Southerners protested that the book was unfair. They pointed out that the author had not lived in the South. Yet Stowe claimed that her book was based on facts. Garrison's paper, *The Liberator*, had often carried stories of the evils of slavery. Frederick Douglass, a former slave, had told similar stories. Ohio newspapers had carried the story of a slave who had fled across the frozen Ohio River to escape slave catchers. When she

was caught by them, she killed her child. Partly as a result of these supporting reports, northerners believed the book. *Uncle Tom's Cabin* increased the hatred and anger on both sides.

Then, in 1857, feelings again rose with the decision of the Supreme Court in the case *Dred Scott* v. *Sanford*. Scott was a Missouri slave taken north by his owner. For four years, he lived in the free areas of Illinois and the Wisconsin Territory. After his return to Missouri, he was sold.

Some abolitionists became interested in helping Dred Scott win his freedom. They also wished to test slavery in the courts. It was arranged for Scott to sue his new master, Sanford, for his freedom. Scott's lawyers argued that he was free because he had lived on free soil from 1834 to 1838.

There was a good deal of disagreement in the Supreme Court about the case. But the most important opinion was written by Chief Justice Roger B. Taney. Taney felt that the Constitution should be interpreted as it was understood in 1789. Taney held that Scott was not only a slave but also a member of a race considered in 1789 an "inferior class of beings . . . whether **emancipated** or not. . . ." Therefore, Scott was not a citizen and could not sue in court. No court could rule on the case.

However, Taney went on to give his opinions on the case itself. He argued that Scott's **status** depended on the laws of his first home, Missouri, not on those of Illinois. He also argued that the federal government had no power to prohibit slavery in the Wisconsin Territory or any other territory. He declared the Missouri Compromise, which did just that, unconstitutional.

A few days after the Court's decision, Dred Scott was freed by his owner. But the decision caused an uproar in the North. For example, the New York *Tribune* called it a "wicked and false judgment." For many years afterward, the Supreme Court had little influence on many Americans. The Dred Scott ruling was very **disappointing** to abolitionists. Opposition to the decision, the Fugitive Slave Act, and slavery itself rose. At the same time, many southerners were very pleased. They demanded that the ruling be followed to the letter.

Harriet Beecher Stowe meant to sway public opinion with *Uncle Tom's Cabin.* Chief Justice Taney probably did not mean to do anything like that. But both people fed the growing conflict.

Library of Congress

A writer and an abolitionist, Harriet Beecher Stowe became famous overnight for her book *Uncle Tom's Cabin.*

COMPREHENSION CHECK

A. Recognizing the Main Idea

This selection as a whole tells you why

1. *Uncle Tom's Cabin* helped ease tension between the North and the South.

2. the Dred Scott decision was disappointing to the South.

3. feelings in the North and South about slavery grew stronger.

4. the conflict over slavery was not very emotional.

B. Selecting Important Details

Choose the ending that best completes each statement.

1. The book *Uncle Tom's Cabin*
   a. made slavery seem not so bad.
   b. was thought to be unfair in the North.
   c. was written by a person who had lived in the South for many years.
   d. had a great impact on people's feelings in the North and the South.

2. Dred Scott claimed freedom because he
   a. had been freed by Sanford.
   b. was freed by the Supreme Court.
   c. had the support of the abolitionists.
   d. had lived in free territory for several years.

3. All of the following points were made in the Dred Scott decision EXCEPT that
   a. neither a slave nor a free black could bring a case to court.
   b. Scott was a member of an "inferior class."
   c. Scott's status depended on the laws of Missouri, his home state.
   d. the federal government had the power to prohibit slavery in the territories.

4. The Dred Scott decision
   a. was disappointing to southerners.
   b. declared the Missouri Compromise unconstitutional.
   c. made northerners less angry at slavery.
   d. weakened the Fugitive Slave Act.

C. True or False

Decide whether each of these statements is true or false.

1. Simon Legree was a slave who suffered in Harriet Beecher Stowe's book.

2. The stories told by Frederick Douglass and written about in *The Liberator* and other newspapers helped northerners believe *Uncle Tom's Cabin*.

3. Chief Justice Roger B. Taney wrote his opinion about *Uncle Tom's Cabin*.

4. The Supreme Court decision declared that no court could rule on Dred Scott's case.

5. Harriet Beecher Stowe supported the Fugitive Slave Act.

D. Vocabulary

Match the words with the definitions.

Words	Definitions
1. emotional	a. against the law
2. emancipate	b. not meeting hopes
3. status	c. full of feeling
4. disappointing	d. position
	e. give freedom
	f. thoughtful

E. Essay Question

Write eight to ten sentences answering the following questions.

What might have happened if the Dred Scott case had been decided in favor of Dred Scott? Would many other slaves have tried to get their freedom in the same way? How would the southern states have reacted?

The Fugitive Slave Act in Action: The Sims Case

No fugitive slave had ever been caught and returned from Boston. The city was a center of abolitionism, but it was also a stronghold of Whig conservatives. These conservatives felt that the Fugitive Slave Act must be obeyed.

In April 1851, a fugitive slave named Thomas Sims was seized in Boston. A month earlier, the abolitionists had rescued another fugitive. Now they tried to save Sims. But this time, the officials took special care to guard the fugitive slave. Sims was put under special police guard in the courthouse. The courthouse was barred with heavy chains to keep out abolitionists.

Many people in Boston were shocked. Henry Wadsworth Longfellow wrote, "When and where will this end?" Other abolitionists pointed to the chains around the courthouse and cried that liberty was being enslaved.

Efforts to free Sims failed, and he was ordered returned to slavery. A guard of 300 men was detailed to move him to a waiting ship. As the men marched to the harbor, the streets rang with cries of "Shame!" and "Where is liberty?" When Sims walked up the gangplank to the ship, a voice from the harbor called out,

"Sims, preach liberty to the slaves!" The fugitive turned and cried, "And is this Massachusetts liberty?"

Boston was bitterly shamed that day. Town bells throughout Massachusetts tolled as a sign of mourning. The Fugitive Slave Act had been upheld, but thousands had now seen with their own eyes the evil of slavery.

After the Sims case, a Boston abolitionist committee posted this warning that the Fugitive Slave Act was in effect.

CAUTION!!
COLORED PEOPLE
OF BOSTON, ONE & ALL,

You are hereby respectfully CAUTIONED and advised, to avoid conversing with the

Watchmen and Police Officers of Boston,

For since the recent ORDER OF THE MAYOR & ALDERMEN, they are empowered to act as

KIDNAPPERS
AND
Slave Catchers,

And they have already been actually employed in KIDNAPPING, CATCHING, AND KEEPING SLAVES. Therefore, if you value your LIBERTY, and the *Welfare of the Fugitives* among you, *Shun* them in every possible manner, as so many *HOUNDS* on the track of the most unfortunate of your race.

Keep a Sharp Look Out for KIDNAPPERS, and have TOP EYE open.

APRIL 24, 1851.

Lesson 6 The Rise of the Republican Party

WORDS TO UNDERSTAND

Discuss the meanings of these words.

dissatisfaction   homestead   arsenal

NEW WORDS IN SENTENCES

1. Some people were not happy with the decision, and there was a great deal of **dissatisfaction** with the court.

2. Farmers wanted a **homestead** law so they could buy low-priced land from the government for their homes.

3. The purpose of the raid was to take guns from the **arsenal.**

AS YOU READ

As you read this selection, try to answer these questions.

1. What groups joined together to form the Republican party?

2. What events affected the growth of the Republican party?

THE READING SELECTION

Since the 1830s, the two major American political parties had been the Democratic party and the Whig party. The Democrats had been pro-slavery. The Whigs had been divided on slavery and had not taken a stand at all. Those Americans who opposed slavery had no major party to speak for them. Several small parties were formed over the years to serve this purpose. Among them were the Liberty party and the Free Soil party. But these parties never gained much power.

In 1854, northern **dissatisfaction** with the Kansas-Nebraska Act weakened the Whig party. Former Whigs and Free Soilers joined with anti-slavery Democrats to form a new party, the Republican party. Republicans included many groups with different interests.

1. Abolitionists and other reformers left the smaller parties. They wanted the Republicans to take a strong anti-slavery stand.

2. Southern Unionists feared southern leaders might try to secede from the Union. They wanted to oppose this.

3. Northern business interests wanted higher tariffs and aid to the railroads.

4. Farmers in free areas of the West wanted a **homestead** law. This would make government land available at low prices.

The first Republican platform appeared in 1854. It called for the repeal of the Kansas-Nebraska Act and the Fugitive Slave Act. It also called for the abolition of slavery in Washington, D.C. In the 1856 presidential election, the Republicans urged congressional control over slavery in the territories. The Republican candidate received nearly 40 percent of the electoral vote.

Between 1856 and 1860, the Republican party was affected by several events. The Dred Scott decision in 1857 led many anti-slavery Americans to join the Republican party. In 1859, a radical abolitionist, John Brown, led a raid on a federal **arsenal** at Harpers Ferry, Virginia. He hoped to obtain guns for a slave revolt that he planned to lead. But Brown and his followers failed. He was tried and hanged by the state of Virginia. The Republican party had not openly supported Brown's actions. However, frightened southerners blamed the party for them. Strong opposition to the Republicans rose in the South. At the same time, the party gained support in the North. The sections were divided sharply in the 1860 presidential election.

The Republicans nominated Abraham Lincoln. Lincoln was known mainly in the Illinois area. However, he had caught the attention of national leaders during his 1858 campaign for the Senate. Lincoln was not a radical. He believed in stopping slavery from spreading. He believed in a slow emancipation of the slaves. He felt that the nation could not exist "half slave and half free." It would have to become completely one or the other.

In his 1858 Senate campaign, Lincoln had run against Stephen A. Douglas, a Democrat and the author of the Kansas-Nebraska Act. In 1860, Lincoln and Douglas opposed each other again, this time for the presidency. The Democrats had nominated Douglas. But Douglas had lost much of the support of pro-slavery southern Democrats. In an 1858 debate, Lincoln had forced Douglas to comment on the effects of the Dred Scott decision. Cornered, Douglas had said that people of the territories could keep slavery out if they wished to. Many southerners did not like this. They walked out of the Democratic convention when it nominated Douglas. These southerners met and chose their own candidate. There were four candidates for the presidency in 1860. The split in the Democratic party could help Abraham Lincoln. But some southerners had threatened secession if Lincoln were elected. The nation waited to see what would happen.

COMPREHENSION CHECK

A. Recognizing the Main Idea

This selection as a whole tells you how

1. the Republican party was formed as the country became more united on the slavery issue.

2. the Republican party was affected by the Dred Scott decision.

3. the Democratic party united against the Republican party.

4. the Republican party was formed as the country became more divided on the slavery issue.

B. Selecting Important Details

Choose the ending that best completes each statement.

1. The Republican party included all of the following groups EXCEPT
   a. northern business interests.
   b. southern leaders who wanted to secede.
   c. abolitionists.
   d. farmers in the free areas of the West.

2. The Republican platform called for all of the following EXCEPT
   a. repeal of the Kansas-Nebraska Act.
   b. abolition of slavery in Washington, D.C.
   c. congressional control over slavery in territories.
   d. support for John Brown's raid.

3. John Brown
   a. was a moderate abolitionist.
   b. led a successful slave revolt.
   c. frightened southerners, who blamed the Republican party.
   d. was openly supported by the Republican party.

4. In a debate with Lincoln, Stephen A. Douglas
   a. said the nation could not exist "half slave and half free."
   b. gained the support of southern Democrats because of his comment on the Dred Scott case.
   c. agreed with Lincoln about slowly emancipating the slaves.
   d. lost pro-slavery support when he said territories could prohibit slavery.

C. True or False

Decide whether each of these statements is true or false.

1. The Dred Scott decision scared people away from the Republican party.
2. Lincoln was a radical abolitionist.
3. The Liberty party and the Free Soil party were pro-slavery.
4. The Democratic party was united behind Stephen A. Douglas in the presidential campaign of 1860.
5. Some southerners threatened secession if Lincoln were elected.

D. Vocabulary

Match the words with the definitions.

Words	Definitions
1. dissatisfaction	a. a poison
2. homestead	b. unhappiness
3. arsenal	c. government land acquired by the person living on it
	d. land that is not used for farming
	e. a storeroom for guns

E. Using Your Knowledge

Many paragraphs are built around a main sentence. The other sentences in the paragraph give details about the idea. Find the eighth paragraph in the Reading Selection. (It is the paragraph that begins: Between 1856 and 1860. . . .) Write down the main idea of the paragraph. Under that, list two important details given about that main idea.

Black Abolitionism

Before the Civil War, there were many people who dedicated their lives to ending slavery in America. Black people and white people joined in this common cause, which became known as the abolition movement.

Blacks had been active in the fight against slavery as early as 1760. They founded a Free African Society to protect the rights of black people and to end slavery. During the 1800s, thousands of slaves fled to freedom in the North. They joined with free blacks to organize more than fifty black anti-slavery societies by 1830. That year, a National Negro Convention was held in Philadelphia to promote the fight against slavery.

Black people were also quick to support their white allies in the abolition movement. When William Lloyd Garrison founded his paper *The Liberator* in 1831, he had only 450 subscribers, of whom 400 were black people. Three years later, about 1,800 of his 2,300 subscribers were blacks.

Black men and women were among the leaders of the abolition movement. Foremost among the black leaders was Frederick Douglass. Other black abolitionists were David Ruggles, Robert Purvis, David Walker, William Still, Harriet Tubman, and Sojourner Truth. The writings of Henry Highland Garnet sounded a call to action when he urged black people, "Let your motto be resistance! resistance! RESISTANCE!"

Chicago Historical Society

Sophia Smith Collection, Smith College

Sojourner Truth (left) was born a slave. She became a powerful speaker for abolition and other reforms. Harriet Tubman (above, at left) escaped from slavery. She was known for courageously leading more than 300 slaves through the Underground Railroad.

Lesson 7 The Election of 1860

WORDS TO UNDERSTAND
Discuss the meanings of these words.

threaten   **restrict**   **stressed**

NEW WORDS IN SENTENCES
1. Southern states began to **threaten,** or give warning, that they would secede.
2. The states did not want the government to **restrict,** or limit, their power.
3. The Constitution **stressed** what was important to the people who wrote it.

AS YOU READ
As you read this selection, try to answer these questions.

1. Who were the four candidates for president in the election of 1860, and what were their platforms?
2. How did the South react to the outcome of the election?

THE READING SELECTION
Review. A series of events in the 1850s showed that the sections were drawing further apart. *Uncle Tom's Cabin,* published in 1852, increased the anger in both North and South. So did the Kansas-Nebraska Act of 1854 and the Dred Scott decision of 1857. John Brown's raid on a Virginia arsenal in 1859 also caused more conflict. During this period, a new party, the Republican party, was formed. It opposed the extension of slavery to the territories. ☆

In 1860, sectionalism broke the nation apart. In that year's election, there were four parties. Their platforms clearly showed the open conflict, especially over slavery.

Democratic candidate Stephen A. Douglas ran on a platform opposing congressional control of slavery in territories. This was not strong enough for some Southern Democrats. They met and nominated John C. Breckinridge of Kentucky for president. Their platform called for open support of slavery in the territories. The few remaining Whigs helped found the Constitutional Union party. Their candidate was John Bell of Tennessee. He ran on a platform opposing sectional parties.

Republican Abraham Lincoln ran on a partly anti-slavery platform. Republicans said they supported the principles of the Declaration of Independence. They opposed extension of slavery to the territories and any effort to reopen

311

the African slave trade. But they stopped short of complete abolition. In fact, they pledged that each state would continue to control its own "domestic institutions." This was meant to assure the South that slavery would be permitted in areas where it already existed.

The rest of the Republican platform was aimed at getting support from both North and West. It offered something for each section.

1. It supported a tariff "to encourage development of industrial interests of the whole country." This was thought to mean support of a high protective tariff. The North would be helped by this.

2. It supported a homestead law. This would provide farmers in the West with low-cost farmland from the government.

3. It supported a program of internal improvements, including a railroad to the Pacific coast. This would help both western farmers and northern industries and banks.

The Republicans were assured of the reform and anti-slavery vote. That vote would go to any party opposing slavery. In addition, the Republicans had the support of northern industrialists and western farmers. There was even reason to believe the new party might win support from many old Whigs in the South.

Radical southerners continued to **threaten** to secede if Lincoln were elected. The rise of a strong Republican political machine could keep the Democrats from winning control of the government for many years. Years of Republican control were sure to **restrict** the political power of the South. Southerners might lose their influence in the federal government.

In the November election, Lincoln did not win a majority of the popular votes. But he won in eighteen free states. He received nearly 60 percent of the electoral vote by winning states with large populations and many electoral votes. Lincoln was elected president.

After Lincoln was elected, South Carolina was the first state to secede from the Union.

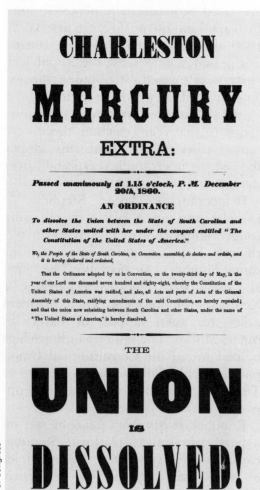

The Presidential Election of 1860

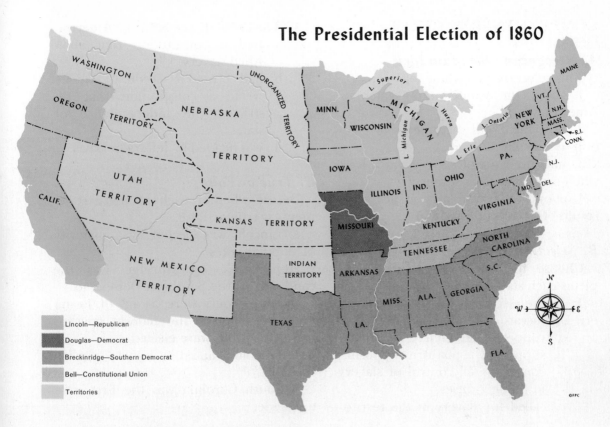

Legend:
- Lincoln—Republican
- Douglas—Democrat
- Breckinridge—Southern Democrat
- Bell—Constitutional Union
- Territories

Lincoln did not receive any popular votes in ten southern states. He was elected by the electoral votes of the North.

But he would not be inaugurated until March 1861.

The South carried out its threat. On December 20, 1860, South Carolina seceded from the Union. Within the next six weeks, six other southern states left the Union. Later, four other states joined them. In all these states, there were people who did not favor such action. However, moderates in both the North and the South failed to prevent secession.

In February 1861, a convention was held in Alabama. It wrote a constitution for the Confederate States of America.

This document **stressed** the independence of the states and protected slavery. A new government was set up, headed by Jefferson Davis.

President James Buchanan had felt he could not stop the secession. The new president, Lincoln, felt he had to act. He again assured the South that he did not support abolition. But Lincoln also declared that no state had the right to leave the Union. He added that there would be no war "unless it be forced upon the national authority."

Before long, events took place that forced a civil war on the nation.

COMPREHENSION CHECK

A. Recognizing the Main Idea

This selection as a whole tells you

1. about the Confederate States of America.

2. how the South accepted the election of Lincoln.

3. how the issue of slavery was solved when southern states seceded.

4. about the candidates, issues, and results of the election of 1860.

B. Selecting Important Details

Choose the ending that best completes each statement.

1. In the election of 1860, the Southern Democrats
   a. supported Stephen A. Douglas.
   b. supported a platform opposing congressional control of slavery in the territories.
   c. called for slavery in the territories.
   d. all of the above.

2. The Republican platform
   a. stopped short of abolition.
   b. would have allowed slavery to continue in areas where it already existed.
   c. opposed extension of slavery to the territories.
   d. all of the above.

3. The Republican platform
   a. had the support of radical southerners.
   b. called for a tariff, a homestead law, and a railroad to the Pacific.
   c. lost the support of farmers.
   d. would have had the support of northern industrialists except for its position on slavery.

4. The Confederate States of America
   a. had a constitution that abolished slavery.
   b. had refused to secede.
   c. wrote a constitution that restricted the independence of states.
   d. was headed by Jefferson Davis.

C. True or False

Decide whether each of these statements is true or false.

1. Lincoln was elected by a majority of popular votes.

2. John C. Breckinridge was the candidate of the Southern Democrats.

3. Southerners were afraid of losing their influence in the federal government if Lincoln were elected.

4. Lincoln wanted a war to abolish slavery.

5. South Carolina was the first state to secede.

D. Vocabulary

Match the words with the definitions.

Words	Definitions
1. threaten	a. give help to
2. restrict	b. place importance on
3. stress	c. give warning
	d. withhold
	e. limit

E. Chronology

Arrange these events in the order in which they happened.

1. Dred Scott decision.
2. South Carolina secedes.
3. End of war with Mexico.
4. Compromise of 1850.
5. Lincoln elected.
6. Kansas-Nebraska Act.

Slavery – Two Southern Views

The slavery issue set the North against the South. But it also set people within each section against one another. Some southerners opposed secession. For years, many in the South had opposed slavery. Some of the most active abolitionists were southerners. Many workers on the Underground Railroad were southerners. The debate raged on.

Thomas Dew was a professor at the College of William and Mary in Virginia. He later became president of the college. He defended slavery as a "positive good." He argued:

> It is the order of nature and of God that the being of superior knowledge, and therefore of superior power, should control those who are inferior. It is as much the order of nature that men should enslave each other as that other animals should prey upon each other.

On the other side was Angelina Grimké. Born and raised on a South Carolina plantation, she was forced to leave the South because of her opposition to slavery. She toured the North, speaking against slavery.

> As a moral being, I feel that I owe it to the suffering slave, and to the mistaken master, to my country and the world, to do all that I can. I must help overturn this system of crimes, built up upon the broken hearts and bodies of my countrymen in chains, and cemented by the blood, sweat and tears of my sisters in bonds.

Library of Congress

Huge profits could be made by raising slaves for market. This photograph shows slaves near their cabins at a plantation in Georgia.

Neither side ever won over the other. Debate did not settle the issue of slavery. Only the Civil War did.

Unit 6 Summary   The Growing Crisis: Slavery

Life Under Slavery

Since its beginning in the 1600s, slavery had been important to the South. It had slowly died out in the North, which now opposed it. The South's economy depended on slave labor. Slaveowners controlled the politics of that section.

The lives of slaves varied. In general, they worked long hours under an overseer. Slaves had only the bare necessities of life. They had no rights and lived under the rules of slave codes. Physical abuse was part of slavery. Some slaves rebelled against this. Others escaped to the North. The issue of slavery began to deeply affect American politics.

Texas and the Mexican War

Many of the Americans settling Texas were slaveowners. When Texas became independent from Mexico, it asked for admission to the Union. The South strongly favored this. The North opposed it, since it would give the slave states more power in Congress. Texas was finally annexed in 1845. War soon began with Mexico over the border of the state. In the treaty ending that war in 1848, Mexico ceded California and much of the Southwest to the United States. The South tried to extend slavery to these lands.

The Sections Draw Further Apart

By the 1850s, earlier efforts to solve the slavery problem had failed. In addition, the abolition movement had gained strength. This made new compromises even harder. California's admission to the Union caused a crisis that was settled by the Compromise of 1850. The compromise provided for a stronger Fugitive Slave Act. It also provided that slavery would be decided in the New Mexico and

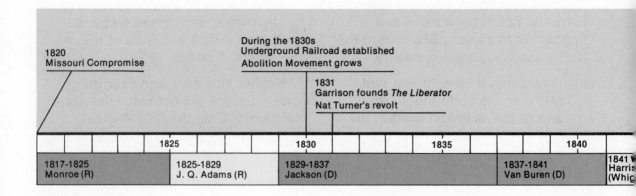

1820
Missouri Compromise

During the 1830s
Underground Railroad established
Abolition Movement grows

1831
Garrison founds *The Liberator*
Nat Turner's revolt

1825   1830   1835   1840

1817-1825
Monroe (R)

1825-1829
J. Q. Adams (R)

1829-1837
Jackson (D)

1837-1841
Van Buren (D)

1841
Harris
(Whig

Utah territories by popular sovereignty. In 1854, popular sovereignty was extended by the Kansas-Nebraska Act. Both of these laws angered the North. The Kansas-Nebraska Act even caused bloodshed in Kansas.

The North was made even angrier by the Supreme Court's decision in the Dred Scott case. The publication of *Uncle Tom's Cabin* also increased tension between the sections.

The Election of 1860

During this time, the Republican party was formed. It opposed extending slavery to territories. In 1860, Abraham Lincoln was the Republican candidate for president. Stephen Douglas was nominated by the Democrats. The Southern Democrats chose their own pro-slavery candidate. The Republicans tried to draw support from both the North and West. As a result, Lincoln carried the electoral college.

Within a month, southern states began to secede. In February, they established the Confederate States of America, headed by Jefferson Davis. Lincoln warned the South that this action could not be accepted.

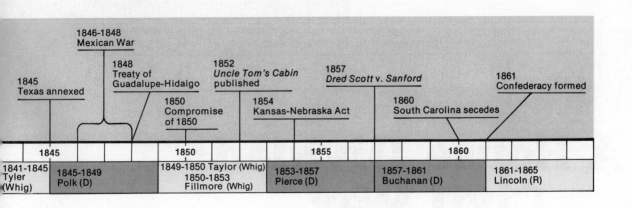

unit 7

Dead Confederate Soldier, May 19, 1864, Library of Congress

Battle of Lookout Mountain by James Walker, U.S. Army photo

A House Divided: Civil War and Reconstruction

Finally, the crisis came to war. Sectionalism and the conflict over slavery could not continue to exist within the Union. The nation broke apart. Everywhere, soldiers went marching off to the Civil War. The bloody battles (above) took a large human toll—from Confederate (left) and Union alike. The war itself took a toll of the nation, leaving destruction and bitterness. For years afterward, Reconstruction programs aimed at putting the pieces back together again.

Lesson 1　Causes of the Civil War

WORDS TO UNDERSTAND

Discuss the meanings of these words.

immediate　　**permanent**
voluntary　　**endure**

NEW WORDS IN SENTENCES

1. There were many reasons for the war, but the **immediate** cause was the attack on the fort.

2. They joined by their own choice, on a **voluntary** basis.

3. Lincoln wanted the states to stay together in a **permanent** union that would last through the years.

4. If a nation is to **endure,** it must continue even when there are disagreements among the people.

AS YOU READ

As you read this selection, try to answer these questions.

1. What were some of the causes of the Civil War?

2. To what extent was slavery a cause of the war?

THE READING SELECTION

Abraham Lincoln was elected president in November 1860. He was not inaugurated until March 1861. There were four months between Lincoln's election and his inauguration. In that time, Southern states moved toward secession.

South Carolina was the first state to secede. It was followed by six other states. In February 1861, the secession leaders met in Alabama and formed the Confederate States of America. They elected Jefferson Davis, a former United States senator from Mississippi, president of the Confederacy.

Soon after President Lincoln took office, he tried to send supplies to Fort Sumter, South Carolina. Earlier attempts to do this had been stopped by Southern troops. When South Carolina learned of Lincoln's plan, its troops opened fire on the fort. After thirty-four hours, the federal forces surrendered. This event marked the beginning of the Civil War.

The firing on Fort Sumter was the **immediate** cause of the Civil War. It was the last in a series of problems that brought about the war. There were political, economic, and social causes of the Civil War.

Differences among the sections of the country had existed since colonial times. With different land, climate, and people, the North and South developed different ways of life. Their economies developed

The attack of Confederate forces on Fort Sumter, South Carolina, signaled the start of the Civil War.

Library of Congress

differently. Their economic needs were linked to their political views. Sectionalism appeared in many parts of American life.

The West and South developed agriculture, while the North developed industry and trade. Both the North and West were interested in developing roads and railroads. The South did not feel a need for new transportation. The North favored high tariffs to protect its industries. The West agreed with the North on tariffs, but the South bitterly opposed them. Tariffs added to the expenses of plantation owners. With low tariffs, the South could trade its cotton for cheaper foreign goods.

The free-labor economy of the North was opposed to the slave economy of the South. The North needed a nation of wage earners to buy its manufactured products. If the millions of Southern slaves were freed, there would be a bigger market for Northern products.

Political differences also existed between the sections. Southerners favored a strict interpretation of the Constitution. This would prevent the federal government from controlling slavery. Most Northerners favored a loose interpretation. This would permit strong ties between government and business. Federal funds and laws could help develop industry and transportation.

A major source of conflict between North and South was the nature of the federal Union. To the South, the federal government was a **voluntary** association of individual states. Southerners felt that states were free to leave this Union when they wanted. The North felt the federal Union was **permanent.** Northerners denied the right of any state to secede.

Political power was very important to the South. As new states and territories joined the Union, the South saw itself losing more and more power in Congress. It was becoming a political minority. Southerners were afraid of a federal government dominated by free states. Such a government could pass laws unfavorable to the slave states. Southern extremists cried out for secession as the only means of safeguarding states' rights. Northern extremists demanded that the South be forced to accept the Northern point of view on most matters. To some extent, extremism on both sides helped bring on the war.

How much did slavery help to cause the Civil War? There has been much dispute over this. But we can say that it played a very important part. The slavery issue had been a major one in the United States for many years. Other issues, such as the tariff, had been settled by compromise. But slavery did not lend itself to compromise. In 1858, Abraham Lincoln had said, " 'A house divided against itself cannot stand.' I believe this government cannot **endure** permanently half slave and half free. . . . I do expect it will cease to be divided. It will become all one thing, or all the other." Three years later, the nation began a war that would settle this issue.

In the Civil War, eleven slave states left the Union and established the Confederate government. Four border states and the western part of Virginia remained in the Union.

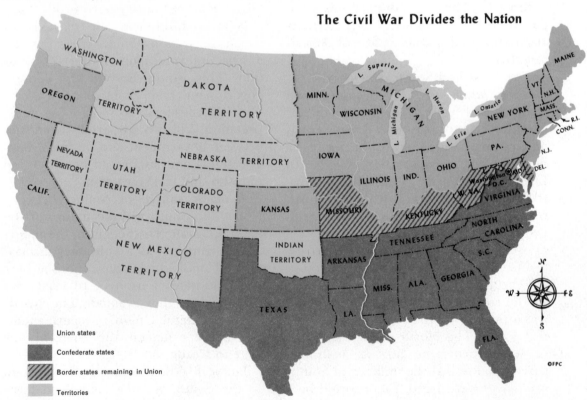

The Civil War Divides the Nation

Union states

Confederate states

Border states remaining in Union

Territories

©FPC

COMPREHENSION CHECK

A. Recognizing the Main Idea

This selection as a whole tells you that

1. Lincoln thought the nation could not endure half slave and half free.
2. Northerners and Southerners compromised on the issue of slavery.
3. the firing on Fort Sumter caused the Civil War.
4. there were political, economic, and social causes of the Civil War.

B. Selecting Important Details

Choose the ending that best completes each statement.

1. The Confederate States of America
    a. elected Abraham Lincoln as its president.
    b. allowed shipments of supplies to Fort Sumter.
    c. elected Jefferson Davis as its president.
    d. tried to stop Southern states from seceding.
2. The North was in favor of all of the following EXCEPT
    a. developing new transportation.
    b. low tariffs.
    c. strong ties between government and business.
    d. a free-labor economy.
3. The South was in favor of all of the following EXCEPT
    a. states' control of slavery.
    b. the right of states to secede from the Union.
    c. low tariffs.
    d. federal funds for industry and transportation.

4. The different political views of the North and South
    a. developed suddenly.
    b. could all be settled by compromises.
    c. were linked to their different economies.
    d. all of the above.

C. Fact or Opinion

A fact is an event or situation that actually happened. It is really true, no matter what someone thinks about it. An opinion is someone's belief or judgment about something. Decide whether each of these statements is fact or opinion.

1. The Confederate States of America was formed in 1861.
2. Lincoln did the wrong thing in sending supplies to Fort Sumter.
3. Federal troops at Fort Sumter surrendered.
4. The South and North disagreed about the interpretation of the Constitution.
5. The only correct interpretation of the Constitution is a loose one.

D. Vocabulary

Match the words with the definitions.

Words	Definitions
1. immediate	a. done by choice
2. voluntary	b. to last
3. permanent	c. foolish
4. endure	d. explanation of the meaning
	e. closest in time
	f. unchanging

E. Ask Yourself

Was slavery the most important cause of the Civil War?

Lesson 2 The Civil War

WORDS TO UNDERSTAND
Discuss the meanings of these words.

strategy   **morale**

NEW WORDS IN SENTENCES
1. The army's **strategy** was a careful plan to slowly weaken the enemy.
2. When a battle is lost, the **morale** of the army goes down.

AS YOU READ
As you read this selection, try to answer these questions.

1. What advantages did the North have over the South?
2. What was the military strategy of the North? of the South?

THE READING SELECTION
Review. The Civil War had many causes. The North and the South had different economic needs. Politically, they disagreed in their views of the Constitution and the federal Union. The slavery issue did not lend itself to compromise and therefore helped to bring on the war. By the time President Abraham Lincoln took office in March of 1861, the Confederate States of America had already been formed. In April, South Carolina troops fired on the federal forces at Fort Sumter. This began the war. ☆

Between April 1861 and April 1865, the United States was torn apart by a civil war. The war was fought by the North, or Union, and the South, or Confederacy. The Confederacy was fighting to keep slavery. It also wanted to win its independence from the North. The Union was fighting at first only to restore the federal Union. Later, the North also fought to free the slaves.

The North had several advantages from the beginning. It had a balanced economy. In other words, it had developed industry and banking along with agriculture. In 1861, about 85 percent of the nation's factories were located in the North. So this section could produce the arms and other materials for war. The South's economy was largely one-sided. It depended on imported manufactured products. The war

Lincoln met with Union officers at Antietam, Maryland. Union forces stopped the Confederate advance at the battle fought here.

cut off this supply. Confederate armies were often short of war materials.

The North also controlled about 70 percent of the nation's railroad tracks and trains. It was able to move troops and supplies to areas in which they were needed. The South's transportation system was less developed. Often, supplies could not be transported to the troops.

Population was another advantage for the North. The Union states had 22 million people. The Confederacy had only 9 million people, of which 3.5 to 4 million were slaves. The North's advantage is seen in these figures for army size during the war.

Year	Union	Confederacy
1862	637,000	401,000
1863	918,000	446,000
1864	860,000	481,000
1865	959,000	445,000

Union military **strategy** had four goals.
1. To capture the Confederate capital of Richmond, Virginia.
2. To blockade Southern ports.
3. To control the Mississippi and Tennessee rivers.
4. To split the Confederacy into sections, using Union armies in both east and west.

Confederate military strategy had three goals.
1. To capture Washington, D.C.
2. To advance into central Pennsylvania. This would split the North into two parts.
3. To defend the South, using the bulk of Southern troops, and to wear down the North gradually.

Early in the Civil War, the Confederacy seemed to be winning. Southern forces won the First Battle of Bull Run. They invaded Maryland. The South also kept control of most of the Mississippi River. The Union did win some victories in Tennessee and at New Orleans. And the blockade of Southern ports grew more and more successful.

By 1862, England and France were considering recognizing the Confederate government. But late that year, the Union forces stopped the Confederate advance at Antietam, Maryland. As a result, England and France decided not to recognize the Confederacy. The Union victory also encouraged President Lincoln to issue the Emancipation Proclamation in January 1863. This document freed all slaves in areas still in rebellion against the federal government.

In 1863, the turning point of the war came. Confederate General Robert E. Lee's advancing army was stopped at Gettysburg, Pennsylvania. Shortly before, Union General Ulysses S. Grant

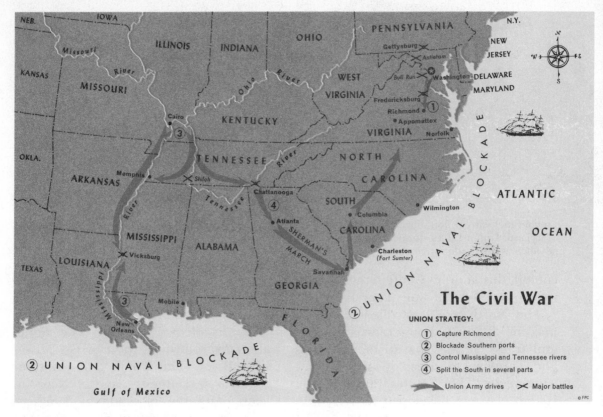

The Civil War

UNION STRATEGY:
① Capture Richmond
② Blockade Southern ports
③ Control Mississippi and Tennessee rivers
④ Split the South in several parts

⟶ Union Army drives   ✕ Major battles

© FPC

This map shows how the North defeated the South. Notice how the Union army drives achieved the goal of splitting the Confederate states into several parts.

had captured Vicksburg, Mississippi. With Vicksburg and New Orleans under the Union flag, the North controlled the Mississippi River.

In 1864, Grant was appointed commander of all Union troops. He moved toward Richmond in a series of battles. Meanwhile, General William Sherman invaded Georgia. Sherman marched his thousands of troops across the state to the ocean. The army captured Atlanta and Savannah. It also destroyed most bridges, railroads, farms, and buildings in its path.

The Confederacy was now split into several parts. Food and other supplies were hard to get. Transportation had broken down. **Morale** was very low. On April 9, 1865, General Lee surrendered his army to General Grant at Appomatox, Virginia. Within weeks, the other Confederate armies surrendered, and the war was over.

The Civil War took a great toll. More than 600,000 Union and Confederate soldiers died, and at least 375,000 were wounded. Much of the South was in ruins. There remained bitterness and anger on both sides.

AMERICANS AT WAR

Both the Confederacy and the Union were served by thousands of brave people. Some were in battle, some behind the lines. Many became famous, such as Confederate General Robert E. Lee (below) and Union General Ulysses S. Grant (bottom left). Others were less well known. Belle Boyd (top left) was a successful Confederate spy. Sarah Edmonds (left) was one of a number of women who disguised themselves as men and served in the Union army.

327

RECORDING THE CIVIL WAR

The Civil War was the first American war to be photographed. Several photographers, among them Mathew Brady, set out to record the action. However, they had problems with their relatively new equipment. For example, the camera was limited. A photograph was clear only if the subject was completely still for several minutes. Movement caused a blur. Thus, battle scenes — such as the one at top left, at Fort Wagner — were left to artists. But photographs did provide a realistic record. Opposite are the dead of the Union's "Iron Brigade." On this page are (from top): Union wounded after the Battle of the Wilderness; a Union strategy meeting (Grant, leaning over the bench, is blurred because he moved); and a Union artillery group.

COMPREHENSION CHECK

A. Recognizing the Main Idea

This selection as a whole tells you how

1. the Confederacy hoped to defend the South and gradually wear down the North.

2. Confederate forces controlled most of the transportation systems.

3. the North defeated the South in a bitter civil war.

4. the South had most of the advantages in the Civil War.

B. Selecting Important Details

Choose the ending that best completes each statement.

1. At the beginning of the war, all of the following were advantages of the North EXCEPT
   a. greater population.
   b. a balanced economy.
   c. control of most transportation.
   d. control of the Mississippi River.

2. General Robert E. Lee's army advanced into Pennsylvania in order to
   a. split the North into two parts.
   b. blockade the Southern ports.
   c. march across Georgia to the sea.
   d. capture the Confederate capital of Richmond.

3. General William Sherman's army
   a. marched across Georgia to the ocean.
   b. split the North into two parts.
   c. was careful not to destroy anyone's property.
   d. surrendered to General Grant's army in Richmond.

4. General Ulysses S. Grant
   a. was commander of all Union troops.
   b. captured Vicksburg, Mississippi.
   c. accepted the surrender of General Lee.
   d. all of the above.

C. True or False

Decide whether each of these statements is true or false.

1. England and France recognized the Confederacy.

2. President Lincoln issued the Emancipation Proclamation before the war was over.

3. The turning point of the war came when General Lee's advancing army was stopped at Gettysburg, Pennsylvania.

4. The Confederacy could always get the food and supplies it needed.

5. The Union blockade of Southern ports was not successful.

D. Vocabulary

Match the words with the definitions.

Words	Definitions
1. strategy	a. group spirit
2. morale	b. type of business
	c. plan of action
	d. study

E. Map Skills

Refer to the map on page 326. Imagine that you had been the commander of the Southern forces. What would have been your strategy to defend the South against the Northern forces?

Blacks in the Civil War

The slavery of black people was a central issue of the Civil War. Yet the North had great difficulty in deciding whether to use black men as soldiers. It was not until late in 1862 that black volunteers were finally accepted in the Union army. Even then, they had to endure prejudice. For a time, black privates were paid only seven dollars a month, while white privates were receiving thirteen dollars.

But nothing could stop a flood of black volunteers from rushing to the colors. More than 186,000 blacks served as Union soldiers, and thousands of others fought in the Union navy.

The 55th Massachusetts Volunteer Regiment was made up entirely of black soldiers. James Monroe Trotter, a sergeant major in the regiment, was a militant black man who spent his life fighting for equal rights. His son, Monroe Trotter, later followed in this same militant tradition.

On August 2, 1864, Sergeant Major Trotter wrote a letter to sixteen-year-old Francis Jackson Garrison, whose brother was one of the white officers in the regiment. Trotter had met young Francis during visits to the home of his father, William Lloyd Garrison, the famed abolitionist. In his letter, Trotter wrote the following words about some of his fellow soldiers.

I am sorry to say that Sergeant Boon, Benj. Griffin and Finlay Rickman are dead. They were foremost in the brave charge on "Fort Wright" on James Island, and they died while nobly battling for country and Freedom. Poor Sgt. Boon! Do you recollect him? He was only Corp'l when at Readville. No one's death has made me feel so sad as his. In truth I loved him. At Readville he could neither read nor write. I spoke to him of the importance of learning, telling him that I would gladly help him, and that when he could read I would recommend him for Sergt. Right manfully he took hold, and before he died he had acted orderly Sergt., and could make out all the papers and written three letters home. He went to James Island with no gun and only side arms. His arm was sore and he could not carry his rifle. But his brave spirit would not rest quiet while his comrades were gone forth to battle and therefore he sought and obtained the permission of his commander to join the expedition. He was wounded by a large grape [shot] in the leg, which was amputated, causing instant death. He was cheerful and brave to the last. In camp, on the hill-side near to where stands the cannon out of which was hurled the ball that caused his death, he is laid.

A while ago I was at the grave. We have placed a board at his head bearing this inscription:

As He died to make man holy
Let us die to make man free

Lesson 3 Politics During the Civil War

WORDS TO UNDERSTAND

Discuss the meanings of these words.

resented   centralize

habeas corpus   conscripted

NEW WORDS IN SENTENCES

1. Congress **resented** the president's use of special powers.

2. The right of *habeas corpus* means that a person cannot be imprisoned without being brought to court.

3. Southern states did not want to **centralize** the Confederacy and give power to one government.

4. Some people had volunteered, but others were **conscripted,** or drafted, into the army.

AS YOU READ

As you read this selection, try to answer these questions.

1. What were some reactions to the use of power by Abraham Lincoln and Jefferson Davis?

2. How did the Civil War affect the presidential campaign of 1864?

THE READING SELECTION

Review. When the Civil War began in 1861, the North had many advantages over the South. It controlled most of the nation's industry, rail transportation, and banking. It also had a much greater population. The North hoped to blockade the South and split it into parts. The South hoped to wear down the North gradually. At first, the South seemed to be winning. But the Northern victory at Antietam in 1862 discouraged foreign recognition of the Confederacy. It encouraged President Lincoln to issue the Emancipation Proclamation. The Union victories at Gettysburg and Vicksburg in 1863 helped turn the tide. Generals Grant and Sherman pushed into the South. In April 1865, Confederate General Lee surrendered. Within a few weeks, one of the costliest American wars was over. ☆

During the Civil War, there were changes in American political parties. There were also changes in the way in which the nation was governed.

The Civil War helped to increase the powers of the president. War often requires quick decisions on many matters. The normal process of legislation may be too slow. The president may be given temporary power to make decisions usually made by Congress. Also, the president is commander in chief of the armed forces. A president has much to say about the conduct of a war.

During the Civil War, there was criticism of President Lincoln's use of special powers. Congress often **resented** the loss of its own power. Some Americans were afraid that freedom and democracy were in danger.

One issue over which there was much debate was the right of *habeas corpus*. The right of *habeas corpus* is used to prevent unfair or illegal arrests. It is guaranteed by the Constitution. During the Civil War, some people in the North opposed the war. These Northerners were often called "Copperheads." They were accused of speaking and acting against the war. In order to prevent this unrest, President Lincoln suspended the right of *habeas corpus* in some places. Some anti-Union leaders were jailed without trials. Lincoln's action drew a great deal of criticism. Supreme Court Chief Justice Taney declared the action illegal, but Lincoln ignored him.

Confederate President Jefferson Davis also tried to cut off the right of *habeas corpus*. He was less successful than Lincoln in carrying out his decision. The Southern states had seceded from a strong federal government. When Davis tried to **centralize** Confederate authority, the states felt threatened again. When he **conscripted,** or drafted, soldiers for the army, many Southerners said he had no power to do so.

Lincoln and Davis both faced political opposition. The Republican party did not exist in the wartime South. However, there were those who opposed President Davis's policies. Both the Republican and Democratic parties continued in the North. The Democrats were weakened by being called sup-

Abraham Lincoln smiles faintly for this photo, taken late in his presidency.

porters of rebellion. However, Union military losses in the early years of the Civil War led to discontent with Lincoln. As a result, the Democrats gained support. The introduction of conscription in the North in 1863 led to riots in Northern cities, especially New York. In the congressional election of 1862, the Democrats showed real gains.

In the presidential campaign of 1864, the Democratic platform called for negotiations with the South to end the war. The Democratic candidate was General George McClellan. He was a former commander of the Union army. McClellan rejected much of the Democratic platform. However, he tried to use Northern disappointment with the war in his campaign against Lincoln.

The Republicans nominated Lincoln again. To win wider support, they chose Andrew Johnson of Tennessee, a former Democrat, for vice-president. They also adopted the name of National Union party. They hoped that this would win the support of former Democrats and other Unionists.

During the summer of 1864, Lincoln seemed to be trailing in the race. However, General Sherman's victories in Georgia in September strengthened the president's position. He won the election with 212 electoral votes to McClellan's 21 votes. Strong support by soldiers of the Union army helped Lincoln win the race.

COMPREHENSION CHECK

A. Recognizing the Main Idea

This selection as a whole tells you about

1. political opposition to Davis and Lincoln.
2. the right of *habeas corpus*.
3. the effects of the Civil War on American politics.
4. Lincoln's popularity.

B. Selecting Important Details

Choose the ending that best completes each statement.

1. President Lincoln ignored the right of *habeas corpus* because he
   a. wanted to conscript soldiers for the army.
   b. did not want to take power from Congress.
   c. was following the ruling of the chief justice of the Supreme Court.
   d. wanted to jail Copperheads without trials.

2. Confederate President Jefferson Davis did all of the following EXCEPT
   a. try to centralize Confederate authority.
   b. cut off the right of *habeas corpus*.
   c. try to establish conscription of soldiers.
   d. lead anti-war protests.

3. During the war, the Republican party
   a. was made up of people opposed to President Lincoln.
   b. did not exist in the South.
   c. did not exist in the North.
   d. was Jefferson Davis's party.

4. In the presidential election of 1864,
   a. the Republican platform called for negotiations with the South to end the war.
   b. Lincoln had the support of all Northerners.
   c. General Sherman's victories influenced the outcome.
   d. George McClellan was the Republican candidate.

C. True or False

Decide whether each of these statements is true or false.

1. Lincoln was criticized for his use of special powers during the war.

2. Copperheads were supporters of President Lincoln.

3. The Civil War increased the powers of Congress because Congress could act more quickly than the president.

4. The Democrats changed their party's name to the National Union party in the presidential election of 1864.

5. The Republican party was strong in the wartime South.

D. Vocabulary

Use a word from this list to complete each sentence.

centralize   *habeas corpus*
strategy   voluntary
resented   conscript

1. The right of _____ is guaranteed by the Constitution.

2. Southern states did not want to _____ Confederate authority.

3. The North needed to _____ soldiers to get enough people to fight the war.

4. Many people _____ the military draft.

E. Essay

Write six to eight sentences answering the following question.

In your opinion, does the government have the right to suspend such liberties as *habeas corpus*, free speech, and a free press in time of war or other emergencies? Explain your answer.

January 1, 1863: Emancipation Day in Boston

President Lincoln issued a preliminary draft of the Emancipation Proclamation on September 22, 1862. In it, he declared that all persons held as slaves in areas in rebellion would be declared free after January 1, 1863.

Because this was only a preliminary draft, it caused much concern in the North. As the date for the emancipation drew near, many Northerners began to fear that the proclamation might not be issued. On December 31, 1862, mass meetings were held by abolition societies in churches all through the North.

One such giant meeting was held in Tremont Temple, Boston. Thousands gathered there to pray together and to listen to abolition leaders denounce slavery and praise President Lincoln. Frederick Douglass, William Lloyd Garrison, and Harriet Beecher Stowe were among those present. As the midnight hour approached, the tension became almost unbearable. The people began singing freedom songs such as:

Oh freedom! Freedom over me!
Before I'd be a slave
I'd be buried in my grave
And go home to my Lord
And be free.

Just before midnight, the message was received that the Emancipation Proclamation would indeed go into effect. As the first minutes of 1863 passed, the meeting joined in a chorus by Handel.

Lesson 4   Foreign Policy During the Civil War

WORDS TO UNDERSTAND
Discuss the meanings of these words.

isolated   envoys
maintain   guerilla

NEW WORDS IN SENTENCES

1. The blockade **isolated** the South so that it had few connections with other countries.

2. Once the blockade had been set up, it was difficult to **maintain** it.

3. The **envoys** were sent by the Confederate government to discuss the war with the governments of France and Britain.

4. A **guerilla** army can defeat a well-supplied traditional army.

AS YOU READ

As you read this selection, try to answer these questions.

1. What were the European points of view about the Civil War?

2. How did the Union prevent Britain and France from helping the South?

THE READING SELECTION

The Civil War greatly affected foreign affairs, particularly those with Britain and France. Both these European nations announced that they would remain neutral during the war. British public opinion was divided on the issue of the war itself. The upper class felt that it had much in common with the large planters of the South. This class tended to support the Confederacy. But in Europe, especially in the working and middle classes, there was strong opposition to slavery. These groups favored the North, particularly after the Emancipation Proclamation was issued.

Although Britain and France were neutral, both countries could have gained from a Confederate victory. In such a case, the United States would have been split into two countries. These new nations would have been smaller and weaker than the old one. They would not have been able to enforce the Monroe Doctrine. Britain would have been able to win more influence in the Americas. The French emperor, Napoleon III, would have been able to expand his empire to include part of the Americas.

The South's hopes for victory in the Civil War rested partly on gaining the support of France and Britain. The South hoped that Britain would need Southern cotton enough to help the Confederacy. But Britain also needed wheat from the North. The North tried to strengthen this link. The Union needed to keep the South **isolated** in order to win the war.

In April 1861, President Lincoln proclaimed a blockade of Southern ports. By that July, the blockade was well under way. It proved very effective. In 1860, about 6,000 ships had reached Southern ports. In the first year of the blockade, only 800 vessels got past Northern patrols.

The North had to **maintain** the blockade without making enemies in Europe. Many European ships were being stopped. There was danger of an incident between a Union warship and a European vessel.

Such an incident led to a crisis early in the war. In 1861, a British ship, the *Trent*, was stopped by a Union warship. The Union captain seized two Confederate officials who were on their way to England. These men, James Mason and John Slidell, were to act as **envoys** of the Confederacy in Europe. They were seeking European aid for the South. The British protested the seizure. There was a threat of war with Britain. Secretary of State Seward finally had the men released, and war was avoided.

There was additional conflict between Britain and the Union over the Confederacy. British shipyards were building ships for the South. Under Confederate command, these ships attacked Northern trading vessels. Many of them, particularly the *Alabama,* seriously damaged Northern trade. Late in the war, ironclad warships were being built in Britain for the South. Lincoln's government threatened open war with Britain if those ships were sold to the Confederacy. The Brit-

ish government finally blocked the sale of the ships. Later, it paid millions of dollars to the United States for the damage done by British-built Confederate ships.

France tended to follow Britain's lead in relations with the United States during the Civil War. But one particular French action posed a new threat. During the war, French troops occupied Mexico. Napoleon III set up a puppet government. It was headed by an Austrian, Prince Maximilian. This was a violation of the Monroe Doctrine. For four years, a Mexican patriot, Benito Juárez, led a **guerilla** fight against the puppet government. The Union government could not stop France, since it could not afford to split its armies between the South and Mexico. It was not until after the Civil War that the United States turned to Mexico. In 1866, it threatened to go to war with France if French troops were not removed from Mexico. The French were faced with both this threat and the continuing struggle with Juárez. They pulled out. Maximilian was captured and put to death by the Mexicans.

The South had needed the help of Britain and France to win the Civil War. The Union had prevented such support. In 1865, the North and the South became one nation again.

COMPREHENSION CHECK

A. Recognizing the Main Idea

This selection as a whole tells you

1. how Britain and France helped the South during the Civil War.

2. how Britain and France helped the North during the Civil War.

3. about the Northern blockade of Southern ports.

4. about relations with Britain and France during the Civil War.

B. Selecting Important Details

Choose the ending that best completes each statement.

1. If the United States had split into two countries
   a. the Monroe Doctrine could have been enforced.
   b. Napoleon III might have been able to extend his empire into America.
   c. Britain would have had less influence in America.
   d. there would have been no effect on Britain and France.

2. The *Trent*
   a. was an ironclad warship.
   b. attacked Northern trading vessels.
   c. was a Confederate ship.
   d. carried two Confederate envoys.

3. After the Civil War, the United States threatened to go to war with France if
   a. France did not pay for damage done to British ships.
   b. Maximilian were killed.
   c. French troops were not removed from Mexico.
   d. all of the above.

4. When French troops occupied Mexico
   a. it was in support of the Monroe Doctrine.
   b. Benito Juárez was in charge of the French government in Mexico.
   c. Prince Maximilian led a guerilla fight.
   d. the Union could not spare troops to fight them.

C. Completion

Fill in the word or words that best complete each sentence.

1. Britain and France announced that they would remain _____ during the Civil War.

2. The working and middle classes in Britain supported the _____ in the Civil War.

3. The Confederate states hoped that Britain would help them because of Britain's need for _____.

4. After the war, Britain paid the United States for damage done by _____ Britain had built for the Confederacy.

5. The French action in Mexico was prohibited by the _____.

D. Vocabulary

Match the words with the definitions.

Words	Definitions
1. isolated	a. irregular warfare
2. maintain	b. large ape
3. envoy	c. alone
4. guerilla	d. someone representing his or her government in another country
	e. keep up

Write eight to ten sentences answering the following questions.

Imagine that you had been an envoy sent by the Confederate government to ask for aid from Britain. How would you convince the British government that it should support the South? What would you ask the British government to do for the South?

Cotton ready for shipping piles up at a Charleston, South Carolina, dock. The Northern blockade almost completely stopped shipping to and from Southern ports.

Courtesy South Carolina Historical Society, Charleston, S.C.

British Support for the North

"Cotton is king" was the slogan of the South. By this, the Southerners meant that Europe, and especially Britain, must have cotton from the South. The Confederacy hoped that Britain would break the Northern blockade to get cotton. But this never happened.

Britain did not interfere in the Civil War for many reasons. For one thing, other sources of cotton became available. For another, Northern wheat was as important to Britain as Southern cotton. Still another reason was the strong support given the North by British working people.

The workers in the British cotton mills suffered greatly because of the war. The Northern blockade kept cotton from coming into Britain. Thousands of people were forced out of work. Yet many of these workers continued to give strong support to the anti-slavery program of the North.

In 1863, when relations between Britain and the United States were very touchy, cotton workers in Manchester, England, held a huge meeting. From this meeting came a message to President Lincoln.

"If you have any ill-wishers here, be assured they are chiefly those who oppose liberty at home. . . . We urge that you complete the erasure of that foul blot upon civilization—chattel slavery."

The resolution of the people at this meeting, and at many others, was important to the North. It kept Britain from hasty action, and it encouraged the North.

Lesson 5 Political and Social Results of the Civil War

WORDS TO UNDERSTAND
Discuss the meanings of these words.

extent   excluded
supremacy   politicians

NEW WORDS IN SENTENCES
1. It was not clear what the **extent,** or range and amount, of federal power should be.
2. The federal government had **supremacy,** or the highest authority, in the country.
3. Some groups were kept out of the room and **excluded** from the meeting.
4. **Politicians** know how to use politics to get what they want.

AS YOU READ
As you read this selection, try to answer these questions.
1. What were some of the political changes that took place in the United States after the Civil War?
2. What were some of the social changes after the Civil War?

THE READING SELECTION
The Civil War, which lasted from 1861 to 1865, resulted in many political and social changes. In some ways, the United States was a changed nation after 1865.

One political result of the Civil War was the strengthening of the federal government. Ever since the debates over the Constitution in 1788, the **extent** of federal power had been in question. Some Americans had argued for an interpretation of the Constitution that would have allowed greater federal power. Others had argued for an interpretation that would have permitted less federal power. The Civil War did not settle this question completely. However, the issue of secession was settled. The **supremacy** of the federal government had been established. In addition, the powers of the president had increased during the war.

The war also brought changes in party politics. The Democratic party was weakened, while the Republican party was strengthened. The Democrats in the North had been linked to secession and had lost support. After the war, the party also lost power in the South. Thousands of former Confederate soldiers could not vote until they took loyalty oaths. Many Confederate leaders were **excluded** from politics. Others had lost the support of the voters when the war was lost. Thus, the Democrats lost both voters and leaders in the

The Confederate flag flying over Fort Sumter was a symbol of
Southern independence. The fort withstood attacks by Union
forces until the last months of the war.

South. Political control of the South was out of the hands of white Southerners.

The Republicans were very strong in the North. They had the support of most former Union army soldiers. Republicans also had the support of the former slaves in the South. To most newly freed blacks, the Republican party was the party of Lincoln. Thus, it was also the party that had given them their freedom. Most former slaves remained loyal Republicans for the rest of their lives. Their votes provided strength for the Republicans in the South.

Great social change went along with the political changes caused by the Civil War. The South in particular was greatly changed.

One important difference was that 3.5 to 4 million slaves were freed. Most had no education. Few of them had homes or possessions. There were shortages of everything in the postwar South — for whites as well as blacks. Southern governments had no money with which to help these people. In March 1865, the federal government established the Freedmen's Bureau. It provided relief for former slaves.

The whole social structure of the South was changed. It had been based on a class system. But now, the slaves, the lowest class, were free. At the same time, the destruction from the war and the end of slavery ended the old plantation system. As a result, the plantation owners were no longer the leaders in the South. The social system the South had known was destroyed.

Many white Southerners felt bitter and defeated. They felt threatened by the free blacks. New leaders began to gain support by appealing to race hatred. Laws called Black Codes were passed in nearly all the Southern states. These codes prevented blacks from voting, holding office, or working in job areas in which they competed with whites.

In the North, also, the war brought many social changes. A new class of rich people was appearing there. For the first time, the nation had a great many millionaires, people who had more than a million dollars. After the war, there was also a new wave of immigration from Europe. Hundreds of thousands of Europeans and Asians were attracted by economic opportunity and political freedom.

Movement westward was encouraged by the passage of the Homestead Act in 1862. The act offered 160 acres of government-owned land in the West to any settler who would work it for five years. Many easterners began to move west of the Mississippi River.

Public education spread throughout the North and West. It was encouraged by government aid. New reform movements began, aimed at greater economic and social equality. At the same time, the importance of the old aristocrats and reformers in politics faded. Politics became more the job of professional **politicians.**

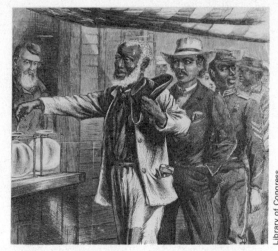

Former slaves vote for the first time. Most voted for the Republican party.

COMPREHENSION CHECK

A. Recognizing the Main Idea

This selection as a whole tells you how the Civil War

1. established the supremacy of the state governments.

2. limited the power of the president.

3. made blacks free and equal to whites under the law.

4. affected the political and social systems of the United States.

B. Selecting Important Details

Choose the ending that best completes each statement.

1. One political result of the Civil War was the

    a. acceptance of a strict interpretation of the Constitution.

    b. loss of federal power.

    c. acceptance of the right of states to secede.

    d. exclusion of Confederate leaders from politics.

2. The Republican party grew strong because it
   a. was linked with secession.
   b. made Republicans take loyalty oaths.
   c. had the votes of former slaves and Union soldiers.
   d. had the support of former Confederate soldiers.
3. In the South, all of the following were effects of the war EXCEPT
   a. destruction of the plantation system.
   b. passage of Black Codes to help former slaves.
   c. bitter feelings on the part of many white Southerners.
   d. freeing of the slaves.
4. In the North after the war,
   a. immigration from Europe and Asia stopped.
   b. the Homestead Act brought settlers to the East.
   c. there were more rich people.
   d. fewer people were getting educations.

C. True or False

Decide whether each of these statements is true or false.

1. The Democrats lost leaders and voters in the South.
2. The Freedmen's Bureau was established to help former slaves.
3. After the war, politics was taken out of the hands of professional politicians.
4. Plantation owners continued to be the leaders in the South after the war.
5. In the years following the Civil War, public education was encouraged by government aid.

D. Vocabulary

Match the words with the definitions.

Words	Definitions
1. extent	a. part of
2. supremacy	b. leave out
3. exclude	c. range and amount
4. politician	d. lawyer
	e. highest authority
	f. person in politics

E. Using Your Knowledge

You know how to find the main idea and the details in a paragraph. An outline is a list of main ideas and details. It often looks like this:

A. Main Idea
   1. Detail
   2. Detail
B. Main Idea
   1. Detail
   2. Detail

Make an outline of the sixth and seventh paragraphs of the Reading Selection. (The sixth is the paragraph that begins, One important difference was that. . . .) You should list one main idea and two details from each paragraph in the form shown above.

The Gettysburg Address

On November 19, 1863, a little over four months after the horrible Battle of Gettysburg, a large crowd assembled at the site of the battle. The people gathered to honor the soldiers who had died there and to dedicate a national cemetery. The highlights of the ceremony were to be an oration by Edward Everett and a speech by President Lincoln.

After an imposing procession and the brief opening ceremonies, Everett began his oration. He was the most famous orator of his day, and his elaborate address lasted two hours. To many present, Lincoln's brief speech—little more than two minutes long—seemed disappointing. Yet today, we recognize it as one of the greatest speeches of all time. Here are his words honoring the dead of the Battle of Gettysburg.

Four score and seven years ago our fathers brought forth on this continent, a new nation, conceived in Liberty, and dedicated to the proposition that all men are created equal.

Now we are engaged in a great civil war, testing whether that nation or any nation so conceived and so dedicated, can long endure. We are met on a great battlefield of that war. We have come to dedicate a portion of that field, as a final resting place for those who here gave their lives that that nation might live. It is altogether fitting and proper that we should do this.

But, in a larger sense, we can not dedicate—we can not consecrate—we can not hallow—this ground. The brave men, living and dead, who struggled here, have consecrated it, far above our poor power to add or detract. The world will little note, nor long remember what we say here, but it can never forget what they did here. It is for us the living, rather, to be dedicated here to the unfinished work which they who fought here have thus far so nobly advanced. It is rather for us to be here dedicated to the great task remaining before us—that from these honored dead we take increased devotion to that cause for which they gave the last full measure of devotion—that we here highly resolve that these dead shall not have died in vain—that this nation, under God, shall have a new birth of freedom—and that government of the people, by the people, for the people, shall not perish from the earth.

Lesson 6 Economic Results of the Civil War

WORDS TO UNDERSTAND

Discuss the meanings of these words.

tenant	transcontinental
sharecropping	greenbacks
cash crop	

NEW WORDS IN SENTENCES

1. The **tenant** paid the landowner for the use of the land.

2. **Sharecropping** meant that a farmer would pay for the use of land, tools, and seeds with part of the crop.

3. A **cash crop** is grown to be sold.

4. The **transcontinental** railroad crossed the American continent from coast to coast.

5. **Greenbacks** were issued by the government to increase the amount of money in circulation.

AS YOU READ

As you read this selection, try to answer these questions.

1. What effects did the end of slavery and the plantation system have on the economy of the South?

2. In what ways did the government favor industrial growth in the North after the war?

THE READING SELECTION

Review. The Civil War brought about a revolution in American politics. The authority of the federal government was established as supreme over that of the states. The right of secession disappeared as an issue in American life and politics. The Republican party emerged greatly strengthened and the Democrats were weakened as a result of the war. All of these were political results of the war.

The war also caused great social changes. It freed 3.5 to 4 million blacks. It also helped destroy the social system of the South and created bitterness and hatred. Many people in the South had nothing left and needed help. In the North, a new, wealthier class was established. At the same time, immigration increased, and more people began to move west. New reform movements called for economic and social equality. ☆

The Civil War also brought about many economic changes. Ways of making a living in the United States were changed by the war. One great revolution was the freeing of the slaves. The ex-slaves, formerly held as personal property in the South, were now free laborers. Millions of people had never been educated. They had never been allowed to hold regular jobs for wages or to live normal family lives. Now they had to find a way to earn a living and provide for their own food and shelter.

This 1865 photograph shows a burned district in Richmond, Virginia. Parts of the South were completely destroyed during the war.

The war had other effects on the economy of the South. The fighting had ruined many areas in the South. Some Southern towns and cities were destroyed. Southern women had worked to keep up farms and cities. They were able to prevent even more damage from being done. But the war had greatly damaged Southern transportation and industry. Also, the freeing of the slaves meant that Southern slaveowners lost what amounted to over 2 billion dollars in property all at once.

The wartime destruction and the end of slavery resulted in the breakup of the Southern plantation system. In its place, there arose a system of **tenant** farming and **sharecropping.** In tenant farming, the owner rented a section of land to a farmer for a regular payment of rent. In sharecrop farming, the owner gave the use of land, seed, tools, and some animals to the farmer in return for a percentage of the crop. Share-cropping became a custom because many poorer whites and newly freed blacks did not have any seed, tools, or farm animals.

Usually the landowner insisted that the farmer plant a **cash crop** for sale, rather than food crops. Often the share-cropper and tenant farmer did not even produce food for themselves. One result of this was that tenants and sharecroppers were often in debt. The cash crop did not bring in enough money to pay for food and the other things they needed. Using mainly cash crops brought another bad result. The chief cash crops in the South were cotton and tobacco. Both of these crops quickly used up the richness of the soil. In addition, some tenants and sharecroppers did not take care of the soil, since they did not own it. All this led to more damage to Southern farmlands.

The Northern economy also was greatly changed by the war. Its industries expanded, and the Republican party took further action to win the support of business and industry. Laws were passed to promote the building of a **transcontinental** railroad. By 1869, the first transcontinental railroad was finished, linking the East and West coasts.

The industrial North was aided also by the passage of high tariff laws. These high tariffs protected American industries from European competition by taxing goods entering the United States. Still more aid to American industry came with the government issue of 450 million dollars in **greenbacks**. Green-backs were paper currency with no gold or silver backing. This put more money into circulation at a key moment. The nation's economy was expanding, and more money was needed. The green-backs were cheap money. They helped some farmers and some business inter-ests. But they also caused some inflation and were opposed by many bankers.

Despite this inflation, the North was far better off than the South. Recon-structing the former Confederate states was the major job facing the nation. For many years, there were programs and policies aimed at this task.

COMPREHENSION CHECK

A. Recognizing the Main Idea
This selection as a whole tells you that

1. the war brought good times to the entire nation.

2. there were small changes in the Southern economy as a result of the war.

3. the industrial growth of the North was held back as a result of the war.

4. both the North and the South underwent great economic changes as a result of the war.

B. Selecting Important Details
Choose the ending that best com-pletes each statement.

1. The freeing of the slaves and the end of the plantation system resulted in

    a. the end of agriculture in the South.

    b. improved use of the land.

    c. the rise of tenant and sharecrop farming.

    d. the strengthening of Southern economic life.

2. The South was greatly affected by
   a. former slaves who had to find a way to make a living.
   b. destruction of land and cities during the war.
   c. cash crops that sometimes damaged farmlands.
   d. all of the above.
3. Greenbacks
   a. were backed by gold.
   b. caused inflation.
   c. were issued by bankers.
   d. hurt all farmers and business owners.
4. The Republican government
   a. helped get the transcontinental railroad built.
   b. protected Northern industries with low tariffs.
   c. opposed issuing greenbacks.
   d. lost the support of business and industry in the North.

C. True or False

Decide whether each of the following statements is true or false.

1. Sharecroppers owned the land they farmed.

2. Cotton and tobacco were the main crops grown in the North.

3. Cash crops always brought in enough money to feed the farmers and landowners.

4. High tariffs protected American industry.

5. Southern farmlands were damaged by cash crops.

D. Vocabulary

Match the words with the definitions.

Words	Definitions
1. tenant	a. crop to be sold
2. sharecropping	b. person who rents
3. transcontinental	c. using farmland in exchange for part of the crop
4. greenbacks	d. paper money not backed by gold or silver
5. cash crop	e. from one continent to another
	f. across a continent

E. Chart Work

Use both Lessons 5 and 6 to make a chart like the one below. Include the political, social, and economic results of the Civil War. List one or two results in each category for both North and South.

	North	South
political		
social		
economic		

The Thirteenth Amendment and the End of Slavery

President Lincoln saw the reuniting of the country as the main task of the Civil War. He expressed this view in a letter in 1862.

> If I could save the Union without freeing any slave, I would do it; and if I could save it by freeing all the slaves, I would do it; and if I could save it by freeing some and leaving the others alone, I would also do that.

Lincoln's feelings were not shared by all people in the North. Abolitionists saw slavery as a terrible evil that was destroying the nation.

On January 1, 1863, Lincoln issued the Emancipation Proclamation. It declared,

> All persons held as slaves within any State . . . the people whereof shall be in rebellion against the United States, shall be then, thenceforward, and forever free.

Not many slaves were immediately set free because of the proclamation. It applied only to those states that had seceded. Slaves in the Northern and border states were not given freedom. Furthermore, the seceded states were under the control of the Confederacy. Most slaves remained under the control of their owners. Many did not hear of the proclamation until much later, when Union forces entered the Confederate states.

The movement for a constitutional amendment to end slavery began in

Library of Congress

Susan B. Anthony was one of the many who fought for the Thirteenth Amendment.

1863. Among the active groups in the campaign was the Women's Loyal National League. This women's group was led by Lucy Stone, Susan B. Anthony, and Elizabeth Cady Stanton. In a little over a year, the group had 2,000 members. The women collected 400,000 names on petitions for an amendment to abolish slavery. These petitions were presented to the Senate together with petitions from other abolition groups. On February 1, 1865, the Thirteenth Amendment was proposed. In a single sentence, it abolished slavery by declaring,

> Neither slavery nor involuntary servitude, except as a punishment for crime whereof the party shall have been duly convicted, shall exist within the United States, or any place subject to their jurisdiction.

Adoption of the Thirteenth Amendment was a requirement for readmission of the seceded states into the Union after the war. The Thirteenth Amendment was ratified on December 18, 1865.

Lesson 7 Debate Over Reconstruction

WORDS TO UNDERSTAND
Discuss the meanings of these words.

lenient   eligible
assassinated guarantee

NEW WORDS IN SENTENCES
1. Lincoln took a **lenient** view rather than a strict one.
2. He was **assassinated** before he could put his plan into effect.
3. Having met the requirements, the state was **eligible** to be readmitted.
4. The state constitutions had to **guarantee** that blacks would be able to vote.

AS YOU READ
As you read this selection, try to answer these questions.
1. What were the differences between Lincoln's plan and the Radical Republican plan for reconstructing the South?
2. How did the Republican party keep political control in the South?

THE READING SELECTION
Review. The Civil War brought about economic changes in both North and South. The South was ruined. Farms, cities, industry, and transportation had been seriously damaged. The breakup of the plantation system led to tenant farming and sharecropping. Freeing the slaves had resulted in a huge unemployed work force. In the North, there had been a great growth of industry. This was aided by high tariffs and the growth of rail transportation. In addition, to make more money available, the government issued greenbacks, currency without gold or silver backing. ☆

Reconstruction, or rebuilding the South, was discussed even while the Civil War was being fought. In 1863, President Lincoln proposed a **lenient** plan for readmitting the Southern states. The plan suggested that when 10 percent of a state's voters took a loyalty oath to the Union, the state would be readmitted.

The Radical Republicans were those who wanted to punish the South. They wanted to treat it as a conquered territory and completely reorganize it. They opposed Lincoln's 10-percent plan in Congress. In 1864, they passed the Wade-Davis Bill. This required a loyalty oath from a majority of a state's voters before readmission. Lincoln used a pocket veto to kill the measure. This angered the Radicals.

In 1865, President Lincoln was **assassinated.** The new president, Andrew

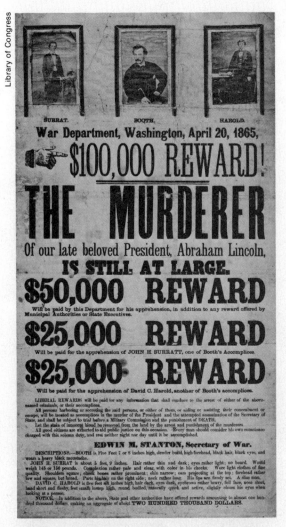

Within two weeks after the assassination, John Wilkes Booth was caught. He died from a bullet wound, but no one knew who killed him. The reward was finally split fifty-three ways.

Johnson, at first favored the Radical view. But he soon accepted Lincoln's ideas. By the end of 1865, he announced that all Southern states were **eligible** for readmission. The Radicals immediately attacked Johnson. They feared that they would lose power to the Southern Democrats. They were also angered by the fact that most Southern states had passed Black Codes. In addition, Georgia had elected a former Confederate official to the United States Senate. The Radicals felt that these actions were insults to the nation.

In 1866, the Radical Republicans gained control of Congress. They passed a series of Reconstruction Acts. These were vetoed by President Johnson but passed by Congress over his veto.

The Reconstruction Acts set two conditions for readmission of Southern states.

1. Each Southern state was to hold a constitutional convention. Elections to this convention were to be open to black as well as white voters. The convention would draw up a new state constitution. Each new constitution was to **guarantee** black men the vote.

2. Each Southern state was to ratify the Fourteenth Amendment to the Constitution before being readmitted to the Union. This amendment declared, in effect, that blacks were citizens and could not be refused the protection of the law. It also prohibited former Confederate leaders from holding office again.

Reconstruction under these acts began in 1867. The entire Confederate area was divided into five military districts. Federal troops were kept in the South until 1877 to protect blacks and to enforce federal laws. By 1870, all the Southern states had been readmitted to the Union. In nearly all, Republicans, supported by blacks, controlled state politics.

President Johnson's opposition to

Radical Reconstruction led to many disputes with the Congress. In 1868, the Radicals impeached Johnson. The House voted to impeach the president, and charges were provided for the Senate trial. Johnson was accused of breaking the Tenure of Office Law, passed by the Radicals in 1867. This law limited presidential power to remove officials. After the Senate trial, the vote fell one short of what was needed to remove Johnson from office.

The effort to remove the president shocked the nation. Had it succeeded, it would have placed even greater power in the hands of the Republican-controlled Congress. By the end of the Civil War, the control of the Republican party had shifted. It had moved into the hands of two main groups. These were the professional politicians and the new class of big business interests. The abolitionists had achieved their purpose, and most of them retired from politics. Many re-

formers gave their support to other new parties. These included the Greenback party and, later, the Populist party. Most of the Union Democrats returned to the Democratic party. This left the control of the Republican party largely in the hands of professional politicians. Their main interest was winning elections.

These politicians found that winning elections could be made easier in several ways. First, they gained the financial support of big business. Business wanted tariff support and other kinds of help from government. It contributed to the party that promised to provide this support. Second, they won the support of most former Union soldiers. Third, they gained control of the South. They did this by excluding many white voters and keeping the support of blacks. Generally, the Republican strategy was successful. Until 1876, Republicans were the leading party in most of the nation.

Radical Republicans failed in their effort to remove President Andrew Johnson (left) from office. But for a while, Johnson's impeachment trial was considered the best show in the nation. Tickets were in great demand.

COMPREHENSION CHECK

A. Recognizing the Main Idea
This selection as a whole tells you

1. why the Democratic party gained strength.

2. about the Radical Republican proposal for a lenient reconstruction plan.

3. about the politics behind the federal plans for reconstruction.

4. how Lincoln was assassinated.

B. Selecting Important Details
Choose the ending that best completes each statement.

1. President Lincoln favored
   a. the Radical Republican plan for reconstruction.
   b. a loyalty oath from 10 percent of the voters in a state before the state could be readmitted.
   c. the Wade-Davis Bill.
   d. treatment of the South as a conquered territory.

2. Andrew Johnson
   a. was assassinated.
   b. vetoed the Radical Republican plan for reconstruction.
   c. was removed from office.
   d. was supported by the Radical Republicans.

3. The Reconstruction Acts
   a. required states to ratify the Fourteenth Amendment before readmission to the Union.
   b. made states eligible for readmission if 10 percent of the voters signed a loyalty oath.
   c. did not require that blacks be guaranteed the vote.
   d. were opposed by the Radical Republicans.

4. The Republicans controlled the country by
   a. excluding black voters in the South.
   b. refusing to support big business.
   c. getting support from Union soldiers, blacks, and businesses.
   d. giving up control of state governments.

C. True or False
Decide whether each of the following statements is true or false.

1. Lincoln wanted a lenient plan for readmitting Southern states.

2. Congress passed the Reconstruction Acts over Andrew Johnson's veto.

3. Federal troops were kept in the South until 1877 to enforce federal laws.

4. All the Southern states were readmitted to the Union.

5. All of the seceded states ratified the Fourteenth Amendment.

D. Vocabulary
Match the words with the definitions.

Words	Definitions
1. lenient	a. murdered
2. assassinated	b. assurance
3. eligible	c. bent over
4. guarantee	d. meeting the requirements
	e. not harsh or strict

E. Essay
Write three or four sentences defending Lincoln's lenient plan for readmission of Southern states. Then write three or four sentences defending the two conditions for readmission set by the Reconstruction Acts.

Lesson 8 Reconstruction in the South

WORDS TO UNDERSTAND

Discuss the meanings of these words.

corruption   bribes
fraud   intimidate

NEW WORDS IN SENTENCES

1. Stealing was one form of **corruption** in government.

2. He was on trial for dishonest acts and was found guilty of **fraud.**

3. Politicians are not supposed to do favors for money and get rich by accepting **bribes.**

4. Blacks were afraid to vote when violence was used to **intimidate** them.

AS YOU READ

As you read this selection, try to answer these questions.

1. Why were white Southerners angry at the state and federal governments during Reconstruction?

2. How did Democrats begin to regain strength in the South?

THE READING SELECTION

Reconstruction of the South began in 1867 under the Radical Republican plan. By 1870, all the former Confederate states had been readmitted to the Union. But the policies and programs of Reconstruction continued until 1877.

The Thirteenth Amendment had already been ratified in 1865. It abolished slavery in the United States. To reinforce their Reconstruction plan, the Radical Republicans passed additional amendments to the Constitution.

The Fourteenth Amendment was ratified in 1868. It granted citizenship to all former slaves. It also stated that no citizen of a state could be deprived of life, liberty, or property without "due process of law." Actually, the due process clause is similar to that of the Fifth Amendment, which requires such due process for citizens of the nation.

The Fifteenth Amendment was ratified in 1870. This amendment stated that citizens could not be denied the right to vote because of race or color or because they had once been slaves.

These amendments helped give blacks political power in the South. The black vote was important to Reconstruction. Since most whites were not allowed to vote, black voters were a majority in many areas. This suited the Republicans, who could count on the black vote. For the first time, black people voted and held office. Hundreds of ex-slaves were elected to state legisla-

Charleston has been rebuilt, and it bustles with activity in this 1872 painting. At center right is an officer of the federal forces that occupied the city during Reconstruction.

tures. Some were elected to the House of Representatives and Senate of the United States. Hiram Revels, a black, was chosen senator from Mississippi. He filled the seat once held by Jefferson Davis, the former president of the Confederacy. Blanche K. Bruce also served as senator from Mississippi. Pinckney B. S. Pinchback became lieutenant governor of Louisiana.

The sight of ex-slaves voting and serving in elected offices was shocking to many white Southerners. After all, it had been only a few years since most blacks had been slaves working as field hands. Many Southerners claimed that black people were not able to understand how government worked. Southerners were also angered by the white politicians who worked with the blacks. Some were Northerners who had moved to the South. Southerners called them "carpetbaggers." Southern whites who worked with them were called "scalawags." Some Southerners argued that blacks were being misled by such white politicians.

Southerners also complained of cor-

ruption in their state governments during Reconstruction. They charged that Republican carpetbaggers and scalawags used **fraud** to win elections and became wealthy from **bribes.** Southern Democrats pointed to increased state debts in the South as proof. Much of this increased debt was a result of rebuilding Southern transportation and providing needed help for the poor. Some claims of corruption were true. Yet corruption in government was not limited to one area or party at that time. Democrats in the North were guilty also. For example, the New York City machine of Democratic boss William Tweed was known for its corruption.

Southern Democrats were determined to regain control of their states. To do this they acted to prevent blacks from voting. Secret organizations like the Ku Klux Klan were founded. These groups used violence to **intimidate** blacks and the whites who supported blacks. Some other whites used economic threats to prevent black tenant farmers and sharecroppers from voting. The Freedmen's Bureau had protected blacks. But it went out of existence in 1872. Congress had passed the Fifteenth Amendment, which guaranteed the black vote. It also passed several laws aimed at controlling white violence.

The Democrats gained strength in most Southern states. Under pressure, Congress restored the vote to most Southern whites in 1872. By 1876, only Louisiana, Florida, and South Carolina remained under Republican control.

In the presidential election of 1876, the Democratic candidate was Samuel J. Tilden. He was opposed by Republican

A cross is burned in a Ku Klux Klan ceremony. Disbanded in 1871, the Klan formed again in 1915.

Rutherford B. Hayes. Tilden won a majority of the popular vote and a possible majority of the electoral vote. However, a dispute arose over the electoral returns from the three Republican states in the South. A special commission was formed to study the issue. The eight Republicans and seven Democrats on the commission worked out a compromise. All the disputed votes went to the Republican, Hayes, making him president. In return, as the new president, Hayes withdrew federal troops from the South.

The withdrawal of these troops in 1877 marked the end of the period of Reconstruction in the South. For many years, Republicans would have little control over the South. And for many years following the end of Reconstruction, blacks in the South would not have equality.

COMPREHENSION CHECK

A. Recognizing the Main Idea
This selection as a whole tells you
1. how scalawags helped the South.
2. about the successful Reconstruction of the South.
3. about the political power struggles during Reconstruction.
4. how ex-slaves gained equality.

B. Selecting Important Details
Choose the ending that best completes each statement.
1. Blacks who voted
   a. made Republicans angry.
   b. supported the Democrats.
   c. elected William Tweed.
   d. often elected black government officials.
2. The Reconstruction plan was
   a. opposed by the Radical Republicans.
   b. reinforced by the Fourteenth and Fifteenth Amendments.
   c. ended after the former Confederate states had been readmitted to the Union.
   d. all of the above.
3. Southern Democrats gained strength when
   a. the Fifteenth Amendment was passed.
   b. whites were prevented from voting.
   c. the Freedmen's Bureau was set up.
   d. Congress restored the vote to Southern whites.

4. The dispute in the presidential election of 1876 was settled by
   a. violence.
   b. giving control of the South to the Republicans.
   c. making Hayes president in exchange for the withdrawal of federal troops from the South.
   d. making the Democratic candidate president.

C. True or False
Decide whether each of the following statements is true or false.
1. The Fifteenth Amendment abolished slavery.
2. Most Southern states remained under Republican control after Congress restored the vote to Southern whites.
3. William Tweed was the Republican boss of New York City.
4. The withdrawal of troops in 1877 marked the end of the Reconstruction period.
5. The Fifteenth Amendment gave citizenship to former slaves.

D. Vocabulary
Write your own sentence for each of these words.

corruption   bribe
fraud   intimidate

E. Ask Yourself
Why do you think there was widespread government corruption in the South after the Civil War? Think of some social, political, and economic causes of corruption that might occur in a country just defeated in a war.

Lesson 9 The Status of Blacks in the Postwar South

WORDS TO UNDERSTAND

Discuss the meanings of these words.

illiteracy   facilities

segregation   lynching

NEW WORDS IN SENTENCES

1. **Illiteracy** was a problem for ex-slaves who needed to know how to read and write in order to get jobs.

2. **Segregation** meant that blacks and whites were to be kept separate in as many ways as possible.

3. Schools, restaurants, hotels, and washrooms are all **facilities** that blacks and whites could not share.

4. **Lynching,** or the illegal hanging of a person by a mob, became more common in the South.

AS YOU READ

As you read this selection, try to answer these questions.

1. How did blacks in the South, with their new freedom, hope to solve the economic problems they faced?

2. What political problems did blacks face in the South?

THE READING SELECTION

One of the main issues during and just after Reconstruction was the status of the former slaves. Three and a half to four million slaves were now free. As slaves, they had no rights. Now, at least according to law, they had equal rights. As slaves, they had been ruled by their owners. Now, they were responsible for themselves.

Freedom did not provide ex-slaves with a way of earning a living. The work that most of them knew best was farm work. But farmers need farmland. The dream of many free blacks was "forty acres and a mule." Few had the money to buy either land or a mule to help work it. Many hoped that either the federal government or the Reconstruction state governments in the South would provide land. Some land was distributed to blacks by state governments. But most blacks were not able to own land. Many ended up as tenant farmers or sharecroppers.

It was also difficult for ex-slaves to earn a living in other ways. Jobs in industry were hard to find, since most industry had been destroyed during the war. In addition, black workers were limited by the Black Codes. These laws prohibited blacks from working at jobs in which they would compete with whites who also needed jobs. Some codes also required that blacks sign contracts that bound them to a job for a period of time.

Black politicians held many positions in the Louisiana government of 1868. As lieutenant governor, Oscar J. Dunne (center) led a fight against government corruption. Pinckney Pinchback (bottom center) later became acting governor. By 1877, Southern whites had regained their political power.

If they left before the time was up, they lost all wages.

Another problem for blacks was **illiteracy.** As slaves, they had been prohibited from learning to read and write. This was a great disadvantage when they had to earn their own living. Education became an important route to equality in the minds of many blacks. Progress was made in this area during Reconstruction. By 1877, about 600,000 blacks were enrolled in free public schools in the South. Free public schools also provided education for many young whites for the first time. Several colleges for black students had been founded. However, in the South, many white people opposed education for blacks. "Schooling ruins the Negro" was a popular idea of the day. As early as 1865, some black schools had been burned and students threatened.

Many blacks hoped that political power would also help them gain equality. The black vote was important to Republicans during Reconstruction. In addition, many blacks held state or local office, although they did not control Southern politics. However, many Republicans were interested mostly in using the black vote to win elections. When Southern whites regained control of their state governments, blacks lost most of their political power.

The end of Reconstruction brought to blacks the fear of a new kind of slavery. In 1875, Tennessee was the first state to adopt Jim Crow laws. Other Southern states followed. Jim Crow laws established legal **segregation** of blacks in the South. The laws provided for separate hotels, restaurants, washrooms, schools, and other **facilities** for blacks. They also provided that blacks be separated from whites on trains—and sometimes even on sidewalks.

Jim Crow was enforced not only by local police but also by unofficial groups like the Ku Klux Klan. **Lynching,** the illegal hanging of a person by a mob, became a common act against Southern blacks. Lynching and other forms of violence remained problems for many years.

There were black leaders who fought Jim Crow laws and other forms of inequality. Some of the early leaders had been active in the abolition movement.

Frederick Douglass. An escaped slave, he had been an abolition leader. He remained active in the black cause until he died in 1895.

Sojourner Truth. Also a former slave and abolition leader, she encouraged blacks to resettle in the West after the Civil War.

Booker T. Washington. He believed that it was most important for blacks to learn the trades. He founded Tuskegee Institute in Alabama, which provided practical education.

Tuskegee Institute

Booker T. Washington was an influential leader and educator. He sought improvements for blacks without radical changes in society.

W. E. B. DuBois. A more radical leader, he criticized Booker T. Washington for seeming to accept segregation and inequality in the South. He felt that full equality was the main goal. He helped found the National Association for the Advancement of Colored People (NAACP) in 1910.

Ida B. Wells-Barnett. Through her newspaper and her other writing, she campaigned against lynching from the 1890s on. She was forced to move to the North, where she worked with DuBois for many years.

COMPREHENSION CHECK

A. Recognizing the Main Idea

This selection as a whole tells you that

1. blacks faced economic and political problems in the postwar South.

2. Jim Crow laws were made to help ex-slaves in the postwar South.

3. blacks controlled Southern politics after the Civil War.

4. blacks could not hold state or local offices after the Civil War.

B. Selecting Important Details

Choose the ending that best completes each statement.

1. Earning a living was hard for ex-slaves because most of them
   a. could get only forty acres and a mule.
   b. were literate.
   c. owned their own land.
   d. could not take jobs that whites wanted.

2. The black vote
   a. was supported by the Ku Klux Klan.
   b. was not important to the Republicans.
   c. gave blacks some political power for a while.
   d. gave Southern Democrats more power.

3. Jim Crow laws
   a. were supported by Booker T. Washington.
   b. established segregation.
   c. made lynching illegal.
   d. were passed by the National Association for the Advancement of Colored People.

4. Segregation meant
   a. resettling in the West.
   b. the end of violence.
   c. moving to the North.
   d. separate facilities for blacks and whites.

C. Fact or Opinion

Decide whether each of these statements is fact or opinion.

1. The government should have given former slaves forty acres and a mule.

2. Slaves had been prohibited from learning to read and write.

3. Jim Crow laws established legal segregation.

4. It is absolutely necessary that blacks and whites be separated.

5. Former slaves should not have owned land.

D. Vocabulary

Match the words with the definitions.

Words	Definitions
1. illiteracy	a. court of law
2. segregation	b. illegal hanging by a mob
3. facility	c. separation
4. lynching	d. a disease
	e. something built or established for a particular use
	f. inability to read or write

E. Ask Yourself

If you had been an ex-slave in the postwar South, you might have found yourself working as a tenant farmer or sharecropper. What differences would owning your own land have made in your life?

A Black Northern Schoolteacher in the South

James Forten was a free black who served in the American navy during the Revolution. Later, his inventions brought him a fortune of $100,000. The Fortens were well-to-do New Englanders who were deeply involved in the fight against slavery. James Forten's granddaughter Charlotte continued the tradition of the family fight for the freedom and equality of blacks.

In the 1860s, Charlotte L. Forten volunteered to teach in ex-slaves' schools in the South. Such schools had been set up in 1862 in areas of South Carolina where the Union army had taken control. Here are some portions from the journal, or diary, kept by the twenty-six-year-old black Northern teacher:

Had my first regular teaching experience, and to you and you only friend beloved, will I acknowledge that it was *not* a very pleasant one. Part of my scholars are very tiny—babies, I call them— and it is hard to keep them quiet and interested while I am hearing the larger ones. . . .

Talked to the children a little while to-day about the noble Toussaint [L'Ouverture]. They listened very attentively. It is well that they should know what one of their own color could do for his race. . . .

To-night gave Cupid a lesson in the alphabet. He is not a brilliant scholar, but he tries hard to learn, and so I am sure he will succeed in time. A man from another plantation came in for a lesson. L[izzie] attended to him while I had Cupid. He knows his letters, and seems very bright. . . .

This morning a large number— superintendents, teachers and freed people—assembled in the little Baptist church. It was a sight that I shall not soon forget—that crowd of eager, happy black faces from which the shadow of slavery had forever passed. "Forever free! Forever free!" Those magical words were all the time singing themselves in my soul. . . .

In B[eaufort] we spent nearly all our time at Harriet Tubman's— otherwise "Moses." She is a wonderful woman—a real heroine. Has helped off a large number of slaves, after taking her own freedom. . . .

Courtesy Prints and Photographic Collection, Moorland-Spingarn Research Center, Howard University

Lesson 10   What Did Reconstruction Accomplish?

WORDS TO UNDERSTAND

Discuss the meanings of these words.

oppressed   **racism**   **reapportioned**

NEW WORDS IN SENTENCES

1. White Southerners felt that the federal government **oppressed** them by using its power to destroy their way of life.

2. Some leaders gained power by promoting **racism,** or the belief that one race is better than another.

3. Voting districts are **reapportioned** so that representation in government matches the populations of various areas.

AS YOU READ

As you read this selection, try to answer these questions.

1. What were the negative sides of Reconstruction?

2. What were the achievements of Reconstruction?

THE READING SELECTION

The value of Reconstruction is still hotly debated today. Many people see the entire period as a series of bad mistakes. Others feel that Reconstruction did accomplish much. They argue that the negative side has received too much attention.

There is no doubt that Reconstruction was affected by the problem of race relations. Efforts to grant citizenship to blacks after the Civil War were resented by many white Southerners and some Northerners. These people were not ready to accept former slaves as equal citizens. Prejudice affected the work of Reconstruction. It has also affected our understanding of the period.

Reconstruction had both positive and negative sides. The negative included a number of problems.

1. The effort of the Radical Republicans to impeach President Johnson was a serious error. In attacking Johnson, the Radicals hurt the image of the office of chief executive. Their constant attacks on that branch of government also threatened the balance of power.

2. Reconstruction angered the South. Many Southerners felt that they were being **oppressed** by the North. Distrust and hatred of the North remained a factor in Southern life for many years.

3. Southern whites came to distrust and fear black voters. Many Southerners felt that blacks were inferior and had re-

sented giving them the vote to begin with. During Reconstruction, many whites felt that the black vote kept the Republicans in power.

4. There was a great deal of corruption in state governments. Taxes rose and state debts increased. Some Reconstruction politicians in the South were honest reformers, but many were not.

5. Fear, hatred, and unsettled conditions in the South led to the rise of corrupt and prejudiced leaders. Many of them relied on race hatred to win. They kept blacks from voting and used **racism** to gain white support.

6. The two-party system in the South was weakened. Southerners turned away from the Republican party. Once the Democrats regained control of Southern governments, they kept it. For many years after 1876, the Democratic party could count on the "solid South."

Despite all this, there were positive sides to Reconstruction. It did produce some improvements.

1. During Reconstruction, the legal basis for black citizenship was established. The Fourteenth and Fifteenth Amendments were passed. For a time, blacks did vote and hold office. The amendments are a legal basis that is still used today in actions to end inequality.

2. New state governments were set up in the South. These governments were based on new state constitutions. Many of these constitutions were modeled on more liberal Northern ones. As a result, certain reforms came to Southern life. For example, local officials were elected, rather than appointed. Representation was **reapportioned** more equally. Areas with greater populations gained representation. Public education was provided for.

3. The record of black officials elected during Reconstruction speaks highly for democracy. Most were honest and hard-working.

4. The railroad system of the South was greatly expanded. Republican state governments gave liberal aid to railroad companies in the South. Sometimes, this led to corruption. But it also helped rebuild a transportation system that had been ruined by the Civil War.

In his second inaugural speech, in March 1865, President Lincoln had said, "Let us strive on to . . . bind up the nation's wounds . . . to do all which may achieve and cherish a just and lasting peace." Reconstruction did not accomplish Lincoln's grand goal. As a program to rebuild the South, or as a program to help the newly freed slaves, it had many weaknesses. In some ways, it failed completely. But in other ways, Reconstruction did succeed.

COMPREHENSION CHECK

A. Recognizing the Main Idea

This selection as a whole tells you that

1. Reconstruction was clearly just a series of bad mistakes.

2. Reconstruction had a negative side as well as a positive one.

3. there were no honest politicians in the South.

4. Reconstruction ended racism.

B. Selecting Important Details

Choose the ending that best completes each statement.

1. Reconstruction was not successful in some ways because
   a. representation in state governments was reapportioned.
   b. most black officials elected during Reconstruction were corrupt.
   c. the Southern railroad system was not rebuilt.
   d. it caused more bad feelings in the South against blacks and Northerners.

2. The effort to impeach President Johnson
   a. gave the chief executive more power.
   b. was made by the "solid South."
   c. was a positive part of Reconstruction.
   d. hurt the image of the presidency.

3. The Fourteenth and Fifteenth Amendments
   a. gave legal basis to black equality.
   b. could not be passed during Reconstruction.
   c. are not important today.
   d. gave women the right to vote.

4. Reconstruction was successful in
   a. stopping corruption.
   b. bringing some reforms to Southern life.
   c. soothing feelings in the South.
   d. ending racism.

C. True or False

Decide whether each of the following statements is true or false. Rewrite the false ones so that they are true.

1. It is clear that Reconstruction was a complete failure.

2. Southern Democrats resented the black vote because it helped keep Republicans in power.

3. Democrats never regained control of Southern governments.

4. Blacks never held office.

5. Some reforms in Southern governments were made during Reconstruction.

D. Vocabulary

Match the words with the definitions.

Words	Definitions
1. oppress	a. redivide representation
2. racism	b. belief in the equality of the races
3. reapportion	c. use power against
	d. remember
	e. belief that one race is better than another

E. Chronology

Arrange these events in the order in which they happened.

1. Firing on Fort Sumter
2. Election of President Lincoln
3. Surrender of General Lee
4. The Emancipation Proclamation
5. Withdrawal of federal troops from the South
6. Passage of Reconstruction Acts

Ida B. Wells-Barnett Fights for Black People

The purpose of Jim Crow laws was expressed by a Southern professor of the time, who summed it up in these points:

The white race must dominate.
This is a white man's country.
There must be no social or
political equality.
Only Southerners understand the
Negro question.
The Negro must be educated to
serve the needs of whites.

Chicago Historical Society

One of the leaders in the fight against Jim Crow was Ida B. Wells-Barnett. She was born a slave in Mississippi in 1862. She attended college and taught in a one-room school before moving to Memphis, Tennessee, at the age of twenty-one. One of her early attacks on Jim Crow laws occurred while traveling on a railroad. She refused to sit in one of the seats reserved for black passengers and had to be moved by force. Ida Wells-Barnett sued the railroad and won her case in a lower court. But the decision was changed in favor of the railroad by Tennessee's supreme court in 1887.

Ida Wells-Barnett lost her job as a teacher in Memphis because of articles she wrote criticizing the schools available for black children. She became editor of a Memphis newspaper called *Free Speech*. In 1892, three of her friends were lynched. Black men in the South were often lynched by people accusing

them of offending white women. Wells-Barnett wrote an article in the *Free Speech* saying that the men were lynched because white storekeepers did not like their competition in business. She began to look into other lynchings and write about them in the newspaper.

Her strong attacks on lynching and Jim Crow won her the praise of other black editors. But she often carried a gun to protect herself from people who were angered by her articles. In 1892, the offices of the newspaper were destroyed, and Wells-Barnett was forced to leave Memphis.

Ida Wells-Barnett moved to New York and worked for a newspaper called the *New York Age*. She continued to write, lecture, and organize groups against lynching and Jim Crow. In 1898, Wells-Barnett was part of a group that went to the White House to protest against a lynching. She also worked in the women's movement and founded the first women's suffrage organization for black women.

Unit 7 Summary   A House Divided: Civil War and Reconstruction

The Civil War

The Civil War had many causes. Economically, the North and the South had developed differently. Therefore, they had different needs. Politically, they disagreed on the interpretation of the Constitution and on the nature of the federal Union. The important issue of slavery did not lend itself to compromise, and it helped bring on the war. By the time President Abraham Lincoln took office in March of 1861, the Confederate States of America had already been formed. In April, South Carolina troops fired on the federal forces in Fort Sumter. This began the war.

The North had many advantages over the South. It controlled most of the nation's industry, rail transportation, and banking. It also had a much greater population. The North hoped to blockade the South and split it into parts. The South hoped to wear down the North gradually. At first, the South seemed to be winning. But the Northern victory at Antietam in 1862 discouraged foreign recognition of the Confederacy. It encouraged President Lincoln to issue the Emancipation Proclamation. The 1863 Union victories at Gettysburg and Vicksburg helped turn the tide. Generals Grant and Sherman pushed into the South. In April 1865, Confederate General Lee surrendered. Within a few weeks, one of the costliest American wars was over.

Results of the Civil War

The Civil War brought about a revolution in American politics. The authority of the federal government was established as supreme over that of the states. The right of secession disappeared as an issue in American life and politics. The Republican party was greatly strengthened and the Democrats were weakened after the war.

The war also caused great social

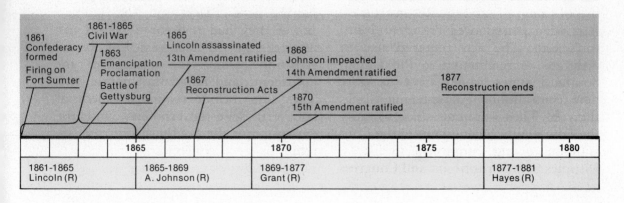

1861 Confederacy formed

Firing on Fort Sumter

1861-1865 Civil War

1863 Emancipation Proclamation

Battle of Gettysburg

1865 Lincoln assassinated
13th Amendment ratified

1867 Reconstruction Acts

1868 Johnson impeached
14th Amendment ratified

1870 15th Amendment ratified

1877 Reconstruction ends

1865   1870   1875   1880

1861-1865 Lincoln (R)   1865-1869 A. Johnson (R)   1869-1877 Grant (R)   1877-1881 Hayes (R)

changes. It freed 3.5 to 4 million black slaves. It helped destroy the social system of the South and created bitterness and hatred. Many people in the South had nothing left and needed help. In the North, a new, wealthier class was established. At the same time, immigration increased, and more people began to move west. New reform movements called for economic and social equality.

There were economic changes both in the North and the South after the Civil War. Farms, cities, industry, and transportation in the South had been seriously damaged. The breakup of the plantation system led to tenant farming and sharecropping. Freeing the slaves meant that there was a huge unemployed work force. In the North, there had been a great growth of industry. This was aided by high tariffs and the growth of rail transportation. In addition, the government issued greenbacks to make more money available.

Reconstruction

President Lincoln was assassinated before he could put into effect his lenient plan for reconstruction in the South. Radical Republicans gained control of Congress, and the Reconstruction Acts were passed over President Johnson's veto. The acts required that in order to be readmitted to the Union, Southern states would have to write new constitutions guaranteeing blacks the vote. They would also have to ratify the Fourteenth Amendment to the Constitution, giving citizenship to blacks. Disputes between Johnson and Congress led to an unsuccessful attempt to remove Johnson from office.

Southerners blamed the debts and corruption in their state governments on carpetbaggers, scalawags, and blacks. They were angered at seeing ex-slaves voting and holding offices. Republicans had political control. They counted on the black vote. Many Southern whites were not allowed to vote. The Democrats regained strength when Congress restored the vote to whites in 1872. The dispute in the presidential election between Samuel J. Tilden and Rutherford B. Hayes was settled when Hayes was given the presidency in exchange for removal of federal troops from the South. The Democrats regained control of the South, and the period of Reconstruction was over.

Blacks in the postwar South faced many social and economic problems. The Black Codes limited their rights, and organizations such as the Ku Klux Klan used violence to intimidate them. Illiteracy, exclusion from many jobs, and the lack of land made it difficult for ex-slaves to earn a living. Jim Crow laws established strict segregation.

Reconstruction failed in that it increased Southern hatred of blacks and Northerners. Blacks lost the political power they had had for a period just after the war. The successes of Reconstruction include the passage of the Fourteenth and Fifteenth Amendments. They also include reapportionment of Southern state governments and the expansion of the Southern railroad system.

PART 3 Change and Challenge: Domestic Affairs, 1865 to the Present

unit
8

Martha Jane (''Calamity Jane'') Canary at Wild Bill Hickok's Grave, 1903, Library of Congress

California Crossing by W. H. Jackson, Thomas Gilcrease Institute of American History and Art, Tulsa, Okla.

A Changing Land and People

It was adventure, new beginning, new hope. It was the frontier.
The westward movement, begun even before the Revolutionary
War, peaked after the Civil War. "Settling the West" was a
romantic ideal and a gritty, hard life. There was often a
common purpose. But there was also frequent conflict.
Railroading, ranching, mining, homesteading—all played a role.
But in the end, the story of the West was its people: from the
huge groups in wagon trains plodding through Indian lands
(above) to bigger-than-life individuals like Calamity Jane (left).

Lesson 1 The Westward Movement

WORDS TO UNDERSTAND

Discuss the meanings of these words.

romantic opportunities

NEW WORDS IN SENTENCES

1. Heroes, adventures, and a special kind of freedom are all parts of the **romantic** image of the West.

2. People moving west were looking for new **opportunities** to make better lives for themselves.

AS YOU READ

As you read this selection, try to answer these questions.

1. What were some of the reasons people moved west?

2. Why were some parts of the West settled before other parts?

THE READING SELECTION

Over the years, Americans have had a very **romantic** image of the West. Did the West in fact make the United States different from other countries? Did it make Americans different from other people? Until 1890, there was always new land lying just beyond the mountains or river. There was a place to begin again. There was a place to strike it rich. For many years, Americans were moving west. They seemed to be more restless and adventurous than other people. They seemed to want more and more progress.

In 1851, an Indiana newspaper writer advised his readers: "Go west, young man." The same advice was given later by Horace Greeley. Americans hardly needed this advice. Young and old, men and women, immigrant and native-born had moved westward. At first, they moved beyond the Appalachian Mountains to the Mississippi River. Later, they began to move west of the Mississippi.

People moved west for many reasons. Many of them went for economic reasons. Some wanted newer, more fertile land. And land in the West could be had easily. Others hoped to strike it rich with gold, silver, furs, or timber. All of these seemed to be in great supply in the West. Other people wanted to find adventure or get a fresh start. The West seemed to offer many **opportunities.** For example, in the period after

In covered wagons, over rough land, people endured the hardships of travel to go west.

mained. They turned to other ways to make a living. Others moved to other parts of the West.

The expansion of the railroad. Transportation brought new people to the West. This helped to tie the new areas to the East. Better transportation helped provide eastern markets for western products, like cattle. In addition, railroads sold a great deal of land to farmers and ranchers. Settlements grew up at railroad and trading centers.

The cattle boom. Cattle ranching had long existed in the Mexican parts of the West. But the growing market for beef brought many new ranchers west. Settlements grew up in ranching areas and in places where cattle were bought and sold.

The development of farm equipment. Improved machinery and equipment helped to make farming in the West possible. Settlements grew in farming areas.

From 1840 to 1870, easterners were moving into the areas just west of the Mississippi River and those around the Great Lakes. But the area west of that, the Plains, lacked water and timber. The new settlers did not continue into that area.

Instead, the discovery of gold in California in 1848 brought them to the Pacific Coast area. By 1870, many other deposits of precious metals had been found along the coast and in Idaho, Colorado, and Nevada. People "skipped over" the Plains and went further west to the mines. So population during this period was growing both in the Far West and in the area near the Mississippi River.

the Civil War, many former slaves left the South. They wanted to own their own land instead of sharecrop. The destruction of the South's economic and social systems also brought many white southerners west. The end of the Civil War brought more European and Asian immigrants, who moved out to settle in the new lands.

The maps in this lesson will help you see the general movement of population westward from 1860 to 1900. You can see that the West was not settled state by state, from east to west. Certain parts of the region were settled more rapidly than others. The growth of areas was linked to several things.

The discovery of gold or silver. Many settlements in the West grew out of early mining communities. When the mines were active, these towns were filled with miners and many others who hoped to get rich quickly. Even after the mines were played out, people sometimes re-

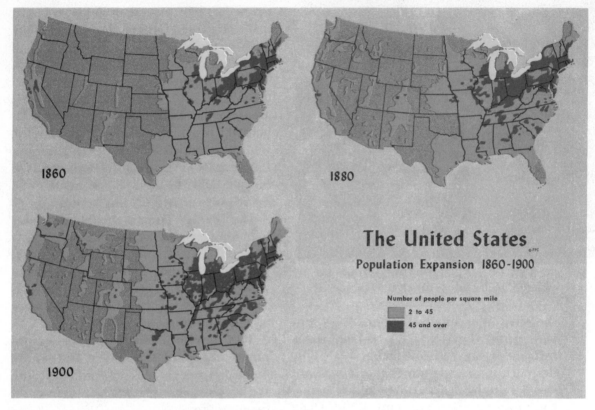

The United States

Population Expansion 1860-1900

1860

1880

1900

Number of people per square mile

■ 2 to 45

■ 45 and over

Western population grew around mining and farming centers. For example, gold was found in southwestern South Dakota in 1874. Compare this area's 1860 and 1880 populations.

The area in between began to fill between 1870 and 1900. People had found ways to deal with the disadvantages of the Plains. Cattle ranches were established in the southern and central areas. Farms producing corn, wheat, and other crops were set up in the central and northern areas.

One important factor in the settling of the Plains was the low cost of the land. The Homestead Act of 1862 offered land at low prices to settlers. There were problems with this law, but between 1862 and 1900, farmers did use it to buy 80 million acres. Five to six times that amount was also sold by the railroads, land companies, and the states. The amount of land held by American farmers doubled between 1860 and 1900.

The story of the westward movement involved several different areas and many different groups of people. It often meant a great change in the lands and great changes for the people who lived there already.

COMPREHENSION CHECK

A. Recognizing the Main Idea
This selection as a whole tells you
1. about the Indians of the West.
2. why people wanted land.
3. how the West was settled.
4. how railroads helped the western settlers.

B. Selecting Important Details
Choose the ending that best completes each statement.
1. The westward movement was helped by all of the following EXCEPT the
   a. Homestead Act.
   b. discovery of gold and silver.
   c. cattle boom.
   d. lack of transportation.
2. The Plains
   a. was the first area to be settled.
   b. had low-cost land available.
   c. grew in population because gold was discovered.
   d. had lots of water and timber.
3. The railroad
   a. could not carry cattle.
   b. could not sell land to farmers.
   c. took western products to eastern markets.
   d. made farming in the Plains impossible.
4. The discovery of gold in California
   a. increased population in the Far West.
   b. brought only a few miners to the Pacific Coast region.
   c. stopped the building of the railroad.
   d. made Americans want to stop moving west.

C. True or False
Decide whether each of the following statements is true or false.
1. The people who moved west were all young men.
2. Improved farm equipment made farming in the West possible.
3. Farmers lost most of their land by 1900.
4. There were few opportunities in the West.
5. The Homestead Act encouraged settlers in the West.

D. Vocabulary
Match the words with the definitions.

Words	Definitions
1. romantic	a. chance
2. opportunity	b. failure
	c. money
	d. adventurous; daring

E. Map Skills
Use the maps in this lesson to answer these questions.
1. In 1860, did most of the West have a large or small population? What changes in population occurred by 1900? How does this prove that the West was being settled?
2. Did the area populated by more than 45 people per square mile increase or decrease between 1860 and 1900? What conclusions could you draw from this about the number and size of cities?

Three Views of the Frontier

An American historian, Frederick Jackson Turner, described the closing of the frontier in these words:

> And now, four centuries from the discovery of America, at the end of a hundred years of life under the Constitution, the frontier has gone, and with its going has closed the first period of American history.

An American writer, John Steinbeck, in his book *The Red Pony,* describes the frontier in the words of an old man who had been a pioneer.

> It wasn't the Indians that were important, nor adventures, nor even getting out here. It was a whole bunch of people made into one big crawling beast. . . . It was westering and westering. . . . When we saw the mountains at last, we cried—all of us. . . . We carried life out here and set it down the way those ants carry eggs. . . . Then we came to the sea, and it was done. . . .There's a line of old men along the shore hating the ocean because it stopped them. . . . But that's not the worst. Westering has died out of the people. Westering isn't a hunger any more. It's all done.

An American poet, Archibald MacLeish, summed up his idea of the frontier in a single sentence.

> West is a country in the mind, and so eternal.

These are three ways in which people have seen the frontier. What are your ideas on the subject?

Excerpt from THE RED PONY by John Steinbeck, copyright 1933, 1937, 1939, 1961, 1965 by John Steinbeck. Reprinted by permission of The Viking Press.

Lesson 2   The Pacific Coast Region

WORDS TO UNDERSTAND
Discuss the meanings of these words.

inhabitants   **tolerance**   **menial**

NEW WORDS IN SENTENCES

1. The **inhabitants** of the area did not want other people to live near them.

2. Without **tolerance** for differences, various kinds of people cannot live together.

3. After he lost interest in the project, the work seemed **menial.**

AS YOU READ

As you read this selection, try to answer these questions.

1. What reasons brought people to the Pacific Coast region?

2. How did the railroad affect the Pacific Coast area?

3. What were relations like among the various peoples who inhabited this region?

THE READING SELECTION

American territory in the Pacific Coast region became the states of California, Oregon, and Washington. The climates and resources of the region are varied. The original Native-American cultures also varied greatly. And the areas developed at different times. But in all of them, gold or other natural riches were responsible for population booms.

California, the first area to begin to grow, was originally part of Spanish Mexico. Spanish priests established missions along the coast. At the missions, priests tried to convert the local Indians to European religion and ways of life. Cities such as Los Angeles, San Francisco, and San Diego all began as Spanish missions. The priests were followed by Mexican landowners, who established huge cattle ranches. But California was isolated from Mexico, and settlement remained limited.

In the treaty ending the war between Mexico and the United States in 1848, California was ceded to the U.S. In that same year, gold was discovered in the Sacramento Valley. Thousands of people poured into California to find riches. The gold rush included whites and blacks from the East, immigrants from Europe, and Mexicans. It also brought large numbers of Chinese to America for the first time.

The new arrivals from the East often came overland, by the California and

Oregon Trails. Others sailed around South America. The more adventurous sailed to Panama and then traveled overland to the Pacific to take another ship.

In later years, many disappointed gold seekers left California. But others stayed or moved further north to continue hunting gold. Old Spanish mission settlements, such as San Francisco, grew into booming cities during the gold rush. By the time of statehood, in 1850, California had 92,000 **inhabitants.**

Gold was also discovered in Oregon and Washington. But the resource that first brought outsiders to the area was furs. Later on, timber became very important. Early in the 1800s, both British and Americans established fur companies in the Oregon Territory—which included both Oregon and Washington. In the 1840s, more and more settlers arrived in long wagon trains along the Oregon Trail. From the 1850s to the 1870s, several gold strikes brought more people.

The new territory of Washington was really opened up in the 1880s by the railroad. It was, in fact, the railroads that opened the entire Pacific Coast region to large-scale growth. The first transcontinental railroad was completed in 1869. Three more transcontinental lines were completed by 1883. These linked the Northwest Coast and California with the East.

Rail transportation made the Pacific Coast area a part of American economic life. Timber, fruit, fish, and other products could be shipped eastward. Eastern manufactured products could be moved by railroad to the West. People traveling westward could do so with greater safety, comfort, and speed than before. In addition, the cities to which the trains traveled became commercial centers. Portland, San Francisco, Sacramento, Los Angeles, and San Diego grew in size. They attracted thousands of inhabitants.

Relations among the various groups of people in the region became tense. The new settlers had gained control of the states, and there was little **tolerance** for Indians, Mexican-Americans, or Chinese. Tribes like the Modoc and Nez Percé were forced off their lands onto reservations. The Mexican landowners in California lost much of their property to squatters. They had little political power in their areas. California schools were even forbidden to teach in Spanish.

The Chinese were looked upon as cheap labor. They were kept in **menial** jobs at low wages. Yet even this worried the American labor movement. It claimed jobs were being taken from Americans. Pressure finally resulted in the Chinese Exclusion Act of 1882, which barred immigration from China. Violence against the Chinese continued. For example, in 1886, the Chinatown in Tacoma, Washington, was burned to the ground. The Japanese, who began arriving in large numbers in the 1890s, also received unfair treatment. They were prohibited by law from owning land. There was an effort to segregate them in public schools in California.

Yet Mexicans and Asians, along with European immigrants and other Americans, were responsible for developing the Pacific Coast area and other areas in the United States.

San Francisco was not prepared for the thousands of people who came to the city during the gold rush. Above, people and animals sink in mud as they try to walk on a San Francisco street after a rain. At left, gold seekers work hard to get riches out of a California mountain stream. Some people went home broke, but others stayed to start businesses or farms.

COMPREHENSION CHECK

A. Recognizing the Main Idea

This selection as a whole tells you that the Pacific Coast area

1. never attracted many people.
2. was easy to get to.
3. was settled by various groups of people seeking economic opportunity.
4. never developed much farming.

B. Selecting Important Details

Choose the ending that best completes each statement.

1. California
   a. attracted mostly fur traders.
   b. was part of Mexico until 1848.
   c. had no gold.
   d. was inhabited by Indians trying to convert the Spanish missionaries.
2. The Oregon Trail
   a. crossed Panama.
   b. opened the Pacific Coast region to large-scale growth.
   c. made the shipping of products to the East easy.
   d. was traveled by settlers in wagon trains.
3. The population of the Pacific Coast area
   a. included Mexicans, Indians, Asians, and black as well as white people.
   b. grew slowly between 1840 and 1890.
   c. was not affected by the railroad.
   d. was not affected by discoveries of gold.

4. Chinese immigrants
   a. took high-paying jobs from white settlers.
   b. lost their land to Mexicans.
   c. were forced to live on reservations.
   d. were excluded by the Chinese Exclusion Act.

C. Fact or Opinion

Decide whether each of these statements is fact or opinion.

1. Spanish priests established missions in California.
2. There should have been more laws like the Chinese Exclusion Act.
3. Gold was discovered in California.
4. Furs and timber were important resources in Oregon and Washington.
5. The European way of life was better than the way of life of most California Indians.

D. Vocabulary

Write your own sentence for each of these words.

inhabitant   tolerance   menial

E. Essay

Write six to eight sentences answering the following questions.

Imagine that you are an easterner in the 1800s. You are trying to talk a friend into going to California with you. You have just heard that gold has been discovered. What might be your friend's reasons for not wanting to go? How would you try to change his or her mind?

The New Americans from China

The first large numbers of Chinese immigrants arrived in the United States in 1850 and 1851. News of the California gold strikes had spread to China. This was welcome news, since life in China was difficult at that time. Floods, drought, and crop failures had brought starvation to many areas of the country. In addition, European nations were forcing the Chinese rulers to give them special rights in China. The Chinese government seemed unable to deal with all these problems.

Thousands of Chinese scraped together the money for the voyage to California. Some contracted to work in America in return for the passage. Most of the immigrants were young men; women were generally prevented from going. Some of the immigrants hoped to earn or find enough gold to bring their families to join them later on. Others planned to return to China with their new riches.

But the California gold fields made few people, including the Chinese, rich. Many of them ended up only working as laborers in other people's mines. When the gold was played out, the Chinese and other workers moved

Chinese immigrants in San Francisco celebrate with music and firecrackers on their way to a festival.

elsewhere. There was a large Chinese community in San Francisco, the main port of entry from Asia. Many miners moved back to either China or San Francisco. Others worked on farms in central California. Still others worked in factories and shops or in the fishing industry.

Many Chinese found work building the western part of the transcontinental railroad. The Central Pacific Railroad was to build a line eastward from Sacramento. It would join the Union Pacific's line somewhere in what is now Utah. The Central Pacific organized thousands of Chinese into work gangs. These gangs were divided into small groups for the backbreaking work over the mountains. Each group's cook prepared Chinese food for the workers. This included fish, poultry, rice, vegetables, and tea. But the Chinese paid a price for their special foods. They received thirty to thirty-five dollars a month in gold. But, unlike other workers, they had to pay for their food.

There was much prejudice against the Chinese and other Asians. For example, in 1872, California took away their right to own land. In 1882, immigration from China was completely cut off. These and other laws remained in effect for many years. Most Chinese were looked upon as cheap labor and were hated and feared by many whites.

Courtesy New York Historical Society

Two Chinese immigrants are among the mixed group at a San Francisco saloon. Mexicans, Easterners, and Europeans also crowded into the booming city.

Why? Partly because negative reports sent back from China influenced Americans before the Chinese even arrived. Partly because they and other Asians seemed even more foreign than European immigrants—and there was prejudice even against Europeans. Yet in the large cities, where most Chinese settled, their culture has become part of city life. They have always retained a pride in their own way of life. By now, it has come to be respected by other Americans as well.

Lesson 3 The Southwest and the Rocky Mountain Regions

WORDS TO UNDERSTAND

Discuss the meanings of these words.

relatively   refrigerated

vaqueros   persecution

NEW WORDS IN SENTENCES

1. Compared with the population of New Mexico, there were **relatively** few settlers in Arizona.

2. *Vaqueros* is the Spanish word for "cowboys."

3. Without **refrigerated** cars on trains, food could not be kept cool enough to ship.

4. A group will sometimes look for a new place to live to escape **persecution** and bad treatment from other groups.

AS YOU READ

As you read this selection, try to answer these questions.

1. What was the importance of cattle to the development of the Southwest?

2. What finally led to the development of the Rocky Mountain region?

THE READING SELECTION

The Southwest area grew into the states of Arizona, New Mexico, Oklahoma, and Texas. The Rocky Mountain region was divided into the states of Colorado, Idaho, Montana, Nevada, Utah, and Wyoming. We often think of these two areas together as part of the "wild West." But the Southwest and the Rockies developed very differently from each other.

The Southwest and the southern tip of the Rockies was the home of very early Indian cultures. People like the Hohokam had developed irrigation to raise crops in the desert environment. Later Indians in the area included both Plains hunters and Southwest farmers. In the 1500s, the Spanish explored the area. And for the next 300 years, most of it was part of the huge Spanish territory of Mexico.

Texas became part of the United States in 1846. The New Mexico Territory (including what is now Arizona) was ceded to the United States in 1848. There were **relatively** few Mexican settlers in Arizona and Texas. But there were about 60,000 Mexicans living in New Mexico. It was the most heavily settled part of the Mexican Southwest.

Most of the Mexican people lived around Santa Fe or further north along the Rio Grande and the Pecos River. They lived in military and administrative towns such as Santa Fe, in small farming towns, or on large cattle ranches. In New Mexico, there were established political and social systems, which less settled areas often did not have. In fact, the Mexicans kept their political power long after new settlers came. They controlled the territorial legislature for many years.

But new settlers from the eastern United States were moving slowly across Texas to New Mexico. Immigrants from older southern states set up cotton plantations in Texas. After the Civil War, plantations in west and south Texas sometimes used Mexican laborers to replace former slaves. But it was large-scale cattle raising that really changed the Southwest.

Easterners adopted the Mexican idea of cattle ranching. The land was well suited for grazing. Mexican *vaqueros* and the newer cowboys (black as well as white) herded thousands of longhorn cattle over the open range. With the end of the Civil War came a cattle boom. The market for beef in the East expanded with the population. At the same time, railroads were reaching west of the Mississippi River. In 1866, the "long drive" became part of cattle ranching. As many as a thousand cattle were herded north to a railroad junction. There they were sold and shipped east. Towns grew quickly along the cattle trails and at the railroads. These wild cattle towns included Abilene, Dodge City, Cheyenne, and Laramie. The invention of the **refrigerated** car in 1875 made it easier to process and ship beef. New settlers poured into the Southwest to join the cattle industry.

There was often conflict between cattle ranchers and sheep ranchers. In some places, like New Mexico, sheep were also an old part of the Mexican economy. But sheep damaged grazing land. The arrival of homesteaders produced even more trouble. Farms fenced in with barbed wire cut down the open range. There were often bitter range wars over grazing lands.

There were also wars with Indians, such as the Apaches, who did not want to lose their lands to either Mexicans or easterners. Leaders like Cochise and Geronimo fought the idea of reservation life. But Indians continued to lose their lands. Oklahoma, for example, had been known as Indian Territory. The Cherokees and other southern tribes had been moved there in the 1830s and 1840s. But after the Civil War, the tribes' lands were cut down. And in 1889, the area was opened to free settlement. Oklahoma City was born in a single day, with a population of 10,000.

Home-seekers rush for land in Oklahoma. Within a day, more than 50,000 people had staked claims.

Paul's Photos

When lightning frightened the cattle, cowboys rode furiously to head off the stampede. If the cattle could be forced to move in a wide circle, the danger would be over.

Settlement of the Rocky Mountain region was encouraged not by cattle but by the discovery of precious metals. In the 1840s, the Mormons, a religious group, had come to Utah to escape **persecution.** They farmed the area and founded Salt Lake City. But the region attracted few other easterners until the 1850s and 1860s. From then on, gold, silver, and copper were discovered in Colorado, Idaho, Montana, Nevada, and Wyoming. Some deposits were small; others were large. Nevada's famous Comstock Lode, for example, produced 500 million dollars worth of gold and silver in twenty years. At first, copper seemed unimportant. But the development of electricity, which used copper wires, provided a new market for the metal. In 1875, only about 20,000 tons of copper were mined in the United States. That total rose to over 300,000 tons by 1900.

The discoveries brought miners and many others to the area. Towns grew up at the sites of the deposits. Places like Virginia City, Nevada, were known as wild and lawless towns. When the mines were finally played out, the people did not always leave. In Nevada, the population did fall from 65,000 in 1880 to 45,000 in 1903, but this was unusual. In more cases, people turned from mining to ranching and farming in the area. Some ranches and farms had already grown to feed the mining areas. These turned to producing crops and beef for eastern markets. The expanding railroads brought this produce to the East—and brought more easterners west.

385

COMPREHENSION CHECK

A. Recognizing the Main Idea

This selection as a whole tells you

1. that black and white settlers were the first people to live in the Southwest area.

2. how cattle ranching developed the Rocky Mountain region.

3. why settlers left the Southwest and the Rocky Mountain region when the mines were played out.

4. how the Southwest and the Rocky Moutain region were developed.

B. Selecting Important Details

Choose the ending that best completes each statement.

1. Mexican settlers
   a. lived mostly in Arizona and Texas.
   b. had established political and social systems in New Mexico.
   c. adopted the eastern idea of cattle ranching.
   d. never had political power in New Mexico.
2. The Southwest was
   a. the home of the Hohokam Indians.
   b. never explored by the Spanish.
   c. never good for cattle ranching.
   d. later called Utah and Wyoming.
3. The long drive refers to the
   a. transcontinental railroads.
   b. trails used by covered wagons.
   c. journeys through the mountain areas.
   d. movement of cattle overland.

4. The Comstock Lode is associated with
   a. land rushes.
   b. silver mining.
   c. copper mining.
   d. the long drive.

C. True or False

Decide whether each of these statements is true or false. Rewrite the false ones to make them true.

1. Cattle ranchers, sheep ranchers, and homesteaders lived without trouble in New Mexico.

2. New Mexico had more Mexican population than any other part of the Southwest.

3. Cochise and Geronimo were in favor of the idea of reservation life.

4. There was not much market for copper until electricity was developed.

5. The Mormons were looking for religious persecution in Utah.

D. Vocabulary

Match the words with the definitions.

Words	Definitions
1. relatively	a. member of the
2. *vaquero*	family
3. refrigerated	b. kept cool
4. persecution	c. comparatively
	d. missionary
	e. cowboy
	f. bad treatment

The Golden Spike Unites the Nation

In the early days of May 1869, a strange sight could be seen in Utah. From both east and west, two snakelike iron rails were stretching toward a meeting point. From the east came the crews laying rails for the Union Pacific Railroad. In the west could be seen the work gangs of the Central Pacific Railroad.

Congress had given its approval for a transcontinental railroad as early as 1862. The outbreak of the Civil War had delayed the work of the Union Pacific. However, the Central Pacific had continued its work. By 1866, both companies were fully engaged in the task of laying tracks across the great stretches of mountain and prairie land.

Visitors to the work camps would have discovered that immigrant labor played an important part in building the first transcontinental railroad. The Union Pacific crews moving westward from Omaha employed thousands of Irish immigrants. Central Pacific crews striking out from California across the mountains were made up of thousands of Chinese laborers.

Laying the tracks was so difficult that completing ten miles a day was outstanding. But despite all hardships, the work went on, with General Grenville Dodge the guiding engineering genius. Then, on May 10, 1869, the two railroad lines met at Promontory, Utah. A golden spike was driven in to unite the two sets of rails and to symbolize the unity of East and West. The transcontinental railroad was finally a reality.

The chief engineers shake hands at the completion of the railroad.

Lesson 4   The Plains Region

WORDS TO UNDERSTAND
Discuss the meanings of these words.

moisture   **insecticides**   **navigable**

NEW WORDS IN SENTENCES
1. Crops need **moisture** from rain in order to grow.
2. Chemicals are used as **insecticides** to kill insects that destroy crops.
3. The boats could not continue up the river because it was no longer **navigable.**

AS YOU READ
As you read this selection, try to answer these questions.

1. What were some reasons for the delay in developing the Plains region?
2. How did the new Plains settlers solve their main problems?

THE READING SELECTION
The Plains region includes what is now the Dakotas, western Nebraska and Kansas, and eastern Montana, Wyoming, and Colorado. It was first the home of the Plains Indians. These tribes had adopted the horse—originally brought to North America by the Spanish—as part of their way of life. They were skilled in using the horse in warfare and in hunting buffalo. The buffalo provided them with most of their needs, though some tribes also farmed.

New settlers moving west reached the region in the 1840s. But they kept going west. They settled instead in the Pacific Coast area and in the Rocky Mountains. It was not until years later that they turned to the Plains.

Why did this happen? Indians had lived in the Plains region for hundreds of years. It was well suited to their way of life. However, to the new settlers, the Plains area seemed like poor farmland. The area had few resources. It was isolated. The climate was harsh. Further settlement of the Plains by non-Indians depended on solving these problems.

The Plains region did not receive enough rainfall to permit the use of normal farming methods. Ways had to be found to bring more water to the fields. One solution was to pump water up from below ground. Settlers drilled 100 to 150 feet below the surface to reach underground streams. This water

Trees were scarce on the Plains. Some Indians and settlers, like
this Nebraska family, built dugout houses with earthen walls.

was then pumped through pipes to the surface, using power supplied by a windmill. In most places, farmers also used a method of farming called "dry farming." The earth was plowed after rain or snow so that it would hold the **moisture.** In addition, farmers planted crops that needed smaller amounts of water. Thus, they learned to live with the lack of water in the Plains region.

But they also needed to deal with the long, hard winters and the tough sod, or soil. New kinds of wheat were developed that were able to grow in colder climates. Wheat was grown in the summer, rather than during the winter, as in other areas. New farm equipment, such as the chilled-iron plow, made it possible to work the thick sod. New **insecticides** were developed to protect the crops from insects.

Yet another difficulty of the environment of the Plains region was the lack of timber. That meant that wooden houses or fences could not be made from local materials. Bringing wood from the East was very expensive. Many settlers solved the housing problem as some Indian tribes had done. They built homes with the thick sod, cutting it and stacking it up like large bricks. The fencing problem was solved with the invention of barbed wire in the 1870s. Farmers could then protect their crops and prevent their livestock from straying.

But the Plains region was also isolated. The area had few **navigable** streams. Transportation depended on the horse. This meant that trade and communication with other parts of the nation was difficult and slow. This problem was solved, as it had been in other areas, by the extension of the railroads. Trains provided links with both the west and east coasts. They speeded transportation of people and goods. Prices of goods brought from other areas fell as the transportation costs were reduced. More new settlers arrived by train. Some of them even came from Europe at the urging of railroad company agents. By 1880, many Europeans were farming in the Plains region. At that time, 73 percent of Wisconsin's population, 71 percent of Minnesota's, 66 percent of the Dakotas', and 44 percent of Nebraska's had foreign-born parents.

However, there was conflict among the settlers over the use of the land. Parts of the region were well suited to grazing cattle. In many cases, the owners turned their cattle loose to roam on public lands. The cattle might stray and damage a homesteader's crops. Or a homesteader might block the route to water with fenced-in fields. The introduction of sheep to the grazing lands added more problems. Cattle owners claimed that sheep ruined the grass for cattle. Lawsuits and violence resulted from these disputes over land and water rights. It took many years for the settlers to learn to live with one another.

Violence also resulted from disputes between the new settlers and the Plains Indians over land use. Homesteads, ranches, railroads, and towns **interfered** with the Indian way of life. The wars between the United States and the Plains tribes were bloody and bitter.

COMPREHENSION CHECK

A. Recognizing the Main Idea
This selection as a whole tells you that
1. transportation was a problem in the Plains region.
2. no one could live in the Plains region.
3. new settlers found ways to solve the problems of living in the Plains region.
4. cattle owners, sheep owners, and homesteaders got along well in the Plains region.

B. Selecting Important Details
Choose the ending that best completes each statement.
1. The new Plains settlers faced all of the following problems EXCEPT
    a. tough soil.
    b. lack of transportation.
    c. lack of wooden fencing materials.
    d. too much rain.
2. Windmills and dry farming helped Plains farmers meet problems caused by
    a. strong winds.
    b. grazing sheep.
    c. lack of rainfall.
    d. cold weather.
3. Indians survived in the Plains region by
    a. building windmills.
    b. developing new farm equipment.
    c. using insecticides.
    d. using horses and hunting buffalo.

4. New people settled the Plains region
   a. before settling in the Pacific Coast area.
   b. when the railroads were extended.
   c. before the Indians.
   d. to avoid war with the Indians.

C. *True or False*

Decide whether each of these statements is true or false.

1. The Plains region includes what is now Kansas, Colorado, and Nevada.

2. Windmills supplied power to water pumps.

3. The railroad companies urged people to settle in the Plains region.

4. There was little conflict among the settlers in the Plains region.

5. The Indians had always used barbed wire for fences in the Plains region.

D. *Vocabulary*

Write your own sentence for each of these words.

moisture   insecticides   navigable

E. *Using Your Knowledge*

Make an outline of the fourth and fifth paragraphs of this reading selection. (The fourth paragraph begins, The Plains did not receive. . . .) Use the form below. Write one main idea and two or three details for each paragraph.

A. Main Idea
   1. Detail
   2. Detail
B. Main Idea
   1. Detail
   2. Detail

F. *Map Skills*

This map shows regions in the United States during the westward movement. Certain areas are labeled with letters. Match each name below with the correct letter. There are two extra letters.

1. Plains region
2. Rocky Mountain region
3. Pacific Coast region
4. Southwest

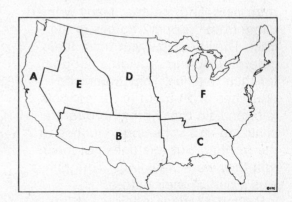

Women of the Frontier

The story of the West is often told through the men who lived there. But women went west also, living the same hard life. There were all kinds of women. As was the case with men, there were fools and wise ones, sinners and people of good will. There were dance-hall hostesses, farmers, reformers, and outlaws. Many women came from "proper" homes in the East. They brought with them their determination to provide a good life for their families. They organized churches and taught in the schools. It is often said that women brought a civilizing and softening influence to the frontier. But this does not mean that they were weaklings. Toughness was a part of their nature.

Bethenia Owens-Adair was born in 1840. She grew up in Oregon and married at the age of fourteen. At eighteen, she divorced her husband, took a job in a laundry, and learned to read and write. Within a few years, she decided to study medicine. At that time, becoming a doctor was nearly impossible for a woman. But in 1880, Owens-Adair finished her studies and opened a practice in Portland.

Mary Elizabeth Lease was another hardworking, tough woman of the West. Born in 1850, she lived in both Texas and Kansas. She and her husband were farmers who knew the problems of those people. She turned to law but soon was too busy to practice. She became involved in organizing farmers to demand higher prices and government support. "Mary Yellin," as she was called, spoke from hundreds of platforms. She urged farmers to fight "Wall Street and the trusts." She was one of the early leaders of the Farmers Alliance movement and the later Populist party.

Martha Jane Canary had a very different kind of life. Born in the 1850s, she and her family went west to Montana in 1865. When she arrived in Deadwood, South Dakota, during the 1876 gold rush, she was already known as Calamity Jane. In later years, she hired out as a teamster. She drifted around Wyoming, Montana, Colorado, and the Dakotas, sometimes associated with such men as Wild Bill Hickok.

Calamity Jane was no gentle spirit. She wore men's clothes, rode well, carried guns, drank, and swore. She was known to curse at the top of her voice, howl like a coyote, and shoot off her guns. But she was not mean or vicious. She volunteered to nurse the sick during a smallpox epidemic in Deadwood in 1878. Calamity Jane captured the imagination of many easterners. Dime novels pictured her as a romantic beauty who faced down villains.

Calamity Jane became, in many minds, a "Western character," along with Wild Bill Hickok and Wyatt Earp. She was doing what most people did not expect women to do. In fact, many women in the West were doing the unexpected.

Lesson 5   Indians and the Westward Movement

WORDS TO UNDERSTAND
Discuss the meanings of these words.

massacred   **assimilation**
resistance   **allotment**

NEW WORDS IN SENTENCES
1. The troops **massacred** almost the entire population of the village.

2. There was strong **resistance** among the Indians to giving up their own ways of life.

3. **Assimilation** of the Indians meant that they were to become part of the culture and society of other Americans.

4. **Allotment** of land to individual Indians meant that the land once shared by the tribe was to be divided up.

AS YOU READ
As you read this selection, try to answer these questions.

1. What were the major events in the conflict between the western Indians and the government?

2. What were the government policies toward the Indians on the reservations?

THE READING SELECTION
Review. The West had several regions, which developed at different times and for different reasons. Parts of the Pacific Coast region and the Southwest had long been settled by the Spanish and Mexicans. From 1840 to 1870, gold and other riches were discovered in the Pacific Coast region and in the Rocky Mountains. Settlers poured in. Many stayed on in these areas. The growth of the Southwest was encouraged by the cattle boom after the Civil War. Cattle ranches and towns grew rapidly. The Plains region was not settled until later, in the 1870s and 1880s. The area had seemed to have too many problems. But the development of better farm equipment and transportation increased homesteads on the Plains.   ☆

The Civil War marked a turning point in the history of the American Indian. By 1806, most tribes east of the Mississippi River had been moved out of the way of white settlement. Very few had retained any of their land. Some tribes had moved into Canada. Others had been moved west of the Mississippi. But the Indians in the Plains region, the Southwest, and the Rocky Mountains were still largely independent. The westward movement that followed the Civil War was to bring an end to their freedom.

The idea of confining the western Indians to definite areas of land dated

Taken in the year after the battle at Wounded Knee, this photo shows soldiers posted at a Sioux camp in South Dakota.

Library of Congress

from 1849. At that time, the commissioner of Indian affairs suggested such reservations. In 1851, the government met with the Sioux, Cheyennes, Crows, Arapahos, Arikaras, and other tribes at Fort Laramie, Wyoming. This meeting established the general area for each tribe.

But the campaign to enforce the reservation policy did not begin until the 1860s. In 1863, war against the Teton Sioux, the western branch of that tribe, began. The war soon expanded to include other tribes that disobeyed reservation rules. In 1864, Colorado militia volunteers under Colonel John Chivington **massacred** a band of peaceful Cheyennes camped under military protection at Sand Creek. This incident

increased **resistance** to the army all over the Plains.

The Indian wars continued until 1890, when the last resistance ended at Wounded Knee, South Dakota. A commission formed in 1867 to make peace with the tribes drew an important conclusion about the wars. "Have we [the United States] been uniformly unjust? We answer unhesitatingly, yes." Yet it is also important to understand that both sides in the wars were sometimes unfair and bloodthirsty. The Cheyennes were massacred at Sand Creek. General George Custer's regiment was massacred by the Sioux in 1876. In the end, the Indians were probably defeated by the railroads and the growing tide of new settlers. They were finally confined on

Red Cloud (top), a Sioux, and Geronimo, an Apache, fought federal attempts to change Indian ways of life.

reservations, often under military guard.

On the reservations, Indians were forced to depend on the government. They were not allowed to hunt or to make war, both of which were important to Plains tribes. Their food and clothing came from the agent on the reservation. All rules were made by the agent or other white officials. This was bad enough. But the agents were often corrupt or simply not concerned about the Indians. Tribes usually lacked proper food, shelter, medical care, and education.

Indian reservation life was shaped by the government's major goal. This was **assimilation,** or absorbing Indians into the culture and society of other Americans. They were no longer to be a separate and different group of Americans. Government policies tried to stamp out traditional Indian life. For years, General John Pope of the U.S. army had urged that livestock raising would be a workable way of life for Plains tribes. But farmers were brought in to teach the Indians agriculture instead. They were stopped from "hunting" what cattle were given to them for food. There were policies against native languages, long hair, traditional dances, holidays, clothing, and painting.

Finally, the goal of assimilation resulted in a policy that aimed at destroying the reservation and the tribe. This was **allotment.** Common ownership and sharing were important Indian traditions. But under the Dawes Act, passed in 1887, the tribe-owned reservation would be broken up and allotted to individual Indians. Any extra land was sold or leased to new settlers. By this time,

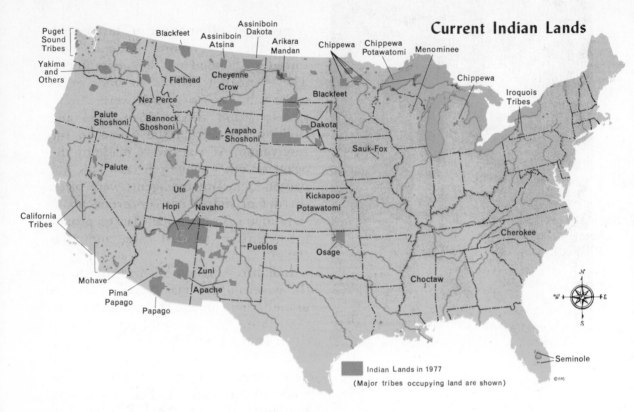

Current Indian Lands

Puget Sound Tribes
Yakima and Others
Blackfeet
Assiniboin Atsina
Assiniboin Dakota
Arikara Mandan
Chippewa
Chippewa Potawatomi
Menominee
Chippewa
Iroquois Tribes
Flathead
Cheyenne Crow
Nez Perce
Blackfeet
Paiute Shoshoni
Bannock Shoshoni
Arapaho Shoshoni
Dakota
Sauk-Fox
Paiute
Ute
Kickapoo Potawatomi
Hopi
Navaho
Osage
Cherokee
California Tribes
Pueblos
Zuni
Choctaw
Mohave
Apache
Pima Papago
Papago
Seminole

Indian Lands in 1977
(Major tribes occupying land are shown)

Most tribes had been moved to reservations by the late 1800s. Today, about half the Indian population lives on reservations.

even some Indians and their supporters believed that assimilation was the best future for the tribes. The Dawes Act had a great deal of support.

Assimilation did not help the Indians. Government policies in general did not. In 1864, Secretary of State Stanton was irritated at the visit of a reformer.

> If he has come here to tell us of the corruption of our Indian system, and the dishonesty of Indian agents, tell him that we know it. But the Government never reforms an evil until the people demand it. Tell him that when he reaches the heart of the American people, the Indians will be saved.

COMPREHENSION CHECK

A. Recognizing the Main Idea

This selection as a whole tells you that the Indians of the Plains, the Southwest, and the Rocky Mountains

1. were moved to Canada by government order.

2. had independent lives on reservations.

3. were forced to live on reservations under unfavorable government policies.

4. were helped by government policies.

B. Selecting Important Details

Choose the ending that best completes each statement.

1. The policy of moving Indians to reservations
   a. allowed Indians to hunt as they had always done.
   b. was suggested, but not enforced until the 1860s.
   c. provided everything they needed.
   d. made Indians independent of the government.

2. Assimilation meant that
   a. Indian cultures could exist alongside other cultures.
   b. Indian tribes would share their land on reservations.
   c. Indians could raise livestock on the reservations.
   d. the government would try to make Indians part of general culture and society.

3. The Dawes Act
   a. had little support.
   b. supported the traditional Indian life.
   c. allotted land to individual Indians.
   d. all of the above.

4. Indians went onto reservations because they
   a. would not massacre new settlers.
   b. were defeated by the new settlers.
   c. wanted to live there.
   d. thought the land would be better.

C. True or False

Decide whether each of these statements is true or false.

1. Plains Indians included the Sioux, Cheyennes, Crows, Arapahos, and Arikaras.

2. A commission in 1867 said the Indians had treated the United States unjustly.

3. Indians on the reservations had to depend on government agents for food and clothing.

4. Indians on the reservations were often under military guard.

5. Allotment of land encouraged the tribal way of life.

D. Vocabulary

Match the words with definitions.

Words	Definitions
1. massacre	a. religious ceremony
2. resistance	b. becoming part of a society
3. assimilation	c. remove from society
4. allotment	d. kill
	e. assigning of an amount
	f. action against a force

E. Map Skills

Use the map on page 396 to find this information. Write down the names of two Indian tribes that have reservations in each of the following areas: the Pacific Coast states, the Southwest states, the Rocky Mountain states, and the Plains states. Refer to Lessons 2, 3, and 4 for information about which states are in each area.

Sarah Winnemucca: The Case for Allotment

Federal Indian policies have often produced debate. Allotment of reservation lands and assimilation of the Indians were two such policies. One of the strongest Indian supporters of allotment was Sarah Winnemucca.

About 1844, Shell Flower was born into the Paiute tribe of Nevada. She was the granddaughter of Chief Winnemucca I. The chief was convinced that the Indians could not defeat the whites. He felt that the Paiutes would have to adopt white ways to survive. Shell Flower was influenced by these ideas and by her childhood contact with whites. It was during a stay with whites that she adopted the name Sarah.

When Sarah Winnemucca returned to her tribe in 1860, she found a changed life. Gold and silver strikes had brought whites to Nevada. A Paiute war had already resulted in the establishment of a reservation at Pyramid Lake.

In 1872, the Paiutes were moved to a new reservation in Oregon. Poor treatment led Sarah to speak out. She began by lecturing in west coast cities. Her message and striking appearance won wide attention. Newspapers responded warmly to her. The opposition called her a liar and worse.

But in 1880, she was invited to Washington. She pleaded her cause before the president and the secretary

Nevada Historical Society

of the interior. She was promised that allotment of land would take place on the Oregon Paiute reservation. She believed strongly in allotment and was pleased with her victory.

But the promise was not kept. Sarah then began a lecture tour in the East. From these lectures came her book, *Life Among the Paiutes*. In 1884, she again seemed to win a victory. Congress passed a bill that would allow allotment for the Paiutes. But the bill was not put into effect.

Under the Dawes Act, allotment was finally carried out. Looking back on it now, it seems to have hurt Indians more than it helped them. But this would have been almost impossible to know at that time. Sarah and others sincerely believed in their cause. She was a courageous fighter, willing to take on the government.

Lesson 6   Did the West Change Our Nation?

WORDS TO UNDERSTAND
Discuss the meanings of these words.

bias   **optimism**

NEW WORDS IN SENTENCES
1. Some people cannot get jobs because of **bias** against their race, sex, or place of birth.
2. There was a great deal of **optimism** on the frontier—people had the feeling that the future would be good.

AS YOU READ
As you read this selection, try to answer these questions.
1. What ideas and attitudes did the American frontier tend to strengthen?
2. What effects did the frontier have on technical progress?

THE READING SELECTION
Review. The policy of confining western Indians to reservations had been formed before the Civil War. But it was not until the 1860s that wars to enforce this policy began. During the wars, both sides were guilty of massacres. By 1890, the tribes were defeated and were kept on the reservations. There, government policies aimed at assimilation. Indian traditions were forbidden. By 1887, the goal of assimilation had resulted in the Dawes Act, which began to break up Indian reservations and tribes.   ☆

In 1890, the superintendent of the census made an official announcement.

> Up to and including 1880 the country had a frontier of settlement, but at present the unsettled area has been so broken into . . . that there can hardly be said to be a frontier line.

The end of the westward movement had been officially declared. Something that had been a part of American history for 300 years had ended. Had it really changed America? How?

One change was obvious. America had been a land of forests, plains, and herds of wild animals. It also had been the land of the American Indian. By 1890, it was the land of newer Americans —Europeans, Africans, Asians, and Mexicans. Many of the animals and forests were gone. In their places were cities, ranches, farms, and railroads.

Some historians think that the frontier experience had other effects as well.

1. The West tended to strengthen American ideas of equality and democracy. Women and men of many races faced the same dangers and hard work on the frontier. There was **bias** against some groups. But in general, there was more democracy than in the more settled East. For example, western states were the first to extend the vote to women. It was clear that pioneer women had made important contributions to settling the West.

2. The frontier encouraged nationalism. Even people who had recently arrived from Europe or Asia began to think of the land as theirs. Everyone was new to the frontier. In addition, the settlers often were dependent on other parts of the country for their needs. They often looked to the government in Washington for help, since local governments might be too new and weak to help them.

3. The frontier provided hope and encouraged **optimism.** The new lands were a kind of safety valve for easterners. They seemed to offer new opportunities to people who were discouraged. They also made people feel optimistic in general about the future of the country. There were great riches waiting to be had.

4. Settling new lands encouraged technical progress. New processes and products were developed. These included agricultural equipment as well as methods of transportation and communication. Often these changes happened very quickly. For example, the Pony Express had been established to carry mail to California in 1860. In 1861, it had already been replaced by the transcontinental telegraph. By 1869, the first transcontinental railroad was completed.

There is still debate over whether or not the frontier really had all these effects. But the 300-year-long westward movement was an experience most nations did not have. In 1902, a future president of the United States, Woodrow Wilson, would write about the effect of the frontier.

This great pressure of a people moving always to new frontiers, in search of new lands, new power . . . had ruled our course and formed our policies like a Fate.

COMPREHENSION CHECK

A. Recognizing the Main Idea

This selection as a whole tells you that the American frontier

1. made America more democratic.
2. helped shape American ideas and development.
3. encouraged the development of the Pony Express.
4. made America more European.

B. Selecting Important Details

Choose the ending that best completes each statement.

1. By 1890
   a. cities had been replaced by forests.
   b. Asians had left the United States.
   c. the Pony Express had replaced the telegraph.
   d. the frontier no longer existed.

2. Some people believe that the frontier encouraged all of the following EXCEPT

    a. technical progress.

    b. optimism.

    c. European traditions.

    d. ideas of equality and democracy.

3. Women in the West

    a. never learned to face hard work.

    b. gained the vote before women in other parts of the country.

    c. could not be optimistic.

    d. did not contribute to the settling of the West.

4. The frontier encouraged nationalism because

    a. it made America like other countries.

    b. it was part of American life for less than ten years.

    c. new settlers looked to the federal government for help.

    d. technical progress slowed down.

C. True or False

Decide whether each of these statements is true or false.

1. America remained the land of the American Indian.

2. The frontier made easterners feel they could always move on to new lands in the West.

3. Few changes were made in agricultural equipment because of the frontier.

4. The frontier was part of American life for 300 years.

5. The frontier strengthened American ideas of democracy and equality.

D. Vocabulary

Match the words with the definitions.

Words	Definitions
1. bias	a. sadness
2. optimism	b. prejudice
	c. fair treatment
	d. feeling that the future will be good

E. Essay

Write six to eight sentences answering the following question.

If there were still an American frontier to settle, would you consider moving there? Give some reasons for your answer.

F. Chronology

Arrange these events in the order in which they happened.

1. Beginning of the Civil War

2. End of the westward movement

3. Discovery of gold in California

4. Completion of the transcontinental railroad

5. Passage of the Chinese Exclusion Act

6. Dawes Act

Chief Joseph of the Nez Percé: "My Heart Is Sick and Sad"

From the 1860s to the 1890s, the United States fought a series of Indian wars. As the frontier moved westward, more and more Indian tribes were forced from their lands and homes. They fought back in any way they could.

The discovery of gold in Oregon and Idaho brought many miners to the lands of the Nez Percé Indians. For fifteen years, the tribe tried to fight off those who moved into the hunting grounds that the Indians held by treaty. Slowly but surely the tribe was defeated. In 1877, they were threatened by United States troops determined to drive them off their lands. The Nez Percés struck out on a desperate 1,500-mile march to try to reach Canada. It was a fighting retreat. But the effort failed when army troops surrounded the Indians just thirty miles from the Canadian border.

Finally, the Nez Percés—like the Sioux, the Crows, the Blackfeet, the Utes, the Apaches, and other tribes—found they had to surrender. Their leader, Chief Joseph, spoke to the general of the army surrounding them.

> I am tired of fighting. Our chiefs are killed. . . . The old men are all dead. . . . It is cold and we have no blankets. The little children are freezing to death. My people . . . have run away to the hills and have no blankets, no food. . . . I want to have time to look for my children and see how many of them I can find. . . . Hear me, my chiefs. My heart is sick and sad. I am tired. From where the sun now stands, I will fight no more forever.

U.S. Signal Corps, the National Archives

Lesson 7 Living in America: New Ways of Life, 1865–1900

WORDS TO UNDERSTAND

Discuss the meanings of these words.

multimillionaires   **feminist**
tenements

NEW WORDS IN SENTENCES

1. **Multimillionaires** have many millions of dollars.

2. Poor people in cities often live in crowded apartment buildings called **tenements.**

3. **Feminist** ideas are voiced by people who argue for the rights of women.

AS YOU READ

As you read this selection, try to answer these questions.

1. How did expanding industry affect rich people and poor people in the United States?

2. What changes took place in the lives of American women?

3. What progress was made toward equality for black people?

THE READING SELECTION

The end of the westward movement did not mean the end of change in the United States. From 1865 through the 1890s, everything seemed to be changing, and it all happened rapidly. There were new people and new places and ways to live.

Population. The United States was becoming a more urban country. The movement from the rural areas to the cities increased each year. In 1870, only about 25 percent of all Americans lived in urban areas. By the end of the 1890s, that figure had risen to nearly 40 percent. The population of New York City rose to 3,400,000 by 1900. Chicago grew from a city of 30,000 in 1850 to one of 1,600,000 in 1900. San Francisco and Los Angeles already had hundreds of thousands of people.

Joining Americans in the cities were millions of new immigrants. Between 1881 and 1900, nearly 9,000,000 people arrived in America. These new immigrants were, to some extent, different from those who had come earlier. There were larger numbers of Japanese, for example. And Europeans were coming more from eastern and southern Europe and less from northern Europe.

The period saw the second large wave of Jewish immigrants arriving. Jews who had arrived earlier, around the 1850s, were largely from Germany. But the Jews entering the United

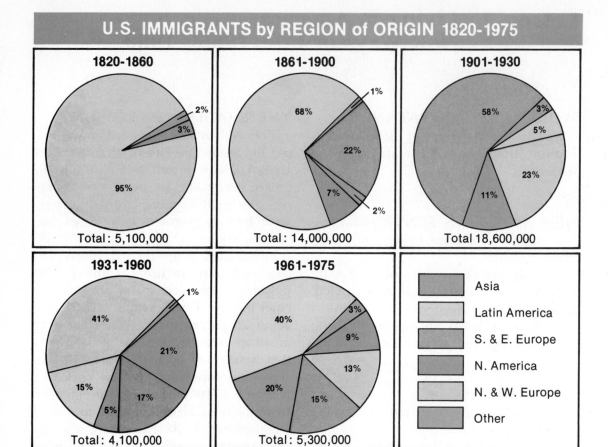

U.S. IMMIGRANTS by REGION of ORIGIN 1820-1975

1820-1860
- 95%
- 3%
- 2%

Total: 5,100,000

1861-1900
- 68%
- 22%
- 7%
- 2%
- 1%

Total: 14,000,000

1901-1930
- 58%
- 3%
- 5%
- 23%
- 11%

Total 18,600,000

1931-1960
- 41%
- 1%
- 21%
- 17%
- 5%
- 15%

Total: 4,100,000

1961-1975
- 40%
- 3%
- 9%
- 13%
- 15%
- 20%

Total: 5,300,000

Legend:
- Asia
- Latin America
- S. & E. Europe
- N. America
- N. & W. Europe
- Other

In what two ways did the wave of immigration between 1861 and 1900 differ from immigration between 1820 and 1860?

States after 1880 were usually from Poland, Russia, and other eastern European countries. From that year until 1930, some 2,250,000 Jews left the Old World for America. Many of them had come to escape religious persecution. Earlier immigrants—Jews and others—had settled across the country, on farms as well as in cities. But most new immigrants remained in the cities, where there were jobs. There were large Jewish communities in New York, Boston, and Chicago. Jewish newcomers, often very poor, were helped by the Jews who were already settled.

Economic life. The jobs that attracted the immigrants and others to the cities were the result of expanded American industry. Following the Civil War, the North saw an industrial boom. The railroads, the oil industry, and steel production all expanded tremendously. This expansion made many new jobs available. In addition, several inventions of the later 1800s expanded jobs in existing fields and added more new ones. The sewing machine, the typewriter, and the telephone were among these. Many of the jobs created by these inventions were taken by women. The number of working women grew during this period.

The expansion of industry also provided opportunities for getting rich. Many people did so. By 1890, there were perhaps 2,000 millionaires. Some were worth hundreds of millions of dollars. For example, when Andrew Carnegie sold his steel company in 1901, he had a fortune of about 500 million dollars. Other **multimillionaires** included J. P. Morgan, a banker, and John D. Rockefeller, a leader of the oil industry.

Society. The rich and near-rich formed a new social class in the cities. Most lived in huge homes with many servants. Their social lives became important to reporters and newspapers. They became known as the Four Hundred—the leaders of American social life. A new aristocracy was created in the United States. It was based on wealth.

But in the cities, there also existed a growing class of poor people. Many of them were immigrants who barely spoke or understood English. They worked for low wages in unsafe factories and lived in crowded, dirty **tenements.** City slums grew larger and larger.

The poor tried to help themselves. Immigrant self-help societies were formed. Unions began to form. They organized strikes to improve working conditions. Both adults and children turned to education as the key to improving their lives. Even older people attended night classes after work to learn English, American history, music, and other subjects. Reformers also tried to help. Lillian Wald, for example, worked in New York City for many years. She helped provide health care in the worst slums.

Many other women worked in settlement houses, classrooms, and business. While many people still felt that "women's place is in the home," more opportunities were opening up. Advanced education for women, for example, was more accepted and more available than it had been before. Business and industry, of course, provided more jobs. At the same time, there was a growing movement aimed at winning the vote for women. By 1898, four western states allowed women to vote in elections. Women got a greater number of legal and economic rights in several states. One **feminist** thinker was Charlotte Perkins Gilman, who argued that the role of women had not kept pace with changes in the industrial world.

But there was little progress for black people during this time. Segregation had become established in many places since the Civil War. And in 1896, the Supreme Court declared segregation constitutional in the case of *Plessy* v. *Ferguson.* The court ruled that facilities could be separate if they were equal. But the fact was that they were rarely equal. And now it seemed that the Supreme Court had approved such a system of inequality. There was much debate about the way in which blacks should work for change. Booker T. Washington stressed getting along with whites. W. E. B. Dubois argued for open opposition to segregation. But changes for this group of Americans would not come for many years.

"THE GILDED AGE"

For some, the 1890s was a time of flashy spending and entertainment. New inventions, bold fashions, and big social events were the news of the day. Millions of New Yorkers (at left) enjoyed the Coney Island Amusement Park, built in 1897. Or, as shown in the photo, they spent time at the beach in "daring" bathing clothes. An aquarium (bottom left) was one of hundreds of exhibits built for the 1893 World's Columbian Exposition in Chicago. Another attraction was the famous circus advertised in this poster (at right). And Buffalo Bill's Wild West show (below) brought some of the exciting old West to audiences in the United States and Europe.

THE BARNUM & BAILEY GREATEST SHOW ON EARTH

AN INTERESTING MOMENT DURING THE PERFORMANCES IN THE MAIN PAVILION.
THREE RINGS SIMULTANEOUSLY OCCUPIED BY HOSTS OF DAINTY
EQUESTRIENNES AND ARENIC EXPERTS EXECUTING THRILLING AND DARING FEATS.

BUFFALO BILL'S WILD WEST
AND CONGRESS OF ROUGH RIDERS OF THE WORLD.

COL. W. F. CODY
BUFFALO BILL
WILL APPEAR
AT EVERY PERFORMANCE

A CONGRESS OF AMERICAN INDIANS. REPRESENTING VARIOUS TRIBES, CHARACTERS AND PECULIARITIES OF THE WILY DUSKY WARRIORS IN SCENES FROM ACTUAL LIFE GIVING THEIR WEIRD WAR DANCES AND PICTURESQUE STYLE OF HORSEMANSHIP.

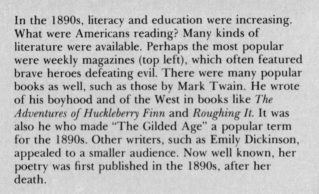

"Look at that mother and her children, sir!" said Fred, "made homeless by your heartless brutality. Your claim is fraudulent, and you know it. Stop this thing instantly, or I'll put you behind prison bars within a week."

In the 1890s, literacy and education were increasing. What were Americans reading? Many kinds of literature were available. Perhaps the most popular were weekly magazines (top left), which often featured brave heroes defeating evil. There were many popular books as well, such as those by Mark Twain. He wrote of his boyhood and of the West in books like *The Adventures of Huckleberry Finn* and *Roughing It*. It was also he who made "The Gilded Age" a popular term for the 1890s. Other writers, such as Emily Dickinson, appealed to a smaller audience. Now well known, her poetry was first published in the 1890s, after her death.

COMPREHENSION CHECK

A. Recognizing the Main Idea

This selection as a whole tells you that after the Civil War,

1. immigrants came to America.
2. there were many changes in population, society, and the economy.
3. everyone got rich because of the expansion of industry.
4. cities got smaller.

B. Selecting Important Details

Choose the ending that best completes each statement.

1. Many rich people
   a. lived in tenements.
   b. formed unions to improve working conditions.
   c. made money from oil, steel, and railroads.
   d. all of the above.
2. Women in the late 1800s
   a. worked only at home.
   b. became less important.
   c. had many jobs connected with the telephone, typewriter, and sewing machine.
   d. never worked in slums.
3. In the case of *Plessy* v. *Ferguson*, the Court ruled that
   a. women could vote.
   b. segregation was unconstitutional.
   c. women should have equal legal and economic rights.
   d. separate but equal facilities were legal.

4. As slums grew,
   a. the poor formed self-help societies.
   b. cities grew smaller.
   c. people stopped wanting education.
   d. there were fewer rich people.

C. True or False

Decide whether each of these statements is true or false.

1. The Four Hundred were the immigrants who came from Japan.
2. New immigrants tended to settle in urban areas.
3. J. P. Morgan was a feminist thinker.
4. Booker T. Washington made millions of dollars in the steel industry.
5. Charlotte Perkins Gilman felt that women should work only at home.

D. Vocabulary

Write your own sentence for each of these words.

multimillionaire   tenement   feminist

E. Ask Yourself

Why did immigrants feel that education was the key to improving their lives? Was education the key for them? Is it today?

F. Graph Skills

Refer to the graph on page 404 to answer these questions.

1. During which period was there the most immigration? During which period was there the least immigration?
2. Did immigration steadily increase from after the Civil War until the present?

Unit 8 Summary A Changing Land and People

The Westward Movement

From 1860 to 1900, the western half of the nation developed quickly. Easterners and new immigrants swelled the population of the area. Many came to find new riches or fertile land. Others came for adventure or opportunity. This growth of the West was affected by four things.

1. Discoveries of gold and silver.
2. Expansion of the railroads.
3. Increasing market for cattle.
4. Improvements in farm equipment.

From 1840 to 1870, most growth was in the areas around the Mississippi River and along the Pacific Coast. It was not until later that the Plains region was settled.

Natural riches were important in developing the Pacific Coast areas. These areas were already settled by Indians and, in some places, by Mexicans. But the supply of furs and lumber in Oregon and the discovery of gold in California and other places brought many new settlers to the area. Some of them were from Asia or Europe. Both black and white Americans came from the East. Cities grew up around the mining areas and former Spanish missions. But conflicts developed between the Americans and the Chinese and Mexicans. There was bias against both minority groups, and immigration from China was stopped for a time.

In the Southwest, cattle ranching was the key to development. Mexicans had long operated huge cattle ranches. The growing market for beef after the Civil War brought new ranchers to the area. Towns grew up near ranches or at railroad junctions where the cattle were sold.

There were few new settlers in the Rocky Mountains until the discovery of gold, silver, and copper in the 1850s

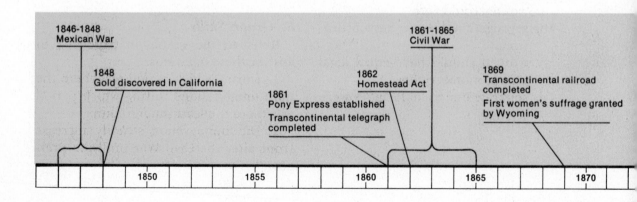

1846-1848
Mexican War

1848
Gold discovered in California

1861
Pony Express established
Transcontinental telegraph completed

1861-1865
Civil War

1862
Homestead Act

1869
Transcontinental railroad completed
First women's suffrage granted by Wyoming

1850   1855   1860   1865   1870

and 1860s. After that, mining towns grew rapidly.

The Plains region had been ignored by new settlers because it seemed to be poor farmland. But improvements in farm equipment and transportation helped solve these problems. As in other areas, the extension of the railroads was important to settlement. The trains carried supplies and new settlers west. They carried western products east.

However, in all these areas, there was conflict with the first inhabitants, the Indians. The idea of keeping western Indians on reservations was not enforced until after the Civil War. This effort brought on wars in which both sides were guilty of massacres. These wars lasted until 1890. On the reservations, government policies aimed at assimilation of the Indians. The Indians were forced to live like other Americans. After 1887, the Dawes Act tried to break up the tribes and reservation lands.

By 1890, the westward movement was over. It had changed the country to a land of ranches, farms, cities, and railroads. Some historians think it had other effects as well.

1. The West strengthened American ideas of equality and democracy.

2. It encouraged nationalism.

3. It encouraged hope and optimism.

4. It led to technical progress in farm equipment, transportation, and communications.

A Changing Society

American society was becoming more urban. Rural Americans and millions of new immigrants moved into the cities. They found jobs in the expanding industries. Industry and business also created a large wealthy class. But growing city slums were filled with the poor. Women were gaining more freedom and working even harder for the vote. But for blacks, there was little change. The Supreme Court upheld segregation in *Plessy* v. *Ferguson* in 1896.

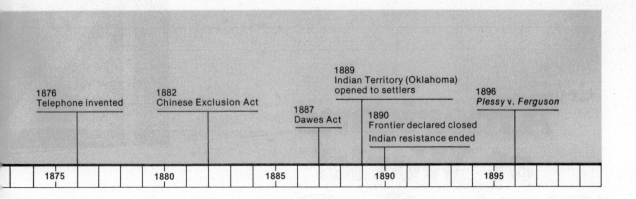

1876
Telephone invented

1882
Chinese Exclusion Act

1887
Dawes Act

1889
Indian Territory (Oklahoma)
opened to settlers

1890
Frontier declared closed
Indian resistance ended

1896
Plessy v. *Ferguson*

1875   1880   1885   1890   1895

unit
9

Garment Workers' Strike, Chicago, 1910, Chicago Historical Society

Why are we Prohibited from Picketing?

WE ARE STRIKING

The Changing West II by Thomas Hart Benton, The New School for Social Research

Americans at Work:
1865 to the Present

The story of farming and labor since 1865 is the story of change in the American economy. It has been a time of problems, from sweatshops to bankrupt farms. It has also been a time of progress: agricultural and industrial revolutions (above), union movements (left), and new government policies.

413

Lesson 1   The Assets of the United States

WORDS TO UNDERSTAND
Discuss the meanings of these words.

assets   **tributaries**
natural resources   **fertile**

NEW WORDS IN SENTENCES
1. Her **assets** included money, a good business, and a new car.
2. Coal and oil are important **natural resources.**
3. The stream was one of the **tributaries** flowing into the river.
4. The land was so **fertile** that anything would grow on it.

AS YOU READ
As you read this selection, try to answer these questions.
1. Why is the geography of the United States one of its major assets?
2. What are some of the minerals that are mined in the United States?

THE READING SELECTION
After 1865, the United States grew to be the greatest industrial nation in the world. It continued to lead all other nations in agricultural production. How did the United States become such a great industrial nation? Part of the answer lies in the many rich **assets** of the country.

Size. The United States is a big country. Being big allows room for the country to grow and change easily. Within this large area are several different climates and many different kinds of land and vegetation. The country also has many **natural resources.**

Geography. The United States may be divided into five main geographical regions. First is the mountain and valley region along the Pacific coast. Next is the Rocky Mountain region. Third is the central plains region, which covers most of the middle of the country. Next comes the Appalachian Mountain region. And fifth is the plains region of the Atlantic coast.

The chief river system of the country is the Missouri-Mississippi. It flows from the far north to the Gulf of Mexico. This river system is fed by a number of **tributaries,** or smaller rivers. These include the Platte, Arkansas, Red, Ohio, and Tennessee rivers. Other major river systems are the Columbia in the Northwest and the Colorado in the Southwest.

The United States has some of the most **fertile** land in the world. Much of

this land is located in the Midwest in what is called the corn belt. There are other fertile valleys and basins in the hilly eastern regions. The United States also has deserts in the West. And there are semitropical regions in the Southeast and Southwest. In addition, there are timberlands in the Northwest, and grasslands in the western high plains.

Different climates and types of soil enable farmers to raise a wide variety of crops and livestock. Wheat, corn, and hogs are raised in the central plains states. Cotton and tobacco are raised in the South. Citrus fruits are grown in the semitropical areas. Apples are a major crop in the Northwest and Northeast. There are dairy farms in the central and eastern sections of the country. Beef cattle are raised all through the plains states. Small farmers in practically every section of the country raise various kinds of vegetables and fruits.

Natural resources. The United States has the many minerals needed for a modern industrial society. Vast supplies of coal and iron allow the United States to supply much of the world's steel. Other resources include oil and natural gas. There are gold and silver as well as copper, aluminum, magnesium, and other industrial minerals.

Water power, coal, and oil are used to produce electricity. Electricity is a major source of power used to turn natural resources to industrial use.

Natural resources are the basis of U.S. industry and agriculture. Water, rich soil, and minerals—such as potash, being mined in bottom picture—have many uses. What are some of these uses?

415

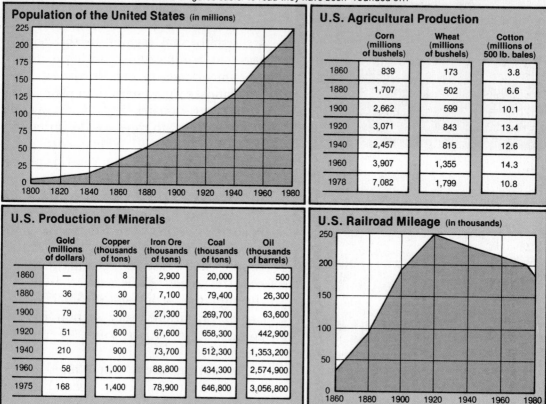

FACTS and FIGURES on ECONOMIC ASSETS

The following figures, or statistics, may help to make even clearer what has been said about America's economic assets. To make the figures easier to read they have been "rounded off."

Population of the United States (in millions)

U.S. Agricultural Production

	Corn (millions of bushels)	Wheat (millions of bushels)	Cotton (millions of 500 lb. bales)
1860	839	173	3.8
1880	1,707	502	6.6
1900	2,662	599	10.1
1920	3,071	843	13.4
1940	2,457	815	12.6
1960	3,907	1,355	14.3
1978	7,082	1,799	10.8

U.S. Production of Minerals

	Gold (millions of dollars)	Copper (thousands of tons)	Iron Ore (thousands of tons)	Coal (thousands of tons)	Oil (thousands of barrels)
1860	—	8	2,900	20,000	500
1880	36	30	7,100	79,400	26,300
1900	79	300	27,300	269,700	63,600
1920	51	600	67,600	658,300	442,900
1940	210	900	73,700	512,300	1,353,200
1960	58	1,000	88,800	434,300	2,574,900
1975	168	1,400	78,900	646,800	3,056,800

U.S. Railroad Mileage (in thousands)

These two charts show increases in U.S. farming and mineral production. What does the top graph show about population? What connection might there be between these two kinds of information?

America has good natural water transportation. The many miles of American coastline contain many good harbors. Boston, New York, Charleston, Mobile, New Orleans, Houston, San Francisco, and Seattle all are important ports. They have made it possible for this nation to become one of the leaders in world trade. In addition, the five Great Lakes and the Ohio and Mississippi rivers are two great inland waterway systems. Heavy, bulky goods such as ore can be moved much more cheaply by water than by rail, truck, or air.

Geography, climate, and natural resources, then, are important reasons for America's industrial power.

COMPREHENSION CHECK

A. Recognizing the Main Idea

In a single sentence, write the main idea of this lesson's reading selection.

B. Selecting Important Details

Choose the ending that best completes each statement.

1. The climate of the United States
   a. is colder than that of most nations.
   b. is mostly either very warm or very cold.
   c. helps produce a wide variety of crops.
   d. greatly limits the ability of the nation to produce crops.

2. America's mineral resources include all the following EXCEPT
   a. rubber.
   b. coal.
   c. iron.
   d. gold.

3. The large amount of steel produced in the United States is due to
   a. the climate of the country.
   b. rich oil deposits.
   c. rich deposits of coal and iron.
   d. many miles of coastline.

4. All of the following are American economic assets EXCEPT
   a. a varied climate.
   b. good shipping ports.
   c. a plentiful supply of electrical energy.
   d. small size.

C. True or False

Decide whether each of these statements is true or false.

1. The United States has few inland waterways.

2. High mountains run through most of the middle of the United States.

3. The five Great Lakes are one of the world's great inland waterways.

4. The United States has a plentiful supply of electrical energy.

5. The Missouri-Mississippi is the chief river system in the United States.

D. Vocabulary

Match the words with the definitions.

Words	Definitions
1. asset	a. able to support much growth
2. natural resources	b. a large river
3. tributary	c. things in nature that people can use
4. fertile	d. a river that feeds into a larger river
	e. something of value
	f. to honor someone

E. Map Skills

Use a map of the United States to help you do the following.

1. Name four states in the area of the Missouri-Mississippi river system.

2. Name one port on the Atlantic coast and one port on the Pacific coast.

3. Choose three of the five geographical regions listed in the reading selection. Name one state from each of these three areas.

Lesson 2   The Industrial Revolution

WORDS TO UNDERSTAND
Discuss the meanings of these words.

industrial   **corporations**   **stock**

NEW WORDS IN SENTENCES
1. After the **industrial** revolution began, most goods were no longer made in the home by hand.
2. **Corporations** are owned by the public.
3. By selling **stock,** corporations can raise large sums of money.

AS YOU READ
As you read this selection, try to answer these questions.
1. How did the Civil War affect the growth of industry?
2. What were some of the important results of the rapid growth of industry?

THE READING SELECTION
The Civil War ended in 1865. The war brought about many important political, social, and economic changes in the country. In politics, the supremacy of the federal government over state governments was established. One great social change was the end of slavery in the South. The biggest economic change was the expansion of the **industrial** system in the North.

Industry in the North had been growing steadily since 1830. The Civil War greatly increased northern industrial power. Uniforms had to be made. Ships had to be built. Guns had to be manufactured. Machines were used to make these products, since the war required so many people in the army and navy.

In the South, the war brought about the beginnings of industrialism. The North had been able to produce everything it needed to fight the war. It was also able to run its railroads and to feed its population. This made a deep impression on the South. Southerners began to realize the need for more industry. Before 1865, the South believed that cotton crops alone could support the people. After 1865, people in the South showed a greater interest in industry.

The industrial revolution came first to the North. It soon affected the whole nation. This rapid growth of industry had a number of effects on the country.

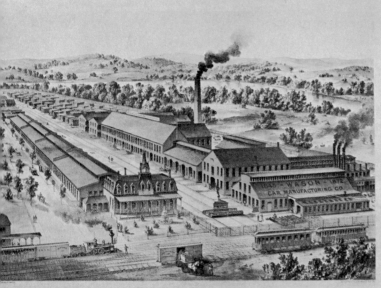

WASON MANUFACTURING COMPANY of SPRINGFIELD, MASS.
RAILWAY CAR BUILDERS.
CAR WHEELS AND GENERAL RAILWAY WORK.

An early blast furnace (above) was used in gun factories. Hot temperatures in the furnace separated iron or other metals from rock. Improved machines and large factories (left) were parts of the industrial revolution.

419

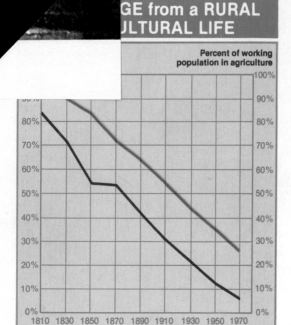

Percent of working population in agriculture

If fewer Americans worked in agriculture, what do you suppose they did for a living?

1. Factories and machines replaced the old way of making goods in the home by hand.

2. Machines made it possible to produce goods in large quantities. This, in turn, meant lower prices. As a result, more people could afford to buy the goods.

3. With the growth of industry came the growth of cities. Many people from farm areas took jobs in city factories.

4. The entire nation took a greater interest in industry and trade. Industry replaced agriculture as the major economic activity of the American people. However, the United States continued to lead the world in agricultural production.

5. Transportation and communica-

tions improved. Soon after the Civil War, railroad lines reached from coast to coast. Also, a national telegraph system was developed.

6. An increasing number of **corporations** were formed. A corporation is a business that sells shares of ownership to the public. The shares are called **stock.** Selling the stock makes it possible to raise large sums of money. The money can then be used to buy machines, build factories, and produce goods.

7. Labor unions began to develop. More and more workers felt the need to form organizations that would protect their interests.

COMPREHENSION CHECK

A. *Recognizing the Main Idea*

This selection as a whole tells you that

1. the South favored industrialism.

2. industrial development brought many changes.

3. industrial development made people rich.

4. industrial development favored the agricultural sections.

B. *Selecting Important Details*

Choose the ending that best completes each statement.

1. The increased use of machines in industry resulted in

    a. higher prices and more goods.

    b. higher prices and fewer goods.

    c. more goods being made by hand at home.

    d. lower prices and more goods.

2. Each of the following was a result of the Civil War EXCEPT
    a. the North depended more upon machines.
    b. the North greatly increased its productive power.
    c. the South turned more to industry.
    d. the South became more industrialized than the North.

3. After the Civil War, the federal government
    a. lost much of its strength.
    b. became as strong as the state governments.
    c. was supreme over the state governments.
    d. was replaced.

4. Corporations
    a. would not use machines.
    b. replaced labor unions.
    c. did not have to sell stock to the public.
    d. raised large sums of money by selling stock to the public.

C. True or False

Decide whether each of these statements is true or false.

1. The growth of industry led to the growth of cities.

2. The development of industry meant there would be fewer labor unions.

3. The industrial revolution started in the South.

4. Agriculture replaced industry as the main economic activity in the United States.

5. People in the North believed that producing cotton alone could support them.

D. Vocabulary

Match the words with the definitions.

Words	Definitions
1. industrial	a. a business that sells stock to the public
2. corporation	b. having to do with factories and business
3. stock	c. a business that does not make money
	d. a share of ownership
	e. having to do with transportation

E. Chart and Graph Work

1. Use the "Economic Assets" chart on page 416 to answer these questions.
    a. In which year was production of gold the highest? Iron ore? Oil?
    b. Did agricultural production increase or decrease between 1860 and 1960?

2. Use "The Change from a Rural Agricultural Life" graph to answer these questions.
    a. What was the last year in which rural population was larger than urban population?
    b. Did the percentage of the population working in agriculture increase or decrease between 1860 and 1960?

3. Look at this answer together with your answer to 1b. What can they tell you about changes in farming methods?

Lesson 3   Government and Business

WORDS TO UNDERSTAND

Discuss the meanings of these words.

regulation   **monopoly**   **consumer**

NEW WORDS IN SENTENCES

1. Government **regulation** of business can prevent some unfair practices.
2. Since the company had a **monopoly** on bottle production, there was no competition.
3. Goods produced by industry are sold to the **consumer.**

AS YOU READ

As you read this selection, try to answer the following questions.

1. What were some points for and against government regulation of business?
2. What were some of the laws passed to regulate businesses?

THE READING SELECTION

As American industry expanded, many small businesses gave way to corporations worth millions of dollars. These huge corporations were able to gain control of whole industries. An example is the Standard Oil Company. It was started in 1870. By 1880, it was refining 95 percent of the oil produced in the country. In 1901, the United States Steel Corporation was formed. It was the first corporation to be valued at $1 billion.

Many corporations also developed tremendous political power. Business interests often influenced members of state legislatures and members of the U.S. Congress. This brought on a demand for some form of **regulation** by the government. Those who argued in favor of regulating business made several points.

1. Business must be regulated to prevent one corporation from controlling a whole industry. This kind of control is called a **monopoly.** It can lead to unfair raising of prices, because a monopoly has no competition.

2. "Price rigging" by groups of corporations in an industry must end. Price rigging means that companies agree among themselves to buy or sell only at a certain price. Such a practice is unfair to the **consumer** and to other businesses.

3. The public must have protection from industrial practices that could

Big business is often wealthy and important to the economy. In this cartoon, what is its relationship to government?

have bad effects on the health of the nation. This was especially true of the methods used in preparing foods.

There were also some Americans who felt that many corporations needed regulation simply because they were too powerful.

Those who were against regulating business made these points.

1. Regulation would give too much power to political groups and parties.

2. The growth of business would be limited or otherwise restricted by regulation.

3. One group of businesses might be favored over another.

4. Regulation would lead to too much government interference in the daily lives of the people.

The effort to regulate industry was helped by the work of a group of writers called "muckrakers." A muckraker is someone who rakes up dirt. The muckrakers wrote about conditions in American life that needed reform in the 1890s and early 1900s.

One famous muckraker was Ida Tarbell. She wrote about the way the Standard Oil Company squeezed out all competition and destroyed many small businesses. Another muckraker was Upton Sinclair. His book *The Jungle* was

In 1880, one company refined 95 percent of the nation's oil.
What does this cartoonist think about that?

about the filth and disease in the meat-packing plants in Chicago. The story he told aroused the nation and brought demands for reform. It was said that Sinclair changed the eating habits of Americans.

The writings of the muckrakers alerted Americans to the necessity for reform. Many people were now aware of the abuses of business and wanted to correct them. The result was a group of laws involving government regulation of business. They included the following.

The Interstate Commerce Act (1887). This law tried to curb problems in the railroad industry. In 1903 and 1906, this law was strengthened. The Interstate Commerce Commission was given the power to set shipping rates.

The Sherman Antitrust Act (1890). Its purpose was to prevent the growth of monopolies in business.

The Meat Inspection Act and the Pure Food and Drug Act (1906). These laws came as a direct result of the conditions exposed in Upton Sinclair's book *The Jungle.*

The Federal Trade Commission Act (1914). It set up a commission to prevent false advertising and unfair competition by means of price fixing.

These are a few examples of government regulation. They played an important part in American life and are still in effect today. The federal government was limited in its actions. Federal regulations applied only to industries that operated across state lines. However, many states also passed laws to regulate industries within their borders.

COMPREHENSION CHECK

A. Recognizing the Main Idea

This selection as a whole tells you that regulation of business

1. is a good thing.
2. is a bad thing.
3. has been going on for too many years.
4. has its good and bad points.

B. Selecting Important Details

Choose the ending that best completes each statement.

1. All the following were arguments in favor of regulation EXCEPT
   a. the public had to be protected.
   b. corporations were too powerful to be allowed complete freedom.
   c. political groups needed more power.
   d. the government had to help prevent unfair monopolies.

2. A strong argument against monopoly in business was that
   a. it could be a bad thing for profits.
   b. it could lead to unfair raising of prices.
   c. it might lead to lowering of prices.
   d. it would make the government too powerful.

3. All of the following were arguments against regulation of business EXCEPT that it might
   a. give too much power to political parties.
   b. favor one business over another.
   c. reduce prices of products.
   d. lead to government interference in the daily lives of people.

4. In the period after 1865
   a. industry did not expand very much.
   b. a few industries expanded.
   c. industry expanded greatly.
   d. only the Standard Oil Company expanded.

C. True or False

Decide whether each of these statements is true or false.

1. Even those who favored government regulation did not think it was needed in the food industry.
2. Price rigging was a benefit to the consumer.
3. Those opposed to government regulation feared it might lead to limiting the growth of business.
4. A monopoly in an industry means that many companies control that industry.
5. The Meat Inspection Act was the result of the conditions exposed in the book called *The Jungle*.

D. Vocabulary

Match the words with the definitions.

Words	Definitions
1. regulation	a. one who sells
2. monopoly	b. one who buys and uses items
3. consumer	c. control by a single company
	d. small business
	e. control by rules

E. Ask Yourself

Do you think it is necessary for government to regulate business today? Why or why not?

Upton Sinclair and *The Jungle*

Upton Sinclair was twenty-eight years old when he published *The Jungle* in 1906. The novel, set in Chicago, told the story of an immigrant family. It described the way the family was cheated and used. Sinclair also included material about conditions in the Chicago stockyards.

Sinclair wrote *The Jungle* to win people over to his political views. His goal was to make Americans more aware of the great gap between the rich and poor classes. The book created a sensation when it appeared. However, it was Sinclair's descriptions of filthy conditions in the meat-packing plants that caused the sensation, not his descriptions of social classes.

The American people wanted to know if the stockyard conditions described in the novel were true. President Theodore Roosevelt appointed a commission to investigate the Chicago stockyards. The commission's report indicated that Sinclair's descriptions were accurate. The government began to work towards cleaning up the meat-packing industry. A meat inspection act was passed, and the first steps towards cleaning the stockyards were taken.

Sinclair had hoped to convert the American people to new political views. Instead, his book led to radical changes in the food industry. He once said, "I aimed my novel for people's hearts but hit them in the stomach." Upton Sinclair may not have accomplished his original goal, but *The Jungle* made him one of the most important muckrakers of the time.

Lesson 4   The Problem of Labor

WORDS TO UNDERSTAND

Discuss the meanings of these words.

arbitration   **mediation**   **picketing**

NEW WORDS IN SENTENCES

1. In **arbitration,** both sides must follow the ruling of a third party, whether they agree with the ruling or not.

2. In **mediation,** both sides work with a third party to reach a compromise they agree on.

3. The **picketing** continued every day during the time the workers were on strike.

AS YOU READ

As you read this selection, try to answer these questions.

1. What were some of the problems facing the first American unions?

2. What are some of the methods labor uses to win its demands?

THE READING SELECTION

Review. Many Americans began to feel that the large corporations ought to be regulated by the government. They felt control was needed to prevent monopolies and price rigging and to protect the quality of food and drugs. Other Americans argued that such regulation gave the government and political groups too much power and could limit or otherwise affect business growth. But federal laws were finally passed. The Interstate Commerce Commission was set up to control railroads. The Sherman Antitrust Act was passed to prevent monopolies. The Federal Trade Commission was set up to prevent false advertising and price rigging. Laws protecting the quality of food and drugs were also passed. ☆

American working people had almost no power in the early 1800s. Wages were low and work hours were long. Even in the late 1800s, most workers put in a twelve-hour day, six days a week. Child labor was common. Women and children were paid less than men, and the result was that men's wages were also kept down. Every few years, there were periods of high unemployment, so that workers could not find jobs. At that time, American workers had no unemployment insurance or old-age pensions.

Working people felt that they were being robbed of their dignity. Working conditions were bad, and workers had few ways to improve them. Those who

427

complained ran the risk of being fired. Any worker could be fired at any time, for any reason.

Attempts to organize workers into unions had had little success. There had been unions since early in the 1800s, but the first effective national union was not formed until 1869. Those who tried to establish unions faced several major problems.

1. Could workers and small employers belong to the same unions? This was a problem in such industries as printing, baking, cigar making, and barbering. These trades were often performed in small shops. An employer and two or three workers often worked side by side.

2. Should only skilled workers be members of unions? What should be done about the many unskilled workers in the factories?

3. What could be done to change the anti-union attitude of the government and the courts? For example, a strike in Philadelphia had been ruled illegal by the courts in 1806.

There had been efforts to organize workers during the 1830s. An organization called the National Trades Union was formed in 1834. It managed to get 300,000 members before it collapsed in 1837. The efforts of working people to win shorter hours won some support from the government. In 1840, President Van Buren ordered a ten-hour day on all work being done for the federal government. The unions even won some support in the courts. In 1842, a Massachusetts court ruled that unions were legal and had the right to strike.

Culver Pictures, Inc.

Some early strikes, such as an 1860 shoemakers' strike (above), were peaceful. Others, such as the Pullman strike (opposite) in 1894, involved conflict and violence.

In 1866, the National Labor Union was set up. This union was never effective and failed in 1873. The first real national union was the Noble Order of the Knights of Labor. It was formed in 1869 by Uriah S. Stephens, a tailor from Philadelphia. Membership in the Knights of Labor was open to all working people except bankers, lawyers, gamblers, and those who sold hard liquor. In 1878, the Knights of Labor came under the leadership of Terence V. Powderly, a Pennsylvania machinist.

The Knights of Labor was opposed to strikes and violence. It favored boycotts and **arbitration.** A boycott is an action to refuse to buy the products of companies that oppose unions. A well-organized boycott can mean considerable loss of money to a company. Arbitration is one of the means of settling disputes

between two parties. A third party is brought in to end the dispute. In arbitration, the decision made by the third party is final. Both the union and the management must accept it. Sometimes the two parties will use **mediation.** A mediator is a third party who tries to help a union and management work out a compromise. In mediation, the third party does not make the final decision.

There were many strikes in the 1880s. Police and militia were often used to halt strikes. The striking workers refused to work at their jobs until the employer met their demands. Workers on strike would parade in front of the factory with signs. This parading is called **picketing.** Its purpose is to keep other workers from taking over the jobs of the strikers.

Strikes and other actions by unions led to tense situations in many parts of the United States. Public opinion turned strongly against unions after a bomb explosion in Chicago's Haymarket Square in 1886. An unknown person threw a bomb at police who came to break up a labor meeting. This incident caused many people to fear unions. The Knights of Labor, along with other labor unions, was blamed for violence and bombings. Actually, the union had little to do with labor troubles in Chicago at the time.

In 1886, the Knights of Labor had about 700,000 members. Within the next few years, that number fell to almost nothing. The Knights of Labor was all but dead. Its place was taken by a new national labor organization called the American Federation of Labor.

COMPREHENSION CHECK

A. Recognizing the Main Idea

1. In a single sentence, write the main idea of this lesson's reading selection.

2. Write two other points that are made in this lesson's reading selection.

B. Selecting Important Details

Choose the ending that best completes each statement.

1. In the early 1800s,
    a. women and children were paid the same wages as men.
    b. workers had unemployment insurance.
    c. national workers' unions were strong.
    d. most workers worked twelve hours a day, six days a week.

2. All the following methods were used by workers to win their demands EXCEPT
    a. strikes.
    b. boycotts.
    c. arbitration.
    d. the militia.

3. One advantage of arbitration and mediation is that they
    a. help win strikes.
    b. bring in the aid of third parties to avoid or settle strikes.
    c. prevent unionism.
    d. favor unionism.

4. All of the following were problems of early union organization EXCEPT
    a. the relationship of skilled and unskilled labor.
    b. the anti-union attitude of the government and courts.
    c. the question of who should be allowed to join unions.
    d. the need to halt strikes.

C. True or False

Decide whether each of these statements is true or false. Rewrite the false ones to make them true.

1. The use of child labor was common in the late 1800s.

2. Gamblers, lawyers, and bankers were members of the Knights of Labor.

3. The Knights of Labor was in favor of using violence.

4. The purpose of picketing is to keep others from entering a factory whose workers are on strike.

5. The labor meeting at Haymarket Square in Chicago in 1886 was peaceful.

D. Vocabulary

Write your own sentence for each of these words.

arbitration   mediation   picketing

E. Ask Yourself

Do you think working conditions would have improved without unions? Why or why not?

The Triangle Shirtwaist Fire

In 1961, the International Ladies Garment Workers Union held a memorial meeting. The meeting was held in memory of 146 workers who had died fifty years before in the terrible fire at the Triangle Shirtwaist Company in New York City.

The Triangle Shirtwaist Company was one of hundreds of garment-making companies in New York. These companies were known as sweatshops because of their bad working conditions. Many were located in huge building lofts. The lofts lacked proper lighting, and little attention was paid to safety measures. Bales of materials were stacked in the halls and piled against exit doors. On March 25, 1911, a fire broke out in the Triangle Shirtwaist loft. It spread rapidly and was soon out of control. Workers who tried to flee the building were trapped by jammed doors. Thousands of people who gathered in the streets helplessly witnessed the deaths of 146 workers, most of them young women.

The fire shocked the entire nation. New York City moved to enact a stricter building code for factories. Labor laws were revised to give better protection to workers. At the same time, additional thousands of garment workers joined unions to win better working conditions.

The terrible tragedy of the Triangle fire had started the movement for better working conditions in the garment industry. At their memorial meeting fifty years later, garment workers could look back upon great progress.

Culver Pictures, Inc.

Lesson 5 The American Federation of Labor

WORDS TO UNDERSTAND

Discuss the meanings of these words.

contracts   **depression**
collective bargaining

NEW WORDS IN SENTENCES

1. The **contracts** provided better wages for the workers.

2. The **collective bargaining** between the employer and the union representatives went on for many weeks.

3. In an economic **depression,** many people are unemployed.

AS YOU READ

As you read this selection, try to answer these questions.

1. How did the American Federation of Labor differ from national unions of earlier times?

2. What were the problems facing working people in the 1930s?

3. How did the Congress of Industrial Organizations differ from the American Federation of Labor?

THE READING SELECTION

In 1886, a new labor organization was formed. It was known as the American Federation of Labor (AFL). Since then, the AFL has been the leading organization of American workers.

The person most responsible for the success of the American Federation of Labor was Samuel Gompers. Gompers was an English-born cigar maker who led the AFL from 1886 until his death in 1924. He and the other AFL leaders built a strong national union by following several basic ideas.

1. The AFL was not to be just a large group of workers. It was to be a collection of separate craft or trade unions. There would be a bakers' union, a carpenters' union, a plumbers' union, and so on. These unions were joined together in a national federation. In this way, each union could control its own affairs and still have the support of the national federation.

2. The AFL would mainly seek to organize the skilled craft workers in each trade.

3. The AFL would not engage in political activity. The purpose of the AFL was to win better working conditions and higher wages for its members. It did not seek to change laws or to reform the government.

4. The AFL unions would seek labor **contracts** with employers. These contracts would make the unions the

Among labor organizers were Rose Schneiderman (above), Samuel Gompers (top right), and Elizabeth Gurley Flynn (right). Flynn worked with the Industrial Workers of the World.

collective bargaining agents for the workers. Collective bargaining means that union leaders speak for all the workers in bargaining with employers.

To better understand how the AFL was organized, we can examine the carpentry trade. Carpenters are skilled workers. In the AFL, they were organized in the International Union of Carpenters and Joiners. Local unions of carpenters were set up in each town and city. Members paid dues to the local unions. The locals elected their own officers.

All the local unions of carpenters were joined together in an international union. This union met every few years to set policies and elect officers. Local unions sent delegates to this international convention. They also paid dues to the international union. The carpenters' international union, in turn, joined with other international craft unions to form the AFL.

The AFL unions had considerable power because they organized the skilled craft workers in each trade. Such skilled workers were not easily replaced in case a strike was called. If the carpenters working in an area went on strike, they could stop all construction work. Skilled carpenters could not easily be replaced by non-union workers. Workers on strike received some money from the union strike fund. This fund was supported by union dues.

AFL membership rose from 500,000 in 1900 to about 2 million in 1914. By 1920, there were about 4 million AFL members. However, the AFL also faced many problems. Its membership made up only a small part of the total American work force. The AFL made almost no attempt to organize the millions of unskilled workers in the steel, auto, mining, and oil industries. The AFL was also weakened by disagreements among unions.

Between 1920 and 1930, membership in the AFL declined by almost a million. After 1929, the United States was in the grip of an economic **depression.** At one point, about one worker out of every four had no job. Craft unions fought one another for jobs for their members. Union membership declined further.

In 1933, the New Deal administration of President Franklin D. Roosevelt began. The attitude of the New Deal was helpful to labor. In 1933, Congress passed the National Industrial Recovery Act (NIRA). One section declared that workers had the right to join unions of their own choice and to bargain collectively.

Some labor leaders began to demand that the AFL do something to organize the millions of non-union workers. These labor leaders proposed that industrial unions be set up. An industrial union organizes all the workers in an industry regardless of the kind of work they do.

In 1935, the Committee for Industrial Organization was set up by a group of AFL unions. This committee won great success in the automobile, steel, rubber, and transportation industries. The AFL leaders feared that the industrial unions would soon become stronger than the craft unions. They ordered the committee to disband. Many of the unions refused, and they were suspended by the AFL.

The suspended unions later formed an independent organization called the Congress of Industrial Organizations (CIO). It was led by John L. Lewis and, later, by Philip Murray. In 1955, the CIO merged with the AFL. Industrial unions had become a more important part of the labor movement.

COMPREHENSION CHECK

A. Recognizing the Main Idea

This selection as a whole tells you about the

1. carpenters' union.
2. organization of unskilled workers into unions.
3. organization and work of the AFL and the CIO.
4. why the AFL and CIO split apart.

B. Selecting Important Details

Choose the ending that best completes each statement.

1. The main idea of organization in the AFL was to
   a. form one big union.
   b. form craft unions and unite them in a federation.
   c. organize unskilled workers.
   d. help promote socialism.

2. Under the AFL plan, the control of union affairs in a trade
   a. belonged to the AFL.
   b. remained in the hands of employers.
   c. belonged to the union within that trade.
   d. belonged to the national federation.

3. The Committee for Industrial Organization
   a. organized skilled workers only.
   b. was successful in a number of industries.
   c. ordered the AFL to disband.
   d. did not organize unskilled workers.

4. The idea behind industrial unionism is that
   a. workers belong to the union of their own craft.
   b. workers join any union they want.
   c. workers join the union of their industry regardless of craft.
   d. workers do not join unions.

C. Completion

Fill in the word or words that best complete each sentence.

1. _____ was a cigar maker who helped build the AFL.

2. The AFL was organized to be a large collection of _____.

3. Strike funds were supported by union _____.

4. The NIRA gave workers the right to join _____ and to _____ collectively.

5. The CIO organized _____ unions rather than _____ unions.

D. Vocabulary

Use a word from this list to complete each sentence.

collective bargaining depression
corporation   contracts

1. The workers wanted better working conditions written into their _____.

2. Without _____, workers had no way of working out contracts with employers.

3. Wages and prices fell during the _____.

E. Using Your Knowledge

If you make an outline before writing an essay, you will see clearly the main idea and the details you want to include. Make an outline for a two-paragraph essay answering the following question: What were the reasons for the way the AFL was organized? Write two main ideas and two details under each idea.

Rose Schneiderman and the Women's Trade Union League

Rose Schneiderman was one of the people caught up in strong reform movements at the beginning of this century. She came to America from Poland in 1890, at the age of eight. Like other Jews who left their countries because of violence and discrimination, the Schneiderman family hoped to make a better life in the United States. The family was very poor, and Rose was only thirteen years old when she went to work.

Her first job was in a large department store. She worked sixty-four hours a week for $2.25. When she was sixteen years old, she took a job as a machine operator making cap linings. In 1903, Schneiderman and another woman organized a women's local of the United Cloth Hat and Cap Makers Union in New York.

In 1905, Schneiderman joined the New York branch of the Women's Trade Union League. The league had been organized a couple of years earlier. The purpose of the league was to bring more women into the labor unions and to improve their working conditions.

Rose Schneiderman worked as an organizer for the Women's Trade Union League. In 1909, she helped lead 25,000 women working in the garment industries out on strike.

The strike was unsuccessful, and conditions at factories did not improve. Three years after the strike, a fire in the Triangle Shirtwaist Company building killed 146 workers, most of them young women. Rose Schneiderman was determined that this would never happen again. She worked hard for the passage of a safety code for factories.

During the 1920s, the Women's Trade Union League had great influence on labor reforms in the state of New York. Rose Schneiderman worked as president of the league and then was appointed secretary of labor for New York in 1937. As the only woman on the Labor Advisory Board of the National Recovery Administration set up under the New Deal, Schneiderman worked, without much success, to make labor laws more fair to women. One example of discrimination against women was that labor unions allowed women to be paid less than men for the same work.

Rose Schneiderman served as secretary of New York's department of labor until 1944. In 1947, at the age of sixty-five, she retired as president of the New York Women's Trade Union League. Rose Schneiderman's view of the trade union movement was best expressed when she wrote

> To me, the labor movement was never just a way of getting higher wages. What appealed to me was the . . . great cause that created fellowship. You wanted the girl or the man working beside you to be treated just as well as you were, and an injury to one was the concern of all.

Lesson 6   Government and Labor

WORDS TO UNDERSTAND

Discuss the meanings of these words.

laissez-faire   **compulsory**
compensation

NEW WORDS IN SENTENCES

1. Making laws to control business practices was against the idea of **laissez-faire.**

2. His **compensation** for a week's work was to be fifty dollars.

3. The **compulsory** school law meant that all children had to attend school.

AS YOU READ

As you read this selection, try to answer these questions.

1. Why did the government take little action on behalf of working people in the 1800s?

2. What laws were passed in the 1900s to benefit working people?

THE READING SELECTION

During most of the 1800s, Americans believed that the government should not try to regulate business or labor. Because of this, the government took little action on behalf of working people. There were a few exceptions. One was the action of the federal government in setting up the Bureau of Labor in 1884.

The federal government did act to control some practices of big business. However, it did little to pass laws protecting workers. This was partly due to the continuing belief in the idea of **laissez-faire.** *Laissez-faire* is a French expression meaning "let alone." Those who believed in laissez-faire did not want the government interfering in relations between employers and workers or in other economic affairs.

Belief in laissez-faire was one reason for government inaction. Another reason was that the American Federation of Labor was not active in politics. The AFL followed the advice of its president, Samuel Gompers, that labor ought to "reward its friends and punish its enemies." The AFL did not try to make itself powerful in any one political party. Nor did it try to form a special labor party as had been done in many countries in Europe. As a result, union leaders had little influence on government.

The government passed very few laws on behalf of working people until the

Employment Agency by Isaac Soyer (1937. Oil on Canvas. 34¼ x 45 inches), Collection of Whitney Museum of American Art

National Archives

In the 1930s, employment agencies were full of jobless people (top). The government finally created some jobs in conservation (above).

1900s. In 1913, the Department of Labor was formed. This meant that a secretary of labor was added to the president's cabinet. The Department of Labor began to collect information dealing with labor and its problems. Such information was important to Congress in preparing new laws.

In 1916, the federal government enacted the Adamson Act. It provided for an eight-hour day for railroad workers. At the time, this was an outstanding government action on behalf of labor. However, most of the labor laws from 1900 to 1930 were passed by state legislatures, not by the federal government. The most important state labor laws were the workers' **compensation** acts. These laws provided that workers be compensated—that is, paid—for injuries suffered as a result of accidents on the job. Many state governments also passed **compulsory** education laws. These laws required children to attend schools. These laws helped take children out of factories.

The federal government began to pass legislation affecting labor after 1933, when Franklin D. Roosevelt was president. One important law was the National Labor Relations Act (NLRA). It was passed in 1935 to replace part of the NIRA, which had been declared unconstitutional. It gave workers the right to join unions of their choice and to bargain collectively with employers. The NLRA also defined unfair practices on the part of employers. It established the National Labor Relations Board to investigate and settle disputes. The act was challenged in court, but in 1937, the Supreme Court held the NLRA to be constitutional. The act proved a great benefit to the union movement.

In 1935, the Social Security Act was passed. The act provided for a system of old-age pensions and for unemployment insurance for workers. In 1938, the government passed the Fair Labor Standards Act. It set up a forty-hour week and a minimum wage of forty cents an hour. These government labor laws represented a new attitude of the government toward the protection of working people.

COMPREHENSION CHECK

A. Recognizing the Main Idea
This selection as a whole tells you

1. about the government's changing attitudes toward labor.

2. why the government never acted on behalf of labor.

3. how the belief in laissez-faire made the government pass laws controlling business practices.

4. why Franklin D. Roosevelt did not approve of laws controlling business practices.

B. Selecting Important Details
Choose the ending that best completes each statement.

1. The government attitude toward business regulation during the 1800s
   a. favored strict regulation.
   b. was linked to a belief in laissez-faire.
   c. opposed laissez-faire.
   d. depended on which party the AFL favored.

2. Most of the federal laws affecting labor were passed
   a. before 1865.
   b. before 1890.
   c. between 1900 and 1933.
   d. after 1933.

3. The workers' compensation acts passed by many states provided for
   a. minimum wages in certain industries.
   b. payment to workers injured on the job.
   c. social security for workers.
   d. the right to join unions.

4. The Social Security Act
   a. gave workers the right to join unions.
   b. set up the forty-hour week.
   c. made minimum wages illegal.
   d. set up a system of old-age pensions and unemployment insurance.

C. True or False

Decide whether each of these statements is true or false.

1. Compulsory education laws helped take children out of factories.
2. The Bureau of Labor was established in the early 1900s.
3. The AFL formed a special labor party in the United States.
4. The NLRA made collective bargaining illegal.
5. The Supreme Court found the NLRA to be constitutional.

D. Vocabulary

Match the words with the definitions.

Words	Definitions
1. laissez-faire	a. required; needing to be done
2. compensation	b. to try
3. compulsory	c. the least possible
	d. payment
	e. let alone

E. Essay

Write a fifty-word essay telling three ways in which the state or federal government affects a worker on a job.

F. Using Your Knowledge

Match the laws with the descriptions.

Laws	Descriptions
1. National Labor Relations Act	a. set up a forty-hour week and minimum wage
2. Fair Labor Standards Act	b. set up an eight-hour workday in railroad industry
3. Adamson Act	c. gave workers the right to join unions of their own choice
4. Social Security Act	d. provided for old-age pensions and unemployment insurance
	e. established the Bureau of Labor

Frances Perkins, Secretary of Labor

Frances Perkins built her career and life's work around improving labor conditions in this country. Her expert skills and knowledge led to her appointment as United States secretary of labor in 1933. Perkins was the first woman cabinet member in the nation's history. But there was opposition to her appointment. Many people felt that the country was not ready for a woman in such a high government position. However, Perkins's accomplishments showed that she was certainly ready to take on the job.

Frances Perkins began her career as a college teacher and then became a social worker. After working in Chicago and Philadelphia, she took a job with the Consumers' League of New York.

For more than twenty years, Frances Perkins served on several New York commissions concerned with industrial safety. She took special interest in studying sanitary conditions and fire prevention in factories and became recognized as an expert in these areas. She worked hard to improve factory safety inspections. Perkins also worked to establish a system of workers' compensation laws. These laws provided that people injured on the job would receive payments so that they could continue to support themselves and their families.

In 1929, Franklin D. Roosevelt was governor of New York. He appointed Frances Perkins to the office of state industrial commissioner. Five years later, when Roosevelt was president, he appointed her United States secretary of labor.

From the day she took office, Frances Perkins was active in the New Deal programs. She helped get Congress to write and pass the Social Security Act in 1935. For the first time, Americans had insurance for unemployed and aged workers. In 1938, the Labor Department helped draw up the Fair Labor Standards Act. It was passed by Congress that same year. The law provided for a minimum wage of forty cents an hour and for a forty-hour work week. It also set a minimum age of sixteen for factory workers. Opposition was strong, but Frances Perkins knew that this law would strengthen the nation.

Perkins was secretary of labor for twelve years under President Franklin D. Roosevelt. Later, she served on the federal Civil Service Commission. Frances Perkins retired when she was seventy-three years old, with a long list of important accomplishments to her credit.

New York Times

Lesson 7   Labor Problems Since 1945

WORDS TO UNDERSTAND
Discuss the meanings of these words.

authorized   **affirmative action**
featherbedding

NEW WORDS IN SENTENCES

1. The strike failed because it was not **authorized** by the union.

2. **Featherbedding** involved union demands that unnecessary workers be hired.

3. **Affirmative action** resulted in a fair representation of minority and women workers in the company.

AS YOU READ

As you read this selection, try to answer these questions.

1. What were some criticisms of labor unions in 1945?

2. Why was the Taft-Hartley Act passed, and what were some of its provisions?

3. What are some problems facing labor and unions in the United States today?

THE READING SELECTION

Labor unions in the United States gained strength in the 1930s. In fact, by 1945, some people feared that the unions were becoming too strong. The people who criticized the labor unions pointed to several failings.

1. It was charged that some of the union leaders were gangsters. These gangsters were said to grow rich on the dues collected by the unions. Some gangsters would "shake down" factory owners. They forced employers to pay for protection against strikes.

2. Unions were sometimes unable to prevent "wildcat" strikes. Wildcat strikes are those not **authorized** by the union.

3. There were often disputes between unions. These fights arose when two unions could not agree on which one should represent the workers in an industry. Such disputes often led to strikes to force employers to recognize one of the unions.

4. Some craft unions limited their membership. It became almost impossible for new workers to enter certain trades. This limited membership was a special problem for women, young people, and minority groups.

5. Unions were accused of **featherbedding.** They often insisted that employers hire workers whose jobs were no longer necessary. For example, the railroad unions have tried to keep extra workers in locomotives even though newer engines require a smaller crew.

6. Some unions were accused of calling too many strikes. Such strikes were costly and often a great public inconvenience.

Just after World War II, there were some strikes in important industries. These strikes made many people feel that labor unions were becoming too powerful. Public opinion began to favor some government control over unions as well as over business. Union officials argued against such control. They felt it would serve the interests of employers rather than the interests of the general public.

The movement to limit the power of unions resulted in the Taft-Hartley Act of 1947. This act amended the National Labor Relations Act, which had been so helpful to labor unions in 1935. The union leaders disliked the Taft-Hartley Act. They referred to it as a "slave labor" law. The Taft-Hartley Act included several provisions.

1. It outlawed a "closed shop" agreement. A closed shop is one in which only union members may be hired to work. However, the law did allow the "union shop" agreement. A union shop agreement allows the employer to hire non-union workers. But each new employee must join the union within a certain time.

2. It prohibited the secondary boycott. In other words, unions could not picket stores or factories that sold or used non-union goods.

3. It required all unions to issue regular financial statements of money received and money spent.

4. It provided for a sixty-day "cooling-off" period before a union could call a strike. In strikes that affected the national

Off-duty New York police demonstrate for a pay raise. Should public-service employees, such as police, have the right to strike?

welfare, this cooling-off period could be extended for another eighty days.

The Taft-Hartley Act has not proved as serious a drawback to labor as most unions had feared. But workers face other, more serious problems than the limits imposed on unions by the Taft-Hartley Act.

For example, workers are directly affected by inflation. In a period of inflation, workers must demand higher pay to meet the rising costs of goods. When workers win these higher wages, businesses pass on the cost to consumers. The resulting higher prices leave workers once again unable to keep up. Since the 1970s, an inflation rate of about 10 percent a year has been a major problem for workers.

Rising unemployment is another serious problem. During the 1960s, about 3 percent of American workers were out of work. By 1981, the figure had risen to about 7 percent and was much higher for

443

black workers, teenagers, and women. Government unemployment insurance has given temporary help to many out-of-work people. But only a big increase in the number of available jobs will help ease the unemployment problem.

Workers and unions also face the problems arising from changes in the types of jobs available. In 1900, about 47 percent of American workers were engaged in making goods. Another 44 percent were in service industries, such as sales, repairs, transportation, and health care. Only about 9 percent of all workers were employed by national, state, or local governments. Today, however, only about 30 percent of American workers are engaged in making goods. Fifty-five percent now work in service industries, and nearly 15 percent are employed by government agencies. These changes mean that workers must now be trained for new types of jobs. And unions are losing members in the goods-producing industries. They now must seek members in the largely non-union service industries and government agencies.

Workers also face the problem of unfair labor practices. For many years, women received less pay than men for doing the same job. A 1963 law makes such unfairness illegal, but there is still much inequality in the labor force.

Women and members of minority groups have supported programs of **affirmative action.** Such programs require employers to hire a certain number of qualified minority or women applicants. Affirmative action programs are designed to give women and minorities a fair representation in labor. However, many people oppose affirmative action

"How Long Has It Been Since You Walked Around Outside?" from *The Herblock Gallery* (Simon & Schuster, 1968)

Union members have sometimes criticized their leaders. What kind of criticism is shown in this cartoon?

programs. They argue that such programs are unfair to qualified white or male workers. Opponents of affirmative action gained support with the election of Ronald Reagan as president in 1980. President Reagan does not favor affirmative action programs.

Clearly, government is involved in current labor issues. But how much should government do? Should it encourage affirmative action? Should it create jobs for the unemployed? And what can it do about inflation?

COMPREHENSION CHECK

A. Recognizing the Main Idea

1. In a single sentence, write the main idea of this lesson's reading selection.

2. Write two other points that are made in this lesson's reading selection.

B. Selecting Important Details

Choose the ending that best completes each statement.

1. Unions were accused of
   a. authorizing wildcat strikes.
   b. refusing to featherbed.
   c. not being powerful enough.
   d. being controlled by gangsters.
2. Some craft unions favored
   a. the Taft-Hartley Act.
   b. limited membership.
   c. a "slave labor" law.
   d. government control over the number of strikes.
3. The Taft-Hartley Act
   a. allowed closed shop agreements.
   b. encouraged secondary boycotts.
   c. provided for a cooling-off period before strikes.
   d. did not permit union shop agreements.
4. In the years since 1900, there has been an increase in the percentage of
   a. service-related jobs and jobs for government workers.
   b. government workers, but a decrease in service-related jobs.
   c. workers engaged in making goods.
   d. all types of jobs.

C. Fact or Opinion

Decide whether each of these statements is fact or opinion.

1. Unions should be controlled by the government.

2. Unions have been accused of featherbedding.

3. The government should create jobs to ease unemployment.

4. Affirmative action programs should be abolished.

5. Rising prices are a problem for workers today.

D. Vocabulary

Write your own sentence for each of these terms.

authorize   affirmative action
featherbedding

E. Essay

Write three or four sentences supporting the following statement. Then write three or four sentences arguing against it.

Affirmative action programs should not be allowed because they sometimes benefit minorities at the expense of other people.

F. Graph Skills

Use the graphs in this lesson to answer these questions.

1. What percentage of the total female population was working in 1940? In 1977?

2. What percentage of working women were managers and administrators in 1970? What percentage were in clerical jobs?

3. In which fields are the median salaries of males greater than the median salaries of females?

WOMEN in the WORK FORCE

Percentage of female adults in the work force

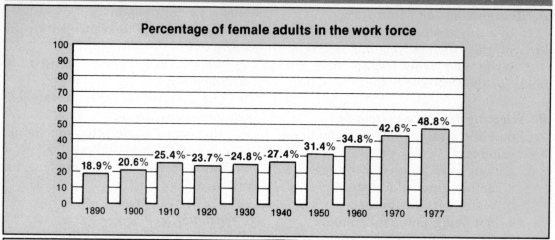

Year	Percentage
1890	18.9%
1900	20.6%
1910	25.4%
1920	23.7%
1930	24.8%
1940	27.4%
1950	31.4%
1960	34.8%
1970	42.6%
1977	48.8%

Median female and male salaries 1975

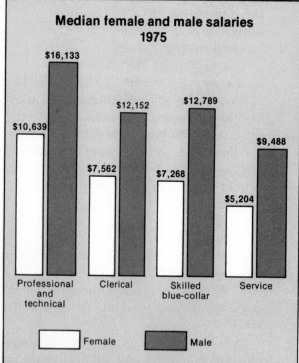

Professional and technical — Female $10,639 — Male $16,133
Clerical — Female $7,562 — Male $12,152
Skilled blue-collar — Female $7,268 — Male $12,789
Service — Female $5,204 — Male $9,488

☐ Female   ■ Male

Percentage of working women in various fields 1978

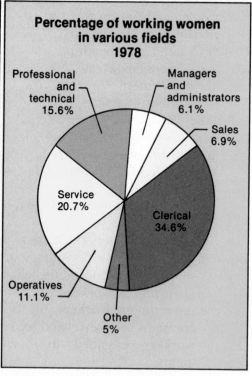

Professional and technical 15.6%
Managers and administrators 6.1%
Sales 6.9%
Clerical 34.6%
Other 5%
Operatives 11.1%
Service 20.7%

The percentage of women working has increased greatly (top graph). How do female and male salaries compare? In which fields do most women work? In which field do the fewest women work?

Women in the Work Force: The Views of Juanita Kreps

Why don't more women have jobs with power and responsibility? Why does the average woman make less money than a man? These are difficult questions. Juanita Kreps, an economist who was appointed secretary of commerce in 1976, has attempted to answer them.

Kreps feels that one problem is that women have often been looked upon as "temporary" workers, who take jobs only until they get married and have families. Thus, companies are less likely to spend time and money training a woman for a higher position, because they feel this effort will be wasted. Men, who are considered permanent wage earners, are felt to be worth such an investment.

New York Times

Kreps points out that most women are not paid for their work as homemakers. It is possible that this low value placed on women's work in the home may carry over to an employer's idea of the value of woman's work in industry and business. Thus, she may be paid less because it is felt that she is worth less. And she may even be willing to accept lower wages because they are at least an improvement over no wages at all.

Kreps argues that education also has contributed to women's lower positions and salaries. The average educational level of women exceeded that of men until 1974. But job training for women differs from that of men. Most technical, industrial, and trade courses are taken by men. Most health, business, and commercial courses are taken by women. As a result, males are better trained for higher paying jobs.

Kreps feels that greater educational opportunities for women will help. She also suggests more flexible working schedules that allow time for women to care for children at home. But clearly what is also needed is a change in the value placed on women's work.

Lesson 8 Unrest Among Farmers

WORDS TO UNDERSTAND

Discuss the meanings of these words.

surplus   interest
credit   cooperative

NEW WORDS IN SENTENCES

1. There were **surplus** products because farmers produced more than they could sell.

2. Buying things on **credit** means you are trusted to pay for them at a later time.

3. The money that banks charge for giving loans is called **interest.**

4. Owners of **cooperative** stores saved money because they bought items direct from manufacturers.

AS YOU READ

As you read this selection, try to answer these questions.

1. What were some things that helped the agricultural revolution?

2. What were the farmers' four main problems?

3. How did farmers try to get relief from their problems?

THE READING SELECTION

Review. Until the 1930s, the federal government provided little protection for workers. This was because the AFL was not active in politics and because there was much belief in the laissez-faire idea of government. After 1900, many states did pass workers' compensation laws, and the U.S. Department of Labor was formed. But the major acts came after 1933. In that year, the National Labor Relations Board was set up by a law that supported unions and limited the power of employers. In 1935, the Social Security system was established. In 1938, the forty-hour week and a minimum wage were enacted into law. ☆

A revolution in industry followed the Civil War. It helped to bring an agricultural revolution to the United States. One result of the industrial revolution was the invention of many new farm machines. These machines included the reaper, harvester, combine, and tractor. They made it possible for one farmer to produce the amount of crops that once would have required dozens of farmers.

The agricultural revolution also benefited from advances in science. Scientists found new ways to plow land. They developed better ways to irrigate lands, and they developed chemical fertilizers. Farmers learned scientific methods of crop growing and animal breeding.

The government played an important part in the agricultural revolution. The

THE TESTING OF THE FIRST REAPING MACHINE NEAR STEELE'S TAVERN. VA. A.D. 1831.

Department of Agriculture was created in 1862 and became a cabinet-level agency in 1889. The Department of Agriculture offered many valuable services to American farmers.

By the end of the Civil War, there was more farmland, and farms were producing much larger crops than before. Farmers were planting mainly cash crops. In earlier times, they had grown only what they needed for their families. Now, they grew such crops as wheat, cotton, and corn, which they sold to make money. They used the cash to support their families and to run their farms. Farmers often produced more than they could sell. This led to the problem of **surplus** farm products. Surpluses drove the prices of crops down.

The agricultural revolution brought more food to more people. However, it left farmers discontented. The farmers had four main difficulties: falling prices, high transportation rates, high tariffs, and a high cost of borrowing money.

Often, the cost to produce a crop was high, but the price received for the crop was low. The costs of fertilizer, seed, and other products were often higher than farmers could afford. Some of these products were sold by companies that had a monopoly on these goods. A company that controlled all the seed sold in a state could charge whatever prices it wanted. In addition, farmers paid high rates to the railroads for carrying their goods to the markets. Farmers also had to pay high rates to the owners of grain elevators. These elevators were used to store grain that could not be sold immediately.

Farmers complained about the high cost of manufactured goods. Clothing, machinery, tools, and household goods were expensive. Some of these items could have been imported from other countries at less cost. However, there was a tariff, or tax, on goods brought into this country. This made the foreign goods as expensive as American goods. Farmers resented having to pay higher costs because of high tariffs.

Farmers often had to borrow money to run their farms. But many farmers could not get loans from the banks. The farmers complained that the banks offered little **credit** and charged high rates of **interest** for loans. Without credit, farmers could not produce.

These problems led to unrest in the years after the Civil War. Farmers formed various organizations to press several demands.

1. The need for a flexible credit system. Farmers wanted loans at reasonable rates of interest.

2. The need for cheap money. Farmers generally wanted the government to issue more paper money. More money in circulation meant higher prices. Higher prices meant farmers could pay their debts more easily with cheap money.

3. The need for regulation of shipping and storage rates. Farmers wanted rates charged by railroads and grain elevators to be fair.

In 1867, an organization known as the Patrons of Husbandry was formed. This soon became known as the Grange. That was the name given to each of the local units. The Granger movement sought to have laws passed in various states to regulate railroad rates. It also organized **cooperative** stores. These stores bought and sold seed, fertilizer, and other items on a cooperative basis. A cooperative store is owned and operated by the customers of the store. They buy direct from manufacturers. The members of cooperatives saved money because they did not have to pay extra money to someone between the manufacturer and themselves. However, the Granger movement began to lose importance after 1886.

Farmers also sought to win relief through the "Greenback movement." During the 1860s, the government had printed about 450 million dollars worth of greenbacks. This paper money was printed without gold or silver to guarantee its value. Most paper currency carried a pledge that it could be exchanged for gold or silver. The greenbackers opposed any plan to take the paper greenbacks out of circulation. In fact, they wanted the government to print more paper money. This would create cheap money and raise prices. The Greenback movement won support for a time, but it began to die out in the middle 1880s.

The Farmers' Alliance movement appeared in the 1880s. The Farmers' Alliance groups also demanded cheap money and higher farm prices. They wanted federal regulation or ownership of railroads, telegraph systems, and grain elevators. The alliance movement was at its height from 1885 to 1892. By 1892, it was replaced by a new political party. This was the People's, or Populist, party.

COMPREHENSION CHECK

A. Recognizing the Main Idea

This selection as a whole tells you that

1. farmers were not able to organize themselves.

2. cheap money was not a good idea for farmers.

3. the agricultural revolution brought many difficulties for farmers.

4. farmers did not need help from the state or federal governments.

B. Selecting Important Details

Choose the ending that best completes each statement.

1. A flexible credit system was important to farmers because it
   a. helped them increase crops.
   b. raised the costs of production.
   c. would make more credit available.
   d. would wipe out the debts of the farmer.

2. One important purpose of cooperative stores was to
   a. end government regulation.
   b. increase profits of manufacturers.
   c. lower the costs of goods farmers had to buy.
   d. bring about cheap money.

3. An important demand of the Grangers was
   a. the regulation of railroad rates.
   b. the end of all government regulation.
   c. higher prices for goods sold to farmers.
   d. the end of cheap money.

4. The Greenback movement wanted
   a. more gold money.
   b. more silver money.
   c. more paper money.
   d. to lower the value of gold and silver.

C. Chronology

Arrange the following in the order in which they were formed.
1. Farmers' Alliance movement
2. the Grange
3. Populist party
4. Department of Agriculture

D. Vocabulary

Write your own sentence for each of these words.

surplus	interest
credit	cooperative

E. Homework

Select one of the following headlines. Then tell in about a hundred words what it might have meant to a farmer in Iowa in the 1880s. Use at least one outside source to prepare your essay.

1. SUPREME COURT RULES GRANGER LAW ILLEGAL IN ILLINOIS

2. GREENBACKERS ACCUSED OF WANTING "FUNNY MONEY"

3. COOPERATIVE STORES ORGANIZED TO MEET FARMERS' NEEDS

Lesson 9   Farmers and the Populist Movement

WORDS TO UNDERSTAND
Discuss the meanings of these words.

minting   demonetized

NEW WORDS IN SENTENCES
1. Unlimited **minting** meant that there would always be a lot of money in circulation.

2. After silver was **demonetized,** it was no longer used to back the nation's currency.

AS YOU READ
As you read this selection, try to answer these questions.

1. What was "free silver"?

2. What were the main demands of the Populist party?

THE READING SELECTION
Review. In the 1870s and 1880s, American farmers banded together in an effort to improve their situation. Their groups included the Grangers, Greenbackers, and Farmers' Alliance. One thing all these groups wanted was cheap money. Cheap money meant inflation, which would help the farmers. Inflation would raise the prices of farm products. This would make it easier for farmers to run their farms and to pay the debts they owed.   ☆

In the 1870s, the issue of cheap money became tied up with the issue of **minting,** or making, silver coins. Until the 1870s, the nation's currency was usually backed by both silver and gold. However, very little silver was presented for minting. In 1873, Congress passed a new coinage act that **demonetized** silver. This meant that the currency of the nation would be based on gold only. But during the 1870s, the silver mines in Colorado and Nevada began producing large amounts of silver. The supply of silver increased greatly. Mine owners then joined with the farmers in demanding that the government buy the silver. The silver could be added to the money already in circulation. Such an increase in money would bring inflation and help the farmers. This "free silver" movement soon became a major issue in American politics.

In 1892, a new political party was

At a Granger meeting in the 1870s, posters call attention to the problems of farmers. The Grangers influenced the government to put controls on railroad and warehouse prices.

formed to represent the interests of the farmers. It was called the People's party, or Populist party. The platform of the Populists included the following demands.

1. The free and unlimited minting of silver. It was proposed that sixteen ounces of silver equal one ounce of gold in value. This would add great value to silver.

2. An increase in the amount of money in circulation. Such an increase would help raise the prices of products that farmers sold.

3. Government ownership of railroads and telephone and telegraph lines. This demand was made because farmers objected to the unfair rates being charged by private owners.

4. A graduated income tax. This meant that persons with higher incomes would pay a higher percentage of their income in tax. For example, a person making $5,000 a year might pay a tax of 15 percent, while a person making $15,000 a year would pay 20 percent. During the Civil War, income taxes had been introduced in the North. But the taxes were dropped after the war.

5. The direct election of U.S. senators. The Constitution provided that senators be chosen by state legislatures. The Populists believed this was undemocratic. They felt that the state legisla-

tures were dominated by big business interests.

6. A single term for the president of the United States. The Populists thought it would be more democratic to limit the term of office of the president. They favored a single four-year period, with no reelection allowed.

The Populists were considered radical in the 1890s. But they do not seem very radical today. Many of their aims have been fulfilled. Through the years, the currency in circulation has been increased and also cheapened. The government does not own the railroads or telegraph and telephone lines. However, it does regulate their operations

closely. There has been an income tax since 1913. Senators are now elected directly, and our president is limited to two four-year terms.

In 1892, the Populists nominated their own candidate for the presidency. He lost, but in 1894, a number of Populist candidates won in congressional elections. In 1896, the Populists joined with the Democratic party in backing William Jennings Bryan for president. He ran on a free-silver platform. Bryan was defeated, and the Populist party soon disappeared from American politics. However, as we have seen, many of their ideas were adopted by the major political parties.

William Jennings Bryan was an unsuccessful candidate for president three times. He spoke forcefully for free silver, the rights of working people, and government control over big business interests.

Library of Congress

COMPREHENSION CHECK

A. Recognizing the Main Idea
In a single sentence, write the main idea of this lesson's reading selection.

B. Selecting Important Details
Choose the ending that best completes each statement.

1. The idea behind the demand for free silver was to
   a. lower the price of silver.
   b. have the government pay nothing for the silver it needed.
   c. stop the use of silver in American currency.
   d. have the government buy silver and turn it into money.

2. The ideas of the Populists
   a. have largely been accepted by the nation over the years.
   b. were never widely accepted in any part of the nation.
   c. were never regarded as radical.
   d. were no different from the ideas of other parties.

3. In the 1890s, Populists were thought of as
   a. conservative.
   b. moderate.
   c. radical.
   d. unfair.

4. Populists backed William Jennings Bryan for president in
   a. 1890.
   b. 1892.
   c. 1894.
   d. 1896.

C. Completion
Fill in the word or words that best complete each sentence.

1. In the 1896 election, the Populists joined with the _____.

2. One important Populist demand was _____ ownership of telegraph lines.

3. Farmers wanted inflation because it would _____ farm prices.

4. The graduated income tax takes a _____ percentage of higher incomes.

5. The Constitution provided that U.S. senators be chosen by _____.

D. Vocabulary
Match the words with the definitions.

Words	Definitions
1. minting	a. issuing paper money
2. demonetize	b. statement of party policies
	c. making money
	d. to stop using as a basis for currency

E. Essay
Write a fifty-word essay arguing for or against at least one point in the Populist platform.

Lesson 10 Major Farm Problems, 1896–1933

WORDS TO UNDERSTAND

Discuss the meanings of these words.

acute　　　**foreclosed**　　　**mortgages**

NEW WORDS IN SENTENCES

1. The workers knew the problem was **acute** because the red danger lights were flashing.

2. When farmers could not make payments, their loans were **foreclosed** and their farms were taken by the banks.

3. The last payments on the **mortgages** are due next year.

AS YOU READ

As you read this selection, try to answer these questions.

1. What events eased farm problems after 1896?

2. What caused new farm problems after World War I?

THE READING SELECTION

During the 1880s and 1890s, farmers took actions to improve their condition. In 1896, the farmers in the Populist party joined with the Democrats. Together they tried to win the election on the issue of free silver. They failed, but conditions for the farmer did improve. There were several reasons for the improvement.

1. A general economic depression in the nation ended after 1896. Business conditions improved. Farmers benefited from a rise in the prices of farm products.

2. The United States went to war with Spain in 1898. The war brought inflation to the country, and farm prices rose. The amount of money in circulation increased as the government bought millions of dollars worth of goods. In addition, gold was discovered in Alaska, Africa, and other places. This increased the amount of gold available to the government. This meant that more gold-backed money could be brought into circulation.

3. Farm prices rose even higher as a result of foreign demand for United States crops. This demand came about because of worldwide crop failures around 1900.

4. The population of the United States increased. This was partly because millions of immigrants came to the United States after 1900. The in-

456

creased population brought a greater demand for farm products.

The farm problem in the United States was not so **acute** in the early 1900s as it had once been. However, it soon grew serious again. Continued improvement of farm machinery made it possible for farmers to bring more land under cultivation. Expansion of the chemical fertilizer industry brought an increase in the amount of crops grown. New methods of scientific farming and animal breeding also helped increase production. Before long, farmers had extra crops, or surpluses. There was no place to sell these surpluses.

Surplus farm production was only one part of the growing farm problem. Another problem came from overexpanding farmland during World War I. In the years between 1914 and 1918, farmers received high prices for their crops. As a result, many farmers bought additional land. The farmers paid very high prices for the land. They expected to pay for this land with the money they received for the crops they raised. However, farm prices fell sharply when the war ended in 1918. And farmers did not make as much money as they thought they would. Thus, many farmers could not make the payments on the land they had bought. They lost that land and often their original farms as well. The 1920s were years of increasing farm crisis in the United States.

Farm surpluses drove down the prices of wheat, corn, hogs, cotton, and tobacco. Prices were so low that it did not pay to bring some products to market for sale. Farmers in Iowa often burned their corn for fuel. The falling prices brought a severe depression to farm areas. Many farmers lost their land when they could not pay their debts. This happened when banks **foreclosed mortgages** for nonpayment of money owed. Thousands of farmers lost everything. They were forced to work as farm laborers or to become tenant farmers on land they had formerly owned. Some farmers went to the cities to look for jobs.

While hard times were taking place on farms, the rest of the nation was enjoying prosperity. The prosperity from 1921 to 1929 resulted in high prices on all products except farm crops. These high prices added to the problem of the farmers. They could not afford to buy such items as clothing, machinery, coal, and fertilizer.

The period of national prosperity ended in 1929, however. It was replaced by a terrible economic depression. Millions of people were thrown out of work. Thousands of businesses were forced to close. This period of depression after 1929 only added to the farmers' problems. Food produced on the farms went unsold, while people went hungry in the cities of the nation.

The farmers' problems were a matter of great concern to the government and to the nation. Unfortunately, government and business leaders at that time still held that the government ought not to interfere in such matters. Some efforts were made to help the farmers. However, these efforts were not made on a large enough scale to solve the problems.

COMPREHENSION CHECK

A. Recognizing the Main Idea

This selection as a whole tells you that

1. the farm problem disappeared after 1900.

2. the farm problem grew less serious after 1900.

3. the farmer is worse off today than in 1900.

4. the farm problem seemed less acute in the early 1900s but worsened after World War I.

B. Selecting Important Details

Choose the ending that best completes each statement.

1. The widespread buying of farmland during World War I
   a. greatly improved the condition of the farmer later.
   b. did not make much difference to the farmer.
   c. resulted in great farm hardships later.
   d. resulted from the need to cut production of food.

2. The war with Spain resulted in
   a. inflation.
   b. an end to inflation.
   c. lower farm prices.
   d. worse farm conditions than ever.

3. All the following helped improve farm conditions after 1896 EXCEPT
   a. increased population of the United States.
   b. the improvement in crop production all over the world.
   c. the discovery of gold in Africa.
   d. crop failures in many parts of the world around 1900.

4. After 1929, economic conditions were
   a. good for farmers but bad for business.
   b. good for farmers and business.
   c. bad for both farmers and business.
   d. bad for farmers but good for business.

C. True or False

Decide whether each of these statements is true or false. Rewrite the false statements to make them true.

1. The period after 1921 brought great prosperity to most farmers.

2. Farm surpluses disappeared because more crops were grown on less land.

3. The war with Spain helped improve the condition of the farmers.

4. Population increase in the United States brought a demand for more farm products.

5. Many farmers bought more land during World War I.

D. Vocabulary

Write your own sentence for each of these words.

acute   foreclose   mortgage

E. Essay Question

Write about twenty-five words telling the story that might go with one of the following headlines.

1. WAR WITH SPAIN BRINGS FARM PROSPERITY

2. GOLD DISCOVERED — FARMERS TO BENEFIT

3. WAR ENDS — FARM PRICES GO DOWN

Lesson 11 Government and Agriculture Under the New Deal

WORDS TO UNDERSTAND
Discuss the meanings of these words.

staple   **parity**

NEW WORDS IN SENTENCES
1. There is always a demand for **staple** crops.
2. **Parity** is the ratio between the price a farmer receives for his crop and the prices he must pay for the goods he buys.

AS YOU READ
As you read this selection, try to answer these questions.
1. How did the New Deal attempt to solve farm problems?
2. What were some problems of the New Deal farm programs?

THE READING SELECTION
Review. The economic depression of 1929 brought hard times to the entire nation. Farmers were hit especially hard because they had been experiencing hard times since 1921. From 1921 to 1929, farmers had suffered from high production and low prices. As farmers produced more crops in an effort to get more income, they increased the surpluses. This, in turn, drove crop prices even lower. Adding to the farmers' problems was the lack of credit. This increased the number of mortgage foreclosures. More and more farmers lost their farms. They were forced to become either tenant farmers or farm laborers or to leave the farms. ☆

During the early depression years, the government did little to aid the farmers. In 1929, President Hoover tried to reduce the farm surpluses by making government purchases. But this had little effect, since production continued to be high.

In 1932, the nation elected Franklin D. Roosevelt as president. The New Deal program was developed under President Roosevelt. It included a full-scale attack on the causes of farm distress. The New Deal farm program received a setback in 1936 when parts of the Agricultural Adjustment Act were declared unconstitutional. However, in 1938, a second law was passed, which the Supreme Court declared constitutional. With this and other laws to aid farmers, the Roosevelt administration tried to solve the farm problem. The New Deal farm program hoped to do several things.

1. Reduce production of many farm crops. The government would pay farmers not to plant crops on certain parts of their land. The main purpose was to cut down production of **staple** crops such as wheat, corn, and cotton.

2. Raise the prices of farm products. Reducing production would tend to raise prices. But the government also would guarantee a fair price level for farm products. This level would be fair in relation to the prices the farmers paid for goods. This relationship is called **parity.** Surplus crops would be bought at parity price by the government, but production was to be limited.

3. Start programs to help save the soil from destruction. The government would pay the farmers to conserve, or save, their land and to plant crops that enriched the soil.

4. Begin a loan program to help farmers own their own land. The government proposed to make long-term loans at low interest rates to help tenant farmers. They could buy their own land with such loans. The program also kept owners from losing their farms through foreclosures.

In the ten years after 1933, farm prices did rise, and farm conditions did improve. However, the New Deal farm program was not a complete success. Following are some of the faults of the program.

1. It was very expensive. It cost the government hundreds of millions of dollars.

2. It led to higher prices for consumers who bought farm products.

3. It gave tremendous powers to the government. The government could now control the amount of farm goods produced.

4. It did not really solve the problem of surpluses. Though the farmers planted fewer acres of land, they produced more crops per acre. This was because they kept improving their farming methods. Surpluses piled up in government warehouses and grain elevators.

In 1939, World War II began in Europe. By December 1941, the United States was in the war. The sudden great need for food at home and abroad resulted in high prices for farm products. The government now encouraged farm production. It guaranteed prices equal to 90 percent of parity. In other words, if the parity price of corn had been set at $2.00 a bushel, the government guaranteed farmers a price of $1.80 a bushel for all the corn they could produce. Of course, production increased tremendously. Again it happened that a war was responsible for economic prosperity.

Drought, dust storms, and low prices brought great poverty to farmers during the 1930s. New Deal programs were set up to help them. The poster at right, made for the Farm Security Administration, shows deep feeling for the farmers' problems.

DEPRESSION

Farmers were especially hard hit by the Depression. Drought turned the West into a "Dust Bowl" (left). Winds simply blew the dried-out soil away. One Kansas farmer said he could count the farms going by outside his window. At the same time, eastern farmers faced huge floods. Everywhere, farmers packed up and left to find work. One family walked 900 miles. In four years, 300,000 people drove to California to find jobs. There they worked for as little as forty-five cents a day. Their hard life was written on their faces (right). In the 1930s, the Farm Security Administration hired photographers to capture the time in pictures. The photos on these pages are part of that record.

COMPREHENSION CHECK

A. Recognizing the Main Idea

This selection as a whole tells you

1. why wheat, corn, and cotton are staple crops.

2. how much money the New Deal programs for farmers cost.

3. about the goals and problems of the New Deal programs for helping farmers.

4. why the New Deal did not include programs for farmers.

B. Selecting Important Details

Choose the ending that best completes each statement.

1. Overproduction of farm goods led to
   a. higher crop prices.
   b. the end of farm problems.
   c. fewer mortgage foreclosures.
   d. lower crop prices.

2. The purpose of guaranteeing a parity price was to
   a. increase the surplus of farm products.
   b. force prices down.
   c. guarantee a fair income for farmers.
   d. make farmers work harder for their money.

3. The New Deal farm program was criticized for
   a. taking power from the government.
   b. costing too much money.
   c. lowering prices of farm products for consumers.
   d. making it harder for farmers to get loans.

4. All the following were parts of the New Deal farm program EXCEPT
   a. soil conservation.
   b. giving land free to farmers.
   c. raising farm prices by fixing parity rates.
   d. payments to farmers to reduce production of crops.

C. Completion

Fill in the word or words that best complete each sentence.

1. The government offered loans to farmers at _____ interest rates.

2. The government hoped to wipe out crop surpluses by _____ the amount produced.

3. Parts of the first Agricultural Adjustment Act were declared _____.

4. Though farmers used fewer acres of land, they were able to produce more crops because of _____ farming methods.

5. A major criticism of the New Deal was that its policies led to higher prices paid by _____.

D. Vocabulary

Match the words with the definitions.

Words	Definitions
1. staple	a. based on a ratio
2. parity	b. unnecessary
	c. type of party
	d. basic

E. Essay

Write a "letter to the editor" in which you either defend or criticize the New Deal farm policies. Write no more than seventy-five words.

Robert F. Wagner, Sr. and New Deal Legislation

Franklin D. Roosevelt's New Deal policies lasted from 1933 until his death in 1945, but most of the major New Deal laws were passed in the first four years of the Roosevelt administration. The man who was responsible for introducing many of these laws was Senator Robert F. Wagner of New York. In fact, he was the sponsor of so many laws that he has come to be called the Father of New Deal Legislation.

Robert F. Wagner, Sr., was born in Germany, but his family moved to New York when he was very young. Like many other immigrants, he made a successful career in his adopted land. He was elected to the New York State Assembly and, later, to the New York State Senate. His interest in labor came from a term of service on the State Factory Investigating Committee in 1911. Later, he served as a judge on the state supreme court. In 1927, he was elected to the United States Senate. He served as a senator for the next twenty-two years.

Senator Wagner was a firm believer in the New Deal policies. He sponsored such bills as the National Industrial Recovery Act, the Social Security Act, the National Labor Relations Act (still called the Wagner Act), and the National Housing Act. These laws brought about better working conditions and better living conditions for the people.

Lesson 12 Farm Problems Since World War II

WORDS TO UNDERSTAND

Discuss the meanings of these words.

overproduction **agribusiness**
efficiency

NEW WORDS IN SENTENCES

1. An **overproduction** of crops meant there were more crops produced than could be used.

2. The **efficiency** of new farming methods allowed farmers to grow more crops on less land.

3. Large-scale **agribusiness** can put small farmers out of business.

AS YOU READ

As you read this selection, try to answer these questions.

1. How does the government try to solve the problems of overproduction in agriculture?

2. What are some problems with the parity price system?

3. What problems do farmers face today?

THE READING SELECTION

Review. Life for farmers in the United States improved somewhat between 1939 and 1945. In those years, World War II created a great need for food and other farm products. The American surplus crop problem almost disappeared during this time. ☆

The end of the war in 1945 brought back many of the farmers' problems. Peace decreased the need for farm products. **Overproduction** and surpluses caused farm prices to fall sharply. Surplus crops and falling prices were once again the major problems of the American farmer.

The government tried to help by limiting production and buying up some surplus farm crops. However, overproduction was not solved by the government's action. The farmers agreed to use fewer acres for production each year. But the new machines and improved farming methods developed during the war increased the farmers' **efficiency.** As a result, their crops were often larger than before, despite their use of less land. Government-bought surplus rose to record high levels.

Farmers faced other problems. The rising inflation after 1945 created higher costs. While farm income often fell, prices of manufactured goods rose steadily. Labor costs also rose. Many farm laborers left the rural areas for higher-paying jobs in the cities. To attract workers, farmers had to raise the

Small farmers have trouble competing with agribusiness. Huge farms like the one shown can more easily absorb rising farm costs. But some small farmers find that they can stay in business by growing special crops aimed at a smaller market.

wages of hired labor. Farmers' incomes were often not large enough to meet increased costs for labor and products.

The problems of farm life continue to this day. Each year, the number of farmers actually working the land goes down. Huge **agribusiness** firms have taken over many smaller farms. These large corporations do more than grow the crops. They also manufacture the farm machines and process, store, and distribute the farm goods. Smaller farmers cannot compete with agribusiness. The energy crisis has increased costs for fuel and fertilizer. Agribusiness can absorb these costs more easily than small farmers can. Many small farmers are being forced off their farms.

Those farmers who remain depend on the government to guarantee a fair price for crops. The government has set up a system of price supports. This system guarantees the farmer a certain price for some crops. This parity price protects the farmer when crop prices fall. In exchange for this guaranteed price, farmers must agree to limit their production to help prevent a surplus. A surplus forces prices down.

After World War II, the government used a system of fixed price supports. The government paid 90 percent of its parity price. In 1948, Congress approved a different system, one with flexible price supports. Under this system, the percentage of parity the government would

467

pay depended on the size of the crops for that year. If the crops were large, the government would pay as little as 60 percent of parity. If the crops were small, the government would pay up to 90 percent. The farmers did not like this system. In 1949, Congress returned to a system of fixed price supports. But many people feel that fixed farm supports make farm items unfairly expensive to city buyers. The support system also costs the government billions of dollars in payments to farmers.

Even a 90 percent fixed support did not seem to help the farmers enough. Many are still unable to earn a fair living. In 1977–78, some farmers went on strike. They demanded that the government pay the full 100 percent of parity price. That demand was not met. In the early 1980s, President Reagan's administration cut sharply into farm support programs to reduce federal spending.

Farm policies have also become an international issue in recent years. In the 1970s, the Soviet Union had a series of crop failures. The grain shortage led the Soviet Union to buy several million tons of American grain. The United States government bought the grain from farmers and sold it to the Soviet Union.

The grain sale brought better prices for American farmers. However, the sale angered many people. Some farmers received higher prices for their grain than others did. Also, the American government sold the grain to the Soviet Union for less money than it had spent to buy it. The United States lost several billion dollars on the sale. Some Ameri-

W. McNamer, Woodfin Camp and Associates, Inc.

cans protested that the Soviet Union was getting the grain more cheaply than American buyers would. In addition, the American taxpayer would end up paying, through taxes, the money the government lost.

The protests succeeded in changing the government's policy. Under the new policy, the government can sell to the Soviet Union and the People's Republic of China. But the sales have to be at market price. Sales under the new policy greatly benefit American farmers by reducing their surplus crops.

FARM PRICES 1869-1976

WHEAT: Average price per bushel received by farmers

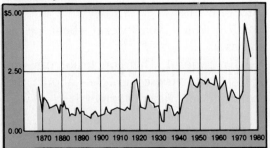

CORN: Average price per bushel received by farmers

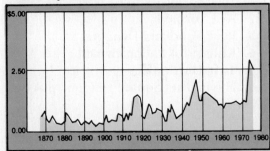

COTTON: Average price per 500 lb. bale received by farmers

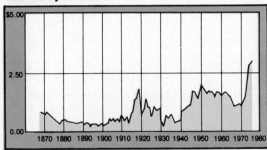

The graphs above indicate that farm prices have been very unstable. How could that lead to the farmers' strike shown opposite?

COMPREHENSION CHECK

A. Recognizing the Main Idea

1. In a single sentence, write the main idea of this lesson's reading selection.

2. Write two other points that are made in this lesson's reading selection.

B. Selecting Important Details

Choose the ending that best completes each statement.

1. All of the following are problems for today's farmers EXCEPT the
    a. high cost of labor.
    b. sale of surplus crops to other countries.
    c. high cost of energy.
    d. low price of crops.

2. Government price supports were set up to
    a. make sure farmers would have less buying power.
    b. encourage overproduction.
    c. guarantee farmers fair prices for their crops.
    d. save money for the government.

3. Increased use of machinery means that
    a. crops will bring higher prices.
    b. larger crops can be raised on smaller acreage.
    c. smaller crops will be raised on greater acreage.
    d. crops will bring lower prices.

4. Some people do not approve of the price support system because it
    a. does not help farmers.
    b. floods the market with surplus goods.
    c. makes money for the government.
    d. costs the government too much.

C. Fact or Opinion

Decide whether each of these statements is fact or opinion.

1. Surplus farm products force prices down.

2. The United States should not sell grain to the Soviet Union.

3. Flexible price supports are better than fixed price supports.

4. The United States cannot sell grain to the People's Republic of China for less than market price.

5. Price supports cost the government money.

D. Vocabulary

Match the words with the definitions.

Words	Definitions
1. overproduction	a. high production with less effort
2. efficiency	b. parity
3. agribusiness	c. creation of surplus
	d. large farming corporations
	e. foreclosure

E. Homework

Imagine that you are a farmer explaining to a city person why the government pays price supports. Write six to eight sentences answering the following questions.

1. What might happen to you if there were no government price support system?

2. Why must the government limit production of a crop before guaranteeing that it will support the price of that crop?

F. Graph Skills

Use the graphs in this lesson to answer these questions.

1. In which three years were cotton prices lowest?

2. In which year were wheat prices highest?

3. In general, what conclusion can you draw from these graphs about the economic security of farmers?

G. Chronology

Arrange these events in the order in which they happened.

1. Social Security Act
2. AFL formed
3. Pure Food and Drug Act
4. Knights of Labor formed
5. Taft-Hartley Act
6. Haymarket Square riot took place

Organizing Migrant Workers

Unions have made many gains for skilled workers since the 1800s. But great numbers of workers have remained unorganized and unprotected by unions. Migrant farm workers were among the unprotected until very recently. Many of the migrant farm workers are Mexican-Americans. They plant and harvest crops across the nation.

During the 1950s, César Chávez and Dolores Huerta became leaders in an effort to organize farm workers. César Chávez had been a farm worker himself. Although Dolores Huerta had not been a farm worker, she had grown up in close contact with the problems of migrant farm workers in California. Huerta and Chávez and a small group of others began the task of bringing to the migrant farm workers some of the rights that other workers in the United States had enjoyed for many years.

Poverty, illiteracy, and the traveling that farm workers do made it difficult to organize a union. Many farm owners threatened to fire workers who joined unions. There were cases of violence against workers and union organizers. But by 1965, the union was strong enough to declare a strike against grape growers in California. Chávez and Huerta stressed the need for a non-violent strike.

A boycott against grapes was called to support the strike. The boycott caught the attention of the public. The support of many people across the nation helped make the strike successful. Contracts were signed by the union with many large growers.

During the next ten years, the United Farm Workers had ups and downs. One of its most serious problems was the teamsters' union. The teamsters sought to undercut the UFW by signing contracts with the growers. Huerta was among those working to win the workers' support. She often debated the issues with teamster representatives right in the fields. There was sometimes fighting between followers of the two unions.

The conflict was finally settled when special legislation was passed in California. Under its provisions, elections were held to let the migrant workers choose between the unions or to vote for no union. The result was a decided victory for the United Farm Workers.

By 1977, the United Farm Workers had become a recognized part of the American union movement and part of the AFL-CIO. Wages and working conditions of migrant farm workers have improved. But there is still much progress to be made.

United Press International

United Press International

Unit 9 Summary Americans at Work: 1865 to the Present

Business and Industry

Industrial growth depended on the natural assets of the United States. The nation has fertile farming and grazing land, mineral resources, and good ports.

The Civil War led to an expansion of industry in both North and South. More goods were made by machine in factories. Larger quantities lowered prices of goods. The growing factories led to larger cities and to the increased importance of industry in the economy.

Poor practices in business, many exposed by muckrakers such as Ida B. Tarbell and Upton Sinclair, led to a cry for government regulation of business. Some Americans opposed giving such power to the government. But laws were finally passed to control businesses such as the railroad and food production industries. The Sherman Antitrust Act was intended to prevent monopolies. The Federal Trade Commission was set up to prevent price rigging and false advertising claims.

Labor Unions

American workers were underpaid and had few rights in 1865. The first effective national labor union was the Knights of Labor, formed in 1869. In 1886, the American Federation of Labor was formed. It was a collection of unions for skilled workers in various crafts and trades. It merged in 1955 with the Congress of Industrial Organizations.

It was not until the 1930s that government did much to protect the worker. In the 1930s, the National Labor Relations Board was set up to settle disputes and support labor. The Social Security system was established. Minimum wages and maximum hours were set.

A movement to limit the growing powers of unions resulted in the passage of the Taft-Hartley Act in 1947. It is still in effect today.

Workers continue to face the problems of rising prices, unemployment, and unfair labor practices. Affirmative action

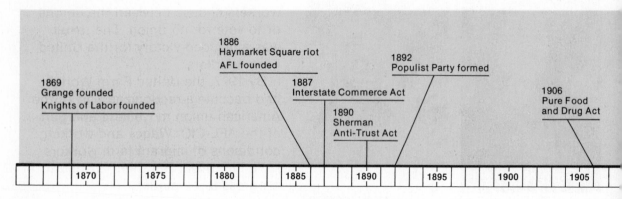

1869
Grange founded
Knights of Labor founded

1886
Haymarket Square riot
AFL founded

1887
Interstate Commerce Act

1890
Sherman
Anti-Trust Act

1892
Populist Party formed

1906
Pure Food
and Drug Act

1870   1875   1880   1885   1890   1895   1900   1905

programs and the Equal Employment Opportunity Commission are meant to ensure fair treatment for workers, especially women and minorities.

Agriculture

The industrial revolution and scientific progress helped produce an agricultural revolution. New machinery made farms more productive, but it often brought the prices for farm products down. Farmers had difficulty meeting the high costs of products and services they had to buy. The Grangers and other groups sought state control of transportation rates and an easier credit system.

In 1892, the Populist party demanded free silver and more money in circulation, as well as other changes. The party disappeared, but many of its ideas have since been adopted.

In the early 1900s, various political factors improved the farmer's life temporarily. By the 1920s, however, growing farm surpluses brought down prices. Farmers who could not pay off their loans lost their farms. The national depression that began in 1929 only made the farmer's position worse.

During the New Deal of the 1930s, two Agricultural Adjustment Acts were passed to reduce production and to raise prices for farm products—if necessary, by government support. The New Deal program had some success, but it was World War II that increased demand for food and thus solved the farmer's problems for a time.

To ease problems of overproduction after the war, the government set up a system of fixed price supports. The government was to buy surplus crops from farmers at 90 percent of the parity price. Flexible supports were tried for one year, but this system was not acceptable to the farmers.

Price supports are controversial, because they make farm items more expensive for city buyers and cost the government a great deal of money. But the rising cost of energy and other high costs have made the problems of farmers worse. Some farmers are demanding that the government pay the full 100 percent of parity price to ease their problems.

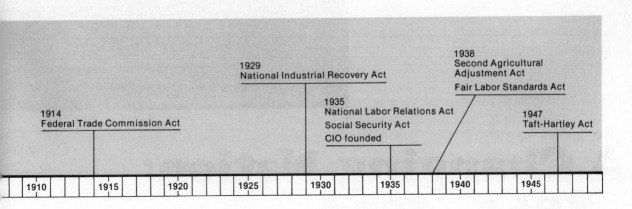

1914
Federal Trade Commission Act

1929
National Industrial Recovery Act

1935
National Labor Relations Act
Social Security Act
CIO founded

1938
Second Agricultural Adjustment Act
Fair Labor Standards Act

1947
Taft-Hartley Act

1910 1915 1920 1925 1930 1935 1940 1945

unit
10

Chicago wall mural, photo by C. R. Bennett

A Changing Nation:
1865–1929

In 1876, the nation celebrated its centennial (above). In 100 years, it had grown to thirty-eight states with a population of 45 million. The Centennial Exposition in Philadelphia looked to the future, highlighting new inventions and machines. Fifty years later, the nation included forty-eight states and 120 million people. The new inventions of 1876 had become a part of daily life. The people had changed, too—especially women and their roles (left). The nation was becoming modern.

475

Lesson 1   Politics After the Civil War

WORDS TO UNDERSTAND
Discuss the meanings of these words.

turmoil   subsidies   censured
scandals   defraud

NEW WORDS IN SENTENCES
1. They rushed about excitedly, creating confusion and **turmoil.**
2. When the **scandals** were uncovered, many dishonest politicians had to face trial.
3. Some farmers receive **subsidies** from the government to help them pay their expenses.
4. The vice-president tried to **defraud** the bank by altering the bank's records and pocketing the money.
5. The principal **censured** the troublemakers, but she did not expel them from school.

AS YOU READ
As you read this selection, try to answer these questions.
1. How did the Civil War weaken the Democratic party?
2. What were some of the scandals of the Grant administration?

THE READING SELECTION
The last half of the nineteenth century was a time of great **turmoil** in American politics. In the years following the Civil War, there were two major political parties. These were the Republican and the Democratic parties. The Civil War greatly weakened the Democratic party. The Democrats were charged with having supported the disloyal Southerners during the war. Slowly, the Democrats regained their strength, but they still faced many problems.

Politicians in both major political parties were guilty of dishonest practices. In many cities and states, a single "boss" controlled the area's political life. Corruption and bribery were fairly common throughout the United States. Dishonest politicians frequently rigged elections. The issue of corruption was to play an important part in many political campaigns after 1865.

In 1865, Andrew Johnson succeeded to the presidency after Lincoln was assassinated. His policies aroused great controversy and brought a split between the Radicals and other Republicans in Congress. Johnson barely escaped conviction after being impeached in 1868. Although he wanted to run for another term as president, Johnson was not nominated by his party.

In the election year of 1868, the Republicans nominated General Ulysses S. Grant. Grant was the great military hero of his day. Hundreds of thousands of Union army veterans supported him. The Democrats nominated Horatio Seymour, former governor of New York. The Republicans made the Civil War a major campaign issue. In their campaign against Seymour, the Republicans called the Democrats the party of disloyalty and war.

In spite of his great popularity, Grant defeated Seymour by only about 300,000 popular votes. But Grant won 214 electoral votes, while Seymour won only 80. About 700,000 former slaves voted for the first time in a presidential election. Their votes undoubtedly provided Grant's popular majority.

Grant was a military leader, not a politician. He had never been active in politics, and he knew very little about most political issues. He made almost no effort to influence Congress or to suggest legislation for the nation. Grant was content to allow Congress to introduce and pass laws. Grant's attitude allowed the legislative branch to grow somewhat stronger than the executive branch. Grant served two terms as president, from 1869 to 1877. During these years, the presidency lost much power to the Congress.

The Grant administration was marked by a number of serious **scandals.** In 1869, a group of speculators, including Grant's own brother-in-law, tried to gain control of the gold market. They failed, but many people were financially ruined. The scandal shocked the American people and weakened their confidence in Grant and the Republicans.

Another scandal of the Grant administration was exposed in 1872. At the time, the federal government was giving millions of dollars to the railroads in various kinds of **subsidies.** In 1862, Congress gave the Union Pacific Railroad the right to build a line westward from Omaha, Nebraska. The promoters of the Union Pacific organized a separate company called the *Crédit Mobilier.* It constructed the rail lines and equipped the railroad. The *Crédit Mobilier* charged very high prices to the railroad for this work. The difference between the high prices and the actual cost of the work went into the pockets of those who controlled the two companies. These people used their companies to **defraud** the United States government and the people who had invested money in the company. Many members of Congress were bribed to go along with the plan. In 1872, an article in the New York *Sun* first exposed the scandal. Congress began an investigation, and many officials were **censured.** The scandal further damaged the reputation of the Republicans and of President Grant.

Nobody believed that Grant himself was dishonest. However, many did feel that he lacked good judgment. Corruption was widespread at the time, and Grant was easily fooled. Many people used their friendship to trick him.

The Democrats were also involved in frauds and scandals. In New York, for example, a democratic politician named William "Boss" Tweed headed the Tweed Ring. This group of corrupt politicians cheated the city out of tens of millions of dollars.

Many people were troubled by the widespread dishonesty in politics. Reformers looked for a candidate who could stand above dishonest policies. In

1872, a group of Liberal Republicans nominated Horace Greeley, a Republican, to oppose Grant. The Democrats also nominated Greeley, but he lost to Grant by a wide margin.

Grant's second term as president was less scandalous than his first. By the end of his second term, however, Grant had lost much of the confidence of the American people. They began to feel that he had not been a wise choice for president. Nonetheless, Grant's popularity as a military hero remained strong.

COMPREHENSION CHECK

A. Recognizing the Main Idea
This reading selection as a whole tells you that

1. the scandal of the *Crédit Mobilier* damaged Grant's reputation.
2. President Andrew Johnson helped restore peace between Northern and Southern states.
3. the period after the Civil War was one of great turmoil in American politics.
4. former slaves could vote for the first time in the presidential election of 1868.

B. Selecting Important Details
Choose the ending that best completes each statement.

1. The Republican candidate for president in 1868 was
   a. Andrew Johnson.
   b. Rutherford B. Hayes.
   c. General Ulysses S. Grant.
   d. James A. Garfield.

2. In the period immediately following the Civil War
   a. the Democratic party gained great strength.
   b. the Republican party lost much of its strength.
   c. both parties were about equal in strength.
   d. the Republican party emerged as the stronger political party.

3. During the Grant administration, the executive branch
   a. grew stronger than Congress.
   b. lost some power to Congress.
   c. overpowered the judicial branch.
   d. was greatly respected.

4. The issue of corruption
   a. was important only in New York.
   b. was a greater problem to Democrats than to Republicans.
   c. was a great problem to both major parties.
   d. concerned only the Republicans.

C. Completion
Fill in the word or words that best complete each of the sentences.

1. _____ was Grant's opponent in the election of 1868.
2. The votes of former _____ helped elect Grant.
3. The *Crédit Mobilier* handled construction work of the _____ Railroad.
4. The _____ nominated Horace Greeley for president in 1872.
5. One scandal during Grant's administration involved _____ speculation.

D. Vocabulary

Write your own sentence for each of these words.

turmoil   subsidies   censure
scandal   defraud

E. Homework

Write a fifty-word essay about any one of the following people. You can look up information about them in the library.

Ulysses S. Grant   James Fisk
Andrew Johnson   Carl Schurz
Horace Greeley   "Boss" Tweed

Jay Gould (left) and James Fisk.

"Black Friday"

Jay Gould and James Fisk were two daring speculators. In 1869, these "robber barons" worked out a plan that would give them control of the available gold supply of the entire United States. Their plan was to buy up the gold that circulated in the open market. Once they had most of this supply of gold, they could force up the price of gold and sell out at a fabulous profit. The only hitch in this plan was the possibility that the government might release some of the gold reserve in the United States Treasury for sale. Such an action would ease the demand for gold, lower its price, and break the speculators' corner on the gold market.

To keep the government from putting its gold on the market, Gould and Fisk enlisted the help of President Grant's brother-in-law. He was to use his influence on the president to keep the government from selling any gold until the corner was secured by the speculators.

Over a period of several weeks, the price of gold rose steadily. Pressure mounted for the government to release treasury gold. When he became aware of the danger of a corner on the gold market, President Grant took immediate action. The government released 4 million dollars of the gold reserve for sale. The result was the breaking of the high gold prices on "Black Friday," September 24, 1869. The plan had failed. But hundreds of investors lost their money, and many businesses suffered losses. Fisk symbolized the spirit of the speculators and the corrupt spirit of the times when he refused to pay his debts. He dismissed these with the comment, "Nothing is lost save honor."

Lesson 2 The Election of 1876

WORDS TO UNDERSTAND

Discuss the meanings of these words.

civil service   **tactics**
implicated

NEW WORDS IN SENTENCES

1. The **civil service** system requires employees to demonstrate their qualifications for government jobs.

2. He was **implicated** in the scandal and later confessed to having been involved in the illegal activities.

3. Advertisers use many **tactics** to persuade people to buy their products.

AS YOU READ

As you read this selection, try to answer these questions.

1. What factors caused a shift in political power after the Civil War?

2. What compromise ended the disputed election of 1876?

THE READING SELECTION

Review. Political control of the United States had been largely in Republican hands after 1865. But by the 1870s, the Republicans were losing out to the Democrats. The shift in political power may be traced to several factors.

1. The Democrats were slowly recovering from the charge of disloyalty. By 1876, the Civil War had been over for more than ten years. The hatred caused by the war was beginning to fade.

2. The Democrats were regaining power in the South. Democrats replaced Republican Reconstruction governments throughout the South. Special laws and threats of violence kept many former slaves from voting. As a result, the Republicans, who counted on the votes of black people, were weakened.

3. The corruption of the Grant administration (1869–1877) had badly damaged the Republican party. The Republican party was split between the reformers and the professional, often dishonest, politicians. In 1872, the reformers broke away from the party. They nominated a Liberal Republican presidential candidate, Horace Greeley. Greeley opposed the regular Republican candidate, General Grant. Although Greeley lost to Grant, the Liberal Republicans kept growing in strength. ☆

One of the major demands of the Liberal Republicans was for a system of **civil service.** Under a civil service sys-

480

tem, federal workers would have to meet certain qualifications to receive their jobs. A system of civil service would remove government jobs from political control. The jobs would go only to persons who could prove their qualifications. The professional politicians of both parties were bitterly opposed to civil service. They wanted to keep their patronage power and the political influence that went along with it.

As the election of 1876 drew near, Democratic strength rose steadily. The Republicans at first supported James G. Blaine of Maine as their presidential candidate. But in 1876, Blaine was **implicated** in some shady dealings with the Union Pacific Railroad. The Republicans decided to look for another candidate. They wanted a candidate who could not be accused of corruption. They chose Rutherford B. Hayes, governor of Ohio.

The Democrats nominated Governor Samuel J. Tilden of New York. Tilden had gained national fame by his efforts

In his first term, President Hayes stressed civil service reform during a period of dishonesty and corruption. In this cartoon, Republicans refuse Hayes the nomination to a second term.

THE CINDERELLA OF THE REPUBLICAN PARTY AND HER HAUGHTY SISTERS.

to break up the corrupt Tweed Ring in New York.

On election day, it looked as if Tilden and the Democrats had won. Tilden had a popular majority of about 250,000 votes. He also seemed to have won a majority of the electoral votes. But there was a dispute over the electoral votes from four states. Without the electoral votes of these states, neither the Democrats nor the Republicans had enough votes to win. The election was sent to the Congress to be settled.

In January 1877, Congress set up a special electoral commission. It was to decide which electoral votes should go to each candidate. There were eight Republicans and seven Democrats on the commission. The members of the commission voted along straight party lines. Since there was a Republican majority on the commission, all the disputed electoral votes were given to Hayes, the Republican. He was declared president-elect.

But the commission's vote did not end the matter. Both houses of Congress still had to approve the commission's decision. For a while, it seemed that there would not be an agreement in time for the March 4 presidential inauguration. Southerners were outraged at the Republican **tactics.** They felt that at least some of the southern electoral votes had been Tilden's. Southerners accused the Republicans of "stealing the election." Republicans responded by accusing the Democrats of using force and violence to keep black citizens from voting. In the end, the parties agreed on a compromise. The Democrats accepted the election of Hayes. In return, the Republicans agreed to withdraw federal troops from the South and to appoint a southerner to the cabinet. The Republicans also promised to make aid available for road and railroad improvement in the South.

The withdrawal of federal troops meant the end of Reconstruction in the South. The Republicans, through the terms of the compromise, indicated that they were giving up the fight to win full civil and legal rights for former slaves. After 1876, the political leadership of the South passed into the hands of the Democrats.

COMPREHENSION CHECK

A. Recognizing the Main Idea

In a single sentence, write the main idea of this lesson's reading selection.

B. Selecting Important Details

Choose the ending that best completes each statement.

1. The first results of the election of 1876 showed
   a. neither candidate to have a majority of the votes.
   b. Hayes to be the apparent winner.
   c. a tie between the candidates.
   d. Tilden to be the apparent winner.

2. The electoral commission set up to decide the 1876 election
    a. was made up entirely of Republicans.
    b. voted without regard to party membership.
    c. voted along straight party lines.
    d. refused to decide the outcome of the election.
3. As a result of the compromise that settled the election of 1876
    a. the Democrats gained control of the presidency.
    b. federal troops were removed from the South.
    c. former slaves won full legal rights.
    d. the Republicans retained control of the South.
4. The object of the civil service reform movement was to
    a. increase the number of government workers.
    b. end Reconstruction governments in the South.
    c. strengthen the political parties.
    d. end political control of federal jobs.

C. Completion
Fill in the word or words that best complete each sentence.
1. A civil service system _____ the power of professional politicians.
2. The Republican who, because of his shady dealings, was not selected as a candidate in 1876 was _____.
3. There were _____ Republicans than Democrats on the electoral commission.

4. An important part of the settlement of the 1876 election was the promise that the next cabinet would include a _____.
5. Another part of the 1876 election settlement was the withdrawal of _____ from the South.

D. Vocabulary
Match the words with the definitions.

Words	Definitions
1. civil service	a. armed forces
2. implicated	b. methods used to achieve a goal
3. tactics	c. convicted
	d. government system requiring workers to meet certain qualifications
	e. named as having been involved in something

E. Using Your Knowledge
In the following paragraph, each sentence is numbered for easy reference. Which sentence contains the main idea? Which sentences contain details to help explain the main idea?

(1) The Democrats began to regain their strength in the 1870s. (2) During these years, they were accused less often of disloyalty. (3) Because many blacks were kept from voting in the South, the Republican Reconstruction governments were replaced by Democrats. (4) The Republican party was weakened nationwide by the corruption of the Grant administration.

Lesson 3 The Democrats Regain Their Power

WORDS TO UNDERSTAND
Discuss the meanings of these words.

merit   pension
bolted   plurality

NEW WORDS IN SENTENCES
1. She got a scholarship to college because of her high grades and outstanding **merit.**

2. Some Democrats who were displeased with the Democratic candidate **bolted** the party and voted for the Republican candidate.

3. The company gave its retired workers a generous **pension** so they could afford to live comfortably.

4. The winning candidate won the election by a **plurality** of only fifty votes, although he received less than half of the votes cast.

AS YOU READ
As you read this selection, try to answer these questions.

1. What major issue separated the Stalwarts and Half-Breeds?

2. How did the election of Grover Cleveland mark a great change in American politics?

THE READING SELECTION
Review. The election of 1876 had shown many weaknesses in the Republican party. For the first time since the Civil War, the Republicans came close to losing the presidency. Only the straight party vote on the electoral commission secured the victory for Rutherford B. Hayes, the Republican candidate.

A compromise had settled the dispute in the election of 1876. As part of the compromise, the Republicans promised

1. to remove federal troops from the South.

2. to appoint a southerner to the cabinet.

3. to help the South build roads and railroads. ☆

Hayes proved himself to be quite capable as president. He established his strength by refusing to give the Republican leaders control over filling federal jobs and choosing the cabinet. President Hayes sided with civil service reformers. He wanted federal jobs assigned on the basis of **merit,** not political influence.

While Hayes was president, the split in the Republican party widened. Some of the Republicans, called "Stalwarts," were against any reform in party politics. Opposing them were the "Half-Breeds." The Half-Breeds favored an end to corruption. They supported some civil service reform.

President Hayes decided not to run

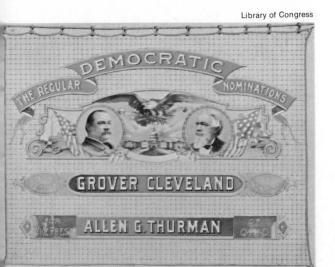

Cleveland was the only president to serve two separated terms of office. This banner is from his 1888 campaign.

for a second term. The Stalwarts wanted the Republican party to nominate a candidate who would not permit further reforms. The Half-Breeds, on the other hand, favored a candidate who would support reform. After much dispute, the Republican party finally named James A. Garfield of Ohio as its candidate. Garfield was a Half-Breed. To balance the ticket, the party named a Stalwart, Chester A. Arthur, as candidate for vice-president.

In the election of 1880, Garfield defeated the Democratic candidate. A few months after his inauguration, Garfield was assassinated. His assassin was a man who had not been given a federal job he had wanted. The slaying of President Garfield shocked the nation. The tragedy showed the dangers of using patronage to fill federal jobs.

Vice-President Chester A. Arthur became president when Garfield died.

The new president had long practiced political patronage. He also had been involved in charges of corruption. Most people expected him to carry out the wishes of the professional party politicians. But Arthur surprised his old political friends. He put the needs of the nation ahead of political considerations and began to support civil service reform. The Pendleton Act, passed in 1883, set up a limited civil service. It required competitive examinations for about 12 percent of all federal jobs. It also provided that future presidents could increase this percentage. Today, over 90 percent of all federal jobs are protected by merit examinations.

By 1884, the Republicans were again badly split over the issue of reform. A third independent reform group arose in the Republican party. These people were called the "Mugwumps." They felt that the Republicans had to press hard for radical reforms.

In 1884, the Mugwumps refused to support the Republican candidate, James G. Blaine. In 1876, Blaine had been implicated in some shady dealings with a railroad company. So the Mugwumps **bolted** the Republican party and gave their support to Grover Cleveland, the Democratic candidate.

The election of 1884 was probably the hardest fought political contest in American history. Both candidates had been involved in scandal. Cleveland's scandal was of a personal nature, while Blaine's was political and financial. In the end, Cleveland won by a narrow margin.

In his first term, Cleveland proved himself able and honest. Guided by his conscience, he vetoed many **pension** bills for Civil War veterans. He felt that most of these bills were not justified. In addition, Cleveland expanded the civil service. This expansion pleased many reformers.

Cleveland greatly strengthened the executive branch by opposing the Senate on the Tenure of Office Act. This act, passed during Andrew Johnson's administration, reduced the president's power to make appointments and dismiss officials. Under Cleveland's leadership, the Tenure of Office Act was repealed in 1887. President Cleveland also helped create the new Department of Agriculture. The secretary of agriculture became a member of the president's cabinet.

In 1888, the Democrats again nominated Cleveland for president. The Republicans chose Benjamin Harrison, grandson of a former president. Harrison received fewer popular votes than Cleveland, but he won a majority of the electoral votes. Harrison, then, became president.

During Harrison's term, Congress passed a veterans' pension bill that Cleveland had vetoed. It also passed the highest protective tariff the nation had known.

The Sherman Antitrust Act was also passed during Harrison's presidency. This law tried to limit the growth of huge monopolies in American industry. The law proved very difficult to enforce. In fact, it was often used against labor unions instead of against big businesses.

Another important act passed during Harrison's term was the Sherman Silver Purchase Act. The act increased the amount of money in circulation and helped raise prices of goods. Many farm groups in the nation favored this act.

In the election of 1892, President Harrison was again opposed by former President Cleveland. In addition, a new party called the People's, or Populist, party was on the ballot. The Populists represented organized farmers who wanted cheaper currency and other reforms. Grover Cleveland won the election by a **plurality** of 400,000 votes. But the Populist candidate had received over a million popular votes and twenty-two electoral votes. Populism was clearly going to be a challenge to the Democrats.

The Democrats, then, had been able to win the presidency in 1884 and 1892. With Cleveland back in office, the Democrats had once again regained their strength.

COMPREHENSION CHECK

A. Recognizing the Main Idea

This reading selection as a whole tells you that

1. the Populist party became a real threat to the Democrats' strength.

2. the Mugwumps further split the Republican party.

3. civil service was formally introduced as law by the Pendleton Act of 1883.

4. the Democrats began to regain their power after 1876.

B. Selecting Important Details

Choose the ending that best completes each statement.

1. Chester A. Arthur was named vice-presidential candidate in 1880 because he was a
   a. Half-Breed.
   b. reformer.
   c. Stalwart.
   d. compromise candidate between Stalwarts and Half-Breeds.
2. The Pendleton Act
   a. decreased the number of federal jobs.
   b. pleased the Stalwarts.
   c. made all federal jobs dependent on merit examinations.
   d. introduced a major reform by establishing a federal civil service.
3. The nomination of Blaine in 1884 caused Republican reformers to
   a. support the party actively.
   b. form a third party.
   c. give their support to the Democrats.
   d. take no action in the campaign.
4. President Cleveland's opposition to the Tenure of Office Act
   a. served to make the Senate more powerful.
   b. caused Congress to pass a stronger act.
   c. resulted in the repeal of the act and the strengthening of the executive branch.
   d. offended the Democrats in Congress.

C. Fact or Opinion

Decide whether each of these statements is fact or opinion.

1. Between 1876 and 1884, the Republican party split into the Stalwarts, Half-Breeds, and Mugwumps.
2. The Mugwumps should have remained loyal to the Republican party.
3. Pension bills for Civil War veterans were not justified.
4. Cleveland vetoed many pension bills for Civil War veterans.
5. The Sherman Silver Purchase Act increased the amount of money in circulation.

D. Vocabulary

Write your own sentence for each of these words.

merit	pension
bolted	plurality

E. Chronology

For each of the following groups, choose the letter of the event that came first in history.

1. a) election of Hayes
   b) election of Grant
   c) election of Garfield
2. a) disputed election of 1876
   b) Reconstruction of the South
   c) assassination of Garfield
3. a) formation of the Republican party
   b) Reconstruction of the South
   c) the Civil War

F. Essay

In an essay of about fifty words, explain who the Mugwumps were and why they bolted their party in 1884.

Lesson 4 From McKinley to Theodore Roosevelt

WORDS TO UNDERSTAND
Discuss the meanings of these words.

advocates industrialized
hoard imperialism

NEW WORDS IN SENTENCES
1. The **advocates** of reform spoke out for an end to corruption in government.
2. The young boy tried to **hoard** all the pennies he found, but his mother made him share them with his brother.
3. For many years, the country was agricultural, but with the coming of machines and factories, it soon became **industrialized.**
4. After strong charges of **imperialism,** the country gave its colonies their independence.

AS YOU READ
As you read this selection, try to answer these questions.
1. How did the silver issue split the Democratic party?
2. How did McKinley's election mark a turning point in American life?
3. Why was Theodore Roosevelt nominated for the vice-presidency?

THE READING SELECTION
In 1892, angry farmers left the Democratic party and organized the People's, or Populist, party. From the beginning, the Populists demanded the free and unlimited coinage of silver. The unlimited coinage of silver would cheapen money by putting more of it into circulation. Cheaper money would raise farm prices and aid the desperate farmers.

Most Republicans had long opposed any cheapening of the currency. The Democrats were divided on the silver issue. Many Democrats, especially those from the South and the West, supported the free-silver program. These Democrats were strong **advocates** of Populist ideas. Some Democrats, including President Cleveland, opposed the free-silver program. These people were called "Gold Bugs."

In 1893, a severe business depression left many people unemployed. Many companies could not afford to stay in business. The high tariff passed during the Harrison administration had resulted in lower government revenues on imports. At the same time, the payment of veterans' pensions used up the treasury surplus. As the federal gold supply was used up, people began to panic. President Cleveland felt he had to halt the loss of gold. He called for repeal of the Sherman Silver Purchase Act. This act allowed people to exchange silver-backed currency for gold. In a panic, many people began to exchange their paper money for gold coins. They began to **hoard** their gold, and soon gold became scarce. Cleveland wanted to stop the exchange of paper money for gold before the treasury was emptied of its reserves.

Cleveland and the Gold Bug members of Congress repealed the Silver Purchase Act in 1893. Although this repeal helped stop the flow of gold from the treasury, it angered many farmers and split the Democratic party.

When the Democrats met in Chicago to select a candidate for the election of 1896, they found their party seriously divided. Some Democrats supported free silver, but others did not. The free-silver group controlled the convention. The youthful William Jennings Bryan became the Democratic candidate. The Populists also threw their support to Bryan. In addition, Bryan picked up the support of some Republicans from the West who favored free silver.

While the Democrats were split, most Republicans united behind William McKinley of Ohio. McKinley was a loyal Republican who favored hard money (gold) and high tariffs to protect American businesses. McKinley had the backing of a million-dollar fund for his campaign. Bryan had seemed a very popular candidate, but he could not bring the Democrats to victory. McKinley's funds helped the Republicans win the electoral votes of the big eastern states and defeat Bryan.

The victory of McKinley was a turning point in American life. The Populists had emphasized the importance of the farmer. After Bryan's defeat, the Populist movement ended. Farmers had to take a secondary place in American life. The United States had become an **industrialized** nation. Soon it would be one of the greatest industrial nations in the world.

President McKinley had the support of the new industrialists. He was entirely devoted to the idea of an industrial nation. McKinley had worked actively for higher tariffs when he was a member of Congress. As president, he strongly supported high tariffs.

Soon after McKinley took office, the free-silver issue died out. High tariffs, however, remained a political issue. Opposition to high protective tariffs was strong even among Republicans. The tariffs were attacked because they kept prices high. By keeping out foreign goods and competition, the tariffs encouraged the growth of monopolies. But the demands for tariff reforms soon came to an end. In 1898, the United States became involved in a war with Spain. Domestic issues gave way to the concerns of war.

The Spanish-American War grew out of American interest in Cuba's revolt against Spain. Many Americans wanted to build a colonial empire. They hoped to take over the Spanish colonies of Cuba, Puerto Rico, and the Philippine Islands. The United States took Cuba's side in the struggle. A few months after the war started, the United States defeated Spain in the Caribbean and the Pacific. The peace treaty brought Puerto Rico, Guam, and the Philippines under United States control. Cuba, however, was given independence.

Wartime prosperity at home and the swift victory made McKinley popular. The Democrats nominated Bryan to oppose McKinley in 1900. The Democrats accused the Republicans of **imperialism,** but this issue failed to win popular support. Even the reports that Filipinos were resisting American forces failed to disturb most Americans. Some Americans did protest, however, when they heard about the brutal treatment some Filipinos got from American army commanders. This protest led to a new policy toward governing the Philippines, but it did not strengthen the Democratic chances for victory.

McKinley and the Republicans scored a huge victory in 1900. Theodore Roosevelt of New York was elected vice-president. When Roosevelt was president of the New York City Board of Police Commissioners, his reform ideas had disturbed many politicians. These politicians were glad to get rid of Roosevelt and bury him in the almost powerless office of vice-president.

In 1901, shortly after his second term began, President McKinley was assassinated. Young Theodore Roosevelt moved up to the presidency of the United States. His political foes had failed to bury him. The nation was about to be launched on a new period of reform.

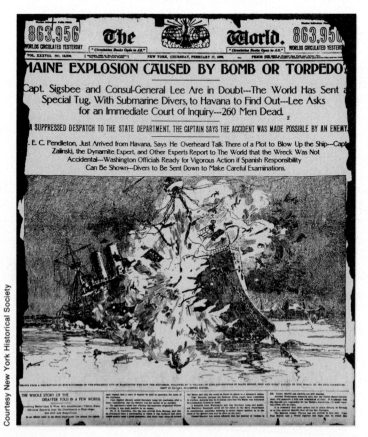

American newspaper accounts of Spanish-Cuban conflict had long been biased against Spain. When the American battleship *Maine* exploded at Havana, Cuba, American newspapers shouted the story. The papers created sympathy for the colony of Cuba and anger against Spain. The slogan "Remember the Maine" built up feelings that led to the Spanish-American War. Powerful newspapers often used biased reporting to influence the public. Publisher William Randolph Hearst once told his artist, "You furnish the pictures, I'll furnish the war."

COMPREHENSION CHECK

A. Recognizing the Main Idea
In a single sentence, write the main idea of this lesson's reading selection.

B. Selecting Important Details
Choose the ending that best completes each statement.

1. Populists supported all of the following EXCEPT
   a. more money in circulation.
   b. unlimited coinage of silver.
   c. Bryan for president in 1896.
   d. McKinley for president in 1896.
2. The Gold Bugs were
   a. mostly Republicans who were opposed to free silver.
   b. found only in the Populist party.
   c. those Democrats who opposed the free-silver program.
   d. in favor of the Sherman Silver Purchase Act.
3. The election of McKinley in 1896 was aided by all of the following EXCEPT
   a. the votes of the eastern states.
   b. the split in the Democratic party.
   c. the split in the Republican party.
   d. the large campaign fund his party raised.
4. The swift victory of the United States in the Spanish-American War
   a. strengthened the Democrats.
   b. had little effect on politics.
   c. strengthened the Republicans.
   d. weakened both parties.

C. True or False
Decide whether each of these statements is true or false. Rewrite the false statements so that they are true.

1. Many farmers were glad to see the Sherman Silver Purchase Act repealed.
2. Cleveland introduced the Sherman Silver Purchase Act in 1893.
3. After 1896, farmers came to occupy a secondary place in American politics.
4. All Republicans were agreed that high protective tariffs were needed.
5. McKinley represented the interests of American business.

D. Vocabulary
Match the words with the definitions.

Words	Definitions
1. advocates	a. declare again
2. hoard	b. supporters
3. industrialized	c. practice of building an empire by controlling colonies
4. imperialism	d. defend
	e. built up with factories and machines
	f. save for oneself; keep greedily

E. Essay
Write a fifty-word essay on one of the following topics.

1. How did McKinley's victory mark a turning point in American life?
2. In 1896, one Populist song declared, *the farmer is the person who feeds them all.* Why might farmers of the time have been bitter about their life? What does this song tell us about the way farmers regarded their position in life?

Clara Barton
and the Red Cross

At age seventy-seven, Clara Barton went to the battlefields of the Spanish-American War. She endured dangerous conditions and extreme weather. Her purpose was to bring badly needed food and medical supplies to the people in the war. With the American Red Cross behind her, she saw to the distribution of provisions valued at a half million dollars. The Spanish-American War was the first war in which the Red Cross played a part. But it was not the first war Clara Barton had seen firsthand.

Clara Barton had been known as the Angel of the Battlefield during the Civil War. She had become aware of the gross lack of medical care and supplies for the wounded. With her own money and money from contributions, she bought supplies. She traveled to hospitals, army camps, and battlefields and became known for providing relief even under the worst conditions.

After the Civil War, Clara Barton went to Europe to recover from an illness. While there, she met the leaders of the International Committee of the Red Cross. The committee was working to bring some humanitarian conditions to war.

Clara Barton returned to the United States in 1873. Against much resistance, she campaigned for the United States to become part of the

Library of Congress

International Red Cross. Finally, in 1882, the United States did so.

The American Red Cross went beyond wartime work. It provided relief in both foreign and domestic disasters. The method of the Red Cross was to get to the location as quickly as possible with food, clothing, medicine, shelter, and materials for rebuilding.

Clara Barton eventually resigned as president of the American Red Cross. She was honored in Europe and in America for her great contributions to peacetime and wartime relief services.

Lesson 5   The Progressive Movement

WORDS TO UNDERSTAND
Discuss the meanings of these words.

sweatshop	dissolved
rebates	conservation

NEW WORDS IN SENTENCES
1. The workers' long hours and unsafe working conditions made the factory seem like a **sweatshop.**

2. The company was condemned for paying **rebates** to some customers when other customers were not getting such refunds.

3. They **dissolved** their partnership because they could never agree.

4. Roosevelt started a program of **conservation** to save the natural resources of the United States.

AS YOU READ
As you read this selection, try to answer these questions.

1. What were some major reform movements of the 1890s?

2. How did the views of the Progressives differ from the laissez-faire views of the early 1800s?

THE READING SELECTION
American reform movements before 1865 had been concerned with several issues. These included free public education, the abolition of slavery, and women's rights.

After 1865, the reform movements expanded to improve more areas of life. The reform movements of the 1890s set out to reform society as a whole. They argued that the United States should offer a better life to all its people.

Reformers during the 1890s sought a wide range of social changes.

1. The Populist revolt of the 1890s sought better conditions for the farmer. Although populism failed, many of its reform ideas were adopted in later years.

2. Reformers sought improvement of housing conditions in the big cities. Many reformers were determined to improve the lives of the poor. Some set up settlement houses in slum areas to try to help poor people. The most famous of these settlement houses was Hull House in Chicago. It was founded by Jane Addams, the pioneer social worker.

3. Reformers worked to eliminate corruption from local politics. Corruption was not limited to any one political party, nor to national politics alone. The political life of many cities was controlled by bosses and their "ma-

chines." Lincoln Steffens shocked the nation with his book *Shame of the Cities*. His book told the story of big city corruption.

4. Reformers sought to end child labor, low wages, and **sweatshop** conditions in the factories.

5. Reformers began to demand better treatment for American Indians.

6. Reformers sought to reduce control of the nation's economy by huge business monopolies.

7. Reformers sought to prevent the sale of impure foods and harmful drugs.

The reform movement found a leader in Theodore Roosevelt. The assassination of President McKinley in 1901 brought Roosevelt to the presidency. He introduced a new reform program based on progressivism. Progressivism was a movement for social, political, and economic reform. The progressives believed in the right of the government to regulate society.

The attitude of the progressives marked a change from earlier times. The earlier national belief had been that a government should stay out of as many areas of life as possible. At the same time, the government had never really kept a "hands-off" policy. The reformers believed that government action should be in the interests of all the people. This belief became the cornerstone of the Progressive movement.

One of the progressives was Senator Robert M. La Follette of Wisconsin. He led the Progressive movement in Congress. Jane Addams fought for govern-

ment aid to people in city slums. Other progressives were Lincoln Steffens and Ida Tarbell. In their books, these writers exposed many social evils.

With Roosevelt as president, the progressives found a leader. In turn, Roosevelt found the public support he needed for his many ideas about reform. The Roosevelt administration introduced reforms in the areas of business, public safety, natural resources, and labor.

Regulation of railroad companies. Railroads often charged different rates to different customers. They gave **rebates** to the frequent rail users like the Standard Oil Company. During the Roosevelt administration, two laws regulating the railroads were passed.

The first of these was the Elkins Act of 1903. This act curbed the policy of giving rebates and charging unfair prices to some shippers. The second was the Hepburn Act, passed in 1906. This act strengthened the Interstate Commerce Commission (ICC). It gave the ICC the power to set maximum railroad rates.

Antimonopoly action. The Department of Justice began to enforce the Sherman Antitrust Act. The Northern Securities Company, made up of several railroad companies, was **dissolved** by the order of a government agency.

Regulation of the food and drug industries. The Pure Food and Drug Act and the Meat Inspection Act of 1906 were the first steps taken to safeguard America's health by outlawing harmful foods and drugs.

Efforts to protect the nation's natural resources. Roosevelt strongly supported a program of land, water, mineral, and forest **conservation.** He set up the government Forest Service to conserve American timberlands. In 1902, the Newlands Act was passed. It raised money for federal irrigation projects. The Roosevelt administration also set aside millions of acres of land for use as national parks, timber and mineral reserves, and water power sites.

A "square deal" for labor. In the 1902 coal strike, the mine owners refused to meet with the union. President Roosevelt stepped in and forced the mine owners to settle the strike with the union. This action differed sharply from the government's treatment of labor in the 1880s and 1890s. In those years, the federal government had often taken action against unions in its support of business owners.

Library of Congress

Culver Pictures, Inc.

Reformers worked both in and outside of the Progressive party. Progressive writer Ida Tarbell (left bottom) exposed the need for reform. Progressive politicians President Roosevelt (far left) and Senator La Follette (left top) changed legislation. Other reformers included W. E. B. DuBois and Lillian Wald (this page). DuBois founded the NAACP, and Wald improved health care programs.

COMPREHENSION CHECK

A. Recognizing the Main Idea

1. In a single sentence, write the main idea of this lesson's reading selection.

2. Write two other points that are made in this lesson's reading selection.

B. Selecting Important Details

Choose the ending that best completes each statement.

1. Progressives believed that the government should
    a. maintain a "hands-off" policy.
    b. support monopolies.
    c. work against labor unions.
    d. work in the interests of all people.

2. Settlement house workers were concerned mainly with
    a. uplifting lives in slum areas.
    b. improving factory conditions.
    c. reform of city politics.
    d. better farm conditions.

3. Reformers worked for all of the following EXCEPT
    a. better treatment for Indians.
    b. the end of government corruption.
    c. protection of natural resources.
    d. rebates for railroad companies.

4. The Elkins Act of 1903 and the Hepburn Act of 1906 were concerned with regulating
    a. monopolies.
    b. conservation.
    c. railroad companies.
    d. labor.

C. Fact or Opinion

Decide whether each of these statements is fact or opinion.

1. Government should stay out of as many areas of life as possible.

2. The nation's economy should be controlled by large monopolies.

3. The Roosevelt administration set aside millions of acres of land for parks.

4. The government should not support business owners over unions.

5. The ICC was given the power to set maximum railroad rates.

D. Vocabulary

Use a word from this list to complete each sentence.

sweatshop   dissolve
rebates   conservation

1. Until the Elkins Act, some railroad companies gave _____ to frequent customers.

2. The national park system is only one part of the government's _____ program.

3. Progressives wanted the government to _____ huge monopolies.

4. The workers complained that their factory was a _____.

E. Essay

Write a fifty-word essay describing the major reform movements of the 1890s. When you finish, try to outline your own essay. If your essay was well organized, you should be able to show the main ideas and the details that support them. If your essay was not well organized, outlining it will show its weaknesses and help you improve it.

Jane Addams of Hull House

Jane Addams was born in 1860 in Cedarville, Illinois. After graduating from college, she attended the Woman's Medical College in Philadelphia for a time. The idea of a woman studying medicine was still an unusual one in the 1880s. But before she completed her studies of medicine, Jane Addams developed an interest in social reforms.

Library of Congress

During a trip to England, she had seen the social work being done in London's slums. In 1889, Addams returned to Illinois and helped establish Hull House in Chicago, one of the first settlement houses in America. Her work over the next forty-five years won her many honors, including the Nobel Peace Prize in 1931.

Hull House became a center for political changes. Addams and her co-workers influenced the passage of laws dealing with child labor, welfare, and education. Hull House people were responsible for getting sweatshops, where many immigrants worked, inspected for safety. They also helped establish the first juvenile court in the country.

Perhaps the best description of the work Jane Addams and others did at Hull House appears in her own words.

> We found ourselves spending many hours in efforts to secure support for deserted women, insurance for widows, damages for injured workers, and furniture from the clutches of installment stores. . . . Another function of the Settlement resembles that of the big brother whose mere presence protects the little one from the bullies.

Jane Addams wrote articles and lectured on the problems in city slums. She also fought for women's suffrage and against political corruption. Addams died in 1935 at the age of seventy-four. She was honored by people all over the world.

Lesson 6   Progressivism and the Election of 1912

WORDS TO UNDERSTAND
Discuss the meanings of these words.

decisive   aggressive
denounced   suffrage

NEW WORDS IN SENTENCES

1. She was sure of her ideas and was able to be **decisive** in resolving conflicts.
2. The people at the meeting **denounced** the speaker's attitude as rude and offensive.
3. They pushed through the crowd in an **aggressive** manner.
4. The women's **suffrage** bill gave women the right to vote.

AS YOU READ

As you read this selection, try to answer these questions.

1. Why did President Taft fail to gain the support of the progressives?
2. What was the New Nationalism?
3. How did the formation of the Bull Moose party guarantee the victory of the Democrats in 1912?

THE READING SELECTION

President Theodore Roosevelt had pledged not to seek office in the 1908 election. Instead, he named William Howard Taft to run as his successor. Roosevelt hoped that Taft would continue his progressive program. Taft was nominated and easily elected to office in 1908.

Although Roosevelt had handpicked Taft, he soon became displeased with his choice. President Taft was not able to win wide support from the progressives. He had trouble filling Roosevelt's shoes. Even though Roosevelt left for a hunting trip in Africa after the election, he remained the leader of the progressives. His personality, even when he was away, overshadowed that of President Taft.

Taft lacked the strong leadership qualities that Roosevelt had used so well. Taft was more likely to follow Congress than to lead it. He was not **decisive,** and he could not control the different elements in his own party. As a result, the party that had been united under Roosevelt became divided under Taft.

Taft came into conflict with the progressives soon after taking office. During his campaign, Taft had promised the progressives that he would lower the tariff rates. Soon after he was elected, a reform tariff bill was introduced in the House. But the Senate stripped the bill of its reforms. By the time the bill reached Taft, it once again called for high tariffs. Nonetheless, Taft signed the bill and thereby broke his promise. This angered many progressives.

But the Progressive movement did accomplish several reforms during Taft's administration.

Passage of the Mann-Elkins Act. This act gave the Interstate Commerce Commission the power to regulate telephone, telegraph, and cable companies.

Passage of the Sixteenth Amendment. This constitutional amendment, ratified in 1913, provided for a nationwide income tax. This measure was proposed under President Taft.

Despite these reform measures, the progressives continued to distrust Taft. The breaking point between President Taft and the progressives was the Pinchot-Ballinger dispute over conservation policies. Chief Forester Gifford Pinchot was a leading progressive and a friend of Theodore Roosevelt. Pinchot accused Secretary of the Interior Richard Ballinger of planning to let business interests take over some federal coal reserves. Ballinger denied this, and Pinchot was dismissed from office. His dismissal was **denounced** by progressives, but Taft supported Ballinger. Public opinion, however, sided with Pinchot. The controversy split the Republican party all the further, and Ballinger was later forced to resign.

In 1910, Roosevelt returned from his travels in Africa and Europe. He was hailed with enthusiasm by progressives in the Republican party. Soon after his return, Roosevelt made a speech calling for a "New Nationalism." He favored an **aggressive** policy of economic reform. Roosevelt thought that the government should protect the interests of the nation as a whole. He wanted more government regulation if necessary. Roosevelt's speech was considered an attack on Taft's more conservative ways. It served

During the progressive era, reformers sought to improve conditions in the big cities and to improve the lives of the poor. Jacob Riis contributed by photographing life in New York tenements, sharply describing conditions in the slums. Immigrants pictured here are trying to sell their wares to passersby.

Library of Congress

to widen the split in the Republican party.

The progressives greeted the call for the New Nationalism with joy. They felt that Taft would never bring about the reforms they demanded. Many progressives supported Senator La Follette of Wisconsin for the presidency. Others hoped that Roosevelt would again seek the Republican nomination.

Roosevelt finally agreed to run for president as the Republican candidate. But Taft was not about to give up the party's nomination to Roosevelt. The fight for nomination brought the final break between Roosevelt and Taft. Through his patronage power, Taft controlled the votes of many of the convention delegates. Taft supporters soon took control of the nominating convention. They barred many Roosevelt delegates, and Taft won the nomination.

Roosevelt's followers refused to accept the convention's choice. They declared Taft's nomination a fraud and called on Roosevelt to lead a third party. About six weeks later, the Roosevelt forces met in Chicago to form the Progressive (Bull Moose) party. The party got its nickname from Roosevelt. He declared that he was ready to run for office and was "as fit as a bull moose." With Roosevelt as their candidate, the Progressives adopted a reform platform. This platform included demands for strict regulation of monopolies and lower tariffs. It also sought the direct election of senators, women's **suffrage,** the end of child labor, and minimum wage standards for working women.

The Democrats chose Governor Woodrow Wilson of New Jersey as their candidate. Wilson had already made a name for himself as a liberal and a reformer. He represented the progressives of the Democratic party. Wilson supported a program called the New Freedom. It proposed as many reforms as Roosevelt's New Nationalism.

In the election of 1912, both Roosevelt and Wilson spoke out strongly for reform. President Taft, the official Republican candidate, had only conservative support. It was soon evident that the contest was between Roosevelt and Wilson.

Wilson won the election of 1912, mainly because the Republican vote was split. Wilson won more than 6 million votes. Roosevelt received about 4 million and Taft about 3.5 million. Wilson did not win a majority of the popular vote. However, he did win 435 electoral votes, while Roosevelt won 88 and Taft only 8. The Democrats also gained control of both houses of Congress.

COMPREHENSION CHECK

A. Recognizing the Main Idea

This reading selection as a whole tells you that

1. the Pinchot-Ballinger dispute split the Republican party.

2. Taft was not a decisive president.

3. Roosevelt called for a New Nationalism.

4. During Taft's presidency, the Republicans split, and the Democrats gained power.

B. Selecting Important Details

Choose the ending that best completes each statement.

1. The Pinchot-Ballinger dispute centered around the issue of
   a. conservation.
   b. labor relations.
   c. railroad regulation.
   d. control of the Progressive party.

2. Roosevelt's program of New Nationalism called for
   a. less reform for the nation.
   b. no government regulation.
   c. regulation wherever necessary for the nation's welfare.
   d. regulation only in emergencies.

3. The Republican convention of 1912
   a. strongly supported Roosevelt.
   b. did not support either Taft or Roosevelt.
   c. was controlled by Roosevelt supporters.
   d. was controlled by Taft supporters.

4. The results of the election of 1912
   a. gave Roosevelt more popular votes than all other candidates.
   b. gave Taft more votes than Roosevelt.
   c. showed Roosevelt and the Bull Moose party the winners.
   d. showed Wilson a winner by a plurality of votes.

C. Completion

Fill in the word or words that best complete each sentence.

1. In his dispute with Pinchot, Ballinger was supported by _____.

2. The election of 1912 was a victory for the _____.

3. The Sixteenth Amendment allowed a national _____.

4. _____ was the Bull Moose candidate in 1912.

5. Wilson's program was called the _____.

D. Vocabulary

Write your own sentence for each of these words.

decisive   aggressive
denounced   suffrage

E. Essay

Write a fifty-word essay in answer to this question: Was Theodore Roosevelt right in agreeing to run as a third-party candidate in 1912? Make sure that you give at least two reasons for your answer.

F. Using Your Knowledge

Complete the following outline of the major issues of the Taft administration.

I. The Taft administration is connected with several progressive reforms.
   A.
   B.

II. Several conflicts with the progressives helped split the Republican party during Taft's administration.
   A.
   B.

Theodore Roosevelt and Conservation

The idea of conserving natural resources did not come easily to most Americans. There was a long tradition of waste in American life. Farmers often used the soil carelessly. After all, there always was new, fresh land farther west. Many farmers cleared trees on their land in a wasteful manner. Lumbering interests destroyed vast resources by their careless logging methods. The government showed little interest in protecting the forest lands. Removal of the forests led to soil erosion and floods because there were no tree roots to hold the soil or absorb the water.

Americans also were careless in the handling of other natural resources. The destruction of wildlife led to the near disappearance of many birds and animals. There was also great waste in the mining of coal and other mineral resources.

From 1901 to 1909, President Theodore Roosevelt made conservation a national issue. He used his power as president to set aside valuable land reserves.

Five national parks, two national game preserves, and fifty-one wild bird refuges were created under Roosevelt's administration. Nearly 150 million acres of forest land and 80 million acres of coal land were set aside in land reserves. This guaranteed that the land would not be subject to careless and wasteful use by private owners. Another 1.5 million

Conservationist John Muir (right) and Roosevelt.

acres of land were set aside for future water projects. Roosevelt knew the importance of water resources, especially in dry western lands. The Forest Service was strengthened as a force for conservation. National forests were transferred to the care of the Department of the Interior. This helped remove some of the constant pressure by logging interests to gain control of the forest lands.

Theodore Roosevelt was a lover of nature and the outdoors. He had an understanding of the importance of natural resources and the need for conservation. And he took action to strengthen the feeling for conservation in the American people.

Lesson 7   Woodrow Wilson and the New Freedom

WORDS TO UNDERSTAND
Discuss the meanings of these words.
trusts   promissory notes   exempted

NEW WORDS IN SENTENCES
1. Business **trusts,** like monopolies, threaten to drive competing firms out of business.
2. When they took out a bank loan, they gave the banker **promissory notes** stating when they would repay the money.
3. The students who had gotten high scores on the test were **exempted** from doing the homework assignment.

AS YOU READ
As you read this selection, try to answer these questions.
1. What were the major reforms of Wilson's New Freedom program?
2. How did the New Freedom movement affect progressivism in the Republican party?

THE READING SELECTION
Review. Taft's presidency proved a disappointment to the progressives. The Pinchot-Ballinger dispute over conservation policies widened the split in the Republican party. When Roosevelt returned from abroad, he once again became a leader for the progressives.

At the Republican nominating convention, Taft's supporters barred Roosevelt's followers from participating. Taft won the Republican nomination. But Roosevelt and his progressive supporters founded a third party. Roosevelt ran for president as the Bull Moose candidate.

With the Republicans split between Taft and Roosevelt, Woodrow Wilson, the Democratic candidate, was able to win the election. He had only a plurality of popular votes, but he won a wide majority of electoral votes. His New Freedom program had won support from many reformers. ☆

The Democratic victory in 1912 helped promote the national reform movement. During the 1880s and 1890s, the Democrats had been the party of reform. Then, when the progressives gained strength in the early 1900s, the Republicans became the reform party. After the election of 1912, Woodrow Wilson's New Freedom represented the reform element in the Democratic party.

Wilson, like Roosevelt, brought strong

leadership to the presidency. He worked hard to get Congress to pass the reform laws he wanted. Most of the reforms passed during Wilson's first term in office concerned the economic life of the country.

Tariff reform. Many people were against high protective tariffs. These tariffs served chiefly to raise prices and aid **trusts.** Trusts are formed when several corporations combine into one large firm. In 1913, Congress lowered the tariffs for the first time since the Civil War. The tariff bill also contained an income tax law. The Sixteenth Amendment, adopted in 1913, had made a national income tax legal.

Banking and financial reform. The Wilson administration established the Federal Reserve System in 1913 to con-

President-elect Wilson and President Taft in the inaugural parade. Democrat Wilson won the election by a large majority over split Republican party candidates Taft and Roosevelt.

trol the currency. Under this system, federal reserve banks were set up in twelve districts. All national banks had to join the system. State banks could join if they wished. Member banks deposited a certain amount of their money in the federal reserve bank in their district. These banks could then cash in their "IOUs," or **promissory notes,** at the reserve banks. The federal reserve banks would give the member banks currency in exchange for the notes. The banks could then use this currency to lend additional money, at a fee, to other people.

The Federal Reserve System made currency available when business conditions demanded it. Later, a similar system was set up for farm loans. Through this system, farm associations could obtain the credit they needed.

Antitrust laws. Congress created the Federal Trade Commission (FTC) in 1914 to prevent the growth of business trusts. In the same year, Congress also passed the Clayton Act. Both the FTC and the Clayton Act tried to tighten the provisions of the Sherman Antitrust Act. Both measures aimed at regulating, not dissolving, trusts. However, like the Sherman Antitrust Act, these reforms proved unable to stop the formation of ever greater business combinations. To this day, regulation of trusts and monopolies remains a problem.

Labor reforms. The Clayton Act sought to curb trusts. But it also protected labor unions. This act declared that labor unions could not be considered as trusts. The Clayton Act therefore **exempted** labor unions from the regulations governing trusts.

Labor received additional support in the Adamson Act. This act established an eight-hour working day for all laborers on interstate railroads. The Adamson Act helped labor in its fight for an eight-hour working day throughout the nation.

Wilson's vigorous actions won many reformers to the side of the Democrats. With Roosevelt unable to take over the Republican party, the progressives had no place to turn for leadership within their party. Many progressives were now ready to support a Democrat who backed their programs.

The reform program was cut short by World War I. In 1914, most of Europe became involved in war. In the last two years of Wilson's first term, the United States was in danger of being involved in the war. National interest had shifted from issues of reform to issues of war. Wilson's reelection in 1916 was not based on his reform policies. The Democratic party campaigned for Wilson with the slogan "He kept us out of war." Just one month after Wilson's inauguration in 1917, the United States became actively involved in World War I. The New Freedom program had to be put aside until the war was over.

COMPREHENSION CHECK

A. Recognizing the Main Idea

1. In a single sentence, write the main idea of this lesson's reading selection.

2. Write two other points that are made in this lesson's reading selection.

B. Selecting Important Details

Choose the ending that best completes each statement.

1. During the period from 1901 to 1912
   - a. the Democrats made up the reform party.
   - b. the two parties were equally in favor of reform.
   - c. the Republicans made up the reform party.
   - d. neither party favored reform.

2. The Clayton Act was concerned with the regulation of
   - a. conservation.
   - b. city life.
   - c. politics.
   - d. monopolies and trusts.

3. The Adamson Act gave strength to
   - a. farmers.
   - b. bankers.
   - c. railroad companies.
   - d. labor.

4. The creation of the Federal Reserve System
   - a. helped break up monopolies.
   - b. kept banks from failing.
   - c. helped control the currency.
   - d. aided trusts.

C. True or False

Decide whether each of these statements is true or false.

1. Woodrow Wilson represented the reform group in the Democratic party.

2. A national income tax was established in 1913.

3. Wilson's program won many progressives over to the Democratic party.

4. The Clayton Act declared that labor unions were to be considered as trusts.

5. The outbreak of World War I strengthened the New Freedom program of the Wilson administration.

D. Vocabulary

Use a term from this list to complete each sentence.

trusts   promissory notes   exempted

1. Business _____ often drive smaller companies out of business.

2. The students who had not disrupted the class were _____ from the punishment.

3. They signed _____ that guaranteed payment by the end of next year.

E. Homework

Write a fifty-word essay on one of the following topics.

1. Why do you think certain people might have opposed the income tax?

2. Explain the purposes of each of the following: the Adamson Act, the Clayton Act, and the Federal Reserve System.

Lesson 8　President Harding and the "Return to Normalcy"

WORDS TO UNDERSTAND
Discuss the meanings of these words.

disillusioned　**prosperity**　**leased**

NEW WORDS IN SENTENCES
1. They started with high hopes but were **disillusioned** by their many failures.
2. Successful businesses and high salaries are often signs of national **prosperity.**
3. The owners **leased** the building to the company for a period of five years.

AS YOU READ
As you read this selection, try to answer these questions.

1. How did the election of Harding affect the movement toward greater government regulation of business?

2. What were the major problems of Harding's administration?

THE READING SELECTION
Review. In the years after 1850, the two major political parties took turns being reform parties. From 1854 through Reconstruction, the newly formed Republican party stood for reform. During the 1880s and 1890s, the Democratic party became the party of reform, though it shared this title with the Populists in the 1890s. From 1901 to 1912, the Republican party was the party of progressivism and reform. When the Bull Moose party split from the Republican party, those Republicans remaining became conservative. In 1912, Woodrow Wilson and his New Freedom program led a Democratic movement for reform.　☆

Wilson's reform program was interrupted by World War I. After 1917, Wilson's main interest was in foreign affairs. He devoted his efforts to a plan for the League of Nations. The League of Nations was to be an international organization that would try to work for world peace.

Americans had entered World War I with enthusiasm. Many Americans felt that they were fighting to "save the world for democracy." At home and overseas, the United States launched a mighty war effort. By the time the war ended, however, Americans were **disillusioned.** Their disillusionment increased when allies of the United States began quarreling among themselves.

The war caused many people to turn away from the Democrats. At the same time, the Progressive and New Freedom movements also lost strength. In the election of 1920, the Republicans nominated Warren G. Harding, a party regular from Ohio. Harding won by a sweeping majority of about 7 million votes.

The election of 1920 was the first time in American history that all women were able to vote for a president of the United States. Women had long sought voting rights. During the war, they had entered the work force in great numbers. This great contribution to the war effort had persuaded many people that women should be given the vote. Shortly before the election of 1920, the Nineteenth Amendment was ratified, and women were guaranteed the right to vote.

Warren Harding did not believe in reform programs. He felt that the country should return to what he called "normalcy." He wanted to see life return to the way it had been before the war. Unlike Roosevelt and Wilson, he favored reducing the government's regulation of business.

Normalcy also suggested a withdrawal from European affairs. Many people believed in isolating the United States from Europe's problems. These people opposed the idea of joining any sort of international organization. The Congress, dominated by Republicans, strongly supported isolationism. President Harding agreed with Congress that the United States should not join the League of Nations, even though the league had been proposed by a previous American president, Woodrow Wilson.

A depression in 1921 strengthened American support for isolationism. Many people blamed Europe and the war for the depression. The tariffs were once again raised with the hope of keeping out low-cost foreign-made goods. Many people believed higher tariffs would help bring back **prosperity.**

Harding's administration was soon hit by a series of scandals. As president, Harding gave government jobs to some personal friends and old political associates from Ohio. Some of these people did not perform their jobs well. Others were guilty of outright corruption.

The chief scandal of the period was the Teapot Dome affair. It involved the Teapot Dome oil reserves in Wyoming. The secretary of the interior, Albert Fall, **leased** these government-owned oil lands to private speculators. For this and other favors, Fall received over $300,000 in bribes.

The nation knew nothing of this scandal or any others until after Harding died in 1923. Harding had hoped to straighten out his scandal-ridden administration before it was exposed to the public. When the scandals were finally exposed, most people agreed that Harding himself had been personally honest. However, they felt he had been a poor judge of character.

Harding died in office. His death brought Vice-President Calvin Coolidge to the presidency. Coolidge generally favored the idea that the government ought not regulate business any more than was absolutely necessary. Coolidge said, "The chief business of the American people is business."

COMPREHENSION CHECK

A. Recognizing the Main Idea

1. In a single sentence, write the main idea of this lesson's reading selection.

2. Write two other points that are made in this lesson's reading selection.

B. Selecting Important Details

Choose the ending that best completes each statement.

1. The disillusionment after World War I
   a. encouraged a spirit of reform.
   b. led to political loss for the Republicans.
   c. had little effect on the political parties.
   d. led to Democratic losses.

2. The Teapot Dome scandal was concerned with
   a. the problem of railroad rebates.
   b. labor problems.
   c. tariffs.
   d. federal oil reserves leased to private business.

3. The return to normalcy involved
   a. seeking greater reforms.
   b. support for the League of Nations.
   c. a return to progressivism.
   d. moving away from reform.

4. In the election of 1920
   a. the Republicans barely won the presidency.
   b. the Democrats held on to the presidency.
   c. the Republicans won the presidency by a large majority.
   d. third parties played an important role.

C. True or False

Decide whether each of these statements is true or false. Rewrite the false statements so that they are true.

1. Warren Harding represented the reform group of the Republican party.

2. During Harding's presidency, the Congress supported Wilson's plan for the League of Nations.

3. A depression in 1921 strengthened support for American isolationism.

4. Harding was himself involved in taking bribes.

5. Coolidge favored greater government regulation of business.

D. Vocabulary

Match the words with the definitions.

Words	Definitions
1. disillusion	a. rent out
2. prosperity	b. depression
3. lease	c. disappoint former hopes and ideals
	d. economic well-being
	e. isolated

E. Essay

Write an essay of about fifty words describing how politics in the United States changed after World War I. Compare ideas on government regulation and reform before the war with those after the war.

The Suffragists and the Nineteenth Amendment

By 1910, there had been more than forty years of hard work to try to win American women the right to vote. Women had won the right to vote in several western states. But women's suffrage leaders felt that the time had come to press for speedier action. A constitutional amendment was needed to grant the vote to women all over the nation. The efforts to get an amendment passed were led by two women who had little use for each other. These suffragist leaders (their critics mockingly called them "suffragettes") had different ideas and methods.

The National American Women's Suffrage Association (NAWSA) was founded in 1890. By 1910, Carrie Chapman Catt was the strongest influence in the organization. At the age of sixty-nine, she was a hard-working leader with strong views. Her greatest skills were as an organizer and an administrator. She felt that the way to gain the vote was to show men, especially politicians, the justice of women's demands. But other women at the time believed in a different kind of action.

Alice Paul was twenty-five years old in 1910. While living in England, she had learned the methods of civil disobedience from militant English suffragists. These methods included protest marches, disruptions of Parliament, and hunger strikes. The NAWSA did not approve of such

In England, suffragists were radical. As women in the U.S. adopted this style, protest marches became common. New organizations such as the National Women's party (displaying banner) involved thousands of women. How many states on this map gave women the vote before 1920?

actions, so Alice Paul formed the National Women's party. In 1913, she and her followers organized a women's suffrage march in Washington, D.C. For the next seven years, Alice Paul led a series of militant actions.

Women picketed the White House— an action almost unheard of at the time. Even as the nation's press wrote editorials against this action, Alice Paul went further. She and other militant suffragists chained themselves to the White House gates. Police had to be called to cut away the chains. The women who were arrested went on hunger strikes in the jails. In the meantime, dozens of meetings and marches were being held across the land.

Alice Paul and her followers kept the issue red hot. At the same time, Carrie Chapman Catt and her followers worked to win over politicians and public figures. It was a two-front attack. And in the end, the Nineteenth Amendment was ratified in 1920. It consisted of one simple statement.

The right of citizens of the United States to vote shall not be denied or abridged by the United States or by any state on account of sex.

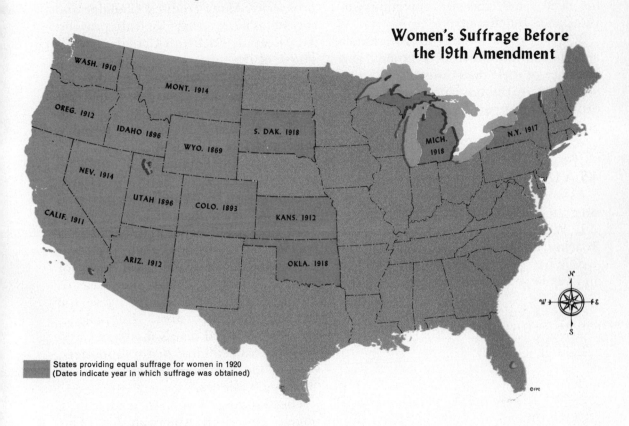

Women's Suffrage Before the 19th Amendment

WASH. 1910
MONT. 1914
OREG. 1912
IDAHO 1896
S. DAK. 1918
WYO. 1869
MICH. 1918
N.Y. 1917
NEV. 1914
UTAH 1896
COLO. 1893
CALIF. 1911
KANS. 1912
ARIZ. 1912
OKLA. 1918

States providing equal suffrage for women in 1920
(Dates indicate year in which suffrage was obtained)

Lesson 9 The Coolidge Prosperity

WORDS TO UNDERSTAND
Discuss the meanings of these words.

characterized   materialism
indefinitely   appointees

NEW WORDS IN SENTENCES
1. Strong leadership and an interest in reform **characterized** the presidency of Theodore Roosevelt.
2. Since everyone disagreed on when to meet again, the next meeting was postponed **indefinitely.**
3. Their great interest in fine clothes and beautifully furnished homes was evidence of their **materialism.**
4. Most of the governor's **appointees** proved worthy of the jobs they were given.

AS YOU READ
As you read this selection, try to answer these questions.
1. What features characterized the Roaring Twenties?
2. What general beliefs did Hoover and Coolidge have about government?

THE READING SELECTION
In 1923, the death of Harding brought Vice-President Coolidge to the presidency. But the change in presidents did not bring any change in policies. Coolidge, like Harding, opposed any government programs of reform.

Coolidge was fortunate to be in office from 1923 until 1929. The postwar depression had ended, and during these years, the nation enjoyed great prosperity. Many credited Coolidge and the Republican party for this prosperity. "Keeping cool with Coolidge" was a slogan of the time.

Republicans nominated Coolidge for reelection in 1924. Progressives had lost faith in both the major parties by 1924. They knew that Coolidge, the Republican candidate, opposed reform. The Democrats also nominated a candidate opposed to reform, John W. Davis. Unhappy with both candidates, progressives once again formed a third party. They nominated Senator Robert M. La Follette of Wisconsin as their presidential candidate. But the good years of national prosperity and the idea of "keeping cool with Coolidge" gave the Republicans the victory. La Follette, however, received nearly 5 million votes. Progressivism still had many supporters, even at the height of prosperity in the "Roaring Twenties."

The Roaring Twenties made up a unique period in American life. This

The lifestyle of the Roaring Twenties reflected changing fun, fads, and fashions. What impressions of the period can you get from this mural?

period was **characterized** by several features.

1. During the 1920s, many new industries developed. These new industries manufactured many new consumer goods, such as automobiles, radios, and electrical appliances. The expanding industries created many new jobs for American workers.

2. Economic prosperity led to many "get-rich-quick" ideas. Millions of Americans believed that prosperity would continue **indefinitely.** They speculated in stocks, bonds, and real estate. To encourage the sale of stocks, people were allowed to pay only a small percentage of the cost of the stock at the time of purchase. The rest of the payment was due at a later date. Most speculators bought stock with the intention of reselling it as soon as the price rose. They therefore did not worry about

paying the remainder of the cost. They never considered what might happen if the price of the stock should fall.

3. The nation was driven by an interest in **materialism.** The old ideals of reform and social service seemed to have faded away. The goal of many people in the 1920s was to obtain some degree of personal wealth and comfort. This materialism was widespread throughout the nation.

4. Organized gangsterism became a part of American life. The Eighteenth Amendment (1917) had helped create this problem. This amendment prohibited the sale of liquor. Soon, it became apparent that the law could not be enforced. Millions of Americans violated the law by buying illegal liquor. The smuggling of illegal spirits became a major business. Rival mobs of gangsters controlled the illegal sale of liquor.

5. There was a breakdown in American ideals. Many Americans distrusted intelligence and original ideas. Their attitude toward intellectual matters came to be known as Babbittry. This name came from the book *Babbitt*, written by Sinclair Lewis. Lewis described George Babbitt, the main character of the book, as a dull businessman. Babbittry infected many Americans with a desire for material comforts and a distrust of intellectuals. Along with Babbittry went a firm belief in a government that does not try to regulate business.

President Coolidge proved to be an honest and fairly able president. He cleaned up government by removing many of Harding's **appointees.** But Coolidge believed in keeping government activities to a minimum. He felt the country was getting along very well without government action.

In 1928, the Republicans named Herbert Hoover as their presidential candidate. Hoover had been a brilliant engineer. After World War I, he had served as an administrator of government aid to Europe. Hoover had also been secretary of commerce under both Harding and Coolidge. Like them, he believed strongly in limiting federal regulation of business.

The Democrats nominated Alfred E. Smith, governor of New York, as their candidate. Smith was a reformer and was also the first Catholic nominated for president. The 1928 campaign was a bitter one, but Hoover won easily. However, the prosperity that had seemed to go along with the Republicans was soon to vanish. One year later, the Great Depression struck.

COMPREHENSION CHECK

A. *Recognizing the Main Idea*

This reading selection as a whole tells you that

1. Babbittry was common in the 1920s.

2. Coolidge led a program of great reform.

3. the 1920s was a time of great prosperity, and Coolidge saw little reason to make reforms.

4. progressives gained strength during the 1920s.

B. Selecting Important Details

Choose the ending that best completes each statement.

1. The program of the Coolidge administration
    a. favored many progressive ideas.
    b. differed from Harding's program.
    c. was the same as Harding's program.
    d. favored increased federal activity and reform.

2. Progressive ideas were represented in the election of 1924 by
    a. none of the political parties.
    b. Republicans.
    c. Democrats.
    d. Senator La Follette.

3. All of the following were features of the Roaring Twenties EXCEPT
    a. increased speculation.
    b. interest in material goods.
    c. desire for more reforms.
    d. growth of new industries.

4. The term *Babbittry* applies to
    a. gangsterism in American life.
    b. regulation of business in the 1920s.
    c. speculation in real estate.
    d. distrust of ideas and intellectuals in the 1920s.

C. True or False

Decide whether each of these statements is true or false.

1. Sinclair Lewis created the character George Babbitt.

2. Herbert Hoover had a reputation for favoring increased federal regulation of business.

3. Organized gangsterism in the U.S. was tied to the smuggling of liquor during the 1920s.

4. The election of 1924 showed that progressivism had no support in the country.

5. Many people bought stock during the 1920s with the intention of selling it as soon as the price rose.

D. Vocabulary

Match the words with the definitions.

Words	Definitions
1. characterized	a. without time limit
2. indefinitely	b. defined by its important features
3. materialism	c. concern with acquiring possessions
4. appointees	d. far off
	e. allowance
	f. people chosen for certain jobs

E. Chronology

Arrange these events in the order in which they happened.

1. Assassination of McKinley
2. 19th Amendment ratified
3. 16th Amendment legalizes income tax
4. Spanish-American War
5. Exposure of Teapot Dome scandal
6. U.S. involvement in World War I

F. Using Your Knowledge

Make an outline of the major features of the Roaring Twenties. Be sure to include details as well as main ideas.

Amelia Earhart: Aviation Pioneer

The 1920s are sometimes known as the Roaring Twenties. It was a time when Americans were driven by a sense of excitement. Speed seemed to be the most important thing. Automobile races, motorboat races, and airplane races were very popular.

Aviation was born when the Wright brothers flew their first engine-driven airplane in 1903. Interest in airplanes grew rapidly during World War I but lost strength after the end of the war in 1918. For the next ten years, aviation attracted mainly military people and a small group of daredevils. In 1927, Charles A. Lindbergh became the first person, flying alone, to cross the Atlantic Ocean nonstop.

From the start, Amelia Earhart set out to show what women could do in aviation. In 1928, she was the first woman to fly across the Atlantic Ocean as a passenger. That same year, she became aviation editor for a national magazine. She wrote two books about flying and prepared herself for a career in aviation. In 1930, Earhart was named vice-president of one of the early passenger airlines.

Amelia Earhart became one of the stars of American aviation. She flew from one part of the country to another piloting many different kinds of airplanes. The newspapers and radio told the story of the records she set for speed and altitude flying. In 1935, she flew alone from Hawaii to the mainland of the United States. Such flights were very dangerous at the time, and great skill was needed by pilots flying long distances. In 1937, Amelia Earhart set out with her navigator on an around-the-world flight. The airplane apparently ran into difficulty over the Pacific Ocean near New Guinea. Radio contact with Earhart was lost, and her plane disappeared on July 2, 1937. No trace was ever found of the airplane or Amelia Earhart and her navigator.

Amelia Earhart was one of the courageous pioneers of aviation. She was a popular part of the Roaring Twenties. And she pointed the way for a place for women in aviation.

Lesson 10 Living in America: Improvements in American Life, 1890 — 1929

WORDS TO UNDERSTAND

Discuss the meanings of these words.

life expectancy   **sewage disposal**
emigrated

NEW WORDS IN SENTENCES

1. If the average **life expectancy** goes up, people expect to live longer.

2. They **emigrated** from Poland to make a new life in the United States.

3. Modern **sewage disposal** systems provide a clean method for removing waste.

AS YOU READ

As you read this selection, try to answer these questions.

1. In what ways was the health of Americans improved after 1890?

2. What inventions helped improve life for Americans?

THE READING SELECTION

The years between 1890 and 1929 brought many changes to the lives of Americans. In almost every area of life, great improvements made people's lives healthier and more comfortable.

Medical care. In 1890, there were about 100,000 doctors and 17,000 dentists. By 1929, however, there were over 150,000 doctors and 71,000 dentists. Medical research and drug preparation also improved. More hospitals were built, and people were given better care. As a result, the average **life expectancy** of Americans rose by about ten years between 1900 and 1929.

Reforms. Government reforms also helped improve the lives of Americans. In 1906, Congress passed the Meat Inspection Act and the Pure Food and Drug Act. These laws helped protect Americans from the dangers of food poisoning and unsafe drugs. The government also began to protect the health of workers, especially children and women. The child labor laws passed during the 1800s had not proved effective. But during the 1900s, federal laws began to prohibit child labor in many industries. These federal laws were often matched by state laws requiring children under a certain age to attend school.

As a result of these laws, school populations rose. In 1900, there were about 17 million pupils in public schools. The number rose to nearly 28 million in 1928. The number of high school graduates also rose from 95,000 to about 600,000.

Population. The population of the United States continued to grow. From 1890 to 1930, the population grew from about 63 million to over 123 million. Continued immigration added to this growth. More than 5 million people from northern and western Europe had **emigrated** to the United States between 1860 and 1880. In the next thirty years, 12 million Europeans emigrated to the United States. Most of these people came from central Europe, Russia and its Polish lands, and Italy.

Everyday life in the United States was changing. Many people moved away from farm areas to live in city areas. In 1900, about 60 percent of Americans lived in rural areas. Twenty years later, more than half of all Americans lived in urban areas.

City life. The quality of life in the city began to improve. Refrigeration made it possible to store many foods safely. Central heating also made city life safer and more comfortable. Steam heating systems replaced fireplaces and coal-burning stoves. City living was also improved by indoor plumbing. After 1890, cast-iron enameled bathtubs and washbasins were installed in many homes. At the same time, the flush toilet was invented. In the cities, bathtubs, washbasins, and flush toilets were linked to **sewage disposal** systems. Because of these improvements in sanitation, the health of the American people improved.

Electricity. Electricity played a great role in improving life. Thomas Edison had invented the electric light bulb in 1879. Within a few years, streets and homes across the country were lighted by electricity. Gas lamps and lanterns were replaced by electric light. By 1929, about

Americans were fascinated by new inventions—such as Edison's phonograph and the Wright brothers' airplane.

68 percent of American homes, most of them in the cities, had electric service.

Communication. Changes in communication greatly improved American lives. The number of telephones in the country rose from about 234,000 in 1890 to 20 million in 1929. People could talk easily to friends and relatives. Businesses had easy communication with one another and with the public.

Transportation. Transportation also changed life in the United States. Electric trolleys replaced horse-drawn trolleys after 1887. The electric trolley provided cities with clean, cheap, and speedy transportation. Underground systems of transportation, called subways, were used first in Boston in 1897. Subways made it possible to move great numbers of people safely and swiftly without clogging the streets.

In 1927, Charles Lindbergh made the first solo flight across the Atlantic Ocean. His flight helped open the airways for passenger travel. In 1928, the airlines were flying four times as many passenger flights as in 1927. The world seemed to be growing smaller.

It was, however, the automobile that brought the greatest change to American transportation. In 1909, Henry Ford's mass-produced Model T automobile led the way for the rest of the automobile industry. In 1910, about 180,000 cars had been sold. In 1929, nearly 4.5 million cars were sold. Concrete and asphalt roads were built all across the country. People greatly enjoyed their freedom to travel about easily by car.

COMPREHENSION CHECK

A. Recognizing the Main Idea

This selection as a whole tells you that

1. American life changed very little between 1890 and 1929.

2. American life between 1890 and 1929 improved in many ways.

3. Americans became very healthy between 1890 and 1929 because of better sanitation.

4. American life improved between 1920 and 1940.

B. Selecting Important Details

Choose the ending that best completes each statement.

1. The health of Americans improved because
   a. the Meat Inspection Act was repealed.
   b. there were fewer indoor plumbing systems.
   c. there were more hospitals and doctors.
   d. the life expectancy went down.

2. Child labor laws were often matched by
   a. improvements in sanitation.
   b. laws requiring children to attend school.
   c. higher tariffs.
   d. regulation of food and drugs.

3. The number of people living in cities after 1900
   a. decreased slightly.
   b. stayed the same as in former times.
   c. increased rapidly.
   d. decreased to less than 30 percent of the 1880 population.

4. The greatest change in American transportation in the early 1900s was brought about by
    a. trolleys.
    b. subways.
    c. airplanes.
    d. automobiles.

C. True or False

Decide whether each of these statements is true or false.

1. By 1929, there were over 150,000 doctors in the United States.

2. Steam heating systems are not as safe as coal-burning stoves.

3. Most of the homes that had electrical service by 1929 were in rural areas.

4. The population of the United States decreased between 1890 and 1930.

5. Federal laws passed in the early 1900s began to prohibit child labor in some industries.

D. Vocabulary

Write your own sentence for each of these terms.
life expectancy   sewage disposal
emigrate

E. Essay

Choose the three improvements discussed in this lesson that you think did the most to make life in America better. Write an essay of seventy-five words explaining your choices.

Famous Immigrants in American Life

Many immigrants found America to be a place where they could develop their skills and use their genius. Among them were Andrew Carnegie, Mary Harris Jones, and Albert Einstein.

Andrew Carnegie was born into extreme poverty in Scotland in 1835. He came to the United States at the age of thirteen. He became a telegraph operator and then took a railroad job and worked his way into a management position. After 1865, he decided to devote his time and money to the iron industry. He acquired coal mines, iron mines, and a fleet of ships to carry the ore to the mills. At the

Well-known immigrants Andrew Carnegie (below), Mary Harris Jones, and Albert Einstein.

Library of Congress

time of his retirement, his wealth from the Carnegie Steel Company was estimated at 500 million dollars. He had started with no money and built a fortune. Carnegie devoted the rest of his life to giving away his millions to support education, public libraries, and the world peace movement.

Mary Harris Jones was born in 1830 in Ireland. She came to the United States with her family at the age of five. Later, "Mother Jones," as she was called, became well known as a labor organizer. She organized mine workers in West Virginia, Colorado, and Arizona. Colorado coal mine owners sent her away from their mines three times in 1913, but she kept returning to the mines in spite of the danger. At the age of eighty-five, she helped in the streetcar and garment workers' strikes in New York City. And she was still organizing mine workers in West Virginia when she was ninety-one years old. Mother Jones's ability to get publicity brought government attention to the problems of workers and of children in factories. Mary Harris Jones died in 1930, having led a life courageously working for better labor conditions.

Albert Einstein was born in Germany in 1879. His genius in the fields of mathematics and physics won him the Nobel Prize in 1921. Because he was a Jew, Einstein was forced to flee the rising Nazi power in Germany. He settled in the United States in 1933 and accepted a position at Princeton University, where he remained for the rest of his life. Although a peace-loving man, he had the task of informing President Franklin D. Roosevelt in 1939 of the possibilities of atomic warfare. In 1940, he became an American citizen. Einstein's theory of relativity changed scientific ideas about time, space, and motion and laid the basis for the splitting of the atom.

These individuals left one home and culture to find their way in another. Their work contributed greatly to the development of the United States.

Unit 10 Summary A Changing Nation: 1865 – 1929

Politics and Federal Power

Since the mid-1800s, the two major political parties in the United States have been the Republican and Democratic parties. The Republican party was formed in 1854, and it captured the presidency in 1860. In the seventeen elections between 1860 and 1928, the Republicans elected thirteen presidents and the Democrats elected four.

One of the most important issues during these years was the proper role of the federal government. For many years, it was generally believed that "that government governs best which governs least." Many people felt that the government should not try to regulate business. But some reformers began to feel that the government should exercise more control. This view gained great popularity when Theodore Roosevelt became president in 1901. Later administrations, especially those of Harding and Coolidge, did not support government regulation, but the issue remained an important one.

The Reform Spirit

The reform spirit has appeared again and again in American history. Toward the end of the nineteenth century and early in the twentieth, reform legislation sought a better life for people of the United States. Political reforms sought to end corruption in government. The introduction of the civil service system in 1883 weakened the patronage system of filling federal jobs. Another political reform provided for the direct election of senators. Economic reforms included regulation of business, banking, and wages and hours for working people. Social reforms sought to end child labor and grant women the right to vote.

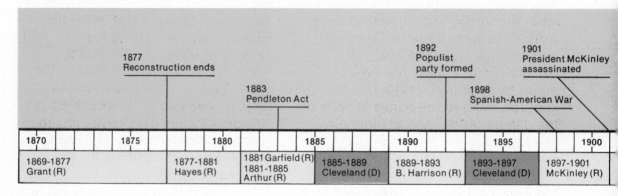

Political Parties and Reform

Originally, the Republican party, with its interest in ending slavery, was the party of reform in American politics. After Reconstruction, the Republicans gradually lost their reputation as reformers. The Democratic party became the party to which the reformers looked for leadership. Third parties, like the Populists, also advanced reform ideas. By 1896, the Democrats had adopted many of the programs of the Populists.

The Spanish-American War interrupted the reform movement in 1898. But the Democrats remained the party of reform until 1901, when Theodore Roosevelt became president. Under Roosevelt's leadership, the progressive wing of the Republican party became the reform group in American politics. Republican reform movements ended when the progressives bolted the party and the Democrats won the election in 1912.

In 1912, the Democrats, led by Woodrow Wilson, took over the cause of reform with the New Freedom. But the outbreak of World War I in 1914 and American entry into the war in 1917 ended the New Freedom program.

The victory of conservative Republicans in 1920 ended the reform movements for a while. The nation enjoyed a period of great prosperity and great industrial growth. Reform seemed unnecessary to many people.

Changing Lives

During the early 1900s, many changes helped improve the quality of American life. Better health care and sanitation helped increase the average life expectancy. Inventions like the light bulb, telephone, radio, and automobile made life easier for the people of the United States.

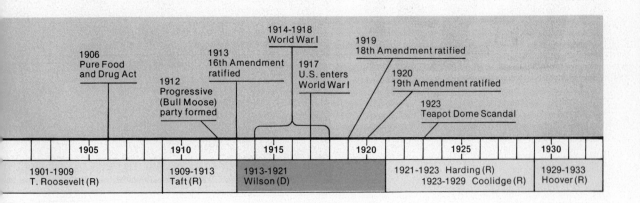

1906
Pure Food
and Drug Act

1912
Progressive
(Bull Moose)
party formed

1913
16th Amendment
ratified

1914-1918
World War I

1917
U.S. enters
World War I

1919
18th Amendment ratified

1920
19th Amendment ratified

1923
Teapot Dome Scandal

1905   1910   1915   1920   1925   1930

1901-1909
T. Roosevelt (R)

1909-1913
Taft (R)

1913-1921
Wilson (D)

1921-1923 Harding (R)
1923-1929 Coolidge (R)

1929-1933
Hoover (R)

unit
11

FDR by Rueben Appel, United Press International

Detail—*Metropolitan Life* by Victor Arnautoff, Coit Tower PWAP, photo by Don Beatty

Modern Challenges:
1929–1970s

From the Depression of the 1930s to the conflict of the 1960s, the time since 1929 has been filled with changes in lifestyles, values, and politics. These changes have been represented in the everyday lives of Americans (above). They have also been represented by individual leaders, from Franklin D. Roosevelt (left), to Martin Luther King, Jr., to Betty Friedan. Before 1929, the nation had faced the challenges of becoming modern. After 1929, it faced the challenges of *being* modern.

525

Lesson 1   The Great Depression

WORDS TO UNDERSTAND

Discuss the meanings of these words.

purchasing power   **expenditures**
recession

NEW WORDS IN SENTENCES

1. People without money have no **purchasing power.**
2. In a period of **recession,** economic activity decreases.
3. Increased federal **expenditures** led to an unbalanced federal budget.

AS YOU READ

As you read this selection, try to answer these questions.

1. What were some reasons for the Great Depression?
2. What was President Hoover's policy toward the economy?

THE READING SELECTION

There had been many economic depressions in the United States before 1929. But the one that began in that year was the worst in the nation's history. The first sign of the Great Depression was the stock market collapse in October 1929. Stock prices dropped suddenly. Thousands of people lost all the money they had invested.

The stock market's "Panic of 1929" has often been blamed for the depression that followed. But the explanation is more complex than that. There were many economic problems that contributed to the Great Depression.

1. Many people had become speculators in the stock market. Stocks had become overpriced.

2. Farmers had not shared in the prosperity of the 1920s. There had been an economic depression in agriculture since 1921. Prices for farm products were very low.

3. It had become difficult to get credit. Farmers and business people often needed credit to operate. Many businesses and farms were lost because owners could not get credit.

4. Industrial production had grown faster than the market for products. Americans' **purchasing power** had not grown fast enough. They did not make enough money to buy the goods produced. When demand for products decreased, factories had to shut down. Many workers were laid off.

5. American protective tariffs decreased foreign trade. They kept foreign goods out of the country. As a result, many foreign nations refused to import American goods. This decreased the market American manufacturers counted on.

6. Thousands of banks had to close because of unsound practices. Many banks had speculated unwisely with their investments. Since there was no deposit insurance, many Americans lost all their money in banks that failed.

7. The depression was worldwide. The American and European economies were closely linked. This made recovery from the depression more difficult.

Recovery from previous depressions had come without government action. Depression and recovery was considered part of the general business cycle. According to one theory, this business cycle has four periods.

1. The first period is prosperity. Wages, prices, and profits are high. Unemployment is low during this time.

2. Prosperity may be followed by a period of **recession.** Wages, prices, and profits begin to fall, and unemployment rises.

3. The period of recession may grow worse and become a depression. At this time, wages and prices fall sharply. There is widespread business failure and unemployment.

The stock market crash brought down much of the American economy with it. Large and small banks lost their money and had to close.

4. Depression may be followed by recovery. In recovery, wages, prices, and profits again increase. Production and employment begin to rise. The economy returns to prosperity.

In this business cycle, depression is a natural stage, which will be followed by recovery. From 1929 to 1932, President Herbert Hoover's administration believed that recovery was just around the corner. Hoover believed that government did not need to take any major steps to help the economy. He preferred the laissez-faire approach.

Hoover did support efforts to strengthen farm credit and raise farm prices. He also tried to help businesses recover. This was done by making more loans available through the Reconstruction Finance Corporation. Hoover also increased federal **expenditures** on public works projects in an effort to provide jobs. But, in general, he preferred private to government action in fighting the depression.

By 1932, millions of people were out of work. Little relief was provided for them. People were dissatisfied. When the Democrats charged that Hoover was to blame for the depression, the voters listened. In the 1932 presidential campaign, the Democratic candidate was Franklin D. Roosevelt. He was governor of New York and a cousin of former president Theodore Roosevelt. He promised a "New Deal" for the American people, including government action if necessary. His promises captured the public imagination and provided hope for the nation. Roosevelt defeated Hoover by winning the electoral votes of forty-two states. His administration would be the longest of any American president. It would also contain some of the most sweeping reforms in American government.

President Hoover called for cooperation among business people and labor leaders to keep wages and prices stable. He did not believe that economic conditions would continue to get worse.

Chicago Historical Society

COMPREHENSION CHECK

A. Recognizing the Main Idea

This selection as a whole tells you

1. why the depression was worldwide.
2. how the stock market caused the Great Depression.
3. about the causes of the Great Depression and Hoover's approach to ending it.
4. why President Hoover wanted government action to fight the depression.

B. Selecting Important Details

Choose the ending that best completes each statement.

1. The Panic of 1929
   a. caused the depression.
   b. started when a bank closed.
   c. caused the recession.
   d. started with a drop in stock prices.
2. Farmers
   a. could get credit to buy land and equipment easily.
   b. had been prosperous in the 1920s.
   c. had to sell farm products at low prices.
   d. had a lot of purchasing power.
3. The protective tariffs
   a. increased foreign trade.
   b. decreased foreign trade.
   c. widened the market for American goods.
   d. had no effect on exports.
4. The Great Depression
   a. put millions of people out of work.
   b. was over by 1931.
   c. happened only in America.
   d. was the first depression.

C. True or False

Decide whether each of these statements is true or false. Rewrite the false statements so that they are true.

1. President Hoover thought recovery would never come.
2. Prosperity, recession, depression, and recovery are the four parts of one general business cycle theory.
3. Government help brought the economy out of previous depressions.
4. Wages, prices, and profits increase during a depression.
5. Hoover increased federal expenditures in order to provide jobs.

D. Vocabulary

Match the words with the definitions.

Words	Definitions
1. purchasing power	a. question
	b. ability to buy
2. recession	c. something spent
3. expenditure	d. setback in the economy

E. Ask Yourself

What happened to farmers in the 1920s when they tried to get loans to buy seed and fertilizer for the next year's crop? Why? Why did many farmers lose their farms?

F. Homework

Try to understand the depression by answering the following questions. Write down your answers.

What happens when there are great quantities of products being produced, but people do not have much money to buy them? What happens to prices? What happens to profits? What happens to wages and employment?

Bessie Smith and the Blues

The 1920s and early 1930s was a time of great activity in the arts by black Americans. Jazz music and the blues were an important part of the art forms of black people.

W. C. Handy, a black trumpeter and composer, made blues music a part of American life. His song "St. Louis Blues" was written in 1914 and remains a classic to this day. Many other black musical artists helped bring blues music to all America. These artists included Mamie Smith, whose recording of "Crazy Blues" in 1920 sold 7,500 records in one week. This was an amazing sale of a recording at that time. Another black singer, Ma Rainey, became known as the Mother of the Blues. But perhaps the best known of the blues singers of the time was Bessie Smith, the Empress of the Blues.

Bessie Smith was born into extreme poverty in Tennessee in 1894. Little is known about her early life. As a young woman, she sang with Ma Rainey in tent shows and carnivals. Later, she toured the black vaudeville circuit singing in the black ghettos of large southern cities.

Bessie Smith made a number of recordings between 1923 and 1933 for Columbia Phonograph Company. Her recordings had remarkable sales and may have brought Columbia out of bankruptcy. She formed her own show and traveled to Boston, New York, Chicago, and the large cities of

Duncan Scheidt

the South, playing mostly to black audiences. She sang without a microphone and was known for her rich voice and expressive style.

Bessie Smith died from injuries she received in an automobile accident in Mississippi in 1937. After her death, her records continued to help spread her name among music lovers in all parts of America. Her style influenced the singing of Billie Holiday and Mahalia Jackson. Today, Bessie Smith is recognized as one of the great classic singers of the songs of sorrow and despair that are called the blues.

Lesson 2   A New Deal for the American People

WORDS TO UNDERSTAND

Discuss the meanings of these words.

reforestation   **concur**

NEW WORDS IN SENTENCES

1. **Reforestation** projects replace the trees cut down for lumber with newly planted trees.

2. When two people share the same ideas, their views **concur.**

AS YOU READ

As you read this selection, try to answer these questions.

1. What were some of the actions President Roosevelt took immediately to bring the country out of the depression?

2. What problems did the New Deal run into?

3. What long-lasting changes in the economic system were made by President Roosevelt?

THE READING SELECTION

Review. The stock market crash in 1929 began the worst depression in the nation's history. Many things helped bring it about. Among them were speculation in stocks, a lack of credit, a decrease in the market for industrial products, and poor banking practices. As the depression worsened, the voters elected Franklin D. Roosevelt president. ☆

Franklin D. Roosevelt took over as president in March 1933. The depression was at its worst point. Unemployment had risen to about 12 million people, or one-fourth of all workers. Two-thirds of the nation's banks had closed. The savings of millions of people were in danger. Farm prices were so low that thousands of farms were being lost through foreclosures. In general, public confidence in the American economic and political systems had slipped.

Roosevelt began to act immediately. The first 100 days of his administration saw an amazing amount of government action, supported by the Democratic Congress.

1. An executive order declared a "bank holiday." A few days later, the Emergency Banking Act was passed. All banks were closed while their finances were inspected.

2. The Civilian Conservation Corps (CCC) Act aimed at both conservation and relief for the unemployed. It estab-

As first lady, Eleanor Roosevelt worked for human rights and took an active part in government. In this photo, she meets with Aubrey Williams and Mary McLeod Bethune of the National Youth Administration. Bethune also served as President Roosevelt's Special Advisor on Minority Affairs.

lished the CCC to provide jobs in **reforestation** and flood-control projects.

3. The Federal Emergency Relief Act (FERA) gave additional funds to state and local governments for unemployment relief.

4. The Truth-in-Securities Act provided a check on stock market activities.

5. The Agricultural Adjustment Act (AAA) established minimum farm prices and government control over farm production. Farmers were paid to reduce production in order to keep prices up.

6. The Tennessee Valley Authority (TVA) Act was passed. It provided flood control and cheap electric power in the Tennessee River valley.

7. The National Industrial Recovery Act (NIRA) established the National Recovery Administration (NRA). The NRA was supposed to encourage cooperation in industry. It set up codes of competition and pledged fair hours and wages for workers.

These early New Deal actions soon were tested in legal cases, some before the Supreme Court. The conservative Supreme Court declared several laws, including the NIRA and the AAA, unconstitutional. The justices felt that the laws went beyond federal power provided for in the Constitution. Roosevelt objected to what he called "horse-and-buggy" decisions. In 1937, he asked Congress to increase the number of justices on the Court. This would allow Roosevelt to appoint a number of justices who would **concur** with his views. Thus, he would influence the Court's future votes. The bill met strong opposition, even from Roosevelt supporters. At the same time, however, the Court began to reverse its conservative stands. Although Roosevelt's "court-packing" bill did not pass, relations with the Supreme Court improved.

President Roosevelt continued to work with the Congress to reform economic weaknesses. From 1933 to 1941, a number of long-lasting changes were made.

Business. To meet the banking crisis, the Federal Deposit Insurance Corporation (FDIC) was established. This insured deposits in member banks. To prevent future stock market crashes, the Securities and Exchange Commission (SEC) was set up to regulate market activities.

Labor. The National Labor Relations Board was established in 1935 by the National Labor Relations Act. It helped settle strikes. It also helped guarantee the right of workers to join independent, rather than company, unions. In addition, the Fair Labor Standards Act set minimum wages and hours.

Agriculture. When the first Agricultural Adjustment Act was declared unconstitutional, a second one was passed. It limited production and fixed minimum prices for farm products.

Unemployment. To combat unemployment, the Works Progress Administration (WPA) and, later, the Public Works Administration (PWA) were set up. Their federal projects provided work for millions of people. The CCC continued to provide work in conservation. And the National Youth Administration (NYA) found part-time work for boys and girls attending school. A special Division of Negro Affairs in the NYA was headed for many years by Mary McLeod Bethune. She worked to make sure that jobs were made available for blacks as well as whites.

Social security. The Social Security System provided old-age pensions and unemployment insurance for the first time. The United States had lagged behind Europe in social legislation. This was because of laissez-faire attitudes in the United States.

Roosevelt's administration in the 1930s was one of the most active in American history. It stirred up a great deal of support — Roosevelt was reelected in 1936 by a huge majority. But it also stirred up bitter opposition and criticism. It is important to consider both of these when looking back at the New Deal.

COMPREHENSION CHECK

A. Recognizing the Main Idea
This selection as a whole tells you that the Roosevelt administration
   1. closed the banks for a "holiday."
   2. had laissez-faire attitudes.
   3. had almost everyone's support.
   4. took action against the depression with the New Deal programs.

B. Selecting Important Details
Choose the ending that best completes each statement.
   1. The early New Deal actions
      a. were "horse-and-buggy" actions.
      b. raised constitutional problems.
      c. had the support of the Republican Congress.
      d. were "court-packing" actions.
   2. The National Industrial Recovery Act (NIRA)
      a. was declared constitutional.
      b. provided for improvements for the Tennessee Valley.
      c. set up jobs in reforestation projects.
      d. set up the NRA.

3. During Roosevelt's administration, workers
   a. lost their unemployment insurance.
   b. were not allowed to join labor unions.
   c. were guaranteed the right to join labor unions.
   d. lost the right to a minimum wage.

4. To prevent future stock market crashes,
   a. the Securities and Exchange Commission was set up.
   b. the Social Security Act was passed.
   c. the Public Works Administration was set up.
   d. the National Labor Relations Act was passed.

C. True or False

Decide whether each of these statements is true or false.

1. There was low unemployment when Roosevelt became president.

2. Roosevelt did not take much action during the first 100 days of his administration.

3. The Supreme Court ruled that Roosevelt wanted "horse-and-buggy" legislation.

4. The Social Security System guarantees workers the right to join unions.

5. The Agricultural Adjustment Administration fixed minimum prices for farm products.

D. Vocabulary

Use a word from this list to complete each sentence.

concur   reforestation
recession   expenditure

1. The logging company planned a _____ project.

2. The justices might not _____ with the opinions of the president.

E. Ask Yourself

What are some arguments against too much government involvement in business, agriculture, and social problems? Does the United States government have a laissez-faire approach to economic and social problems today? Do you think it should?

F. Map Skills

Use the map below to answer these questions.

1. Which states had dams built in them as part of the TVA?

2. Which states now have nuclear plants?

3. Which states have steam plants?

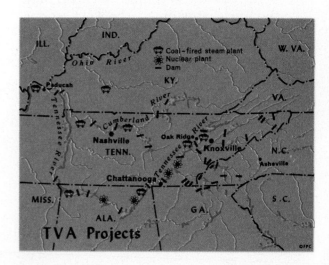

TVA Projects

The Tennessee Valley Authority

At the end of World War I, the government was faced with the problem of what to do with an electric power plant in Alabama. A dam and the plant had been built by the government to produce chemicals for weapons. The plant, at a place called Muscle Shoals on the Tennessee River, was offered for sale to private investors. Before it could be sold, it became a political issue through the action of Senator George W. Norris of Nebraska.

Senator Norris, a former Progressive Republican supporter of Theodore Roosevelt's Bull Moose campaign, proposed government operation of the power plant. Norris led a fight in Congress that lasted for fifteen years. His bills were vetoed by Presidents Coolidge and Hoover, who were against putting a government power plant in competition with those run by private industry.

Senator Norris refused to be discouraged. In 1933, he interested President Franklin D. Roosevelt in the project. The area of the Tennessee Valley had been in a sad condition since the Civil War. Forests had been destroyed by loggers and fires. Farmland had been robbed of its richness by the flooding of the Tennessee River every year. Few farms had electricity, there was little industry, and there was little that local governments could do for the area. Thousands of people lived in poverty, and disease had become widespread.

What finally came as a result of Senator Norris's efforts was the Tennessee Valley Authority (TVA). There was opposition to the TVA because the federal government had never before undertaken such a big project to help one area of the country. Some people thought that there was no way that a big plan by a government far away could solve the problems of the Tennessee Valley without creating new ones.

The TVA set up an agency to build dams and power plants along the Tennessee River in seven southern states. These states would produce chemical fertilizer and also sell electricity to areas without power. The rates set for electricity by the government would be used as a yardstick for judging rates of private power companies.

But the TVA did more than build dams and power plants in the Tennessee Valley. It brought new prosperity to the area through reforestation projects, flood control, soil conservation, recreation area development, and improved agricultural methods. It was a great triumph for George Norris, and one of the dams is appropriately named Norris Dam.

Lesson 3   What Was the Value of the New Deal?

WORDS TO UNDERSTAND
Discuss the meanings of these words.

bureaucracy	purge
civilian	discrimination

NEW WORDS IN SENTENCES

1. A big government **bureaucracy** can be very expensive.

2. **Civilian** workers are not part of the military.

3. Leaders sometimes want to **purge** an organization so that no one who disagrees with their policies has power.

4. **Discrimination** keeps people out of jobs or housing because of their race or sex.

AS YOU READ

As you read this selection, try to answer these questions.

1. What were some of the arguments against the New Deal?

2. What were some of the accomplishments of the New Deal?

THE READING SELECTION

Review. In the first 100 days of his New Deal, President Roosevelt and the Congress acted to provide jobs and relief for the unemployed. They also acted to regulate banks, the stock market, farm prices, and industry. When some of these measures were declared unconstitutional, Roosevelt tried unsuccessfully to "pack" the Supreme Court. His effort received strong criticism. But the Court did begin to reverse its conservative stands on its own. The important legislation of the New Deal included business regulation of banks and the stock market, guarantees of the right to unionize, and guarantees of minimum wages and hours. The New Deal also guaranteed minimum farm prices, provided millions of federal jobs, and began Social Security.   ☆

The New Deal had much in common with the New Nationalism of Theodore Roosevelt and the New Freedom of Woodrow Wilson. All these programs abandoned the traditional American laissez-faire attitude. In its place, these programs established governmental regulation and reform.

The New Deal programs and Roosevelt's striking personality affected Americans strongly. After a few years, the nation was divided on the New Deal. Support for it came from big-city voters and labor unions. The opposition included Republicans and conservative Demo-

President Roosevelt was both a loved and a hated man. Many thought his policies would destroy the American economic system. Others saw him as a great leader and a humanitarian.

crats. Critics raised several arguments against the New Deal.

1. The New Deal was based on a strong federal government. Its legislation gave broad powers to the government. This was based on a loose interpretation of the Constitution. Many people did not agree with this interpretation.

2. The New Deal increased the federal **bureaucracy.** The number of **civilian** federal employees more than doubled between 1931 and 1941. To many people, this symbolized the hated big government.

3. The New Deal was expensive. The national debt rose from about $19 billion in 1932 to about $43 billion in 1940.

4. The New Deal did not end the depression. Nor did it manage to solve the problem of unemployment. In 1939, there were still about 8 million unemployed.

5. President Roosevelt was accused of trying to win too much power for himself. His effort to "pack" the Supreme Court raised this criticism. So did his request that the voters **purge** legislators in Congress who opposed his program.

Supporters of the New Deal felt that it accomplished several things.

1. It helped preserve the American economic system by helping to rebuild confidence in it. Most New Deal reforms remained based on private ownership of business and industry. The government did begin to take a hand in the economy. But it did not take it over, as governments in some other nations had done.

2. New Deal programs raised the national income, along with the national debt. This income almost doubled between 1932 and 1939.

3. The American farmer was helped. The problems of production and prices did not disappear, but they were eased.

4. New Deal legislation made the lives of most Americans more secure. Working people obtained new rights and benefits. Badly needed reforms and protection were introduced into banking and the stock market.

5. Jobs were provided for many unemployed people. At the same time, many of these jobs furthered conservation and local improvements, as did those in the TVA and the CCC.

6. During Roosevelt's New Deal, women and blacks were brought into official government circles in larger numbers than ever before. Some were informal advisors, but many had formal posts. Frances Perkins, for example, the secretary of labor, was the first woman to serve in the cabinet.

The New Deal was finally ended by World War II. Reform legislation largely disappeared during the war. One exception was the creation of the Fair Employment Practices Commission (FEPC), which acted to stop **discrimination** against minorities. Roosevelt went on to be elected to third and fourth terms, the first and only president to achieve this.

Many people still see the New Deal as a dangerous period of big government. In response to that argument, Roosevelt said in 1936, "Better the occasional faults of a government that lives in the spirit of charity than the consistent omissions of a government frozen in the ice of its own indifference."

So what was the New Deal worth? When you weigh these two sets of arguments, which side seems stronger?

COMPREHENSION CHECK

A. Recognizing the Main Idea

1. In a single sentence, write the main idea of this lesson's reading selection.

2. Write two other points that support this main idea.

B. Selecting Important Details

Choose the ending that best completes each statement.

1. All of the following were arguments against the New Deal EXCEPT
   a. it increased the federal bureaucracy.
   b. the presidency lost power.
   c. it did not end the depression.
   d. the federal debt increased.

2. All of the following were arguments for the New Deal EXCEPT
    a. American farmers were helped.
    b. the national income was raised.
    c. working people gained new rights and benefits.
    d. the government took over business and industry.
3. At the time of World War II,
    a. the New Deal ended.
    b. the Fair Employment Practices Commission ended.
    c. President Roosevelt's administration ended.
    d. reform legislation began.
4. New Deal reforms
    a. were based on a strict interpretation of the Constitution.
    b. solved all the problems of the American farmers.
    c. helped encourage discrimination against minorities.
    d. rebuilt confidence in the American economy.

C. True or False

Decide whether each of these statements is true or false.

1. The New Deal reduced the number of civilian employees.

2. President Roosevelt wanted to purge the government of legislators who did not support his programs.

3. More women and blacks worked in the Roosevelt administration than in previous administrations.

4. The New Deal got most of its support from conservatives.

5. Roosevelt was elected president four times.

D. Vocabulary

Match the words with the definitions.

Words	Definitions
1. bureaucracy	a. get rid of unwanted people
2. civilian	b. prejudiced action
3. purge	c. polite
4. discrimination	d. equal treatment
	e. not military
	f. organization of people carrying out government programs

E. Essay

Roosevelt felt that a government that took action, even if it made mistakes, was better than a government that did nothing.

Write three or four sentences in support of his view. Then write three or four sentences telling whether or not you agree with this view. Give reasons for your opinion.

F. Homework

Ask two or three older people what they remember most about the Great Depression, President Franklin D. Roosevelt, and the New Deal. If they seem willing to talk, get them to remember as much as they can about those years. Take notes to bring back to class.

Lesson 4   Living in America: The Era Between the Wars, 1920 – 1945

WORDS TO UNDERSTAND
Discuss the meanings of these words.

prohibition   resources
speakeasies

NEW WORDS IN SENTENCES
1. Liquor was illegal in the United States during the years of **prohibition.**
2. People went to **speakeasies** to drink liquor and hear music.
3. Most of the **resources** of the country went to the war effort.

AS YOU READ
As you read this selection, try to answer these questions.

1. What were some forms of popular entertainment in America before and after the stock market crash in 1929?
2. What difficulties did minorities and women face?
3. How did the depression and World War II affect the lives of Americans?

THE READING SELECTION
The years between 1920 and 1945 were filled with great contrasts. From boom to bust to war—the lives of Americans changed with the times.

The Jazz Age. World War I had left many Americans bitter. Isolationism and intolerance were high. Many people blamed Communists for the union disturbances in 1919–1920. The Ku Klux Klan, a secret group devoted to hatred of minority groups, attracted 5 million new members in the 1920s.

The twenties were also the years of **prohibition.** But the Eighteenth Amendment could not keep people from drinking. **Speakeasies,** secret nightclubs where liquor was sold, attracted many people. At speakeasies, people danced to jazz music. Some of the greatest jazz musicians of the day belonged to King Oliver's Creole Jazz Band. One of them, Louis Armstrong, made musical history with his cornet. Jazz, first the music of blacks, soon became popular with whites. Phonographs, developed in the late 1800s, sold well in the 1920s and brought jazz and other music into the home.

Radio also brought entertainment into homes. By 1922, there were over 600 radio stations. Sports, drama, and music were brought to the people. The nation became hooked on radio.

In general, the nation was having good times—there was not much social change. Blacks were faced with

Jim Crow laws and a strong Ku Klux Klan. The women's movement lost unity after the passage of the Nineteenth Amendment. In 1923, Alice Paul proposed an Equal Rights Amendment. But it was opposed by many unionists who favored protection for women workers.

Federal Indian policy, however, did change. In 1924, Indians were given citizenship. In 1934, the Indian Reorganization Act ended the huge loss of Indian lands under the 1880s allotment policy. It also reversed previous national policy by recognizing the tribes as political units with limited powers of self-government.

Asian- and Mexican-Americans continued to face problems. A 1924 law reinforced the ban on Asian immigrants. The anti-Asian sentiment behind this law resulted in segregation of Asians and violence against them. On the other hand, Mexican immigration had been encouraged in order to provide cheap labor for the mines, ranches, and railroads of the West. Yet strikes and riots resulted from poor living conditions. And economic depression finally led to mass deportations.

The depression years. The beginning of this economic depression was marked by the stock market crash of 1929. The Jazz Age was replaced by a period of hunger and hopelessness. In 1933, the national unemployment rate reached 25 percent. Many people were forced out of their homes. They camped for the night wherever they could. "Hobo jungles" became a common sight. "Hoovervilles," camps where people built shacks from scraps and cardboard, sprang up in many cities. Some charities offered soup and bread to the hungry. Long lines formed for these meals. Some people sold apples on the street to try to earn enough money for food.

The nation looked to entertainment for escape from the woes of the depression. Radio remained very popular. Eddie Cantor, Burns and Allen, Fanny Brice, Edgar Bergen, Jack Benny, Fred Allen, and Kate Smith helped keep up the spirit of the nation.

Movies became more and more popular. "Talkies" replaced silent movies. By the mid-1930s, nearly 60 percent of all Americans went to the movies once a week. For only a dime a seat, people could see their favorite stars. Movies and radio drew audiences away from the theaters. Still, some of Broadway's liveliest musicals were written in the thirties. Another sort of music, "swing," also caught on.

The war years. After the United States entered World War II, life in America changed quickly. Manufacturing for war needs greatly boosted the nation's economy. For the first time in a long while, most people had jobs and money to spend. Women joined the work force by the millions. But many workers found they had less to spend their money on. The government, to conserve **resources** for the war, had rationed many goods. Some foods, coffee, gasoline, shoes, and other goods were available only in limited supplies. Children collected scrap metal to help the war effort. Cities dimmed their lights to help conserve power. Government posters urged, "Use it up—wear it out—make it do!" Nationwide, people pitched in.

542

GOOD & NOT-SO-GOOD TIMES

World War I was over, and Americans were glad
to turn their attention to playing hard and
moving fast. In the 1920s, all kinds of
entertainment were popular, from joyriding in
cars to dancing the Charleston to watching stars
like Charlie Chaplin in the movies (left page).
The 1930s depression cut in on the good times,
but didn't stop them (this page). The public still
loved movie and sports stars—crowds still
watched Jack Dempsey box. The steps changed
but dancing stayed—marathon contests often
lasted a week or more. Some said Americans
were escaping from their economic problems.
Perhaps that was true.

Everson Museum of Art

Dempsey and Firpo by George Bellows, 1924 (oil on canvas, 51 x 63¼ inches),
Collection of Whitney Museum of American Art, photo by Geoffrey Clements

COMPREHENSION CHECK

A. *Recognizing the Main Idea*
This selection as a whole tells you

1. about movies during the depression.
2. about Indians during the depression.
3. why people joined the Ku Klux Klan in the 1920s.
4. about life in America between 1920 and 1945.

B. *Selecting Important Details*
Choose the ending that best completes each statement.

1. Before the stock market crash of 1929
   a. radios had not been invented.
   b. phonographs had not been invented.
   c. jazz was popular.
   d. swing music was popular.
2. During the depression
   a. talkies replaced silent movies.
   b. few people went to the movies.
   c. only sad songs were written.
   d. most people had money to spend.
3. Alice Paul proposed the
   a. Indian Reorganization Act.
   b. Eighteenth Amendment.
   c. Nineteenth Amendment.
   d. Equal Rights Amendment.
4. A 1924 law regarding Asians
   a. banned segregation.
   b. guaranteed fair wages for workers in the West.
   c. opened the door for further Asian immigration.
   d. reinforced the ban on Asian immigrants.

C. *Fact or Opinion*
Decide whether each of these statements is fact or opinion.

1. Indians were given citizenship in 1924.
2. Movies were good for America because they offered an escape from troubles.
3. The government was wise to ration limited resources during the war.
4. The Ku Klux Klan is a group opposed to most minorities.
5. The Eighteenth Amendment was a mistake.

D. *Vocabulary*
Match the words with the definitions.

Words	Definitions
1. prohibition	a. a useful material or skill
2. speakeasy	b. outlawing of liquor
3. resource	c. when jazz was illegal
	d. nightclub selling liquor during the 1920s
	e. social problem

Pearl Buck
Brings China to America

Immigrants to the United States came from many cultures. Many of these cultures were not understood by other Americans. Perhaps one of the least understood was that of China. It was not until the 1900s that Americans really began to understand China and its people. One of those who increased this understanding was a famous author, Pearl Buck.

Pearl Buck was born in the United States, but she went to China with her missionary parents. She learned to speak the Northern Chinese dialect perfectly. She grew up in two cultures—those of China and the United States. She attended college in America but returned to China. She taught there for many years. Even the Chinese civil war forced her to leave China for only a few years. By the time she was forty years old, she had spent about thirty-two years in China.

When she was thirty-eight, Pearl Buck began to write about the country that she loved so much and knew so well. Her first book, *East Wind, West Wind* (1930), told the story of a young Chinese girl's disappointment in love. During the next year, her most famous book, *The Good Earth,* was published. It centered around the fight of a Chinese peasant to keep his land. It showed many Americans a view of China that they had never seen before. Buck's writing not only gave Americans information on the Chinese

United Press International

ways of life. It also showed Buck's readers people about whom they cared, whose stories mattered to them. It was beginning to help overcome bias against the Chinese. *The Good Earth* was a great success and won a Pulitzer Prize in 1932.

Pearl Buck's fame as a writer continued to grow. She gained an international reputation. In 1938, she was awarded the Nobel Prize for literature, a great honor. One of the speakers at the prize ceremony praised her highly.

You have . . . advanced the understanding and appreciation in the Western world of a great and important part of mankind, the people of China. You have taught us by your works to see the individuals in this great mass of people . . . and you have given us Westerners something of China's soul.

Lesson 5   The Postwar Period

WORDS TO UNDERSTAND

Discuss the meanings of these words.

transition   **stabilize**   **communism**

NEW WORDS IN SENTENCES

1. The **transition** from a wartime economy to a peacetime economy can be difficult.

2. Something must be done to **stabilize** prices if they rise and fall too much.

3. Many Americans were afraid that **communism** would replace the American system of government.

AS YOU READ

As you read this selection, try to answer these questions.

1. How did Truman's administration try to solve the postwar problems?

2. Why were Truman's plans not completely carried out?

THE READING SELECTION

Franklin D. Roosevelt died in April 1945, shortly after he began his fourth term. He was succeeded by Harry S. Truman. The following month, World War II in Europe ended. In August, the war in Asia was over.

During World War II, the nation's attention had been on the struggle with the enemy. Economic action had been aimed at converting production to the needs of war. In fact, it was World War II that finally ended the depression of the 1930s. Social action or reform had been largely put aside. Domestic affairs had taken a back seat to foreign affairs.

In 1945, all this changed. President Truman faced two main problems. The first was concerned with the millions of men and women who had been in the service during the war. They needed jobs, education, and housing. Fortunately, the "G.I. Bill of Rights" had been passed in 1944, under President Roosevelt. It provided unemployment insurance for veterans, loans for home-building and businesses, and money for education. About 12 million ex-service people used the G.I. Bill to get an education.

The second main challenge for President Truman was the **transition** from a wartime economy to a peacetime one. Wartime needs had led to shortages of consumer goods. Prices shot up after wartime price controls were removed.

Dewey was expected to win the presidency in 1948. The final winner, Truman was amused at an early edition headline.

Millions of women had taken over men's jobs during the war. What was to be done with this work force? Shortly after the war, there was also an increase in labor unrest and strikes.

In the election of 1946, the Republicans won control of Congress. Their conservative opposition to Truman's Democratic administration would continue for many years. In 1947, the Congress passed the Taft-Hartley Act, which limited union power. When Truman vetoed it, it was passed over his veto. The Republicans were so strong that Truman seemed headed for defeat in the presidential election of 1948. Splits in the Democratic party seemed to guarantee victory for Republican Thomas E. Dewey. But Truman upset Dewey.

Truman then presented his own program, which he called the "Fair Deal." The legislative proposals sent to Congress asked for a number of things.

1. The repeal of the Taft-Hartley Act. Labor had continued to oppose what it called a "slave labor bill."

2. An increase in the minimum wage. Rising prices had made the original forty cents an hour unrealistic.

3. A program to **stabilize** farm prices so that farmers would have a steady income.

4. A program to provide housing. During the depression and the war, there had been little home-building. This resulted in a serious shortage of housing and an increase in slums.

5. A civil rights program. As part of this program, segregation in army units was to be ended.

Opposition to the Fair Deal by Republicans and conservative Democrats limited Truman's success. In 1950, the United States became involved overseas in the fighting in Korea. This drew some attention away from reform at home. The president's program was only partly carried out.

The minimum wage was raised to seventy-five cents an hour. The National Housing Act provided cities with funds for clearing slums and building low-income housing. The Social Security Act was extended to provide benefits for an additional 11 million people.

However, most of the Fair Deal civil rights program was rejected. The Taft-Hartley Act was never repealed, though it was modified. Truman's farm program was also rejected. However, price supports did continue

Domestic affairs of the late 1940s and early 1950s were affected by the "cold war." This was the name for increased tensions between the United States and the Soviet Union. Americans became more and more concerned about **communism** in the United States. Investigations into the backgrounds of government workers led to many charges and dismissals. In 1951, Congress passed the Internal Security Act over President Truman's veto. This required Communists to register with the government and limited their rights in many ways. Senator Joseph McCarthy of Wisconsin made many charges of communism in government circles. Fear over internal security, or "McCarthyism," as it was called, was reaching its peak as President Truman left office in 1953.

COMPREHENSION CHECK

A. Recognizing the Main Idea

This selection as a whole tells you that

1. there were shortages of consumer goods after the war.
2. Truman had the support of Congress for his postwar plans.
3. Truman's Fair Deal programs for solving postwar problems were only partially put into effect.
4. foreign affairs became more important than domestic affairs after the war.

B. Selecting Important Details

Choose the ending that best completes each statement.

1. The Taft-Hartley Act
   a. limited union power.
   b. had Truman's support.
   c. was vetoed by Congress.
   d. was part of the Fair Deal.

2. All of the following were problems of transition from wartime to peacetime EXCEPT
   a. shortages of consumer goods.
   b. high prices.
   c. unemployment.
   d. the G.I. Bill of Rights.

3. All of the following were part of Truman's Fair Deal EXCEPT
   a. an increase in the minimum wage.
   b. a program to provide housing.
   c. a program to stabilize farm prices.
   d. a program to continue segregation in the armed forces.

4. Truman's plans were only partially put into effect because
   a. a civil rights program was accepted.
   b. the Taft-Hartley Act was repealed.
   c. of opposition from liberal Democrats.
   d. of opposition from Republicans and conservative Democrats.

C. True or False

Decide whether each of these statements is true or false.

1. The cold war was the war between Democrats and Republicans.
2. President Truman supported the Internal Security Act.
3. Joseph McCarthy was a Communist.
4. None of Truman's plans were carried out after the war.
5. Truman wanted to put an end to segregation in the military.

D. Vocabulary

Write your own sentence for each of these words.

transition   stabilize   communism

E. Ask Yourself

Is communism still an important issue in American politics?

The G.I. Bill of Rights

In 1944, while World War II was in full swing, the Congress passed legislation to provide for the future of the millions of men and women in uniform. The idea behind this action was to help those who had served their nation to adjust again to civilian life. Many had given up jobs or interrupted their education and would need aid in picking up the thread of their civilian lives.

The legislation soon was nicknamed the "G.I. Bill of Rights." The initials G.I. stand for "government issue" and were stamped on many pieces of government armed forces property. In time, G.I. came to be a slang name for the soldiers who "belonged" to the army.

The G.I. Bill carried a proposal to aid those who were returning to seek jobs after the war. It guaranteed payment of $20 a week for one year to returning veterans who might have trouble finding work. A key part of the G.I. Bill was its provision for payment of tuition fees, plus living expenses, for veterans attending colleges or, in many cases, completing their high school training. Great numbers of veterans returned to colleges and went on to advanced training with the help of the G.I. Bill.

Veterans of later wars also won benefits under the bill. Those returning from Korea in the 1950s and Vietnam in the 1960s and 1970s have been helped. However, in recent years, many veterans have felt that their benefits, which are overseen by the Veterans Administration (VA), are too small and too bogged down in red tape. The chief of the VA in the late 1970s, Max Cleland, is a disabled Vietnam veteran. He is working to reform the system to meet our modern needs.

Veterans Administration

Lesson 6 Politics of the 1950s

WORDS TO UNDERSTAND

Discuss the meanings of these words.

coalition   violated
flexible   desegregation

NEW WORDS IN SENTENCES

1. The groups had more strength when they joined together in a **coalition.**
2. The price supports were to be **flexible** so that they could change as the economy changed.
3. The laws had to be changed because they **violated** the Constitution.
4. Areas that had been segregated were required by law to begin **desegregation.**

AS YOU READ

As you read this selection, try to answer these questions.

1. What were the domestic policies of the Eisenhower administration?
2. What two crises occurred during the Eisenhower administration?

THE READING SELECTION

Review. Harry S. Truman succeeded to the presidency in 1945. During the next seven years, he tried to solve post-war problems with his Fair Deal. Men and women leaving military service were helped to return to normal lives by the G.I. Bill. A peacetime economy was reestablished. Truman had hoped to establish strong civil rights, housing, farm, and labor programs. He achieved only partial success. The issues of internal security and civil rights were unsolved when he left office.   ☆

During most of the 1950s, the Republican party controlled the White House. In 1952, the Democrats lost the presidency they had held since 1933. President Truman decided not to run for reelection. The party nominated Governor Adlai E. Stevenson of Illinois. The Republicans nominated General Dwight D. ("Ike") Eisenhower. He was the popular former commander of Allied troops in Europe during World War II.

Eisenhower was so popular that he won strong victories in both 1952 and 1956 against Stevenson. He managed to do this even though Republican candidates for Congress were not very successful. For most of Eisenhower's administration, the Democrats controlled Congress. However, the Republicans continued the **coalition** with southern Democrats that they had formed during Truman's term of office. This coalition supported Eisenhower's programs with

On television, Senator McCarthy outlined his idea of
Communist party organization in the U.S. He accused the
Army of "coddling Communists."

enough votes to overcome the opposition.

The Eisenhower program proved to be generally moderate. It sought to limit the expanding powers of the federal government in favor of state or private control. However, it made use of federal powers when necessary. Eisenhower did not return to laissez-faire policies. After World War II, Republicans and Democrats disagreed mainly on the degree of federal involvement.

Federal programs were reduced under Eisenhower. Farm price supports were made **flexible** instead of fixed. This often lowered the amount of federal money spent on farms. The public-housing program was limited to one year. Taxes were reduced, and the budget was smaller. The number of federal officeholders and the amount of money spent on foreign aid were cut back. The administration encouraged private, rather than federal, development of energy resources. In general, the Eisenhower government returned more power to states and private business.

But the 1950s are probably remembered best for two political crises. Both happened in the early years of Eisenhower's administration. These crises concerned internal security and racial segregation.

The issue of internal security had existed for several years. Some Americans feared that Communists were trying to take over the nation. This fear had already led to laws against Communists. It led also to investigations of charges that Communists held government posts.

The leader of the anti-Communists was Republican Senator Joseph McCarthy of Wisconsin. He and his staff accused thousands of people in government and in private life of being Communists. McCarthy made it seem as if the country were in immediate danger of falling to communism. He gained great power because people were afraid to speak out against him. Many people lost their jobs and were ruined because of charges that could never be proved. Finally, in 1954, McCarthyism was stopped when the Senate voted to condemn McCarthy for his actions.

In the same year, a new crisis began. This one was in civil rights for blacks. Segregation in public schools and other facilities had long existed in the South and parts of the North. In 1896, the Supreme Court had ruled that segregation was constitutional. But in 1954, in *Brown* v. *Board of Education of Topeka,* the Court overturned the previous ruling. It held that separate and unequal public facilities **violated** the Fourteenth Amendment. The Court ordered **desegregation** to begin.

The order brought a storm of protest in the South. But blacks, backed up by the federal government, began to enter white public schools. Several serious incidents occurred when local or state officials tried to block desegregation—in

Little Rock, Arkansas, for example. Federal power won out in the long run. Full integration was not accomplished. However, it was the beginning of a strong drive for civil rights that continued into the 1960s.

As 1960 approached, the Republicans were faced with a problem. Eisenhower had served the two terms allowed under the recent Twenty-second Amendment. They could no longer count on his popularity to win the White House for them. Yet they decided to run on the record of his administration. They nominated his vice-president, Richard M. Nixon, for the presidency. Nixon pledged to continue Eisenhower's policies.

Jim Crow segregation laws began after the Civil War. They continued until federal policies in the 1950s and 1960s forced states to change.

United Press International

COMPREHENSION CHECK

A. Recognizing the Main Idea
This selection as a whole tells you

1. how Eisenhower returned to laissez-faire economic policies.

2. why the courts blocked desegregation in the 1950s.

3. about Joseph McCarthy and internal security.

4. about the issues and problems faced by the Eisenhower administration.

B. Selecting Important Details
Choose the ending that best completes each statement.

1. Eisenhower's programs were supported by
   a. a coalition of liberal Democrats and Republicans.
   b. a coalition of Republicans and southern Democrats.
   c. moderates.
   d. only Republicans.

2. All of the following happened in Eisenhower's administration EXCEPT
   a. cutbacks in foreign aid.
   b. a return of power to states and private business.
   c. cutbacks in taxes.
   d. encouragement of federal, rather than private, development of energy resources.

3. Senator Joseph McCarthy
   a. always proved his charges against people.
   b. was a Communist leader.
   c. was condemned by the Senate.
   d. opposed laws against Communists.

4. Desegregation
   a. was illegal.
   b. caused protests in the South.
   c. made separate facilities legal.
   d. violated the Fourteenth Amendment.

C. True or False
Decide whether each of the following statements is true or false.

1. Eisenhower brought a return to laissez-faire economic policies.

2. Eisenhower commanded Allied troops during World War II.

3. The Supreme Court ruled that segregated facilities were constitutional.

4. Nixon pledged to continue Eisenhower's policies.

5. The Republicans and the southern Democrats continued their coalition during Eisenhower's administration.

D. Vocabulary
Match the words with the definitions.

Words	Definitions
1. coalition	a. enemy
2. flexible	b. groups joined together
3. violate	c. changeable
4. desegregation	d. undoing segregation
	e. fixed
	f. break

E. Using Your Knowledge
Make an outline of the reading selection. List four main points of the lesson. Under each main idea, list two or more details found in the selection.

Incident in Little Rock

In 1954, the Supreme Court issued one of its most important decisions. It ruled that previous court actions allowing "separate but equal" schools were not in accord with the current understanding of the Constitution or with the realities of segregation. The Court ruling meant that any form of segregated school was illegal and that blacks must be accepted for admission to all public schools when they applied.

In 1957, several black students applied for admission to a white high school in Little Rock, Arkansas. A state court had forbidden the school board to integrate the school, but a federal judge overruled the lower state court. The governor of Arkansas then called out the state's National Guard and state police. These forces, in effect, acted to keep the black students out of the school. Some rioting broke out in Little Rock, and this led to action by the federal government.

President Eisenhower acted swiftly and forcefully. He converted the Arkansas National Guard to federal service and so took them out of the control of state officials. Next, the president sent 1,000 U.S. Army paratroopers to enforce order in the city. The safe conduct of the black students was then guaranteed, and they continued to attend the school. The armed forces were slowly withdrawn, and the process of integration in the school continued.

President Eisenhower's action was resented by some people in the nation, but it met the approval of those who believe that good public education must be available to all Americans.

A black student tried to attend high school in Little Rock, Arkansas, while white students shouted insults. The entrance was blocked by the Arkansas National Guard until the troops were nationalized.

Wide World

554

Lesson 7   Democratic Programs of the 1960s

WORDS TO UNDERSTAND

Discuss the meanings of these words.

climaxed   emphasized
idealism   overwhelming

NEW WORDS IN SENTENCES

1. The high points of the year were the television debates that **climaxed** the presidential campaign.

2. As people grow older, they sometimes lose their **idealism** and the belief that they can make the world better.

3. The demands were **emphasized** when letters arrived from all over the country.

4. There could be no argument about who had won the election, because it was an **overwhelming** victory.

AS YOU READ

As you read this selection, try to answer these questions.

1. What were the main characteristics of Kennedy's administration?

2. How did Johnson continue Kennedy's domestic programs?

3. How did the war in Vietnam affect the presidential election of 1968?

THE READING SELECTION

The election of 1960 was a hard-fought one. The Republican candidate, Richard M. Nixon, ran on the record of the popular President Eisenhower. The Democrats had chosen Senator John F. Kennedy of Massachusetts, an Irish-Catholic. At first, there was concern that bias against Catholics would hurt Kennedy. But the issue turned out to be a minor one.

The platforms of both parties supported civil rights, medical care for the aged, and a strong foreign policy. Once again, however, they differed on the degree of federal involvement in local affairs. The campaign was **climaxed** by a series of four televised debates. This was the first time that presidential candidates had argued issues face to face. These debates seemed to give Kennedy an edge over Nixon. Kennedy won the election by a small margin of the popular vote, though his electoral vote victory was greater.

At his inauguration, Kennedy said, ". . . the torch has been passed to a new generation of Americans. . . ." For many people, his administration was one of youth and **idealism.** He captured the imagination of Americans.

However, he did not capture Congress. Kennedy had a good deal of trouble getting his "New Frontier" program approved. He did succeed in increasing the minimum wage and in getting aid for economically poor areas.

President Kennedy (middle right) meets with advisors, including the future president Johnson (second from left).

The Peace Corps was established to provide person-to-person help for developing nations. However, medical care and farm programs met defeats. A "freedom march" of 200,000 people in Washington in 1963 **emphasized** demands for further civil rights action. As a result, Kennedy requested sweeping civil rights legislation from the Congress.

In November 1963, President John Kennedy was killed in Dallas, Texas. It was the fourth assassination of an American president. The nation was shocked and saddened. But within two hours of Kennedy's death, Vice-President Lyndon B. Johnson was sworn in as president.

President Johnson pledged to continue Kennedy's programs. He called them the programs of the "Great Society." Johnson had been majority leader of the Senate for many years. His experience there helped him succeed in getting several of Kennedy's programs through Congress.

One example was Medicare. Kennedy's medical care program had been defeated. Under Johnson, a bill providing care for the aged was passed. He also succeeded in establishing a department of urban affairs (the Department of Housing and Urban Development—HUD), which had been rejected under Kennedy.

Johnson went on to establish his own programs. He declared a "war on poverty." Billions of dollars were spent on anti-poverty programs in both urban and rural areas. The Job Corps was set up to provide training for young workers. Programs of financial aid to education were established. They aimed at expanding school services to include more of the poor.

The Civil Rights Act of 1964 was yet another federal attempt to support the increasing demands for racial equality. It went further than any legislation before it to end segregation and discrimination. Among other things, the Civil Rights Act required that federal funds be withdrawn from programs that practiced discrimination. It also set up an agency to aid in the desegregation of schools. The act gave the attorney general more power to protect citizens from discrimination in voting and education.

There were many sit-ins and other demonstrations, mostly in the South, to protest inequality. The Reverend Martin Luther King, Jr., came to be identified with peaceful protest. But in some cases, the response by whites, including the Ku Klux Klan and even the police, was violent. Police dogs were unleashed on many demonstrators, and some civil rights workers were killed. The federal government provided what support it could, but in many cases, it could not interfere with state affairs. By the late 1960s, racial tensions had led to riots in several northern cities. Many were in response to the assassination of King in April 1968. However, the period did produce progress. Blacks, openly backed by federal laws, were gaining more control of their own lives. Their movement was also encouraging other minorities and women to openly demand change.

Despite racial problems, the Johnson domestic program was largely success-

Job and housing discrimination often force blacks to live in run-down sections of cities, such as Watts in Los Angeles. High unemployment and the feeling that nothing could be done against such discrimination helped lead to the 1964 Watts riot. Much of the area was burned and looted in what was only one of many riots in city ghettos.

Wide World

557

Some people have argued that Lyndon Johnson was a good president who had one problem — a bad war. What does this cartoonist think about the effect of the Vietnam War on Johnson's career?

© 1967 Punch/Rothco

ful. Johnson was reelected to his own term as president in 1964 by an **overwhelming** majority. It was assumed he would run and win again in 1968.

But Johnson ran into trouble with his foreign policy. American aid had long been sent to the anti-Communist side in the Vietnamese civil war. Begun under President Eisenhower, this support had been increased by both Kennedy and Johnson. By 1968, over 500,000 American troops were in Vietnam, and 25,000 Americans had died in the war. Opposition to the war grew, and Johnson's popularity dropped. He was challenged for the 1968 Democratic nomination by Senator Eugene McCarthy and, later, by Senator Robert Kennedy, both of whom were opposed to the war. He was also challenged by Alabama conservative George C. Wal-

lace. In March 1968, the president chose not to run again.

The 1968 Democratic convention, held in August in Chicago, was stormy. Senator Robert Kennedy had been assassinated a couple of months before the convention. Senator Eugene McCarthy and Vice-President Hubert H. Humphrey struggled for the nomination. Outside the convention hall, antiwar demonstrators tangled with the police. In the end, Humphrey won the nomination. He hoped to win on the domestic record of President Johnson. This same strategy had been used in 1960 by Vice-President Richard M. Nixon. Oddly enough, the Republican candidate facing Humphrey in 1968 was Richard Nixon. He had been nominated again by the Republican party.

COMPREHENSION CHECK

A. Recognizing the Main Idea

1. In a single sentence, write the main idea of this lesson's reading selection.

2. Write two other points that support this main idea.

B. Selecting Important Details

Choose the ending that best completes each statement.

1. All of the following were part of President Kennedy's New Frontier program EXCEPT
    a. an increased minimum wage.
    b. the Peace Corps.
    c. aid for economically poor areas.
    d. the war on poverty.

2. President Johnson
    a. was assassinated.
    b. had a popular foreign policy.
    c. was never elected president.
    d. succeeded in getting programs passed where Kennedy had failed.

3. Reverend Martin Luther King, Jr.,
    a. was assassinated.
    b. led the Ku Klux Klan.
    c. was an Alabama conservative.
    d. thought violence was the way to gain black equality.

4. The Democratic convention of 1968
    a. was calm.
    b. nominated Hubert H. Humphrey for president.
    c. nominated Richard M. Nixon for president.
    d. nominated Lyndon B. Johnson for president.

C. True or False

Decide whether each of these statements is true or false.

1. Kennedy defeated Nixon by an overwhelming majority in 1960.

2. President Johnson chose not to run for president a second time.

3. The Civil Rights Act of 1964 supported black demands for equality.

4. The movement for black rights was relatively quiet during the 1960s.

5. The Democratic and Republican platforms in 1960 both supported federal involvement in local affairs.

D. Vocabulary

Match the words with the definitions.

Words	Definitions
1. climax	a. make weaker
2. idealism	b. highest point
3. emphasize	c. completely overpower
4. overwhelm	d. run away
	e. make stronger or more obvious
	f. high hopes and beliefs

E. Essay

Write six to eight sentences answering the following questions.

Imagine that you are president of the United States and that you want the country to become a "great society" under your leadership. What would you do to make this society great? What changes would you try to make? Do you think you would be able to accomplish all your goals?

The Twenty-fifth Amendment in Action

The Constitution states that whenever a president dies in office, the vice-president becomes president. But until 1967, whenever a vice-president became president, died, or had to leave office, the country was left without a vice-president. This problem was solved by the Twenty-fifth Amendment to the Constitution, ratified in 1967. The Twenty-fifth Amendment gives the president the power to appoint a vice-president with the approval of Congress.

The Twenty-fifth Amendment was put to use twice within seven years of ratification. Vice-President Spiro T. Agnew resigned his office in 1973. President Nixon, in accordance with the Twenty-fifth Amendment, sent Congress his nominee for the office. This was Congressman Gerald Ford of Michigan. Congress voted to approve Ford. He then became the vice-president of the United States.

One year later, in 1974, President Nixon resigned his office. Vice-President Ford moved up to the position of president. The new president sent the name of his nominee for vice-president to the Congress. Ford's choice was Nelson Rockefeller, former governor of New York. The two houses of Congress approved the nomination, and Rockefeller became vice-president.

In 1975, the Twenty-fifth Amendment seemed to have passed its first tests. Under its provisions, the Congress had approved the appointment of two new vice-presidents, Ford and Rockefeller. Ford had succeeded a vice-president who had resigned the office. Rockefeller succeeded Ford when the vice-president became president. Americans were satisfied with the qualifications of the new president and vice-president. Both were popular, hard-working, and honest.

The amendment seemed to work smoothly, but one thing troubled many Americans. By 1975, the United States had both a president and a vice-president who had not been elected to office. President Ford and Vice-President Rockefeller owed their high offices to a process of selection rather than election. This seemed a bit undemocratic to some Americans. There was a suggestion of a new amendment to provide special elections for replacing a president or vice-president. But would this be efficient? What other solution could there be?

Sidney Harris

"REMEMBER, IN THIS GREAT COUNTRY ANYONE — GIRL OR BOY — CAN GROW UP AND BE APPOINTED PRESIDENT."

560

Lesson 8   Conformity and Controversy

WORDS TO UNDERSTAND
Discuss the meanings of these words.

controversy   conformity

ghettos   lobbied

NEW WORDS IN SENTENCES

1. The **controversy** arose because the two sides could not reach an agreement.

2. Most large American cities have **ghettos**, or parts of the city where members of minority groups live.

3. **Conformity** includes dressing, speaking, and thinking the same way as most people.

4. Some people **lobbied** to try to convince public officials to end the war in Vietnam.

AS YOU READ

As you read this selection, try to answer these questions.

1. What were some probable causes of conformity in the early 1950s?

2. What were some probable causes of controversy during the 1960s?

THE READING SELECTION

Review. President John F. Kennedy captured the imagination of the American people. But he had trouble getting his programs approved by Congress. When Lyndon Johnson took over after Kennedy's assassination, he was more successful. Part of his Great Society program was the passage of Medicare and legislation to fight poverty. These efforts included aid to education, job training, and civil rights laws. The 1960s was a time of racial tension, as blacks demonstrated for their rights. They were often led by Martin Luther King, Jr. Though his domestic program worked, Johnson's foreign policy in Vietnam was unpopular. He chose not to run again, and Vice-President Hubert H. Humphrey ran against Republican Richard M. Nixon in 1968. ☆

During the 1960s, American life seemed torn by **controversy.** Civil rights workers were jailed and attacked in the South. Black leaders talked of "black power" and black revolution. There were fires and riots in the **ghettos.** Thousands of people marched against the Vietnam War. Young men fled to Canada to avoid the army. Federal agencies such as the Federal Bureau of Investigation kept secret files on many Americans.

The events of the decade shocked, angered, and worried many people. The 1950s, they said, had been so quiet.

Why had there been this sudden change?

Most Americans of the 1950s had lived through the depression of the 1930s. At that time, millions of Americans had lost their homes, jobs, savings, and pride. Material goods and financial security became very important. Many of these people would not want to take risks that would put these things in danger again.

Americans of the 1950s had also developed certain ideas about government. The American system was good. Our government was usually right. Governments and people who opposed our system were usually bad. For example, the Nazis were a very clear enemy in World War II. Questioning our government was linked to being an enemy.

As a result, the 1950s saw a great deal of **conformity.** Social and financial security seemed to lie in being and doing what others expected. Many men in business even wore the same kind of clothing—the gray flannel suit. Women and minorities quietly took a back seat.

Conformity during the 1950s was strengthened by the cold war, the Korean War, and McCarthyism. Disputes between the Soviet Union and the United States led to the cold war. It made Americans distrust any criticism of their government or way of life. The Korean War, from 1950 to 1953, helped encourage the spirit of conformity. Criticism of government or industry was called un-American.

Not many people protested investigations by Senator Joseph McCarthy and other anti-Communists. They feared losing their jobs and reputations.

Marches and demonstrations involved hundreds of thousands of people in the 1960s. The 1963 march on Washington was a peaceful call for civil rights (opposite). A 1,000-mile California march brought attention to farm workers (right). But sometimes protest was violent, as at the 1968 Democratic National Convention (above).

This happened to many of those who did stand up to McCarthyism.

By 1960, things were different. The changes began with the minorities. Blacks were no longer willing to conform to what whites expected. The first hint had come in 1954. The NAACP had taken the *Brown* v. *Board of Education of Topeka* case all the way to the Supreme Court. Boycotts and sit-ins swelled into the large nonviolent protest movement led by Martin Luther King, Jr. Northern whites—many of them students—joined the protest.

By 1967, civil rights protest was joined by protest against the Vietnam War. Most members of this movement were white and middle-class. Many were college students. For many of them, this turn against conformity included things besides politics. Long hair, beards, blue jeans, and other casual clothing became popular.

There were several kinds of anti-war protest. The most obvious was the large demonstration. But there was also more traditional political work. Students and others **lobbied** in Congress and campaigned for candidates against the war. Finally, there was individual, illegal action. Draft cards and records were destroyed. "Draft dodgers" fled to Canada—10,000 by 1968.

Such protest had not existed in the early 1960s, but it grew quickly. In 1967, there were 35,000 people in a march in Washington. Two years later, there were 250,000. In 1968, Senator Eugene McCarthy had strong support for his anti-war stand. Later in the year, radical students fought with police outside the Democratic convention to demonstrate their feelings against the war. Year by year, the protest seemed to grow. In 1970, four Kent State University students were killed by the National Guard during a protest.

The deaths were a product of the emotions of the times. There was often violent reaction to both civil rights and anti-war demonstrations. There was fear and hatred on all sides of these questions. There was name-calling, shouting, and worse.

But it all ended. Large-scale protest generally disappeared after about 1970. Why does the decade of the 1960s stand out from those before and after it?

The conformity of the 1950s did not disappear entirely. The majority of Americans never became involved in protests. And those who did protest were under pressure not to do so.

Yet conformity did decrease. There were certainly more Americans willing to take risks to question established policies. Why? The young people of the 1960s had not been strongly influenced by the depression or World War II. Many were even too young to remember the pressure to conform in the 1950s. The risks of not conforming might well have seemed very small to them. Yet, why did protest disappear in the early 1970s?

There are many questions. We are still too close to the 1960s to be able to answer any of them definitely.

COMPREHENSION CHECK

A. Recognizing the Main Idea

1. In a single sentence, write the main idea of this lesson's reading selection.

2. Write two other points that support this main idea.

B. Selecting Important Details

Choose the ending that best completes each statement.

1. During the 1950s, the need for conformity
   a. disappeared.
   b. encouraged criticism of the government.
   c. was fought by Joseph McCarthy.
   d. was linked to the need for social and financial security.

2. Boycotts and sit-ins for the rights of black people
   a. did not include whites.
   b. were part of the nonviolent movement led by Joseph McCarthy.
   c. showed that blacks were willing to conform to what whites expected.
   d. were part of the nonviolent movement led by Martin Luther King, Jr.

3. For many Americans, the 1960s were years of
   a. questioning.
   b. protest.
   c. violence.
   d. all of the above.

4. Anti-war protest
    a. involved the majority of Americans during the 1960s.
    b. took many forms.
    c. was similar to the protest against McCarthyism.
    d. was all done in demonstrations.

C. True or False

Decide whether each of these statements is true or false. Rewrite the false statements so that they are true.

1. Living through the depression of the 1930s generally made people willing to take risks.

2. During the 1950s, questioning the government was thought of as a good way to improve American life.

3. Many anti-war protesters were middle-class college students.

4. Public protest and large-scale demonstrations were common in the 1960s.

5. Most Americans were involved in protests during the 1960s.

D. Vocabulary

Write your own sentence for each of these words.

controversy   conformity
ghetto   lobby

Dr. Martin Luther King, Jr.: A Man with a Dream

In 1955, the twenty-six-year-old Dr. Martin Luther King, Jr., a black minister, won national attention as the leader of the boycott that ended bus segregation in Montgomery, Alabama. During the next ten years, King became one of the most respected leaders of the civil rights movement. He was awarded the Nobel Peace Prize in 1964.

King's message was simple and direct. He sought to enlist black and white Americans in massive, non-violent protests against racism and inequality. His great courage, calmness, and appeal to reason and common sense touched the hearts of many Americans. But he was also attacked by white racists who looked upon him as a "troublemaker" and by more militant black leaders who felt he was too moderate.

Criticism, harsh words, and threats could not stop Dr. King. He continued to fight with words and deeds for racial equality. In 1963, Martin Luther King spoke these words to 200,000 Americans gathered at the foot of the Lincoln Memorial in Washington, D.C.

I have a dream. I have a dream that one day this nation will rise up and live out the true meaning of its creed: "We hold these truths to be self-evident, that all men are created equal."

I have a dream that one day, on the red hills of Georgia, sons of former slaves and sons of former slaveowners will sit down together at the table of brotherhood.

I have a dream that one day my four children will live in a nation where they will not be judged by the color of their skin, but by the content of their character.

In 1968, King gave his support to black garbage workers in Memphis, Tennessee, who were striking for better pay and improved working conditions. There had been rioting in Memphis during the strike, and there was talk of violence. It was reported that King was marked for death. But on April 3, he talked to the striking workers.

. . . death doesn't matter to me now because I've been to the mountaintop. And I've looked over, and I've seen the promised land. So I'm happy. I'm not fearing any man. Mine eyes have seen the glory of the Coming of the Lord.

The next day, King was killed by a rifle shot fired by a hidden assassin. His body was taken home to be buried in Atlanta. A shocked nation watched the funeral services on television and heard the words of one of his sermons.

Wide World

If any of you are around when I meet my day, I don't want a long funeral. . . . I'd like someone to mention that day that Martin Luther King, Jr., tried to give his life serving others . . . that I did try to feed the hungry . . . that I did try in my life to clothe the naked . . . that I did try in my life to visit those who were in prison. And I want you to say that I tried to love and serve humanity.

Lesson 9 Republicans in the 1970s

WORDS TO UNDERSTAND

Discuss the meanings of these words.

deficit   subpoenas
prosecutor   amnesty

NEW WORDS IN SENTENCES

1. The national government has a budget **deficit,** because it spends more money each year than it takes in.
2. The **prosecutor** had the job of carrying out the investigation on behalf of the government.
3. The court sends out **subpoenas** when it wants someone or something to appear in court.
4. The president had the power to give **amnesty,** or pardons, to the people who had avoided service during the war in Vietnam.

AS YOU READ

As you read this selection, try to answer these questions.

1. What were some of the domestic programs of the Nixon administration?
2. Why did Nixon resign from the presidency?
3. What actions did Gerald Ford take when he became president?

THE READING SELECTION

The election of 1968 was close. Both Hubert Humphrey and Richard Nixon pledged to end the American involvement in Vietnam. In November, Nixon received less than 44 percent of the popular vote. But he won 301 electoral votes to Humphrey's 191.

President Nixon wanted to reduce taxes and the expenses of the federal government. He also wanted to slow down the increasing rate of inflation. Nixon had little success, however. By 1973, the total national **deficit** had risen to over $400 billion. In that same year, prices rose at the fastest rate since 1947.

Other domestic policies, however, were more successful. As part of his "New Federalism," Nixon proposed that the federal government share revenues with the states. The Democratic Congress passed this measure. It also passed legislation to establish a lottery system for the military draft. It reformed federal tax laws. In 1969, Congress passed an act that gave the government power to act against those responsible for polluting. In 1970, the Environmental Protection Agency was established.

During Nixon's administration, the Supreme Court acted again to desegregate schools. Its decision to allow busing of children met opposition from the administration and from the public. The Nixon years also saw a peak in the American space program begun under

Kennedy. In 1969, two U.S. astronauts were the first human beings to land on the moon.

But it was foreign policy on which Nixon prided himself. He withdrew American troops from Vietnam, although not until 1973. He also visited the People's Republic of China and tried to improve relations with the Soviet Union.

In 1972, President Nixon defeated the Democratic candidate for president, Senator George McGovern, by a landslide. Shortly before the election, several burglars had been arrested at Democratic headquarters in the Washington, D.C., buildings called Watergate. They were later convicted of intending to steal private papers and leave "bugging" devices. This was to be Nixon's undoing.

Investigations by the *Washington Post* linked the burglars to Nixon's reelection committee and then to top White House aides. The Watergate affair held the nation's attention for two years. A special Senate committee looked into it, as did a special **prosecutor.** Many high officials, including Nixon's former attorney general, John Mitchell, were convicted of breaking the laws.

The president at first claimed he was innocent. He refused to obey **subpoenas** for tape recordings of White House conversations. In October 1973, the House Judiciary Committee began impeachment hearings. Nixon again refused to provide the tapes. He argued that the president had the executive privilege of withholding information from the public if necessary. But in July 1974, the Supreme Court decided that no American was above the law.

On July 30, the House Judiciary Committee recommended impeachment for three reasons. First, Nixon had tried to cover up the illegal Watergate activities. Second, he had misused his office and other federal agencies, violating citizens' rights. Third, he had violated the Constitution by disobeying the subpoenas. Committee member Elizabeth Holtzman argued, "We found presidential conduct that was sorry and disgraceful . . . [a] web of misconduct."

On August 5, Nixon admitted he had not told the whole truth. The information on the tapes was finally released. It cost him his last bit of support. On August 9, 1974, Richard Nixon resigned.

Vice-President Gerald Ford was sworn in the same day. He had been appointed by the president in 1973 when Vice-President Spiro Agnew resigned under charges of bribery. Ford, a conservative Republican, had been a member of the House of Representatives for many years. He hoped to calm the nation after the Nixon scandal. However, his pardon of the former president raised criticism again. In another effort to heal old wounds, President Ford established a limited **amnesty** program for those who had avoided service in the Vietnam war.

President Ford's main concern was the economy. Inflation was a major problem. Also in 1974, a period of recession began, and unemployment increased greatly. Ford introduced legislation to lower taxes and to provide public service jobs for the unemployed. Both these measures were approved by Congress.

In 1975, the economy began to recover. However, it remained an issue in

Nixon tried to satisfy the Watergate investigation by releasing "edited" parts of the tapes (behind him, above). But it did not work. After he resigned, Gerald and Betty Ford (right) took over the White House

the 1976 presidential election. Jimmy Carter of Georgia was the Democratic candidate. The Republicans nominated President Ford. This campaign, like the one in 1960, featured televised debates between the candidates. The public was apparently ready for a whole new administration. Carter won a narrow victory over Ford in November. After eight years, the Democrats had regained the White House. In addition, the Democrats expanded their control of both houses of Congress.

COMPREHENSION CHECK

A. Recognizing the Main Idea

This selection as a whole tells you

1. about the Democrats during the 1970s.

2. why Nixon's domestic programs were successful.

3. what happened at Watergate.

4. about the policies and problems of the Republicans during the 1970s.

B. Selecting Important Details

Choose the ending that best completes each statement.

1. President Nixon tried to do all of the following EXCEPT
   a. reform tax laws.
   b. slow down inflation.
   c. improve relations with the People's Republic of China and the Soviet Union.
   d. establish an amnesty program.

2. Nixon's administration
   a. established the Environmental Protection Agency.
   b. established a lottery for the military draft.
   c. started the sharing of federal revenues with states.
   d. all of the above.

3. Impeachment of Nixon was recommended by the House Judiciary Committee for all of the following reasons EXCEPT
   a. trying to cover up illegal activities.
   b. misusing his office to violate citizens' rights.
   c. making tapes of White House conversations.
   d. disobeying court subpoenas.

4. President Ford
   a. refused to pardon Nixon.
   b. resigned under charges of bribery.
   c. established an amnesty program.
   d. defeated Jimmy Carter in the election of 1976.

C. Fact or Opinion

Decide whether each of these statements is fact or opinion.

1. Hubert Humphrey would have ended the war in Vietnam sooner than Nixon did.

2. Nixon's economic policies did not reduce inflation.

3. The burglars caught at the Democratic headquarters at Watergate were linked to top White House aides.

4. Ford was correct to give Nixon a pardon.

5. The Supreme Court ruled that the president is not above the law.

D. Vocabulary

Write your own sentence for each of these words.

deficit
prosecutor
subpoena
amnesty

E. Chart Work

Make a chart of the presidents of the United States starting with Herbert Hoover. In columns next to their names, write down their political party, the years they were president, and two or three important events or policies of each administration.

Media Responsibility and Freedom of the Press

Freedom of speech and the press are rights guaranteed by the First Amendment to the Constitution. Newspapers, magazines, radio, television—all the sources of information known as the "media"—have this guarantee. But along with freedom goes responsibility.

Newspapers, radio, and television have the responsibility of informing people in an accurate and unbiased manner. They also have great power, because they reach millions of people. Public opinion and the course of events are often influenced by the media.

There have been many cases of the media having to balance rights and responsibilities. One of the most challenging cases arose in 1972 in the Watergate affair. At the center of the story was the newspaper, the *Washington Post.* Two young reporters for the newspaper looked into the attempt to burglarize the national Democratic party headquarters at Watergate. Their investigation kept uncovering facts that seemed to involve White House officials in the burglary.

The management of the *Washington Post* was uneasy with the investigation. President Nixon and the entire government would be put under a cloud of suspicion if the Watergate story were printed as it was uncovered. All the facts could not be known in advance. And there was a chance that much might never be known for

The Washington Post

certain. Should the newspaper continue its efforts to uncover information? Suppose it turned out that the suspicions were not justified? The government and the president would remain smeared with the suggestion of guilt. And the newspaper would be responsible for undermining faith in the government.

Katherine Graham, the publisher and head of the company that owned the newspaper, had to make the final decision. The reporters and newsroom editors of the *Washington Post* did not want to be timid about reporting the truth, even though it involved the newspaper, and perhaps the nation, in serious risks. Katherine Graham made the decision to continue the story.

The result of Graham's decision was the uncovering of much of the wrongdoing in the Watergate affair. This set off a national crisis and led to the resignation of President Nixon. But the nation was able to absorb this crisis in government. The newspaper had used its constitutional right to report the news in a responsible way.

Lesson 10   Living in America: Society Since World War II

WORDS TO UNDERSTAND

Discuss the meanings of these words.

suburbia   bicentennial
atomic

NEW WORDS IN SENTENCES

1. Life in **suburbia** is different from life in the city.

2. An **atomic** war could be more destructive than any war in history.

3. Two hundred years after it was founded, the United States celebrated its **bicentennial.**

AS YOU READ

As you read this selection, try to answer these questions.

1. How did people fill their leisure time in the 1950s?

2. Why was the 1960s a period of soul-searching for Americans?

3. What changes in the U.S. seemed to be beginning in the 1980s?

Artist Robert Rauschenberg completed this piece of art in 1964. Do you think he was making a statement about the United States specifically during the 1960s, or a general statement about the nation? What idea or ideas do you think he is trying to communicate?

THE READING SELECTION

The United States has changed in many ways since World War II. Each decade, or ten-year period, brought new changes.

The 1950s. After World War II, there was a sudden increase in the number of births. Along with the "baby boom" came the growth of **suburbia.** Between 1947 and 1954, nearly 9 million people moved to the suburbs. Movement to the suburbs continues to this day.

By 1950, most people had to work only forty hours a week. In 1950, the American people spent five times more money on ways to fill their leisure time than on medical care.

The introduction of long-playing records and hi-fi equipment boosted the recording industry. During the mid-1950s, Elvis Presley became the superstar of rock 'n' roll music. This new music form replaced the jazz and swing music forms favored in the 1940s.

Americans also found time to read more than ever. Paperback books became very popular, but hardback books continued to sell very well. Listening to the radio remained a popular leisure-time activity. In 1959, nearly 50 million American homes had at least one radio. In addition, there were radios in millions of American automobiles. Although radio was popular, it was losing ground to television. By 1959, there were TV sets in 44 million homes.

During the 1950s, the United States and the Soviet Union became involved in what was called "the race for space." It began in October 1957, when the Soviet Union launched the first space satellite, Sputnik I.

The 1960s. During the 1960s, the United States took the lead in space exploration. In July 1969, the spaceship Apollo 11 took two astronauts to the moon. Millions of people watched on television as the astronauts planted the American flag on the moon. It was a day of triumph for the United States.

The sixties were also years of troubled soul-searching for Americans. Demonstrations across the country protested both U.S. involvement in the Vietnam conflict and social injustices at home. Many black Americans voiced their protests and demanded an end to racism and inequality. Women's groups gained a wide following in their efforts to gain full economic and legal rights for all women. Spanish-speaking Americans, Indians, and other minority groups sought an end to discrimination.

Many young people questioned the beliefs and values of the older generation. The youth movement used music to express its values and protest social wrongs. Rock music festivals attracted tens of thousands of young people.

The 1970s. With the end of the Vietnam conflict, anti-war feeling gave way to a spirit of reform. Anti-pollution groups sought to protect the environment and endangered wildlife. Concern for the environment also led some groups to oppose the use of nuclear power as a source of energy or as a weapons system.

The 1970s also saw a demand for reform in government. Americans were shocked by the Watergate scandal and the resignation of President Nixon. The Watergate events helped bring about a demand for honesty and openness in politics.

The 1970s were also years of revolution in electronics. Commercial television expanded into the areas of videotape recorders, video discs, and cable television. The development of the silicon

Some people thought them just scruffy, but they were followed by screaming crowds. The Beatles and their influence were a mark of the 1960s.

United Press International

574

chip gave even small computers, or microcomputers, a great capacity for storing information. Microcomputers became widely used in small businesses, homes, and classrooms.

The 1980s. The start of the 1980s promised great change. The liberal political views of the previous forty years began to give way to a more conservative outlook. The landslide election of Ronald Reagan as president in 1980 was one sign of this new conservative feeling. President Reagan began leading the nation away from New Deal liberalism toward a conservatism he described as the "New Federalism."

COMPREHENSION CHECK

A. Recognizing the Main Idea
This selection as a whole tells you
1. about President Reagan's conservative program.
2. about changes and developments in American life since World War II.
3. why the 1960s were years of protest.
4. about American astronauts since World War II.

B. Selecting Important Details
Choose the ending that best completes each statement.
1. During the 1950s, many Americans used their leisure time to
  a. protest the war in Vietnam.
  b. sing protest songs.
  c. study the Watergate scandal.
  d. watch television.

2. The 1960s saw
  a. the start of the space race.
  b. a baby boom.
  c. the Watergate scandal and the resignation of a president.
  d. none of the above.
3. The 1970s saw
  a. the revolution in electronics and computers.
  b. efforts to save endangered wildlife.
  c. the closing out of the Vietnam conflict.
  d. all of the above.
4. During the 1980s, the United States seemed to
  a. become more conservative.
  b. remain as liberal as ever.
  c. change little in its political views.
  d. be in a period of troubled soul-searching about equal rights for all.

C. Completion
Fill in the word or words that best complete each sentence.
1. During the years from 1947 to 1954, nearly 9 million Americans moved to _____.
2. In the 1950s, _____ listening lost ground to _____ viewing as a leisure-time activity.
3. Apollo 11 took the first people to the _____.
4. The youth movement used _____ to express values and protest wrongs.
5. The silicon chip gives the small _____ a greater capacity for storing information.

D. Homework

Use the library to find out more about a topic in this lesson. Choose either the 1950s or the 1960s. Find additional information about music, *or* television and movies, *or* politics in that period. Organize the information into a brief outline.

E. Chronology

Arrange these events in the order in which they happened.
1. Watergate scandal
2. baby boom
3. election of Ronald Reagan as president
4. World War II
5. space flight to moon

F. Using Your Knowledge

What might have been the story behind each of the following headlines? Write at least twenty words about each headline.

1. SOVIETS LAUNCH SPUTNIK I
2. BLACKS, WOMEN, INDIANS DEMAND FULL RIGHTS
3. WATERGATE SCANDAL SHOCKS NATION
4. REAGAN LEADS CONSERVATIVE VICTORY

Today's Women's Movement

On August 26, 1977, more than 3,000 women gathered to march to the White House. Many of them were dressed in white. The parade and the white clothing were in honor of the fifty-seventh anniversary of the Nineteenth Amendment. They were also in honor of an earlier march—one held in 1913.

In 1913, the women were hissed and booed on their route to the White House. Groups of men along the way broke up the parade before it ever reached its goal. Sixty-four years later, it was a different story. The 1977 marchers were cheered along the way. Their leaders were met at the White House by President Jimmy Carter, who again pledged his support for the Equal Rights Amendment. At his side was Hazel H. Hallinan, a veteran of the 1913 march.

Many things have changed in the women's movement since 1913. The main concern in the early days was winning the vote. Now, women are using their votes, the courts, unions, government, and economic pressure to reach wider goals.

One basic concern is greater economic opportunity. Equal pay for equal work is still a primary goal. In addition, members of the women's movement reject the idea that certain fields "belong" to men. Women now serve in the police and armed forces. They work in construction, drive buses, and mine coal. They are overcoming opposition to becoming executives, doctors, and lawyers.

The women's movement has drawn many women together with some common goals. But some people feel that the women's movement is destructive to valuable traditions in American life. Ideas about men's roles, family responsibilities, and women's place in society are being questioned and changed.

Ken Regan, Camera 5

To gain equality, women need college and university education. They also need opportunities as apprentices in labor union programs. The women's movement supports affirmative action programs to increase the number of women and minorities in education and labor.

The women's movement is also concerned with sexism in many areas. Sexism refers to discrimination on the basis of sex. The women's movement holds fast to the belief that sexism is unfair to both women and men.

In 1981, the women's movement celebrated a major breakthrough when President Reagan named Judge Sandra Day O'Connor to be a justice of the Supreme Court. Liberal and conservative women voiced their approval of Judge O'Connor, a conservative. In October 1981, Justice O'Connor became the first woman justice of the Supreme Court.

Although President Reagan named a woman to the Supreme Court, he remained opposed to the Equal Rights Amendment. By the end of 1981, the amendment had been approved by thirty-five states. But it appeared that it would not receive the required approval of thirty-eight states by June 30, 1982. That was the final date by which the Equal Rights Amendment had to gain approval. But leaders of the women's movement pledged to continue their efforts for an equal rights amendment.

Lesson 11   Current Issues: Housing, Health Care, Education, and Equality

WORDS TO UNDERSTAND

Discuss the meanings of these words.

urban renewal   **parochial**
socialized medicine

NEW WORDS IN SENTENCES

1. **Urban renewal** seeks to build new buildings to replace old, unsafe ones.

2. A **parochial** school is a school that is run by a religious group.

AS YOU READ

As you read this selection, try to answer these questions.

1. How has the government tried to solve housing problems?

2. How has the government tried to solve national health-care and education problems?

3. How is the government trying to eliminate discrimination?

4. How has the election of President Reagan affected government social programs?

THE READING SELECTION

Since 1933, the government has tried to help provide good housing, health care, and education for all Americans. It has also made efforts to promote equal treatment for blacks, women, and other minority groups.

These social efforts have had the general support of every administration, Democratic or Republican, for nearly fifty years. But by the late 1970s, there was a general feeling that many programs were too costly and ought to be cut back. That feeling, and a voter "revolt" against high taxes, helped lead to a Republican victory in 1980. Ronald Reagan was elected president and took office in 1981. His election and the aid given him by Republicans and conservative Democrats have led to changes in government social programs.

Housing. A serious housing shortage has existed for many years. Rising housing costs and the high interest rates on mortgage loans have made home ownership difficult for most middle-class Americans. At the same time, rents have risen steadily and caused hardships for people who live in rented housing.

The federal government has programs to ease the housing problem. One of these programs provides banks the government's guarantee on loans made to people buying homes. Federal money has also supported public housing programs for low-income tenants.

What problems and benefits are there in city life? In suburban life? How can government help create good living environments?

Some public housing programs have involved tearing down slum buildings to make room for new dwellings. These programs are among those called **urban renewal.** Urban renewal programs have been criticized for destroying long-established neighborhoods. They are also very costly. President Reagan's effort to reduce spending will probably limit future public housing programs.

Many middle- and high-income families have moved away from the inner cities to outlying areas. The people remaining in the inner city are often poor. The cities are weakened as tax income falls off. As a result, the quality of education and city services often goes down. Roads and bridges are not kept in repair. Garbage collection becomes spotty, and the city often takes on a tired and dirty look.

Federal programs to aid cities have had some success. They have also been criticized as being costly. Some have been riddled with graft and politics. The budget-cutting policies of the Reagan administration have reduced federal aid to cities since 1982.

Health care. One federal program to help people pay medical bills is called Medicare. In this program, the federal government pays a large share of medical costs for persons over the age of sixty-five. Another program is called Medicaid. It extends government aid for health care to people who cannot afford it, regardless of age. These programs have helped the elderly and the poor. But they are very costly and grow more expensive each year. In 1979, the government paid nearly 17 billion dollars for Medicaid and well over 25 billion dollars for Medicare. One of the challenges of the budget-cutting effort is to reduce spending without hurting the sick and needy.

The high costs of health care have led to greater interest in preventing illness. Recent research has shown that there are many harmful agents in the products we use. Some people feel that the government should ban harmful products to reduce the risk of disease. Others believe that requiring warning labels on dangerous products is all the government should do.

Education. The power to control education resides with the states. Local school boards are responsible for raising money to run the schools. Because of rising costs, today's school districts are able to cover only about half of the cost of education. State governments help out with most of the remaining costs. Federal funds support programs designed to help pupils with special needs, such as those with handicaps or learning problems.

Many people want more federal aid for schools. Others fear that increased federal aid would be a threat to local control of public schools. The general effort to reduce federal spending has led to demands for less federal aid to the schools.

There are many private schools in the United States. Most of these are **parochial** schools, run by religious groups. Rising costs present a serious problem to these private schools. The parents of children attending private schools pay tuition as well as the taxes that support public schools. They argue that they deserve some form of tax credit or federal

Parents in San Francisco protested against busing students for integration (top). The march in Boston was for it. What arguments can you think of for and against busing?

aid. But the Supreme Court has ruled that direct aid to parochial or private schools is unconstitutional. At present, federal aid to private schools is for limited purposes, such as for textbooks.

The federal government has the power to require schools to provide equal opportunities for all students. In 1954, the Supreme Court ruled all segregation in public schools illegal. The courts have ordered some cities to bus students from one school to another to achieve racial balance.

Opponents of forced busing argue that the government has no right to require busing. They also argue that its cost places an additional burden on taxpayers. People supporting busing feel it is necessary to end school segregation. Americans are divided over the issue. But opponents of busing won strength with the election of President Reagan.

Equality. Recent federal laws have made most forms of discrimination illegal. Laws now prohibit unfair housing practices that for many years kept minorities from living in certain areas. Federal laws also guarantee the right of all people to an equal education. The federal government is even trying to reduce financial inequality by helping the poor, aged, and disabled.

There are limits to what the government can do. A fair housing law will not give people the money to buy or rent a home. Affirmative action programs cannot instantly provide many people with the needed experience they may lack because of years of discrimination. Laws and programs, however well-intentioned, cannot solve many social problems. Conservative Americans believe that govern-

COMPARISONS of
WHITE and NON-WHITE POPULATIONS 1975

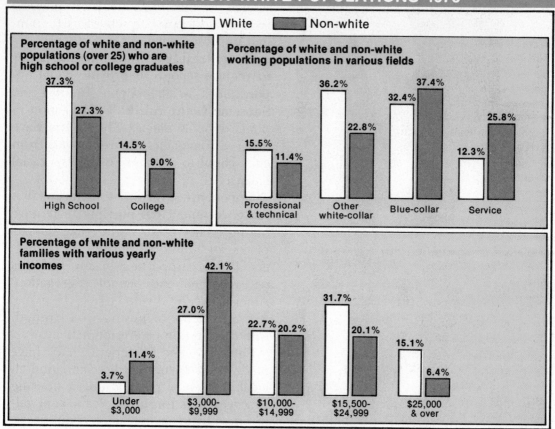

☐ White   ■ Non-white

Percentage of white and non-white populations (over 25) who are high school or college graduates

High School: 37.3% (White), 27.3% (Non-white)
College: 14.5% (White), 9.0% (Non-white)

Percentage of white and non-white working populations in various fields

Professional & technical: 15.5% (White), 11.4% (Non-white)
Other white-collar: 36.2% (White), 22.8% (Non-white)
Blue-collar: 32.4% (White), 37.4% (Non-white)
Service: 12.3% (White), 25.8% (Non-white)

Percentage of white and non-white families with various yearly incomes

Under $3,000: 3.7% (White), 11.4% (Non-white)
$3,000–$9,999: 27.0% (White), 42.1% (Non-white)
$10,000–$14,999: 22.7% (White), 20.2% (Non-white)
$15,500–$24,999: 31.7% (White), 20.1% (Non-white)
$25,000 & over: 15.1% (White), 6.4% (Non-white)

Notice the differences in education between whites and non-whites, shown above. Then study the information on the income and jobs of each group. How could education affect income and jobs? How could we end the gaps between the two groups?

ment actions achieve little and cost too much. They strongly support the efforts of President Reagan to limit the activities of government in American life. The conservative view is opposed by liberals, who see the need for continued government action to help solve social problems.

COMPREHENSION CHECK

A. Recognizing the Main Idea

1. In a single sentence, write the main idea of this lesson's reading selection.

2. Write four other points that are made in this lesson's reading selection.

B. Selecting Important Details

Choose the ending that best completes each statement.

1. The government tries to solve housing problems by doing all of the following EXCEPT
   a. guaranteeing home loans for low-income buyers.
   b. building apartments for low-income tenants.
   c. encouraging the flight to the suburbs.
   d. funding urban renewal projects.

2. Government health care costs for the elderly and poor
   a. have been ended in recent years.
   b. have declined in recent years.
   c. have remained steady in recent years.
   d. have risen steadily over the years.

3. Federal aid to public schools
   a. is unconstitutional.
   b. helps meet rising costs.
   c. gives more control to local school boards.
   d. covers more than half of the school costs.

4. Busing students
   a. is intended to maintain segregated schools.
   b. is supported by everyone.
   c. has often been ordered by the courts.
   d. is intended to encourage racial discrimination.

C. True or False

Decide whether each of these statements is true or false. Rewrite the false statements so that they are true.

1. Federal laws can do nothing to prevent discrimination in housing.

2. Conservative Americans favor increased spending in government programs designed to help solve problems.

3. One problem with urban renewal is that it sometimes drives people out of their communities.

4. Discrimination is quickly eliminated when laws are passed making it illegal.

5. President Reagan is opposed to forced busing.

D. Vocabulary

Use each of these vocabulary words in a sentence that differs from the sentence in which it appears in the selection.
urban renewal   parochial

E. Ask Yourself

The Reagan administration is pledged to reduce spending in order to cut taxes. President Reagan believes that lower taxes will help stimulate the economy. A stronger economy, in turn, will provide more jobs and will let people afford to care for themselves. But lowering taxes means reducing federal aid for housing, education, and health care. Which do you think is more important, lower taxes or continued aid to the social programs listed above? State your reasons in an essay of at least forty words.

From President Carter to President Reagan

In January 1977, Jimmy Carter, former governor of Georgia, was inaugurated as president. He had narrowly beaten President Gerald Ford, the Republican candidate.

Critics soon accused President Carter of being "all form and no substance." In fact, the president did seem to have problems handling many of the complex issues of his high office. Some of President Carter's proposals and appointments ran into trouble with Congress. His budget director faced a difficult Senate investigation of earlier financial actions and eventually resigned.

President Carter's greatest achievement may have been arranging the Camp David meeting of President Sadat of Egypt and Prime Minister Begin of Israel. Aided by President Carter, these two former enemies agreed to the terms of a peace treaty.

President Carter's success at the Camp David meeting was short-lived. His administration was troubled by economic problems that included high inflation rates and a sluggish economy. They combined to create a condition that became known as "stagflation."

The president's problems worsened as a result of the Iranian crisis (see p. 674). Many Americans saw themselves as helpless in times of crisis, and they blamed President Carter.

The 1980 presidential election saw President Carter, the Democratic candidate, opposed by the Republican candidate, Ronald Reagan. Mr. Reagan

Candidates Carter and Reagan held a televised debate before the 1980 presidential election.

advanced a program that was markedly conservative in its views of government economics and foreign affairs. Mr. Reagan was swept into office by a landslide vote. The Republicans also gained control of the Senate.

The "Reagan revolution" of 1981 involved these changes.

1. Passage of tax laws cutting taxes by 25 percent over a three-year period. The president declared his intention of cutting 750 billion dollars in taxes in a five-year period. Such tax cuts were designed to stimulate savings and business investment.

2. Sharp cuts in the budget that would add up to 130 billion dollars in five years. These cuts meant the reduction of many social programs.

3. Increased spending for national defense.

Economists differed on the possible results of the Reagan program. But they agreed that it would bring many changes.

Lesson 12　Current Issues: Conservation and Energy

WORDS TO UNDERSTAND

Discuss the meanings of these words.

renewable　　　　　　　**recycling**
endangered species　　**solar**

NEW WORDS IN SENTENCES

1. **Renewable** resources can replace themselves naturally.

2. **Endangered species** are types of animals that are close to becoming extinct.

3. **Recycling** materials means reusing them in the same or different forms.

4. **Solar** energy is the energy that can be obtained from the sun.

AS YOU READ

As you read this selection, try to answer these questions.

1. Why must Americans try to conserve resources?

2. How has the government tried to regulate the use of resources?

THE READING SELECTION

Both state and federal governments are responsible for preserving and protecting our nation's natural resources. Some of our natural resources, such as air, soil, trees, and water, are **renewable.** With care, they can be reused or replaced many times. Other resources, including oil, coal, copper, and iron, are non-renewable. Once used, they are gone forever.

Conservation of forests. Protecting forests from fire, diseases, pests, and careless cutting is very important. Forests provide timber to make many products. In addition, forests also provide a home for wildlife.

The federal and state governments work to protect our forests. State governments even regulate the cutting of private timberland. Careful methods of harvesting and replanting help keep a good supply of timber available.

Soil conservation. The United States loses millions of acres of fertile topsoil each year. This loss is caused by wind and water, poor farming methods, and unwise use of dry lands. Many crops wear out the soil.

Farm organizations, scientists, and the government work together to conserve the soil. Farmers are usually willing to use new chemicals and farming methods in conservation. However, they are not as willing to plant less or to allow some lands to rest. To encourage

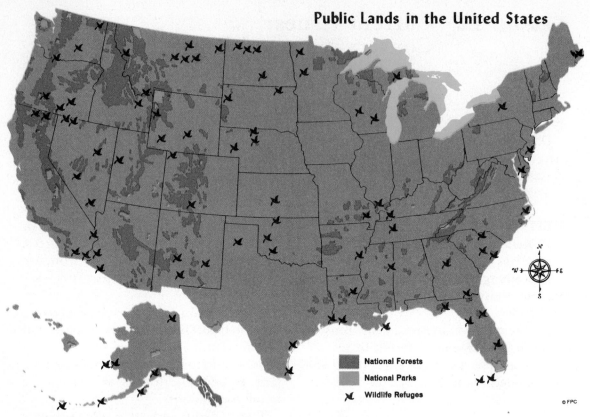

Public Lands in the United States

National Forests
National Parks
Wildlife Refuges

© FPC

Many national parks depend on support from visitors. But too many people could spoil the wilderness and frighten the wildlife. Most parks solve that problem by allowing visitors to travel only in limited areas.

them, state soil conservation districts distribute local and federal aid to farmers who participate in soil conservation programs. All levels of government cooperate in this effort.

Wildlife conservation. Yet sometimes, disputes break out between state and federal governments over the responsibility for conservation. For example, in 1976, Alaska announced a plan to shoot most of the wolves on certain federal lands in the state. The wolves were said to be attacking caribou, popular game for hunters. The caribou population was uncomfortably low. However, many kinds of wolves are extinct, and others are **endangered species.** The federal government opposed the state of Alaska's plan. After legal battles, a court ruled in 1977 that the federal government, not the state, had control over wildlife on federal land. The case is one example of recent efforts to protect wildlife. These efforts are important. By the mid-1970s, more than 60 kinds of American animals had already become extinct, and 130 more were considered endangered.

Conservation of air and water. The government is also involved in conservation of our air and water. Federal and state laws now limit the amount of pollutants that can be dumped into waters. The federal Environmental Protection Agency (EPA) has won the right to regulate industrial pollution. State governments, along with the federal government, have budgeted huge sums of money for cleaning up water.

Air pollution is another problem. Industries and automobiles pour millions of tons of chemical gases into the air. Many states and communities have air control laws. Some of these laws require industries to install devices to reduce air pollution. But air and water pollution affect large areas. Pollution in Indiana soon becomes a problem for Illinois. For this reason, the federal government has had to set certain national standards for clean air and water.

Mineral conservation. Americans are only slowly starting to conserve their non-renewable mineral resources. Products made of copper, iron, steel, and lead continue to use up limited resources. Reusing, or **recycling,** these products could help conserve mineral resources.

Energy. The United States, like the rest of the world, faces a serious energy crisis. American oil production is very high but does not meet the needs of the nation. By the late 1970s, the United States was importing 40 percent of the oil it used.

The federal government is trying to encourage people to use less gasoline and fuel oil. It has suggested that other fuels, especially coal, could be used.

However, this could require that air pollution laws be weakened. There is often a conflict between energy and conservation. For example, the Alaskan pipeline brings us 600,000 barrels of oil each day. But it seems to harm wildlife.

New energy. Researchers are seeking to develop new sources of energy. **Solar** energy offers some hope for the future. However, it needs to be developed. Some people feel that the government should support this development. Nuclear energy is another source of power. Several hundred nuclear plants are already producing electrical energy. However, some scientists believe that the dangerous nuclear waste products cannot be safely disposed of. They also fear that nuclear power plants harm the environment. The government must weigh the benefits and the dangers and decide how much it should regulate nuclear plants.

Many Americans are worried that government involvement in energy and conservation may hurt private business in these areas. Others feel that such involvement is necessary to protect our resources. Americans are not yet agreed on the government's role in these areas and in many others.

L.L.T. Rhodes, Van Cleve, Inc.

Which is more important, conservation or energy? Sometimes the two are in conflict. For example, the nation depends on oil. But oil can harm the environment. It can spill from tankers or offshore wells. Then it kills animals that become covered with it (below left). And the Alaskan pipeline (below) was opposed by conservationists who felt it would harm both soil and wildlife. Perhaps the solution lies in new forms of energy. Devices to collect and store solar energy for use (left) may provide safe energy for the future.

United Press International

Steve McCutcheon

588

COMPREHENSION CHECK

A. Recognizing the Main Idea

1. In a single sentence, write the main idea of this lesson's reading selection.

2. Write two other points that are made in this lesson's reading selection.

B. Selecting Important Details

Choose the ending that best completes each statement.

1. Forests are destroyed by all of the following EXCEPT
   a. fires.
   b. pests.
   c. livestock.
   d. careless harvesting.

2. Fertile topsoil is ruined by all of the following EXCEPT
   a. poor farming methods.
   b. wind and water.
   c. crops that use up the soil.
   d. soil banks.

3. The federal government has tried to stop air pollution by
   a. causing an energy crisis.
   b. making sure that cars give out pollutants.
   c. setting national standards for clean air.
   d. encouraging industry to put chemical gases into the air.

4. Mineral resources
   a. can be conserved by recycling.
   b. are renewable.
   c. meet all the energy needs of the country.
   d. are unlimited.

C. True or False

Decide whether each of these statements is true or false. Rewrite the false statements so that they are true.

1. Farmlands must be planted every year to keep the soil fertile.

2. Soil conservation districts give aid to farmers who take part in programs to conserve soil.

3. Nuclear power plants may present a risk to the environment.

4. There is nothing that can reduce air pollution from factories.

5. Nearly 200 kinds of American animals are extinct or endangered.

D. Vocabulary

Use a term from this list to complete each sentence.

renewable   recycle
endangered species   solar

1. Americans must learn to _____ many products.

2. Animals close to extinction are members of _____.

3. Some resources are not _____.

4. _____ energy taps the sun's power.

E. Ask Yourself

If Americans do not conserve resources and limit pollution now, how might our lives be affected in the future?

F. Map Skills

Use the map in this lesson to answer these questions.

1. Which part of the country has the most national parks and forests?

2. If the government had not set aside forests, parks, and refuges, what might have happened to wildlife?

Rachel Carson: Pioneer in Ecology

The importance of the conservation of forests, soil, and mineral resources began to be appreciated around 1900. However, it took many years to enact conservation laws, and some of these laws still are very weak. The understanding of ecology and its importance has been a more recent accomplishment. Ecology is a branch of the science of biology. It deals with the relationships living things have to one another and to their environment.

Much of the credit for making the American people understand ecology belongs to Rachel Carson. Carson was a marine biologist and science writer. She worked for most of her life as a scientist for the United States Fish and Wildlife Service. This government agency works to protect the nation's wildlife. Two books written by Rachel Carson helped make ecology a part of the vocabulary of the people.

Rachel Carson wrote *The Sea Around Us* in 1951. In this book, she dealt with the biology, chemistry, and history of the world's oceans and seas. Her clear form of writing helped many people better understand the interrelationships among living things. For the first time, many people understood that the living things of the oceans are part of a food chain that supports the human race.

Rachel Carson's second book, *Silent Spring,* was written in 1962. It proved more startling than her study of the seas. In *Silent Spring,* she dealt with the growing dangers of pesticides.

A pesticide is a poison used to kill insects that are harmful to plant life. The use of pesticides had grown sharply during the 1940s and 1950s. They seemed highly effective in killing insects that were harmful to various crops. Rachel Carson pointed out in her book that many chemicals used as pesticides also kill animals, birds, and fish by poisoning their food supply. In addition, pesticides get into the human food supply, where they are harmful to people.

Rachel Carson died in 1964 at the age of fifty-seven. She had the satisfaction of knowing that her books had alerted the world to the science of ecology. Today, there are dozens of national groups that are concerned with the problems of ecology. Many laws have been passed limiting air and water pollution.

Unit 11 Summary   Modern Political Challenges: 1929 – 1970s

The Depression

The worst depression in American history began in 1929. It was brought on by several problems. Among them were speculation in stocks, lack of credit, and poor banking practices. There was also a drop in the market for industrial products.

In 1932, President Franklin Roosevelt began his New Deal. He acted quickly to provide jobs and relief for the unemployed. He also regulated banks, the stock market, farm prices, and industry. The New Deal supported unions and workers and established the Social Security System.

The New Deal was expensive, and it increased the bureaucracy. The federal government became bigger and more powerful. However, it helped rebuild the American economy and eased the lives of the unemployed as well as working people.

The Postwar Period

Harry S. Truman became president in 1945. His Fair Deal tried to solve postwar problems. The economy was changed back into a peacetime one. Returning veterans were helped by the G.I. Bill. But opposition limited Truman's success in domestic reform.

Republican President Dwight D. Eisenhower tried to limit the expanding federal powers. He gave more power back to states and private ownership. Federal expenses were cut.

In the 1950s, opposition to communism grew in the United States. Senator Joseph McCarthy led investigations of government officials, professors, and writers. The panic did not end until 1954. Then a new crisis began over civil rights. The Supreme Court had ordered desegregation in *Brown* v. *Board of Education of Topeka*. Federal power was used to enforce the decision.

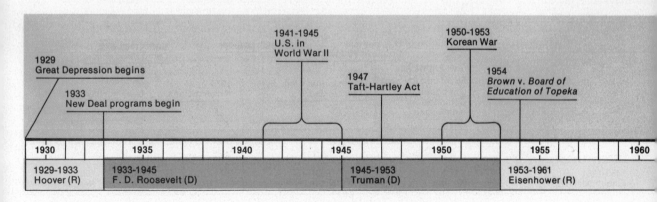

1929
Great Depression begins

1933
New Deal programs begin

1941-1945
U.S. in
World War II

1947
Taft-Hartley Act

1950-1953
Korean War

1954
Brown v. *Board of Education of Topeka*

| 1930 | 1935 | 1940 | 1945 | 1950 | 1955 | 1960 |

1929-1933
Hoover (R)

1933-1945
F. D. Roosevelt (D)

1945-1953
Truman (D)

1953-1961
Eisenhower (R)

Since 1960

Democratic presidents were in office from 1961 to 1969. President John F. Kennedy, elected in 1960, sought to extend the New Deal through his New Frontier program. His assassination in 1963 brought Vice-President Lyndon B. Johnson to the presidency. Johnson was elected to a full term in 1964. His Great Society program included Medicare, a war on poverty, and civil rights legislation. Liberals supported Johnson's domestic program but opposed his Vietnam policies.

Richard M. Nixon, a Republican, took office in 1969. He was forced to resign in his second term because of the Watergate scandal. Vice-President Gerald Ford took over and faced the problems of inflation and economic recession. In 1976, he was defeated for the presidency by Jimmy Carter. President Carter lost to Ronald Reagan in 1980. President Reagan took office in 1981 with a program aimed at cutting taxes and government costs.

Society and Culture Since 1920

The jazz age of the 1920s came to a close with the stock market crash of 1929. The American economy remained depressed until the early 1940s. Then World War II war orders helped put many people back to work.

After World War II, many Americans moved to the suburbs. Paperback books, radio, and television were popular. Rock 'n' roll replaced swing music.

The 1960s saw assassinations, protests against the fighting in Vietnam, and the rise of the black protest movement.

In the 1970s, the Watergate scandal led to efforts to reform politics. Strong efforts were also made to end discrimination based on race or sex. The government developed regulations for energy, natural resources, and pollution.

The efforts of the government in behalf of social causes lost popularity in the late 1970s and early 1980s. Tax-revolt movements and an outcry against the costs of "big government" seemed to indicate a turning away from liberalism.

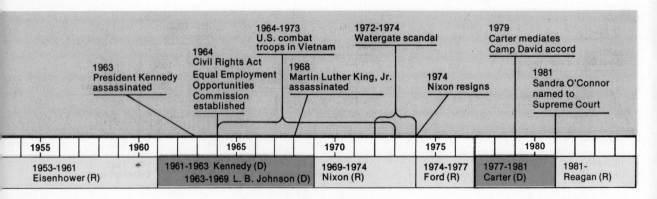

PART 4 World Power: Foreign Affairs to the Present

unit
12

Crimean Conference, U.S. Army photo

Perry's Arrival in Japan, Library of Congress

New World Power: Foreign Policy Through 1945

In 160 years, the United States rose from a weak nation in international affairs to a major force. The change was gradual. In 1783, few European countries expected the new nation to survive—and much early foreign policy was isolationist. But by the mid-1800s, the nation was actively establishing relations with such countries as Japan (above). And by 1945, when the "Big Three" Allied powers met at Yalta (left), the United States was one of the two most powerful nations in the world. It was an amazing change over such a short span of time.

Lesson 1 The Making of Foreign Policy

WORDS TO UNDERSTAND

Discuss the meanings of these words.

diplomats   **partisan**   **recognition**

NEW WORDS IN SENTENCES

1. Many foreign **diplomats** visit the United States to promote goodwill for their countries.

2. The president was accused of **partisan** politics after her attack on the opposing party.

3. When the new country won its independence, it sought **recognition** in the United Nations.

AS YOU READ

As you read this selection, try to answer these questions.

1. What are the general goals of United States foreign policy?

2. How has our foreign policy changed over the years?

THE READING SELECTION

Each nation of the world must establish a foreign policy. There are several general goals of the foreign policy of the United States.

1. Establishing relations between the United States and other nations.

2. Protecting the rights of United States citizens and interests in foreign lands.

3. Developing trade relations with other nations.

4. Settling disputes between the United States and other nations. These disputes often concern boundary lines or the terms for repaying debts. They may also arise over rights on the high seas. Disputes may be settled by war or by peaceful negotiation. The United States has settled many of its disputes with other nations through negotiation.

The president of the United States is responsible for setting the foreign policy of the nation. United States foreign policy is administered by the secretary of state, a member of the president's cabinet. The secretary of state is in charge of our ambassadors and **diplomats** in all parts of the world.

Congress also plays an important part in foreign policy. The president may make treaties with foreign nations, but the Senate must approve them by a two-thirds majority. The president appoints ambassadors, but again, the Senate must approve them. Most important, it is up to Congress to appropriate the money required for the various needs of foreign policy.

The foreign policy of the United States has often been **partisan.** Each political party has had its own idea of what our foreign policy should be. In recent years, many people have tried to develop a bipartisan foreign policy. With a bipartisan foreign policy, both parties agree on the basic policy. This means that U.S. relations with other countries would not change when a different political party comes to power.

The general goals of United States foreign policy have remained the same through the years. But the specific goals have often changed with the times. When the United States won independence in 1783, it faced special problems. One of the important goals of early foreign policy was to establish the United States as an independent nation. United States representatives and ambassadors to other countries had to gain **recognition.** United States citizens in foreign lands had to be assured of protection. In addition, our early foreign policy had to settle border disputes with British Canada and Spanish Florida.

Finally, early foreign policy sought to avoid involvement in European wars and disputes. The United States wanted to remain neutral, especially in the wars between Britain and France after 1789.

As the United States grew, its foreign policy changed. The United States began to seek new lands wherever possible. The idea of manifest destiny guided the United States in its efforts to extend from the Atlantic to the Pacific. There were often many boundary disputes over the newly acquired lands. United States foreign policy had to settle these disputes with foreign powers.

In the 1800s, United States foreign policy sought to keep any European nation from gaining too strong a foothold in the New World. Such European colonization would have threatened the strength and security of the United States.

The power of the United States grew steadily through its foreign policy. From the days of struggle for recognition, the United States gradually grew into a major world power. As a world power, it expanded its foreign policy goals to include protecting the ideal of freedom at home and abroad.

COMPREHENSION CHECK

A. Recognizing the Main Idea

This selection as a whole tells you about

1. foreign policy in early days.
2. border disputes.
3. the president's role in foreign policy.
4. the making of foreign policy and its goals.

B. Selecting Important Details

Choose the ending that best completes each statement.

1. Setting up foreign policy for the United States is the responsibility of
   a. the citizens.
   b. Congress.
   c. the president.
   d. the cabinet.

2. All treaties with foreign nations must receive approval by
   a. both houses of Congress.
   b. a majority of the Senate.
   c. a majority of the House.
   d. a two-thirds majority of the Senate.

3. Foreign policy in the early days of the United States concerned all of the following EXCEPT
   a. settling boundary disputes.
   b. avoiding involvement in the affairs of Europe.
   c. becoming a world power.
   d. winning recognition as an independent nation.

4. United States foreign policy is administered by
   a. the president.
   b. the cabinet.
   c. foreign diplomats.
   d. the secretary of state.

C. True or False

Decide whether each of these statements is true or false. Rewrite the false statements so that they are true.

1. Bipartisan foreign policy has always been the rule in the United States.

2. The Senate must approve the appointment of all ambassadors.

3. The United States did not want to remain neutral in the wars between Britain and France.

4. The idea of manifest destiny guided the United States in its desire for new lands.

5. In the 1800s, the United States encouraged European countries to colonize in the New World.

D. Vocabulary

Write your own sentence for each of these words.

diplomats   partisan   recognition

E. Homework

Write a fifty-word essay in answer to this question: how has the foreign policy of the United States changed with the times?

Lesson 2   Foreign Policy: The First 100 Years

WORDS TO UNDERSTAND
Discuss the meanings of these words.

entangling   prestige

cargoes   ceded

NEW WORDS IN SENTENCES
1. The ball of yarn was **entangling** the playful kitten.
2. The ships from Colombia carried mainly coffee, but the ships from Sweden had many different **cargoes.**
3. His **prestige** grew considerably when he won the debate.
4. Our nation grew bigger when Mexico **ceded** some areas of land to the United States after defeat in the Mexican War.

AS YOU READ
As you read this selection, try to answer these questions.
1. In what ways did the United States seek to stay out of European conflicts?
2. How did the prestige of the United States grow?

THE READING SELECTION
Review. In the years immediately after 1783, United States foreign policy was concerned with several goals.

1. Winning recognition of the rights of the United States as an independent nation.
2. Settling boundary disputes.
3. Remaining neutral in European conflicts.

As the nation grew, foreign policy expanded to include new goals.

1. Acquiring new lands.
2. Achieving status as a world power.
3. Keeping Europeans from colonizing the New World.
4. Defending the ideal of freedom at home and abroad. ☆

As first president of the United States, George Washington tried to avoid involvement in European affairs. He issued a proclamation of neutrality in the British-French wars. The United States and Britain tried to ease their relations with Jay's Treaty. This treaty failed to solve the issue of our nation's right to freedom of the seas. As a result, the Jay Treaty was unpopular with many Americans.

American relations with Spain had a much better start. Pinckney's Treaty of 1795 settled the boundary between the United States and Spanish Florida. It also granted the United States free navigation of the Mississippi River.

When President Washington left office, he delivered his famous farewell ad-

dress. In it, he warned against form-ing **entangling** alliances with European nations. His warning influenced U.S. foreign policy for many years.

After Washington, Presidents Adams and Jefferson also worked to keep the United States neutral in Europe's wars. But the wars in Europe, especially those between Britain and France, soon in-volved the United States.

Both Britain and France violated American neutrality. Both nations stopped United States ships on the high seas and seized their **cargoes.** The British, with their superior navy, seized U.S.

ships far more often than did the French. Yet, during the administration of John Adams, it was the French ac-tions that angered many Americans. President Adams sent negotiators to discuss the issue with France. But the French representatives demanded bribes before they would begin discussing the problem. The United States negotiators refused to pay. The XYZ affair, as this incident came to be called, caused bitter feeling toward France. For a while, there was danger of war. But France and the United States gradually settled their differences peacefully.

In its earlier years, the U.S. often remained neutral in foreign conflicts. It took such a position during the war between Texans and their government in Mexico. However, when the bloody defeat of Texans at the Alamo (left) was reported by survivor Susana Dickinson (right), sympathy for Texas grew. An independent Texas was finally admitted to the Union in 1845. Soon afterward, a border dispute led to the Mexican War.

University of Texas at Austin

To help avoid entanglement in European wars, President Jefferson imposed the Embargo Act. This act prohibited United States ships from sailing to European ports. Jefferson's aim was to keep United States ships out of the war areas. However, the embargo crippled U.S. commerce and later had to be repealed.

Under President Madison, the United States continued its efforts to keep out of European conflicts. It also sought to win recognition of its rights. During this time, Napoleon was emperor of France. He set out to conquer many countries and soon controlled much of Europe. Britain opposed Napoleon. As a result, Napoleon barred British trade from Europe. With its main source of trade cut off, Britain often seized United States ships and captured U.S. sailors. These seizures finally led to the War of 1812, between Britain and the United States.

The war, however, did not settle the issues of neutral rights or freedom of the seas. In fact, the treaty ending the war did nothing more than restore the two countries' relations to what they were before the war. But the United States gained **prestige** through some of its victories at sea. It also won a great land victory at New Orleans. After Napoleon's defeat in 1814–1815, Britain no longer needed to seize cargoes and sailors. The United States then had greater freedom of the seas.

Two diplomatic moves soon helped improve the relations between the United States and Britain. In 1817, the Rush-Bagot Agreement was signed. It provided for a demilitarized United States–Canadian border. In 1818, the boundary between Canada and the United States from the Great Lakes to the Rockies was settled. The forty-ninth parallel became the boundary that settled the dispute. It is called the Line of 1818.

Other major boundary disputes were settled in various ways. In 1819, Spain **ceded** Florida to the United States. In return, the United States paid 5 million dollars to some of its citizens who had claims against Spain. The dispute with Britain over the Oregon country was settled by negotiation in 1846.

As part of the United States effort to gain strength and security, President Monroe issued the Monroe Doctrine in 1823. It declared that no new colonization by Europeans was to be allowed in the Western Hemisphere. Great Britain supported the Monroe Doctrine.

The Monroe Doctrine aided the United States in its desire for new lands. Victory in the Mexican War (1846–1848) brought the United States new territories, including California. The purchase of Alaska from Russia further expanded American territory.

The prestige of the United States grew with its size. Prestige was a main issue in foreign policy during the Civil War period. France violated the Monroe Doctrine by setting up an emperor in Mexico in 1864. Because the United States was fighting its Civil War, it could do nothing to prevent this violation. But after the Civil War, the United States forced France to remove its troops. The French-backed emperor was executed by the new Mexican government.

The Civil War raised other issues involving the prestige of the United States. During the war, the British had given aid to the Confederacy. In 1872, a court handling international disputes decided that Britain must pay 15.5 million dollars to the United States for damages. This decision strengthened the prestige of the United States.

COMPREHENSION CHECK

A. Recognizing the Main Idea

1. In a single sentence, write the main idea of this lesson's reading selection.

2. Write two other points that support this main idea.

B. Selecting Important Details

Choose the ending that best completes each statement.

1. Jay's Treaty was made with
   a. Spain.
   b. France.
   c. England.
   d. Canada.

2. The XYZ affair nearly led to war with
   a. England.
   b. Spain.
   c. Canada.
   d. France.

3. The purpose of the Embargo Act was to
   a. promote trade with Europe.
   b. help France.
   c. help England.
   d. avoid entanglement in Europe's wars.

4. When the French put an emperor in Mexico, they violated the
   a. rights of Spain.
   b. neutrality of the United States.
   c. Monroe Doctrine.
   d. concept of manifest destiny.

C. Completion

Fill in the word or words that best complete each sentence.

1. _____ settled the boundary between the United States and Spanish Florida.

2. French negotiators in the XYZ affair demanded _____ before they would begin discussions.

3. President _____ imposed the Embargo Act.

4. The Rush-Bagot Agreement provided for a _____ United States–Canadian border.

5. The Monroe Doctrine barred _____ of the Western Hemisphere by Europeans.

D. Vocabulary

Match the words with the definitions.

Words	Definitions
1. entangling	a. give up
2. cargoes	b. status
3. prestige	c. negotiation
4. cede	d. causing complicated involvements
	e. goods carried by ships
	f. embargo

Lesson 3 Imperialism and the Spanish-American War

WORDS TO UNDERSTAND

Discuss the meanings of these words.

superiority   **sensational**   **rebellion**

NEW WORDS IN SENTENCES

1. He recognized her **superiority** in tennis when she easily won the match.

2. The newspapers were criticized for their **sensational** stories about murder and brutality.

3. When the king's rule became unjust, the people planned a **rebellion.**

AS YOU READ

As you read this selection, try to answer these questions.

1. Why were many people attracted to the idea of imperialism in the 1880s?

2. What were the major causes of the Spanish-American War?

3. What were the main results of the war?

THE READING SELECTION

Review. In the period following 1783, the foreign policy of the United States was aimed at several goals.

1. Achieving recognition as a nation.

2. Building national prestige.

3. Settling boundary disputes.

4. Acquiring new nearby territories.

5. Avoiding involvement in European conflicts.   ☆

During the 1880s, these goals expanded to include the winning of colonies. Many Americans became interested in the idea of imperialism. Britain, France, and other European nations owned colonies and built empires in distant lands. These European nations often claimed to have racial and national **superiority** over the people of the colonies. They claimed that they were helping the colonies develop. Actually, the colonies were important to European nations for economic reasons. The industrial revolution in Europe demanded a constant supply of raw materials such as iron, tin, oil, cotton, and wool. In many cases, European countries could obtain these raw materials cheaply by seizing colonies that had a ready supply. Colonies also provided a market for the finished products.

Before the 1880s, the United States had little interest in imperialism. The nation was engaged mainly in expanding westward and in building industries at home. The United States followed a policy of isolationism. But by the end of the 1880s, the United States showed more interest in imperialism.

One reason for this change of view was that the United States wanted greater prestige. Gaining colonies across the world would strengthen the prestige of the United States.

Also, the closing of the United States frontier in the 1880s and 1890s released energy for new projects. Much of this energy was directed to the industrial revolution.

The industrial revolution had brought new wealth to Americans. Many investors had surplus money to invest in foreign lands. After the 1880s, there was a steady flow of United States money to foreign territories. Imperialism appealed to these investors as a way to protect their interests in foreign lands.

Another reason for the new interest in imperialism in the United States was the need for raw materials. New colonies would be sources for raw materials. At the same time, these colonies would be markets for surplus manufactured goods.

In the late 1800s, the United States began to acquire colonies. Hawaii and

By 1900, the U.S. had become a colonial power. On this map, find at least five territories of the U.S. In what part of the world were most of the territories?

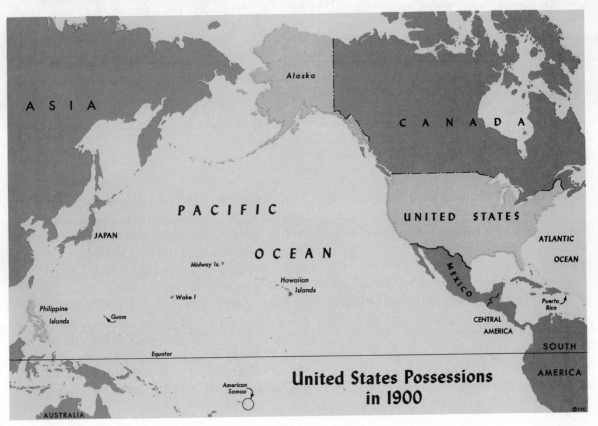

United States Possessions in 1900

The advance up San Juan Hill in Cuba—part of it led by
future president Theodore Roosevelt—was costly but important
for the U.S. This victory helped win the Spanish-American War.

some islands of Samoa were annexed by
the United States in the late 1890s. However, it was the Spanish-American War
in 1898 that made the United States a
colonial power.

Spanish mismanagement of its colony
of Cuba had long angered many Americans. The Cubans fought many times for
independence from Spain. American
newspapers, especially the "yellow journals," sided with the Cubans. These
yellow journals were known for their
bold headlines and **sensational** stories.
They stirred up feelings for war against
Spain. Also, some people had economic
reasons for wanting to end Spanish control of Cuba. They wanted the United
States to take Cuba as a colony.

In January 1898, the United States
sent the battleship *Maine* to Havana to
protect U.S. citizens and property in
Cuba. In February, an explosion sank
the *Maine*. The United States blamed
Spain and, two months later, declared

war. U.S. naval and land forces moved into action. They attacked not only Cuba but also the Spanish-owned Philippine Islands in the Pacific. The United States won victories in both the Caribbean and the Pacific. Spain was forced to agree to a treaty that ended the war. The treaty had several terms.

1. Cuba was given its freedom from Spain. For a time, the United States controlled Cuba. The U.S. withdrew direct control in 1902.

2. Spain ceded the Philippine Islands to the United States for 20 million dollars.

3. The islands of Guam and Puerto Rico were taken by the United States.

After the war with Spain, the United States became a world colonial power. It had new, important possessions in both the Pacific and the Caribbean areas. But the United States soon found that imperialism created problems. American soldiers had to put down the **rebellion** in the Philippines, which continued to demand independence. Many people began to feel that imperialism violated the ideals of democracy.

The U.S. must "uplift and civilize" Filipinos, said President McKinley. However, many Filipinos did not agree. Rebels (below) fought a three-year guerilla war with U.S. troops.

COMPREHENSION CHECK

A. Recognizing the Main Idea

This selection as a whole tells you that

1. Cuba was a colony of Spain.

2. the industrial revolution was in full force.

3. yellow journals sided with the Cubans.

4. imperialism became a goal of United States foreign policy.

B. Selecting Important Details

Choose the ending that best completes each statement.

1. Imperialism was promoted by all of the following EXCEPT

    a. the need for raw goods.

    b. a belief in racial superiority.

    c. a desire for peace.

    d. the need for new markets.

2. During the 1890s, the United States gained control of

    a. Panama and the Samoan Islands.

    b. Mexico.

    c. Colombia.

    d. Hawaii, Cuba, and the Philippines.

3. All of the following were causes of the Spanish-American War EXCEPT

    a. yellow journalism.

    b. the sinking of the *Maine.*

    c. manifest destiny.

    d. a strong interest in imperialism.

4. As a result of the Spanish-American War, the United States took over

    a. Panama and the Philippines.

    b. the Philippines, Guam, and Puerto Rico.

    c. Puerto Rico, Guam, and Hawaii.

    d. the Philippines, Guam, and Samoa.

C. True or False

Decide whether each of these statements is true or false.

1. Isolationist feeling was strong in the United States in the early 1800s.

2. The idea of imperialism was very popular among Americans in the early 1800s.

3. The industrial revolution helped promote the idea of imperialism.

4. The Spanish-American War made the United States a world colonial power.

5. Yellow journalism helped stir up feelings against war.

D. Vocabulary

Use a word from this list to complete each sentence.

superiority   rebellion

sensational   cargoes

1. He lost his air of _____ when he failed several of his exams.

2. The police tried to crush the _____, and many people were imprisoned.

3. The _____ news stories played on people's fears.

E. Homework

Write a fifty-word essay explaining the main causes of the Spanish-American War and three important results of the war.

F. Using Your Knowledge

Make an outline of U.S. foreign policy from 1783 to 1898. Use the goals of foreign policy during these years as the major headings in your outline. Fill out your outline with specific events that helped achieve those goals.

The Problems of Imperialism

The end of the Spanish-American War produced changes in the foreign policy of the United States. The treaty ending the war gave the Philippine Islands, Puerto Rico, and Guam to the United States. It also gave the United States temporary control over Cuba. The United States thus became a real colonial power. Imperialism became an important part of the nation's foreign policy. But imperialism brought problems with it.

Imperialism was often linked to a very strong feeling of nationalism. Unfortunately, this often developed into a belief that the citizens of the United States were superior to the people of the new colonies. This was a form of racism. Racism was not new in the United States. It had long been directed against blacks, both free and slave. Sometimes, it had also been connected with the idea of manifest

destiny. American Indians and Mexicans had often been considered inferior people. After 1900, racism directed against the people of the new colonies increased. This troubled many Americans.

Administering the new colonies also created problems. One example was the Philippines. The Filipino people had fought for independence from Spain for a long time. When Spain was defeated, they felt they should become independent. Many rebelled when they learned the islands would become a colony of the United States. Defeating this rebellion took several years. There were many instances of brutality against Filipinos by the American army. Within the United States, opposition to the policies in the Philippines grew stronger.

Cuba presented another problem. The United States had entered the Spanish-American War pledging to help Cuba win its independence. Congress passed the Teller Resolution, which promised not to annex Cuba. Yet after the war, some Americans suggested violating this pledge. The promise was kept after all. However, for many years the United States kept the right to intervene in Cuban affairs.

United States imperialism was often resented by the people in the colonies. It often created disputes at home. Yet for at least one period in our history, it was a vital part of our foreign policy.

Lesson 4 Foreign Policy in the Western Hemisphere

WORDS TO UNDERSTAND

Discuss the meanings of these words.

intervened   **corollary**

NEW WORDS IN SENTENCES

1. When the prisoners began to fight, the guards **intervened** and broke the fight up.

2. His own generous donation was a **corollary** to his fund-raising speech.

AS YOU READ

As you read this selection, try to answer these questions.

1. How did the Roosevelt Corollary expand the Monroe Doctrine?

2. Why did U.S. citizens fear an unstable Mexican government in the early 1900s?

3. What was the Good Neighbor policy?

THE READING SELECTION

As the United States became a world power, it was no longer interested in isolationism. The United States began to be actively involved in the affairs of other countries. The meaning of the Monroe Doctrine of 1823 expanded as the United States became involved in Latin American affairs.

The Monroe Doctrine was seriously challenged only once in the 1800s. During the 1860s, the French government tried to establish Maximilian as emperor of Mexico. It sent troops to support Maximilian's rule. This action violated the Monroe Doctrine. In 1867, the United States forced France to remove its troops from Mexico. Maximilian was overthrown, and the Mexicans returned Benito Juárez to the presidency. The Maximilian affair showed that the United States intended to enforce the Monroe Doctrine.

Between 1895 and 1904, the Monroe Doctrine was expanded. In 1895, a boundary dispute between Venezuela and the British colony of Guiana threatened to break into war. Secretary of State Richard S. Olney involved the United States in the dispute. By so doing, he stretched the meaning of the Monroe Doctrine. He declared that the United States had the right to involve itself in any dispute in the Western Hemisphere. The boundary issue be-

The U.S. went to great lengths to build a canal across Panama. It even supported a revolution. Find Panama on the map above. Why did it seem such a good place for a canal?

tween Venezuela and British Guiana was finally settled by arbitration.

Several years later, the Monroe Doctrine was expanded further. In 1902, Venezuela failed to pay its debts to some European investors. Britain, Italy, and Germany threatened to send warships to collect the debts. Once again,

the United States **intervened.** The United States insisted on the use of arbitration. The European nations agreed, and the crisis passed.

The issue of debts arose again in 1904, when the Dominican Republic was unable to pay. President Theodore Roosevelt took a bold new step. He announced a **corollary,** or extension, of the Monroe Doctrine. The Roosevelt Corollary gave the United States the right to serve as "an international police power" for disputes in the Caribbean. As a police power, the United States would guarantee the payment of debts and keep peace in Latin America. The corollary remained a part of foreign policy for the next twenty-five years.

The United States became actively involved in Latin American affairs. One of the most important goals of U.S. foreign policy in the early 1900s was to build a canal across the isthmus between North and South America. The United States asked Colombia, which controlled the Panama territory, for the right to build the canal. The Colombian government rejected the request.

President Roosevelt, however, was determined to build the canal. He soon let it be known that he would support an independent Panama. A revolution broke out in Panama against Colombia. The United States Navy moved in to prevent Colombian troops from landing in Panama. With the help of the United

Library of Congress

"I took the Canal," Teddy Roosevelt once boasted, "and let Congress debate." He made it sound so easy. But for a time, it seemed that getting the land in Panama was much easier than building the canal. Special sanitation and medical programs had to be set up to fight yellow fever and malaria. In addition, building the forty-mile canal was often difficult. The work, finally completed in 1914, cost 365 million dollars. This picture shows construction of one of the locks.

In 1867, the U.S. helped Benito Juárez (above) end foreign interference in Mexico. But in the 1900s, the U.S. itself sent troops to Mexico to end a revolt by Pancho Villa (below).

States, the revolution was a success. In 1903, the new government of Panama signed a treaty with the United States. This treaty gave the United States permanent control of a ten-mile-wide strip of land across Panama. It also gave the United States a right to be involved in Panama's affairs to help ensure a stable government. In return, the United States paid Panama 10 million dollars. It also paid a rental fee of $250,000 a year to Panama.

The canal was completed in 1914. But Roosevelt's interference in Panama left ill feelings among Latin Americans. Latin Americans began to feel that the United States had interfered too much in their affairs.

Many people also objected to the involvement of the United States in Mexico. Many United States citizens had invested great sums of money in businesses in Mexico. These investors, especially those

who had developed Mexico's oil deposits, wanted to make sure their interests were protected.

Several revolutions in 1911 and 1913 were said to threaten the security of the United States. President Wilson refused to recognize the Mexican government that had come to power in 1913. In 1914, he sent troops to occupy the Mexican city of Vera Cruz.

Pressure from the United States finally forced a change of government in Mexico. That new government, however, soon faced a rebellion led by Pancho Villa. His forces were accused of raiding several United States towns near the Mexican border. As a result, the U.S. government sent troops into Mexico to capture Villa. They did not succeed. By this time, United States interference in Mexican affairs was creating much ill will between the two nations.

The involvement of the United States in World War I helped end U.S. military actions in Mexico. However, relations between Latin American countries and the United States remained strained for the next twenty years.

The tensions between the United States and Latin America eased greatly during the 1930s under the leadership of President Franklin D. Roosevelt. He developed a Good Neighbor policy toward Latin America. This policy recognized the right of Latin American nations to work with the United States in settling problems. The United States agreed to cooperate with Latin American countries in forming policies and making decisions.

COMPREHENSION CHECK

A. Recognizing the Main Idea

1. In a single sentence, write the main idea of this lesson's reading selection.

2. Write two other points that support this main idea.

B. Selecting Important Details

Choose the ending that best completes each statement.

1. Until its successful revolt, Panama was a part of
   a. Mexico.
   b. France.
   c. Spain.
   d. Colombia.

2. The Roosevelt Corollary
   a. limited United States power in Latin America.
   b. granted European powers limited rights in Latin America.
   c. established the United States as an international police power in the Caribbean.
   d. reduced the power of the Monroe Doctrine.

3. The right of the United States to intervene in any dispute in the Western Hemisphere was established by
   a. the idea of manifest destiny.
   b. the Roosevelt Corollary.
   c. the Monroe Doctrine.
   d. Olney's expansion of the Monroe Doctrine.

4. The Good Neighbor policy was introduced by
   a. President Washington.
   b. Secretary of State Olney.
   c. Theodore Roosevelt.
   d. Franklin D. Roosevelt.

C. True or False

Decide whether each of these statements is true or false. Rewrite the false statements so that they are true.

1. The Venezuelan boundary dispute of 1895 was settled by arbitration.

2. President Theodore Roosevelt's foreign policies were strongly approved of by most Latin American people.

3. The United States became more involved in Latin American affairs to obtain the right to build the Panama Canal.

4. The United States supported Pancho Villa as president of Mexico.

5. Benito Juárez was returned to power after Maximilian was overthrown.

D. Vocabulary

Match the words with the definitions.

Words	Definitions
1. intervene	a. modify
2. corollary	b. logical extension
	c. violate
	d. become involved in

E. Essay

Write a fifty-word essay explaining why Olney's expansion of the Monroe Doctrine and the issuing of the Roosevelt Corollary might have angered Latin Americans.

F. Map Skills

This map shows the Caribbean area. Certain areas are labeled with letters. Match each description below with the correct letter.

1. Country that owned Panama until 1903.

2. Country unable to pay its debts in 1904.

3. Country with which British Guiana had a boundary dispute in 1895.

4. Area in which a canal was completed in 1914.

5. Country in which U.S. troops fought Pancho Villa.

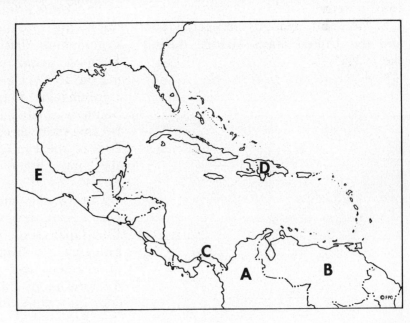

Lesson 5 Foreign Policy in the Far East

WORDS TO UNDERSTAND
Discuss the meanings of these words.

suppress   **indemnities**

NEW WORDS IN SENTENCES
1. The governor tried to **suppress** the angry mob by sending in the National Guard.

2. The nation was forced to pay **indemnities** for damages it caused during the war.

AS YOU READ
As you read this selection, try to answer these questions.

1. What was the purpose of the Open Door notes?

2. How did relations between Japan and the United States change during the 1930s?

THE READING SELECTION
Review. After 1898, the foreign policy of the United States was increasingly concerned with the Caribbean area and the Far East. The United States had acquired the colonies of Guam, the Philippine Islands, and Puerto Rico as a result of the Spanish-American War. These U.S. territories made events in the Far East and the Caribbean very important to the nation. In the Caribbean area, our foreign policy centered around expanding the meaning of the Monroe Doctrine. This expansion often took the form of U.S. intervention in Latin American affairs. During the 1930s, this policy was replaced by the Good Neighbor idea of cooperation. ☆

The United States had been active in the Pacific since the 1850s. An American, Commodore Matthew Perry, opened the Japanese islands to trade in 1854. During the 1850s, United States clipper ships were engaged in trade in China and the South Seas. After 1890, the United States became more directly involved in the affairs of the Far East. In the late 1890s, the United States acquired Pacific territories.

During the mid-1800s, China and Japan were not strong world powers. But Japan soon came under Western influence. It began to strengthen its government and develop its industry. As a result of this strength, the Japanese were able to keep imperialist pow-

In the 1800s, many nations' flags flew over warehouses in Canton, China. China's rulers were weakened by such foreign interference.

ers from dominating their nation. The Chinese were less fortunate. From 1840 on, they were partly controlled by several European powers.

England and France were the first to win special trading rights from the Chinese. They were soon joined by other nations, including Germany and Russia. By 1890, control of the Chinese mainland was divided among several of the big powers. Each imperialist power controlled trading privileges within a particular area of China. These European powers each had a "sphere of influence" in China. The United States was late in its interest in developing trade with China. It found that Europeans had a monopoly on such trade. In

President James Buchanan officially greets a visiting Japanese delegation. The first Japanese ports were opened to U.S. trade in 1854. Additional agreements during Buchanan's administration expanded relations.

Brown Brothers

many cases, the Europeans controlled the port cities of China.

In 1899, Secretary of State John Hay issued a statement on China. It was called the Open Door note. Hay sent Open Door notes to Germany, England, and Russia. Later, he also sent notes to Japan, Italy, and France. These notes declared that all nations ought to have equal trading rights in China. They also implied that all nations ought to respect China's independence. Hay asked the nations receiving these notes to agree to the Open Door policy. The responses were vague. No nation wanted to agree completely and give up any of its sphere of influence. At the same time, no nation wanted to refuse outright and run the risk of war. Despite the vague answers, the Open Door policy did succeed in creating a new feeling in the Far East. Through the Open Door notes, the United States informed the world that it would not be locked out of Far Eastern affairs.

In 1900, the United States became directly involved in Chinese affairs. United States and European troops were sent to China to **suppress** the Boxer Rebellion. The Boxer Rebellion was an outbreak of violence against foreigners in China. The Boxers were a group of Chinese people who objected to the control of China by foreigners. With the help of U.S. troops, the rebellion was put down. China was forced to pay **indemnities,** or damages, to those nations whose citizens had been killed or injured, or whose property had been destroyed.

In 1905, the United States once again became involved in the affairs of the Far East. Japan asked President Theodore Roosevelt to mediate in the dispute between Japan and Russia that had led to war. As a result of the peace terms, Japan became a strong power. From that time on, the United States was watchful of Japan's growing power.

As Japan grew more aggressive, the United States and Japan often opposed each other. Japanese aggression against

China in the 1930s drew sharp criticism from the United States. A crisis arose when Japan took over the Chinese area of Manchuria. The United States reacted by refusing to recognize Japan's right to the territory.

In 1941, the tensions between Japan and the United States led to war. The attack on Pearl Harbor by the Japanese was followed by their conquest of the Philippines and other Pacific islands. After four years of fighting, the United States defeated Japan. The defeat of Japan helped restore the independence of China. By 1945, the Far East was no longer a distant area to the people of the United States. It had become a key area for preserving the security of the United States in a troubled world.

The Japanese drive for more land led to war with the U.S. On this 1939 map, what areas are already under Japanese control?

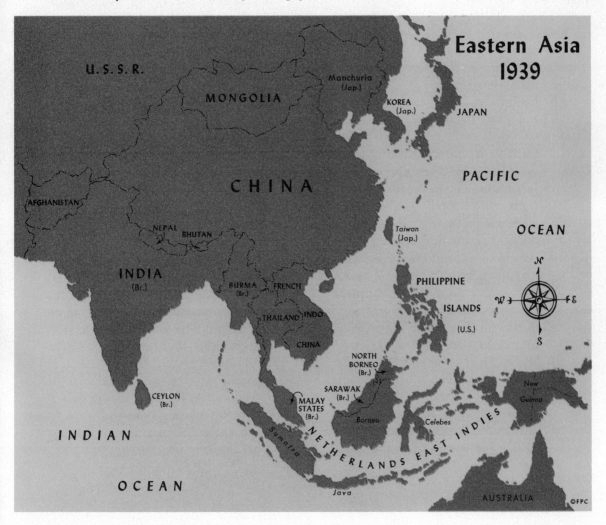

Eastern Asia 1939

COMPREHENSION CHECK

A. Recognizing the Main Idea

This selection as a whole tells you about

1. foreign policy in the Caribbean.
2. the Boxer Rebellion.
3. past foreign policy in the Far East.
4. the Open Door policy.

B. Selecting Important Details

Choose the ending that best completes each statement.

1. The Boxer Rebellion was an attack on foreigners in
    a. Japan.
    b. Manchuria.
    c. the Philippines.
    d. China.
2. The Open Door policy declared that
    a. European spheres of influence in China should be expanded.
    b. Japan should have no trading rights with China.
    c. all nations should have equal trading rights in China.
    d. the Boxers should be given military support.
3. When Japan seized the Chinese territory of Manchuria
    a. President Roosevelt intervened to end the war.
    b. Secretary of State Hay issued the Open Door policy.
    c. the United States recognized Japan's right to the territory.
    d. the United States refused to recognize Japan's right to the territory.

4. Commodore Perry was responsible for opening trade with
    a. China.
    b. the Philippines.
    c. Japan.
    d. the South Seas area.

C. Fact or Opinion

Decide whether each of these statements is fact or opinion.

1. The U.S. criticized Japan for attacking China.
2. It was best for China to be dominated by European countries.
3. The Boxers should not have rebelled against foreigners in China.
4. Disputes in the Far East have nothing to do with the security of the U.S.
5. Japan and the United States went to war in 1941.

D. Vocabulary

Write your own sentence for each of these words.

suppress   indemnities

E. Using Your Knowledge

Each of these events directly involved China, *or* Japan, *or* both countries. For each event, write one or two sentences telling which country was involved, when it occurred, and why it was important.

1. Commodore Matthew Perry opened trade
2. Manchuria taken over
3. Spheres of influence established
4. Boxer Rebellion put down
5. Open Door note sent
6. Pearl Harbor attacked

Lesson 6 The United States and World War I

WORDS TO UNDERSTAND

Discuss the meanings of these words.

perished   **resume**   **armistice**

NEW WORDS IN SENTENCES

1. The animals **perished** because they were not given food or water.

2. She put aside her studying but promised to **resume** it after dinner.

3. The **armistice** ended the fighting between the two nations.

AS YOU READ

As you read this selection, try to answer these questions.

1. What events led to the entry of the United States into World War I?

2. Why did the United States refuse to enter the League of Nations?

THE READING SELECTION

Review. Before 1890, much of United States foreign policy was based on isolationism. The nation was concerned mainly with domestic affairs in those years. After 1890, the people of the United States developed great interest in the Far East. At the same time, the United States also developed greater interest in the Caribbean and Latin America. The meaning of the Monroe Doctrine expanded along with U.S. interest in foreign areas. But the people of the United States were still strongly in favor of isolationism.   ☆

The outbreak of World War I did not, at first, seem to involve the United States. Germany, Austria-Hungary, and Turkey were allied as the Central Powers. They opposed Great Britain, France, Russia, and later, Italy, which were known as the Allies. The war between these powers arose over conflicts in imperialist and nationalist interests. The Central Powers and the Allies turned to war to settle their conflicts.

From the beginning of World War I, the United States sought to remain neutral. President Woodrow Wilson issued a proclamation of neutrality. His administration made serious efforts to keep the country at peace. In fact, Wilson campaigned for reelection in 1916 on the slogan "He kept us out of war."

In spite of its neutrality, the United States was slowly drawn into the Euro-

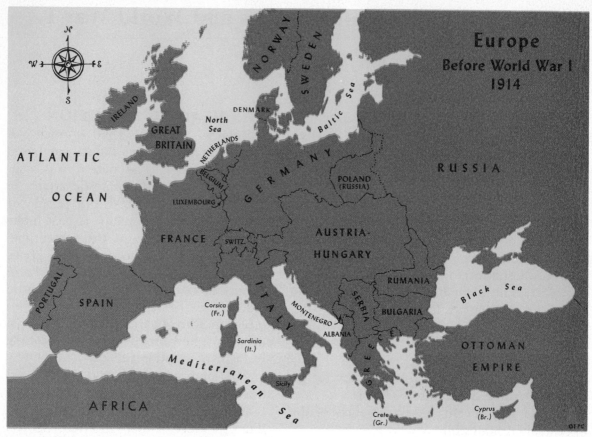

In World War I, the Central Powers—Germany, Austria-Hungary, and Turkey—faced the Allied Powers—France, Britain, and Russia. In 1915, Italy joined the Allies.

pean conflict. Most citizens felt a sympathy for the English-speaking British. In addition, many people were angered when Germany violated the neutrality of Belgium. Germany also lost sympathy when it began using submarines. The submarines often sank ships without warning. The people of the United States were especially angry when U.S. ships were sunk. The German use of poison gas in warfare also angered many people.

In 1915, German submarines sank the British passenger ship *Lusitania.* More than 100 U.S. citizens were among those who **perished.** In the following year, Germany pledged that it would not sink merchant and passenger ships without warning. But in 1917, the British uncovered a note written by Germany's foreign secretary, Alfred Zimmermann. This secret note revealed Germany's intention to **resume** unrestricted submarine attacks. It also pro-

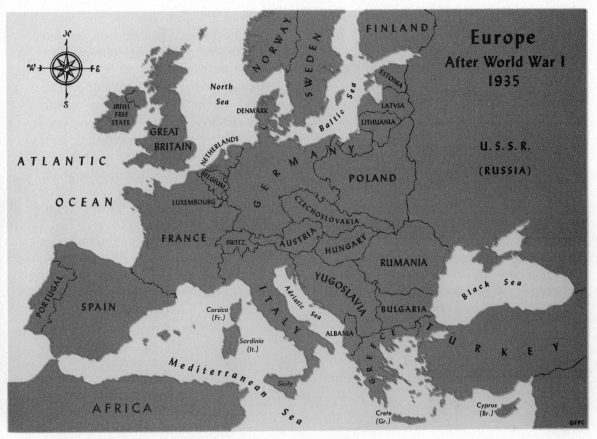

Compare this map with the one on the opposite page. What happened to Germany's territory after it lost World War I? What happened to its ally, Austria-Hungary?

posed an alliance between Mexico and Germany in the event that the United States declared war on Germany. In return for the alliance, Mexico would receive Texas and the Southwest. These were lands Mexico had lost to the United States in the Mexican-American War. Soon after the Zimmermann note was revealed, the United States declared war on Germany.

The United States was in the war for only eighteen months, but it played an important part. General John J. Pershing led the American Expeditionary Force to fight in France. More than 2 million United States troops were in France by the end of the war. At General Pershing's insistence, the United States troops fought as a distinct unit rather than as replacements for British and French troops. The United States lost over 126,000 soldiers. Over 230,000 U.S. soldiers were wounded. These were light losses compared to the 5 million who died in the other Allied armies. However, the U.S. troops were active in only a few battles. They suffered heavy losses in these engagements. Another 60,000 U.S. soldiers and sailors died of disease during the war. The Central Powers lost over 3.3 million soldiers in World War I.

By November 1918, the Germans were forced to seek an **armistice.** The United States had by now become a world power. President Wilson was a recognized world leader. He attended the peace treaty meetings in France. President Wilson proposed the establishment of a new international organization, the League of Nations. He declared that the League of Nations would serve to end the threat of future wars.

However, Wilson's plan for the League of Nations was not supported by the people of the United States. The Senate even refused to ratify the peace treaty of Versailles. The end of the war had led to many disputes among the Allies. People in the United States were disillusioned with the cause for which they had fought. As the nation moved into the 1920s, people were less concerned with idealism and more concerned with material things. They returned to their old isolationist views as they began to feel their borders once again secure against attack from foreign sources.

The people of the United States had another reason for returning to their support of isolationism. The Russian Revolution in 1917 created a fear among many people of spreading communism. Many Americans believed that they must never again become involved in the world's problems.

COMPREHENSION CHECK

A. Recognizing the Main Idea

1. In a single sentence, write the main idea of this lesson's reading selection.

2. Write two other points that support this main idea.

B. Selecting Important Details

Choose the ending that best completes each statement.

1. The Central Powers included all the following EXCEPT
    a. Germany.
    b. Austria-Hungary.
    c. Spain.
    d. Turkey.

2. The Zimmermann note involved German promises to
    a. the United States.
    b. Italy.
    c. the Central Powers.
    d. Mexico.

3. The proposal for the League of Nations came from
    a. France.
    b. England.
    c. the United States.
    d. Russia.

4. All the following were reasons for American entry into World War I EXCEPT
    a. isolationism.
    b. unrestricted submarine warfare by Germany.
    c. American sympathy for the British.
    d. American sympathy for the Belgians.

C. True or False

Decide whether each of these statements is true or false.

1. Germany was a member of the Central Powers.

2. Italy was a member of the Allies in World War I.

3. The Zimmermann note proposed an alliance between Germany and Mexico.

4. President Wilson's proposal for the League of Nations was supported by the people of the United States.

5. The United States moved back to isolationist thinking after World War I.

D. Vocabulary

Match the words with the definitions.

Words	Definitions
1. perished	a. unrestricted
2. resume	b. agreement to stop fighting
3. armistice	c. begin again
	d. summarize
	e. died

E. Ask Yourself

Was the United States justified in entering World War I?

F. Map Skills

Use the maps on pages 622 and 623 to answer these questions.

1. Which countries gained land after World War I?

2. Which new countries were created?

AS WE GO MARCHING ON

THE WAR TO END WAR

Woodrow Wilson asked Congress to declare war in 1917, arguing that "the world must be made safe for democracy." Congress agreed strongly. So for the first time, Americans marched off to war in Europe. In all, forty-two infantry divisions were sent to France, along with arms and ammunition. Women also served in the war effort, both in Europe and at home, releasing men for the armed forces. For the United States, the war was fortunately short. But it was not, as many had hoped, "the war to end war."

Lesson 7 American Isolationism and World Affairs in the 1930s

WORDS TO UNDERSTAND

Discuss the meanings of these words.

remote	totalitarian
fascists	dictatorial

NEW WORDS IN SENTENCES

1. He lived in a **remote** part of the country, far from all cities and towns.

2. **Fascists** believe that a strong central government is more important than the individual rights of the people.

3. In a **totalitarian** state, leaders of a single party control every aspect of life in that country.

4. People living under a **dictatorial** government are not allowed to express their disapproval of their leader.

AS YOU READ

As you read this selection, try to answer these questions.

1. How did acts of aggression in the 1930s affect U.S. isolationism?

2. How did the United States change its neutrality laws after World War II began?

THE READING SELECTION

For the first hundred years of its history, the United States sought to remain free from involvement in European affairs. President Washington's farewell address helped create this isolationist spirit. The people of the United States were concerned with their own domestic problems, such as the tariff, slavery, and westward expansion.

During the late 1800s, people in the United States felt secure against attack by any foreign power. The United States had huge oceans on both its eastern and western borders. Its neighbors to the north and south were not very aggressive. Most people in the United States felt safe.

Isolationist feeling in the United States grew stronger during the 1920s. Many people were disillusioned by the results of World War I. They felt that they had been cheated by the British and French. These former allies could not repay the war debts they owed the United States government. The European Allies had great disputes among themselves about the terms for peace. They had trouble agreeing on how to divide the spoils. Their disputes decreased American interest in European affairs.

At the same time, a fear of communism began to grow. People feared that the communism of the Soviet Union would extend to other countries. This fear strengthened isolationist thinking in the United States. The spirit of the Roaring Twenties also contributed to isolationism. People were concerned with obtaining material comforts and increasing their incomes. Europe and Asia were far away. Their problems seemed **remote** to most people in the United States.

Although isolationism was popular in the United States, the many changes in Europe during the 1920s and 1930s could not be ignored. After World War I, one European nation after another changed its form of government. In 1917, Communists took control of Russia. With Mussolini as their leader, **Fascists** seized control of Italy in 1922. Fascists value the good of the nation or race above the good of the individual. In fascist governments, a single party with one strong leader has control over the whole country. Fascist leaders control all areas of a country's life, including business, religion, and politics. Fascists generally use a police force to crush all those who oppose them.

In 1933, the National Socialist German Workers' Party (Nazis), led by Adolph Hitler, came to power in Germany. The Nazis, like the Italian Fascists, believed in a **totalitarian** form of government. Hitler had gained widespread support among the German people after he helped Germany recover from a depression. The Nazis soon had complete control in Germany. Under Hitler, the Nazis sought to extend German military control to other areas of the world as well.

Many smaller countries of Europe also moved toward **dictatorial** governments. People in the United States began to express concern about the spread of anti-democratic ideas in Europe. They realized that the United States might not be as secure in its isolationism as they had imagined. Yet, the United States held fast to its policy of isolationism.

The Nazis had begun a campaign of terror against their opponents. Many thousands of Germans were imprisoned, and some were put to death. They included liberals, intellectuals, and many others. The Nazis also launched a brutal campaign against German Jews. Nazis believed that Jews threatened the "purity" of the German race. By 1934 and 1935, hundreds of German Jews had fled the terror of the Nazis. Among those who left Germany was Albert Einstein, world-famous scientist and Nobel Prize winner. The Germans who were able to escape the Nazis told of the arrests, beatings, and killings going on in Germany. Many people urged the United States to permit people fleeing from Nazi Germany to enter as immigrants. The United States, however, refused to change its immigration limits. Thousands of German Jews were unable to get out of Germany. They were thrown into Nazi camps, and many died. In spite of the stories of Nazi terror, the United States refused to become involved.

COMPREHENSION CHECK

A. Recognizing the Main Idea

This selection as a whole tells you about

1. Hitler's rise to power.
2. isolationism in the first 100 years of United States history.
3. U.S. isolationism and European affairs before World War II.
4. fascist governments in Europe.

B. Selecting Important Details

Choose the ending that best completes each statement.

1. German Nazis wanted
   a. a democracy.
   b. freedom of thought.
   c. to get rid of opponents.
   d. to defeat totalitarianism.
2. In 1922, Mussolini became the leader of
   a. Germany.
   b. Japan.
   c. Russia.
   d. Italy.
3. All of the following statements describe a fascist government EXCEPT
   a. it controls all areas of life.
   b. it depends heavily on a government police force.
   c. one leader has most of the power.
   d. its officials compete with members of other parties in open elections.
4. During the 1920s, the United States
   a. changed its immigration policies for people fleeing Germany.
   b. wanted to be involved in European affairs.
   c. no longer wanted to be isolated.
   d. kept to a policy of isolationism.

C. Completion

Fill in the word or words that best complete each sentence.

1. After World War I, Britain and France could not _____ their debts to the United States.
2. Nazis believed in a _____ form of government.
3. Hitler had gained support by helping the Germans recover from a _____.
4. The United States refused to change its _____ rules and let the fleeing Jews into the country.
5. After World War I, many people began to fear that Soviet _____ would extend to other countries.

D. Vocabulary

Write your own sentence for each of these words.

remote   totalitarian
fascists   dictatorial

E. Essay

Write a seventy-five-word essay explaining why isolationism was a part of foreign policy in the 1930s.

F. Chart and Graph Skills

Make a chart contrasting the features of a fascist government with those of a democratic government. Divide a sheet of paper into two columns. Label the column on the left "Democracy." Label the column on the right "Fascism." Under each column, make a list of characteristic features.

Lesson 8   The Beginning of World War II

WORDS TO UNDERSTAND
Discuss the meanings of these words.

surrender   quotas

NEW WORDS IN SENTENCES
1. The invasion of troops forced the natives to **surrender** their land.

2. **Quotas** set limits on the number of people admitted.

AS YOU READ
As you read this selection, try to answer these questions.

1. What were the events that led to World War II in Europe?

2. How did the United States become directly involved in the war?

THE READING SELECTION
Review. Isolationism was strong in the United States following World War I. Despite their support of isolationism, Americans grew concerned over changes in European governments and politics. Mussolini and his Fascists were in control of Italy. Hitler and the Nazis were gaining power in Germany.   ☆

During the 1930s, a series of aggressive actions by some nations aroused even greater concern.

1. Japan invaded and conquered Manchuria in 1931. The Chinese government was powerless to prevent this conquest. The United States issued a note of strong protest to Japan and refused to recognize Japan's right to Manchuria. However, neither the United States nor any other nation took effective action against Japan.

2. In 1935, the Italian army attacked the African nation of Ethiopia. Once again, the world seemed unable to prevent aggression. After a brave struggle, Ethiopia was finally conquered by Italian troops.

3. In 1936, the German and Italian governments formed an alliance known as the Rome-Berlin axis. That same year, both nations interfered actively in the Spanish civil war. They aided the forces of General Francisco Franco, who shared their political views. The newly created Spanish republic was defeated by Franco and his Fascist and Nazi allies.

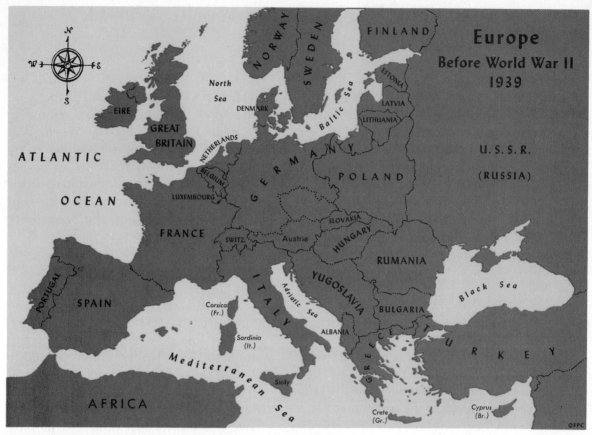

Between 1938 and 1941, the Axis won control of most of Europe, from France to eastern Russia and from Norway to Greece.

4. In 1938, Germany took control of Austria. That same year, the Germans demanded that Czechoslovakia **surrender** part of its territory to Germany. Neither France nor England was able to challenge Hitler over this territory. Hitler promised, however, to let the rest of Czechoslovakia remain free. Hitler broke this promise in 1939, and the rest of Czechoslovakia fell to Germany.

5. In 1937, Japan invaded China. Three years later, Japan joined Germany and Italy in forming the Rome-Berlin-Tokyo axis.

6. In 1939, Germany invaded Poland. As a result, Britain and France, as allies of Poland, declared war on Germany. World War II had begun.

During this entire period, the League of Nations had protested the many acts of aggression. But the league had never had any real power to enforce its protests.

When war threatened in the 1930s, the United States tried to protect its neutral status. The Roosevelt administration passed a neutrality act in 1935. This act kept the United States from lending or selling arms to nations at war. But by 1937, it became clear that such neutrality aided the aggressor nations. So Congress passed another neutrality act in 1937. This act included a cash-and-carry plan. The plan permitted nations to buy arms for cash if they shipped them in their own vessels. Because the British fleet was very large, this plan helped the British. In 1941, the United States went even further. The Lend-Lease Act was passed. It permitted the United States to lend or lease arms to democratic nations. In the words of Franklin Roosevelt, the United States was now doing "its full part in creating an adequate arsenal of democracy."

At first, the war was between Germany and the alliance of France, Brit-

The excitement of a Nazi rally at Nuremberg (above) contrasts with the murder of millions of Jews (below).

ain, and Poland. Fascist Italy was Germany's ally, but it did not enter the war immediately. The Soviet Union had signed a non-aggression pact with Germany in 1939 and was not yet involved in the war.

Germany quickly defeated Poland and then overran France. After the defeat of France, Italy joined the war on Germany's side. By mid-1940, Britain was fighting alone against Germany and Italy. The defeat of France had brought war to the shores of Great Britain. Great Britain was in danger of invasion. But the British were finding it increasingly difficult to pay cash for weapons. The Lend-Lease Act of 1941 helped Britain acquire weapons. Before long, United States merchant ships were carrying goods overseas.

The first two years of World War II brought victories to Nazi Germany. As the German armies conquered most of Europe, they extended their campaign of terror against Jewish communities. In the United States, a Jewish leader, Rabbi Stephen S. Wise, warned President Roosevelt that 2 million Jews had already been killed. In spite of this warning, the United States refused to suspend immigration **quotas** to allow Jews fleeing Germany to enter in greater numbers than before.

In 1941, Germany attacked the Soviet Union. Late that same year, the Japanese attacked the United States naval base at Pearl Harbor in Hawaii. This attack brought the United States into the war against the Axis powers. The spirit of isolationism vanished as the United States declared war, first against Japan and then against Germany.

COMPREHENSION CHECK

A. Recognizing the Main Idea

1. In a single sentence, write the main idea of this lesson's reading selection.

2. Write two other points that support this main idea.

B. Selecting Important Details

Choose the ending that best completes each statement.

1. The United States entered World War II when Pearl Harbor was attacked by
    a. Germany.
    b. Italy.
    c. Japan.
    d. Czechoslovakia.

2. The attack on Ethiopia was an act of aggression by
    a. Germany.
    b. Japan.
    c. Russia.
    d. Italy.

3. The cash-and-carry plan passed in 1937 favored
    a. neither side in the war.
    b. mostly the Axis powers.
    c. mostly the British.
    d. Italy.

4. The expression "arsenal of democracy" is most accurately associated with
    a. the neutrality acts of 1935 and 1937.
    b. the cash-and-carry plan.
    c. strict isolationism.
    d. the Lend-Lease Act of 1941.

C. Completion

Fill in the word or words that best complete each sentence.

1. The first two years of World War II brought many victories to _____.

2. The United States entered World War II after the attack on _____ in late 1941.

3. After Japan seized _____ in 1931, the United States took no effective action against Japan.

4. The Rome-Berlin axis aided _____ in the Spanish civil war.

5. France and Britain entered World War II when Germany invaded _____.

D. Vocabulary

Use a word from this list to complete each sentence.

surrender   quotas   armistice

1. The immigration _____ specified how many people from each area of the world could move to the United States.

2. With defeat almost certain, the enemy was forced to _____.

E. Chronology

Review this lesson to find the events that led to World War II. On a separate sheet of paper, copy the following dates. Write the events leading to World War II under the appropriate dates.

1935   1936   1939   1941

Making America an Arsenal of Democracy

By December 1940, Britain was facing desperate conditions in its fight against the Nazis. France had fallen, most of the British equipment had been lost in the fighting in France, and Britain had been heavily pounded by the Nazi air forces. The British found themselves short of money to buy arms and ammunition from the United States. Prime Minister Winston Churchill said, "Give us the tools, and we will finish the job."

President Roosevelt proposed to help the British get the tools to use in the fight. He urged that the United States supply the materials of war to the British without regard to payment. In the early months of 1941, Congress hotly debated the proposed lend-lease bill. A sum of 7 billion dollars was proposed to be used to aid those who were in danger of attack or under actual attack.

The isolationists argued that such an act would involve us in war. The president declared that only by such aid could we hope to avoid ultimate war with aggressive nazism. In March 1941, a lend-lease bill was passed. The Lend-Lease Act provided that the president could sell, transfer, exchange, lease, or lend materials of war to allies.

President Roosevelt declared to the nation on radio, "Our nation is going to be what our people have proclaimed it must be—the arsenal of democracy." With this act, the U.S. was no longer neutral in the war.

This is Nazi brutality

RADIO BERLIN.--IT IS OFFICIALLY ANNOUNCED:--
ALL MEN OF LIDICE - CZECHOSLOVAKIA - HAVE BEEN SHOT:
THE WOMEN DEPORTED TO A CONCENTRATION CAMP:
THE CHILDREN SENT TO APPROPRIATE CENTERS-- THE
NAME OF THE VILLAGE WAS IMMEDIATELY ABOLISHED.
6/11/42/115P

Lesson 9 The United States in World War II

WORDS TO UNDERSTAND
Discuss the meanings of these words.

offensive   **consequences**
concentration camps   **casualties**

NEW WORDS IN SENTENCES
1. At first, the troops were just defending their territories, but soon they launched an **offensive** attack.

2. The Nazis forced Jews into **concentration camps,** where millions of people died.

3. One of the **consequences** of eating too much sugar is a greater risk of tooth decay.

4. The U.S. **casualties** from World War II included 300,000 killed and 700,000 wounded.

AS YOU READ
As you read this selection, try to answer these questions.

1. How did the United States solve the problem of fighting a war on two fronts?

2. What were some of the consequences of World War II?

Throughout the war, the U.S. government used posters to persuade Americans to do many things—from volunteering for the service to growing home vegetables to buying war bonds.

THE READING SELECTION
Review. World War II began in 1939, when Nazi Germany invaded Poland. France and Britain came to the aid of Poland. The United States tried to stay out of the war. It had passed neutrality acts. These neutrality laws had, at first, prevented the United States from aiding the warring nations. Isolationist feeling was still quite strong in the United States. In spite of this, President Franklin D. Roosevelt urged a program of aid to nations opposing the Nazis. In 1937, the cash-and-carry plan was introduced. Later, the United States passed the Lend-Lease Act. The United States became an "arsenal of democracy."

At first, Germany fought against France, Britain, and Poland. In 1940, Britain was fighting alone against Germany and Italy. The defeat of France had brought war to the shores of Great Britain. The United States entered the war in 1941, after the Japanese attacked Pearl Harbor. ☆

Isolationism in the United States disappeared after the attack on Pearl Harbor. When the United States entered the war, it joined the Allied forces. The Soviet Union had also joined the Allies. Germany had violated the Soviet-German non-aggression pact in 1941 by invading Russia.

In the first months after the attack on Pearl Harbor, the United States suffered many defeats. Japan conquered the Philippines and several other islands in the Pacific. The United States prepared for a long war. With enemies in both the Pacific and Europe, the Allies had to plan their strategy carefully. Military leaders decided to concentrate their efforts on the European fight until Germany was defeated. Then the Allies could turn to war in the Far East.

General Dwight D. Eisenhower led the Allied forces in North Africa. Later, he served as supreme commander of the Allied invasion of Europe. The Far East commander was General Douglas MacArthur. At first, MacArthur's forces fought to hold back Japanese advances in the Pacific until the Allies were ready to take the **offensive.** By 1944, the Allied forces were beginning to defeat the Japanese. The United States Navy also won victories over the Japanese in a series of battles at sea.

During the war, Americans continued to hear stories of terror about the Nazis. In August 1943, the *New York Times* produced evidence of a list of nearly 2.5 million people starved or killed by the Nazis. Many people tried to arrange payment to the German government for release of large numbers of people in Nazi **concentration camps.** But nothing was done by the Allied governments.

In 1944, a Treasury Department official accused the State Department of neglecting the problem of help for Europe's Jews. President Roosevelt at this point agreed to take limited action. He approved of trying to help Jews in Europe move to Palestine. But British officials who controlled Palestine turned the plan down. They feared it might cause conflicts with Arabs in the region. Once again, nothing was done.

In mid-1944, Allied troops landed in France. They swept in from the west while Russian troops moved toward Germany from the east. Germany was forced to surrender in May 1945. Allied soldiers who captured the German concentration camps could hardly believe what they saw. The Nazis had killed more than 9 million people in their death camps, including 6 million Jews. They had used firing squads, brutal beatings, and poison gas chambers to kill their prisoners. They used huge ovens to burn the dead. Their object, in their own words, was a "final solution" to the Jewish "problem." That final solution was to be the total destruction of the world's Jews.

The Nazis did not succeed in their plan for a final solution. They did, however, destroy much of the once famed and thriving Jewish culture of Eastern Europe. They killed 3 million Polish Jews, 1.5 million Russian Jews, and 750,000 Jews in Hungary and Rumania. Entire communities were wiped out. The survivors of the death camps told the story of their fight for survival to a shocked world.

The surrender of Germany did not end the war. In August 1945, the United States dropped atomic bombs on Hiroshima and Nagasaki in Japan. These bombs were unlike others used before. They produced terrible death and destruction. Japan was forced to surrender. After six terrible years of war, the nations of the world could finally begin programs of reconstruction and peace.

When you ride ALONE you ride with Hitler!

Join a Car-Sharing Club TODAY!

Culver Pictures, Inc.

Gasoline was one of many items that were rationed at home in order to increase supplies needed in the war. This government poster was meant to encourage Americans to use car pools. How does it communicate that idea?

In 1945, the United States had been at war for four years. The war had many important **consequences.**

1. The national debt of the United States rose from 43 billion dollars in 1940 to 258 billion dollars in 1945. The nation had spent about 330 billion dollars on the war—ten times more than it had spent on World War I. The war also cost many human lives. Of the 12 million men and women in the U.S. forces, about 1 million had been **casualties.** Nearly 300,000 had been killed.

2. The United States and the Soviet Union emerged as the two leading world powers.

3. Isolationism faded away. The United States was now deeply committed to the idea of world cooperation to preserve peace.

640

THE BIG WAR

If any war is remembered, it is the Second World War. The globe was torn apart. The war seemed to be everywhere, to touch everything and everyone. Like any war, it was the story of the dead and the living. The dead were soldiers in faraway places, from Pearl Harbor to the Battle of the Bulge —and they were the unburied dead of the concentration camps. But there were survivors—of all those battles, of all those camps. And there were survivors at home: American women building planes, Berlin women rebuilding their city. It is survivors who help us remember.

641

COMPREHENSION CHECK

A. Recognizing the Main Idea

1. In a single sentence, write the main idea of this lesson's reading selection.

2. Write two other points that support this main idea.

B. Selecting Important Details

Choose the ending that best completes each statement.

1. All of the following were consequences of World War II EXCEPT

  a. an increase in the national debt of the United States.

  b. the emergence of the United States as a world power.

  c. the return of the United States to isolationism.

  d. the strong involvement of the United States in world cooperation.

2. The Nazi campaign against the Jews resulted in all of the following EXCEPT

  a. the destruction of much of Eastern European Jewish culture.

  b. the death of 6 million Jews in camps.

  c. many Jewish communities being totally wiped out.

  d. the total destruction of the world's Jews.

3. General Dwight D. Eisenhower was the United States commander

  a. in the Far East.

  b. in both Europe and the Far East.

  c. first in North Africa, then in the Far East.

  d. first in North Africa, then in Europe.

4. The Allied military leaders decided to concentrate their first efforts on

  a. Japan.

  b. South Africa.

  c. Europe.

  d. the Philippines.

C. True or False

Decide whether each of these statements is true or false.

1. The Nazis killed over 9 million people in death camps.

2. Great Britain and the Soviet Union were allies of the United States in World War II.

3. In the first months after the attack on Pearl Harbor, the United States scored immediate victories.

4. While the Allies swept toward Germany from the west, the Russian troops moved in from the east.

5. Japan dropped an atomic bomb on Pearl Harbor.

D. Vocabulary

Write your own sentence for each of these words.

offensive   casualties
consequences   concentration camps

E. Chronology

Arrange these events in the order in which they happened.

1. Monroe Doctrine

2. War between the United States and Britain

3. U.S. entry into World War I

4. Boxer Rebellion

5. Spanish-American War

6. U.S. entry into World War II

General Eisenhower Orders D-Day

In the late hours of June 5, 1944—in England—an important decision faced General Dwight D. Eisenhower. The supreme commander of Allied forces had to decide whether to order a full-scale invasion of the Normandy coast of France. Tens of thousands of Allied soldiers were aboard a giant fleet of over 5,000 vessels ready to launch the invasion. Just across the English Channel were the mighty forts of the Nazi armies. Any invasion would be a risky business, but the risk was made greater by dismal, rainy weather.

Bad weather meant less effective air cover by Allied airplanes. It meant that land targets would be difficult to spot from battleships aiding the invasion.

Finally, it meant great difficulties in landing paratroops, glider troops, and other soldiers in the assault ships.

A decision had to be made within the next few hours. To delay meant that the invasion would have to be postponed several weeks. But could General Eisenhower risk a disaster by invading in poor weather?

The German generals watching the weather assumed that there was no danger ahead. But in the late hours, General Eisenhower received word that the weather might improve soon. He boldly took the risk and gave the order to proceed with the invasion. A few hours later, the first paratroops were landing in French territory behind German lines. By dawn on June 6, 1944, the Allied armies were storming the German forts in the first step to victory in Europe.

Unit 12 Summary A New World Power: Foreign Policy Through 1945

The Making of Foreign Policy

The foreign policy of the United States has four general goals. These are: establishing relations with other nations, protecting U.S. rights and citizens in foreign lands, developing trade with foreign countries, and settling disputes with foreign powers.

The president of the United States is charged with shaping the nation's foreign policy. The secretary of state is responsible for carrying out the foreign policy of the president. The president cannot make foreign policy alone. The Senate must approve all treaties with foreign powers by a two-thirds majority. It must also give majority approval to the president's appointments of ambassadors. Also, Congress has the power to appropriate the funds for foreign policy.

Early Foreign Policy

In the early days of the republic, the foreign policy of the United States had three main purposes. They were: to obtain recognition by European nations, to settle boundary problems, and to avoid getting involved in European wars.

The United States and Britain set the boundary between Canada and the United States from the Great Lakes to the Rockies in 1818. The Oregon boundary was settled with Britain in 1846. The border dispute with Spain was settled in 1819 when Spain ceded Florida to the United States. In 1848, the Mexican War settled the border disputes between Mexico and the United States.

The nation tried to avoid involvement in European disputes. President Jefferson's Embargo Act tried to halt trade with warring nations, but this ruined U.S. commerce and was repealed. British seizures of American ships and sailors led to the War of 1812. This war ended in 1814. It helped establish the strength of the United States.

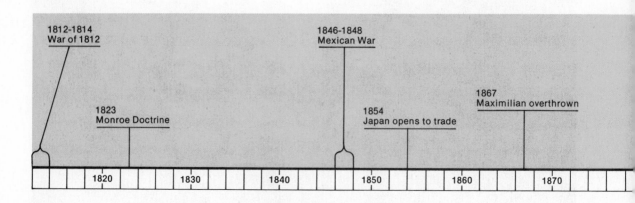

1812-1814
War of 1812

1846-1848
Mexican War

1867
Maximilian overthrown

1823
Monroe Doctrine

1854
Japan opens to trade

1820   1830   1840   1850   1860   1870

The Monroe Doctrine

The War of 1812 did not solve the problems of U.S. neutrality rights. But with the defeat of Napoleon, the problem of British seizures of American ships came to an end. In 1823, the United States introduced the Monroe Doctrine. The Monroe Doctrine declared that the United States would permit no further European colonization of the Western Hemisphere.

The Monroe Doctrine was seriously challenged in Mexico. The effort by France to set up Maximilian as emperor of Mexico was unsuccessful. The United States showed its intention to enforce the Monroe Doctrine.

Imperialism and Isolationism

As a result of the war with Spain in 1898, the United States took over the colonies of Puerto Rico and the Philippine Islands. President Theodore Roosevelt expanded the Monroe Doctrine with the Roosevelt Corollary. The corollary stated that the United States had the right to intervene in Latin American affairs. Many Latin Americans resented this policy. They also resented U.S. actions in securing the Panama Canal.

Despite its interest in imperialism, the United States maintained a policy of isolationism. In the first years of World War I, the United States was neutral. But it joined the Allies against Germany in 1917. After the war, the belief in isolationism grew stronger. The United States refused to join the League of Nations.

World Cooperation

President Franklin D. Roosevelt brought a gradual change to the foreign policy of the United States. He introduced the Good Neighbor policy toward Latin America. When World War II broke out in 1939, the United States tried to remain neutral. But when Japan attacked Pearl Harbor in 1941, the United States entered the war as part of the Allied forces fighting Germany, Italy, and Japan.

Victory in World War II helped the United States become a leading world power. The old idea of isolationism gave way to a spirit of cooperation among nations.

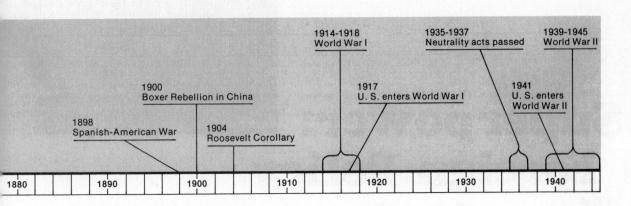

unit
13

Vietnam War protest, 1969, Wide World

Superpower: Foreign Policy Since 1945

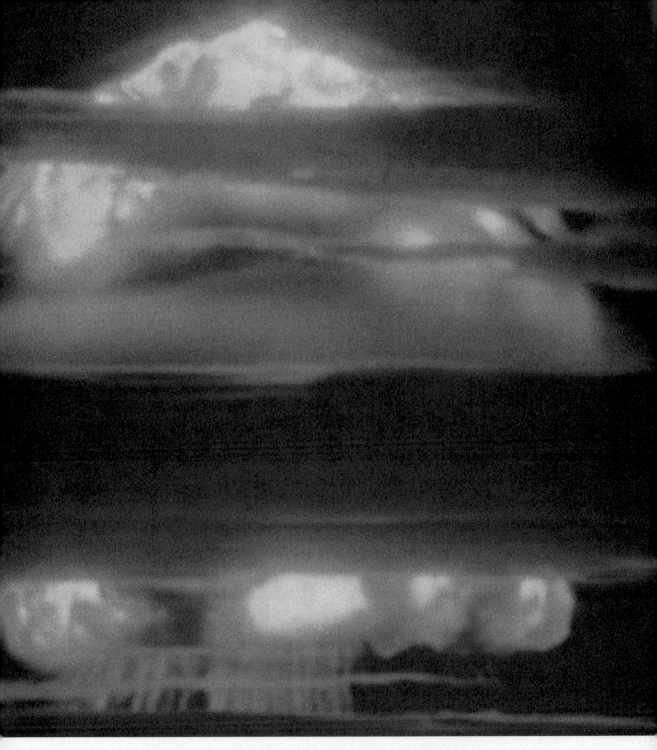

The bomb. Since 1945, nuclear weapons (above) have changed
the world and international affairs. The threat of such
destruction has influenced the foreign policies of the United
States and other nations. American policies toward many areas
of the world have also been influenced by changing attitudes
(left). It is a different world, and often a difficult one.

647

Lesson 1   World War II Changes the World

WORDS TO UNDERSTAND
Discuss the meanings of these words.

ammunition   **occupation**
chaos   **developing nations**

NEW WORDS IN SENTENCES
1. The guns were useless without **ammunition.**
2. The traffic accident resulted in **chaos** on the highway.
3. After the war, the defeated nation was under **occupation** by enemy troops.
4. **Developing nations** often look to developed nations for agricultural and industrial techniques.

AS YOU READ
As you read this selection, try to answer these questions.
1. Why was there chaos in some countries after World War II?
2. How were the Axis powers governed after the war?
3. How did the war change the balance of power in Europe and Asia?

THE READING SELECTION
From 1939 to 1945, most of the world was involved in fighting World War II. From 1941 on, the United States played a key role in defeating the Axis—Germany, Italy, and Japan. During the war, American industry produced vast amounts of food and war materials, such as ships, tanks, planes, guns, and **ammunition.** The United States helped keep Allied troops well supplied. At the same time, American ground, naval, and air forces carried the war to the enemies' homelands. Toward the end of the war, the United States used the atomic bomb against Japan.

Both the winners and the losers suffered during the war. The massive fighting brought destruction to many nations.

The human cost. Between 30 and 60 million soldiers and civilians lost their lives in the war. Millions of them died in concentration camps and prison camps. The Nazis had deliberately destroyed millions of men, women, and children in death camps. These people were not enemy soldiers or criminals. They were Jews, Catholics, gypsies, or political opponents of the Nazis. Over 6 million Jews alone died in camps.

Physical destruction. There was heavy damage to many areas of Britain, France, Germany, Poland, Italy, and the Soviet Union. China suffered much

Ben Shahn used art to speak out about war and politics. What contrasts are there in this 1945 painting, *Liberation*?

from the Japanese invasion. And two Japanese cities, Hiroshima and Nagasaki, were almost totally destroyed by the atomic bombs dropped on them. The destruction of cities, farms, factories, and railroads left many nations in a state of economic **chaos.** Millions of people faced death from starvation or disease.

Allied occupation of Axis nations. The Allied victory shattered the totalitarian political systems of the Axis nations. Italy established a democratic system of government. But Germany and Japan came under **occupation** by Allied nations. The four major Allied powers—Britain, France, the Soviet Union, and the United States—shared the occupation of Germany. The Soviet Union occupied the nations of Eastern Europe that had earlier been taken over by the Nazis. It encouraged the establishment of Communist governments in these areas. Japan was governed by the Allied military, headed by an American, General Douglas MacArthur. Under American influence, a new Japanese constitution was written.

Political effects. World War II brought lasting changes to the world. Many political effects of the war have remained until the present.

The "balance of power" in Europe was totally changed. France was no longer a major power. Even Britain was thought of as a "former" world power. The Soviet Union became the strongest power in Europe. In the years after the war, the Soviet Union made remarkable industrial gains. Politically, it soon began to oppose its former allies. This opposition often brought it into conflict with the United States.

Associated Press

Populations shifted and borders changed in much of Europe after World War II.

Over twenty high Nazi officials were tried for war crimes by the Allies in the Nuremberg trials.

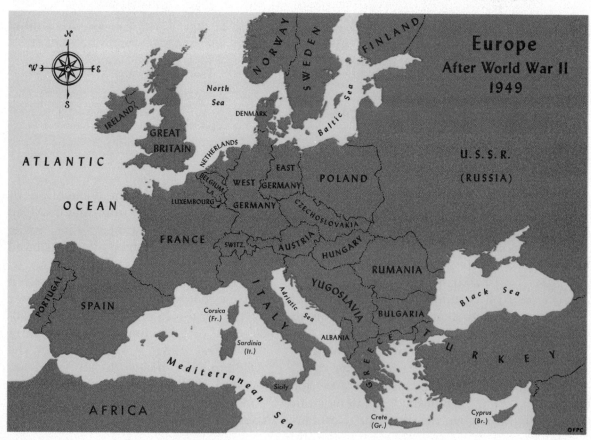

Europe
After World War II
1949

NORWAY
SWEDEN
FINLAND
North Sea
DENMARK
Baltic Sea
IRELAND
GREAT BRITAIN
ATLANTIC
NETHERLANDS
EAST GERMANY
POLAND
U.S.S.R.
(RUSSIA)
BELGIUM
WEST GERMANY
OCEAN
LUXEMBOURG
GERMANY
CZECHOSLOVAKIA
FRANCE
SWITZ.
AUSTRIA
HUNGARY
RUMANIA
PORTUGAL
SPAIN
ITALY
Adriatic Sea
YUGOSLAVIA
BULGARIA
Black Sea
Corsica (Fr.)
ALBANIA
GREECE
TURKEY
Sardinia (It.)
Mediterranean Sea
Sicily
AFRICA
Crete (Gr.)
Cyprus (Br.)
©FPC

The United States had also become a leading world power as a result of the war. A return to the isolationism of the 1930s seemed impossible. In the early years of the nation, foreign policy had been based on the idea of remaining separate from Europe's quarrels. But since World War II, the United States has been actively involved in international affairs. It became the strongest opponent of communism.

In Asia, the United States became particularly concerned about the spread of communism because of events in China. The Japanese occupation of China had led to a truce between Mao Tse-tung's Communist forces and Chiang Kai-shek's supporters. After the war, the struggle began again. In 1949, the Communists gained control of the Chinese mainland, establishing the People's Republic of China. The largest nation in Asia was now Communist.

Western nations were concerned that communism would spread to other parts of Asia and to Latin America and Africa. In these areas, there were growing movements for independence from European colonial governments. New nations were coming into being. Many of them were still building up their economies and political systems. Competition grew between Communist and Western nations for the loyalty of these **developing nations.**

In general, international politics after World War II became more complex. There were new alliances. There were both new nations and old nations taking on new roles. It was in this atmosphere that the United Nations began its work.

COMPREHENSION CHECK

A. Recognizing the Main Idea

1. In a single sentence, write the main idea of this lesson's reading selection.

2. Write two other points that support this main idea.

B. Selecting Important Details

Choose the ending that best completes each statement.

1. The atomic bomb
    a. was dropped by Germany.
    b. killed 6 million Jews.
    c. killed only soldiers.
    d. destroyed Hiroshima and Nagasaki.

2. During World War II, the United States did all of the following EXCEPT
    a. use the atomic bomb.
    b. produce arms and ammunition.
    c. use naval and air forces.
    d. put Jews and Catholics in concentration camps.

3. After World War II, Germany and Japan
    a. were occupied by Allied nations.
    b. had civil wars.
    c. gained control of the Chinese mainland.
    d. restored their totalitarian governments.

4. After World War II, the United States
    a. returned to isolationism.
    b. supported the spread of communism.
    c. lost its place as a world power.
    d. remained involved in international affairs.

C. True or False

Decide whether each of these statements is true or false. Rewrite the false statements so that they are true.

1. General Douglas MacArthur headed the military government in China.

2. Britain and France remained major world powers after the war.

3. Mao Tse-tung headed the government of Japan.

4. International politics after the war became more complex.

5. There was economic chaos in many European countries after the war.

D. Vocabulary

Match the words with the definitions.

Words	Definitions
1. ammunition	a. type of food
2. chaos	b. total confusion
3. occupation	c. completely avoid
4. developing nations	d. areas growing in industry and agriculture
	e. military control of an area
	f. materials used in fighting

E. Map Skills

Compare the map of Europe after World War II on page 650 with the map of Europe in 1939 on page 632. Then answer these questions.

1. Name three countries next to one another that no longer existed by 1949. What countries took over their lands?

2. What happened to Germany after the war?

3. What nation gained the most territory as a result of the war?

Detention Camps in America

In 1945, Americans tended to look back on their part in World War II with pride. One aspect of the war, however, did not inspire pride. War often brings out the worst in people. During the war, Americans at home had been overcome by fear and hatred. The hatred of an enemy can easily spread to hatred of groups at home associated with that enemy. During World War II, Japanese-Americans were victims of this fear and hatred.

There had long been bias against the Chinese and Japanese in America. During the war, this rose to a fever pitch. The Japanese attack on Pearl Harbor angered Americans. It was called "sneaky," and the Japanese were considered evil. Japanese victories in the Pacific and an attack on the West Coast by a Japanese submarine further increased American fear.

Few people felt that Italian-Americans or German-Americans were traitors. But many people felt that Japanese-Americans were still loyal to the government in Tokyo. These people argued that the Japanese-Americans would betray the United States to the enemy. Some people feared that they would help Japanese soldiers invade the West Coast.

Innocent Japanese-Americans were picked up and held by officials for questioning. Newspaper editorials stirred up hatred and fear. Finally, in 1942, a federal order forced all

Japanese-Americans from the West Coast. They had to quickly sell their homes, businesses, and possessions. They were shipped to special camps, where they were often guarded by the army. The camps were actually concentration camps. The Japanese-Americans were not abused while there, but all their freedom was taken from them. The camps were dreary, crowded, and generally unpleasant.

The federal order made no distinction between recent Japanese immigrants and "Nisei," Japanese-Americans born in this country. They were all sent away. There was not even one proved case of Japanese-American disloyalty. Yet 59 percent of Americans questioned in a 1942 poll favored the camps. The camps even had the approval of the president and the Supreme Court.

About the only way for a Japanese-American man to get out of the camps was to sign a loyalty oath and volunteer for the armed forces. Two special regiments of Nisei were formed, the 100th Infantry and the 442nd Infantry. Both were sent to Europe. The 442nd served in Italy and was the most decorated regiment in World War II.

By the time these soldiers returned home, almost all Japanese-Americans had been released from the camps. Yet the fact remains that while they were fighting in Europe, their relatives and friends were imprisoned in America, simply because of their ancestry.

Japanese-Americans board trains for relocation camps in the western deserts and the Arkansas swamplands. More than 110,000 Japanese-Americans were taken from their West Coast homes. Why did the courts order this relocation policy?

United Press International

Lesson 2 The United Nations

WORDS TO UNDERSTAND

Discuss the meanings of these words.

entanglements   procedural
sanctions   substantive

NEW WORDS IN SENTENCES

1. Being a major world power meant having **entanglements** with the governments of foreign countries.

2. To show their opposition to racism in South Africa, some nations used economic **sanctions** against the country.

3. Deciding which day the election would be held was a **procedural** matter.

4. Whether or not the country would go to war was a **substantive** question.

AS YOU READ

As you read this selection, try to answer these questions.

1. What were some reasons for the failure of the League of Nations?

2. How is the United Nations organized?

3. What are some weaknesses of the United Nations?

THE READING SELECTION

Review. When World War II ended in 1945, between 30 and 60 million people had been killed. Millions died in Nazi concentration camps. The destruction of cities, farms, factories, and railroads in many countries brought about economic chaos. Allied nations occupied Germany and Japan. The war changed the balance of power totally. The Soviet Union and the United States became the leading world powers. They often were in conflict over the spread of communism. When China became a Communist nation, the People's Republic of China, Western nations were fearful that communism would spread to the newly independent nations in other areas of the world. ☆

The period after 1945 saw a change in American foreign policy. Two world wars had shown the impossibility of avoiding foreign **entanglements.** The oceans separating the United States from Europe and Asia no longer protected the nation against modern warfare. Isolationism could not play an important part in foreign policy. The United States and other nations saw that an international organization was needed. Such an organization could help prevent a third world war—one that could be fought with atomic weapons.

There had been previous efforts to establish international organizations. President Woodrow Wilson had proposed the League of Nations after

World War I. The league was formed in 1920. But it was largely a failure for several reasons.

1. Many important nations, including the United States, were not members of the league. The Soviet Union was a member only from 1934 to 1939. Germany, Italy, and Japan all left the league in the 1930s.

2. The league required unanimous approval of proposed actions. This approval was almost impossible to get.

3. League actions were limited. The league was not able to use military strength to enforce its decisions. It could only ask for international **sanctions** (trade boycotts) against offending nations. These were not very effective.

Despite the failure of the League of Nations, many people still believed that such an international group was needed. During World War II, the Allied nations pledged support for such an organization. In April 1945, representatives of many nations met in San Francisco. They drew up a charter for the

Land for the UN building in New York was donated by the U.S.

Wide World

new United Nations (UN). In June, fifty nations signed the charter. Since then, more than ninety other nations have joined the UN.

The chart with this lesson shows the basic organization of the UN. The central unit is the General Assembly. Each member nation is represented in the General Assembly with a vote. The General Assembly serves as a place for debate on world problems. It often refers action to the Security Council. But it can act in a crisis if the Security Council has failed to act.

The Security Council has fifteen members. Five of these are permanent—the United States, the Soviet Union, France, Britain, and China. They are sometimes called the "Big Five." The other ten seats are filled by various other UN member nations for a period of two years. The Security Council has the main responsibility for keeping world peace. It investigates disputes, suggests settlements, and determines UN action in a world crisis. **Procedural** matters can be approved by a majority of nine of the fifteen nations. **Substantive** decisions on important issues must be approved by all fifteen nations. Each of the five permanent members has the power to veto many Security Council actions or decisions.

In addition to the Security Council, there are four other main UN divisions, which are responsible to the General Assembly.

The Trusteeship Council. Its job is to help prepare former colonies for independence.

The International Court of Justice. It settles legal disputes among nations. It can appeal to the Security Council for enforcement of its decisions.

The Economic and Social Council. It works to improve economic and social conditions around the world.

The Secretariat. It is responsible for the daily running of the UN. The Secretariat is headed by the secretary general of the UN.

The organization of the United Nations is similar to that of the earlier League of Nations. However, it is stronger than the league was in two ways. First, all major powers, and almost all nations of the world, are members. Second, the UN has more power to make decisions and to enforce them than the league had. For example, it can take military action, as it did in Korea in the early 1950s.

However, the UN still has weaknesses. The veto power in the Security Council can be overused by a permanent member. A veto can prevent any action by the council. In addition, the UN has not been able to prevent many regional conflicts. For example, it was not able to stop the fighting in Vietnam.

Yet the UN offers hope for preventing a future atomic war. It can also be a place in which nations work together on issues that affect all of them, such as protection of the world's environment and resources, or the use of outer space.

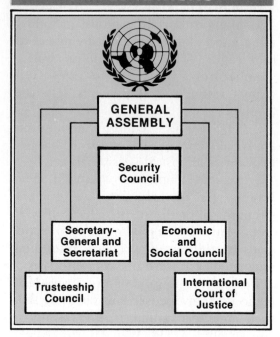

ORGANIZATION of the UNITED NATIONS

COMPREHENSION CHECK

A. Recognizing the Main Idea

1. In a single sentence, write the main idea of this lesson's reading selection.

2. Write two other points that support this main idea.

B. Selecting Important Details

Choose the ending that best completes each statement.

1. The United Nations includes all of the following agencies EXCEPT the
   a. Security Council.
   b. Economic and Social Council.
   c. International Court of Justice.
   d. Council for the Promotion of Isolationism.

2. The League of Nations
   a. could enforce its decisions with military strength.
   b. was ignored by many important nations.
   c. demonstrated by its failure that international organizations could not work.
   d. could not ask for economic sanctions against a nation.
3. Strengths of the United Nations include all the following EXCEPT
   a. membership by all major world powers.
   b. ability to act without unanimous support.
   c. limitation of membership to only the major powers.
   d. ability to use military force.
4. The Security Council
   a. cannot act in a crisis.
   b. has more members than the General Assembly.
   c. has a representative from each member nation.
   d. has fifteen members.

C. Completion
Fill in the word or words that best complete each sentence.
1. Colonies are prepared for independence by the _____ Council of the United Nations.
2. Any of the five permanent members of the Security Council can _____ decisions.
3. The secretary general of the United Nations heads the _____.

4. The Security Council's permanent members are Britain, the United States, France, China, and _____.
5. Legal disputes between nations can be settled by the _____.

D. Vocabulary
Use a word from this list to complete each sentence.

entanglements   procedural
sanctions   substantive
ammunition

1. A _____ decision should be made only after a great deal of thought has been given to the matter.
2. Several countries agreed to economic _____ against the country that started the violence.
3. The issue was only a _____ question, so there was little debate.
4. _____ with other nations could no longer be avoided by the United States.

E. Ask Yourself
What are some arguments for and against the veto power of the five permanent members of the Security Council?

F. Homework
Look in an encyclopedia for information about each of these parts of the United Nations. Write one or two sentences about each item.
1. World Health Organization
2. World Bank
3. International Labor Organization
4. UNESCO

UN Delegate:
Eleanor Roosevelt

In 1945, when the first meeting of the new United Nations General Assembly took place in London, one of the delegates was already very well known. She was Eleanor Roosevelt.

Eleanor Roosevelt had been an unusual "First Lady." Her public career before and during Franklin D. Roosevelt's administration was unlike that of any other president's wife. She had long been active in social reform movements, and she became a champion of the needy. She lectured, wrote a popular newspaper column, and often gathered information for the president. By 1939, *Time* magazine called Eleanor Roosevelt the most influential woman in America. Many people wondered if her career would be over when FDR died in 1945.

It was not—not if Harry Truman had anything to say about it. The new president was determined not to waste Eleanor Roosevelt's talents. She was appointed a delegate to the new United Nations.

The newspapers were once again filled with pictures of "Eleanor." She traveled all over the world in the cause of peace. Her visits to India, Israel, Britain, France, and other nations involved more than lunches with diplomats. She continued her tradition of seeking out and talking to "ordinary" people. She met students, labor leaders, scientists, and people on the streets.

In 1946, Eleanor Roosevelt chaired the commission on human rights of the UN's Economic and Social Council. She helped draft the Universal Declaration of Human Rights. This document marked the first international acceptance of the idea of basic human rights. Yet the issue of such rights, Eleanor Roosevelt once wrote, was most important at the personal level.

Where, after all, do universal rights begin? In small places, close to home—so close and so small that they cannot be seen on any maps of the world. Yet they are the world of the individual persons; the neighborhood . . . the school . . . the factory. . . . Unless these rights have meaning there, they have little meaning anywhere.

Eleanor Roosevelt retired from the UN in 1952, though she returned for one more year as delegate in 1961. Shortly before she died in 1962, she made a statement that summarized her outlook.

This I know. This I believe with all my heart. If we want a free and peaceful world, if we want to make the deserts bloom and man to grow to greater dignity as a human being—*we can do it!*

Lesson 3   Foreign Policy in Europe

WORDS TO UNDERSTAND

Discuss the meanings of these words.

propaganda   **disarmament**

containment   **détente**

NEW WORDS IN SENTENCES

1. A nation may use **propaganda** to twist information to its own advantage.

2. The policy of **containment** tried to limit communism to the countries in which it already existed.

3. A **disarmament** agreement would limit the supplies of weapons kept by both sides.

4. The relaxing of strained relations between countries is called **détente.**

AS YOU READ

As you read this selection, try to answer these questions.

1. What were the purposes of the Truman Doctrine, the Marshall Plan, and the North Atlantic Treaty Organization?

2. What were some of the main events of the cold war?

3. What problems remain in the European foreign policy of the United States?

THE READING SELECTION

During World War II, Nazi Germany seemed to be the main threat to the world. In order to defeat Nazi Germany, the Western nations and the Soviet Union overlooked their differences and became allies. But when Germany ceased to be a threat in 1945, the temporary alliance broke down. Since then, United States foreign policy has been influenced by the struggle for power with communism.

The period following the war and extending into the 1960s has been called the time of the cold war. This was not a declared war, fought between armies. It was a struggle that used **propaganda,** foreign aid, and other strategies instead of guns. Both the democracies and the Communist nations tried to bring more countries over to their sides.

The cold war in Europe began right after World War II. Soviet troops occupied most of eastern Europe—areas that had been under German control. Germany itself was split into four zones of occupation. The eastern part of the country was occupied by the Soviet Union. The western part was occupied by the United States, Britain, and France. The city of Berlin, which was in the Soviet zone, was also split into four zones of occupation. These occupations were supposed to be temporary. However, the two sides could not reach agreement on the reuniting of Germany. In 1948, the Soviets tried to force the Western nations out of Berlin by blockading the city. This effort failed. The Western powers used an "airlift" to fly supplies into the city, and the blockade was broken. But the Soviets would not give up their control over occupied areas in Germany and Berlin. In 1948, France, Britain, and the United States gave up their control and combined their zones into the German Federal Republic. The Soviets set up Communist governments in the eastern part of Germany and in other nations they occupied. These governments were generally under the control of the Soviet Union.

The United States took steps to stop the further growth of Soviet power. In 1947, it had adopted the policy of **containment** proposed in the Truman Doctrine. President Harry S. Truman had pledged economic and military aid to any nation threatened by an outside power. This aid was specifically intended for Greece and Turkey. By 1948, the United States extended its aid to all of Europe. Americans believed that communism could be defeated in strong and stable Western nations. So the United States began to supply aid to Europe to help it recover from the destruction of World War II. The Marshall Plan, proposed by Secretary of State George C. Marshall, provided 12 billion dollars in aid to Europe.

An additional effort to stop the Soviet Union was taken in 1949 with the formation of the North Atlantic Treaty

Under the Marshall Plan, the U.S. sent over 12 billion dollars of aid to Europe—including this flour shipment to Yugoslavia.

Organization (NATO). The twelve member nations were from Western Europe and the North Atlantic. They agreed to join in a common defense against aggression. Joint military forces were established, and the United States provided 6 billion dollars worth of military aid. The Soviet Union and other Communist countries responded by establishing the similar Warsaw Pact in 1955.

The United States has encouraged European economic as well as military strength. In 1957, the European Economic Community (EEC), or Common Market, was formed. Its purpose has been to help develop trade among its members.

By the mid-1950s, Europe had largely recovered from the effects of World War II. But Western relations with the Soviet Union remained rocky. In 1955, hopes for improved relations had grown. The Geneva Summit Conference opened up the possibility of **disarmament** on both sides. But conflicts between Western nations and Communist nations increased tensions again. In 1956, revolts in both Poland and Hungary were put down by Soviet troops. In 1961, East Germany and the Soviet Union again created a crisis in Berlin. The Communists sealed off East Berlin from the western section of the city with a high wall. Hopes for reuniting Berlin and the rest of Germany faded.

Yet in the 1970s, relations again showed some improvement. The relaxed tensions have been called **détente.** Trade between the Soviet Union and the United States increased. For exam-

Associated Press

Relations with the U.S.S.R. in the 1950s were often complicated by Premier Nikita Khrushchev's moods. He is shown here in the UN, following an outburst in which he pounded the desk with his shoe.

ple, the United States made large sales of grain to the Soviet Union. Scientific cooperation resulted in joint American-Soviet space missions. Presidents Richard Nixon and Gerald Ford both visited the Soviet Union, and Soviet chief Leonid Brezhnev visited the United States.

Some problems remain, however.

When President Carter met with NATO heads of state, he promised to "join with Europe" to "strengthen the alliance—politically, economically, and militarily." Carter also indicated that NATO would remain the "heart" of U.S. foreign policy.

Arms limitation has continued to be a difficult issue. In 1969, Strategic Arms Limitation Talks (SALT) began, producing agreements signed in 1972. But further agreements have been hard to establish. In recent years, there has also been tension over Soviet policies on human rights. Several Soviet protesters have gained the support of the West in their struggle to win more civil rights in the Soviet Union. The West has also tended to support the right of Russian Jews to emigrate. The Soviet Union has argued that its domestic affairs are not the business of other nations. It has warned that continued Western support for opposition groups in the Soviet Union could threaten détente.

663

COMPREHENSION CHECK

A. Recognizing the Main Idea

1. In a single sentence, write the main idea of this lesson's reading selection.

2. Write two other points that support this main idea.

B. Selecting Important Details

Choose the ending that best completes each statement.

1. All of the following were United States efforts toward containment EXCEPT

    a. the Truman Doctrine.

    b. the Marshall Plan.

    c. the Warsaw Pact.

    d. NATO.

2. The European Economic Community is

    a. a military alliance.

    b. an alliance of protesters.

    c. a result of disarmament.

    d. an economic alliance.

3. Soviet protesters

    a. oppose Western interference in Soviet domestic affairs.

    b. have strong Western support.

    c. oppose more civil rights in the Soviet Union.

    d. all of the above.

4. Berlin is

    a. in the western part of Germany.

    b. a Communist city.

    c. divided by a wall.

    d. occupied entirely by France, Britain, and the United States.

C. Completion

Fill in the word or words that best complete each sentence.

1. The _____ Plan provided billions of dollars in aid to Europe after World War II.

2. Western nations and the Soviet Union have twice come into conflict over access to the city of _____.

3. _____ is a common defense agreement among twelve Western nations.

4. Improved relations with the _____ include grain sales, cooperation in space, and visits by heads of state.

5. Soviet troops put down _____ in Poland and Hungary.

D. Vocabulary

Match the words with the definitions.

Words	Definitions
1. propaganda	a. U.S. policy to limit communism
2. containment	b. relaxed tensions
3. disarmament	c. information that is twisted to persuade
4. détente	d. U.S. policy toward protesters
	e. reduction of weapons production

E. Homework

What might happen if détente between the United States and the Soviet Union cannot be maintained?

Prepare an outline that explains your ideas. Your outline should include at least two main ideas, with two or more details under each one.

Write an essay of two or more paragraphs using your outline for a guide.

Lesson 4 Foreign Policy in Asia

WORDS TO UNDERSTAND

Discuss the meanings of these words.

erupted   subtle

domino theory bloc

NEW WORDS IN SENTENCES

1. The conflicts had been present for many years, and they finally **erupted** in a war.

2. The **domino theory** held that Communist control over one nation could influence other nations around it to become Communist.

3. The struggle went on in ways that were more **subtle** than open warfare.

4. The **bloc** of nations voted together on most issues.

AS YOU READ

As you read this selection, try to answer these questions.

1. What were the effects of Japan's occupation by the United States?

2. What have been the policies of the United States toward the two Chinas?

3. How has the domino theory influenced foreign policies of the United States?

THE READING SELECTION

Review. After 1945, the alliance between the Soviet Union and the Western powers broke down. The Soviets established Communist governments in the areas they occupied. The United States tried to contain communism and provided aid to Europe under the Marshall Plan. Western cooperation was established in NATO and the EEC. The 1950s and 1960s saw much conflict between communism and the democracy of Western nations. But with greater cooperation in the 1970s, relations seemed to improve. ☆

Since World War II, United States foreign policy has been more concerned with Asia than before. Asia is important for two reasons. First, Japan and China are both strong, independent nations. Their actions can have great effects on the United States and the world. Second, American involvement in developing nations has increased. Many of these nations are in Asia.

After World War II, Japan was occupied mainly by the United States. The occupation resulted in political, economic, and social reforms in Japan. The occupation ended in 1951. Since then, Japan has continued its economic growth. Its exports are a challenge to many Western economies. However, Japan is now a strong ally of the United States.

During its occupation of Japan, the United States began to face another foreign policy issue in Asia. The conflict with communism spread from Europe to Asia. In the 1930s, a civil war had **erupted** in China. Communist forces led by Mao Tse-tung were challenging Chiang Kai-shek's Nationalist forces for control of the nation. After World War II, the fighting broke out again. The United States supported Chiang's forces. But by 1949, Mao's troops had won control of the mainland. Nationalist forces withdrew to the island of Taiwan.

Both Mao and Chiang claimed to represent the "true" China. Their claims created the diplomatic problem of two Chinas. The Nationalist government, the Republic of China, held China's seat on the United Nations Security Council. The Communist nation, the People's Republic of China, demanded this representation. For many years, the United States refused to recognize Communist China and blocked its admission to the UN.

The United States was afraid of Communist expansion in Asia. U.S. foreign policy was based on a belief in the **domino theory.** This theory held that if one nation became Communist, surrounding nations would also fall to communism, much as a line of dominoes falls.

War in Korea added to American fears. After World War II, Korea was divided into two sections. The Soviet Union controlled the north, the United States the south. In 1950, North Korean troops crossed the border into South Korea. The United States led the UN in condemning this action. The UN sent troops to support South Korea. U.S. troops made up the bulk of these

"What's Our Firm, Unswerving Asia Policy This Week?"

forces. The fighting lasted until 1953. About 33,000 Americans were killed in combat. The Communists were defeated, and Korea is still divided.

In the 1960s, history seemed to repeat itself. The United States became involved in a conflict in Vietnam. After World War II, the French colony of Indochina was divided into the new nations of Laos, Cambodia, and Vietnam. Civil war broke out in Vietnam, and French troops were forced out by Vietnamese pro-Communists. The nation was divided into two sections. The north was held by the Communists, led by Ho Chi Minh. The south was held by an anti-Communist government. An

The cartoon opposite had a good point: policy toward communism in Asia changed greatly from the 1950s to the 1970s. In the 1950s, the U.S. fought communism in Korea. In 1961, it continued this anti-communist policy by increasing the number of U.S. troops in Vietnam (above). The peak was reached in 1968. Suddenly in the 1970s, change could be seen. Troop levels dropped. In 1972, Richard Nixon was the first president to visit China (left). And in 1973, the last American troops left Vietnam. The old anti-communist policies had softened.

667

U.S. foreign aid to the Far East and Pacific greatly increased from 1950 to 1960 to 1970 (see chart). Partly because of this aid, Japan was able to establish itself as a major industrial nation. Now Japan is exporting its industries to other countries. One example is this Sony plant in San Diego, California.

Sony Corporation

election was to decide which government would control the entire country. But this election was never held.

Pro-Communists in South Vietnam, the Vietcong, began a guerilla war against the anti-Communist government. United States support of the South Vietnamese government increased. By 1971, over 500,000 American troops were fighting in Vietnam. These troops were finally withdrawn in 1973. In 1975, the Communists won control of the whole nation. Laos and Kampuchea also became Communist.

The United States had lost its struggle in Southeast Asia. But at the same time, relations with Communist China were improving. In 1972, President Richard Nixon visited the People's Republic, and moves toward full diplomatic relations were begun. The U.S.

withdrew its opposition to Communist China's representation in the UN, and the People's Republic replaced Taiwan. Yet American aid to Taiwan continued to trouble relations between the U.S. and the People's Republic.

The contest between communism and democracy continues in Asia. But it is often on a more **subtle** level now. Many developing nations, such as India, refuse to take sides. Often these nations want to use aid from both sides. The United States has increased its total foreign aid since World War II. Asia has received a large portion of this funding. Developing nations in Asia and other areas now make up a "Third World" **bloc** in the UN. Both Communist and Western nations are trying to influence the votes of the bloc.

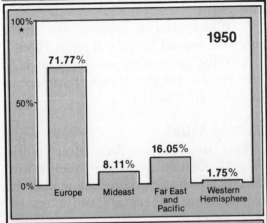

CHANGES in TOTAL U.S. FOREIGN AID

1950

- 100%*
- 71.77% Europe
- 8.11% Mideast
- 16.05% Far East and Pacific
- 1.75% Western Hemisphere
- 50%
- 0%

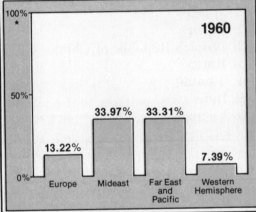

1960

- 100%*
- 13.22% Europe
- 33.97% Mideast
- 33.31% Far East and Pacific
- 7.39% Western Hemisphere
- 50%
- 0%

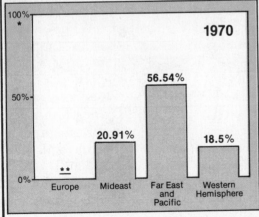

1970

- 100%*
- ** Europe
- 20.91% Mideast
- 56.54% Far East and Pacific
- 18.5% Western Hemisphere
- 50%
- 0%

* small amounts of aid not listed given to other areas of world

** returned money exceeded aid given

COMPREHENSION CHECK

A. Recognizing the Main Idea

1. In a single sentence, write the main idea of this lesson's reading selection.

2. Write two other points that support this main idea.

B. Selecting Important Details

Choose the ending that best completes each statement.

1. In the civil war in China,
   a. the United States supported Mao Tse-tung.
   b. Chiang Kai-shek led the Communist forces.
   c. Chiang Kai-shek's forces withdrew to Taiwan.
   d. Mao Tse-tung's forces withdrew to Taiwan.

2. Third World nations
   a. are not allowed in the United Nations.
   b. do not accept foreign aid from Communist countries.
   c. are important to both Communist and Western nations.
   d. want to be controlled by the major powers.

3. The United States and the UN sent troops to Korea because
   a. North Korea requested it.
   b. the Vietcong crossed the border into South Korea.
   c. the United Nations condemned South Korea.
   d. North Korean Communist troops crossed the border into South Korea.

4. For many years, the admission of the People's Republic of China to the United Nations was blocked
    a. by the Soviet Union.
    b. by Mao Tse-tung.
    c. by the United States.
    d. because of its small size.

C. Fact or Opinion

Decide whether each of these statements is fact or opinion.

1. Vietnam should not be a Communist country today.
2. The United Nations condemned North Korea for sending troops into South Korea.
3. Third World nations will never be advanced industrial nations.
4. Laos, Cambodia, and Vietnam were once the French colony of Indochina.
5. Communism is not good for China.

D. Vocabulary

Match the words with the definitions.

Words	Definitions
1. erupt	a. cruel
2. domino theory	b. united group
	c. explode suddenly
3. subtle	d. Western expansion theory
4. bloc	e. theory concerning the spread of Communism
	f. not obvious

E. Graph Skills

Use the graphs in this lesson to answer these questions.

1. Which area or areas of the world received the most U.S. foreign aid in 1950? In 1970?

2. Which area or areas of the world received increasing percentages of aids between 1950 and 1960? Between 1960 and 1970?

3. Which area or areas of the world received less aid in 1970 than in 1950?

4. What percentage of the total U.S. foreign aid did the Middle East receive in 1950? In 1960?

F. Map Skills

This map shows Asia after World War II. Certain areas are labeled with letters. Match each name below with the correct letter. There are two extra letters. Refer to the map on pages 702–703 for help.

1. Japan
2. People's Republic of China
3. Korea
4. Taiwan
5. India
6. Vietnam

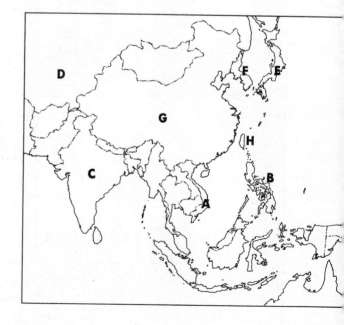

Lesson 5 Foreign Policy in the Middle East

WORDS TO UNDERSTAND
Discuss the meanings of these words.

access partition terrorism
Zionism refugee

NEW WORDS IN SENTENCES
1. Losing **access** to oil would be hard on industrial nations.
2. The movement to set up a Jewish state in Palestine was called **Zionism.**
3. After the **partition,** there were two countries instead of one.
4. Danger forced the man to leave his country and become a **refugee.**
5. **Terrorism** often involves surprise attacks and acts of violence that create fear.

AS YOU READ
As you read this selection, try to answer these questions.
1. What are the aims of American foreign policy in the Middle East?
2. How was Israel established? What problems exist between Israel and the Arab nations?
3. What was the importance of the Camp David agreement between Israel and Egypt?

THE READING SELECTION
The Middle East includes areas of land in southwestern Asia and northeastern Africa. Some of the nations within the Middle East are Libya, Egypt, Saudi Arabia, Israel, Jordan, Lebanon, Syria, Turkey, Iran, and Iraq. Judaism, Christianity, and Islam all had their beginnings in the Middle East. Today Islam is the main religion, but more than 1½ million Christians live in Lebanon. And about 3 million Jews live in Israel.

The Middle East has been important in American foreign policy since World War II for two main reasons. First, the industrial nations of the world need the oil produced in the Middle East. Second, the Middle East has been the scene of tension and conflict since the end of World War II. This conflict has at times threatened to involve both the United States and the Soviet Union.

American foreign policy in the Middle East has generally had three aims.

1. It has tried to block expansion of Soviet influence in the region.

2. It has sought to expand its own influence in the region. The United States has long had a close relationship with Israel. In recent years, the United States has also sought to improve relations with Arab nations of the region.

3. It has tried to maintain **access** to the oil produced in the Middle East.

Conflict in this region centers on the

671

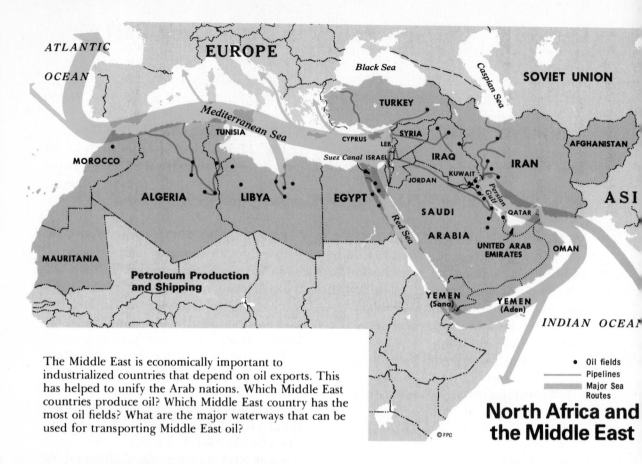

The Middle East is economically important to industrialized countries that depend on oil exports. This has helped to unify the Arab nations. Which Middle East countries produce oil? Which Middle East country has the most oil fields? What are the major waterways that can be used for transporting Middle East oil?

Legend:
- Oil fields
- Pipelines
- Major Sea Routes

North Africa and the Middle East

existence of Israel, a Jewish nation. Originally, the area was called Palestine and was shared by Jews and non-Jews. Centuries ago, most Jews were driven out. They began to return in the late 1800s, encouraged by a movement called **Zionism.** Nazi persecution of Jews in Europe in the 1930s and 1940s caused thousands of Jews to flee to Palestine.

During World War II, the Nazis killed more than 6 million Jews in special death camps. Most of the Jews left alive after the war moved from Europe. Tens of thousands went to Palestine. Arabs of the region feared the effects of Jewish immigration, and conflicts soon arose.

The United Nations proposed a **partition** of Palestine into Arab and Jewish sections. The plan went into effect in spite of Arab objections.

On May 14, 1948, the Jewish sections of Palestine became the independent state of Israel. The new state was quickly recognized by the United States and the Soviet Union. On May 15, Israel was attacked by troops from its Arab neighbors. The Arabs were defeated and lost control of their own areas. But they kept control of the city of Jerusalem. Many Arabs remained in Israel, but hundreds of thousands fled to neighboring Arab countries. At the same time thousands of Jews whose families had lived in Arab lands for centuries were forced to flee. More than 450,000 Jews left Arab lands in the years from 1948 to 1957. The great majority of these Jews settled in Israel.

Jewish **refugees** found a new home and a new life in Israel. Arab refugees were less fortunate. Most were forced to live in makeshift refugee centers in Jordan, Syria, and other Arab nations. Some Arab refugee families have lived in these camps for more than thirty years. The years of exile have made many refugees bitter. Militant groups of Palestinian refugees have organized to try regaining the lands now under Israeli control. The most powerful Arab militant group is the Palestine Liberation Organization (PLO). The PLO and other Arab groups have often used **terrorism** to oppose Israel. Often these attacks bring on counterattacks by Israel.

From 1948 until 1974, Egypt led the Arab struggle against Israel. Egypt was joined in the actual fighting by troops from Syria, Jordan, and Iraq. The Arab armies, in spite of equipment and advice from the Soviet Union, lost wars in 1956 and 1967. In 1967, Israel occupied the Golan Heights in Syria, the west bank of the Jordan River in Jordan, and the Sinai Peninsula in Egypt. Israel also took over the city of Jerusalem, a holy place for Jews, Christians, and Moslems.

In October 1973, Egypt, Syria, Iraq, and Jordan attacked Israel. The war became known as the "Yom Kippur War" because the Arab attack was launched on the Jewish High Holy Day known as Yom Kippur. The Arab armies, supplied with modern weapons by the Soviet Union,

came close to victory. But the Israeli army and air force, with the help of supplies from the United States, beat off the attacks. Israeli forces pushed across the Suez Canal, cut off a large Egyptian army group, and threatened all of Egypt. At this point the UN, with the support of the United States, established a ceasefire. A neutral area was set up east of the Nile River and in the Golan Heights region.

The American support of Israel in the war angered the Arabs. Leaders of the oil-producing Arab nations organized an oil embargo against the United States and other nations friendly to Israel. The success of the embargo encouraged the Arab nations and their allies in the Organization of Petroleum Exporting Countries (OPEC) to use oil as an economic and political weapon. The price

In a peace effort, Sadat (right) met with Israeli Prime Minister Begin to bring down the "psychological wall" between their countries.

United Press International

673

OPEC members meet regularly to decide how much oil
to sell for how much money.

of oil rose from less than $5 a barrel in
1973 to more than $35 a barrel in 1981.

Tensions between Israel and Egypt
were eased when President Anwar El-
Sadat of Egypt visited Israel in 1977. He
was the first Arab leader to visit Israel
since its formation. Soon after this visit,
the United States took an active part in
trying to settle Israeli-Egyptian differences. In 1978, President Sadat and
Prime Minister Menachem Begin of
Israel met in the United States. The
meeting was arranged by President
Jimmy Carter and was held at the presidential lodge in Pennsylvania known as
Camp David. With the help of President
Carter, a peace treaty was agreed upon
at Camp David. It seemed a great victory
for American foreign policy, but problems soon arose.

The Camp David agreement did not
win the approval of most Islamic nations.

They accused Egypt of selling out the
Palestinians. The United States was accused of favoring Israel and doing
nothing to help the Palestinians.

During the late 1970s, the United
States was involved in one crisis after
another in the Middle East. In November
1979, the American embassy in Teheran,
Iran, was seized by Iranian militants.
Americans were seized and held as hostages for more than a year. The Iranian
crisis may have led in part to President
Carter's defeat in the 1980 presidential
election. The hostages were finally set
free on the day Carter left office.

Ronald Reagan, the newly elected
president, faced new problems when
President Sadat was assassinated in October 1981. Sadat's successor, Hosni
Mubarak, pledged to continue the Sadat
policies, but the future of the Middle
East seemed more clouded than ever.

COMPREHENSION CHECK

A. Recognizing the Main Idea

1. In a single sentence, write the main idea of this lesson's reading selection.

2. Write two other points that support this main idea.

B. Selecting Important Details

Choose the ending that best completes each statement.

1. All of the following are aims of American foreign policy in the Middle East EXCEPT

    a. limiting the influence of the Soviet Union in the area.

    b. giving all of Palestine back to the Arabs.

    c. maintaining access to the petroleum of the Middle East.

    d. seeking to expand its own influence in the region.

2. Israel was created by the

    a. Six-Day War.

    b. Palestine Liberation Organization.

    c. United States.

    d. United Nations.

3. Arab nations

    a. receive no support from the Soviet Union.

    b. always accepted the existence of Israel.

    c. can use oil to influence other nations.

    d. suggested the Palestine partition plan to the UN.

4. The United States

    a. created OPEC.

    b. tries to maintain relations with both Israel and the Arab nations.

    c. has not been affected by higher oil prices.

    d. has refused to act as mediator in the Arab-Israeli conflict.

C. Completion

Fill in the word or words that best complete each sentence.

1. The _____ and other Arab groups have often used terrorism to oppose Israel.

2. Thousands of _____ are living in refugee camps.

3. The _____ proposed partition of Palestine into Arab and Jewish sections.

4. _____ is an organization that controls oil prices.

5. Israel does not want to give up the land it gained in the _____ War.

D. Vocabulary

Match the words with the definitions.

Words	Definitions
1. access	a. successful war
2. Zionism	b. homeless person
3. partition	c. movement to establish a Jewish state
4. refugee	d. use of violent scare tactics
5. terrorism	e. a way out
	f. division
	g. opportunity to use

E. Essay

Write six to eight sentences answering the following questions.

Why is oil extremely important to industrial nations? How might the importance of oil to these nations affect the future of Israel?

F. Homework

Is the Middle East still in the news? Bring in a news clipping that tells about some event in the Middle East during the past week. Be prepared to discuss the importance of that event.

G. Using Your Knowledge

What might have been the story behind each of the following headlines? Write at least thirty words about each headline.

1. PLO SAYS IT SPEAKS FOR PALESTINIANS

2. OIL EMBARGO LEADS TO LONG LINES AT GAS PUMPS

3. SADAT AND BEGIN PLEDGE NEW START AT CAMP DAVID

4. NEW PROBLEMS FOR MIDDLE EAST AFTER DEATH OF SADAT

Middle East Hopes and Perils: Camp David and Recent Crises

The world watched with hope and interest when the Camp David meeting of Egyptian and Israeli leaders opened on September 6, 1978. The meeting ended eleven days later, on September 17. During that week and a half, there were many meetings between President Sadat and Prime Minister Begin. President Carter and his secretary of state, Cyrus Vance, were also present and served as go-betweens.

The Camp David agreement set forth these main points.

1. Egypt and Israel were to sign a peace treaty in three months. Actually, the treaty was signed six months later.

2. Israel was to begin withdrawing its military forces from the Sinai Peninsula three to nine months after the treaty was signed. All Israeli troops were to be out of the Sinai two to three years after the treaty was signed. The Sinai was to become an area free of military forces.

3. Israel agreed to negotiate the future of the West Bank and Gaza areas. Israel had won these lands from Arab neighbors and was to plan their future with Egyptian, Jordanian, and Palestinian representatives. But as yet Israel has refused to deal with the PLO and regards it as a terrorist organization. The PLO, in turn, has refused even to recognize Israel's right to exist.

While Camp David promised hope, a crisis in Iran brought great dismay.

In 1951, the United States had

helped restore the ruler, or shah, of Iran to the throne. In the next twenty years, Iran became a major oil-producing nation of the Middle East. The shah used Iran's wealth to modernize the nation and its armed forces. Iran became one of the most powerful Middle East nations and a strong ally of the United States. But Iran also suffered from corruption by people close to the shah. Unrest was widespread among students, the middle class, and Islamic religious leaders.

In January 1979, the shah was overthrown and forced to flee Iran. A new government took power, led by a former exiled religious leader, the Ayatollah Khomeini. The new government was very anti-American. It blamed the United States for the many cruel acts that had been committed by the shah's police.

In November 1979, Iranian militants seized sixty-five Americans and held them as hostages in the embassy building. A rescue effort by an American military task force in April 1980 failed to free the hostages.

President Carter took economic measures to try to punish Iran. These efforts had some effect. Iran had become involved in a war with Iraq and was suffering many economic and political problems. Finally, in January 1981, an agreement between Iran and the United States led to the freeing of the hostages.

The election of Ronald Reagan as president in 1980 brought changes to American policies in the Middle East. President Reagan declared the United

Black Star

Iran's Ayatollah Khomeini is a religious leader with great political influence. He and his followers call for a strict obedience to the laws of Islam.

States would never again permit Americans to be held hostage. He followed his stern warning with a request that Congress increase spending for the armed forces. At the same time President Reagan set out to win allies in the Arab world. As part of this new policy, the United States criticized the Israelis for bombing a nuclear reactor in Iraq in 1981. Soon after, the United States supported the UN in condemning the Israelis for bombing a civilian area of Beirut, Lebanon. And, over strong Israeli protest, the United States agreed to sell several billion dollars worth of American military equipment to Saudi Arabia.

Lesson 6   Foreign Policy in Africa

WORDS TO UNDERSTAND
Discuss the meanings of these words.

apartheid   **reluctant**

NEW WORDS IN SENTENCES
1. The policy of **apartheid** (pronounced ə-pär′-tāt), or strict segregation of the races, has been strongly criticized.
2. Most rulers are **reluctant** to give up power.

AS YOU READ
As you read this selection, try to answer these questions.
1. Why is Africa important to the industrial nations of the world?
2. How have the activities of the Soviet Union and Cuba affected events in Africa?
3. How does the African policy of President Reagan differ from the policy of President Carter?

THE READING SELECTION
The African continent is divided by the great Sahara Desert. The lands above the Sahara are known as North Africa. The Islamic religion and the Arab culture are accepted by nearly all the people of North Africa. North Africa is linked more often with the Middle East than with areas south of the Sahara.

Most of Africa lies south of the Sahara and is called sub-Saharan Africa. The lands directly south of the Sahara were long known as the Sudan. The name comes from the Arabic words *bilad al sudan,* or "land of the black people." Sub-Saharan Africa is mainly linked to the cultures and religious beliefs of black Africa. However, the Islamic religion is an important force in some parts of sub-Saharan Africa.

Before 1945, almost all of Africa was held or controlled by European nations. Great Britain, France, Italy, and Portugal were the colonial powers in Africa. Germany had lost its African colonies in World War I (1914–1918). World War I had also set in motion a sense of nationalism in Africa. World War II (1939–1945) brought a full-blown spirit of nationalism to all of Africa. The United States, and the newly created United Nations, supported the African nationalist movement. It resulted in independence for almost all of Africa.

Africa has become important economically and politically to the United States. Africa's economic importance is a result

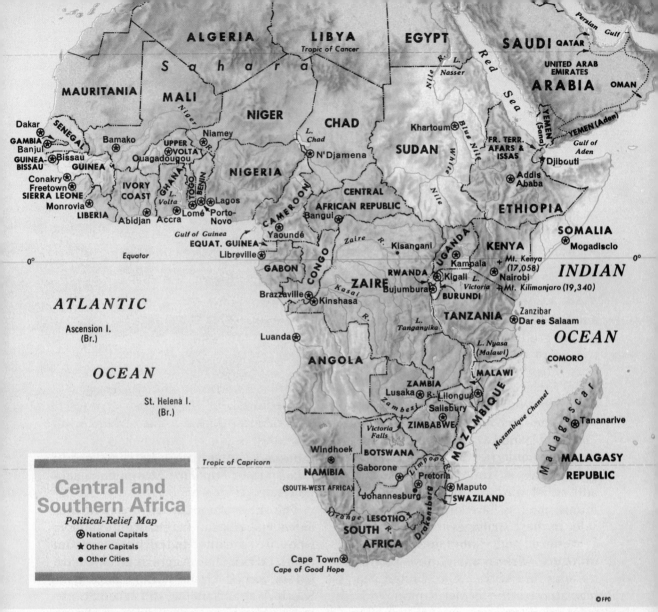

The Sahara Desert separates Northern Africa—often considered part of the Mideast—from Central-Southern Africa.

of its great natural resources. These resources are important to many industrialized nations. The United States, the Soviet Union, and most of Europe import African raw materials for their industries. Africa supplies most of the world's industrial diamonds. It is an important source of copper ore, gold, iron,

oil, and other minerals. Africa also is a large market for the industrial products of other nations.

Africa's political importance has grown since World War II. More than forty new African nations have replaced the colonies once held by European powers. The African nations in the UN have joined with Middle Eastern, Asian, and Latin American nations to form a powerful Third World voting group.

In most sub-Saharan African nations, black people are now black-ruled. Independence and nationalism in many of these countries have been linked to anti-colonialism. Many new African nations dislike any form of foreign influence, which they associate with colonialism. African feelings have sometimes made relations between the United States and African governments more difficult.

African nationals often face the problem of unifying very different and hostile groups. Many new African countries were formed with old colonial borders. These borders were often different from tribal or geographic zones. Thus, opposing groups often find themselves within the same country. Kenya, Angola, Zaire, Uganda, Tanzania, Rwanda, Burundi, and the Central African Republic have all suffered from civil war and tribal warfare. Western and Communist nations have supported different sides in these struggles for power.

Western and Communist efforts to influence African affairs have produced tensions in Africa. The United States has accused the Soviet Union and its allies of interfering in African affairs. Both the United States and the Soviet Union have given economic and military aid to some African nations. The pro-Communist government of Cuba has been especially active in Africa. Cuban troops have helped establish friendly African governments in Ethiopia and Angola. The presence of Cuban troops in Africa has been severely criticized by the United States. In Angola, several

Dwight W. Follett

thousand Cuban troops helped a group called the Popular Movement gain power.

The new Angolan government has aided guerrillas in neighboring Namibia who are seeking independence from South Africa. The Angolan actions have led to armed clashes with troops from South Africa. Namibia, still called South-West Africa by the white-led South African government, was a German colony before 1914. After World War I, it was put under the control of South Africa, which was then a British colony. South Africa became an independent nation in 1961, controlled by a white minority. It kept control over the Namibian area in spite of efforts by the UN to establish an independent Namibia. Black Namibians seeking inde-

Africa has retained many of its customs and traditions while making rapid progress. The modern face of Africa is shown at left. The Cocoa Tower in Nigeria (left) is a symbol of the continent's growing commerce and agriculture. Yet in some ways, Africa has remained the same. Outdoor marketplaces (above) are still popular and are often the center of activity in villages. And while Africa's famous animal population has decreased, it is now protected.

pendence have been aided by Cuba and the Soviet Union as well as by Angola.

In spite of many existing tensions, the African nations have tried to develop unity. The Organization of African Unity (OAU) was founded in 1963. It seeks to bring together African nations and advance their interests. One area in which black African nations are strongly united is their opposition to the Republic of South Africa. That nation, led by a white minority, is viewed as an enemy of black Africa.

South Africa, and its northern neighbor, Rhodesia, were British colonies until the 1960s. Black people, the majority of the population, had few rights in both white-ruled colonies. South Africa became an independent republic in 1961, and Rhodesia declared its independence in 1965. Great Britain protested that the action by the white Rhodesian minority was illegal. However, neither Britain nor the UN was able to stop the action of the Rhodesians.

The new South African and Rhodesian governments took steps to keep control in the hands of the white minority. The United States often expressed its disapproval of actions by South Africa and Rhodesia. American protests had little effect. But conditions in Rhodesia were finally changed as a result of guerrilla activity by black nationalists. Several thousand people died in the fighting before a cease-fire was arranged. An election was held in which black people were given the full right to vote. The result was the election of a black majority in the parliament of Rhodesia. The new government dropped the name Rhodesia and chose the name Zimbabwe. Zim-

babwe was the name of a black African kingdom of the area in the 1400s.

The establishment of a black-led government in Rhodesia left only South Africa with a white minority government. South Africa took harsh measures against guerrilla groups in its own borders and in nearby Namibia. The South African government also continued to maintain its policy of **apartheid,** or segregation of the races. The United States has been under great pressure to oppose South Africa's government. But some Americans have been **reluctant** to interfere in what they see as a South African domestic civil rights issue.

During President Jimmy Carter's term of office (1977 – 1981), the United States often protested South Africa's racist policies. These protests were in line with President Carter's stress on human rights. The election of President Ronald Reagan in 1980 brought a change in American policies in Africa. President Reagan has put the main stress upon the dangers of communism in Africa and other parts of the world. As a result, the United States has softened its attitude toward South Africa.

COMPREHENSION CHECK

A. *Recognizing the Main Idea*

1. In a single sentence, write the main idea of this lesson's reading selection.

2. Write two other points that support this main idea.

B. *Selecting Important Details*

Choose the ending that best completes each statement.

1. The European colonial nations in Africa after World War I were
   a. Britain and Germany.
   b. Britain, France, Italy, and Portugal.
   c. Germany and France.
   d. Portugal and Germany.

2. African nationalism
   a. led to European colonization.
   b. prevents acceptance of aid from other countries.
   c. led to the independence of many African nations.
   d. has kept African nations out of the United Nations.

3. Various African nations have received economic and military aid
   a. from the UN.
   b. from neither the Soviet Union nor the United States.
   c. from both the United States and the Soviet Union.
   d. from South Africa.

4. **Apartheid** is a policy followed today in
   a. most of Africa.
   b. Zimbabwe.
   c. Angola.
   d. South Africa.

C. *True or False*

Decide whether each of these statements is true or false.

1. Most of Africa is still under colonial control.

2. Most of the people in South Africa are black.

3. Election in Rhodesia resulted in a white majority in parliament.

4. President Reagan does not see a danger of communism in Africa.

5. Most sub-Saharan nations today are ruled by black people.

D. *Vocabulary*

Use a word from this list to complete each sentence.

apartheid   access   reluctant

1. Many people are _____ to change old ways of doing things.

2. Black and white people do not mix at all in African countries that have _____ policies.

E. *Essay*

Write three or four sentences arguing in favor of the following statement and three or four sentences arguing against it.

The United States should take a strong stand against governments that do not allow people civil rights.

Use the map in this lesson to answer these questions.

1. This nation lies on the coast of the Atlantic Ocean. Its neighbors are Guinea, the Ivory Coast, and Sierra Leone. It was established for former slaves from the United States who wanted to return to Africa. What is its name?

2. This nation, with a capital named Lagos, is in the western part of Africa. It has the largest population of all African nations and is a leading oil producer. What is its name?

3. This nation borders both Lake Victoria and the Indian Ocean. Its capital is Dar es Salaam. Africa's highest mountain, Kilimanjaro, and one of its most famous wild animal preserves, Serengeti National Park, are in this country. What is it?

4. This nation lies between Rhodesia and Zaire. It has always been black ruled. Once called Northern Rhodesia, it opposed unification with what was then called Southern Rhodesia, a white-ruled country. What is this nation's name now?

Black Americans and African Policy

In the 1930s, Countee Cullen, a black American poet, wrote a poem called "Heritage" about Africa. He tried to determine what ties remained between himself and the land his people had originally come from.

> *One three centuries removed*
> *From the scenes his fathers loved,*
> *Spicy grove, cinnamon tree,*
> *What is Africa to me?*

This question has become more and more important to American blacks. When Africans were brought to America as slaves several hundred years ago, they were forced to break many of the ties to their native land. For example, their African names were immediately replaced with European ones. They were expected to speak European languages and adopt the Christian religion. After a few generations, Africa seemed far away. In fact, James Baldwin, another black writer, has argued that American blacks are now totally different from Africans.

Yet links between black Americans and Africa have grown stronger during this century. The first of several Pan-African congresses was held in 1919. These meetings brought together delegates from Africa and America. In the 1920s, a "back to Africa" movement became popular for a time in the United States.

The success of African nationalism after World War II increased the interest of black Americans in the

Demonstrations such as this one in Nashville, Tennessee, protest discrimination practices in South Africa. Several sports associations, including the Olympics, have expelled South Africa.

continent. Delegates to the UN from the newly independent nations were often asked to speak in black communities. Books on Africa and the black heritage became big sellers. Some black Americans adopted African clothing. African languages, art, and culture were studied by many.

White minority rule in African countries reminds many black Americans of the slavery under which their people lived in the United States. The black community in this nation has strongly supported the causes of blacks in Rhodesia, South Africa, and Namibia, where whites still rule. The Congressional Black Caucus has often voiced its position to the press and the president. In recent years, other black leaders have toured Africa and called for a strong United States policy against white rule. There have been pro-Africa demonstrations to emphasize these views.

How much has all this really affected American foreign policy in Africa? That is hard to measure. But it is probable that black Americans have influenced the United States stand against white rule in Africa.

Lesson 7   Foreign Policy in the Western Hemisphere

WORDS TO UNDERSTAND

Discuss the meanings of these words.

stability   **multilateral**   **regimes**

NEW WORDS IN SENTENCES

1. The government does not undergo violent changes when there is **stability** in the country.
2. The **multilateral** agreement called for action by many nations.
3. **Regimes** did not last long because new people kept taking over the government.

AS YOU READ

As you read this selection, try to answer these questions.

1. How has the United States foreign policy in the Western Hemisphere caused resentment?
2. What has the United States done to improve relations with Latin America?
3. What have been the major events in United States relations with Cuba?

THE READING SELECTION

American foreign policy in the Western Hemisphere dates back to the Monroe Doctrine in 1823. For many years, the United States took on a major role in the hemisphere. It often interfered with the affairs of other American nations in order to protect its own interests.

In more recent times, the United States has changed its policy. Its aim has been to build good relationships with its neighbors. A first step was the Good Neighbor policy of the 1930s. Current foreign policy in the Western Hemisphere has two purposes.

1. The United States wants to protect its borders and security at home. This is part of foreign policy in any region, but it is especially important in our nation's own hemisphere.
2. The United States wants to encourage peace, **stability,** democracy, and well-being in other nations of the Western Hemisphere. Our nation is concerned about economic growth in the area and about the spread of communism.

Since World War II, the United States has proposed making the Monroe Doctrine a **multilateral** doctrine. Thus, all countries in the Western Hemisphere would be responsible for enforcing it. In 1948, the United States and Latin American nations established the Organization of American States (OAS). OAS members are pledged to aid one

Latin American cities—old and new. A village in Bolivia (left) is built on a hillside along the Andes. Modern Rio de Janeiro (above) is one of the most beautiful cities in the world.

another in defense and to solve their own problems peacefully. The OAS is the main source of multilateral action on the Monroe Doctrine.

In 1961, the United States proposed an "Alliance for Progress." This program is designed to support economic and social improvements in Latin American nations. It is supported by the OAS, which also oversees many of its activities. The alliance has had some success, but not enough. Many Latin American nations continue to have economic and social problems and have moved away from democracy. The United States has often criticized Latin American governments for not respecting human rights. Since 1981, the Reagan administration has softened this criticism. Today the United States places

687

its main stress upon the importance of strong, anti-Communist governments in Latin America.

There have also been important changes in the relations between the United States and Mexico. The illegal entry of thousands of Mexicans into the United States has long been a problem. Many Mexican people enter illegally in order to find work or become permanent residents. Efforts to find these illegal immigrants and deport them have caused bad feelings in the past. Today, the United States and Mexico are working out arrangements for temporary work permits and citizenship for longtime residents.

One of the main problems of United States policy in Latin America has been relations with Cuba. In 1950, a revolution overthrew the existing dictator. The leader of the revolt, Fidel Castro, established the first Communist government in the Americas. Thousands of Cubans who opposed Castro emigrated to the United States.

The United States was worried about a Communist government ninety miles from its own shores. It imposed a trade embargo against Cuba. But since Cuba was receiving aid from other Communist nations, the embargo did not work.

Cuba was the center of two crises in the 1960s. A 1961 invasion of Cuba by anti-Castro Cubans was quietly supported by the United States, but it failed. American support of the invasion led to a worsening of Cuban-American relations. Then, in 1962, the United States discovered that the Soviet Union had set up long-range missiles in Cuba. The United States demanded the removal of the missiles. After several tense days, the Soviet Union withdrew the missiles, and tensions were eased.

Relations with Cuba improved slightly in the late 1970s. In late 1977, each nation established "interest offices" in the other. This was a step toward full diplomatic relations. President Castro argued that complete removal of the embargo was necessary for full relations. Presi-

The UN Security Council met in an emergency session on the Cuban missile crisis. Here, U.S. Ambassador to the UN Adlai Stevenson questions Soviet delegate Valerian Zorin on the placement of Soviet missiles in Cuba.

Wide World

UNITED STATES

President John F. Kennedy was in a showdown with Soviet Premier Nikita Khrushchev and Cuban Prime Minister Fidel Castro in the Cuban missile crisis. What is reflected by the size of the characters in the cartoon? What stereotypes can you see in the cartoon?

dent Carter claimed that improving human rights in Cuba was also necessary. He also protested the presence of Cuban troops in Africa. Cuban troop involvement in several African nations, including Ethiopia and Angola, continues to strain the relations between Cuba and the United States.

Human rights were a major concern of the Carter administration's policy in Latin America. Previously the United States had supported many military **regimes** in Latin America as long as they were anti-Communist. The Carter administration sought to stress democracy rather than anti-communism. In this way, it hoped to encourage governments in Latin America to become more democratic. The Reagan administration has generally avoided criticism of anti-Communist governments in Latin America.

An important part of the new United States policy in Latin America concerns the Panama Canal. The canal was built in the early 1900s by the United States. Under a treaty with the new nation of Panama, land for the canal was leased to the U.S. However, Panamanians and other Latin Americans resented United States presence in the area. In 1977, two new treaties to change canal ownership were signed by Panama and the United States. These treaties will turn about half of the Canal Zone over to Panama. The United States will operate the canal until the year 2000, but Panama will get a share of the revenues from it. Along with the canal treaties went a separate agreement by which the United States will provide loans and credits to Panama. The U.S. Senate approved these treaties in March and April 1978.

COMPREHENSION CHECK

A. *Recognizing the Main Idea*

1. In a single sentence, write the main idea of this lesson's reading selection.

2. Write two other points that support this main idea.

B. *Selecting Important Details*

Choose the ending that best completes each statement.

1. The United States has tried to improve relations with Latin America through all of the following EXCEPT the
   a. Good Neighbor policy.
   b. support for the Cuban invasion.
   c. Alliance for Progress.
   d. Organization of American States.

2. The Reagan administration has stressed the importance of
   a. human rights and democracy in Latin America.
   b. social improvements in Latin America.
   c. anti-communism in Latin America.
   d. all of the above.

3. Long-range missiles were set up in Cuba in 1962 by
   a. the United States.
   b. the OAS.
   c. the Soviet Union.
   d. Mexico.

4. The Panama Canal
   a. increased the popularity of the United States in Latin America.
   b. was built by Panama.
   c. was built on land originally part of the United States.
   d. was built by the United States on land leased from Panama.

C. *True or False*

Decide whether each of these statements is true or false. Rewrite the false statements so that they are true.

1. The Organization of American States does not include the United States.

2. Fidel Castro is head of the government in Panama.

3. Illegal immigration is a problem in United States relations with Mexico.

4. OAS members are pledged to aid one another in defense.

5. Alliance for Progress is mainly a form of military alliance.

D. *Vocabulary*

Use a word from this list to complete each sentence.

multilateral	stability
regime	propaganda
bloc	

1. The new _____ tried to make improvements in the country.

2. Action by one nation would not be as effective as _____ action.

3. The crisis threatened the _____ of the country's government.

E. *Ask Yourself*

Why does the United States worry about the possible spread of communism in Latin America?

F. *Homework*

Use the library or newspapers and magazines to find information on some topic related to Latin America. Write an essay of at least fifty words on the topic you have chosen.

Lesson 8   The United States and World Peace

WORDS TO UNDERSTAND

Discuss the meanings of these words.

nuclear   **ballistic missile**
radioactive fallout

NEW WORDS IN SENTENCES

1. The use of **nuclear** weapons could destroy much of the world.

2. Atomic explosions put tiny particles called **radioactive fallout** into the air.

3. A **ballistic missile** does not need a pilot to carry bombs to the target.

AS YOU READ

As you read this selection, try to answer these questions.

1. How have modern weapons increased the costs of war?

2. What actions have been taken by the United States and the Soviet Union to try to reduce the threat of nuclear war?

3. How involved should the United States become in regional wars?

THE READING SELECTION

The United States has been involved in four wars since 1917. World War I (1917–1918) and World War II (1941–1945) were wars declared by Congress. The wars in Korea (1950–1953) and Vietnam (1964–1973) were undeclared. American troops were in Korea and Vietnam under the orders of the president of the United States.

Wars are costly in terms of both human lives and money. American casualties in these four wars amounted to more than 630,000 dead and 1,280,000 wounded. Since 1917, more than 764 billion dollars has been spent on war. These heavy financial costs have contributed to our national debt and inflation.

The dangers of war today are greater than ever before. **Nuclear,** or atomic, weapons can kill tens of millions of people. Modern warfare can even affect nations other than those at war. People thousands of miles away from the attack area may still be in danger from the **radioactive fallout,** poison gases, or deadly germs that are part of modern weapons systems.

In 1945, the United States was the only nation able to make the nuclear bomb. But American scientists knew it would not be long before other countries developed nuclear weapons. Many felt that some system of international control was needed to prevent a race for atomic supremacy.

In 1946, the United States offered the Baruch Plan to the United Nations. The Baruch Plan proposed disarmament and the control of nuclear materials. The Soviet Union offered a different plan, also calling for disarmament. The nations could not agree on international inspection. Therefore, no treaty was signed.

By 1949, the Soviet Union had developed its own nuclear bomb. It was followed by Great Britain, France, the People's Republic of China, and India.

By 1960, the United States and the Soviet Union had tested more powerful hydrogen bombs. One of the huge hydrogen bombs developed in 1961 was 3,000 times more powerful than the first atom bomb. Hydrogen bombs produced great amounts of dangerous radioactive fallout during testing. The threat of hydrogen bombs led to the Nuclear Test Ban Treaty, signed in 1963 by the Soviet Union, Great Britain, and the United States. To reduce the danger of fallout, this treaty allowed only underground testing.

As nations developed systems for dropping nuclear bombs on targets, new threats to peace arose. A number of **ballistic missile** systems were developed. These used rocket missiles to carry nuclear bombs. The main ballistic systems belonged to the United States and the Soviet Union. Both nations also developed an anti-ballistic missile (ABM) system. The ABM system sought to destroy enemy ballistic missiles before they hit their targets. Other systems were then developed to destroy the ABM weapons. The cycle seemed endless. Finally, in the 1970s, the United States and the Soviet Union held talks (SALT) to limit the use of ABMs and offensive weapons. This has helped to ease the arms race. Of course, improving relations between Western and Communist nations also helps ease tension that might lead to wars.

One possible trouble area that remains, however, is that of wars between smaller nations. These nations may not have nuclear arms, but larger nations that do could be drawn into their wars. The United States and other nations oppose the extension of nuclear arms to most smaller nations. But the actual role of the United States — and the Soviet Union — in many of these regional wars remains in question.

For example, by 1973, most Americans felt that our involvement in Vietnam was too great. In 1977, the United States did not become involved in a civil war in Angola, an African nation. The U.S. argued that no outsiders ought to be involved. But at the same time, Americans are continuing to try to mediate between Arab nations and Israel. Do we want to try to prevent wars by becoming involved ourselves? What kinds of risks are we taking when we do this? Is political involvement, such as mediation, "safe," and military involvement "unsafe"? How much involvement is too much? On the other hand, can we return to isolationism and not involve ourselves in regional disputes? These are questions that need to be answered as we develop a definite policy on involvement.

One other question relating to world peace is the role of the United Nations. Many people claim that the UN is not effective, that it really has no role in preserving peace. If this is true, then what can be done to strengthen the UN? Is there a likely replacement for it?

The issues surrounding world peace and the role of the United States in preserving it are complex. The answers are not easy. But these questions are certainly ones to which we need answers.

COMPREHENSION CHECK

A. Recognizing the Main Idea
1. In a single sentence, write the main idea of this lesson's reading selection.
2. Write two other points that support this main idea.

B. Selecting Important Details
Choose the ending that best completes each statement.
1. The Baruch Plan
   a. was proposed by the Soviet Union to encourage ABMs.
   b. proposed extension of nuclear arms to small countries.
   c. called for disarmament and the control of nuclear materials.
   d. was proposed by the United Nations to end the war in the Middle East.
2. The Nuclear Test Ban Treaty
   a. was not signed by the United States.
   b. bans all testing of nuclear bombs.
   c. was intended to limit the development of ballistic missiles.
   d. allows underground testing of nuclear bombs.
3. The SALT agreements deal with
   a. limits on ballistic missile systems.
   b. limits on involvement of the United States in regional wars.
   c. Vietnam and Angola.
   d. underground testing of ballistic missile systems.
4. Nuclear weapons
   a. will always be limited to a few big countries.
   b. can be made only in the United States and the Soviet Union.
   c. cannot kill many people.
   d. make modern warfare different from wars of the past.

C. True or False
Decide whether each of these statements is true or false. Rewrite the false statements so that they are true.
1. American scientists thought it would be a long time before other nations developed nuclear weapons.
2. The Soviet Union offered a plan calling for disarmament in the 1940s.
3. One hydrogen bomb that was developed was 3,000 times more powerful than the first atomic bomb.
4. The United States and the Soviet Union never get involved in the wars of small nations.
5. Some people feel that the United Nations is not strong enough to preserve peace.

D. Vocabulary
Write your own sentence for each of these terms.

nuclear   ballistic missile
radioactive fallout

E. Essay

Write about seventy-five words answering these questions.

Should the United States be involved at all in disputes between other nations? What kind of involvement is best? How do we decide when to limit such involvement?

F. Chronology

Arrange these events in the order in which they happened.
1. Nuclear Test Ban Treaty
2. New Panama Canal treaties written
3. Israel established
4. American troops withdrawn from Vietnam
5. Truman Doctrine
6. Korean War

Puerto Rico

Puerto Rico is an island about 900 miles southeast of Florida. Spanish is the main language of the island, although many people also speak English. The island's population is descended from a mixture of Spanish, Indian, and African peoples. Puerto Rico is part of the United States. The people of Puerto Rico are United States citizens.

Puerto Rico was a Spanish colony for over 350 years. After the Spanish-American War in 1898, Spain ceded the island to the United States under the terms of the peace treaty. Congress set up a government in the new territory, with a governor appointed by the president. In 1917, Puerto Ricans became citizens of the United States. The people of Puerto Rico elected their own governor in 1948. Four years later, Puerto Rico adopted a constitution and became a self-governing commonwealth of the United States.

As a commonwealth, the island has a special relationship with the rest of the United States. It has special trade and tax arrangements that encourage economic growth. The people of Puerto Rico govern themselves. They cannot vote for the president while iiving on the island. But the people of the island elect a non-voting representative to Congress.

Puerto Rico is a crowded island with a rapidly growing population. Many people have been moving from rural areas to urban centers. A large

Columbus claimed Puerto Rico for Spain in 1493. In English
the name means rich port, referring to San Juan (above).

number of Puerto Ricans moved from the island to New York and other mainland cities, especially after World War II. They were looking for better economic opportunities. But many Puerto Ricans on the mainland have had problems dealing with language and culture differences, discrimination, and the lack of jobs. The number of people moving to the mainland dropped off after the early 1950s as economic conditions improved on the island.

During the last thirty years, Puerto Rico has made great gains in industry, agriculture, and education. There is a growing controversy over the status of the island. Some Puerto Ricans want the island to remain a commonwealth of the United States. They believe that the present relationship with the United States government is beneficial. Others want the island to become a state so that it will have the same rights and powers as other states. A rising nationalist movement wants the island to become an independent country. This movement is supported by people who value the separate cultural and economic identity of Puerto Rico. In 1967, a majority of Puerto Ricans voted to remain a commonwealth. The future of Puerto Rico will be determined by its people.

Unit 13 Summary Superpower: Foreign Policy Since 1945

The End of World War II

The Second World War brought death and destruction to many nations. Between 30 and 60 million soldiers and civilians lost their lives. Millions of them died in concentration camps. The destruction of farms, cities, transportation, and industry brought economic chaos. The war also had some lasting political effects.

The Soviet Union and the United States became the leading world powers. They often came into conflict over the spread of communism, especially in developing areas of the world.

The war also made it clear that isolationism could no longer be a part of American foreign policy. The United States helped found the United Nations to help nations work together. The UN is more successful than the earlier League of Nations. Its membership is larger and its powers are greater.

Relations with Europe

After 1945, the Soviet Union established Communist governments in the areas it occupied. The United States formed a policy of containment of such expansion. Under the Marshall Plan, it sent aid to rebuild Europe. Western military and economic cooperation were encouraged through NATO and the EEC.

The 1950s and 1960s saw a cold war between the Communist and Western nations. However, relations began to improve in the 1970s. There was increased cooperation, though arms limitation and human rights remained serious issues.

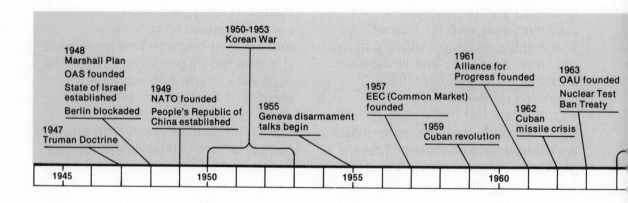

1947
Truman Doctrine

1948
Marshall Plan
OAS founded
State of Israel established
Berlin blockaded

1949
NATO founded
People's Republic of China established

1950-1953
Korean War

1955
Geneva disarmament talks begin

1957
EEC (Common Market) founded

1959
Cuban revolution

1961
Alliance for Progress founded

1962
Cuban missile crisis

1963
OAU founded
Nuclear Test Ban Treaty

1945 1950 1955 1960

Relations with the Third World

The Third World has received more attention from the United States since World War II. The developing nations in these areas are now an important voting bloc in the UN. Many of these countries also control important natural resources. The United States has opposed communism in all of these areas. It has also increased its foreign aid in order to help these nations develop.

In Asia, Japan has been the strongest ally of the United States since World War II. The United States has only recently begun to establish normal relations with Communist China. In the 1950s and 1960s, the United States fought wars against communism in Korea and Vietnam. It is now trying to prevent neutral nations from becoming Communist.

In the Middle East, the United States has supported the Jewish state of Israel since 1948. However, it also has a great need for oil produced by the Arab nations. Recently, it has tried to balance these aims by mediating the conflict between Israel and its neighbors.

In Africa, the United States has tried to establish good relations with the many black nations that have become independent since World War II. However, the white minority government in South Africa has been a problem for American foreign policy. The United States is under pressure to oppose such minority rule.

In the Western Hemisphere, the United States is changing its policies. Its main goal until recently has been the protection of its own security. Now, it is balancing this goal with that of treating other nations in the region as equals. It is trying to reduce conflict with Communist Cuba. Multilateral cooperation has been encouraged through the OAS and the Alliance for Progress.

World Peace

Maintaining world peace is both more important and more difficult than ever before. Modern weapons make war more dangerous. The United States has been involved in efforts to control nuclear weapons and other arms. The American role in disagreements between other nations can be an important factor in world peace.

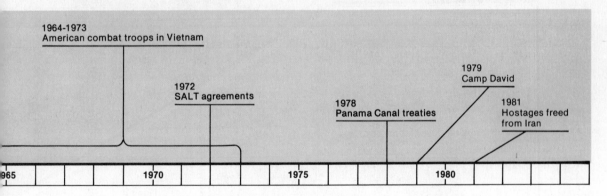

1964-1973
American combat troops in Vietnam

1972
SALT agreements

1978
Panama Canal treaties

1979
Camp David

1981
Hostages freed from Iran

965   1970   1975   1980

PACIFIC OCEAN

135°　130°　125°　120°　115°　110°　105°

50°　49°　45°

BRITISH COLUMBIA
Cape Flattery
Vancouver Island
Vancouver
Calgary

ALBERTA
Regina

CANADA
SASKATCHEWAN

Tacoma
Seattle
Spokane
Olympia
WASHINGTON
Mt. Rainier (14,410 ft.)
Columbia
Snake
Columbia Plateau

Great Falls
Fort Peck
Missouri River
Reservoir
Yellowstone River
NORTH

Willamette R.
Portland
Salem
Cascade R.
Columbia R.
OREGON

Helena
Butte
MONTANA
Bitterroot Range
Billings
Billings

Boise
IDAHO
Snake River
Pocatello
WYOMING

Rapid City
Black Hills
SOUTH

Coast Ranges
Sierra Nevada
Sacramento R.
Central
Humboldt River
Reno
Carson City
NEVADA
Great Basin
Great Salt Lake
Salt Lake City
Ogden
Provo
UTAH

Casper
Laramie
Cheyenne
NE

Great Plains

Sacramento
San Francisco
Oakland
CALIFORNIA
San Joaquin Valley
Fresno
Coast Ranges
Mt. Whitney (14,495)
Death Valley

Denver
Pikes Peak (14,110)
Colorado Springs
Pueblo
COLORADO
Arkansas R.

Point Conception

Las Vegas
Lake Mead
Grand Canyon
Colorado
Colorado
Plateau
Wasatch Mts.

Mohave Desert
Salton Sea
Colorado River
ARIZONA
Gila R.
NEW MEXICO
Sangre de Cristo Mts.
Santa Fe
Albuquerque
Canadian River
Amaril

Los Angeles
Long Beach
San Diego
Mexicali
Phoenix
Salt R.
Roswell
Pecos River

Tucson
El Paso
Ciudad Juárez
MEXICO
Rio Grande
San

698

120°　115°

ARCTIC OCEAN
70°　170°　160°　150°　140°　70°　130°

SOVIET UNION
Bering Strait
65°
Brooks Range
Arctic Circle
River
66½°　65°

Seward Pen.
Nome
ALASKA
CANADA

Bering Sea
Yukon
Fairbanks
Tanana
Alaska Range
Mt. McKinley (20,320)

Pribilof Islands
Anchorage
Mt. St. Elias (18,008)
Juneau

Aleutian Range
Kodiak Island
Gulf of Alaska
SCALE
Ketchikan

55°
Aleutian Is.
Alaska Peninsula
PACIFIC OCEAN

Miles
0　100　200　300　400　500
Kilometers
0　200　400　600　800
One inch—about 470 miles

160°　150°　140°

160°　158°　156°

Kauai
22°
Oahu
Honolulu
Molokai
Maui
HAWAII

PACIFIC OCEAN
20°
Hawaii
Hilo

SAME SCALE AS MAIN MAP
160°　158°　156°

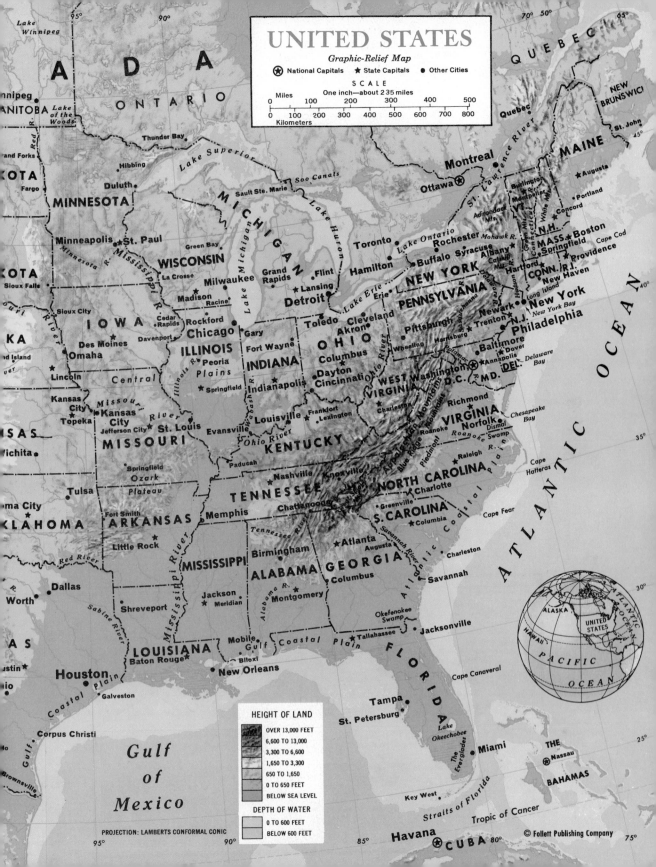

UNITED STATES

Graphic-Relief Map

⊛ National Capitals ★ State Capitals ● Other Cities

SCALE
One inch—about 235 miles

Miles 0   100   200   300   400   500
Kilometers 0 100 200 300 400 500 600 700 800

HEIGHT OF LAND

OVER 13,000 FEET
6,600 TO 13,000
3,300 TO 6,600
1,650 TO 3,300
650 TO 1,650
0 TO 650 FEET
BELOW SEA LEVEL

DEPTH OF WATER

0 TO 600 FEET
BELOW 600 FEET

PROJECTION: LAMBERTS CONFORMAL CONIC

© Follett Publishing Company

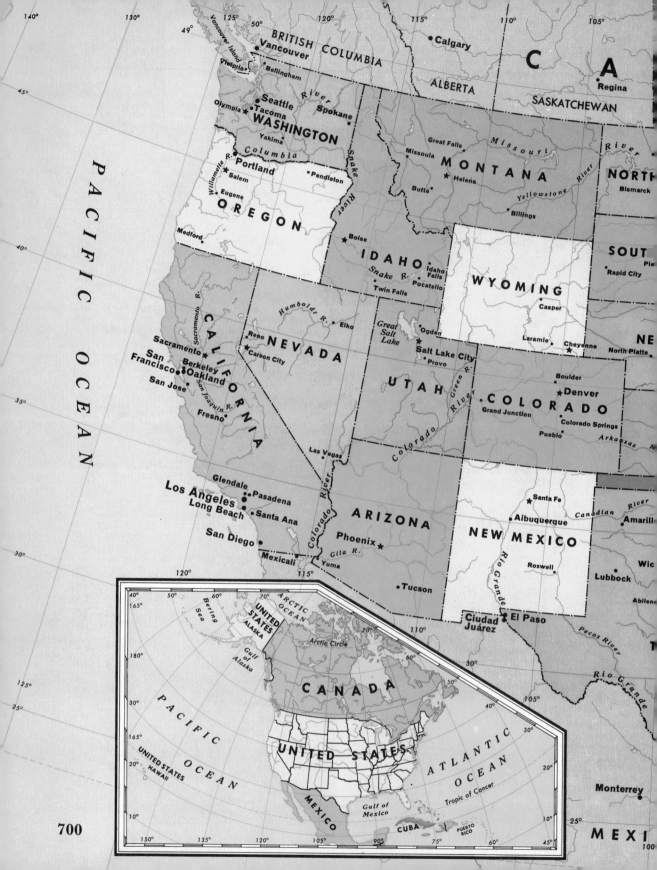

The World
Political Map

⊛ National Capitals
★ Other Capitals • Other Cities

SCALE
One inch–about 1660 Miles

Miles
0 500 1000   2000   3000   4000   5000
0   2000   4000   6000   8000
Kilometers

Projection Modified Van Der Grinten

ARCTIC OCEAN

Franz Josef Land

Svalbard
Spitsbergen
(Nor.)

Severnaya
Zemlya

Laptev
Sea

New Siberian
Islands

East Siberian
Sea

International Date Line

Barents
Sea

Kara
Sea

Novaya Zemlya

North Cope

Wrangel I.

U.S.S.R.
ALASKA
Bering Strait

Murmansk

Nome

St. Lawrence I.

Arctic Circle

UNION OF SOVIET

Archangel

Ob

Yenisei

Lena
River

Kolyma

Bering Sea

Pribilof
Islands

SWEDEN
FINLAND

SOCIALIST REPUBLICS

River

Kamchatka Peninsula

Sea of
Okhotsk

Aleutian Islands

Helsinki

L. Ladoga
Leningrad

Gorki
Sverdlovsk

Omsk

Novosibirsk

Irkutsk

Lake
Baikal

Amur
River

Khabarovsk

Sakhalin

Kuril Islands

NORTH

Stockholm

Riga

Moscow

Chelyabinsk

A S I A

Sea of
Japan

Hokkaido

Baltic

POLAND

Kharkov

Kiev

Saratov

Karaganda

Lake
Balkhash

MONGOLIAN
REPUBLIC

Ulan Bator

Mukden

Vladivostok

N. KOREA

Honshu

JAPAN

CZECH.
AUST.

E U R O P E

Warsaw

Volgograd

Rostov

Astrakhan

Aral
Sea

Tashkent

Peking
Tientsin

Seoul

S. KOREA

Nagoya

Tokyo

PACIFIC

HUNG.
RUM.
YUGO.
BULG.
ALB.
GREECE

Odessa

Black Sea

Istanbul

Ankara

TURKEY

Tbilisi
Caspian Sea
Baku

Amu Darya
Syr Darya

Kashgar

CHINA

Ho

Hwang

Yangtze

Nanking

Shanghai

Wuhan

Osaka
Yokohama
Kyushu

Bonin Islands
(Japan)

Sicily
Crete
Athens
CYPRUS
Mediterranean Sea
LEB.
ISR.
SYRIA
Benghazi
Alexandria
Cairo

Tehran

IRAN

AFGHANISTAN

Kabul
Islamabad
Lahore

KASHMIR

TIBET

Lhasa

NEPAL

Delhi

BHUTAN

Klang

Chungking

Canton

East
China
Sea

MACAO
(Port.)

HONG
KONG
(Br.)

TAIWAN
(Formosa)

Ryukyu Is.

Tropic of Cancer

OCEAN

LIBYA

EGYPT

JORDAN
IRAQ

Baghdad

KUWAIT
QATAR

Persian Gulf

U.A.E.

Riyadh

SAUDI

Mecca

OMAN

PAKISTAN

Karachi

New
Delhi

Ganges

INDIA

BURMA

Rangoon

LAOS

Hanoi

South
China
Sea

VIETNAM

Luzon

Quezon City

Manila

PHILIPPINES

Mindanao

Mariana
Islands

Guam
(U.S.)

Wake Island
(U.S.)

Marshall
Islands

Bombay

Arabian
Sea

Bay of
Bengal

THAILAND

Bangkok

KAM.

Saigon

TICA

CHAD

Khartoum

SUDAN

Addis
Ababa

ETHIOPIA

SOMALIA

ARABIA

YEMEN
(Sana)

YEMEN (Aden)

Socotra
Yemen (Aden)

Hyderabad

Madras

Andaman
Islands
(India)

Laccadive
Islands
(India)

MALDIVES

SRI LANKA

Colombo

MALAYSIA

Kuala Lumpur

SINGAPORE

Borneo

Celebes

TRUST TERRITORY OF
Caroline Islands
THE PACIFIC ISLANDS
(U.S.)

Gilbert
Islands
(Br.)

NAURU

OCEAN

CENTRAL
AFRICAN
REP.

RWANDA
BURUNDI

ZAIRE

Kinshasa
Brazzaville

UGANDA

Nairobi

KENYA

TANZANIA

Zanzibar
Dar es Salaam

Victoria

L. Tanganyika

SEYCHELLES

Equator

Sumatra

INDONESIA

Java

East Indies

Moluccas

Jakarta

WEST
IRIAN

PAPUA
NEW GUINEA

Port
Moresby

Bismarck
Arch.

Solomon
Islands
(Br.)

New
Hebrides
(Br. & Fr.)

FIJI

Tuvalu
Islands
(Br.)

ANGOLA

ZAMBIA

MALAWI

L. Nyasa

COMORO

Tananarive

MAURITIUS

INDIAN

Timor

Timor Sea

Darwin

Arafura Sea

Coral
Sea

New
Caledonia
(Fr.)

ZIMBABWE

Salisbury

MOZAMBIQUE

Madagascar

MALAGASY
REPUBLIC

Tropic of Capricorn

AUSTRALIA

Brisbane

NAMIBIA
SOUTH-WEST
AFRICA

BOTSWANA

Pretoria
Johannesburg

Maputo

SWAZILAND

OCEAN

Perth

SOUTH
AFRICA

LESOTHO

Durban

Cape Town
Cape of
Good Hope

Port Elizabeth

Adelaide

Melbourne

Tasmania

Hobart

Sydney

Canberra

Tasman
Sea

Auckland
North
Island

Auckland Is.
(N.Z.)

South
Island

Wellington
Christchurch

NEW
ZEALAND

Antarctic Circle

Follett Publishing Company

TICA

Glossary

In this Glossary, you will find all the vocabulary terms listed in this book, as well as some additional terms. You may use the Glossary as you would a dictionary. However, only the word meanings that will be most helpful in studying this book have been included here. You can find more meanings in a dictionary.

Abolish Do away with; put an end to.

Abolition The ending of something, often of slavery.

Abomination A shameful or evil thing.

Abuse Harsh or unfair treatment; to treat harshly.

Access Way or means of approach; opportunity to use.

Acute Demanding immediate attention.

Adjourn To end a session or meeting for a time.

Administration The managing of a business or government; the group of people in charge.

Advanced More developed than others.

Advocate A person who supports or speaks in favor of something.

Affirmative action Positive action; program to increase opportunities for women and minorities, in order to encourage equality.

Agency An office or division of government.

Aggressive Forceful; willing to put oneself forward.

Agribusiness Large-scale farming business that also often controls sources of supplies and distribution of products.

Alien A person who is not a citizen of the country in which he or she lives.

Allegiance Loyalty to a country, person, or cause.

Alliance An agreement between two or more parties to work or fight together.

Allotment Division of a whole into parts and distribution of each part, as in allotment of Indian land.

Ally A friend or supporter.

Ambassador A person who represents a government in a foreign nation.

Amendment A change in, or addition to, a law, rule, or constitution.

Ammunition Anything that can be hurled or fired at a target; military supplies.

Amnesty A general pardon.

Annex To take over an area and join it to a larger area.

Apartheid A policy of strict racial segregation in every aspect of life.

Appeal To ask for another, more favorable decision in a higher court.

Appointee A person chosen to hold a certain job.

Apprenticeship Method of learning a trade, skill, or art by working under a trained person.

Appropriation Money set aside for a certain use.

Arbitration The settling of a dispute by a third party.

Aristocracy Any class that is considered superior because of birth, culture, or wealth; the nobility.

Armistice An agreement to stop fighting.

Arsenal A place where military equipment is made and stored.

Assassinate To murder by a surprise or secret attack.

Asset Something of value.

Assimilation Absorption of one thing or group by another.

Assume To take upon oneself or take over.

Atomic Having to do with atoms, the tiny particles in matter; a kind of weapon or energy.

Authority The power or the right to force obedience.

Authorize To give power or approval.

Bail Money deposited with a court to free a prisoner from jail until trial, meant to guarantee the prisoner's appearance at trial.

Ballistic missile A rocket used to carry nuclear warheads.

Bias A tendency to feel or act in a certain way without good reason; prejudices.

Bicentennial The anniversary of 200 years.

Bill of attainder A document that declares a person guilty of a crime without a court trial.

Bloc A unified group of people or nations.

Blockade Control of traffic into or out of a place by the military.

Bolt To break away from a political party or organization.

Boycott A refusal to buy certain goods or products; refusal to buy from a certain source.

Bribe A gift or reward given to obtain a dishonest or illegal favor.

Bureaucracy Officials working for and in government.

Cabinet The group of people who advise the head of a government.

Candidate A person running for office.

Cargo Goods carried by a ship, plane, or other vehicle.

Cash crop A crop grown to be sold rather than used by the farmer.

Casualty A person wounded, killed, or lost in war.

Caucus A closed political meeting at which candidates and/or policies are decided on.

Cede To give up, or give away, something.

Censure To criticize or blame; to condemn.

Census An official count of the population.

Centralize To bring under one control; to gather together.

Ceremony Formal actions for a special occasion.

Chaos Complete confusion and disorder.

Characterize To define or describe something by its most important features.

Circumnavigate To travel completely around something, such as the earth.

Civilian Not belonging to the military.

Civilization A highly developed culture.

Civil service Government employment other than military, legislative, or judicial.

Clan A group of related people or families.

Climax To reach the highest or most exciting point.

Coalition An alliance or union of two or more groups.

Collective bargaining Meetings between employer and union representatives to work out differences over wages and working conditions.

Colonization The establishment of settlements in foreign lands.

Colony A settlement outside an established nation, controlled by that nation.

Commerce The buying and selling of goods; trade.

Commission A written paper giving certain powers, privileges, or duties.

Communism A political theory that aims at doing away with private property; a totalitarian system of government in which the state owns all means of production.

Compensation A price paid in return for a service; a price paid to make up for something lost or damaged.

Competition A contest with another for some gain or reward.

Compromise To settle a disagreement by arranging for both sides to give up part of what they want; a settlement.

Compulsory Required or forced.

Concentrate To collect in one place.

Concentration camp A camp in which political opponents and/or minorities may be held prisoner or killed.

Concur To agree; to have the same opinion.

Concurrent Happening or existing at the same time.

Confederacy A political unit or government made up of several smaller units or governments.

Confirm To approve; to make definite.

Conformity The adjusting of thoughts or behavior to fit in with other people.

Conscript To draft; to force into military service.

Consent Agreement; permission.

Consequence A result.

Conservation Avoidance of waste; preservation, often with reference to natural resources.

Consumer A person who buys and uses goods.

Containment The act of keeping something within limits; the U.S. policy of trying to stop the spread of Communism after World War II.

Contender A person competing for a position or office.

Continent One of the seven large land masses of the world.

Contract A written agreement that can be legally enforced.

Controversy A dispute or argument.

Convention A large meeting held for some special purpose.

Convict To prove or declare guilty.

Cooperative A business owned and operated by its customers, who share in the profits or losses.

Copyright The sole right to reproduce, publish, and sell a written or artistic work.

Corollary A reasonable result or extension.

Corporation A business that sells shares of ownership.

Corruption Evil conduct; dishonesty.

Credit Trust that a person or business will pay for purchased goods at a later time.

Crisis A serious problem needing immediate attention; a turning point.

Criticize To find fault with.

Culture The beliefs, knowledge, customs, and activities of a group of people.

Custom The way something is usually done by a person or group of people.

Decisive Settling something firmly; showing a decision clearly.

Decline A decrease.

Deficit Shortage of money; the amount by which money spent exceeds money available.

Defraud To cheat or take something away by deceit.

Demarcation The setting of limits or boundaries.

Demilitarization The removal of military units from an area.

Demonetize To stop using as a basis for currency.

Denounce To speak against; to give information against.

Deport To send an alien out of a country.

Depression A period of low economic activity and high unemployment.

Descendant An offspring: child, grandchild, great-grandchild, etc.

Desegregation To do away with the separation of races.

Deserter A person who leaves military service without permission.

Détente The relaxing of tension.

Developing nation A nation working to build and strengthen its economy.

Dictatorial Having to do with a person who has absolute power; overbearing.

Diplomat A person who handles official business between nations.

Disappointing Failing to meet hopes or wishes.

Disarmament The reduction of military supplies.

Discourage To try to prevent; to take away hopes.

Discrimination Making a distinction in favor of, or against, a particular group of people; often, prejudicial action.

Disillusion To disappoint high hopes or ideals.

Dispute To argue; an argument.

Dissatisfaction Unhappiness; lack of contentment.

Dissolve To put an end to; to break up.

Domestic Having to do with the internal affairs of a nation.

Dominant Stronger, controlling.

Domino theory The theory that if communism took over one nation, it would also take over surrounding nations.

Double jeopardy Being tried again for a crime after having been found innocent of it.

Duel A formal fight between two people to settle a quarrel.

Duplicate An exact copy.

Economic Having to do with making, distributing, and using wealth.

Efficiency The ability to work without wasted time or effort.

Electoral college The special group of officials elected to choose the president and vice-president of the United States.

Eligible Qualified; meeting all requirements.

Emancipate To set free.

Embargo A government order stopping trade.

Emigrate To leave one country to settle in another.

Emotional Appealing to or arousing feelings.

Emphasize To call attention to; to stress.

Empire A large number of different territories or nations controlled by a single government.

Encourage To give hope or courage.

Endangered species A kind of wildlife that is in danger of dying out completely.

Endure To continue to exist; to survive.

Enforce To carry out; put into effect.

Entangle To involve or tangle up.

Entanglement Deep involvement that is difficult to get out of.

Enumerate To name one by one; to list.

Environment The world around us; conditions that affect living things.

Envoy A representative or messenger sent by one government to another.

Erupt To burst out or to explode suddenly.

Excise tax An internal tax on the manufacture, sale, or use of an item within a country.

Exclude To shut out; to keep from taking part.

Execute Put to death.

Executive The branch of government that carries out the laws; an official.

Exempt To make free from requirements.

Expenditure Something spent.

Expire To end.

Export An article sent out of one country for sale in another.

Ex post facto After the fact. An ex post facto law makes it possible to punish a person for an earlier act that was not a crime when it was committed.

Extent Space, degree, or amount included; the range.

External tax A government duty placed on goods imported into a country.

Extradition The turning over of a prisoner by one authority to a different authority that has the right to try the suspect.

Extremist A person who favors radical, or extreme, political ideas, methods, or practices.

Facility Something built for a particular use.

Fascist Having to do with a political system in which a strong central government controls all parts of life in a nation; a person who supports such a system.

Featherbedding Requirement that an employer maintain more workers than are actually needed.

Federal Having to do with the government of a nation formed by the union of several states or units.

Federation A group or collection of organizations or governments joined together for a special purpose.

Feminist Having to do with the belief in the equality of women; one who holds that belief.

Fertile Able to support the growth of plants or crops; able to grow.

Financial Having to do with money.

Flexible Capable of being changed; easily adapted.

Foe An enemy.

Foreclose To take back a mortgage, usually by taking over property given as security.

Fraud Dishonesty or trickery; something that is done to trick or cheat.

Fugitive A person who is trying to escape.

Fundamental Forming a basis; basic.

Ghetto An area largely populated by one or more minorities.

Greenbacks Paper money not backed by gold or silver.

Guarantee To pledge or promise; a promise backed with something given as security.

Guerilla Warfare carried on by bands of people not part of a regular army; a fighter in such a band of people.

Habeas corpus A legal order that forces an authority to charge a prisoner with a specific crime, in the presence of a judge.

Hoard To store up; to keep greedily.

Homestead A house and the land and buildings connected with it; a piece of land acquired from the government by living on it.

Humanitarian Concerned with the welfare of people.

Idealism Acting according to high hopes and beliefs.

Illegal Against the law.

Illiteracy Inability to read and write.

Immediate Nearest or most directly connected; closest in time.

Immigrant A person from one country who settles in another.

Immigration Coming into a country or region to live.

Impeach To formally accuse a public official of wrongdoing in office.

Imperialism The practice of building an empire by establishing and controlling colonies.

Implicate To show to be involved in, or connected with.

Import To bring goods from one country into another.

Impress To force someone to serve.

Inalienable Cannot be given, or taken, away.

Inaugurate To install into office with ceremony.

Income tax Money paid out of people's earnings to support their government.

Indefinitely Without a time limit; vaguely.

Indemnity A payment to make up for loss, damage, or expense.

Indentured Bound by contract to work for a period of time in order to pay a debt.

Industrial Having to do with factories and manufacturing.

Industrialized Built up with factories and machines.

Inferior Less important or valuable; lower in quality or position.

Inflation An economic situation in which credit and money in circulation increase and prices rise.

Inhabitant One who lives in an area.

Insecticide A substance that kills insects.

Interest Money paid in return for the use of money.

Interfere To block or hinder.

Internal tax A government duty placed on goods produced within a country.

Interpret To explain the meaning of.

Interpretation An understanding or explanation.

Interstate Having to do with two or more states.

Intervene To become involved in a dispute in order to help settle it.

Intimidate To influence someone's actions with fear.

Intolerable Unbearable.

Invalid Without force or power.

Invention An item or process developed from study and experiments.

Isolate To separate from others.

Isolationism A national policy of keeping out of foreign affairs.

Isthmus A narrow strip of land (between two bodies of water) that connects two larger land areas.

Judicial Having to do with the courts or with judges; the branch of a government that interprets the laws.

Judicial review The power of courts to decide if an existing law is constitutional.

Jurisdiction The issues or area over which authority extends.

Justice A system for deciding fair treatment of people suspected of crime.

Justify To show to be right or reasonable.

Laissez-faire The idea that government should not involve itself in business and economic affairs.

Lease To rent; a written rent agreement.

Legislative Having to do with making laws; the branch of government that makes the laws.

Legislature A lawmaking group.

Leisure Time free from work or duty.

Lenient Not harsh or strict.

Libel An untrue statement that damages someone.

Life expectancy The number of years a person can expect to live.

Lobby To try to influence lawmakers.

Loyalist A colonist who supported England before or during the Revolution.

Lynching Unlawful hanging of a person, often by a mob.

Maintain To keep or keep up; to carry on.

Majority More than half of a total.

Manifest destiny The belief that nothing could stop the United States from expanding its area west to the Pacific Ocean.

Manufacture To make goods, especially by machine.

Massacre To kill the helpless in large numbers.

Materialism Concern with acquiring possessions; often placing greater value on objects than on ideas or feelings.

Mediation Attempt by a third party to work out a compromise in a dispute.

Menial Unpleasant and lacking dignity.

Mercantilism An economic policy aimed at strengthening a nation by building up its supply of gold and other precious metals, often by controlling trade with colonies.

Mercenary A soldier serving for pay in a foreign army.

Merit Worth or value; good or bad quality.

Method The way something is done.

Migrant A person who moves from one place to another.

Militia A state or local military force.

Minimum Least possible; lowest.

Mint To make coins.

Missionary A person who works to convert people to a religion.

Moderate Favoring middle-of-the-road political positions rather than extreme ones.

Modification A change or alteration.

Moisture A small amount of water; wetness.

Monopoly Control of an industry or the supply of an item by one group or company; a group that has such control.

Morale The spirit or mental state of a group or person.

Mortgage A loan to buy property for which the security is the property itself.

Muckraking The finding and exposing of corruption or bad conduct in business or government.

Multilateral Involving several nations or groups.

Multimillionaire A person who has many millions of dollars.

Nationalism Loyalty to, and pride in, a nation, often favoring one's nation over all others.

Natural resources Useful materials in nature, such as minerals, timber, etc.

Navigable Permitting passage of ships or boats.

Navigator A person who plans and guides the route of a ship or airplane.

Negotiate To discuss and arrange the terms of an agreement.

Neutral On neither side in a quarrel or war.

Nominate To name as a candidate for election or appointment.

Nuclear Having to do with the nucleus, or central part, of an atom; a kind of weapon or energy.

Null and void Not in effect; having no legal force.

Nullification The act of making a law void or not binding.

Obligation A responsibility, duty, or debt.

Occupation Military control of an area.

Offensive An aggressive attack; having to do with attack.

Opportunity A good chance.

Oppose To be against; to act, fight, or struggle against.

Oppress To crush or control by harsh or cruel authority.

Optimism A feeling that the future will be good; hopefulness.

Ordinance A law.

Outmoded Out of date or style.

Overproduction Production of more than is needed or can be sold.

Overrule To reverse, or set aside, a decision made by someone having less authority.

Overseer A boss or supervisor, especially on a plantation.

Overwhelm To completely overpower.

Parity The ratio between the price a farmer receives for crops and the prices of goods the farmer must buy; the state of being equal.

Parochial Having to do with a church or religious group.

Partisan Strong or blind loyalty to a political party or cause.

Partition Division into parts.

Patent A document that gives a person the sole right to make, use, and sell an item for a certain number of years.

Patriotism The feeling of pride in, and loyalty to, a country.

Patronage Distribution of government jobs on a basis other than merit.

Pension Payment to a person who is not working but who has earned support because of past service.

Perish To die; to be destroyed.

Permanent Lasting or intended to last for a long time.

Persecution Repeated bad treatment or harm.

Picketing The parading by striking workers.

Platform A statement of the beliefs and future actions of a political party or candidate.

Plurality The larger number or amount, but less than half of the total.

Political Having to do with government or politics.

Politician Person whose profession is politics and/or government.

Popular sovereignty The right of residents of an area to make decisions or govern for themselves, especially with reference to the slavery issue.

Popular vote The votes of the public in an election.

Precedent An action or decision that can serve as a model for later ones.

Prejudice An opinion formed without thought or judgment.

Preside To lead or conduct a meeting.

Prestige Importance or status in the eyes of others.

Procedural Having to do with the methods of, or rules for, taking care of routine business.

Proceedings Happenings; events.

Profitable Bringing a gain; bringing in money.

Progressive Having to do with progress, improvement, moving forward; a member of the reform movement called Progressivism.

Prohibit To forbid.

Prohibition The outlawing of the production and sale of alcoholic drinks.

Promissory note A written promise to pay a certain sum of money at a fixed future time.

Propaganda Efforts to convince people of opinions or beliefs; information that may be twisted to serve a purpose.

Proportion One thing in relation to another.

Proprietary Owned and controlled by a private person or group.

Prosecutor A lawyer who argues the case against an accused person.

Prosperity Financial well-being.

Protective Guarding against harm.

Provision A condition or specific statement in a law or contract.

Purchasing power Ability to buy.

Purge To force unwanted members from a group.

Qualifications Requirements for a job.

Quota A minimum or maximum number of people or things.

Racism Belief that a race of people is either better than, or worse than, others.

Radical Supporting great changes or reforms.

Radioactive fallout Dust particles produced in an atomic explosion that give off radiation.

Rate A payment fixed according to an established scale.

Ratify To confirm; to approve.

Ration A fixed allowance or share of something; to divide something into shares.

Realistic True to life; based on fact.

Reapportion To reorganize or redivide; especially to redivide political districts according to population.

Rebate A return of part of a payment.

Rebellion An uprising against an authority; a revolt.

Recession A period of decreased economic activity.

Recognition Formal acknowledgement of existence.

Recycle To re-use; to process again for re-use.

Reforestation The planting of new trees to replace trees cut down.

Refrigerated Kept cold.

Refugee A person who flees home to reach safety.

Regain To get again.

Regime The government or group in power.

Registered Entered on an official list.

Regulation Control by rules or laws; a rule or law.

Relatively Comparatively; compared to.

Reluctant Unwilling; slow to act.

Remote Far away; far off.

Removal Taking or moving away; the policy of moving Indians away from their land.

Renewable Able to be made like new again; capable of being replaced naturally.

Repeal To take out of effect; to remove legal force from.

Republic A form of government in which citizens elect representatives to govern for them.

Resent To feel ill will and anger.

Resident A person who lives in an area.

Residual Remaining; left over.

Resistance Opposition to, or action against, a force.

Resource A useful material or skill.

Restore To give back.

Restrict To keep within limits; to limit.

Restriction A limiting condition or rule; a limitation.

Resume To go on, especially after an interruption.

Retribution Something given or required in repayment, especially punishment.

Revenue Money coming in; income.

Rival One who tries to defeat or outdo another.

Romantic Having heroic, adventurous, or imaginative appeal.

Rumor An unproved story or statement.

Rural Having to do with the country and farmland; opposite of urban.

Sanction A penalty; an action taken by a group of nations against another nation.

Sanitary Having to do with health, especially cleanliness.

Scandal Shameful action that brings public disgrace.

Secede To withdraw from a group or nation.

Secession A withdrawal from a group or nation.

Sectionalism The favoring of the interests of one section over those of the country as a whole.

Sedition Speech or action causing rebellion against a government.

Segregation Separation; the setting apart from others, as of racial groups.

Self-rule Rule of an area by the area's own government and people.

Sensational Exciting or startling; causing excitement.

Sewage disposal The carrying off of waste matter in special drains and pipes.

Sharecropping Tenant farming in which the farmer pays the landowner a share of the crop in exchange for the use of land and equipment.

Slate A list of candidates in an election.

Socialized medicine Health care controlled by government and paid for with taxes.

Solar Having to do with the sun.

Solution An answer; a way to work out a problem.

Source The origin or starting place.

Speakeasy Club or restaurant selling liquor during Prohibition.

Spoils system The practice of giving government jobs in return for political support.

Stability Steadiness; firmness.

Stabilize To make firm or steady.

Staple Most important or basic; the most important crop or product.

Status A person's condition or position in society.

Stock A share of ownership in a corporation.

Strait A narrow waterway connecting two larger bodies of water.

Strategy A plan of action.

Stress To place importance on; to emphasize.

Subpoena A written order requiring the presence of a person or of certain information in court.

Subsidy A grant or contribution of money to help support something.

Substantive Having real importance or important content.

Subtle Hard to see or recognize.

Suburbia The smaller communities around a city.

Succeed To take over a job or position when it becomes vacant.

Sue To seek justice by bringing a disagreement to a court of law.

Suffrage The right to vote.

Superiority Higher and better quality.

Suppress To stop by force or put down; to keep or hold back.

Supremacy Having the highest authority or power.

Surplus An extra amount beyond what is needed.

Surrender Give up; yield.

Sweatshop A factory or business in which employees have bad working conditions and low wages.

Tactics Procedures or methods of action to reach a goal.

Tariff A tax on goods imported into a country.

Technical Having to do with useful knowledge or skills, or with the methods of science or industry.

Temporary For a short time only.

Tenant A person who pays rent in return for using a building or a piece of land.

Tenement An apartment house, especially one in bad condition and occupied by the poor.

Tension Strain between people or groups.

Terrorism The use of violence and fear, usually to gain a political goal.

Textile Cloth.

Threaten To promise a negative action; to give warning of trouble to come.

Tolerance Willingness to put up with people, beliefs, and ways different from one's own.

Totalitarianism Having to do with a political system in which an individual or a party holds all power and has complete control.

Transcontinental Extending across a continent.

Transition The change from one condition or thing to another.

Treason Action against one's government.

Treaty A formal agreement between two or more governments or independent political units.

Tributary A river or stream that flows into a larger river.

Trust A group of companies that controls much of a particular business.

Trustee The person or persons legally responsible for the property or affairs of another person or group.

Turmoil Commotion; confusion; great disturbance.

Tyranny Government by a harsh and unfair ruler.

Unanimous In complete agreement; without a single opposing vote.

Uncivilized Undeveloped; not cultured.

Uniform All alike.

Unity A state of being completely together; in total agreement.

Urban Having to do with cities or towns.

Urban renewal The improvement of run-down parts of a city.

Utopia An ideal or perfect society.

Vaquero Spanish word for cowboy.

Vast Very large; huge.

Vested Given certain powers or rights.

Veto To reject or refuse to approve; a rejection.

Violate To disobey; to break a law or rule.

Violence Rough or harmful action.

Voluntary Done by choice; not forced.

Writ of assistance A legal order allowing unlimited search by officials.

Zionism The movement to make a Jewish homeland in Palestine.

Index of Maps, Charts, and Graphs

Index

This index includes references to material in all four parts of *American History, 6th Edition.* The text is divided into parts as follows:

Part 1: pages 1–192
Part 2: pages 193–368
Part 3: pages 369–592
Part 4: pages 593–696

In the index entries, a page with an illustration is indicated by *p.*, one with a map by *m.*, one with a chart by *c.*, and one with a graph by *g.*

Cover painting:
  View of St. Louis, 1846 by Henry Lewis,
  The St. Louis Art Museum (Detail),
  Purchased: Eliza K. McMillan Fund